Copyright © 2013 by Paul L. Rein
All rights reserved. No part of this book may be used or reproduced in any manner whatsoever without written permission of the author. Published 2013.

Printed in the United States of America.
ISBN: 978-1-59571-913-3

Designed and published by
Word Association Publishers

205 Fifth Avenue
Tarentum, Pennsylvania 15084
www.wordassociation.com
1.800.827.7903

FULL & EQUAL ACCESS:
Disabled Rights Litigation In California

Paul L. Rein, ATTORNEY AT LAW
Edited by Aaron Clefton

WORD ASSOCIATION PUBLISHERS
www.wordassociation.com
1.800.827.7903

TABLE OF CONTENTS

1. DEDICATION AND ACKNOWLEDGMENT 1

   A. THANK YOU TO MY OFFICE ALLIES 1

   B. REMEMBERING KEITH KELLUM 2

   C. CALIFORNIA SET AN EXAMPLE FOR NATIONAL (ADA) ACCESS COMPLIANCE 3

   D. ED ROBERTS, "GODFATHER" OF THE DISABILITY RIGHTS MOVEMENT 3

2. FOREWARD: A PERSONAL NOTE 5

3. LEGAL DISCLAIMER: NO PERSONAL LEGAL ADVICE IS INTENDED BY THIS BOOK 7

4. INTRODUCTION 8

   A. PREFACE: CALIFORNIA LAWS AND THE FEDERAL ADA STANDARDS PROVIDE TOOLS TO OBTAIN DISABLED ACCESS 8

   B. PURPOSE OF THIS BOOK 11

   C. THIS BOOK ADDRESSES CALIFORNIA LAW DISABLED ACCESS ISSUES, INCLUDING INCORPORATED ADA VIOLATIONS, BUT WILL NOT COVER ADA TITLE I OR OTHER "EMPLOYMENT" ISSUES 13

   D. BE AWARE OF NEW "SB1608" LEGISLATIVE CHANGES IN CALIFORNIA LAW, EFFECTIVE JANUARY 1, 2009, AND SB 1186, EFFECTIVE JANUARY 1, 2013. 15

   E. STRUCTURE OF THIS BOOK 16

   F. NOTE ON CIVIL CODE § 55 ATTORNEY FEES THREAT AGAINST PLAINTIFFS: DISTRICT COURT IN OLIVER V. IN-N-OUT BURGERS FOLLOWS HUBBARD V. SOBRECK RATHER THAN JANKEY IN FEDERAL COURT. 16

I. CALIFORNIA LAW - ENFORCING CALIFORNIA'S DISABLED ACCESS
    REQUIREMENTS THROUGH PRIVATE LAWSUITS 17

    A. LIABILITY: THE RIGHT TO "FULL AND EQUAL ACCESS" UNDER
       CALIFORNIA LAW 17
       1. INTRODUCTION: THE PROBLEM OF ACCESS DENIAL 19

       2. CASE LAW SUPPORTS USE OF PRIVATE LAWSUITS TO OBTAIN
          ACCESS IN CALIFORNIA 17

       3. PRIVATE LAWSUITS ARE NEEDED TO ENFORCE
          ADA TITLE III IN CALIFORNIA 20

       4. CALIFORNIA'S PUBLIC POLICY IS TO MAXIMIZE ACCESS. 21
          a. POLICY IS TO MAXIMIZE INTEGRATION OF DISABLED PERSONS
             INTO ALL SOCIAL AND ECONOMIC ASPECTS OF OUR SOCIETY,
             INCLUDING ANY STATE FUNDED PROGRAM OR ACTIVITIES 21

          b. ENCOURAGING PRIVATE LAWSUITS ENFORCES THIS CALIFORNIA
             PUBLIC POLICY 22

          c. OBJECTIVES OF COMPLAINT: INJUNCTION, DAMAGES AND FEES ... 23

          d. STATUTORY DAMAGES ARE AVAILABLE 23

       5. PLAINTIFF DOES NOT HAVE TO PROVE WRONGFUL "INTENT" 24
          a. BECAUSE PUBLIC POLICY IS TO MAXIMIZE DISABLED ACCESS-
             IBILITY IN COMMERCIAL BUILDINGS, NO PROOF OF WRONGFUL
             INTENT IS REQUIRED FOR VIOLATION OF CIVIL CODE §§ 54 AND
             54.1, THE DISABLED PERSONS ACT 24

          b. AN "UNRUH ACT" (SECTION 51 CIVIL CODE) VIOLATION DOES <u>NOT</u>
             REQUIRE PROOF OF WRONGFUL "INTENT," AS FINALLY DECIDED
             BY THE CALIFORNIA SUPREME COURT IN MUNSON V. DEL TACO,
             JUNE 2009 25

    B. CALIFORNIA STATUTORY SCHEME FOR DISABLED ACCESS 26
       1. PUBLIC POLICY AND PURPOSE OF REGULATIONS:
          TO MAXIMIZE ACCESSIBILITY AND USABILITY FOR DISABLED
          PERSONS 26
          a. INTERPRETATION OF STATUTES: CALIFORNIA PUBLIC POLICY
             REQUIRES A BROAD INTERPRETATION OF STATUTES RELATING
             TO PROTECTING "HANDICAPPED" PERSONS/INDIVIDUALS WITH A
             DISABILITY AND THEIR RIGHT TO USE PRIVATE LAWSUITS TO
             ENFORCE ACCESS COMPLIANCE 26

- b. CALIFORNIA STATUTES AND DECLARATIONS OF POLICY SUPPORT BROAD INTERPRETATIONS OF PROTECTIONS FOR DISABLED PERSONS 28
    - (1) GOAL: TOTAL INTEGRATION OF DISABLED PERSONS INTO MAINSTREAM SOCIETY 28
    - (2) CIVIL CODE §§ 51, 54 AND 54.1 PROVIDE PROTECTIONS FOR DISABLED PERSONS 28
    - (3) THE TERM "ACCESSIBLE TO AND USEABLE BY" SET FORTH IN THE STATUTES REFLECTS THE GENERAL <u>PURPOSE</u> OF ACCESS <u>RATHER</u> THAN THE SPECIFIC IMPLEMENTING REQUIREMENTS FOR ACCESS COMPLIANCE; THESE WERE SET BY THE ASA AS "<u>MINIMUM</u> STANDARDS" (FOR 1968-1981, BEFORE TITLE 24) 30
- c. PURPOSE OF STANDARDS: ASA AND TITLE 24 REGULATIONS FOCUS ON MAXIMIZING ACCESSIBILITY AND USABILITY 31
- d. GOVERNMENT CODE §§ 4450 et seq. REQUIREMENTS WERE ADOPTED BY HEALTH & SAFETY CODE §§ 19955-19959 FOR ALL PRIVATELY OWNED PUBLIC FACILITIES CONSTRUCTED OR ALTERED AFTER JULY 1, 1970, AND SET <u>MINIMUM</u> STANDARDS FOR COMPLIANCE 32

2. ALL "ALTERATIONS, STRUCTURAL REPAIRS, OR ADDITIONS" TO A BUILDING TRIGGER DISABLED ACCESS UNLESS EACH ITEM OF WORK IS SPECIFICALLY "EXCEPTED" BY TITLE 24 REGULATIONS AND PROCEDURES 33
    - a. CALIFORNIA'S STATUTORY SCHEME OF REQUIREMENTS INCLUDES THE HEALTH & SAFETY CODE, GOVERNMENT CODE, AND TITLE 24 - THE STATE BUILDING CODE (THE "STATE ARCHITECT'S REGULATIONS") 33
        - (1) CALIFORNIA STATUTORY SCHEME SUMMARIZED 33
        - (2) "ALTERATIONS" TO EACH "FACILITY" TRIGGER ACCESS 34
        - (3) "ACCESSIBILITY" IS DEFINED BY THE TITLE 24 REGULATIONS IN EFFECT AT THE TIME OF ALTERATIONS 35
        - (4) INVESTIGATION AND DISCOVERY WILL DETERMINE THE CONSTRUCTION AND ALTERATION HISTORY 35
        - (5) CONSULT THE RELEVANT YEAR'S REGULATIONS AND "STATE ARCHITECT'S MANUAL" 37
    - b. 1970-1982 ALTERATIONS WERE CONTROLLED BY CALIFORNIA STATUTES AND THE "ASA," THE REGULATIONS OF THE "AMERICAN STANDARDS ASSOCIATION" WHICH CONTAINED "PATH OF TRAVEL" AND PRIMARY ENTRANCE REQUIREMENTS. 37

    c. FOR ALL CALIFORNIA CONSTRUCTION OR ALTERATIONS PERMITTED FROM 1982 TO THE PRESENT, TITLE 24 REGULATIONS DEFINE THE PURPOSE OF ACCESS REGULATIONS, AND THE SCOPE OF ACCESS REQUIREMENTS TRIGGERED BY ALTERATIONS 39

       (1) POST 1982 STANDARDS ARE SET BY TITLE 24 39

       (2) THE TITLE 24 STATEMENT OF "PURPOSE" IS RELEVANT TO INTERPRETATIONS 40

       (3) TITLE 24 APPLIES TO BOTH PUBLICALLY AND PRIVATELY FUNDED BUILDINGS 40

    d. ALL "ALTERATIONS" TRIGGER ACCESS <u>EXCEPT</u> THOSE SPECIFICALLY EXCEPTED BY THE TITLE 24 CODE PROVISIONS (§2-105(B)11A(7) (1984 Code) 41

    e. THE OPERATIVE STANDARD FOR TRIGGERING ACCESS IS "ALTERATIONS, STRUCTURAL REPAIRS, OR ADDITIONS," AS SPECIFIED IN §19959 HEALTH & SAFETY CODE AND THE TITLE 24 REGULATIONS 43

    f. THE BURDEN OF PROOF TO SHOW AN "EXCEPTION" GENERALLY RESTS ON THE PARTY "WHO CLAIMS ITS BENEFITS" 44

3. PUBLIC POLICY REQUIRES ACCESS, INCLUDING PATH OF TRAVEL TO THE AREA OF ALTERATION, WHENEVER ALTERATIONS ARE MADE AND MONEY IS SPENT FOR BUILDING IMPROVEMENTS 45

4. AN UNREASONABLE "HARDSHIP" EXCEPTION MAY BE AVAILABLE, BUT ONLY WHEN SPECIFIED CONDITIONS ARE MET, INCLUDING PROVIDING "EQUIVALENT FACILITATION" 46

5. ACTUAL "ACCESSIBILITY" IS REQUIRED IN ORDER FOR EQUIVALENT FACILI-TATION TO BE SUFFICIENT TO JUSTIFY ANY HARDSHIP EXCEPTION 48

6. ALL ALTERATIONS TRIGGER ACCESS UNLESS A FORMAL HARDSHIP EXCEPTION (1) IS FORMALLY GRANTED, (2) COMPLIES WITH CODE RE-QUIREMENTS (HEALTH & SAFETY CODE § 19957; § 2-422(C) TITLE 24); AND (3) IS SUPPORTED BY WRITTEN FINDINGS ENTERED IN PUBLIC RECORDS ... 49

    a. THE BURDEN OF PROOF FOR AN EXCEPTION IS ON THE DEFENDANT 49

    b. GOVERNMENT CODE §§ 4450ff WAS INCORPORATED INTO HEALTH & SAFETY CODE §§ 19955 - 19959; § 4451(d) GOVERNMENT CODE AND § 19957 HEALTH AND SAFETY CODE BOTH REQUIRE "EQUIVALENT FACILITATION" AS A CONDITION FOR AN "EXCEPTION" 49

      c. ALTERATIONS TRIGGERED ACCESS UNLESS AN <u>UNREASONABLE</u> HARDSHIP EXCEPTION IS PROVEN 50

      d. <u>EQUIVALENT FACILITATION</u> IS A MANDATORY REQUIREMENT, PER STATUTE AND REGULATIONS, WHEN ANY HARDSHIP EXCEPTION IS GRANTED 51

      e. SINCE 1982 TITLE 24 HAS REQUIRED COMPLIANCE WITH FIVE FACTORS, INCLUDING SPECIFIC <u>WRITTEN FINDINGS</u> BY THE BUILDING DEPARTMENT, AS A CONDITION FOR GRANTING A "HARDSHIP" EXCEPTION 51

C. CALIFORNIA CASE LAW HAS ESTABLISHED: THE RIGHT TO ENFORCE ACCESS REQUIREMENTS BY PRIVATE LAWSUIT; THAT NO WRONGFUL INTENT IS REQUIRED; AND THAT IT IS NO DEFENSE THAT ACCESS STANDARDS WERE NOT ENFORCED BY THE LOCAL BUILDING DEPARTMENT 52

  1. LEADING APPELLATE CASES ESTABLISH THE RIGHT TO ENFORCE ACCESS BY A PRIVATE LAWSUIT 52

  2. NO WRONGFUL INTENT NEEDS TO BE PROVEN FOR A VIOLATION OF CIVIL CODE §§ 54 AND 54.1 53

  3. A BUILDING DEPARTMENT'S LACK OF ENFORCEMENT IS NOT A DEFENSE 54

  4. THE UNIFORM BUILDING CODE SPECIFICALLY PROVIDES THAT ISSUANCE OF A BUILDING PERMIT DOES <u>NOT</u> APPROVE VIOLATION OF ANY ACCESS REQUIREMENTS 54

D. ACCESSIBLE "PATH OF TRAVEL" REQUIREMENTS UNDER THE "ASA" (1970 - 1981) AND TITLE 24 STANDARDS (1982 - PRESENT) 54

  1. AN ACCESSIBLE "PATH OF TRAVEL" IS NEEDED TO MAKE AN AREA "ACCESSIBLE" 54

  2. AN ACCESSIBLE "PATH OF TRAVEL" IS NECESSARY IN ORDER TO MAKE AN AREA "ACCESSIBLE TO AND USEABLE BY" DISABLED PERSONS UNDER THE ASA 56

  3. A 1979 CALIFORNIA LEGISLATIVE COUNSEL'S OPINION RECOGNIZED THAT AN ACCESSIBLE PATH OF TRAVEL TO AN AREA WAS IMPLICITLY REQUIRED IN ORDER FOR THIS AREA TO BE CONSIDERED "ACCESSIBLE" 56

  4. FROM 1970 UNTIL THE 1982 ADOPTION OF THE STATE ARCHITECT'S TITLE 24 REGULATIONS, HEALTH & SAFETY CODE §19959 AND THE "ASA" REGULATIONS REQUIRED AN ACCESSIBLE PATH OF TRAVEL TO ANY AREA OF ALTERATION, IN ORDER FOR THIS AREA TO BE MADE "ACCESSIBLE" 58

5. PEOPLE EX REL. DEUKMEJIAN V. CHE, INC. (1983) 150 CAL.APP.3D 123 APPLIED THE ASA STANDARDS, TRACED THE LEGISLATIVE HISTORY, AND OUTLINED IMPORTANT POLICY CONSIDERATIONS FOR STATUTORY CONSTRUCTION 59
    a. THE CHE CASE SPELLED OUT THE STATUTORY HISTORY OF CALIFORNIA DISABLED ACCESS LAWS AND THE INTERRELATION OF STATUTES AND REGULATIONS FROM 1968 TO 1981 59
    b. CHE FOUND THE 1981 TITLE 24 REGULATIONS "CLARIFIED" THE PRIOR "ASA" REGULATIONS IN SPECIFYING PATH OF TRAVEL REQUIREMENTS 62

6. PATH OF TRAVEL REQUIREMENTS UNDER THE 1970-1981 "ASA" STANDARDS (DONALD V. SACRAMENTO VALLEY BANK (1989) 209 CAL. APP. 3d 1183) 64

7. "PATH OF TRAVEL" IS EXPLICITLY DEFINED IN THE 1982 STATE ARCHITECT'S REGULATIONS ("TITLE 24") THE 1984 STATE ARCHITECT'S INTERPRETIVE MANUAL, AND THE 1984 AND 1989 REGULATIONS 65

8. ARNOLD V. UNITED ARTISTS CONFIRMED THE VALIDITY OF THE STATE ARCHITECT'S REGULATIONS AND THE "GREAT WEIGHT" TO BE GIVEN TO THE STATE ARCHITECT'S INTERPRETATIONS 67

9. SEPTEMBER 17, 1992 OPINION OF CALIFORNIA ATTORNEY GENERAL DAN LUNGREN, A STATEWIDE DIRECTIVE TO ALL CALIFORNIA BUILDING OFFICIALS, CONFIRMED THE "PATH OF TRAVEL" REQUIREMENTS 68

10. THE ADA SPECIFIES THAT DISABLED PERSONS ARE ENTITLED TO BOTH ADA AND CALIFORNIA STATE LAW PROTECTIONS, AND TO WHICHEVER STATUTE PROVIDES "GREATER OR EQUAL PROTECTION" 69

11. PATH OF TRAVEL REQUIREMENTS INCLUDE AN ACCESSIBLE, SAFE AND PRIMARY PUBLIC ENTRANCE 69
    a. "PATH OF TRAVEL" ACCESS THROUGH THE FRONT ENTRANCE, REQUIRING SAFETY FEATURES AT THE FRONT ENTRANCE, ARE TRIGGERED BY ANY ALTERATION INSIDE A RESTAURANT OR OTHER PUBLIC BUILDING 69
    b. ALTERATIONS MAY TRIGGER THE NEED TO CORRECT ANY CONTINUING DANGER TO DISABLED PERSONS AT A FRONT ENTRANCE, A LANDING, AND/OR AN ACCESS RAMP 70
    c. COMPLIANCE IS GOVERNED BY THE SPECIFIC REQUIREMENTS SPECIFIED IN THE REGULATIONS, NOT BY ANY "EXPERT'S" NOTION OF "ACCESSIBLE AND USEABLE" 71
    d. ARE CROSSWALKS REQUIRED FOR A SAFE AND ACCESSIBLE "PATH" OF TRAVEL FROM PARKING AREAS TO STORE ENTRANCES? 72

E. "CONSTRUCTION DIMENSIONAL TOLERANCES" IS NOT A DEFENSE WHEN (A) THERE IS NO SHOWING OF STRUCTURAL IMPRACTICABILITY, OR (B) WHERE REGULATION REQUIRES SPECIFIC MAXIMUM OR MINIMUMS 73

    1. STRICT COMPLIANCE WITH ADAAG STANDARDS IS REQUIRED "UNLESS THE INFEASIBILITY EXCEPTION APPLIES" 74

    2. CALIFORNIA TITLE 24 REQUIREMENTS DO NOT ALLOW APPLICATION OF "CONSTRUCTION TOLERANCE" STANDARDS WHERE THE CODE ALREADY STATES A "RANGE" WITH SPECIFIC MINIMUM AND MAXIMUM END POINTS 74

    3. POSSIBLE USE OF "HANDBOOK OF CONSTRUCTION TOLERANCES" 75

    4. EXAMPLE: REASONS FOR REQUIRING COMPLIANCE WITH "TECHNICAL" DISABLED PARKING PLACE "SIDE SLOPE" REQUIREMENTS 75

F. ACCESSIBLE PUBLIC RESTROOMS ARE GUARANTEED BY LAW FOR "THE PUBLIC, CLIENTS OR EMPLOYEES" BY HEALTH AND SAFETY CODE § 19955 AND TITLE 24 REGULATIONS (§ 2-105(B)11B(2) IN 1984) 76

    1. HEALTH AND SAFETY CODE §19955 AND TITLE 24 REGULATIONS (§2-105(b)11B(2) IN 1984) REQUIRE ACCESSIBLE SANITARY FACILITIES FOR EMPLOYEES AS WELL AS PATRONS 76

    2. THE PRACTICAL RESULT, WHEN A RESTROOM EXIT DOES NOT MEET "TECHNICAL REQUIREMENTS" MAY BE TO TRAP A DISABLED PERSON IN THE REST ROOM 76

    3. MAXIMUM DOOR OPENING FORCE OF 5 POUNDS MUST BE PROVIDED 77

G. ANY VIOLATION OF THE ADA ALSO VIOLATES CIVIL CODE §§ 54(C) AND 54.1(D) BY SPECIFIC STATUTORY INCORPORATION, UNDER BOTH OF THESE STATUTES 77

    1. CALIFORNIA LAW EFFECTIVELY ADDS "DAMAGES" AS A REMEDY FOR ANY ADA VIOLATION WHICH DAMAGES OR DETERS A DISABLED PERSON 77

    2. THE ADA'S INCORPORATION INTO CALIFORNIA STATUTES DOES NOT CREATE FEDERAL JURISDICTION 78

    3. THE FEDERAL COURT RETAINS DISCRETIONARY JURISDICTION OVER PLAINTIFF'S STATE LAW CLAIMS 79

    4. SECTION 51 (f) CIVIL CODE ALSO INCORPORATES ANY VIOLATION OF THE ADA, ADDING MINIMUM DAMAGES PER VIOLATION REMEDY 79

H. REBUTTING DEFENSES ASSERTED BY BUILDING OWNERS AND OPERATORS 79

1. CALIFORNIA STANDARDS FOR ENFORCING DISABLED ACCESS REQUIREMENTS BY PRIVATE LAWSUIT DO NOT ALLOW "EXCEPTIONS" TO PROVIDING DISABLED ACCESS UNLESS EQUIVALENT FACILITATION IS PROVIDED 79

2. NON-ENFORCEMENT OF THE LAW BY BUILDING DEPARTMENTS IS NOT A VALID DEFENSE 81
   a. ENFORCEMENT BY PRIVATE LAWSUIT OF DISABLED ACCESS REQUIREMENTS IS APPROPRIATE WHEN BUILDING DEPARTMENTS HAVE ISSUED PERMITS WITHOUT ENFORCING STATUTORY ACCESS REQUIREMENTS 81

   b. ENFORCEMENT OF DISABLED ACCESS REQUIREMENTS IS NOT THE EXCLUSIVE DOMAIN OF THE BUILDING DEPARTMENT 82

   c. FAILURE TO COMPLY WITH DISABLED ACCESS STATUTES IS NOT EXCUSED BY "APPROVAL" BY THE BUILDING DEPARTMENT; NEITHER THE BUILDING DEPARTMENT, THE STATE NOR PRIVATE DISABLED PERSONS ARE "ESTOPPED" FROM ENFORCING THE LAW 83

   d. THERE IS NO CALIFORNIA EVIDENCE CODE § 664 "PRESUMPTION" THAT THE ACCESS LAW WAS PROPERLY ENFORCED BY THE BUILDING DEPARTMENT, ESPECIALLY WHEN ANY VARIANCE IS GIVEN WITHOUT PROVIDING "EQUIVALENT FACILITATION AND PROTECTION" FOR THE DISABLED 85

   e. THE UNIFORM BUILDING CODE PROVIDES THAT ISSUANCE OF A PERMIT, APPROVAL OF PLANS, OR SUBSEQUENT APPROVAL AS THE RESULT OF AN INSPECTION, DO NOT CONSTITUTE APPROVALS FOR VIOLATION OF ANY ORDINANCE 86

   f. DISABLED PERSONS' RIGHTS CAN'T BE INVALIDATED BY A BUILDING OFFICIAL'S MISTAKE 86

3. BUILDING OFFICIALS' PRIOR FAILURE TO REQUIRE ACCESS UPGRADES SHOULD NOT LEAVE A BUILDING IN LESS THAN A LEGALLY ACCESSIBLE CONDITION 87
   a. DEFENDANTS CANNOT PROPERLY OBTAIN A HARDSHIP EXCEPTION WITHOUT COMPLYING WITH § 422'S REQUIREMENTS 87

   b. A BUILDING OFFICIAL MAY NOT GIVE A "RETROACTIVE" HARDSHIP EXCEPTION WITH-OUT COMPLYING WITH § 422(c) OF TITLE 24 88

   c. CASE LAW HAS REJECTED RELIANCE ON BUILDING DEPARTMENT PERMITS WHICH IMPROPERLY ALLOWED ALTERATIONS WITHOUT PROVISION OF ACCESS 88

      d.   ANY LOCAL REGULATIONS WHICH CONFLICT WITH STATE BUILDING CODE REQUIREMENTS ARE INVALID AS PRE-EMPTED 89

4. THE COURTS, NOT THE LOCAL BUILDING DEPARTMENT, ARE THE FINAL AUTHORITY FOR ENFORCEMENT OF DISABLED ACCESS UNDER CALIFORNIA AND FEDERAL LAW 90

5. SUCCESSOR OWNER LIABILITY: SUCCEEDING OWNERS AND OPERATORS ARE LIABLE FOR ALTERATIONS BY PRIOR OWNERS WHICH TRIGGERED ACCESS 90
   a. LACK OF ACCESS IS A PUBLIC <u>NUISANCE</u> WHICH "RUNS WITH THE PROPERTY"; RESPONSIBILITY PASSES TO ANY SUCCESSIVE OWNER .. 90
   b. TWO ORDERS BY NORTHERN DISTRICT CHIEF JUDGE VAUGHN WALKER ESTABLISHED LIABILITY OF A SUCCESSOR OWNER 92
   c. ALTERATIONS BY ANY PREVIOUS OWNER AFTER JULY 1, 1970 TRIGGERED A HEALTH & SAFETY CODE ACCESS REQUIREMENT WHICH PASSES WITH OWNERSHIP 93
   d. ANALOGIES FROM TOXIC WASTE CASES SUPPORT A CONTINUING DUTY TO PROVIDE ACCESS 94
   e. BOTH LANDLORD AND TENANT ARE LIABLE TO THE DISABLED PLAINTIFF, ALTHOUGH THEY MAY ARRANGE INDEMNITY THROUGH LEASE AGREEMENTS 95

6. HARDSHIP, ETC. "EXCEPTIONS" ARE ONLY VALID WHEN THEY MEET STATUTORY REQUIREMENTS, PROVIDE EQUIVALENT FACILITATION, AND PROVIDE WRITTEN FINDINGS PER TITLE 24 CRITERIA 96
   a. "HARDSHIP" "EXCEPTIONS" MUST MEET THE REQUIREMENTS OF HEALTH & SAFETY CODE § 19957 AND § 422(c) OF TITLE 24 REGULATIONS 96
   b. "ABUSE OF DISCRETION" TO GRANT PERMIT WITHOUT COMPLIANCE 97
   c. THE POLICY OF THE LAW IS TO BROADLY CONSTRUE REQUIREMENTS FOR DISABLED ACCESS 98
   d. NO HARDSHIP EXCEPTION WITHOUT EQUIVALENT FACILITATION 98
   e. A COURT CANNOT "PRESUME" THAT BUILDING INSPECTORS GRANTED HARDSHIP EXCEPTIONS, BECAUSE TITLE 24 REGULATIONS REQUIRE WRITTEN AND RECORDED FINDINGS OF UNREASONABLE HARDSHIP 99
   f. THE "TWENTY PERCENT RULE," ORIGINATED IN THE APRIL 1994 TITLE 24 REGULATIONS, REQUIRES THAT A SUM EQUAL TO TWENTY

PERCENT OF <u>TOTAL</u> CONSTRUCTION COSTS IS THE <u>MINIMUM</u> TO BE SPENT ON ACCESS FEATURES, AND <u>ONLY</u> WHEN A "HARDSHIP" IS ESTABLISHED 100

  g. NO "RETROACTIVE" HARDSHIP EXCEPTION IS AVAILABLE YEARS AFTER ALTERATIONS HAVE TRIGGERED ACCESS REQUIREMENTS ... 101

  h. THERE IS NO SPECIAL "EXCEPTION" FOR "KITCHEN" ALTERATIONS .. 103

   (1) ALTERATIONS OF EITHER OF TWO LEVELS OF A GIVEN FLOOR REQUIRES THAT THEY BE JOINED BY A RAMP OR LIFT 103

   (2) ALTERATIONS TO A KITCHEN (A "FOOD PREPARATION AREA") SPECIFICALLY TRIGGER ACCESS PER §611(d) 6 OF TITLE 24 (1984 CODE) 104

   (3) KITCHEN FACILITIES ARE NOT EXCEPTED FROM ACCESS REQUIREMENTS; ALTERATIONS IN THE KITCHEN AREA TRIGGER AN ACCESSIBLE PATH OF TRAVEL FROM THE SIDEWALK THROUGH THE FRONT DOOR.. 104

 7. IN OPPOSING EFFORTS TO LIMIT ACCESS, PLAINTIFF SHOULD NOTE THAT PUBLIC POLICY IN CALIFORNIA CALLS FOR A BROAD INTERPRETATION OF PROTECTIONS FOR DISABLED PERSONS.................. 105

  a. STATUTES AND DECLARATIONS OF POLICY: IN INTERPRETING ACCESS ISSUES, THE COURT SHOULD APPLY THE STRONG PUBLIC POLICY TO MOST FULLY PROTECT THE NEEDS OF PERSONS WITH DISABILITIES 105

  b. THE POLICY OF THE LAW IS TO BROADLY CONSTRUE REQUIREMENTS FOR DISABLED ACCESS 107

  c. CALIFORNIA STATUTES, CASE LAW, AND BUILDING REGULATIONS FOCUS ON MAXIMIZING ACCESS FOR DISABLED PERSONS 107

  d. DISABILITY ACCESS LAWS SHOULD BE INTERPRETED SO AS TO "MAXIMIZE INCENTIVES FOR COMPLIANCE" 108

 8. NO EXCEPTION FOR SECOND FLOOR ACCESS UNLESS SPECIFIC STATUTORY CRITERIA MET... 109

 9. A BUSINESS' <u>POLICY</u> MAY VIOLATE CIVIL CODE § 54.1 EVEN IF THERE ARE NO ILLEGAL ARCHITECTURAL BARRIERS 110

I. INJUNCTIVE RELIEF IS REQUIRED UNDER CALIFORNIA LAW FOR VIOLATIONS OF "FULL AND EQUAL" ACCESS.. 111

 1. AN ORDER FOR INJUNCTIVE RELIEF IS REQUIRED UNDER CALIFORNIA LAW... 111

2. INJUNCTIVE RELIEF MAY BECOME "MOOT" WHEN A DEFENDANT SUPPLIES ACCESS AFTER A COMPLAINT IS FILED 112
   a. THE ISSUES OF INJUNCTIVE RELIEF MAY BECOME "MOOT" FOR INJUNCTIVE RELIEF PURPOSES WHEN DEFENDANTS FINALLY PROVIDE "ACCESS" DURING LITIGATION; IF SO, A PLAINTIFF MAY BECOME A PREVAILING PARTY UNDER CALIFORNIA LAW STANDARDS AND BECOME ENTITLED TO CIVIL RIGHTS ATTORNEY FEES AS A "CATALYST," BUT ONLY IF THE PLAINTIFF MADE A <u>PRE-LITIGATION</u> OFFER TO SETTLE 112

   b. SHOWING A NEED FOR AN ORDER THAT DEFENDANTS "MAINTAIN" ACCESSIBLE FEATURES MAY AVOID A FINDING OF "MOOTNESS" 113

   c. IN <u>HANKINS v. EL TORITO</u>, THE COURT FOUND THAT ACCESS WAS PROVIDED BECAUSE OF PLAINTIFF'S LETTERS (BUT CAVEAT <u>GRAHAM</u> AS TO "CATALYST" THEORY LIMITATIONS) 114

3. WHEN LIFTS ARE INSTALLED, THEY SHOULD USUALLY BE INDEPENDENTLY OPERABLE BY DISABLED PERSONS 115
   a. THE "LOCKED LIFT" ISSUE: THE <u>HANKINS</u> APPELLATE DECISION FAILED TO RESOLVE WHETHER DEFENDANTS MUST UNLOCK THE LIFT 115

   b. A RAMP IS PREFERABLE TO A LIFT IN MOST SITUATIONS 116

   c. UNDER SOME CIRCUMSTANCES THE "INDEPENDENT OPERATION" REQUIREMENT MAY BE INAPPLICABLE AS A PRACTICAL MATTER; BUT A RAMP MAY BE A BETTER SOLUTION 116

4. SEPARATE ACCESSIBLE MEN'S AND WOMEN'S RESTROOMS MAY BE REQUIRED (UNLESS AN ACCESSIBLE UNISEX RESTROOM IS ALLOWED AS AN "EQUIVALENT FACILITATION" UNDER A "HARDSHIP" EXCEPTION) 117

5. PROVISION OF TWO SINGLE ACCOMMODATION UNISEX RESTROOMS, WITH ONLY ONE ACCESSIBLE, <u>MAY</u> WORK AS A PRACTICAL SOLUTION AS "READILY ACHIEVABLE" UNDER THE ADA OR UNDER CALIFORNIA LAW WHERE A "HARDSHIP" EXCEPTION IS GIVEN 119

6. SPECIAL STANDARDS OF ACCESSIBILITY FOR BUILDINGS WITH HISTORICAL SIGNIFICANCE 120

J. DAMAGES: PURSUANT TO CALIFORNIA CIVIL CODE §§51, 52, OR, ALTERNATIVELY, 54.1 AND 54.3, A DISABLED PERSON DENIED "FULL AND EQUAL ACCESS" IS ENTITLED TO DAMAGES FOR DENIAL OF CIVIL RIGHTS 120
   1. STATUTORY AND COMPENSATORY DAMAGES ARE AVAILABLE PER CIVIL CODE §§ 52 and 54.3 120

a. CIVIL CODE § 54.3 PROVIDES DAMAGES FOR VIOLATIONS OF CIVIL CODE §§ 54 or 54.1 120

b. STATUTORY <u>MINIMUM</u> DAMAGES ARE $1,000 PER CIVIL CODE §54.3 VIOLATION, BUT MORE MAY BE APPROPRIATE BASED ON THE FACTS 121

    (1) <u>DONALD V. CAFÉ ROYALE</u> (1990) 218 CAL.APP.3D 168 121

    (2) <u>BOTOSAN V. MCNALLY REALTY, ET AL.</u> (9TH CIRCUIT) (2000) 216 F.3D 827 122

    (3) <u>BOEMIO V. LOVE'S RESTAURANT</u> (S.D. CAL. 1997), 954 F.SUPP. 204 122

    (4) <u>HANKINS V. EL TORITO RESTAURANTS, INC.</u> (1998) 63 CAL.APP. 4TH 510 AWARDED SUBSTANTIALLY MORE DAMAGES THAN THE STATUTORY "MINIMUM" 122

    (5) <u>LONBERG V. CITY OF RIVERSIDE</u> (C.D.CAL.) 2007 WL2005177 ("LONGBERG II") AWARDED DAMAGES FOR EACH LACKING CURB CUT ENCOUNTERED 122

c. STATUTORY MINIMUM DAMAGES OF $4,000 PER CIVIL CODE § 51 VIOLATION, PER § 52(a) 123

d. AUTHORITIES <u>WERE</u> SPLIT ON WHETHER DISCRIMINATORY INTENT WAS REQUIRED FOR CIVIL CODE § 51 VIOLATION; THE CALIFORNIA SUPREME COURT IN <u>MUNSON v. DEL TACO</u> FINALLY HELD (7-0) THAT <u>NO "INTENT"</u> WAS REQUIRED TO BE PROVEN 125

    (1) <u>GUNTHER V. LIN</u> (NOW <u>OVERRULED</u>), A STATE COURT DCA OPINION, HAD HELD THAT A PLAINTIFF MUST PROVE DISCRIMINATORY INTENTION FOR A § 51 VIOLATION 125

    (2) IN <u>WILSON V. HARIA AND GOGRI CORP. DBA JACK IN THE BOX, ET AL.</u> (E.D.CAL.) JUDGE KARLTON REJECTED <u>GUNTHER</u> 125

    (3) IN <u>MUNSON</u> (2009) THE CALIFORNIA SUPREME COURT SETTLED THE ISSUE: NO "INTENT" IS NEEDED (7-0) 125

e. CIVIL CODE §§51, 52 AND 54.1, 54.3 ALLOW DAMAGES BASED ON DETERRENCE 126

f. EFFECTIVE JANUARY 1, 2009, CIVIL CODE SECTION 55.56 LIMITS RECOVERY OF DAMAGES TO PERSONS ACTUALLY ENCOUNTERING OR DETERRED BY A CODE VIOLATION, AND INCLUDES THOSE SUFFERING DIFFICULTY, DISCOMFORT OR EMBARRASSMENT AS A RESULT 127

      g. A "CONSTRUCTION RELATED ACCESSIBILITY CLAIM" IS NOW DEFINED BY CODE 129

2. DAMAGES COMPUTATION CASE PRECEDENTS 129
      a. <u>TALLARICO V. TRANS WORLD AIRLINES</u> 129

      b. <u>HANKINS V. EL TORITO RESTAURANTS</u> 130

      c. <u>H'S LORDSHIPS</u> 130

      d. THE <u>"PIERCE COLLEGE"</u> CASE 131

      e. <u>WILSON V. HARIA AND GOGRI CORP. (DBA JACK IN THE BOX)</u> HELD <u>EACH</u> VISIT <u>MAY BE</u> A COMPENSABLE VIOLATION 131

3. DAMAGES FOR DISCRIMINATORY POLICY, CIVIL CODE §§51 AND 54.1; <u>HANKINS V. EL TORITO</u>, (1998) 63 CAL.APP. 4TH 510 132
      a. DAMAGES TO MARK HANKINS FOR DISCRIMINATION AGAINST A DISABLED PERSON PER CIVIL CODE §§ 51 AND 54.1 132

      b. PUBLIC POLICY REQUIRES A BROAD INTERPRETATION OF THE UNRUH ACT (CIVIL CODE §§ 51 ET SEQ) 133

      c. A POLICY OF REFUSING USE OF AN AVAILABLE FIRST FLOOR EMPLOYEE'S RESTROOM TO DISABLED PERSONS UNABLE TO CLIMB STAIRS TO THE SECOND FLOOR PUBLIC RESTROOMS WAS HELD TO BE A DIRECT VIOLATION OF THE UNRUH ACT AND RESULTED IN SUBSTANTIAL DAMAGES 133

      d. DISABILITY DISCRIMINATION IS ANALOGOUS TO TO RACE OR SEX DISCRIMINATION AS TO THE DAMAGE CAUSED 135

      e. DAMAGES EXAMPLE: HANKINS' TESTIMONY REGARDING DEFENDANTS' DISCRIMINATORY TREATMENT AND HIS RESULTING ANGER, EMBARRASSMENT, AND PHYSICAL PAIN 135

      f. "FULL AND EQUAL ACCESS" IS REQUIRED 135

      g. DAMAGES STANDARD: THE COURT SHOULD AWARD GENERAL DAMAGES FOR A DEFENDANTS' DISCRIMINATORY TREATMENT AND FOR THE SPECIFIC PHYSICAL, MENTAL AND EMOTIONAL PAIN AND SUFFERING, ANGER AND HUMILIATION SUFFERED BY A DISABLED PLAINTIFF 136

      h. PUBLIC POLICY SUPPORTS LIABILITY AGAINST NON-COMPLYING BUSINESSES 138

4. TREBLE DAMAGES POTENTIAL 139
   a. PER CIVIL CODE §§ 52 AND 54.3 139

   b. WHILE PROVING WRONGFUL INTENT IS NOT NEEDED TO PROVE
      LIABILITY UNDER CIVIL CODE §§ 54 AND 54.1, EVIDENCE OF "BAD
      INTENT" MAY SHOW A BASIS FOR TREBLE DAMAGES OR EVEN
      PUNITIVE DAMAGES IN AN EXTREME CASE; BUT CAVEAT
      CALIFORNIA SUPREME COURT LIMITATIONS.. 140

5. ARE <u>DAILY</u> STATUTORY DAMAGES AVAILABLE? 141
   a. ARGUMENT FOR <u>DAILY</u> STATUTORY DAMAGES FOR CONTINUING
      AND KNOWING VIOLATION, PER CIVIL CODE §54.3 141

   b. A 90 DAY COMPLIANCE PERIOD IS SET BY CODE 142

   c. <u>BOTOSAN V. FITZHUGH</u> ALLOWED PLEADING DAILY DAMAGES 142

   d. DAILY DAMAGES ON A DETERRENCE BASIS 143

   e. CAVEAT USE OF DAILY DAMAGES CLAIM AS CONDEMNED BY 9TH
      CIRCUIT IN <u>MOLSKI v. EVERGREEN DYNASTY CORPORATION</u>,
      BASED ON IMPROPER "LITIGATION STRATEGY" 143

6. STATUTORY DAMAGES ON A "PER VISIT" BASIS 144

7. PUNITIVE DAMAGES - AVAILABILITY AND STANDARDS 143
   a. LAW: PLAINTIFF MAY BE ENTITLED TO PUNITIVE DAMAGES
      UNDER THE CRITERIA OF CIVIL CODE § 3294 WHERE OPPRESSION,
      FRAUD, MALICE OR CONSCIOUS DISREGARD FOR THE RIGHTS
      OF DISABLED PERSONS HAVE BEEN PROVEN IN ADDITION TO
      VIOLATIONS OF THE CIVIL RIGHTS ACTS 144

   b. PUNITIVE DAMAGES <u>MAY</u> BE AVAILABLE PURSUANT TO CIVIL CODE
      §3294 FOR ACTIONS WHICH WERE EITHER 1) MALICIOUS OR IN
      CONSCIOUS DISREGARD OF THE RIGHTS OF DISABLED PERSONS
      2) OPPRESSIVE, OR 3) FRAUDULENT 145

   c. APPELLATE CASES HAVE UPHELD AWARDING OF CIVIL CODE
      §3294 PUNITIVE DAMAGES IN CASES WHERE STATUTORY
      COMPENSATORY DAMAGES WERE AWARDED FOR SEXUAL
      DISCRIMINATION, RACIAL DISCRIMINATION, AND AGE
      DISCRIMINATION 148

   d. USE OF "90 DAY" COMPLIANCE PROVISION OF GOVERNMENT
      CODE § 4452 SHOWING TIME IS OF THE ESSENCE 149

   e. IN <u>TOM FISHER v. MILLENNIUM BANK</u> HON. SAUNDRA ARMSTRONG
      OF THE NORTHERN DISTRICT COURT UPHELD A DISABLED
      PLAINTIFF'S RIGHT TO SEEK CIVIL CODE §3294 PUNITIVE DAMAGES

		FOR CONSCIOUS DISREGARD; BUT SEVERAL YEARS LATER THIS COURT HELD PLAINTIFF <u>MAY</u> BE LIMITED TO CIVIL CODE § 54.3 TREBLE DAMAGES 150
	f.	THE AMOUNT OF PUNITIVE DAMAGES SHOULD BE SET TO DETER FRAUDULENT, OPPRESSIVE, OR MALICIOUS CONDUCT, AND SET AN EXAMPLE FOR OTHERS 151
	g.	PLAINTIFF'S ATTORNEYS SHOULD CONSIDER THE POLICIES BEING ENFORCED IN DETERMINING <u>WHETHER</u> TO PLEAD AND SEEK PUNITIVE DAMAGES 151
	h.	IN <u>STATE FARM v. CAMPBELL</u> AND <u>EXXON</u> THE U.S. SUPREME COURT HAS PLACED LIMITS ON PUNITIVE DAMAGES 152

8. REBUTTING CERTAIN DAMAGE DEFENSES 153
   a. "PLAINTIFF WAS <u>ABLE</u> TO GET IN." PLAINTIFF WAS DENIED "FULL AND EQUAL ACCESS" PER CIVIL CODE § 54.1 EVEN THOUGH HE WAS "ABLE" TO GET IN TO THE PUBLIC FACILITY; NEW CIVIL CODE SECTION 55.56 CLARIFIES THIS 153

   b. IT IS NOT A "DEFENSE" THAT PLAINTIFF HAS PREVIOUSLY SUED OWNERS OF OTHER FACILITIES FOR ACCESS 155

   c. THE <u>MOLSKI</u> 9TH CIRCUIT OPINION CRITICIZED ABUSES BUT MADE CLEAR THAT "SERIAL" LAWSUITS MAY APPROPRIATELY BE USED TO OBTAIN ADA ACCESS 156

   d. THE NUMBER OF PLAINTIFF'S PRIOR SUCCESSFUL LAWSUITS SHOULD NOT BE USED TO QUESTION A DISABLED PERSON'S "CREDIBILITY" OR "STANDING" TO SUE 158

   e. PLAINTIFF SHOULD RESIST DISCOVERY OF PAST SETTLEMENTS AS IRRELEVANT; OR, AT WORST, COULD STIPULATE TO MINIMUM STATUTORY DAMAGES 160

9. PROTECTIONS FOR DISABLED PERSONS ASSISTED BY SERVICE ANIMALS 161
   a. MULTIPLE FEDERAL AND CALIFORNIA STATUTES AND REGULATIONS PROHIBIT DISCRIMINATION AGAINST DISABLED PERSONS WITH SERVICE ANIMALS 161

   b. CALIFORNIA PENAL CODE § 365.5(b) MAKES IT A CRIME TO REFUSE SERVICE TO A DISABLED PERSON AND HIS/HER SERVICE ANIMAL ... 161

   c. CIVIL CODE §§ 54.1 AND 54.2(a) PROTECT THE RIGHTS OF DISABLED PERSONS TO BE ACCOMPANIED BY A SERVICE DOG 162

- d. THE ADA, 28 C.F.R. 36.302, AND DOJ REGULATION SECTION 35.136 PROHIBIT EXCLUSION OF SERVICE ANIMALS 162
- e. EXAMPLES OF LITIGATION PROTECTING THE USE OF SERVICE DOGS 164
- f. SAMPLE COMPLAINT: SEE APPENDIX, § IX-G 164

10. TWO YEAR STATUTE OF LIMITATIONS 165

11. POINT OF SALE MACHINE MAY VIOLATE STATUTORY PROTECTIONS FOR DISABLED USABILITY 166

K. CALIFORNIA'S STATUTORY ATTORNEY FEES 166
 1. STATUTES OFFERING ATTORNEY FEES 166
    - a. FEDERAL LAW FEES, PER ADA § 505, TO "PREVAILING PARTY," WITH NO REQUIREMENT FOR ANY "PRE-LITIGATION DEMAND" 166
    - b. STATE LAW FEES PER CIVIL CODE §§ 52, 54.3 AND 55; CODE OF CIVIL PROCEDURE § 1021.5; HEALTH & SAFETY CODE § 19953 167
    - c. CALIFORNIA PUBLIC POLICY PROVIDES FOR AN AWARD OF ATTORNEY'S FEES UNDER THE DPA AND UNDER CODE OF CIVIL PROCEDURE § 1021.5 168
    - d. "ADA" PLAINTIFFS ARE CARRYING OUT IMPORTANT PUBLIC POLICIES AS "PRIVATE ATTORNEY GENERALS" 169
    - e. PLAINTIFFS ARE ALSO ENFORCING IMPORTANT PUBLIC POLICY UNDER CALIFORNIA LAW 169
    - f. PER MORENO, ATTORNEY FEES MUST BE SET AT DISTRICT'S MARKET RATE FOR ATTORNEYS WITH SIMILAR QUALIFICATIONS ... 169

 2. CALIFORNIA "CATALYST" FEES SURVIVE, BUT ONLY WHEN PRE-LITIGATION OFFER TO SETTLE WAS PREVIOUSLY MADE BY PLAINTIFF 170
    - a. GRAHAM V. DAIMLERCHRYSLER ALLOWED LIMITED "CATALYST" THEORY 170
    - b. NO PRELITIGATION NOTICE OR PRELITIGATION SETTLEMENT EFFORTS ARE RELEVANT UNLESS PLAINTIFF SEEKS FEES ON A "CATALYST" BASIS 172
    - c. WRITTEN SETTLEMENT OFFERS MAY BE RELEVANT PER CIVIL CODE SECTION 55.55 [SEE § I-L, INFRA] 173

 3. RELEVANT AUTHORITY ON FEE ISSUES 173
    - a. PUBLIC POLICY REQUIRES A FEE AWARD INCLUDING COMPENSATION FOR ALL HOURS REASONABLY INCURRED,

        ESPECIALLY WHEN PLAINTIFF HAS OBTAINED "EXCELLENT RESULTS" 173

    b. THE FEE AWARD MUST BE LARGE ENOUGH TO ENTICE COMPETENT COUNSEL TO UNDERTAKE DIFFICULT PUBLIC INTEREST CASES 174

    c. UNDER CALIFORNIA LAW A MULTIPLIER "ENHANCEMENT" OF THE LODESTAR MAY BE EARNED FOR THE "RISK" OF HANDLING A CIVIL RIGHTS CASE ON A CONTINGENT FEE BASIS 175

        (1) KETCHUM V. MOSES SET THE STANDARD 175

        (2) SOME EXAMPLES OF REASONS FOR "RISK" MULTIPLIER AWARD . 177

    d. WHERE ATTORNEY FEES HAVE BEEN DELAYED, THE COURT MAY AWARD FEES AT HIGHER, CURRENT RATES 178

    e. DEFENDANTS' ATTORNEYS' HOURS SPENT ARE NOT A PROPER CRITERIA FOR MEASURING THE REASONABLENESS OF PLAINTIFF'S ATTORNEYS' HOURS 179

    f. PLAINTIFF'S ATTORNEY IS ENTITLED TO COMPENSATION FOR ALL HOURS REASONABLY SPENT, AND MAY ESTABLISH THOSE HOURS BY VERIFIED TIME STATEMENTS 180

4. THE AMOUNT OF DAMAGES RECOVERED CANNOT SERVE AS A CAP OR LIMITATION ON THE AMOUNT OF FEES AWARDED, ESPECIALLY IN SITUATIONS IN WHICH DEFENDANTS' RESISTANCE DRIVES UP THE AMOUNT OF A PLAINTIFF'S FEES 180
    a. NO CAP OR LIMITATION ON AMOUNT OF FEES 180

    b. DEFENDANTS' CONDUCT DRIVING UP FEES 181

    c. PLAINTIFF IS ENTITLED TO FEES FOR ENFORCING COMPLIANCE WITH AN INJUNCTION OR CONSENT DECREE 183

    d. NO EFFORTS ARE "DUPLICATIVE" WHEN THEY ARE REASONABLY MADE TOWARD A COMMON GOAL OR TASK 185

    e. PLAINTIFF'S ATTORNEYS ARE ENTITLED TO SPEND THE TIME REASONABLY NECESSARY TO AFFORD PLAINTIFF "QUALITY REPRESENTATION" 186

    f. DEFENDANTS' CHALLENGES TO PLAINTIFF'S STAFFING DECISIONS AND "BILLING JUDGMENT" WERE REJECTED BY JUDGE PATEL IN CHABNER V. UNITED OF OMAHA LIFE INS. CO., 1999 WL 33227443 (N.D.CAL. 1999) AND BLACKWELL V. FOLEY, *supra*, AND BY JUDGE THELTON HENDERSON IN CHAVEZ V. CHEVY'S, C01-4322 TEH (N.D.CAL. 2003) 187

5. IF DEFENDANT "MOOTS" A FEDERAL COURT ADA ACTION BY FULL ACCESS COMPLIANCE OR BY CLOSING THE SUBJECT FACILITY, FORCING PLAINTIFF TO REFILE THE ACTION IN STATE COURT TO OBTAIN DAMAGES AND FEES, PLAINTIFF'S ATTORNEY' FEES, LITIGATION EXPENSES, AND COSTS INCURRED IN THE U.S. DISTRICT COURT ACTION SHOULD BE RECOVERABLE IN THE STATE COURT ACTION 187

6. PLAINTIFF'S ATTORNEY FEES SHOULD BE SET AT "MARKET" RATES, AND AT CURRENT RATES TO OFFSET DELAY IN PAYMENT 189

7. NO FEES ARE AWARDED TO "PREVAILING PARTY" DEFENDANTS AGAINST A "GOOD FAITH" CIVIL RIGHTS PLAINTIFF, EVEN UNDER CALIFORNIA LAW: HUBBARD V. SOBRECK, LLC (9th CIRCUIT, 2009) 554 F.3d 742 [BUT CAVEAT JANKEY V. LEE, *INFRA*, AT SECTION I-K-10] 190

8. IN THE 2011 TURNER DECISION, A CALIFORNIA APPELLATE COURT HELD THAT NO ATTORNEY FEES COULD BE AWARDED TO A PREVAILING DEFENDANT UNDER CIVIL CODE SECTION 55 BECAUSE THIS WOULD CONFLICT WITH PUBLIC POLICY SET BY THE LEGISLATURE IN SECTIONS 52 AND 54.3, WHEN HOURS WORKED WERE INTERTWINED 192

9. [SEE ALSO SECTION IV-J, *INFRA* RE U.S. SUPREME COURT'S FOX V. VICE (2011) DECISION] 193

10. JANKEY V. LEE, 55 Cal. 4th 1038 (CAL. DEC. 17, 2012) - NEW DECISION UPHOLDING "REVERSE" ATTORNEY FEES AND POSSIBLY CHILLING DISABLED RIGHTS LITIGATION 193

11. THE SAME PUBLIC POLICIES PROTECTED BY THE CHRISTIANBURG DOCTRINE SHOULD APPLY TO CALIFORNIA LAW CIVIL RIGHTS ACTIONS 195

12. "CAVEAT" - POSSIBLE TACTIC TO AVOID NEED TO PLEAD CIVIL CODE § 55, IN LIGHT OF JANKEY V. LEE 195

L. EFFECT OF SB 1608 AND NEW CALIFORNIA CIVIL CODE § 55.55: WRITTEN SETTLEMENT OFFERS NOW RELEVANT 196

M. STATUTE OF LIMITATIONS: IN CALIFORNIA SOL IS NOW TWO YEARS FROM THE DATE WHEN PLAINTIFF SUFFERED INJURY, UNLESS A GOVERNMENT TORT CLAIM IS INVOLVED 197
   1. TWO YEAR STATUTE OF LIMITATIONS FROM DENIAL OF ACCESS/INJURY .. 197

   2. IF A GOVERNMENT ENTITY MAY BE INVOLVED, PLAINTIFF MUST MEET SIX MONTH CALIFORNIA DEADLINE FOR FILING A GOVERNMENT CLAIM TO OBTAIN STATE LAW DAMAGES, AND MUST FILE LAWSUIT WITHIN SIX MONTHS OF CLAIM DENIAL 197

3. NO STATE LAW GOVERNMENT CLAIM IS REQUIRED TO OBTAIN DAMAGES DIRECTLY UNDER ADA TITLE II, BUT PROBABLY IS REQUIRED IF PLAINTIFF SEEKS TO USE AN INCORPORATED "ADA" VIOLATION AS THE BASIS FOR VIOLATION OF SECTION 51(f), 54(c), OR 54.1(d) CALIFORNIA CIVIL CODE AND SEEKS STATE LAW DAMAGES 198

N. SB 1186 (2012) MADE MAJOR CHANGES IN CALIFORNIA DISABILITY RIGHTS LAWS 198
   1. CAVEAT: NEW LEGISLATION EFFECTIVE IMMEDIATELY (AT LEAST FOR STATE COURT ACTIONS) 198

   2. LEGISLATIVE COUNSEL'S DIGEST OF SB 1186 199

   3. COMMENTARY ON PASSAGE OF SB 1186 203

II. GOVERNMENT ENTITIES - OBTAINING ACCESS TO PUBLIC BUILDINGS UNDER CALIFORNIA LAW AND ADA TITLE II 204
  A. CALIFORNIA LAW ACCESS REQUIREMENTS APPLY TO ALL GOVERNMENTAL CONSTRUCTION AND ALTERATIONS SINCE 1968 204
    1. GOVERNMENT CODE § 4450ff ET SEQ APPLY TO ALL GOVERNMENTAL CONSTRUCTION AND ALTERATION, STRUCTURED REPAIRS AND ADDITIONS TO EXISTING BUILDINGS SINCE NOVEMBER 1968. 204

    2. PUBLIC POLICY REQUIRES ACCESS, INCLUDING AN ACCESSIBLE PATH OF TRAVEL TO THE AREA OF ALTERATION, WHENEVER ALTERATIONS ARE MADE 205

    3. ALL CONSTRUCTION AND ALTERATIONS TRIGGER ACCESS REQUIREMENTS 207

    4. FOR ALTERATIONS AFTER JULY 1, 1982, "PATH OF TRAVEL" IS EXPLICITLY DEFINED IN THE 1982 STATE ARCHITECT'S REGULATIONS ("TITLE 24") AND THE 1984 STATE ARCHITECT'S INTERPRETIVE MANUAL 207

    5. FROM 1970 UNTIL THE 1982 ADOPTION OF THE STATE ARCHITECT'S TITLE 24 REGULATIONS, GOVERNMENT CODE § 4450 ET SEQ., HEALTH & SAFETY CODE §19959 AND THE "ASA" REGULATIONS ALL REQUIRED AN ACCESSIBLE PATH OF TRAVEL TO ANY AREA OF ALTERATION, IN ORDER FOR THAT AREA TO BE MADE "ACCESSIBLE"... 209

    6. CHE FOUND THE 1981 TITLE 24 REGULATIONS "CLARIFIED" THE PRIOR "ASA" REGULATIONS IN SPECIFYING PATH OF TRAVEL REQUIREMENTS 211

    7. A 1979 CALIFORNIA LEGISLATIVE COUNSEL'S OPINION RECOGNIZED THAT AN ACCESSIBLE PATH OF TRAVEL TO AN AREA WAS IMPLICITLY REQUIRED IN ORDER FOR THIS AREA TO BE CONSIDERED "ACCESSIBLE" UNDER THE ASA STANDARDS AND UNDER THE STATE ARCHITECT'S

       (TITLE 24) REGULATIONS THEN BEING FORMULATED 213

    8. GOVERNMENT CODE § 11135, ESTABLISHED IN 1977, ALSO REQUIRES "FULL AND EQUAL ACCESS" 214

    9. CAVEAT: SIX MONTH GOVERNMENT CLAIM REQUIRED FOR DAMAGES UNDER CALIFORNIA LAW 215

B. SECTION 504 OF THE REHABILITATION ACT OF 1973, THE FEDERAL PREDECESSOR TO THE ADA, REQUIRED REMOVAL OF BARRIERS AND PROVISION OF ACCESS FOR ALL RECIPIENTS OF FEDERAL FINANCIAL ASSISTANCE 215

C. ADA TITLE II COVERS ALL SERVICES, PROGRAMS AND ACTIVITIES OF STATE AND LOCAL GOVERNMENT AGENCIES 215
    1. TITLE II COVERS BOTH BUILDINGS AND SERVICES (BUT THIS BOOK WILL FOCUS ON BUILDINGS, AND SERVICES PROVIDED BY ACCESSIBLE BUILDINGS) 215

    2. INJUNCTIVE RELIEF IS AVAILABLE TO OBTAIN ACCESSIBLE COURTHOUSES, VETERANS BUILDINGS, LIBRARIES, PUBLIC COLLEGES AND UNIVERSITIES, AND ALL OTHER GOVERNMENTAL BUILDINGS, AND TO "MAINTAIN" ACCESSIBLE FEATURES 219

    3. AFFIRMATIVE STEPS BY THE GOVERNMENT ENTITY ARE REQUIRED TO AVOID DISCRIMINATION 221

    4. TRANSPORTATION SERVICES ARE ALSO COVERED BY TITLE II, BUT WILL NOT BE COVERED IN THIS BOOK 224

    5. ANY VIOLATION OF THE ADA, INCLUDING TITLE II, IS INCORPORATED AS A VIOLATION OF CALIFORNIA LAW, PER. CIVIL CODE §§ 51(f) 54(c), AND 54.1(d) 224

    6. NO CALIFORNIA LAW "GOVERNMENT CLAIM" IS NEEDED TO BRING A TITLE II ACTION, BUT TITLE II DAMAGES ARE LIMITED TO "INTENTIONAL" DISCRIMINATION WHEREAS SECTION 54.3 CIVIL CODE DAMAGES FOR VIOLATIONS OF SECTIONS 54 AND 54.1 PROBABLY ARE NOT SO LIMITED 224

    7. DAMAGES: ADA TITLE II REQUIRES "INTENTIONAL" DISCRIMINATION FOR RECOVERY OF DAMAGES 224
       a. PROOF OF CONDUCT IN CONSCIOUS DISREGARD OR "DELIBERATE INDIFFERENCE" TO DISABILITY RIGHTS 224

       b. LIABILITY FOR INJUNCTIVE RELIEF UNDER TITLE II DOES NOT REQUIRE "INTENTIONAL" DISCRIMINATION WHERE A GOVERNMENT POLICY HAS A DISPARATE IMPACT ON DISABLED PERSONS ... 226

  c. NO PUNITIVE DAMAGES AGAINST A GOVERNMENT AGENCY (GOV. CODE SECTION 818) 226

 8. PUBLIC ENTITIES COVERED BY TITLE II: COURTHOUSES, COLLEGES, JAILS, PUBLIC PARKING LOTS AND PUBLIC PROPERTY RENTED TO PRIVATE TITLE III ENTITIES 226
  a. COURTHOUSE CASES AND TENNESSEE V. LANE 226

  b. COLLEGES 227

  c. PUBLIC PROPERTY RENTED TO PRIVATE PUBLIC ACCOMMODATIONS .. 227

   (1) BARNES & NOBLE AT JACK LONDON SQUARE 228

   (2) CITY LIABLE AS OWNER, OPERATOR, LESSOR, OR LESSEE 228

  d. JAILS 228

 9. TITLE II REGULATIONS ESTABLISH THAT DEFENDANT PUBLIC ENTITIES HAVE THE BURDEN OF PROVING THE EXISTENCE OF ANY AFFIRMATIVE DEFENSES 230

 10. ATTORNEYS FEES, LITIGATION EXPENSES AND COSTS ARE AVAILABLE PER ADA § 505 231

III. ADA TITLE III STANDARDS AND INTERRELATION WITH CALIFORNIA LAW 232
 A. ADA "ACCESS" REQUIREMENTS <u>ADD</u> TO EXISTING LIABILITY BASES UNDER CALIFORNIA LAW 232
  1. BOTH NEW CONSTRUCTION AND ALTERATION AND "READILY ACHIEVABLE" ACCESS REQUIREMENTS UNDER THE ADA PROVIDE SEPARATE BASES FOR INJUNCTIVE RELIEF AND ATTORNEY FEES 232

  2. EXPLANATION OF ADA, ITS PURPOSES, ITS SUPREMACY OVER ANY STATE REQUIREMENTS; NO PREEMPTION OF STATE LAW REMEDIES 234

  3. ENFORCEMENT OF TITLE III IS PRIMARILY BY PRIVATE LAWSUITS; ADA PLAINTIFFS ACT AS PRIVATE ATTORNEY GENERALS 235
   a. AS ADA COMPROMISE, PRIMARY ENFORCEMENT IS BY PRIVATE LAWSUITS 235

   b. PUBLIC POLICY TO ENCOURAGE PRIVATE ATTORNEY GENERAL ACTIONS 236

  4. ANY VIOLATION OF THE ADA ALSO VIOLATES CIVIL CODE §§ 51(f), 54(c) AND 54.1 (d) AND EARNS DAMAGES PER §§ 52 AND 54.3 237

  5. CAVEAT REMOVAL TO FEDERAL COURT: PLEADING AN ADA VIOLATION IN STATE COURT COMPLAINT MAY RESULT IN REMOVAL TO FEDERAL COURT 238

        a. MAY BE TACTICAL CHOICE WITH MANY FACTORS TO CONSIDER. 239

        b. TIME LIMITS FOR REMOVAL IN ACCORDANCE WITH SECTIONS 1141, 1146 AND 1369. 240

    6. SUPPLEMENTAL JURISDICTION OVER STATE LAW CLAIMS; PLAINTIFF MUST RE-FILE IN STATE COURT WITHIN 30 DAYS OF ANY "DISCRETIONARY" DISMISSAL 240

B. "READILY ACHIEVABLE" BURDEN OF PROOF 241
    1. DEFENDANTS HAVE THE BURDEN OF PROOF TO SHOW "NOT READILY ACHIEVABLE"... 241
        a. BURDEN OF PRODUCTION AND BURDEN OF PROOF TO SHOW "NOT READILY ACHIEVABLE" ARE BOTH UPON DEFENDANTS IN THE 9TH CIRCUIT 241

        b. PRECEDENTIAL ANALOGOUS CIVIL RIGHTS CASE LAW SUPPORTS SHIFTING THE BURDEN OF PROOF TO DEFENDANTS 247

        c. <u>WILSON V. HARIA AND GOGRI CORP. DBA JACK IN THE BOX, ET AL.</u> (2007) HELD THAT THE BURDEN OF PROOF WAS UPON DEFENDANTS, AND THAT THEY WAIVED THIS DEFENSE BY NOT PLEADING "NOT READILY ACHIEVABLE" AS AN AFFIRMATIVE DEFENSE 248

        d. PLAINTIFF'S POSITION: DEFENDANTS HAVE THE BURDEN OF PROVING THAT EACH AND EVERY ACCESS FEATURE WAS NOT READILY ACHIEVABLE 248

        e. IS BURDEN ON DEFENDANT <u>BY STATUTE</u> TO "DEMONSTRATE" NOT READILY ACHIEVABLE? 249

    2. "READILY ACHIEVABLE" STATUTORY STANDARDS INCLUDE COMPARISON OF ACCESS COSTS WITH ALL RESOURCES, INCLUDING THOSE OF ANY PARENT COMPANY 250
        a. <u>PINNOCK</u> UPHELD THE ADA'S CONSTITUTIONALITY AND SET CERTAIN STANDARDS 250

        b. DISCOVERY MAY BE NEEDED TO COMPARE THE COSTS OF PROVIDING ACCESS AGAINST THE "OVERALL FINANCIAL RESOURCES" OF EACH DEFENDANT 252

        c. <u>CAVEAT</u> DEFENSES BASED ON "MOM AND POP" FINANCIAL FACTORS WHICH MAKE BARRIER REMOVAL MORE DIFFICULT 253

        d. <u>BOTOSAN V. MCNALLY</u> REALTY SET THE 9TH CIRCUIT STANDARD FOR THE "NOT READILY ACHIEVABLE" DEFENSE 253

        e. PARENT COMPANY'S OVERALL FINANCIAL RESOURCES ARE RELEVANT AND DISCOVERABLE 254

      f. ADAAG SECTION 4.1.7 (ADA ACCESSIBILITY GUIDELINES) SETS THE STANDARDS FOR EVALUATING "READILY ACHIEVABLE" 256

   3. EVEN IF BARRIER REMOVAL IS "NOT READILY ACHIEVABLE," A BUSINESS MAY BE LIABLE FOR FAILING TO MAKE FACILITIES AVAILABLE THROUGH "ALTERNATIVE METHODS" 256

   4. A BUSINESS'S POLICY MAY ALSO VIOLATE ADA TITLE III IN SETTING INSURANCE RATES OR IN NOT PROVIDING ACCURATE TRAVEL AGENCY INFORMATION 258

   5. EXAMPLES AND PRIORITIES IN DOJ REGULATIONS: 28 CFR § 36.304 "REMOVAL OF BARRIERS" 258

C. SECTION 503 PROHIBITS ACTIONS WHICH RETALIATE AGAINST OR PUNISH A PLAINTIFF OR HIS LEGAL REPRESENTATIVES FOR ENFORCING THE ADA 260
   1. SECTIONS 503 (a) AND (b) PROHIBIT BOTH RETALIATION AND HARASSMENT 260

   2. DAMAGES ARE AVAILABLE FOR EITHER HARASSMENT OR RETALIATION 262

   3. BURDEN OF PROOF STANDARD 263

   4. DOJ REGULATIONS PROTECT AGAINST RETALIATION 263

   5. DISCOVERY AIMED AT QUESTIONING PRIOR SUCCESSFUL ADA LAWSUITS BY A PLAINTIFF MAY ITSELF BE A VIOLATION OF SECTION 503 264

D. PUBLIC POLICY IS TO PROTECT THE RIGHTS OF DISABLED PERSONS TO ENFORCE THE ADA AND <u>ENCOURAGE</u> "PRIVATE ATTORNEY GENERAL" ACTIONS 264

E. "STANDING" TO BRING A TITLE III ADA ACTION FOR INJUNCTIVE RELIEF REQUIRES HAVING ENCOUNTERED AT LEAST ONE BARRIER TO ACCESS OR HAVING BEEN DETERRED FROM DOING SO, AND AN INTENT TO USE THE FACILITY AFTER ACCESS HAS BEEN SUPPLIED 265
   1. PROVING "STANDING" FOR A TITLE III ADA ACTION IN FEDERAL COURT: TITLE III, § 308(a) OF THE ADA SPECIFICALLY GRANTS PLAINTIFF <u>STANDING</u>, TO SEEK <u>INJUNCTIVE RELIEF</u> FOR <u>CONTINUING</u> ARCHITECTURAL BARRIERS WHICH DENY ACCESS TO PERSONS WITH DISABILITIES 265

   2. PUBLIC POLICY REQUIRES A BROAD INTERPRETATION OF "STANDING": AS A MATTER OF PUBLIC POLICY CONGRESS SPECIFICALLY WROTE INTO THE AMERICANS WITH DISABILITIES ACT OF 1990 A BROAD RIGHT TO "STANDING" FOR ANY DISABLED

PERSON WHO KNEW THAT HE WOULD BE DISADVANTAGED BY VISITING AN INACCESSIBLE PUBLIC FACILITY, AND TO ALLOW HIM TO BRING A LEGAL ACTION TO OBTAIN ADA COMPLIANT ACCESS WITHOUT GOING THROUGH THE "FUTILE ACT" OF ACTUALLY VISITING THE FACILITY 267

3. CONGRESSIONAL INTENT IS CLEAR IN SECTION 308(A)(1) OF THE ADA THAT STANDING TO SUE TO REQUIRE READILY ACHIEVABLE ACCESS TO A PUBLIC FACILITY IS GRANTED TO ANY DISABLED PERSON WITHOUT THE "FUTILE GESTURE" OF VISITING A FACILITY KNOWN TO BE INACCESSIBLE 268

4. PUBLIC POLICY SUPPORTS A BROAD VIEW OF CONSTITUTIONAL STANDARDS; PRIVATE ENFORCEMENT IS THE PRIMARY METHOD OF OBTAINING ADA COMPLIANCE 268

5. §36.501 OF THE ADAAG REGULATIONS ALSO SPECIFIES THAT STANDING WITHOUT A "FUTILE GESTURE" VISIT IS AVAILABLE FOR <u>ANY</u> VIOLATION OF TITLE III, NOT SIMPLY §303 CASES 269

6. TACTICS: THE STRONGER CASE MAY STILL REQUIRE A PERSONAL VISIT ATTEMPT TO ASSURE DAMAGES PER CIVIL CODE SECTION 55.56 272

7. <u>SKAFF V. MERIDIEN NORTH AMERICA BEVERLY HILLS, LLC</u> (9TH CIR. 2007) CLARIFIED FEDERAL "STANDING" STANDARDS REGARDING SEEKING INJUNCTIVE RELIEF AND STATUTORY PREVAILING PARTY ATTORNEY FEES 272

8. A BROAD STANDING HOLDING WAS ISSUED BY THE 9TH CIRCUIT IN <u>DORAN V. 7-ELEVEN, INC.</u> (2008) GIVING STANDING TO REQUIRE REMEDIATION OF ALL BARRIERS TO PERSONS WITH PLAINTIFF'S DISABILITIES 273

9. THE 9TH CIRCUIT REAFFIRMED <u>DORAN V. 7-ELEVEN</u>'S BROAD "STANDING" STANDARDS IN <u>WILSON V. KAYO OIL CO.</u> AND IN THE EN BANC <u>CHAPMAN</u> DECISION (2011) 275

10. A DISABLED PERSON HAS STANDING TO COMPLAIN ABOUT DENIAL OF "COMPANION SEATING" IN A THEATER OR SPORTS ARENA 276

F. THERE IS NO "EXHAUSTION OF ADMINISTRATIVE REMEDY" OR PRE-FILING "NOTICE" REQUIREMENT UNDER TITLE III OF THE ADA 276
1. IN <u>BOTOSAN V. MCNALLY REALTY</u> THE 9TH CIRCUIT HELD THERE WAS NO "NOTICE" REQUIREMENT 276

2. IN <u>SKAFF V. MERIDIEN NORTH AMERICA BEVERLY HILLS, LLC</u>, THE 9TH CIRCUIT HELD THERE IS NO PRE-SUIT NOTICE REQUIREMENT 276

3. DEFENDANT'S FAILURE TO PLEAD THE "NOTICE" ISSUE UNDER §2000a-3(c) MAY WAIVE THIS DEFENSE 277

4. PLAINTIFF <u>COULD</u> VOLUNTARILY PROVIDE WRITTEN NOTICE TO THE CALIFORNIA OR UNITED STATES ATTORNEY GENERAL'S OFFICES, OR LOCAL BUILDING OFFICIALS 278

5. THE CODE SECTION THAT DEFENDANTS <u>USED TO</u> RELY UPON, 42 USC § 2000a-3(c), IS <u>NOT</u> INCORPORATED INTO THE AMERICANS WITH DISABILITIES ACT OF 1990 (ADA) 278

6. SEVERAL "PRE-<u>BOTOSAN</u>" DISTRICT COURTS IN CALIFORNIA REJECTED ANY NOTICE REQUIREMENT IN WELL-REASONED OPINIONS 279

7. COURTS SHOULD GIVE CONSIDERABLE WEIGHT TO THE ADMINISTRATIVE DETERMINATION BY THE DEPARTMENT OF JUSTICE THAT THE NOTICE REQUIREMENTS OF §2000a-3(c) DO <u>NOT</u> APPLY TO TITLE III ACTIONS UNDER THE ADA 281

8. DEFENDANTS CANNOT SHOW ANY PREJUDICE FROM LACK OF PRIOR NOTICE TO AN APPROPRIATE LOCAL AUTHORITY 281

G. BOTH LANDLORD AND TENANT OF A BUSINESS PROPERTY REMAIN JOINTLY RESPONSIBLE TO A DISABLED PLAINTIFF REGARDLESS OF ANY INDEMNITY AGREEMENTS 282

H. LIABILITY OF LANDLORD AND TENANT FOR PLAINTIFF'S ATTORNEY FEES IS ALSO "JOINT AND SEVERAL" 283

I. SERVICE ANIMALS HAVE SPECIFIC ADA PROTECTIONS 284

J. THE FEDERAL COURT SHOULD MAINTAIN SUPPLEMENTAL JURISDICTION WHERE STATE LAW CLAIMS ARE BASED ON SAME FACTS AS THE ADA CLAIM 285

K. THEATER "LINE OF SIGHT" CASES: FEDERAL AND CALIFORNIA REQUIREMENTS 285

IV. ATTORNEY FEES UNDER THE ADA 288
A. PREVAILING PARTY STANDARD RE: ATTORNEY FEES, LITIGATION EXPENSES AND COSTS TO A PREVAILING PLAINTIFF 288
1. ADA ATTORNEYS FEES, LITIGATION EXPENSES AND COSTS MAY BE AWARDED PER SECTION 505 [42 USC 12205] 288

2. PREVAILING PARTY PLAINTIFF IS ENTITLED TO STATUTORY ATTORNEY FEES, WITHOUT ANY PRE-LITIGATION DEMAND, IF HE OBTAINED A COURT ENFORCEABLE SETTLEMENT AGREEMENT 288

B. GRAHAM V. DAIMLER-CHRYSLER PRESERVED "CATALYST" ATTORNEY FEES UNDER CALIFORNIA LAW ONLY UNDER NEW REQUIREMENT FOR A PRE-LITIGATION EFFORT TO SETTLE; NO PRE-LITIGATION EFFORT IS NEEDED WHEN PLAINTIFF IS THE PREVAILING PARTY 290

C. PUBLIC POLICY CALLS FOR ENCOURAGING TITLE III ADA LAWSUITS 291
   1. ADA TITLE III ENFORCEMENT IN CALIFORNIA BY PRIVATE LAWSUITS ... 291
   2. ENTITLEMENT TO REASONABLE ATTORNEY FEES EVEN WHEN DAMAGES AWARDED ARE MINIMAL 291
   3. ADA PLAINTIFFS ARE ENFORCING THE PUBLIC INTEREST, SEEKING TO VINDICATE A POLICY OF THE "HIGHEST PRIORITY" 292
   4. ADA § 503 PROTECTS BOTH DISABLED PERSONS AND THEIR REPRESENTATIVES AGAINST RETALIATION OR INTIMIDATION 293

D. ADA TITLE III PLAINTIFFS ARE ACTING AS "PRIVATE ATTORNEY GENERALS" IN THE PUBLIC INTEREST 294

E. "LAWYERS MUST EAT" - ENFORCEMENT OF CIVIL RIGHTS DEPENDS ON ADEQUATE ATTORNEY FEES AWARDS 296

F. FEES MUST BE SET AT MARKET RATES USING "MORALES" FACTORS: PLAINTIFF'S ATTORNEY FEES RATES MUST BE BASED ON THE ATTORNEYS' EDUCATION, EXPERIENCE AND LEGAL SKILLS 298

G. A COURT SHOULD NOT "SECOND GUESS" PLAINTIFF'S "STAFFING DECISIONS" 299

H. NO ATTORNEY FEES CAN BE AWARDED AGAINST A "GOOD FAITH" CIVIL RIGHTS PLAINTIFF (CHRISTIANSBURG RULE) [AT LEAST UNDER FEDERAL LAW] 300
   1. CHRISTIANSBURG RULE IS INCORPORATED INTO §505 OF THE ADA 300
   2. RULE ALSO APPLIES TO LITIGATION EXPENSES AND COSTS IN 9TH CIRCUIT (BROWN V. LUCKY STORES) 301
   3. THE DEPARTMENT OF JUSTICE SECTION-BY-SECTION ANALYSIS: TITLE III [28 C.F.R. PT. 36, APP. B, §36.505] CLARIFIES THAT "LITIGATION EXPENSES" INCLUDE EXPERT WITNESS FEES AND TRAVEL EXPENSES, AND THAT PLAINTIFFS ARE PROTECTED BY THE "CHRISTIANBURG" STANDARDS. 302
   4. A DEFENDANT'S DEMAND FOR ATTORNEY FEES AGAINST A

      DISABLED PLAINTIFF MAY CONSTITUTE A THREAT WHICH VIOLATES §503(b) OF THE ADA 302

5. THERE IS NO EXCEPTION TO THE CHRISTIANSBURG RULE SIMPLY BECAUSE ONE ADA PLAINTIFF HAS FILED MULTIPLE PREVIOUS LAWSUITS, SO LONG AS THE INSTANT LAWSUIT IS NOT "FRIVOLOUS" .. 304

6. IN MOLSKI V. EVERGREEN DYNASTY CORP. (9TH CIR. 2007), THE 9TH CIRCUIT SPECIFIED THAT EVEN "SERIAL PLAINTIFFS" MAY BE JUSTIFIED 306

7. IN HUBBARD V. SOBRECK 2009, THE 9th CIRCUIT EXTENDED THE CHRISTIANBURG PRINCIPLES TO DENY CALIFORNIA CIVIL CODE § 55 ATTORNEYS' FEES TO A PREVAILING DEFENDANT AGAINST A "GOOD FAITH" DISABLED PLAINTIFF [BUT CAVEAT JANKEY v. LEE, DECEMBER 17, 2012, WHERE CALIFORNIA SUPREME COURT "DISAGREED"] 307

I. IN 2011 HARRIS REITERATED THE CHRISTIANBURG PRINCIPLES, HOLDING NO FEES AGAINST PLAINTIFF EXCEPT FOR "FRIVOLOUS" CLAIMS, AND ONLY FOR WORK "ATTRIBUTABLE EXCLUSIVELY TO PLAINTIFF'S FRIVOLOUS CLAIMS" 307

J. IN FOX V. VICE THE UNITED STATES SUPREME COURT DETERMINED THAT A PREVAILING DEFENDANT COULD ONLY RECOVER FEES FOR COSTS DEFENDANT WOULD NOT HAVE INCURRED BUT FOR ANY FRIVOLOUS CLAIMS BY A CIVIL RIGHTS PLAINTIFF 308

K. LANDLORD AND TENANT MAY BE JOINTLY AND SEVERALLY LIABLE FOR ATTORNEY FEES 309

L. ATTORNEY LICENSED IN ANY STATE CAN PRACTICE IN FEDERAL COURTS OF OTHER STATES 310

V. PRACTICAL APPROACHES: NOTICE, COOPERATION AND SETTLEMENT 311
   A. INTRODUCTION: CONSIDER EARLY COMMUNICATION WITH DEFENDANTS .. 311

   B. PROMPTLY INFORM DEFENDANTS OF THE VALUE OF AN EARLY SETTLEMENT 312

   C. PROTECT THE PUBLIC INTEREST AS PRIME OBJECTIVE 312

   D. CONGRESS' ATTORNEY FEE PROVISIONS ARE A MESSAGE TO NON-COMPLYING BUSINESSES, AND SUPPORT THE PURPOSES OF THE ADA 312

   E. PLAINTIFF'S ATTORNEYS SHOULD CARRY OUT EARLY INVESTIGATION, RESEARCH AND PREPARATION SO THAT THEY ONLY FILE MERITORIOUS AND "GOOD FAITH" CASES 313

   F. "SEND ME A LETTER, THE SOONER THE BETTER" - WHILE NO ADVANCE NOTICE IS LEGALLY REQUIRED UNDER FEDERAL OR CALIFORNIA LAW,

THERE MAY BE TACTICAL OR PRACTICAL REASONS FOR DOING SO IN SOME CASES 314
   1. WHILE NO ADVANCE NOTICE IS REQUIRED, THERE MAY BE TACTICAL OR PRACTICAL REASONS TO DO SO IN A PARTICULAR CASE 314

   2. DISCUSSING GOALS AND TACTICAL ALTERNATIVES WITH CLIENT 315

   3. REJECT LEGISLATIVE EFFORTS TO REQUIRE MANDATORY 90 DAY NOTICE 316

   4. HAVE DEFENDANTS ALREADY BEEN PUT ON NOTICE OR ARE THEY PART OF A LARGER COMPANY THAT HAS PREVIOUSLY BEEN PUT ON NOTICE? 316

   5. TACTICAL USE OF ADVANCE NOTICE 317
      a. USING ADVANCE NOTICE AS A POSSIBLE BASIS FOR TREBLE DAMAGES UNDER CALIFORNIA CIVIL CODE SECTION 52 OR 54.3 317

      b. ADVANCE NOTICE ALSO USEFUL FOR POSSIBLE "CATALYST" ATTORNEY FEES UNDER CALIFORNIA LAW 319

      c. IS FILING A GOVERNMENT CLAIM A "REASONABLE PRE-LITIGATION OFFER TO SETTLE"? 321

      d. NEITHER ADVANCE NOTICE NOR SETTLEMENT EFFORTS ARE NEEDED UNDER CODE OF CIVIL PROCEDURE § 1021.5 OR THE ADA FOR ATTORNEY FEES TO PLAINTIFF AS PREVAILING PARTY 321

G. IN LITIGATION, APPROACH DEFENDANT EARLY 321
   1. SEEK "WIN-WIN" EARLY SETTLEMENT 321

   2. IN THE NORTHERN DISTRICT OF CALIFORNIA, GENERAL ORDER 56 REQUIRES EARLY DISCLOSURES, SITE INSPECTION, AND MEDIATION PROCEDURES 322

   3. ASK EARLY COOPERATIVE, SITE INSPECTION 322

   4. IF POSSIBLE, PLAINTIFF SHOULD CONSULT A QUALIFIED EXPERT BEFORE FILING A LAWSUIT, AND SHARE THE EXPERT'S PRELIMINARY CONCLUSIONS WITH DEFENDANTS DURING AN EARLY STAGE OF LITIGATION 322

   5. INSIST ON PROVISION OF PROPER ACCESS AS A CONDITION OF ANY SETTLEMENT OF FINANCIAL ISSUES (DAMAGES AND FEES) 323

H. RESIST "CONFIDENTIALITY" AS A CONDITION OF SETTLEMENT 324
   1. RESIST CONFIDENTIALITY 324

   2. PLAINTIFF DOES NOT HAVE TO AGREE! IF DEFENDANT FIGHTS

<u>INSTEAD</u> JUST BECAUSE PLAINTIFF WON'T SIGN CONFIDENTIALITY AGREEMENT, THE ULTIMATE PUBLICITY MAY BE COUNTER PRODUCTIVE TO DEFENDANT 324

    3. CONFIDENTIALITY IS USUALLY AGAINST PUBLIC POLICY; AND IN SOME CIRCUMSTANCES MAY BE UNETHICAL 325

    4. DISABLED PERSONS AND THEIR ATTORNEYS SHOULD PRESERVE THEIR OWN RIGHTS OF FREE SPEECH 326

    5. PLAINTIFFS SHOULD RESIST CONFIDENTIALITY BEING A CONDITION OF SETTLEMENT 327

  I. SETTLEMENT PROCEDURES: GENERAL ORDER 56 IN NORTHERN DISTRICT OF CALIFORNIA AND ITS MEDIATION PROGRAM 328

VI. OTHER REMEDIES FOR DISABILITY DISCRIMINATION 331
  A. SMALL CLAIMS COURTS 331

  B. CLASS ACTIONS 332

    1. INTRODUCTION / DISCLAIMER 332

    2. A CLASS ACTION COULD BE BROUGHT UNDER THE ADA FOR INJUNCTIVE RELIEF AND ATTORNEY FEES ONLY, WITHOUT A CLAIM FOR DAMAGES EXCEPT AS TO THE NAMED PLAINTIFF 333

    3. UNDER THE ADA, CLASS ACTIONS ARE LIMITED TO INJUNCTIVE RELIEF AND ATTORNEY FEES 333

    4. EXAMPLES OF ACTIONS BROUGHT WITH DRA WHICH OBTAINED MAJOR INJUNCTIVE RELIEF AT MULTIPLE BUSINESSES, BUT LEFT DAMAGES ISSUES TO INDIVIDUAL PLAINTIFFS 333
      a. 232 DENNY'S RESTAURANTS (<u>JORGENSEN V. FLAGSTAR</u>) 334

      b. 1,400 JACK IN THE BOX RESTAURANTS (<u>JORGENSEN V. JACK IN THE BOX/FOODMAKER, INC.</u>) 334

      c. 150 BP SERVICE STATIONS (<u>HODGES V. BP OIL</u>) 334

      d. ALL CALIFORNIA GREYHOUND BUS STATIONS (<u>IMPERIALE, POTTER V. GREYHOUND</u>) 335

    5. <u>CAVEAT</u> CLASS ACTION EFFECT ON EXISTING OR SUBSEQUENT INDIVIDUAL ACTIONS 335
      a. INDIVIDUAL ACTIONS MAY BE PUT ON HOLD WITH STAY ON DISCOVERY (<u>TACO BELL</u> EXAMPLE) 335

      b. WATCH FOR QUESTIONABLE CLASS ACTIONS THAT ATTEMPT TO

        INSULATE DEFENDANTS FROM OTHER LAWSUITS BUT DO NOT PROTECT THE PUBLIC INTEREST OR THE RIGHTS OF INDIVIDUAL DISABLED PLAINTIFFS. 335

  C. PUBLICIZING THE VIOLATION MAY HAVE A POSITIVE EFFECT 337

VII. ARE THERE "ABUSES" OF THE ADA? WE CAN PROTECT "GOOD FAITH" BUSINESSES WITHOUT WEAKENING THE ADA OR CALIFORNIA'S LAWS PROTECTING THE DISABLED 338

  A. INTRODUCTION - IS "SERIAL" ADA LITIGATION "ABUSIVE" ? OR ARE ATTORNEY FEE AWARDS CONGRESS' INCENTIVES TO <u>ENCOURAGE</u> ENFORCEMENT OF THE ADA? 338

  B. ANYONE WHO COMMITS FRAUD UNDER THE GUISE OF THE ADA OR OTHERWISE SHOULD BE PUNISHED FOR THE FRAUDULENT CONDUCT, UNDER CURRENTLY AVAILABLE LEGAL REMEDIES; NO AMENDMENTS TO WEAKEN THE ADA ARE NECESSARY 341

  C. EFFORTS TO WEAKEN DISABILITY ACCESS LAWS BY PROVIDING A 90 DAY NOTICE REQUIREMENT WOULD DESTROY ENFORCEABILITY OF THE ADA AND RELATED CALIFORNIA LAWS 342

    1. REQUIRING ADVANCE NOTICE WOULD DESTROY INCENTIVE FOR BUSINESSES TO PROVIDE ACCESS, AND ALLOW THEM TO DELAY DOING SO UNTIL FORMAL COMPLAINTS ARE RECEIVED 342

    2. THE CALIFORNIA ATTORNEY GENERAL ADDRESSED THIS ISSUE IN A 2003 LETTER OPINION WHICH FOUND NO REASON TO REQUIRE ADVANCE "NOTICE" BEFORE A LAWSUIT 343

  D. SOME COURTS HAVE CREATED THEIR OWN REMEDIES TO PUNISH WHAT THEY FOUND TO BE UNETHICAL OR "ABUSIVE" CONDUCT 344

    1. <u>MOLSKI</u> 9TH CIRCUIT DECISIONS/ORDERS 344

    2. THESE CASES ARE EVIDENCE THAT THE COURTS ALREADY HAVE REMEDIES FOR "ABUSES;" THERE'S NO NEED TO WEAKEN CIVIL RIGHTS LAWS IN ORDER TO DETER "MISUSE" 345

  E. JUDGE KARLTON'S DECISION IN <u>WILSON V. PIER 1 IMPORTS</u>, HELD THAT DEFENDANTS DON'T HAVE STANDING TO COMPLAIN ABOUT WHAT PLAINTIFF MAY HAVE DONE IN <u>OTHER</u> CASES, ESPECIALLY WHEN DEFENDANTS ARE NOT "BLAMELESS" AS TO ADA VIOLATIONS 346

  F. FILING A LARGE NUMBER OF LAWSUITS DOES NOT, BY ITSELF, SHOW THE LAWSUITS ARE "FRIVOLOUS" OR "VEXATIOUS" 347

  G. FILING MULTIPLE ADA LAWSUITS IS <u>NOT</u> VEXATIOUS, NOR IS USE OF "BOILERPLATE" COMPLAINTS, SO LONG AS THE ALLEGATIONS IN EACH RE SUPPORTED BY THE FACTS 347

H. DO DEFENDANTS IN ONE CASE HAVE "STANDING" TO COMPLAIN ABOUT PLAINTIFF'S FILING OF OTHER LAWSUITS? 348

I. ADA SECTION 503 MAY PROHIBIT ATTACKS ON DISABLED PLAINTIFFS WHO HAVE FILED PRIOR ADA LAW SUITS [SEE SECTION I-J-8-b, III-C, AND IV-C-4, *supra*] 348

J. SB 1608 (effective 1/1/09) CHANGED CALIFORNIA STATUTES TO GIVE PROCEDURAL ASSISTANCE TO "GOOD FAITH" BUSINESSES IN STATE COURT PROCEEDINGS 348

K. TRUE DISABLED ADVOCATES SHOULD JOIN IN CRITICIZING UNETHICAL CONDUCT BY PLAINTIFFS AS WELL AS DEFENDANTS 349

L. A POSSIBLE CHECKLIST OF ISSUES TO HELP DETERMINE WHETHER AN ATTORNEY'S ACTIONS IN BRINGING A LAWSUIT OR MAKING A DEMAND UPON A BUSINESS IS "ABUSIVE" 349

VIII. CONCLUSION 351
A. OPPOSING DISABLED ACCESS: MONEY, PREJUDICE, AND IGNORANCE 351

B. THE NEW ATTACK ON DISABLED RIGHTS 353

C. PROVIDING ACCESS CAN BE A "WIN-WIN" SITUATION 356

IX. APPENDIX 357
A. LEADING CASES 357
  1. People ex rel. Deukmejian v. CHE, Inc. (1983) 150 Cal.App.3d 123
  2. Donald v. Sacramento Valley Bank (1989) 209 Cal.App.3d 1183
  3. Donald v. Café Royale (1990) 218 Cal.App.3d 168
  4. Hankins v. El Torito Restaurants, Inc. (1998) 63 Cal. App.4th 510
  5. Walker and Adams v. Carnival Cruise Lines (2000) 107 F.Supp.2d 1135
  6. Skaff v. Meridien North America Beverly Hills, LLC, 506 F.3d 832 (9th Cir. 2007)
  7. Blackwell v. Foley, 724 F. Supp. 2d 1068 (N.D. Cal. 2010)

B. CALIFORNIA GOVT. CODE § 4450 AND 4451, EFFECTIVE 11/13/68 APPLIED TO NEW CONSTRUCTION AND ALTERATION INCLUDING "BUILDINGS AND FACILITIES UNDER CONSTRUCTION" AT THAT TIME. 361

C. ASA REGULATIONS (EFFECTIVE NOVEMBER 13, 1968, TO JANUARY 1, 1982, PER GOVERNMENT CODE §§ 4450 AND 4451 (1968) AND CALIFORNIA HEALTH & SAFETY CODE § 19956 (1970) 363

D. OFFICE OF LEGISLATIVE COUNSEL, OPINION OF MARCH 31, 1979 RE: PATHS OF TRAVEL REQUIREMENTS UNDER ASA REGULATIONS 375

E. ATTORNEY GENERAL'S OPINIONS 382
  1. SEPTEMBER 17, 1992 STATEWIDE DIRECTIVE TO CALIFORNIA BUILDING OFFICIALS (SEE § II.D.9) 382

2. 1993 OPINION THAT ADA ENFORCED ONLY BY THE DOJ AND BY PRIVATE LAWSUITS (NO. 93-203) 391

3. AUGUST 4, 2003 OPINION LETTER BY CHIEF DEPUTY ATTORNEY GENERAL STEVE COONY ON BEHALF OF CALIFORNIA ATTORNEY GENERAL BILL LOCKYER (RE: NO "ADVANCE NOTICE LAWS" NEEDED) ..399

F. RESOURCES FOR DISABLED PERSONS 358

G. COMPLAINT SAMPLE - FOR FEDERAL COURT: TITLE III AND CALIFORNIA LAW: SERVICE DOG EXCLUSION (PLUS PHYSICAL BARRIERS) (DARREN K. V. XYZ RESTAURANTS 402

H. GENERAL ORDER 56 (AS OF MAY 29, 2012 AMENDMENTS) FOR NORTHERN DISTRICT, CALIFORNIA. 420

I. CONSENT DECREE SAMPLE- "METREON THEATER" CASE 423

J. SACRAMENTO COMMUNITY THEATER (COMPOSITE PHOTO) 435

K. TEXT OF SENATE BILL NO. 1186 (2012) 436

IINDEX 477
   INDEX OF APPENDIX 488

   INDEX OF PEOPLE 489

TABLE OF AUTHORITIES

1. Aikins, et al. v. Enterprise Rent-A-Car, et al., (2000) 79 Cal. App. 4th 1127

2. Antoninetti v. Chipotle Mexican Grill, Inc., 643F.3d 1165 (9th Cir. , 2010) Cert. Denied 131 S.Ct. 2113.

3. AMC see United States v. AMC

4. Arnold v. United Artists Theater Circuit, Inc., et al. (N.D.Cal. 1994) 866 F.Supp 433

5. Armstrong v. Schwarzenegger, (9th Cir. 2010) 2010 DJDAR 14177.

6. Barry Atwood v. El Torito Restaurants, et al., Alameda Cty. Sup. Ct., Action No. 677858-1

7. Barden v. City of Sacramento (9th Cir. 2002) 292 F.3d 1073

8. Barrios v. California Interscholastic Federation, et al. (9th Cir. 2002) 277 F. 3d 1128

9. Beasley v. Wells Fargo Bank (1991) 235 Cal.App.3d 1407

10. Berne v. City of Oakland, Case No. C07-0505 MMC (N.D. Cal. 2007)

11. Blackwell v. Foley, 724 F.Supp.2d 1068 (N.D.Cal. 2010)

12. BMW v. Gore 517 U.S. 559; 116 S.Ct. 1589

13. Boemio v. Love's Restaurant (1997) 954 F.Supp 204

14. Botosan v. Fitzhugh (1998) 13 F.Supp.2d 1047

15. Botosan v. McNally Realty, et al. (9th Cir. 2000) 216 F.3d 827

16. Brown v. Lucky Stores, Inc., et al. (9th Cir. 2001) 246 F.3d 1182

17. Brown-Booker and Overbo v. Loews California Theaters Inc., et al. (N.D. Cal. 2007) Case No. C07-05368 MHP

18. Buckhannon Board & Care Home, Inc., et al. v. West Virginia Dept. of Health & Human Services, et al. (2001) 121 S.Ct. 1835

19. Californians for Disability Rights v. Mervyn's LLC. 165 CA 4th 571 (2008)

20. Camacho v. Schafer (1987) 193 Cal.App.3d 718

21. Christine Burke v. Heavenly, et al. (E.D.Cal.) Case No. CIV-S04-0957 DFL/PAN

22. Chabner v. United Of Omaha Life Insurance Co., 1999 WL 33227443 (N.D.Cal.) C95-0447 MHP (Opinion of October 12, 1999)

23. Chabner v. United Of Omaha Life Insurance Co., 225 F.3D 1042 (9th Cir. 2000)

24. Chapman v. Pier 1 Imports, 631 F.3d 939 (9th Cir. 2011)

25. Chapman v. Pier 1 Imports (U.S.) Inc., 870 F. Supp. 2d 995 (E.D. Cal. 2012)

26. Chipotle (See Antoninetti above)

27. Chavez v. Chevy's Order Granting Attorney Fees, March 27, 2003, N.D. C01-4322 THE

28. "CHE" People ex rel Deukmajian v.CHE, Inc. (1983) 140 Cal. App 3d 123

29. Christiansburg Garment Co. v. Equal Employment Opportunity Comm. (1978) 434 U.S. 412

30. Coles v. City of Oakland: Attorney Fee Order, 2007 WL 39304 (N.D. Cal.)

31. Crommie v. State of California, et al.,(1994) 840 F. Supp. 719

32. Mangold; Crommie v. California Public Utilities Comm'n et al. (9th Cir. 1995) 67 F.3d 1470

33. Crowder v. Kitigawa, Chairman Hawaiian Bd. of Control (9th Cir. 1996) 81 F.3d 1480

34. Hollynn D'Lil v. Best Western Encina Lodge and Suites, (9th Cir. 2008) 538 F.3d 1031.

35. Hollynn D'Lil v. Ramada Ltd., (C.D. Cal) 2004 WL 3674244

36. James Donald v. Café Royale (1990) 218 Cal.App.3d 168

37. James Donald v. Sacramento Valley Bank (1989) 209 Cal.App.3d 1183

38. Doran v. Del Taco, Inc., et al. (C.D.Cal. 2005) 373 F.Supp.2d 1028

39. Doran v. Del Taco, Inc. (9th Cir. 2007) 534 F.3d 1034.

40. Doran v. 7-Eleven, Inc. (9th Cir. 2007) 506 F.3d 1191

41. Duvall v. County of Kitsap, 260 F.3d 1124 (9th Cir. 2001)

42. Exxon Shipping Co. v. Baker, (2008) 554 U.S 471; 128 S.Ct. 2605

43. Fadhl v. City and County of San Francisco (9th Cir. 1988) 859 F.2d 649, 651

44. Fischer v. SJB-P.D. Inc. (2000) 214 F.3d 1115

45. Fisher v. Bank of the West, C92-4356 FMS (N.D. Cal)

46. Tom Fisher v. Millennium Bank, Calprop Enterprises Ltd. (N.D.Cal.) Case No. C96-00800 SBA

47. Fox v. Vice (2011) 131 S.Ct. 2205

48. Furtyune v. American Multi-Cinema, Inc., 364 F.3d 1075 (9th Cir. 2004)

49. Gates V. Deukmejian (9th Cir. 1992) 987 F.2d 1392

50. George v. BART, 577 F.3d 1005 (9th Cir. 2009)

51. Graham v. DaimlerChrysler Corp. (2004) 34 Cal.4th 553

52. Greene V. Dillingham Construction N.A., Inc. (2002) 101 Cal.App.4th 418

53. Gunther v. Lin, 50 Cal.Rptr.3d 317 (Cal.Ct.App. 2006)

54. Guzman v. Denny's, Inc., et al. (1999) 40 F. Supp.2d 930

55. Peni Hall v. Orpheum Theater, et al. (N.D. Cal.) Case No. C96-1173 CW

56. People ex rel Deukmejin v. CHE, Inc., (1983) 150 Cal.App.3d 123.

57. Mark Hankins v. El Torito Restaurants, Inc., et al. (1998) 63 Cal. App.4th 510

58. Harris v. Maricopa Co. Superior Ct., 631 F.3d 963 (9th Cir. 2011)

59. Helen L. v. DiDario (3rd Cir. 1995) 46 F.3d 325, 335

60. Hensley v. Eckerhart (1983) 461 U.S. 424, 103 S.Ct. 1933

61. Sue Hodges v. BP Oil, et al. (N.D. Cal.) Case No. C95-02215 JLQ

62. Hodges v. El Torito (N.D. Cal) 1998 WL95398, Order of Feb. 23, 1998

63. Hubbard v. Sobrec, LLC, 554 F.3d 742 (9th Cir. 2009)

64. Marvin Huezo v. Los Angeles Community College District (Los Angeles Pierce College), (C.D.Cal.) Case No. CV04-9772 MMM/JWJx, Docket No. 166 (11/17/08 Order re: Attorney Fees)

65. Marvin Huezo v. Los Angeles Community College District (Los Angeles Pierce College), 672 F.Supp 2d 1045 C.D. Cal. (2008) (Order for Permanent Injunction)

66. Marvin Huezo v. Los Angeles Community College District (Los Angeles Pierce College), (C.D.Cal.) Case No. CV04-9772 MMM/JWJx, Docket No. 80 (2/27/07 Order re: Summary Judgment)

67. Independent Living Resources v. Oregon Arena Corporation (1998) 1 F.Supp. 2d 1159

68. Jankey v. Song Koo Lee, 55 Cal. 4th 1038 (2012)

69. Jankey v. Poop Deck, (9th Cir. 2008) 537 F.3d. 1122

70. Concetta Jorgensen v. Denny's, Inc., Case No. 745658-9 (Alameda Sup. Ct.)

71. Concetta Jorgensen v. Jack in the Box Restaurants, et al., Case No. C95-0406 SAW (N.D. Cal. 1995).

72. Keith Kellum v. Silver Dragon Restaurant, Alameda Co. Sup. Ct. (1975).

73. Ketchum v. Moses (2001) 24 Cal.4th 1122

74. Kemp v. Regents of Univ. of Cal., C-09-4687 PJH, 2010 WL 2889224 (N.D. Cal. July 22, 2010)

75. Kittock v. Leslie's Poolmart Inc., (E.D. Cal. 2009) 687 F.Supp.2d 953

76. Kittock v. Ralphs Grocery Co., (C.D. Cal.) 2009 WL 2603096.

77. Lane v. Tennessee (See Tennessee v. Lane)

78. Lawson v. Shell, Alameda Superior Court [Date]

79. Leiber v. Macy's West (N.D. 1999) 80 F. Supp. 2d 1065

80. Judith Leiken v. Squaw Valley Ski Corp., Alex Cushing (E.D. Cal.) Case No. CIV-S-93 505 LKK/GGH Order of June 29, 1994.

81. Lentini v. California Center for the Arts (9th Cir. 2004) 370 F.3d 837

82. Lipsett v. Gumersindo Blanco (USCA, 1st District) 975 F.2d 934

83. John Lonberg v. City of Riverside, (C.D. Cal) 2007 WL 2005177

84. Madden v. Del Taco 2007 DJDAR 5843, C051641, 3rd Dist. Ct. of Appeal (4/25/07)

85. Mannick v. Kaiser Foundation Health Plan, Inc. (N.D.Cal.) Case No. C03-5905 PJH (Attorney fees Order of 9/28/07)

86. Martin v. Cavalier Oceanfront Resort, et al (C.D.Cal.) Case No. CV-02-02259 AHM

87. Carolyn Martin v. Goodin Trust, et al., Case No. CV-02-7305 CAS/VBK

88. McPhee v. Sunset View Cemetery Ass'n, C9502728 WHO (N.D. Cal. 1995)

89. Mervyn's, see Californians for Disability Rights v. Mervyn's LLC

90. Molski v. Evergreen Dynasty Corp. (9th Cir. 2007) 500 F.3d 1047

91. Molski v. Evergreen Dynasty Corp. (9th Cir. 2008) 521 F.3d 1215

92. Molski v. Foley Estates Winery, (9th Cir. 2008) 531 F.3d 1043

93. Molski v. Gleich (9th Cir. 2003) 318 F.3d 937

94. Molski v. M.J. Cable, Inc. (D.C. No. CV-03-04809-DT)

95. City of Moorpark v. Sup. Ct. (1998) 18 Cal.4th 1143

96. Michael Pachovas v. County of Alameda, City of Berkeley, Alameda County Superior Ct. Action No. 713973-8 (1996)

97. Moreno v. City of Sacramento, (9th Cir. 2008) 534 F.3d 1106

98. Munson v. Del Taco, Inc., 46 Cal.4th.661 (2009).

99. O'Campo v. Chico Mall, 758 F.Supp.2d 976 (E.D. Cal. 2010)
Oliver v. In-n-Out Burgers (S.D. Cal. 2013) 2013 WL1927121

100. Overbo, et al. v. Loews California Theatres, Inc. dba AMC Loews Metreon 16 IMAX, et al., C07-5368 MHP, Docket No. 93 (N.D.Cal. Order of Sept. 17, 2010)

101. Parr v. L&L Drive Inn, et al. (2000) 96 F.Supp 2d 1065

102. Paulick v. Bavarian Lion Vineyard Dev., LLC, C 08-04860 CW, 2009 WL 691123 (N.D. Cal. Mar. 10, 2009)

103. People ex rel Deukmajian v.CHE, Inc. (1983) 140 Cal. App 3d 123

104. Pickern, et al. v. Holiday Quality Foods, Inc. (9th Cir. 2002) 293 F.3d 1133

105. Pinnock v. Int'l House of Pancakes, et al.(1993) 844 F. Supp. 574

106. Presta v. Peninsula Corridor Joint Powers Bd. (N.D.Cal. 1998) 16 F.Supp.2d 1134

107. Red Bull Associates, et al. v. Best Western International, Inc. (1998) 862 F.2d 963

108. Richard S. v. Dept. of Developmental Services (9th Cir. 2003) 317 F.3d 1080

109. Rosler v. Stanford University (N.D. Cal.) NO. C03-03579 JF.

110. San Francisco v. Grant Co., (1986) 181 Cal. App.3d 1085

111. Serrano v. Priest (1977) 20 Cal.3d 25

112. Serrano v. Unruh (Serrano IV) (1982) 32 Cal.3d 621

113. Shute v. Carnival Cruise Lines, Inc. (1991) 499 U.S. 585

114. "Silver Dragon" related case: State of California ex rel Department of Rehabilitation v. Superior Court (City of Oakland Real Party in Interest), 137 Cal.App.3d 282 (1st DCA 1982)

115. "Sobreck" see Hubbard v. Sobreck.

116. Skaff v. Meridien North America Beverly Hills, LLC (9th Cir. 2007) 506 F.3d 832

117. Spector v. Norwegian Cruise Line LTD (2005) 125 S.Ct. 2169

118. Squaw Valley see Leiken.

119. State of California, See "Silver Dragon"

120. State Farm v. Campbell, (2003) 538 U.S. 408; 123 S.Ct. 1513.

121. Steger v. Franco, Inc. (8th Cir. 2000) 228 F.3d 889

122. Stevens v. Premier Cruises, Inc. (2000) 215 F.3d 1237

123. Richard Stickney v. McDonald's Corp., et al. (N.D.Cal.)Case No. C99-00558 VRW (1/24/00 Order)

124. Stokus v. Marsh (1990) 217 Cal.App.2d 647

125. Sundance v. Municipal Court (1987) 192 Cal.App.3d 268

126. Tallarico v. Trans World Airlines (8th Cir. 1989) 881 F.2d 566

127. Tennessee v. Lane (2004) 541 U.S. 509, 124 S.Ct. 1978

128. Tipton-Whittingham, et al. v. City of Los Angeles (2004) 34 Cal.4th 604

129. Turner v. Ass'n of Am. Med. Colleges, 193 Cal. App. 4th 1047 (2011)

130. United States Football League v. N.F.L. (2d Cir. 1987) 887 F.2d 408

131. United State v. AMC Entertainment Inc., (9th Cir. 2008) 549 F.3d 760

132. Bernard Walker and Christina Adams v. Carnival Cruise Lines, et al. (1999) 63 F. Supp.2d 1083

133. Bernard Walker and Christina Adams v. Carnival Cruise Lines, et al. (2000) 107 F.Supp.2d 1135

134. Wallace v. Consumer Co-op of Berkeley, Inc., 170 Cal. App.3d 836

135. Wander v. Kaus (9th Cir. 2002) 304 F.3d 856

136. Weissman v. Terranova Industries, Specialty Restaurant Corporation, dba H's Lordships Restaurant, et al., Alameda County Superior Ct. Action No. 636384-4

137. Wilshire Financial Tower v. City of Los Angeles (1990) 217 Cal. App.3d 119

138. Wilson v. Haria and Gogri Corp. dba Jack in the Box, et al. (E.D.Cal.) 479 F.Supp. 2d 1127.

139. Ronald Wilson v. Kayo Oil Co. (9th Cir. 2009) 563 F.3d 979

140. Wilson v. Murillo (2008) 163 Cal App. 4th 1124

141. Zum Brunnen v. Mission Ranch, Clint Eastwood, et al., U.S.D.C., N.D.Cal., Case No. C97-20668 JW (2000)

ARTICLES AND BOOKS CITED

1. Richard Pearl, California Attorney Fee Awards, 2nd Edition (CEB)

2. Samual R. Bagenstos, "The Perversity of Limited Civil Rights Remedies: The Case of 'Abusive' ADA Litigation," 54 UCLA L. Rev. 1 (2006).

3. Arlene Meyerson, Americans with Disabilities Act Annotated (4 Volumes)

PHOTOS

1. "Full and Equal Access?" xliv
2. "Keith Kellum" 2
3. "Erma Rein" 6
4. "Jim Donald" 58
5. "Oakland Bandstand" 118
6. "Sacramento Community Theater" 435

[1]Entrance to Oceanview Restaurant: restrooms located at top of stairs on second floor.

DISABLED ACCESS LITIGATION

1. DEDICATION AND ACKNOWLEDGMENTS

   To the memories of Keith Kellum (1940-1990), and James Donald (1945 -2003), for their pioneering work as advocates for disability rights and as pioneer plaintiffs in cases testing court enforcement of California's disability rights laws in the 1970s and 1980s; and to my mother, Erma Rein (1915-1990), for her courage, love and inspiration; and to my "co-conspirator," the late Ed Roberts (1939 - 1995), the "godfather" of disability rights and awareness. I must also express my appreciation for the efforts of attorneys Bryce Anderson, John Burris, Catherine "Cat" Cabalo, Sid Cohen, Brian Gearinger, Anthony Goldsmith, Celia McGuinness, and Gary Gwilliam, who have each co-counseled cases with me and have been friends, supporters of my work, and partners in litigation over many years. Other attorneys and disabled activists who have been and remain my allies in the continuing fight for "Full & Equal Access" include Jonathan Adler, Connie Arnold, Barry Atwood, Patricia Barbosa, Hollyn D'Lil, Matthew Dietz, Russ Handy, Dave Hicks, Peter Margen, Jordon Metz, Julie Ostil, Larry Paradis, Lisa Rein, Sierra Rein, Bob Schock, Richard Skaff, Daniel U. Smith, Jim Sturdevant, Tim Thimesch, and Sid Wolinsky. I am also grateful to all of my pioneering clients, including (but not limited to) Christina Adams, Connie Arnold, Patty Berne, Nicky Brown-Booker, "Maggie" Dowling, Tom Fisher, Sue Hodges, Marvin Huezo, "B" Johnson, Guy Jones, Concetta Jorgensen, Peter Mendoza, Andi Orsini, Jana Overbo, Steve Potter, Bonnie Regina, Jean Riker, Donna White, Steve White, Zach Woodford. My closest friends, John and Julie Kolar, and Deborah and Sandy Abbley, have always "been in my corner." Thank you also to my publishers, Tom Costello and Steve Mobley at Word Association Publishers.

   A. THANK YOU TO MY "OFFICE ALLIES"

      In my office, my senior paralegal, Aaron Clefton, has been immensely valuable in creating this book. He's worked with me on every aspect of these materials over the past eight years and I could not have created this book without his help. My lawyer partners and friends, Celia McGuinness and Catherine "Cat" Cabalo, have been of great support and assistance, as has our support "staff," Holly Jaramillo and Catherine "Taffy" Castro (now retired), and my daughter, Lisa Rein.

      This book is also dedicated to one of the true "unsung heroes" of the Disability Movement, my brother, Steven Rein, our office manager for the "Rein Law Offices." For the past 28 years he has managed my law office, handled myriad tasks as my secretary, transcribed dictation tapes, corrected my drafts on letters, pleadings and articles, and kept me from giving up on an infinite number of occasions! Thank you, Steve!

B. REMEMBERING KEITH KELLUM (1940 - 1990)

Keith Kellum was an inspiration to those who knew him. Keith was the "handicapped" person who started me into the field of "disabled access" by allowing me to represent him in one of the earliest (1975) successful test cases using a private lawsuit to compel disabled access enforcement in California by injunction and damages: Keith Kellum v. The Silver Dragon Restaurant, Alameda County Superior Court, approximately 1975-1978. [See F.N. 18, §I-G-2-d, *infra*, on Keith Kellum v. Silver Dragon.] Keith was an "able-bodied" classmate of mine at the "Boalt Hall" School of Law (now also called "Berkeley Law") from 1965 to 1968. We both joined the Alameda County Public Defender's office in 1969. Keith developed multiple sclerosis but continued as an active trial lawyer despite his physical condition deteriorating over the years so that he required use of a cane, walker, and finally a motorized wheelchair. Continuing to practice law, he was frustrated when blocked by a new restaurant's steps from having lunch in Oakland's "Chinatown" area with other public defenders. He was especially frustrated because restaurants were newly built without access even after California access laws were enacted in 1970. I was honored in 1975 when Keith chose me to represent him in a pioneer disabled access case. I was a young lawyer, just entering the field of civil litigation after seven years doing criminal defense. I asked Keith, "You know hundreds of lawyers. Why do you want me to represent you?" He answered, "Paul, I want you because you're the meanest, nastiest son-of-a-bitch I know!" With such praise, how could I resist?

Keith Kellum originated the idea that private lawsuits could be used to enforce violations of building code that were not being properly enforced by many building officials during the 1970's. Keith suggested that we enforce section 54.1 Civil Code's guarantee of "full and equal" access in combination with section 19955ff Health and Safety code, which applied access requirements to all new construction to the commercial buildings after July 1, 1970, or alterations after 1972. Our first application of this theory was to sue Oakland's Silver Dragon restaurant, newly constructed in 1973 with steps at its only entrance and with inaccessible restrooms inside. We were successful in obtaining access at the Silver Dragon (in approximately 1978). Our legal analysis of California's statutory requirements was first endorsed by a published appellate opinion in Donald v. Sacramento Valley Bank, 209 Cal.App.3d 1183 (1989).

C. CALIFORNIA SET AN EXAMPLE FOR NATIONAL (ADA) ACCESS COMPLIANCE
Before the ADA was enacted in 1990, some of the individual states had access laws, but California, with laws protecting disabled persons in both governmental buildings (since 1968) and privately owned public accommodations (since 1970) was a pioneer in providing access. Today, according to federal governmental statistics, more than 2.7 million Americans age 15 and older use a wheelchair and another 9.1 million "use an ambulatory aid such as a cane, crutches, or walker."[2]

The number of disabled persons in our society is rapidly increasing, due to increased life spans for aging "baby-boomers," and others factors, such as an increased number of wounded veterans returning from the Iraq and Afghanistan wars. As Ed Roberts, the "godfather" of the disability rights movement used to remind us, "Disability is an Equal Opportunity Employer!"

D. ED ROBERTS, "GODFATHER" OF THE DISABILITY RIGHTS MOVEMENT
The late Ed Roberts (1939 - 1995) was a friend and collaborator. He founded the Berkeley Center for Independent Living in 1969 after going through Cal as its first severely disabled student. Ed required sleeping in an iron lung at Cal's Cowell Hospital each night and operating a motorized wheelchair (with one operable finger) while breathing through a respirator by day. His mother, Zona Roberts, told me some stories about Ed's fighting with the California Department of Rehabilitation after he was transformed by Polio from an athletic 14 year old baseball player into what some newspapers characterized as a "helpless cripple." His mother's efforts to obtain assistive services from the California Department of Rehabilitation were rejected because Ed was "too disabled" to benefit from the Department's programs. Told that he would be "nothing but a vegetable," Ed said he "decided to be an artichoke- soft on the inside but prickly on the outside!" And some 20 years after his rejection by the Department, Governor Jerry Brown appointed Ed to be the Director of the California Department of Rehabilitation in 1975, a post he held through 1983. In 1983 he founded the World Institute on Disability, in Oakland.

---

[2] Americans with Disabilities: 2002 report at http://census.gov/press-release/www/releases/archives/aging population/006809.html

In 2010, a major specially designed building, the "Ed Roberts Campus" was opened in Berkeley as the central headquarters for a number of leading advocacy and assistance organizations for persons with disabilities. These include: DREDF (Disability Rights Education and Defense Fund); the Center for Independent Living (co-founded by Ed Roberts in Berkeley as the first C.I.L. in the United States (1969)); "Through the Looking Glass," and other important organizations and resources for disabled persons. (See Appendix, Section IX-F, *infra*) The July, 2011, New Mobility magazine featured an article about the "dedication ceremony for the Ed Roberts Campus, a multimillion dollar project named for the founder of the disability movement."

2. FOREWORD: A PERSONAL NOTE

Starting 38 years ago, I've chosen to devote my law practice to representation of physically disabled persons in civil rights cases challenging architectural barriers and other forms of disability discrimination. A major motivation has been observing the obvious <u>courage</u> of many of my disabled clients. Many physically disabled persons face <u>daily challenges</u> unthinkable to able-bodied persons; yet many are still able and willing to use their time and energy to work in the public interest to improve conditions for others.

For two weeks in 1984 I served as the "personal attendant" for a quadriplegic friend so he could travel to and attend a "World Conference" for disability leaders in Kingston, Jamaica (sponsored by the Disabled Persons International (DPI) organization). My friend (and sometimes client) was Jim Donald, an active Sacramento attorney who was serving as the United States representative to DPI. Working as the attendant (substituting on a last minute, "emergency" basis) for an active quadriplegic gave me a unique opportunity to realize some of the real personal physical difficulties that persons with severe physical disabilities have to face.[3] This was particularly so when flying with Jim to a "Third World" (and even <u>less</u> accessible) country, and there attending meetings and educational and social events. Although Jim used a motorized wheelchair, he was well known for traveling all over the world to investigate conditions affecting disabled persons, for example visiting (and complaining about treatment of disabled persons in) Japan's prisons, mental hospitals and medical facilities.

I also had an opportunity to observe disability close at hand when my mother, Erma Rein, suffered a stroke and subsequent brain surgery in 1984. Rendered hemiplegic and aphasic, she fought back to regain her abilities to speak, read, live an independent life, and enjoy another six years of life. Ironically, my mother had emotionally and financially supported my work pioneering private enforcement of California's disability access laws since the mid 1970s, before incurring her own disability. Erma Rein helped financially to keep my office afloat while I handled early cases on a mostly "volunteer" basis, until I began earning sufficient statutory attorney fees from public interest access cases to fully support our work. Our mother was very pleased during the remainder of her life that both her sons (myself and my brother, Steve) were working to achieve better access for disabled persons. Her support was inspirational.

---

[3] Although Jim told me that I was the "worst attendant" that he'd ever had!

Erma Lubar Rein (1915-1990) pictured here with Paul and brother Steve at Steve's wedding in 1988

ODE TO ERMA

Always open, warm and loving
helping and giving
To friends in need
She's the one they called on
when feelings needed fixing
She's the one who was there
for everyone else
And when she was afflicted
Some helped, but some drifted off
To nurse their own problems
"How quickly we forget"
But her courage and determination
carried her through and brought
her back
She fought to be with us
And now she's independent
So tough and proud
Her "limitations" minimized
in her own consciousness
She's still there to love and to help,
Still there when we need her
Still someone to admire.
Her daily life an inspiring reminder
That each of us has the power
To be more of what we can be
To make the best of life's challenges
To live the great adventure
To be free while part of the whole
To love and care
To help and share
Integrity and character
A life by the Golden Rule
Once a champion bowler,
Now a steady roller -
Make way for Erma
Our Favorite Rolling Role Model!

3. LEGAL DISCLAIMER: NO PERSONAL LEGAL ADVICE IS INTENDED BY THIS BOOK

This book is intended to give the author's personal interpretation of the law, and is <u>not intended to give any individual reading it personal legal advice on his or her case or potential case</u>, either as a disabled plaintiff, a defendant being sued, a potential defendant, or as an attorney or representative for any of the above categories- <u>or anyone else</u>! This book also doesn't touch on employment issues, transportation issues, or the laws of any state other than California, including interpretation of ADA law by other jurisdictions outside of the 9th Circuit, except the United State Supreme Court. Further, new legislation and case law come down every day. Attorneys should review and shepardize any statute or case law referred to in this book for possible updates on the issues presented here.

NOTE: FOR RESEARCH USE THE DETAILED TABLE OF CONTENTS

4. INTRODUCTION

   A. PREFACE: CALIFORNIA LAWS AND THE FEDERAL ADA STANDARDS PROVIDE TOOLS TO OBTAIN DISABLED ACCESS

   "The state of California estimates the number of disabled individuals living in California at 6.2 million" and approximately one million of these individuals are mobility impaired.[4]

   California leads the nation in statutory and case law precedents protecting the rights of disabled persons to "full and equal access" to public buildings and facilities. To this extent, advocates in other states can use the California statutes and experience as a model. Yet, in 2013, <u>45 years</u> after California first enacted laws to protect the rights of "handicapped" persons to "full and equal access" at public facilities, and 23 years after enactment of the historic Americans with Disabilities Act of 1990, disabled persons <u>still</u> encounter access problems at many public facilities in California. These barriers effectively deny many employment, social, cultural, and recreational opportunities to the disabled. These barriers are reminders to the disabled that, in many ways, they <u>still</u> face economic and social discrimination, and are still treated as "second class" citizens.

   Our society, through state and federal laws, has decided that the benefits of disabled access are so important that businesses must be required to make their premises accessible, <u>even if it costs money</u>. Disabled persons should not have to apologize for the cost of this public benefit, any more than we expect an apology from anyone else who enjoys "full and equal" access under the law.

   Public enforcement of access laws is of primary importance, and has been steadily improving; however, far more needs to be done. The lack of sufficient building official enforcement has been of great concern to the disabled community, although it has greatly improved over the last 30 years. However, building officials in California are not authorized to enforce the federal Americans with Disabilities Act of 1990 and there is no federal bureaucratic enforcement. This means that the ADA must be enforced by private lawsuits. It also means that a business cannot rely on any "safe harbor" because a building department did not require access at the time that any building permits were issued: Access may still be required today, for example, on a "readily achievable" basis under federal law (Title III, § 302, etc., of the ADA), or by using a private lawsuit to enforce the state regulations that the building department "missed."

   Conscientious building officials must be willing to <u>revisit</u> situations where buildings were erroneously <u>allowed</u> to be built without access; such officials cannot be "estopped" from enforcing the law. (<u>San Francisco v. Grant Co.</u> (1986) 181 Cal.App.3d 1085.) The

---

[4] <u>Molski v. Gleich</u> (9th Cir. 2003) 318 F.3d 937, at 954, footnote 23, citing "quick facts: services to Californian with Disabilities, available at http:/www.ca.gov.

California Health and Safety Code places primary responsibility for enforcement of the laws prohibiting barriers in places of public accommodation upon local building officials (Health and Safety Code § 19958). Local and state authorities, including the district attorney, city attorney, county counsel, and attorney general, are also empowered to bring actions to enjoin any violation of access laws. (Health and Safety Code § 19958.5; see also Civil Code § 55.1) However, due to the lack of full enforcement of building codes in the past by many local building departments (particularly during the 1970's when building code requirements regarding access were apparently not fully understood by many officials), many public facilities were erroneously granted building permits for construction or alterations despite their inaccessibility. Enforcement cannot depend on the chance that public officials will discover and correct access violations, particularly violations triggered by alterations carried out in the past, sometimes without benefit of a building permit.

The lack of major access litigation during the 1970s may also have been a factor. In recent years publicity about private lawsuits and about the ADA has awakened public consciousness, including the consciousness of building officials. Building officials were also encouraged to enforce access laws by letters of notification sent by the California Attorney General's Office. (See for example Appendix IX-E-1, a, September 17, 1992 directive to California Building Officials from the California Attorney General.)

Because of past lax enforcement of California's Code requirements, inaccessible facilities will continue in perpetuity to exclude disabled persons unless those disabled persons who have been discriminated against fight back with private enforcement lawsuits. The "readily achievable" provisions of Title III of the ADA require access when it is "not very expensive" to provide access regardless of the age of the building. But Title III is enforced only by private lawsuits; there is no bureaucratic agency enforcement of Title III's "readily achievable" barrier removal requirements.

Once a lawsuit is filed, a defendant owner or operator must show that it is "too expensive" to provide access, for example, by specific comparisons of the cost of a ramp or lift or accessible restroom with the owners' and operators' "overall financial resources." This is the test of what is "readily achievable," per ADA section 301(9) (Botosan v. McNally Realty, et al. (2000) 216 F.3d 827) Most often this defense burden cannot be met, and access will be required. The burden of proof should be on the defendant owner. Wilson v. Haria and Gogri Corp. dba Jack in the Box, 479 F.Supp.2d 1127 (2007); Molski v. Foley Estates Vineyard (2008) 531 F.3d 1043, 1048; Rodriguez v. Barrita, Inc., C 09-04057 RS, 2012 WL 3538014 (N.D. Cal. Mar. 1, 2012). Further "not readily achievable" is not a defense to access requirements triggered by the construction or alteration history of a building.

Ironically, private enforcement actions under the ADA were effectively <u>encouraged</u> by former California Attorney General Dan Lungren, a conservative Republican.[5] On July 14, 1993, Attorney General Lungren issued a directive to all California Building Officials that it was their job to enforce California's state building code laws and regulations, including Title 24, but <u>not</u> to enforce the ADA. Enforcement of the ADA was designated by Congress to be the responsibility only of the United States Department of Justice and by <u>private lawsuits</u>. (See Appendix, IX-E-2, *infra*.)

While we welcome any efforts that state authorities may take to enforce the ADA in California, we agree with former Attorney General Lungren that private lawsuits are the main means of enforcing the Title III requirements as to all businesses which fail to self-police themselves. Enforcement is needed to ensure (1) provision of reasonable accommodations for disabled persons; (2) adjustment of policies to maximize access; and (3) removal of all physical barriers to access which are "readily achievable." The threat of damages and attorney fees may encourage "voluntary" compliance without any lawsuit - actually a win-win situation for the business and the disabled community - a "community" comprised of persons who may become customers of the business <u>once it becomes accessible.</u>

Expanded public agency enforcement of the ADA, either through a change in California policy or by creation of a federal agency enforcement mechanism, would indeed be a welcome supplement. Former California Attorney General Bill Lockyer reminded local building officials under his jurisdiction during his term in office that several California statutes, including Civil Code §§ 54(c) and 54.1(d), <u>incorporate</u> any violation of the ADA as a concurrent violation of California law. Since the California statutes are enforceable by state officials, including the state Attorney General, County Attorneys and District Attorneys (see Health & Safety Code § 19958.5), they would appear to have jurisdiction to enforce "incorporated" ADA violations because these also violate California law.

Access is an important civil right. When businesses and governmental agencies fully recognize that enforcement of this right is essential to disabled persons being able to function on an equal level in our society, and that access cannot be denied on the basis of disability any more than it can be denied on the basis of race or gender, the movement toward "full and equal access" will be greatly accelerated.

However, "private" lawsuits remain the most important source of enforcement. While some businesses have complained that the awarding of damages and attorney fees under California law has the effect of "punishing" defendants, Courts have made clear that private lawsuits are the instrument chosen by Congress and the California legislature for <u>enforcing</u> civil rights

---

[5] Unfortunately Dan Lungren, now a Southern Californian Congressman, introduced (2011) proposed legislation to greatly weaken the ADA!

laws protecting the disabled. Without private lawsuits, the burden of enforcing the law would have to be shifted to major bureaucratic agencies paid for by tax-payers, rather than paid by the responsible business owners (sometimes including recalcitrant scofflaws) whose refusal to "voluntarily" obey the law has made enforcement by lawsuits necessary.

Even prior to the ADA, Donald v. Café Royale, 218 Cal.App. 3d 168 (1990) held that the purpose of disability rights lawsuits under statutes allowing an award of damages and attorney fees for "prevailing party" disabled plaintiffs is to enforce the law, not to "punish:"

> The Legislature's purpose in imposing increased penalties and additional enforcement methods is to guarantee compliance with equal access requirements. The impediments to the physically handicappeds' interaction in community life is the inequity which section 54 et seq. and section 19955 et seq. seek to prevent. Id. at 179-180.

B. PURPOSE OF THIS BOOK

Both the 1961 American Standards Association (ASA) and California's Title 24 (the 1982 State Architect's Regulations, also known as the "California Building Code") commence with a statement of "Purpose." (See § II.A.2.a.(3), *infra*) Similarly, it is appropriate to start this book with a statement of "purpose." For the last 38 years our office has brought lawsuits to enforce the civil rights of physically disabled persons to "full and equal access" to public facilities. I now wish to share with my fellow attorneys and others who support the rights of the disabled, an outline of the law and other tools for obtaining better access for the more than two million ADA "qualified" disabled persons who live in California. These materials may also be of use to public officials, and to businesses that seek to comply with the law, and to their attorneys.

By adopting the "ASA" standards as regulations incorporated into California law in 1968 (per Government Code § 4456) as to governmental public buildings, and in 1970 (per California Health & Safety Code §§ 19955 et seq.) as to privately owned public accommodations, California adopted ASA § 1.2's "purpose": "To make all buildings and facilities used by the public accessible to and functional for the physically handicapped, to, through and within their doors..." Later statutes substituted the word "disabled" for the now archaic "handicapped," and this term was used to frame the landmark federal "Americans With Disabilities Act of 1990," the "ADA."

This book is intended to give a general outline of the law regarding access to public accommodations for disabled persons under California laws first passed in 1968. This book will also address aspects of the ADA which may be applied to governmental buildings and facilities or privately owned public accommodations in California, under ADA Title II and Title III. This is particularly necessary as California law has now incorporated "any violation" of the ADA as a per se violation of California's disability rights laws, including Civil Code sections 51(f), 54(c), and 54.1(d). Although the ADA, Title III, does not have its own damages remedy, an ADA violation may trigger the damages remedies of Civil Code sections 52 and 54.3 under state law, due to incorporation by sections 51(f), 54(c) and 54.1(d) of any violation of the ADA. This adds the potential of a damages award to the other enforcement mechanisms of the ADA.

We will also share some tools and techniques to assist attorneys and advocates in obtaining disabled accessible public accommodations. While I also invite defense counsel to read and benefit from the book, I cannot and do not give "defense" advise. I have never represented or advised businesses, government entities or defendants involved in disabled access lawsuits, and do not consider myself qualified to give any such advice, which must come from a different perspective. There are many qualified lawyers and access consultants (especially those "CASp" certified) who can properly advise actual or potential defendants, businesses and government personnel on their legal obligations. Moreover, taking proactive steps to provide proper access before any lawsuit is needed will be a win-win situation both for businesses and for their disabled patrons and potential customers. Some "practical" suggestions may be of use to defendants as well as plaintiffs, and to their respective attorneys.

To the extent I display a "bias" towards assisting disabled persons to obtain maximized disabled access, both the United State Congress in adopting the ADA, and the California legislature by its progressive statutes (starting 20 years ahead of the ADA), have expressed similar "bias" in establishing as public policy the goal of maximizing "full and equal" access for all disabled persons. This public policy will be discussed throughout this book, and is relevant to "interpretations" of statutory intent.

Portions of the book outline some legal precedents that may be of use to disabled persons - and their attorneys and supporters - when they decide to take action to enforce their rights to "full and equal access" to public accommodations. Individual private lawsuits are necessary to ensure that state and federal access laws are properly enforced. Each action may also have a "ripple effect" which will benefit every disabled person who is later able to use the improved facilities, and a further ripple effect if it motivates "voluntary" access improvements by building owners and/or their tenants.

Attorneys bringing access cases in state court should be aware that pleading an ADA cause of action will give defendants a jurisdictional basis to remove the case to federal court. While seeking injunctive relief based on the federal ADA in a case filed in state court can result in the case being removed to federal court, a lawsuit which only seeks California law damages on the basis that a violation of the ADA is now incorporated into California law, has been held by the 9th Circuit to be insufficient to establish a basis for federal court jurisdiction. (Wander v. Kaus (2002) 304 F.3d 856.) On the other hand, many of the procedural benefits granted to building owners by SB 1608 (2008) are only available in California state court. (O'Campo v. Chico Mall, 758 F.Supp. 2d 976 (E.D. Cal, 2010): California law cannot govern federal court procedures.)

The California laws protecting the rights of the disabled have been "on the books" since the 1968 adoption of Civil Code §§ 54 and 54.1, the Disabled Persons Act. California Health & Safety Code §§ 19953-19959, first adopted in 1970, specified access requirements upon new construction or alteration of existing commercial facilities.

Although this book is written with California litigation as its focus, in other states which have - or will have over the coming years - adopted state statutes for damages for violation of a disabled person's right to "full and equal access," the complaint models and legal principles may be used as examples that may be adapted to the other states' "state law" requirements. The federal ADA requirements should be similar in all states. However, the 9th Circuit (covering the "West") may have been more protective of disabled rights than certain other circuits.

C. THIS BOOK ADDRESSES CALIFORNIA LAW DISABLED ACCESS ISSUES, INCLUDING INCORPORATED ADA VIOLATIONS, BUT WILL NOT COVER ADA TITLE I OR OTHER "EMPLOYMENT" ISSUES

This book outlines some of the leading cases on California disabled access law and gives a summary of ADA access standards as applied to and incorporated into California law, but will leave to others a more detailed description of the nation-wide application of the ADA. However we encourage any practitioners who do not have an "airtight" case solely under California law, and are seeking to make premises accessible for disabled persons, to also include a cause of action to obtain accessible public accommodations under the "readily achievable" standards of the ADA. The ADA may require provision of access through "readily achievable" "barrier removal" regardless of a facility's construction and alteration history, so long as the cost of provision of access is "readily achievable," i.e., can reasonably be absorbed by the owners, operators, lessors and lessees of a public accommodation based on the factors listed in ADA § 301(9) (42 USC § 12181(a)). Most significantly, these factors include a comparison of all defendants' "overall financial resources" as compared with the costs for removal of each of the access barriers. (See Botosan v. McNally Realty (9th Cir. 2000) 216 F.3d 827, 836) (This may provide an inviting area for a plaintiff's use of "discovery" during litigation.) Used together, these California and federal ADA statutes should provide the basis for obtaining access to virtually all major public facilities in California, commercial and governmental.

While practicing in Federal Court may seem more demanding than state court, once its procedural details are learned, it may can be an excellent forum for disability rights litigation. (See discussion, *infra*, Section V-G-2 of "General Order 56" procedures in the Northern District). A lawsuit under the ADA may be filed in either state court or federal court. However, because the ADA is a federal statute, each state court defendant has a right to <u>remove</u> any "ADA" action to federal court, if they so choose. This must be done within 30 days of service. 28 USC 1441. Also, while many federal judges may have a reputation for being more "conservative," they may also be more experienced in handling ADA cases than many state court judges.

This book does <u>not</u> cover employment discrimination against disabled persons under either state law or under ADA Title I. Some "public services" issues covered by ADA Title II are discussed, but <u>not</u> the requirements for <u>public transportation</u> (by planes, buses, trains, etc.).[6] However, we do note specific laws prohibiting denial of access to individuals with service animals (such as taxi drivers refusing to pick up blind persons with guide dogs or businesses rejecting qualified service dogs!) While historically most litigation has involved issues of access for mobility impaired persons - including those using wheelchairs, walkers, canes, crutches or leg prostheses - the "access" laws also protect visually disabled persons, hearing impaired persons, and other forms of disabilities.[7]

This book is largely limited to physical barrier removal and access policy violation issues. Other disability related issues are equally important and are treated by other writers, including access to education, transportation, and employment. Each of these subject matter areas includes the need for physical access. For example, we've successfully sued more than fifteen colleges and universities which refused voluntarily to modify areas of their campuses so that wheelchair users could enter and use classrooms, libraries, restrooms, parking facilities, etc., as needed to effectively learn as a student. We've also achieved access improvements to sports arena facilities including the Stanford Maples Pavilion basketball stadium, and the Stanford Football Stadium- (the "old" stadium, recently replaced). (Despite being a Cal "Bear" graduate, I've also been required to sue the U.C. Regents on several occasions, although we've worked out certain other access issues on a voluntary and cooperative basis).

Employment opportunities for mobility disabled persons also depend upon being able to get into a business: if the entrance is blocked by stairs, neither disabled patrons nor prospective employees can get in. That's why this book is focusing on "architectural barriers": we can design public paths of travel without subjecting physically disabled people to the burden of trying to get their wheelchairs up a flight of stairs, or through a narrow doorway.

With proper planning, disabled access in the design and construction of a commercial or

---

[6] Access to government buildings under California law (since 1968) and Title II ADA is discussed in section II, infra.
[7] Section 3 of the ADA (42 USC 12102) defines the "disability": The term "disability" means, with respect to an individual- (A) a physical or mental impairment that substantially limits one or more of the major life activities of such an individual; or (B) a record of such impairment; or (C) being regarded as having such an impairment.

governmental building can cost little or nothing extra to the builder. When considered as part of the design of a new building, access may cost as little as 1-2% of the total cost.

D. BE AWARE OF NEW "SB 1608" LEGISLATIVE CHANGES IN CALIFORNIA LAW, EFFECTIVE JANUARY 1, 2009, AND SB 1186, EFFECTIVE JANUARY 1, 2013

SB 1608, a bill originating in the California Senate and making major changes in the conduct of disability access litigation in California, was signed into law by the Governor on September 28, 2008. It's provisions were effective as of January 1, 2009. Enacted with <u>bipartisan</u> sponsors, including Republican State Senator Tom Harmon and Democratic State Senators Ellen Corbett and Darryl Steinberg, this bill had the support of an unusual coalition which included the California Chamber of Commerce and the state trial lawyers' organization (Consumer Attorneys of California, CAOC). Intended to avoid a possible initiative battle, SB 1608 was passed by unanimous votes in both the California Assembly, and Senate, and signed into law by the Governor.

As noted by <u>O'Campo v. Chico Mall</u> 758 F.Supp.2d 976 (E.D. Cal., 2010), the <u>procedural</u> requirements of these state law changes are <u>not</u> applicable in federal courts. For example, "stays" of proceedings for businesses declaring a "CASp" evaluation cannot be imposed upon federal district courts. Other changes, such as those to sections of the Disabled Rights Acts, Civil Code §§ 54, 54.1, 55 et seq., dealing with <u>damages</u> standards would seem applicable in all courts. Other <u>procedural</u> requirements for courts, including requirements for "notices" to be served on defendants with the summons and complaint, are inapplicable to federal court because of the supremacy of federal law. On its face, procedural aspects of SB1608 are directed to cases before "superior court judges and commissioners." The new <u>state court</u> provisions require specific notice to be served on defendants along with complaint and summons, advising them of their rights to certain new procedures, under specified circumstances, where they have hired and received a report from a "Certified Access Consultant"(CASp Certified) <u>before being sued</u>. Any attorney practicing in this field, whether representing plaintiffs or defendants, should become familiar with the new statutes enacted by SB 1608.

Practitioners should also be aware of new California Civil Code section 55.56, defining what is required for proof of <u>damages</u>, and section 55.55, allowing "<u>written</u> settlement offers, and rejection by the parties" to be considered during attorney fees litigation, "along with other relevant information."[8] (Emphasis added)

Brand new legislation (40 pages) entitled SB 1186, effective January 1, 2013, was just enacted, creating major requirements for disability rights attorneys sending letters or filing complaints in state courts (the new legislation is included herein below as Appendix K to this book).

---

[8] However all communications related to "mediations" presumably remain privileged under both state and federal law.

Attorneys should also be aware of, (and perhaps also "beware" of) a brand new threat of attorney fees against a disabled person who seeks injunctive relief under Civil Code section 55 and loses, even in a good faith lawsuit: Jankey v. Song Koo Lee, 55 Cal. 4th 1038 (2012). Both the new legislation and Jankey are discussed in the Conclusion, section VIII-B, *infra*.

E. STRUCTURE OF THIS BOOK

I have attempted to make this book easier to use by being "repetitious" in certain respects: I've tried to make certain sections of the book "self-contained" where I have included certain information or references which I've already noted earlier in the book, but am repeating for clarity in context.

This is my personal view of the law defining disability access rights, based on my more than 38 years of practice in this area. It is meant to be a start in analyzing any legal issues, not a guide or solution. Reading and Shepardizing the lead cases regarding any issue should help a conscientious researcher and writer toward finding the latest statutes and case law relevant to determining what the current state of the law is - or sometimes- "should be."

F. NOTE ON CIVIL CODE § 55 ATTORNEY FEES THREAT AGAINST PLAINTIFFS: DISTRICT COURT IN OLIVER V. IN-N-OUT BURGERS FOLLOWS HUBBARD V. SOBRECK RATHER THAN JANKEY IN FEDERAL COURT.

This book has numerous references to the California Supreme Court's decision in Jankey v. Song Koo Lee, 55 Cal. 4th 1038 (2012), and its "disagreement" with the Ninth Circuit's decision in Hubbard v. Sobreck, LLC, 554 F.3d 742 (9th Cir. 2009), which held that federal law preempts Civil Code § 55. On May 10, 2013, Oliver v. In-N-Out Burgers, __ F.Supp.2d __ (2013), 2013 WL 1927121 (S.D.Cal., May 10, 2013), followed SoBreck rather than Jankey: Judge Marilyn L. Huff, held,

> The Ninth Circuit in Hubbard v. SoBreck, LLC held that federal law preempts section 55. 554 F.3d 742, 745–47 (9th Cir.2009). Specifically, the Ninth Circuit held "to the extent that Section 55 does authorize the award of fees to a prevailing defendant on nonfrivolous CDPA state claims that parallel nonfrivolous ADA claims, there is a conflict and the ADA preempts Section 55 of the CDPA." Id. at 747. Therefore, a federal district court may not impose fees pursuant to section 55 unless the court determines that the plaintiff's action was frivolous. See id. at 747.

Oliver, at p.*5.

Rejecting In-N-Out's argument that Jankey should be the "supreme authority on the interpretation of California state statutes," Oliver held that:

> "California Civil Code § 55 may be a state statute, but whether a state statute is preempted by federal law is a question of federal law. . .. Therefore, the Court is bound by the Ninth Circuit's decision in Hubbard." (Oliver at p.*5.)

This opinion should protect good faith plaintiffs from the threat of prevailing party attorney fees against them if they sue in federal court.

I. CALIFORNIA LAW - ENFORCING CALIFORNIA'S DISABLED ACCESS REQUIREMENTS THROUGH PRIVATE LAWSUIT<u>S</u>

   A. LIABILITY: THE RIGHT TO "FULL AND EQUAL ACCESS" UNDER CALIFORNIA LAW

   1. INTRODUCTION: THE PROBLEM OF ACCESS DENIAL

   More than 40 years ago the problem of denial of access to wheelchair users was clearly recognized in the United States as a civil rights issue:

   > "As clearly as 'NO IRISH ALLOWED' and 'WHITE ONLY' the stairways, narrow doors and sidewalk curbs of our society indicate to handicapped persons their exclusion from the centers of our social life."

   <u>1967 Report of the National Commission on Architectural Barriers to Rehabilitation of the Handicapped</u>

   While statutes formerly referred to the need for protection of "the handicapped," and today's nomenclature refers to "disabled" persons, the issues are identical. Courts have recognized that discrimination against physically disabled persons is as destructive and humiliating to them as racial discrimination is to persons of color. As recognized by the California Supreme Court:

   > Disability discrimination is indistinguishable in many ways from race and sex discrimination. Specifically, it can "attack the individual's sense of self-worth in much the same fashion as race or sex discrimination."

   <u>City of Moorpark v. Sup. Ct.</u> (1998) 18 Cal.4th 1143, 1160.

   California has been the state leading the way in recognizing this problem. The issue of discrimination against the "handicapped" was addressed by the California Legislature and signed into law in the late 1960s, more than four decades ago. The California legislation included the Disabled Rights Acts, Civil Code §§ 54, 54.1, 54.3, and 55 which went into effect between 1968 and 1970; the addition of requirements for new construction and alteration entitled "Access to Public Accommodations for Physically Handicapped Persons," Health & Safety Code §§ 19955 - 19959 (effective July 1, 1970); and adding "physically disabled persons" to the categories of persons protected by the Unruh Civil Rights Act, California Civil Code §§ 51-52 (in 1987).

   Even though California passed most of these laws for protecting the disabled more than 40 years ago, (20 years <u>before</u> passage of the "Americans With Disabilities Act of 1990" (the "ADA"), these laws have never been fully enforced by the government.

   Today, despite the existence of these statutory protections, the owners and operators of many large public facilities are still <u>resisting</u> providing the legally required "full and equal" access rights to disabled persons. Political attacks over the last twenty years have continued efforts to weaken disability rights protections on both the state and national level. Lobbying groups including the U.S. Chamber of Commerce, the California Chamber of Commerce, the California Hotel Association, and the California Restaurant Association, have been working on the national and state levels to weaken existing laws and turn back the clock against the established rights of physically disabled persons. Only time will tell whether the well-intentioned passage of SB 1608 in 2008 by a unanimous California legislature will have the effect of strengthening or weakening enforcement efforts.[9]

Businesses which "save money" by violating the law and refusing to provide the legally required disabled access, effectively seek to create an unfair competitive advantage over other businesses - the vast majority of businesses in California - which have complied with the law.[10] Yet, ironically, when disabled accessible features are incorporated into new construction, the additional cost is usually negligible, at most only 1% to 2% of the total construction costs. While the cost of barrier removal from existing commercial buildings may vary, in many cases such cost will be offset by the additional customers - including both the disabled and their families - that accessible businesses will attract as new customers, once they learn that accessibility has been improved .

"Tort reformers" and certain big business lobbyists have continued their efforts to weaken the Americans With Disabilities Act of 1990 and the similar state laws which have protected disabled persons in California since 1968. One threatened "remedy" which would prejudice disabled rights is the repeatedly proposed "90-day notice" requirement, preparatory to filing suit, as a condition precedent for later winning damages or attorney fees. (See article, "Go Ahead, Make My 90 Days: Should Plaintiffs be Required to Provide Notice to Defendants Before Filing Suit Under Title III of the Americans with Disabilities Act?" by (the late) Professor Adam Milani, Wisconsin Law Review (Vol. 2001, No. 1). While the efforts of certain District Court judges to add their own "notice" requirements have been soundly rejected by the Ninth Circuit (cf. Skaff v. Meridien North America Beverly Hills, LLC (9th Cir. 2007) 506 F.3d 832), advocates for the disabled must be vigilant in opposing efforts to weaken legal protections for the disabled. Fortunately the "ADA Notification Act" (H.R. 2804 in 2005) (popularly known as the "Foley Act"), lost most of its momentum after its chief Congressional sponsor, Rep. Mark Foley of Florida, resigned from Congress in October, 2006, after accusations that he had shown an improper interest in Congressional page boys. In

---

[9] SB 1608 was supported by an unusual coalition of influential lobbying groups: the California Chamber of Commerce, California Hotel Association, California Restaurant Association and the Consumer Attorneys of California.
[10] In Californians for Disability Rights v. Mervyn's LLC, 165 CA 4th 571 (2008) plaintiff's state court complaint was based on section 17200 Business and Professions Code, alleging that Mervyn's failure to comply with the ADA constituted an unfair business practice. The trial court's judgment for defendants was reversed on appeal. Section 17200 et seq, combined with Code of Civil Procedure 1021.5 public interest attorneys fees may provide tools for enforcing disability access rights.

2000 actor/director Clint Eastwood supported this bill in congressional hearings, but lost interest after a lawsuit against his "Mission Ranch" Resort was litigated and eventually "settled!"

2. CASE LAW SUPPORTS USE OF PRIVATE LAWSUITS TO OBTAIN ACCESS IN CALIFORNIA

The right to file a "private" disabled access enforcement lawsuit based upon California civil rights laws and architectural barriers laws, and necessitated by a defendant's failure to provide legally required "full and equal access" to a public facility at the time of construction or alteration, was confirmed by the publication of James Donald v. Sacramento Valley Bank (1989) 209 Cal.App.3d 1183. The right of access to all levels of a given restaurant floor, and the right of a disabled person to recover damages and attorney fees under existing California law, were confirmed by James Donald v. Café Royale (1990) 218 Cal.App.3d 168, and Mark Hankins v. El Torito Restaurants, (1998) 63 Cal. App.4th 510. Café Royale also confirmed the right to mandatory statutory minimum damages and attorney fees, per Civil Code § 54.3, and held that no "wrongful intent" was needed to prove a violation of Civil Code § 54.1. Hankins v. El Torito, *supra*, also upheld a trial court's award of $80,000 damages for a single disability access violation (refusal to allow a disabled man to use an available "employees" first floor restroom where the public restroom was up a flight of stairs and physically inaccessible).

Hankins also upheld a trial court award of $403,000 statutory attorney fees. An additional $323,000 fees were awarded to plaintiff's attorneys by the trial court after remand, including a 1.4 public interest "multiplier" enhancement, after defendants' unsuccessful appeals to the First District California Court of Appeals and the California Supreme Court. The threat of paying plaintiff's attorney fees has continued to be a positive incentive for businesses to comply with disabled access laws.

"'The fee-shifting statutes reflect a judgment that civil rights laws will be underenforced unless private lawyers are given financial incentives to bring cases under those laws.' Bagenstos, *supra*, 54 U.C.L.A. L.Rev. at 30.[11] Defense counsel cannot assert these very incentives as a reason to deny the statutorily conferred right they were designed to bring. 'That plaintiffs' lawyers want to be paid the 'reasonable' attorneys' fees authorized by statute should provide no basis for objecting to their litigation practices.'"
Kittok v. Leslie's Poolmart, (E.D. Cal. 2009) 687 F.Supp.2d 953, at 959.

Although the "Americans with Disabilities Act of 1990" (ADA) created national laws protecting the civil rights of physically disabled persons, the California laws, on the books

---
[11] The Perversity of Limited Civil Rights Remedies: The Case of 'Abusive' ADA Litigation, 54 U.C.L.A. L.Rev. (2006).

since July 1, 1970, specifically require access whenever any commercial new construction or building "alterations" are made after that date. (See Health & Safety Code §§ 19955-19959, and § 19953 regarding injunctive relief.) The ADA did not require construction related and alteration related access until January 26, 1993. See ADA § 303 [42 USC 12183].

Individual civil rights enforcement actions are absolutely necessary: there is no federal or state administrative agency designated to enforce Title III of the ADA, and California building department enforcement of California laws was particularly ineffective for new construction and alterations occurring during the 1970s and 1980s. Because building department enforcement has historically been less than perfect, without private enforcement actions, businesses that illegally altered their premises without providing disabled access would be allowed to operate in perpetuity without "full and equal" access for physically disabled persons.

This historical analysis is also one reason why the courts have held that the current owner and operator are responsible for access-triggering alterations that occurred during a predecessor's ownership. (See opinions by Northern District Chief Judge Vaughan Walker in Stickney v. McDonald's (N.D.Cal.) Case No. C99-0558 VRW, Order of January 23, 2000, and Hodges v. El Torito Restaurants, Inc. (N.D.Cal.) (WL 95398, Order of February 24, 1998.) Without successor liability, "businesses would be able to circumvent California's various accessibility requirements through sham sales and transfers." Id.

3. PRIVATE LAWSUITS ARE NEEDED TO ENFORCE ADA TITLE III IN CALIFORNIA

Indeed, private (individual, non-governmental) actions are virtually the only effective mechanism for enforcement of disabled rights in California under Title III of the ADA. Title III, § 302(b)(2)(A)(iv), adds the "readily achievable" barrier removal protections to those set into effect by new construction or "alterations" regulated under California law. [42 USC 12182.] ("Readily achievable" is defined by § 301(9).) Since building officials are not currently authorized under California law to enforce "readily achievable" requirements under the ADA, and as there is no federal administrative agency enforcing ADA Title III, without private lawsuits there would be virtually no enforcement. In 1993, California Attorney General Dan Lungren[12] issued Opinion No. 93-203: that the ADA would not be enforced in California by local building departments and that the "primary responsibility for enforcement of the ADA access requirements through legal action rests with private litigants and the United States Attorney General."

---

[12] See Appendix, infra, section IX-E-2, Opp. Cal. A.G. 93-203, at p. 7. Unfortunately, nearly 20 years later, in 2011-2012, Dan Lundgren, now a Southern California Congressman, is sponsoring legislation to weaken ADA enforcement and add a "90 day notice" requirement similar to the one pushed by Clint Eastwood and Florida Congressman Mark Foley in 2000.

Unfortunately, Department of Justice enforcement actions were rare under the George W. Bush administration (2001-2008). Indeed, in at least one access lawsuit, filed against BART (Bay Area Rapid Transit) on behalf of visually disabled persons, the "Civil Rights" Division of the DOJ actually intervened in defendant's appeal to <u>oppose</u> the rights of visually disabled persons! (<u>George, et al. v. Bay Area Rapid Transit</u> (N.D.Cal.) Case No. C00-02206 CW)(summary judgment for plaintiff under the ADA <u>reversed</u> and remanded in <u>George, et al. v. BART</u>, (9th Cir. 2009) 577 F.3d 1005), later satisfactorily settled because the appellate court had allowed plaintiff to proceed on an alternate state law theory).

Arguably the incorporation of any violation of the ADA as also constituting a violation of California disability rights statutes - Civil Code §§ 51(f), 54(c) and 54.1(d), subjecting offending businesses to the remedies of Civil Code §§ 52, 54.3 and 55 - also subjects such offenders to state enforcement ("an action to enjoin any violation of section 54 or 54.1") by the California Attorney General and any City Attorney or District Attorney. (See Civil Code § 55.1 and California Health & Safety Code § 19958.) Certainly, more public enforcement would necessitate <u>fewer</u> private lawsuits; but that would be a win-win situation for everyone involved, wouldn't it?

In reality, Title III of the ADA was passed in 1990 as a compromise, relying on private enforcement actions to avoid the alternative of a possibly expensive federal "enforcement bureaucracy." (This was apparently necessary to get ADA Title III support from certain Republicans, and the signature by President George H.W. Bush, July 26, 1990.) There is no local governmental enforcement for ADA Title III, the privately operated "public accommodations" section. While "you can't always get what you want," passage of Title III potentially enabled disabled persons to "get what [they] need," i.e. tools to oppose barrier discrimination by remedies of private law suits for injunctive relief and attorney fees.

Although Title III includes no provision for payment of damages, in 1996 California amended Civil Code §§ 51(f), 54(c) and 54.1(d) to incorporate any ADA violation as a violation of California law as well. In this way, California effectively <u>created damages remedies</u> for ADA violations, per Civil Code § 52 for any violation of § 51(f), and per § 54.3 for any violation of §§ 54(c) or 54.1(d).

4. CALIFORNIA'S PUBLIC POLICY IS TO MAXIMIZE ACCESS

   a. POLICY IS TO MAXIMIZE INTEGRATION OF DISABLED PERSONS INTO ALL SOCIAL AND ECONOMIC ASPECTS OF OUR SOCIETY, INCLUDING ANY STATE FUNDED PROGRAM OR ACTIVITIES
   California's strong public policy declaration, (per Government Code §19230), is to maximize the integration of disabled persons into all social and economic aspects of our

society. Providing a damages remedy, including a potential treble damages remedy, as well as statutory attorney fees (per Civil Code §§ 52, 54.3 and 55) added incentives for compliance. (See policy discussion in Donald v. Café Royale, *supra*.) Per California Government Code § 19230:

> Legislative declaration: State policy:
>
> The Legislature hereby declares that (a) It is the policy of this State to encourage and enable individuals with a disability to participate fully in the social and economic life of the State and to engage in remunerative employment.

Further, discrimination on the basis of disability in any program or activity conducted by or receiving state funding, has been prohibited since 1977 by California Government Code § 11135. This code currently reads (in relevant part):

> § 11135. Programs or activities funded by state; discrimination on basis of race, national origin, ethnic group identification, religion, age, sex, sexual orientation, color, or disability; federal act; definitions; legislative findings and declarations
>
> (a) No person in the State of California shall, on the basis of race, national origin, ethnic group identification, religion, age, sex, sexual orientation, color, or disability, be unlawfully denied full and equal access to the benefits of, or be unlawfully subjected to discrimination under, any program or activity that is conducted, operated, or administered by the state or by any state agency, is funded directly by the state, or receives any financial assistance from the state. Notwithstanding Section 11000, this section applies to the California State University.
>
> (b) With respect to discrimination on the basis of disability, programs and activities subject to subdivision (a) shall meet the protections and prohibitions contained in Section 202 of the Americans with Disabilities Act of 1990 (42 U.S.C. Sec. 12132), and the federal rules and regulations adopted in implementation thereof, except that if the laws of this state prescribe stronger protections and prohibitions, the programs and activities subject to subdivision (a) shall be subject to the stronger protections and prohibitions.
>
> (c) (1) As used in this section, "disability" means any mental or physical disability, as defined in Section 12926.

b. ENCOURAGING PRIVATE LAWSUITS ENFORCES THIS CALIFORNIA PUBLIC POLICY

Because of this public policy, in the past the California Attorney General's Office has encouraged the use of private lawsuits to enforce disabled access rights. The Attorney General's office (under Attorney General John van de Camp) joined

Plaintiffs' attorney Paul Rein as amicus curiae in two published cases upholding the use of private lawsuits to protect disabled rights by injunction and compensation for violations of those rights by money damages: James Donald v. Sacramento Bank (1989) 209 Cal.App.3d 1183 and James Donald v. Café Royale (1990) 218 Cal.App.3d 168, "stressing the limited resources of its Civil Rights Division and supporting the need for private lawsuits to enforce disabled access.". Blackwell v. Foley 724 F. Supp. 2nd 1068.[13]

c. OBJECTIVES OF COMPLAINT: INJUNCTION, DAMAGES AND FEES
A complaint regarding alleged disability access violations by a privately owned public accommodation may seek injunctive relief and/or damages potentially awardable under three causes of action under California law, in addition to remedies under the ADA: (1) Violation of statutory protections for disabled persons, Health & Safety Code §§ 19955-19959 (an injunction is specified per § 19953, with statutory "prevailing party" attorney fees); (2) Denial of full and equal access under the Disabled Persons Act, which allows liability for a denial of access without any need to show any form of "intent" (cf. Donald v. Café Royale, *supra*), per Civil Code §§ 54 and 54.1, enforced by damages and attorney fees per § 54.3 and by injunctions and attorney fees per § 55; and (3) Violation of the Unruh Civil Rights Act, Civil Code § 51, enforced by damages and attorney fees per § 52. General damages including emotional distress damages are available, alternatively, under Civil Code §§ 52 and 54.3, with $4,000 and $1,000 minimum statutory damages available, respectively. Café Royale and subsequent case law citing it appear to hold that to prove damages a disabled person must have actually tried to use a facility on a specific occasion, or have been deterred from trying because they had learned about the inaccessibility. (Arnold v. United Artists Theater Circuit, Inc., et al. (N.D.Cal. 1994) 866 F.Supp 433) (See 2008 codification of this standard as part of SB 1608 legislation and new Civil Code § 55.56, effective January 1, 2009.) Civil Code § 52(h) defines "actual damages" as "special damages and general damages;" and presumably this definition also applies to § 54.3 "actual damages." [See § I-"I", *infra*, re: damages.]
While damages up to $7,500 are also available in small claims court, small claims court does not have jurisdiction for injunctive relief. (See §VI-A, *infra*)

d. STATUTORY DAMAGES ARE AVAILABLE
Statutory damages are available per Civil Code §§ 52 and 54.3, with minimum damages, respectively, of $4,000 and $1,000 per violation. (There is no statutory

---

[13]Donald v. Sacramento Valley Bank, *supra*, originally an "unpublished" opinion by the Third District Court of Appeals, was ordered published by a 7-0 vote of the California Supreme Court in 1989.) (Both Donald cases were decided before passage of the ADA in 1990, and did not involve ADA issues.)

maximum damages.) $80,000 general damages - specifically <u>without</u> the court awarding any treble damages - were awarded at a San Mateo County bench trial and upheld on appeal in <u>Hankins v. El Torito Restaurants</u> (1998) 63 Cal. App 4th 510. These two statutes each also authorize imposition of <u>treble</u> damages. Punitive damages <u>may</u> be available per Civil Code § 3294, upon proof that defendants acted in conscious disregard for the rights or safety of plaintiff and other disabled persons, or otherwise acted fraudulently, maliciously or oppressively. (However, some <u>courts</u> have held that the treble damages provisions of § 54.3 Civil Code are for "punishment," preempt the field, and preclude reliance on § 3294 in an action based on violations of sections 54 or 54.1.)

In a 1989 Alameda County Superior Court jury trial, then DREDF attorney Sid Wolinsky obtained major damages against a restaurant chain and its C.E.O. when the chain carried out a $250,000 remodel at H's Lordships Restaurant in Berkeley, <u>without</u> providing a ramp so that disabled wheelchair users could reach the dining area without being "carried" down stairs. Plaintiff Julie Weisman, a quadriplegic law student taking her parents to dinner, was humiliated to have to be physically <u>carried</u> down the stairs. Defendants' contractor testified that he'd offered to construct a ramp for $15,000, but the president of the restaurant corporation refused to spend more than $10,000, and so provided no access! The jury awarded $35,000 compensatory damages, $250,000 punitive damages (per section 3294 Civil Code) against the corporation and another $250,000 punitive damages against the corporation president sued as an individual defendant! <u>Weisman v. Specialty Restuarants, et al</u> (1989). (The trial judge, Hon. Winton McKibben also added $175,000 statutory attorney fees upon post-trial motion.)

5. PLAINTIFF DOES NOT HAVE TO PROVE WRONGFUL "INTENT"

   a. BECAUSE PUBLIC POLICY IS TO MAXIMIZE DISABLED ACCESSIBILITY IN COMMERCIAL BUILDINGS, NO PROOF OF WRONGFUL INTENT IS REQUIRED FOR VIOLATION OF CIVIL CODE §§ 54 AND 54.1, THE DISABLED PERSONS ACT

   In <u>Donald v. Café Royale</u>, *supra*, the trial court had entered judgment against the disabled plaintiff, access pioneer Jim Donald (a quadriplegic attorney), because plaintiff failed to prove that the restaurant operator - who had illegally installed all "tiered" seating up stairs that a disabled wheelchair user couldn't climb - had done so with an improper <u>"intent" to discriminate</u>. The Court of Appeals reversed the trial court, tracing the legislative history and <u>purpose</u> of the disabled access legislation, and found that, because the purpose of the legislation was to require access, adding an element of "intentionality" would be inconsistent with that purpose:

   It is plain to see the Legislature's purpose in imposing increased penalties and additional enforcement methods is to guarantee compliance with equal access requirements. The impediments to the physically handicappeds' interaction in community life is the inequity which section 54 et seq. and section 19955 et seq. seek to prevent. This goal is not met by adopting an interpretation of section 54.3 which would include an element of intentional violation. Such a construction ignores the express language of the statute, its apparent purpose, and the public policy goal of the legislation. The level of compliance would diminish, a result that is clearly repugnant to the statutory purpose. Donald v. Café Royale, *supra*, at 179-180.

Similarly, the 9th Circuit interpretations of Title II and Title III of the ADA have rejected any "intentionality" requirement. (Crowder v. Kitigawa, Chairman Hawaiian Bd. of Control (9th Cir. 1996) 81 F.3d 1480; Helen L. v. DiDario, 46 F.3d 325, 335 (3d Cir. 1995).) (However, a violation of Title II requires proof of wrongful intent for an award of damages under federal law. See section II-C-7, *infra*.)

b. AN "UNRUH ACT" (SECTION 51 CIVIL CODE) VIOLATION DOES NOT REQUIRE PROOF OF WRONGFUL "INTENT," (AS FINALLY DECIDED BY THE CALIFORNIA SUPREME COURT IN MUNSON V. DEL TACO, 2009)

While no "intent" proof is required for a violation of the "Disabled Persons Act" (Civil Code §§ 54 and 54.1, with remedies under §§ 54.3 and 55) (cf. Donald v. Café Royale, *supra*), federal and state courts had come to conflicting results as to the same issue under the Unruh Act, Civil Code § 51 (with remedies under §§ 52). The federal courts had held that, where the violation of § 51 was based on an incorporated violation of the ADA (i.e., by § 51(f)), there should be no "intent" required. The federal courts reasoned that if the ADA can be violated without wrongful "intent" (Cf. Crowder v. Kitigawa, Chairman Hawaiian Bd. of Control (9th Cir. 1996) 81 F.3d 1480, and Helen L. v. DiDario, 46 F.3d 325, 335 (3d Cir. 1995)), no intent should be needed under a California statute which incorporates any violation of the ADA as a per se violation of the state law (Civil Code §§ 51(f) et seq.). (See Wilson v Haria, discussed below)

Arnold v. United Artists Theater Circuit, Inc., et al. (N.D.Cal. 1994) 866 F.Supp 433, had previously held that § 51 could be violated without proof of wrongful intent when it was based on a violation of the ADA, even as to a class of disabled patrons who had been "deterred." This is consistent with other cases which held the ADA could be violated without wrongful intent. Crowder v. Kitigawa, *supra*; Helen L. v. DiDario, *supra*. However, a 2006 California "intermediate" appellate court in Gunther v. Lin, 144 Cal.App.4th 223, 50 Cal.Rptr.3d 317 (Cal.Ct.App. 2006), temporarily added an "intent" requirement back into Civil Code § 51, even when the Civil Code violation was based on incorporation of an "ADA" violation.[14] The Gunther court relied on a

California Supreme Court decision in a non-disability case decided before § 51(f)'s incorporation of the ADA was added by the California legislature in 1992. At least one federal District Court declined to follow Gunther v. Lin: Judge Lawrence Karlton's decision in Wilson v. Haria and Gogri Corp. dba Jack in the Box, et al. (E.D.Cal. 2007) 479 F.Supp.2d 1127, rejected Gunther because it felt the California Supreme Court would not have come to the same conclusion on this state law issue. Wilson held that Gunther was wrong, and as a decision of an intermediary appellate court on a matter of state law rather than of the California Supreme Court, Gunther was not binding on federal district courts. (Wilson v. Haria, et al., *supra*.) In Wilson v. Haria, *supra*, at 1137, Judge Lawrence Karlton reasoned:

> Every court to have considered the issue with the exception of Gunther has read Section 51(f) as not requiring proof of intent. See, e.g., Lentini, 370 F.3d at 847; Presta, 16 F.Supp.2d at 1136; Hubbard v. Twin Oaks Health and Rehabilitation Ctr., 408 F.Supp.2d 923, 928-29 (2004) (Karlton, J.); Boemio, 954 F.Supp. at 208.

In 2008 this issue was certified by the 9th Circuit to the California Supreme Court, as an issue of state law. In June 2009 the California Supreme Court held that Judge Karlton was correct in his Wilson v. Haria analysis, and that no wrongful intent need be proven for a violation of the Unruh Act (section 51ff California Civil Code). Munson v. Del Taco, Inc., 46 Cal.4th 661 (2009) concluded:

> We conclude that a plaintiff proceeding under section 51, subdivision(f) may obtain statutory damages on proof of an ADA access violation without the need to demonstrate additionally that the discrimination was intentional.

> Id. at 670.

B. CALIFORNIA STATUTORY SCHEME FOR DISABLED ACCESS

1. PUBLIC POLICY AND PURPOSE OF REGULATIONS: TO MAXIMIZE ACCESSIBILITY AND USABILITY FOR DISABLED PERSONS

   a. INTERPRETATION OF STATUTES: CALIFORNIA PUBLIC POLICY REQUIRES A BROAD INTERPRETATION OF STATUTES RELATING TO PROTECTING "HANDICAPPED" PERSONS/INDIVIDUALS WITH A "DISABILITY" AND THEIR RIGHTS TO USE PRIVATE LAWSUITS TO ENFORCE ACCESS COMPLIANCE

   California's public policy toward its disabled citizens is established by Government

---

[14]The California appellate court in Gunther v. L in, *supra*, arguably ignored the public policy of maximizing access compliance, as found by the 1990 Court of Appeal decision in Donald v. Café Royale, *supra*, in regard to finding no intent needed under Civil Code § 54.3.

Code § 19230: "The Legislature hereby declares that: (a) It is the policy of this state to encourage and enable individuals with a disability to participate fully in the social and economic life of the state and to engage in remunerative employment." This provision has been cited by courts which have broadly construed statutes intended to help the disabled. [See §§ I.A.4, *supra*, on California's public policy.] In Greater Los Angeles Council on Deafness, Inc. v. Zolin (9th Cir. 1987) 812 F.2d 1103, at 1114, the 9th Circuit considered the important policy considerations involved when interpreting statutes relating to protecting "handicapped" persons, holding that these statutory rights could be enforced by "private lawsuits":

> Also important to our decision is California's stated policy to achieve, in so far as possible, the "total integration of handicapped persons into the mainstream of society." In re Marriage of Carney, 24 Cal.3d 725, 740... (1979) (citing section 11135 as one example of the state legislature's effort in this regard). Cal. Gov't Code §11139 (West 1980), for example, mandates construing section 11135 and related civil rights provisions so as not to frustrate their purpose. Further, among the numerous handicapped rights statutes scattered throughout California Codes is an unequivocal statement that it is California's policy "to encourage and enable disabled persons to participate fully in the social and economic life of the state..." Cal. Gov't Code §19230(a) (West 1980). Refusing handicapped people an opportunity to vindicate their rights through private lawsuits would, in our view, be inconsistent with these statements of policy from California's legislature and courts.

In People Ex Rel. Duekmejian v. C.H.E., Inc. (1984) 150 Cal.App.3d 123, at 133, an access enforcement action by the California Attorney General, the court traced the legislative schemes establishing handicapped access requirements in California and noted,

> The underlying legislative intent of these statutory schemes is to require affirmative conduct so as to guarantee access to the physically handicapped upon construction of new facilities or with the repair or alteration of existing facilities. (Emphasis added)

An array of legislative schemes was set out by the court in Donald v. Sacramento Valley Bank (1989) 209 Cal.App.3d 1183, a pre-ADA California decision which confirmed the use of private lawsuits to enforce statutory building code requirements for provision of access. This case specified the incorporation of the Government Code §§ 4450 et seq. standards for government buildings (1968) into Health & Safety Code §§ 19955-19959 (1970), which applied these same construction and alteration standards to privately financed public accommodations.

This case also recognized that the 1961 ASA (American Standards Association) standards (also known as "ANSI") specified the building code regulations applicable under Health & Safety Code § 19959, from 1970 to 1982, when Title 24 (the California Building Code) was adopted. (These architectural industry standards were thus adopted into law). The court applied Health & Safety Code § 19959's "alteration" provisions to require an accessible path of travel under the ASA regulations to an automated teller machine (ATM) installed in 1975 on the exterior of a bank that was otherwise constructed before 1970. The ATM was constructed at the top of five stairs. When defendants objected that the 1961 ASA standards didn't <u>specify</u> application to construction of an "ATM" facility, the court noted that the law applied to <u>any</u> public facility, especially as ATMs had not even been invented until well after 1961. Since virtually all ATM facilities had been installed after the July 1, 1970 effective date of Health & Safety Code § 19959, the court's ruling effectively required that every ATM constructed in California had to be placed in an accessible location! A publication of the banking industry complained that this ruling would cost banks in California more than $43 million in remediation expenses.

b. CALIFORNIA STATUTES AND DECLARATIONS OF POLICY SUPPORT BROAD INTERPRETATIONS OF PROTECTIONS FOR DISABLED PERSONS

(1) GOAL: TOTAL INTEGRATION OF DISABLED PERSONS INTO MAINSTREAM SOCIETY
Obtaining accessible public facilities is an important feature in the legislative effort to end discrimination against the disabled. Per <u>People Ex Rel Deukmejian v. CHE</u> (1983) 150 Cal. App.3d 123:

The prohibition against discrimination of the handicapped within Civil Code section 54 et seq., the enactment of Government Code section 4450 et seq. and section 19955 et seq., and the incorporation by reference of the phrase "primary entrance" within applicable specifications, reflect a legislative sensitivity to the hardships suffered by those afflicted with a wide range of physical disabilities. They are part of an expanding legislative effort to attain "the commendable goal of total integration of handicapped persons into the mainstream of society." (Id., at 135)

(2) CIVIL CODE §§ 51, 54 AND 54.1 PROVIDE PROTECTIONS FOR DISABLED PERSONS
The Unruh Civil Rights Act (Civil Code §§ 51-52) and the Disability Rights Act (Civil Code §§ 54 and 54.1), give important legal remedies for disabled persons. In addition to damages, available pursuant to §§ 52 and 54.3, injunctive relief for §51 violations is provided by §52(c) and injunctive relief for §§ 54 and 54.1 violations is offered by § 55. Attorney fees and costs may be recovered per §§ 52, 54.3 and 55. Effective 1988, the Unruh Civil Rights Act, Civil Code §§ 51 and 52, added "disabled persons" to the

protected categories of persons against whom discrimination is forbidden.[15]

Civil Code § 54 provides that:
> Individuals with disabilities . . . have the same right as the general public to the <u>full and free</u> use of the streets, highways, sidewalks, walkways, public buildings, medical facilities, including hospitals, clinics, and physicians' offices, public facilities, and other public places. [Emphasis Added]

Section 54.1(a)(1) guarantees that:
> Individuals with disabilities shall be entitled to <u>full and equal access</u>, as other members of the general public, to accommodations, advantages, facilities, medical facilities, including hospitals, clinics, and physicians' offices, and privileges of all common carriers, airplanes, motor vehicles, railroad trains, motorbuses, streetcars, boats or any other public conveyances or modes of transportation (whether private, public, franchised, licensed, contracted, or otherwise provided), telephone facilities, adoption agencies, private schools, hotels, lodging places, places of public accommodation and amusement or resort, and other places to which the general public is invited, subject only to the conditions and limitations established by law, or state or federal regulations, and applicable alike to all other persons. (Emphasis added)

Section 54.1(d) further states that, "Full and equal access" includes,
> ... access that meets the standards of Titles II and III of the Americans With Disabilities Act of 1990 and federal regulations adopted pursuant thereto, except that, if the laws of this state prescribe higher standards, it shall mean access that meets these higher standards.

Both the Legislature and the Supreme Court have made clear that courts should construe this language in the broadest possible manner in order to facilitate integration of people with disabilities into all aspects of mainstream society.

The California statutory scheme and its purpose to eliminate barriers to the integration of people with disabilities into the mainstream of community life were described in <u>Café Royale</u>, *supra*; <u>James Donald v. Sacramento Valley Bank</u>, *supra*, at 1191; <u>City and County of San Francisco v. Grant</u>, 181 Cal. App.3d 1085, 1092 (1986); and <u>People Ex Rel. Deukmejian v. CHE, Inc.</u> 150 Cal.App.3d 123, 131 (1983).

In <u>Arnold v. United Artists Theater Circuit, Inc., et al.</u> (N.D.Cal. 1994) 866

---

[15] See "Public Interest Law and Attorney's Fees: Using the New Civil Rights Statutes for Handicapped Persons and Others," May, 1989, Vol. 19, No. 4, CTLA Forum, p. 155, by Paul L. Rein.

F.Supp 433, Judge Thelton Henderson cited <u>Donald v. Café Royale</u>, *supra*, at 808-811, for the "presumption in favor of a broad interpretation in order to further the statute's remedial purpose" being "applied in Civil Code § 54.1 cases." Similarly, the court held that the "California courts have applied the canon of broad construction to civil rights statutes generally, and to § 51 and § 54.1 in particular," citing the California Supreme Court's decision "to interpret the [Unruh] Act's coverage 'in the broadest sense reasonably possible.' " <u>Isbister v. Boys' Club of Santa Cruz</u>, 40 Cal.3d 72, 75-76.

(3) THE TERM "ACCESSIBLE TO AND USEABLE BY" SET FORTH IN THE STATUTES REFLECTS THE GENERAL <u>PURPOSE</u> OF ACCESS <u>RATHER</u> THAN THE SPECIFIC IMPLEMENTING REQUIREMENTS FOR ACCESS COMPLIANCE; THESE WERE SET BY THE ASA AS "<u>MINIMUM</u> STANDARDS" (FOR 1968 - 1981, BEFORE TITLE 24)

<u>Donald v . Sacramento Valley Bank</u>, *supra*, and <u>Donald v. Café Royale</u>, *supra*, held that private persons could file suit to enforce Health & Safety Code § 19955 et seq., and that a violation of § 19955 et seq. resulting in a disabled person being denied access gave that person the right to sue for damages and injunctive relief under Civil Code § 54.1's guarantee of "full and equal access." In federal court, <u>Arnold v. United Artists Theater Circuit, Inc., et al.</u>, *supra*, extended the right to sue under § 54.1 to all those deterred from visiting or utilizing public facilities due to access violations.

While the "purpose" of Government Code § 4450 and of the access policy provisions subsequently incorporated into Health & Safety Code §§ 19955 et seq. is to render buildings and other related public facilities "accessible to and usable by" the physically handicapped, these general statutes did not take the place of specific regulations.[16] Government Code §§ 4450, 4451 and 4452 <u>each</u> referred to future <u>regulations</u> which would be developed "as the State Architect determines are necessary to assure access and usability for the physically

---

[16] Indeed, this was the holding of the (now outdated) decision in <u>Marsh v. Edwards Theatres</u> (1976) 64 Cal.App.3d, 134 Cal. Rptr. 844, based on a 1968 theater visit, that no violation of Civil Code § 54.1 could occur without violation of specific standards. These standards (for alterations and new construction) were set out effective July 1, 1970 in Health & Safety Code §§ 19955-19959. Moreover, as noted by the Court in <u>Donald v. Sacramento Valley Bank</u> (1989) 209 Cal.App.3d 1183, 1189, "In response to the Marsh case, the Legislature added Civil Code § 55, authorizing a private cause of action to enjoin statutory violations of section 54.1." Health & Safety Code § 19953 is an additional statutory basis for injunctive relief. <u>Hankins v. El Torito Restaurants</u>, (1998) 63 Cal. App.4th 510, held that a policy denying "full and equal access" - a policy prohibiting disabled persons from using an available "employees only" restroom when they were unable to climb stairs to a second floor "public" restroom - violated § 54.1 directly, without need to show violation of any other statute or regulations. As another form of "policy" violation, telling a wheelchair user to leave a store because of concern that the wheelchair "might" scratch furniture, would be a "facial" violation of § 54.1's right to "full and equal access" without need to show any "regulation" was violated. Similarly, telling a person disabled by facial disfigurement to stay out of a grocery store because his appearance made other customers uncomfortable, was a direct violation of both sections 51 and 54.1. (This intentional discrimination costs defendants $75,000 in damages plus payment of plaintiff's attorney fees. See <u>Daniel Holbea v. Shamrock Liquors</u>, N.D. Cal, Case No. C00-3369 MEJ)

handicapped." Per Government Code § 4451(d), <u>until</u> these regulations were promulgated (in what became "Title 24," the "State Architect's Regulations, in 1982), the "ASA" Specifications A117.1/1961 were to be used. (See § II.A.2.a.(3), *infra*.) Per Government Code § 4452, a facility is "accessible" only it if meets specific <u>minimum</u> building standards, <u>minimum requirements</u> to insure that buildings, structures and related facilities covered by this chapter are accessible to and functional for the physically handicapped to, through and within their doors... [Emphasis added]

c. PURPOSE OF STANDARDS: ASA AND TITLE 24 REGULATIONS FOCUS ON MAXIMIZING ACCESSIBILITY AND USABILITY

The earliest guidelines used to set access standards were the 1961 "American Standards Association" (ASA) Standards (also known as the "ANSI" standards). These were adopted in California in 1968 by Government Code §§ 4450-4454, and subsequently adopted into the requirements of Health & Safety Code § 19955 from July 1, 1970 to July 1, 1982 (as explained in <u>Donald v. Sacramento Valley Bank</u> (1989) 209 Cal.App.3d 1183, at 1192, 1194). The ASA Standards applied to all construction and alterations between July 1, 1970 and July 1, 1982 when the State Architect's Regulations (Title 24, Part 2) finally went into effect. These regulations may become important in litigation as many building departments did not fully enforce the access laws during this time period when approving permit applications for construction.

ASA §1.2 is captioned "<u>Purpose,</u>" and this purpose should be considered whenever an "interpretation" is required:
> This standard is <u>intended to make all buildings and facilities used by the public accessible to and functional for the physically handicapped, to, through, and within their doors</u>, without loss of function, space or facility where the general public is concerned. [Emphasis added.]

Similarly, the <u>purpose</u> of Title 24, California Code of Regulations, the State Architect's Regulations (also known as the California Building Code), is stated in its (1982) Preamble:

> To assure that barrier-free design is incorporated into all buildings, facilities, site work and other improvements to which this code applies; to assure that these improvements are accessible to and useable by physically disabled persons.

Any "interpretation" of these regulations which purports to <u>limit</u> access, contrary to the <u>purpose</u> of access regulations to <u>maximize accessibility</u>, should be questioned and/or rejected. We should ask, among alternatives, <u>which</u> interpretation will better serve to ensure that facilities "are accessible to and useable by physically disabled persons?"

d. GOVERNMENT CODE §§ 4450 et seq. REQUIREMENTS WERE ADOPTED BY HEALTH & SAFETY CODE §§ 19955-19959 FOR ALL PRIVATELY OWNED PUBLIC FACILITIES CONSTRUCTED OR ALTERED AFTER JULY 1, 1970, AND SET <u>MINIMUM</u> STANDARDS FOR COMPLIANCE

Government Code § 4450 stated the law's <u>purpose</u>, and authorized the State Architect to adopt implementing regulations, for all governmental public buildings:

> It is the <u>purpose</u> of this chapter to ensure that all buildings, structures, sidewalks, curbs, and related facilities... <u>shall be accessible to and usable by the physically handicapped</u>. The State Architect shall adopt and submit proposed building standards for approval.... and shall adopt other regulations for making buildings, structures, sidewalks, curbs, and related facilities accessible to and usable by the physically handicapped. (Emphasis added)

Basic California policy and law regarding requirements of access at privately owned facilities which serve the public are set out in Health & Safety Code §§ 19955 through 19959. A detailed discussion of the requirements of Health & Safety Code § 19955 and the <u>interrelation</u> of § 19955 to the regulations of Title 24 of the California Administrative Code (the State Building Code), the State Architect's Regulations, and their <u>incorporation</u> into Government Code § 4452 (as explained in more detail hereinbelow) are set out in <u>Donald v. Sacramento Bank</u> (1989) 209 Cal.App.3d 1183.

Health & Safety Code § 19955, effective July 1, 1970, states its <u>"purpose"</u> is to ensure that all public accommodations or facilities constructed in this state with private funds adhere to the provisions of Chapter 7 (commencing with section 4450) of division 5 of Title I of the Government Code.

Government Code § 4450, enacted in 1968, applied new construction and alteration access requirements only to <u>government buildings</u>. However, as of July 1, 1970, Health & Safety Code §§ 19955 et seq. were enacted to <u>incorporate</u> Government Code § 4450's requirements and apply these requirements to <u>all privately owned public "facilities"</u> including restaurants, hotels, retails stores, and other commercial facilities.

Government Code § 4452 specified the intention of the Legislature to use these standards as <u>minimum standards,</u> and set a 90 day compliance standard:

> It is the <u>intent of the Legislature</u> that the building standards published in the State Building Standards Code relating to access by the physically handicapped and the other regulations adopted by the State Architect

pursuant to § 4450 shall be used as <u>minimum requirements</u> to <u>insure</u> that buildings, structures and related facilities covered by this chapter are <u>accessible to and functional for the physically handicapped to, through and within their doors</u>, without loss of function, space or facility where the general public is concerned. <u>Any unauthorized deviation</u> from such regulations or building standards <u>shall be rectified by full compliance within 90 days after discovery of the deviation</u>. (Emphasis added)

The issue of <u>how long</u> it should take a business to remove barriers and comply with the law when an existing statutory violation is "discovered," is addressed by this code section. Health & Safety Code §§ 19955 et seq. adopted Government Code §§ 4450 et seq., and applied these standards to privately financed public facilities. Certainly this § 4452 specification requiring "full compliance within 90 days of notice," should be a prima facie presumptive standard for timely compliance with legal disabled access requirements. When, during litigation, a defendant seeks an <u>unreasonable</u> delay in compliance, this section could be asserted as setting the presumptive "timeliness" standard. Particularly if a building is shown to be out of compliance with the law, there should be no delay in providing a remedy. Indeed, "time is of the essence." If a building owner, etc., did not previously know the building was in violation of the law, he or she certainly "discovered" this when served with a lawsuit! Since lack of access to entry or restrooms effectively excludes plaintiff and other disabled persons from use of a public facility, and continues to discriminate against plaintiff on a day-to-day basis until barriers are removed, time must be "of the essence."

2. ALL "ALTERATIONS, STRUCTURAL REPAIRS, OR ADDITIONS" TO A BUILDING TRIGGER DISABLED ACCESS UNLESS EACH ITEM OF WORK IS SPECIFICALLY "EXCEPTED" BY TITLE 24 REGULATIONS AND PROCEDURES
   a. CALIFORNIA'S STATUTORY SCHEME OF REQUIREMENTS INCLUDES THE HEALTH & SAFETY CODE, GOVERNMENT CODE, AND TITLE 24 - THE STATE BUILDING CODE (THE "STATE ARCHITECT'S REGULATIONS")

   (1) CALIFORNIA STATUTORY SCHEME SUMMARIZED
       The California statutory scheme, effective since 1970, is contained in Health & Safety Code §§ 19955 - 19959 and Civil Code §§ 54 - 55. As summarized by the appellate court in <u>James Donald v. Sacramento Bank</u> (1989) 209 Cal.App.3d 1183, at 1190-1193, California law requires that all public accommodations or facilities with new construction <u>or</u> any "alterations, structural repairs or additions" after July 1, <u>1970</u>, be fully accessible to disabled (or "handicapped")

---

[17] Because the State Architect did not publish these standards until 1981, effective July 1, 1982, the ASA regulations controlled in the interim. See Donald v. Sacramento Valley Bank, *supra*.

persons, and that disabled persons are entitled to "full and equal access" to public facilities. Title 24 of the California Administrative Code contains the specific regulations, promulgated by the State Architect, pursuant to Government Code § 4450 controlling the manner of design and construction required to carry out the statutory mandate for access requirements. Per Government Code sections 4450ff, passed in 1968, the State Architect's (Title 24) Regulations were to impose the same requirements for buildings and structures as were contained in pertinent provisions of the latest edition of the Uniform Building Code as well as <u>additional requirements</u> that the <u>State Architect determined were necessary</u> to assure access and usability for the physically handicapped.[17]

Today the state architect's regulations are generally known as "Title 24" or the "California Building Code" (Title-24)

(2) "ALTERATIONS" TO EACH "FACILITY" TRIGGER ACCESS

Building permit and construction document evidence offered by Plaintiff may demonstrate that Defendants were in violation of disability access requirements by virtue of "<u>alterations, structural repairs, or additions</u>" (§ 19959 Health & Safety Code) which occurred on the premises over the years since the "handicapped" access statutes of Health & Safety Code § 19955 et seq. went into effect July 1, 1970. If a public facility was originally constructed prior to this deadline, Health & Safety Code § 19959 required that access be supplied upon <u>any subsequent</u> "alterations, structural repairs or additions":

> § 19959. Alteration of existing public accommodations
> Every existing public accommodation constructed prior to July 1, 1970... shall be subject to the requirements of this chapter when any alterations, structural repairs or additions are made to such public accommodation. This requirement shall only apply to the area of specific alteration, structural repair or addition and shall not be construed to mean that the entire building or facility is subject to this chapter."

Because Health & Safety Code § 19959 applied, inter alia, to <u>all "facilities,"</u> the Court of Appeals held that it applied to all California "ATM" facilities, even though "ATMs" were not specifically listed in the (1961) ASA specifications. <u>Donald v. Sacramento Valley Bank</u>, *supra*, at 1193 recognized that "at the time these [ASA Regulations] were promulgated [1961] ATMs were only a gleam in some banker's eye". This case held that an "accessible" (at least <u>level</u>, "uninterrupted" by steps) path of travel must lead to each facility, including an ATM. (A 1989 industry newsletter asserted that this case and its ATM access facilities would cost the banking industry an estimated $43 million to correct non-complying routes of travel to California ATMs.)[18]

(3) "ACCESSIBILITY" IS DEFINED BY THE TITLE 24 REGULATIONS IN EFFECT AT THE TIME OF ALTERATIONS

To be "accessible," the specific area modified must be (1) reachable by an accessible <u>primary entrance</u>; (2) connected by an accessible <u>path of travel</u> to the area from public sidewalks outside the facility; and (3) must be served by <u>accessible restrooms</u>, public telephones (if otherwise available) and water fountains. This common sense interpretation is spelled out in the Title 24 Regulations of the State Architect (as adopted pursuant to Health & Safety Code §§ 19955-19956 and Government Code § 4452).

While there have been some minor changes in Title 24 since its 1982 adoption, most provisions have been relatively stable. The legal standards discussed regarding Title 24 have been kept very similar from initial adoption effective July 1, 1982 to the present, although numbering has changed considerably. When there might be a question of changing standards, the applicable legal standards for "alterations, structural repairs and additions" are those Title 24 regulations <u>in effect at the time each relevant building permit was issued.</u> However, alterations to provide access today should apply current standards, unless there is a "hardship" finding by the enforcing agency.[19]

(4) INVESTIGATION AND DISCOVERY WILL DETERMINE THE CONSTRUCTION AND ALTERATION HISTORY

It may sometimes be determined by attorneys - either through investigation or upon discovery - that some "alteration" work was done (illegally) <u>without</u> a permit, as occasionally happens. For this reason, and because building department records are often incomplete, plaintiff's attorneys should seek to review all available building department records before a suit is filed, then subpoena and copy these records once litigation commences. Defense counsel will also want this information. Plaintiff should also seek all relevant alteration records on discovery, through a request for production of documents. Individual owners and corporate "persons most knowledgeable" should be questioned on this and other areas at issue.

Either side should disclose this information as part of their federal court "disclosure" obligations, either pursuant to local rules or FRCP § 26. General

---

[18] "The Nilson Report" May, 1989.
[19] As discussed, *infra* at section I-B-2-b, the ASA regulations (also called "ANSI" regulations) were in effect from 1968 to July 1, 1982.

Order 56, which is applied now to all Title II and Title III ADA cases filed in the Northern District of California, requires provision of relevant building records by defendants to plaintiff seven days before a mandatory "cooperative" site inspection, in any case in which the defendants have denied that the construction and alteration history triggered requirements for barrier removal. Per General Order 56, paragraph 2,[20]

> Initial disclosures required by Federal Rule of Civil Procedure 26(a) shall be completed no later than seven days prior to the joint inspection required by ¶ 3. If defendant intends to dispute liability based on the construction or alteration history of the subject premises, defendant shall disclose all information in defendant's possession or control regarding the construction or alteration history of the subject premises.

Plaintiff's discovery should also demand from defendants, as Requests for Production of Documents per FRCP 34, copies of all construction and alteration records in the possession of or under the control of relevant defendants - the building's current owners and operators (as well as "lessors and lessees," if applicable). Interrogatories and questions at deposition should also seek the nature and cost of each "alteration" of any kind between July 1, 1970 and the present date (of the responses or deposition). Depositions of corporations or governmental entities should include a "person most knowledgeable" deposition on this category of "pmk" designees). If relevant, deponents should be questioned, year by year, on any work done to the facility, with or without a permit. (Per section 301(a) ADA, discovery should also include requests for all documents relevant to proving "overall financial resources" of the defendants.)

There may be more than one set of owners and operators, for example, if the building has been sold between the time of plaintiff's visit and denial of access, and the time of the lawsuit being filed and discovery served. The owners and operators at the time of plaintiff's visit may be responsible for damages; but, as to injunctive relief, only the current owners and operators, lessors and lessees have the control of the premises to provide the necessary changes to effect injunctive relief. Thus, these defendants may all be responsible, in one way or another. Further, the current owners, etc., of a building are responsible for the access "triggered" by alterations by a prior owner. (Stickney v. McDonalds (N.D. Cal) Case No. C99-0058 VRW, Order of January 24, 2000; Hodges v. El Torito Restaurants, Inc., C-96-2242 VRW, 1998 WL 95398 (N.D. Cal. Feb.

---

[20] See Appendix, *infra*, at section IX-H (last modified 05/29/12). General Order 56 is relevant to all complaints filed in federal court in the Northern District of California under the ADA as a cause of action. For this reason, General Order 56 requires an explanation by defendants if they deny barrier removal is "readily achievable."

23, 1998), under California law. For public policy reasons, the same should be true under the ADA (but caveat certain district court decisions to the contrary).

(5) CONSULT THE RELEVANT YEAR'S REGULATIONS AND "STATE ARCHITECT'S MANUAL"

The relevant year "State Architect's Manual" should be consulted. For example, the regulations in effect from 1985 to 1988 are those in the 1984 State Architect's Disabled Access Regulations, Title 24, California Code of Regulations, as set out in the State Architect's 1984 Title 24 "Interpretive Manual." (The Manual contains both the text of the Regulations and the interpretations by the State Architect, which are separately designated.) Case law states that the interpretations by the State Architect of its own regulations are entitled to "great weight." (See Arnold v. United Artists (N.D.Cal. 1994) 158 FRD 439, at 447; 866 F. Supp 433.)

"Alteration" was defined in the Uniform Building Code ("UBC"). For example, per § 402 of the 1991 UBC:

> ALTER or ALTERATION is any change, addition or modification in construction or occupancy.
>
> (Thus a "change in occupancy" - nature of business allowed by permitting agency- may constitute an access-triggering "alteration," i.e. when a residence becomes a business.)

UBC § 420 (1983) defines "Structural repair":

> STRUCTURE is that which is built or constructed, an edifice or building of any kind, or any piece of work artificially built up or composed of parts joined together in some definite manner.
>
> REPAIR is the reconstruction or renewal of any part of an existing building for purposes of its maintenance. [Emphasis added]

b. 1970-1982 ALTERATIONS WERE CONTROLLED BY CALIFORNIA STATUTES AND THE "ASA," THE REGULATIONS OF THE "AMERICAN STANDARDS ASSOCIATION" WHICH CONTAINED "PATH OF TRAVEL" AND PRIMARY ENTRANCE REQUIREMENTS

As explained in Donald v. Sacramento Valley Bank (1989) 209 Cal.App.3d 1183, prior to the adoption of the State Architect's Regulations effective July 1, 1982) § 4451(d) Government Code required that facilities subject to § 19955 et seq. Health & Safety Code, "shall conform to the American Standards Associations specifications A117.1/1961" (also known as the "ASA" or American National Standards Institute "ANSI" regulations).

James Donald v. Sacramento Valley Bank (1989) 209 Cal.App.3d 1183, and People ex rel. Deukmejian v. CHE, Inc. (1983) 150 Cal.App.3d 123, both involved enforcement of access requirements under the ASA (for 1975 and 1976 alterations, respectively). As pointed out in James Donald v. Sacramento Valley Bank, *supra*, the ASA standards were originally formulated in 1961 and did not make any reference to an "automatic teller machine" - or many other specific types of "facilities." Yet, Donald v. Sacramento Valley Bank held that an ATM was clearly a "facility" and it was the intention of the ASA, as adopted by the Legislature, to provide access to all public facilities. (See "Purpose," ASA § 1.2, *supra*, at § II.B.1.c.)

People ex rel. Deukmejian v. CHE, Inc. (1983) 150 Cal.App.3d 123, established that building owners and operators are obligated under the statutes and regulations in effect during 1970 -1982 to provide access to any restaurant, hotel, or other public facility constructed or altered during this period. In CHE the court specifically found a requirement for proper access through the front door of an "altered" second story restaurant under California Statutes and the ASA/ANSI requirements; a secondary entrance through the kitchen could not be justified as a form of the "equivalent facilitation" required as a condition of any "hardship exception" allowed under Health & Safety Code § 19957. (CHE at p.134) The court explained why public policy required such an interpretation, to avoid second class treatment and segregation from able-bodied patrons:

> Because we find the required primary entrance must necessarily be burdened by a substantial flow of pedestrian traffic, a public restaurant entrance used by no patrons other than the physically handicapped cannot realistically be a "primary entrance."
>
> The prohibition against discrimination of the handicapped within Civil Code section 54 et seq., the enactment of Government Code section 4450 et seq. and section 19955 et seq., and the incorporation by reference of the phrase "primary entrance" within applicable specifications, reflect a legislative sensitivity to the hardships suffered by those afflicted with a wide range of physical disabilities. They are part of an expanding legislative effort to attain "the commendable goal of total integration of handicapped persons into the mainstream of society ...." In re Marriage of Carney, *supra.*, 24 Cal.3d 725, 740.) The Legislature has declared "[i]t is the policy of this state to encourage and enable disabled persons to participate fully in the social and economic life of the state ...." (Gov. Code, § 19230, subd. (a).) These legislative responses are designed to lessen their entire burden, by guaranteeing equal and full access to public buildings, facilities, and accommodations, without jeopardizing their safety. We believe the law is intended to promote accommodation of the physically handicapped by insuring them access to public restaurants without facing the unnecessary, adverse psychological impact of being separated from

regular customer traffic and shunted through secondary entrances.

CHE at p.135.

c. FOR ALL CALIFORNIA CONSTRUCTION OR ALTERATIONS PERMITTED FROM 1982 TO THE PRESENT, TITLE 24 REGULATIONS DEFINE THE PURPOSE OF ACCESS REGULATIONS, AND THE SCOPE OF ACCESS REQUIREMENTS TRIGGERED BY ALTERATIONS

(1) POST 1982 STANDARDS ARE SET BY TITLE 24

July 1, 1982 and subsequent alterations are controlled by California statutes and "Title 24," the State Building Code, which contain "path of travel" and primary entrance requirements and which require that access be provided regardless of the valuation of the underlying work.[21] The Title 24 building code specifications were required to be incorporated into any new construction or alterations to an existing building, by Health & Safety Code §§ 19955 and 19959.

The legal standards for "alterations, structural repairs and additions" (Health & Safety Code § 19959) from July 1, 1982 to the present include those in the State Architect's Disabled Access Regulations, Title 24, California Code of Regulations. The regulations for many years are set out in the State Architect's Title 24 "Interpretive Manual." (Each Manual contains both the text of the Regulations and the interpretations by the State Architect, which are separately designated.)

Some standards can be found in the Uniform Building Code (UBC), although not all portions of this code have been "adopted" by California. Although there have been modifications from time to time of Title 24 provisions, by and large the changes are relatively minor. Litigants should apply the "1984" Title 24 provisions, for example, as the regulations that were in effect at the time of any 1985 construction/alteration work.

Defendants were obligated to provide access when alterations, structural repairs, or additions triggered disabled access, regardless of the cost of the underlying alterations, structural repairs, or additions, except in those rare occasions when a "hardship" exception has been properly applied for and formally granted by the local building department. (See Health & Safety Code § 19957 and Donald v. Café Royale, *supra*, regarding

---

[21] There is conflicting authority as to whether 1/1/82 or 7/1/82 is the effective date. Per People ex rel. Deukmejian v. CHE, Inc. (1983) 150 Cal.App.3d 123, at 134-135, Title 24 regulations were "effective 12/31/81." However legislative history favors July 1, 1982.

formal requirements for a "hardship exception," including provision of "equivalent facilitation.")¹⁹ Mere non-enforcement of the law by a building department is not an "exception" and does not constitute a defense. (c.f. Donald v. Café Royale, *supra* and section 303(c) of the Uniform Building Code, discussed *infra* at section I-C-4) In this regard, the applicable regulations are hereinafter discussed, primarily using the 1984 regulations for as examples.

(2) THE TITLE 24 STATEMENT OF "PURPOSE" IS RELEVANT TO INTERPRETATIONS

The 1984 Title 24 (or 24-2) Regulations, commence with a statement of "purpose," which is relevant in interpreting the application of the regulatory scheme to any particular situation. "Minimum" standards were set to ensure actual "accessibility."

Purpose - Sec. 2-101.
(a) Standards. To provide minimum standards to safeguard life or limb, health, property, and public welfare and by regulating and controlling the design, construction, quality of materials, use and occupancy, location and maintenance of all buildings and structures within the scope of this Code.

(b) Incorporation. To assure that barrier free design is incorporated in all buildings, facilities, site work and other developments to which this Code applies to assure that they are accessible to, and usable by, physically handicapped persons. (Emphasis added)

(3) TITLE 24 APPLIES TO BOTH PUBLICALLY AND PRIVATELY FUNDED BUILDINGS

Title 24, § 2-105(b)11B describes access requirements for "publicly funded buildings." These requirements are also incorporated into the requirements for "privately" funded buildings. (See § 2-105(b)11B(4), at p.12, of the manual.) § 2-105(b)11B requires that access be provided in:

(5) All existing [publicly funded] buildings and facilities when alterations, structural repairs or additions are made to such buildings or facilities. This requirement shall apply only to area of specific alteration, structural repair or addition and shall not be construed to mean that the entire structure or facility is subject to this Code. Compliance shall require:

---

[22] See section I-H-6 *infra* regarding Title 24 requirements for a valid hardship exception, involving detailed written findings by the building department.

a. That a <u>primary entrance</u> to the building or facility and the <u>primary path of travel to the specific area</u> shall be accessible to and usable by handicapped persons.

b. That <u>sanitary facilities</u>, drinking fountains and public telephones <u>serving the remodeled area</u> shall be accessible to and usable by handicapped persons. (Emphasis added)

<u>Every alteration, structural repair or addition triggers access requirements</u>, including an accessible primary entrance, an accessible path of travel to the specific area altered, and accessible sanitary facilities serving the area altered, <u>regardless of the valuation of the job</u>. The "interpretation" portion of § 2-105(b)11A(5) of the 1984 State Architect's Manual explains:

<u>Existing Buildings - Very Important</u>

This is the section that details the extent to which an existing building must comply if an addition, alteration or repair is made. Full compliance in an existing building incorporates the following work only:

1. The area of remodel must comply.

2. A path of travel to the remodeled area must comply and

3. Bathrooms, telephones and drinking fountains serving the remodeled area must comply.

"These requirements apply to all remodeling jobs <u>regardless of the valuation of the job</u>." (Emphasis in original)

Title 24 further makes clear, in Section 105(b)11B(4), at page 12 of the Manual, that the requirements referred to in section 11(A)(5) apply to <u>privately funded</u> buildings as well as those that are publicly funded:

(4) All existing privately funded public accommodations when alterations, structural repairs or additions are made to such public accommodations as set forth under 11(A)(5) above.

Very important! The requirements for existing privately funded buildings that are to be remodeled are the same as for publicly funded. So you are referred to the publicly funded sections to get this information.

d. ALL "ALTERATIONS" TRIGGER ACCESS <u>EXCEPT</u> THOSE SPECIFICALLY EXCEPTED BY THE TITLE 24 CODE PROVISIONS (§ 2-105(B)11A(7)) (1984 CODE)

Any alteration triggers access, "regardless of the valuation of the job." (1984 State Architects Manual, p.9), unless there is a formal "exception" granted: The only "exception" is when the facility owner applies for and is formally granted an "unreasonable hardship" exception, as required by Health & Safety Code § 19957 and § 422 of the (1984) Title 24 regulations. These required and still require respectively (1) provision of "equivalent facilitation," an alternative form of useable access, as a condition of any "exception" being granted and, (2) specified written findings by the building department.

Businesses have sometimes argued that although they carried out certain "alterations," these were not of some specific nature which "triggered" the access requirements. However, if an "alteration" exists, it should trigger "access" unless it falls within an "exception." For example, § 2-105(b)11A(7) of the 1982 Code, (in 1984 State Architect's Manual, p.11), defined the only exceptions to "alterations" triggering access when Title 24 was adopted:

(7) Alterations, structural repairs or additions consisting of one of the following shall be limited to the actual work of the project:

(a) Altering one building entrance to meet handicapped requirements.
(b) Altering one existing toilet facility to meet handicapped requirements

(c) Altering existing elevators to meet handicapped requirements.

(d) Altering existing steps to meet handicapped requirements.
(e) Altering existing handrails to meet handicapped requirements.
Exception: Projects which consist only of heating, ventilating and air conditioning of existing space are not alterations projects for the purposes of handicap accessibility and shall not be subject to this code.

After this section, the State Architect's interpretation added:

The point here is that certain jobs may be done without triggering any other access requirements. Those jobs are listed in this section. (Emphasis added)

These "exceptions" simply mean that work that is done "only" for the purpose of improving certain "handicapped" access features may not of itself, "trigger" additional requirements.

Note that there are no exceptions for "electrical" work or "mechanical" work in the 1984 (or 1987) Code or Manual. The first appearance of any exception for electrical work was in 1989, and even then the exception was only for work "not involving placement of switches or receptacles." The exception for "cosmetic work that does not affect access, such as painting, carpeting, etc." also first appeared in the 1989 Code and Manual, (Exception No. 3 to § 110A(b)11A(5)).

e. THE OPERATIVE STANDARD FOR TRIGGERING ACCESS IS "ALTERATIONS, STRUCTURAL REPAIRS, OR ADDITIONS," AS SPECIFIED IN §19959 HEALTH & SAFETY CODE AND THE TITLE 24 REGULATIONS

Sometimes a defendant may assert that no access was triggered by alterations which did not constitute "structural" modifications. While "structural modifications" may also constitute a "structural repair" (a lesser standard per UBC definitions), and thus fall within the statutory "structural repair" rubric, other "alterations" and "additions" also trigger access. The standards are set by the language of Health & Safety Code § 19959 and § 2-105(b)11A(5) of Title 24 (1984 numbering). The applicable standards are those in effect as of the permit date of the subject "remodel." Both the statute and the regulation specify that access is triggered by an "alteration, structural repair or addition," except those specified in § 2-105(b)11A(7), discussed *supra*. By specifying these "Exceptions," it seems clear that any other forms of "alteration projects" do trigger access requirements.

It is important to note the date any alteration was "permitted" (i.e., a permit was issued by the relevant building department), and to review the specific State Architect's Regulations then in effect. For example, a defendant relying upon a 1989 code may take the position that: "The regulations do not apply to electrical, mechanical work that is cosmetic."

However, in the 1984 Code, in effect at the time of any 1985 or 1986 alterations, the exceptions were much more limited than this. Per the 1984 "exception" to § 2-105(b)11A(7):

> Exception: Projects which consist only of heating, ventilating, and air conditioning of existing space are not alteration projects for the purpose of handicapped accessibility and shall not be subject to this code. [Emphasis added]

The fact that the 1984 Codes were in effect in 1985 and 1986 is emphasized by a comparison with the same section in the 1987 Interpretive Manual, (Second Printing, July 19, 1987). In this code, per §2-110(b)11A(7), (at page 10), "Exception: "Projects which consist only of heating, ventilating, and air conditioning of existing space are not alteration projects for the purpose of disabled accessibility and shall not be subject to this code." However, even in the 1987 Code, there was no mention of any exception for "electrical" work.

f. THE BURDEN OF PROOF TO SHOW AN "EXCEPTION" GENERALLY RESTS ON THE PARTY "WHO CLAIMS ITS BENEFITS"

In a 2007 order in the (still pending as of 2012) Taco Bell class action (August 8, 2007 "Order Denying in Part and Granting in Part Plaintiffs' Motion for Partial Summary Judgment"), Northern District Judge Martin Jenkins[23] discussed the "burden of proof" issue when applied to defendant's obligation in trying to prove an alleged "unreasonable hardship exception":

> The unnecessary hardship exception applies where compliance with the building standard at the time of construction would make a construction project "unfeasible" based on, among other factors, the cost of providing access, and the cost of all construction contemplated. See Title 24-1981 § 2-422(c); Title 24-1984 § 2-422(c); Title 24-1987 § 2-422 at 29; Title 24-1989 § 422(c); Title 24-1994 § 422(c); Title 24-1999 § 222-U at 28; Title 24-2001 § 222-U at 22-23. According to California's Office of the State Architect, which promulgated the Title 24 access regulations, the undue hardship exception applies only where compliance would be "difficult or impossible because the cost of providing access is too high in relationship to the total cost of the job." Cal. Gov't Code § 4450(b); Office of the State Architect, California State Accessibility Standards Interpretive Manual § 110A(b)11A at 11 (3d ed.1989) (interpreting "unreasonable hardship"). Here, consistent with the rules of statutory construction, the burden of proving the unreasonable exception applies falls on Defendant...; see also N.L.R.B. v. Ky. River Cmty. Care, Inc., 532 U.S. 706, 711, 121 S.Ct. 1861, 149 L.Ed.2d 939 (2001) (discussing " 'the general rule of statutory construction that the burden of proving justification or exemption under a special exception to the prohibitions of a statute generally rests on one who claims its benefits.'" (Citation omitted.)).
>
> In the current case, Plaintiffs have produced evidence indicating that certain architectural elements of Defendant's restaurants are in violation of Title 24... Having satisfied their initial burden, Plaintiffs have shifted the burden to Defendant to present specific facts showing that there is a genuine issue for trial. Fed.R.Civ.P.-56(e); Celotex, 477 U.S. at 324. In response Defendant has failed to identify evidence from which the Court could find: (1) that any of the occupancy permits for any of the restaurants at issue were based on a hardship exception; or (2) that any such hardship exception was merited. Defendant's conjecture that the building inspectors may have applied the hardship exception is insufficient to create a material issue of fact to defeat Plaintiffs' motion for partial summary judgment. Anderson, 477 U.S. at 247-48.

---

[23] In approximately 2009 Judge Jenkins voluntarily left the Federal Bench to accept appointment to the California Court of Appeals. The Taco Bell class action was reassigned to Northern District Judge Phyllis Hamilton.

<u>Moeller v. Taco Bell, Corp.</u>, 2007 WL 2301778 (N.D.Cal. August 8, 2007) (See also section III-B, *infra*, re: ADA "readily achievable" burden of proof)[24]

3. **PUBLIC POLICY REQUIRES ACCESS, INCLUDING AN ACCESSIBLE PATH OF TRAVEL TO THE AREA OF ALTERATION, WHENEVER ALTERATIONS ARE MADE AND MONEY IS SPENT FOR BUILDING IMPROVEMENTS**

Since "handicapped access" legislation was passed into law as to privately owned public facilities, effective July 1, 1970, California has protected the rights of "full and equal access" for disabled persons, including wheelchair users and other with mobility limitations. Government Code §19230(a) sets the policy of the state: "It is the policy of the state to encourage and enable disabled persons to participate fully in the social and economic life of this state." <u>In re Marriage of Carney</u>, 24 Cal.3d 725, 740 (1979) quoted this statute in further finding that "Both the state and federal governments now pursue the commendable goal of total integration of handicapped persons into the mainstream of society." <u>Donald v. Café Royale, Inc.</u>, 218 Cal.App.3d 168, 173 (1990) further supported this important public policy: "The various legislative pronouncements of our state's policy leave no doubt that the <u>purpose of section 54 et seq</u>. ... is to reduce or eliminate the physical impediments to participation in community life by the physically handicapped." (Emphasis added)

Consistent with that purpose, and the specific purposes stated in the "purpose" section of the laws and regulations enacted to provide "access," making an area "accessible" has always required provision of an accessible "path of travel" <u>to</u> the "area of alteration" in any public facility, <u>from</u> the "outside" public sidewalk.

As previously noted, the very <u>purpose</u> of all access codes, starting with the earliest 1961 American Standards Association (ASA) Regulations, per § 1.2, was to make public buildings "<u>accessible to, through and within their doors</u>." Any "interpretation" of regulations and codes must be consistent with this purpose. A detailed policy discussion, as to "ascertaining the intent of the Legislature so as to effectuate the law" and applying that policy to the interpretations of "handicapped access" law is found in <u>Donald v. Sacramento Valley Bank</u>, *supra*, at 1191-1192. The court's "construction of the legislative schemes commences with Civil Code section 54, et seq.... which declares... that physically handicapped persons are entitled to the same right as the able-bodied to full and free use of public facilities and places." <u>Donald v. Sacramento Valley Bank</u>, *supra*, involved a challenge by access pioneer Jim Donald to require an accessible path of travel to an ATM installed in 1975, up five stairs on the exterior of

---

[24] In 2011 Judge Phyllis Hamilton granted partial summary judgment to plaintiff's class, Moeller v. Taco Bell Corp., C 02-5849 PJH, 2011 WL 4634250 (N.D. Cal. Oct. 5, 2011)

a Sacramento bank.[25] (A previous partial settlement with the building owners in the same lawsuit installed a ramp which accomplished access into all portions of a 12 story office building, where previously access to the elevators could be reached only by stairs, effectively blocking wheelchair access to the entire building. However, the defendant bank fought the case rather than install an extension of the building's ramp to its ATM for a total cost of $7000, even when Jim and I offered to waive any damages and attorney fees against the bank. Jim Donald v. Park Executive Bldg., Sacramento Valley Bank et al, Sacramento Superior Court, approximately 1986.

4. AN UNREASONABLE "HARDSHIP" EXCEPTION MAY BE AVAILABLE, BUT ONLY WHEN SPECIFIED CONDITIONS ARE MET, INCLUDING PROVIDING "EQUIVALENT FACILITATION"

Inequities of possible disproportion between the cost of the alteration and the cost of providing access are provided for by an "exception" process for "unreasonable hardships," per Health & Safety Code § 19957: Exceptions from literal requirements of standards and specifications in hardship, etc., cases:

> In cases of practical difficulty, unnecessary hardship, or extreme differences, a building department responsible for the enforcement of this part may grant exceptions from the literal requirements of the standards and specifications required by this part or permit the use of other methods or materials, but only when it is clearly evident that equivalent facilitation and protection are thereby secured. (Emphasis added)

It should be kept in mind that § 19957 is the "enabling statute," against which any regulations allowing "hardship" exceptions must be measured. Several conditions precedent must be shown by building owners seeking such "unreasonable hardship" exceptions in order to justify an "exception," including the following:

> (1) The "total construction cost of alterations, structural repairs or additions" must "not exceed a valuation threshold" of [$58,725 in 1984, per § 2-105(b)11A(6) of 1984 Title 24 regulations and State

---

[25] Jim Donald, as a "qualified" disabled person, was plaintiff in a number of precedent setting California access cases. Jim was a prominent Sacramento attorney who attended U.C. Davis School of Law after breaking his neck in an auto accident and becoming quadriplegic while attending U.C. Berkeley as an undergraduate. Jim was Legal Affairs Director of the California Department of Rehabilitation until 1982, serving while the "godfather" of the disability rights movement, Ed Roberts, was Director of the "CDR." Jim and Ed helped to form an international organization of leaders of disability organizations, Disabled People International (D.P.I.). In 1984 I attended a D.P.I. "World Conference" in Kingston, Jamaica, traveling with Jim and serving as his attendant. (The experience was intensely educating for me, although Jim complained that I was the "worst attendant" he ever had.) Representativesof disability rights organizations from more than 50 countries attended. From talking to representatives of other countries, Jim and I found that although some countries had laws requiring access for disabled persons, these laws were not being adequately enforced by local building officials. It appeared that California was the only jurisdiction where access laws could be enforced by private lawsuit (this was 6 years before the 1990 ADA). Jim Donald passed away in 2003 after practicing law for more than 30 years.

Architect's commentary, p.10 of 1984 <u>Interpretive Manual</u>; in 2011 well over $100,000.[26] If it exceeds this threshold, accessible features <u>must</u> be provided. (§ 2-105(b)11A(6) of the 1984 Title 24 regulations refers to "<u>total</u> construction costs" as the costs to include in determining the "threshold" above which no hardship exception can even be considered. The total costs of the project are counted toward this threshold amount if the project <u>includes</u> alterations, structural repairs or additions. Further, since the April 1994 Title 24 Regulations, a building owner with total construction costs below this threshold must still spend at least 20% of his total construction costs on disabled access improvements in order to be <u>eligible</u> to seek an "unreasonable hardship" finding. "<u>Equivalent facilitation" must always be provided</u>.

(2) "<u>Equivalent facilitation and protection</u>" for disabled persons must still be provided even if an exception from the "literal requirements" is granted. Health & Safety Code § 19957. "Equivalent facilitation" was defined by § 2-406(c) of the 1984 Title 24 Regulations as,

> "an <u>alternative means of complying</u> with the literal requirements of these standards and specifications that provides access in terms of the <u>purpose</u> of these standards and specifications."
> (Emphasis added)

Any claim that a business doing alterations can attempt later to obtain a "retroactive" hardship exception - especially if applied for after a lawsuit is filed - should be looked on with disfavor. The September 17, 1992 California Attorney General's Order to Local Building Officials Re: Enforcement of California Disabled Access Standards (enclosed in full at appendix, section IX-E-1, *infra*.) posited the possibility of a retroactive hardship exception, <u>but only</u> if the conditions existing at the time of the triggering alteration are met. These include whether the total job costs at the time of the triggering alteration were under the Title 24 "valuation threshold." The text of the Attorney General's Standards were included at page 1 of the Appendix to that letter:

> <u>Granting of Retroactive Hardship Exceptions</u> - As a general rule, applications for exceptions must be made prior to construction. If owners were allowed to freely apply for exceptions after

---

[26] Per access consultant Jonathan Adler, "the ENR valuation threshold for the year 2009 was: $126,764."

construction was completed and deviations were discovered, exceptions would swallow up access requirements. However, retroactive hardship exceptions may be granted post-construction under very limited circumstances. A hardship exception may be granted post-construction where the owner establishes that under the facts that existed at the time the relevant building plans were approved, a exception would have been granted.[27] Of course, each of the five criteria noted above would have to be considered. Of critical importance is that the cost of meeting the literal requirements of the access feature at issue is the cost of meeting the same at the time of original plan approval and not the cost of meeting the literal requirements at the time of the application for the retroactive hardship exception. (Emphasis added)

This letter is important as it is the only known authority for granting "retroactive" hardship exceptions. During the Court Trial of Atwood v. El Torito (Alameda County Superior Court, Action No. 677858-1) defendants went back to the building department to get a purported "retroactive hardship exception" after the trial court (Hon. Joseph Carson) had already ruled that defendants were in violation of California law. Thereafter Judge Carson ruled that there was no basis for a "retroactive" hardship claim, and, further, that the building department could not overrule a judge!

5. ACTUAL "ACCESSIBILITY" IS REQUIRED IN ORDER FOR EQUIVALENT FACILATATION TO BE SUFFICIENT TO JUSTIFY ANY HARDSHIP EXCEPTION

To be "accessible," the area constructed or modified must be reachable by an accessible primary entrance and connected by an accessible path of travel to the area from the public sidewalk outside the facility, and must be "served" by accessible restrooms. This common sense interpretation is spelled out in the Title 24 Regulations of the State Architect (as adopted pursuant to Health & Safety Code § 19955 and Government Code § 4452).

The Legislature has continually required - ever since the effective date of Health & Safety Code § 19959, July 1, 1970 - that when money was spent for "alterations," money should also be spent to provide handicapped access. The Legislature also provided that if this would be financially unfair to the owners, (i.e., create an "unreasonable hardship," not just an additional financial obligation) exceptions could be granted by the building department, "but only when it is clearly evident that equivalent facilitation and protection are thereby secured." (Health & Safety Code § 19957) Unless "equivalent facilitation" is provided, i.e. some "alternative means of complying" in order to provide

---

[27] See section I-H-6 a-e, *infra*, re: five written criteria required.

access to a facility, the granting of any "hardship exception" by a building official would be improper. Any granting of such an "exception" may be found by a court to constitute an "abuse of discretion" by the building official and therefore be void. (People ex rel. Deukmejian v. CHE, Inc. (1983) 150 Cal.App.3d 123). If found void, such purported "exceptions" should not be recognized by the courts as a valid defense when building owners are later sued.

6. ALL ALTERATIONS TRIGGER ACCESS UNLESS A FORMAL HARDSHIP EXCEPTION (1) IS FORMALLY GRANTED, (2) COMPLIES WITH CODE REQUIREMENTS (HEALTH & SAFETY CODE § 19957; § 2-422(C) TITLE 24); AND (3) IS SUPPORTED BY WRITTEN FINDINGS ENTERED IN PUBLIC RECORDS

   a. THE BURDEN OF PROOF FOR AN EXCEPTION IS ON THE DEFENDANT
   An exception is by definition an affirmative defense, and it is defendant who has the burden of proof to show it was granted on exception, not plaintiff's burden to disprove a negative. (See N.L.R.B. v. Ky. River Comty Care, Inc., 532 U.S. 706, 711 (2001), *supra*, discussing "the general rule of statutory construction that the burden of proving justification or exemption under a special exception to the prohibitions of a statute generally rests on one who claims it benefits.") [See §§ III.B.1., *infra*, as to burden of proof under the ADA]

   b. GOVERNMENT CODE §§ 4450ff WAS INCORPORATED INTO HEALTH & SAFETY CODE §§ 19955 - 19959; § 4451(d) GOVERNMENT CODE AND § 19957 HEALTH AND SAFETY CODE BOTH REQUIRE "EQUIVALENT FACILITATION" AS A CONDITION FOR AN "EXCEPTION"
   The standards of Government Code § 4450ff apply to "privately owned" public facilities because these standards were incorporated in 1970 into Health & Safety Code §§ 19955ff. Any "impracticability" or "hardship" exception can be obtained only by meeting the standards of Health & Safety Code § 19957, including providing equivalent facilitation:

   > § 19957: Exceptions from literal requirements of standards and specifications in hardship, etc., cases
   >
   > In cases of practical difficulty, unnecessary hardship or extreme differences, a building department responsible for the enforcement of this part may grant exceptions from the literal requirements of the standards and specifications required by this part or permit the use of other methods or materials, but only when it is clearly evident that equivalent facilitation and protection are thereby secured.

   Government Code § 4451(d) also requires "equivalent facilitation." It allows "exceptions from the literal requirements of building standards" "but only when it is clearly evident that equivalent facilitation and protection are thereby secured," an identical requirement to that in Health & Safety Code § 19957. Exceptions require application for and granting of a formal written exception by the building department; no "informal" approval - "across the counter" verbal approval (or any governmental "failure to enforce" the access requirements) would suffice as an excuse. James Donald v. Café Royale (1990) 218 Cal.App.3d 168. (See also section 303(c) of Uniform Building Code: the granting of a permit does not excuse violations, as noted in section I-C-4, *infra*).

Even relatively "minor" alterations triggered access unless Defendants sought, made application for, and were granted a formal written "hardship" exception per the requirements of Health & Safety Code § 19957: a formal application and written granting of an exception are required. (See James Donald v. Café Royale (1990) 218 Cal.App.3d 168). From 1982 on, this was codified, initially by § 2-422(c) of 1984 Code (Manual, p.32), regarding criteria for a finding of "unreasonable hardship." This code cataloged 5 separate factors which must be evaluated by the enforcing agency before granting a "hardship exception."[28]

Further, these specified requirement for written findings:
> The details of any finding of unreasonable hardship shall be recorded and entered in the files of the enforcing agency. (§ 422(c))
> [See also Opinion of Attorney General Dan Lungren, 9/17/92. "To Local Building Officials, Re: Enforcement of California Disabled Access Standards," Section IX, Appendix E -1 of this Book]

The files of the local Building Department regarding most public facilities will usually reflect that there has never even been any application for a "hardship" exception, much less formal findings on the record. Had any exception been granted, this would also have required provision of "equivalent facilitation" per Health & Safety Code § 19957. (People ex rel. Deukmejian v. CHE, Inc.(1983) 150 Cal.App.3d 123) If there is no "equivalent facilitation" provided, no claimed "exception" can be valid!

c. ALTERATIONS TRIGGERED ACCESS UNLESS AN UNREASONABLE HARDSHIP EXCEPTION IS PROVEN

For example, per page 9 of the 1984 State Architect's Manual, (which outlines the regulations in effect at the time of any 1985 and 1986 alterations) any alteration triggers access, "regardless of the valuation of the job." The only exception is when the owner of the business applies for and is formally granted an "unreasonable hardship"

---

[28] See § I-B-6-e, *infra*.

exception. As an "exception" to a public Health & Safety Code requirement, the burden of proving any exception is upon the defendant. [For a similar burden of proof on defendants for the affirmative defense that removing access barriers is <u>not</u> "readily achievable" under the ADA see § III-B-1, *infra*]

d. <u>EQUIVALENT FACILITATION</u> IS A MANDATORY REQUIREMENT, PER STATUTE AND REGULATIONS, WHEN ANY HARDSHIP EXCEPTION IS GRANTED

<u>Any</u> hardship exception requires "equivalent facilitation." Health & Safety Code § 19957 sets the standards to "grant exceptions" "but only when it is clearly evident that equivalent facilitation and protection are thereby secured." Similarly, allowance in Title 24 of any exception to the § 2-611(d) requirement that "Dining, banquet and bar facilities shall be made accessible," contains the limitation, at "Exception No. 1," that, "when an enforcing agency finds" an "unreasonable hardship, an exception shall be granted <u>when equivalent facilitation is provided</u>." (Emphasis added)
[See also § I.B.6.b, *supra*.]

Certain Title 24 regulations appear to purport to excuse even "equivalent facilitation" on the basis that the cost for providing access would be "disproportionate" to the cost of the new alteration. I would respectfully suggest that any <u>regulation</u> purporting to give an "exception" which does not comply with the "enabling legislation" of section 19957 Health and Safety code and purports to give any exception without providing "equivalent facilitation" as a condition, should be found to be <u>invalid</u> by the court. (See also <u>People ex rel Duekmajian v. CHE</u>, *supra*, which reiterates that <u>no</u> claimed "<u>exception</u>" can be valid without equivalent facilitation (<u>CHE</u> at 134) and that granting such "exception" would be an "abuse of discretion" by the building department.

e. SINCE 1982, TITLE 24 HAS REQUIRED COMPLIANCE WITH FIVE FACTORS, INCLUDING SPECIFIC <u>WRITTEN FINDINGS</u> BY THE BUILDING DEPARTMENT, AS A CONDITION FOR GRANTING A "HARDSHIP" EXCEPTION

Since 1982, Title 24 has required compliance with 5 specific conditions for a building department to issue a valid "unreasonable hardship" exception to access requirements. Per the 1986 State Architect's manual (given here as an example, although <u>each</u> relevant year must be checked), the five required factors are found in the text of and commentary to § 2-422(c), which defines "unreasonable hardship":

Sec.2-422.
(c) Unreasonable Hardship: An unreasonable hardship exists when the enforcing agency finds that compliance with the building standard would make the specific work of the project affected by the building standard unfeasible, based upon an overall evaluation of the following factors:

A. The cost of providing access.

B. The cost of all construction contemplated.

C. The impact of proposed improvements on financial feasibility of the project.

D. The nature of the accessibility which would be gained or lost.

E. The nature of the use of the facility under construction and its availability to handicapped persons.

The details of any finding of unreasonable hardship shall be recorded and entered in the files of the enforcing agency.

This is a biggie! As you peruse through the regulations, you will find exceptions from the literal requirements of these regulations for existing buildings. Many of these exceptions may only be incorporated when it is found that an unreasonable hardship would exist if compliance is provided. Each exception from the requirements granted because of unreasonable hardship refers you to this definition. It is the intent that <u>in order to find unreasonable hardship the enforcing authority must make an evaluation based on the five criteria incorporated herewith and to document those findings</u>. Unreasonable hardship is to be determined on a case by case basis."

[Italics in original.](Underline emphasis added)

C. CALIFORNIA CASE LAW HAS ESTABLISHED: THE RIGHT TO ENFORCE ACCESS REQUIREMENTS BY PRIVATE LAWSUIT; THAT NO WRONGFUL INTENT IS REQUIRED; AND THAT IT IS NO DEFENSE THAT ACCESS STANDARDS WERE NOT ENFORCED BY THE LOCAL BUILDING DEPARTMENT

1. LEADING APPELLATE CASES ESTABLISH THE RIGHT TO ENFORCE ACCESS BY A PRIVATE LAWSUIT

Legal standards applicable for requirements of disabled access in public facilities and the right to bring an action for damages and injunctive relief under California law are found in <u>James Donald v. Sacramento Valley Bank</u> (1989) 209 Cal.App.3d 1183, 260 Cal.Rptr. 49, (3rd DCA). This case held that a bank's "ATM's" were public facilities and could not be installed with a path of travel that included inaccessible stairs. An amicus curiae brief by the California Attorney General stressed, inter alia, the importance of private lawsuits for effective enforcement of access laws.[29] (This opinion of the 3rd DCA, originally

---

[29] See Blackwell v. Foley, 724 F.Supp.2d 1068 (N.D. Cal 2010) at p. 1075-1076.

"unpublished" was ordered published by a 7-0 vote of the California Supreme Court.)

James Donald v. Café Royale (1990) 218 Cal.App.3d 168, 180, held, inter alia, that no discriminatory "intent" need be proven to show a violation of Civil Code §54.1's "full and equal access" requirements, and that at least statutory minimum damages and statutory attorney's fees must be awarded for a denial of "full and equal access" at a public restaurant or other public facility.

2. NO WRONGFUL INTENT NEEDS TO BE PROVEN FOR A VIOLATION OF CIVIL CODE §§ 54 OR 54.1

Donald v. Café Royale, *supra*, does create "strict liability," in that an owner of a public facility may be found liable without proof of any wrongful intent. In doing so, the court found that a lack of full and equal access (Civil Code § 54.1) may cause damages to a disabled person regardless of the owner's intent.

> The public policy interest in providing physically handicapped persons with equal access to public facilities warrants the enactment of a statute prescribing liability for denial of access without reference to the violator's intent. (Id. at 180)

On the other hand, the intentional denial of "full and equal accommodations, advantages, facilities, privileges or services in all business establishments" (Civil Code § 51) may be a separate basis for liability.[30] In Hankins v. El Torito,(1998) 63 Cal. App.4th 510, a restaurant's policy of refusing the use of an employees' restroom, even to a disabled person who could not climb stairs to the only public restroom, was held to violate both §§ 51 and 54.1. However, by footnote 4 at Hankins v. El Torito, *supra*, at 520, the court followed Café Royale in holding that no proof of wrongful intent is required to prove an access violation under § 54.1 (In Hankins the policy was also an "intentional" violation of section 54.1).

Under federal law it has also been repeatedly held that the ADA may be violated without proof of any wrongful intent. (Crowder v. Kitigawa, Chairman Hawaan Bd. of Control (9th Cir. 1996) 81 F.3d 1480; Helen L. v. DiDario, 46 F.3d 325, 335 (3d Cir. 1995).) In Arnold v. United Artists Theater Circuit, Inc., et al. (N.D.Cal. 1994) 866 F.Supp 433, Judge Thelton Henderson ruled that when a violation of California Civil Code § 51(f) is based on an incorporated violation of the ADA, no wrongful intent is required. Because of a California Court of Appeal decision in Gunther v. Lin (2006) 144 Cal. App.4th 223, holding "intent" was an element of Civil Code § 51 liability, this issue was up in the air until a unanimous 2009 decision by the California Supreme Court in Munson v. Del Taco, Inc, 46 Cal. 4th 661. Munson held that the Gunther decision was

---

[30] If the violation is of section 51(f) based on incorporation of an ADA violation, liability may also be found without the need to show wrongful intent. Munson v. Del Taco, Inc., 46 Cal. 4th 661 (2009).

wrong; that the federal courts were right; and that no "wrongful intent" was needed for a section 51(f) California Civil Code violation based on a violation of the ADA.

3. A BUILDING DEPARTMENT'S LACK OF ENFORCEMENT IS NOT A DEFENSE
San Francisco v. Grant Co. (1986) 181 Cal.App.3d 1085, held that the granting of a building permit by local building officials does not "estop" even the building officials (or others) from suing to enforce the law.

People Ex Rel Deukmejian v. CHE, Inc. (1983) 150 Cal.App.3d 123, upholding a lawsuit based on both Civil Code § 54.1 and Health & Safety Code § 19955, held that even if a formal variance ("exception") from compliance was issued by a building department, such variance could be challenged in litigation as an "abuse of discretion" where the variance was improperly given, because the permit failed to include an "equivalent facilitation" requirement, per Health & Safety Code § 19957. (CHE, *supra*, 150 Cal.App.3d 123, 137).

4. THE UNIFORM BUILDING CODE SPECIFICALLY PROVIDES THAT ISSUANCE OF A BUILDING PERMIT DOES NOT APPROVE VIOLATION OF ANY ACCESS REQUIREMENTS
Per Section 303(c) of the Uniform Building Code, Validity of Permit. The issuance or granting of a permit or approval of plans, specifications and computations shall not be construed to be a permit for, or an approval of, any violation of any of the provisions of this code or of any other ordinance of the jurisdiction. Permits presuming to give authority to violate or cancel the provisions of this code or other ordinances of the jurisdiction shall not be val Id. (Emphasis added)
[See also section I-H-2-e, *infra*]

D. ACCESSIBLE "PATH OF TRAVEL" REQUIREMENTS UNDER THE "ASA" (1970 - 1982) AND TITLE 24 STANDARDS (JULY 1, 1982 TO THE PRESENT)

1. AN ACCESSIBLE "PATH OF TRAVEL" IS NEEDED TO MAKE AN AREA "ACCESSIBLE"
This issue has arisen in the past because statutory disability access codes were often not properly enforced during the 1970s and 1980s by building departments that misunderstood or ignored the "new" access requirements initiated July 1, 1970.

An area cannot be considered "accessible" under the ASA unless it can be reached by an accessible route. Donald v. Sacramento Bank (1989) 209 Cal.App.3d 1183, and People ex rel Deukmejian v. CHE, Inc. (1983) 150 Cal.App.3d 123, both applied access requirements under the ASA, and showed why an "accessible" "path of travel" has always been an implicit requirement to make an area "accessible to and usable by" disabled persons. While there is no use of the phrase "path of travel" in the ASA, there are analogous requirements in the ASA that all <u>walkways</u> be accessible, as held in <u>Donald v. Sacramento Bank</u>, *supra*.

The ASA requirements for an accessible path of travel, in light of public policy and the purpose of the statutes involved, have been established by the court's interpretation in <u>People ex rel Deukmejian v. CHE</u>, *supra*. This case treated Title 24, the successor to the ASA, as a "legislative amendment" which "merely <u>clarified</u> the existing law." Title 24's <u>explicit</u> requirement for an "accessible" path of travel was held to be an <u>implicit</u> access requirements of Health & Safety Code § 19959 even under the previous "ASA" regulations.[31]

The "path of travel" concept recognizes that in order to make an area inside a building "accessible to," "useable by" and "functional for" disabled members of the public, these persons must be able to <u>travel to the "accessible" area</u> from the adjoining public property. For example, if a new wall is built inside a restaurant, use by disabled persons of the areas adjacent to the "wall" requires <u>getting to</u> these areas; otherwise the concept of "accessibility" is meaningless.

The need to discuss this issue has arisen only because of efforts by certain defendants seeking to avoid providing disabled access. Their efforts included trying to interpret the enabling statutes as <u>limiting</u> rather than <u>expanding</u> access for disabled persons. Health & Safety Code § 19959 (originally passed in 1971 and not modified since 1974) states:

> Every existing public accommodation constructed prior to July 1, 1970, which is not exempted by Section 19956, shall be subject to the requirements of this chapter when any alterations, structural repairs or additions are made to such public accommodation. This requirement shall only apply to the area of specific alteration, structural repair or addition and shall not be construed to mean that the entire building or facility is subject to this chapter.

However, making an area of alteration "accessible" includes creating an accessible <u>entrance</u> to the facility; an accessible <u>path of travel</u> to the "altered" area; and "accessible <u>sanitary facilities, drinking fountains, and public telephones serving the remodeled area</u>..." For example, the 2002 Title 24 Regulations on "Accessibility for Existing Buildings" spelled out the requirements for the types of access triggered by "renovation, structural repair, alterations and additions to existing buildings":

---

[31] See § I-D-3, *infra*.

SECTION 1134B – ACCESSIBILITY FOR EXISTING BUILDINGS

1134B.1 Scope. The provisions of this division apply to renovation, structural repair, alteration and additions to existing buildings, including those identified as historic buildings. This division identifies minimum standards for removing architectural barriers, and providing and maintaining accessibility to existing buildings and their related facilities.

1134B.2 General. All existing buildings and facilities, when alterations, structural repairs or additions are made to such buildings or facilities, shall comply with all provisions of Division I, New Buildings, except as modified by this division. These requirements shall apply only to the area of specific alteration, structural repair or addition and shall include those areas listed below:

1134B.2.1 A primary entrance to the building or facility and the primary path of travel to the specific area of alteration, structural repair or addition, and sanitary facilities, drinking fountains, signs and public telephones serving the area.

2. AN ACCESSIBLE "PATH OF TRAVEL" IS NECESSARY IN ORDER TO MAKE AN AREA "ACCESSIBLE TO AND USEABLE BY" DISABLED PERSONS UNDER THE ASA

ASA Provision 1.2, entitled "Purpose," stated in part that "This standard is intended to make all buildings and facilities...<u>accessible to and functional for the physically handicapped to, through and within their doors</u>." (Emphasis added). In addition ASA Sections 4.1 (Site Development), 4.2 ("Walkway"), 5.2.1 ("Doors") and 5.6 ("Toilets") are relevant. For illustrative purposes, provision 5.6 states that "It is essential that an appropriate number of toilet rooms...be made accessible to and useable by the physically handicapped." How could this be achieved unless there is an accessible "path of travel" to the toilet rooms? For example, one fine San Francisco restaurant added an elegant rear dining area with restrooms which were individually somewhat "accessible" - except the only way to reach the restrooms was to climb four stairs! (<u>Berne v. Garibaldi's</u> (N.D. Cal 2009) (To their credit, defendants promptly made the entire restaurant fully accessible after being sued.)

3. A 1979 CALIFORNIA LEGISLATIVE COUNSEL'S OPINION RECOGNIZED THAT AN ACCESSIBLE PATH OF TRAVEL TO AN AREA WAS IMPLICITLY REQUIRED IN ORDER FOR THIS AREA TO BE CONSIDERED "ACCESSIBLE"

"Path of travel" requirements have always been a basic component for making any area "accessible" to disabled persons. As early as March 31, 1979, a California Legislative Counsel's opinion recommended that the "path of travel" concept be <u>spelled out</u> in the

State Architect's Regulations (then in the planning stages, but not issued and effective until July 1, 1982, as Title 24, Part 2).[32]

The Legislative Counsel concluded, as to the July 1, 1970 to June 30, 1982 period when the ASA regulations were in effect,

> Thus it is our opinion that when a public building or facility that was constructed prior to November 13, 1968 is structurally remodeled after March 4, 1972, Section 4456 [Gov't Code] requires that a path of travel from the exterior of the structure to the remodeled area, a path of travel from any key facilities serving the remodeled area of the structure to the remodeled area, (where such key facilities are required for the physically handicapped), and the key facilities themselves be accessible to the physically handicapped to the same extent that the remodeled area of the structure is to be so accessible.

Government Code §§ 4450-4456 (adopted in 1968) have the same "accessibility" requirements for government buildings, upon alteration, as those of Health & Safety Code sections 19955 - 19959, adopted two years later (as of July 1, 1970) for privately owned public facilities. Health & Safety Code § 19955 et seq. adopts and incorporates the requirements of Government Code §§ 4450 et seq., and adopts these requirements to privately owned public buildings.

Such a "path of travel" requirement was implicit in the concept of "accessibility," and consistent with the stated "purpose" of Government Code § 4450, which is to ensure that "public buildings are to be accessible to and usable by the physically handicapped." [Emphasis added] The 1979 Legislative Counsel's opinion explained why a path of travel was a necessary component of usability for an accessible location:

> It is our opinion that the specific limitation in Section 4456, which requires only the providing of accessibility to, and usability by, the physically handicapped to that portion of the public building or facility constructed prior to November 13, 1968, which is altered, repaired or added after March 4, 1972, does not exempt the administrative authority of the building or facility from also making a path of travel from the exterior of the structure to the remodeled area, a path of travel from any key facilities serving the area to the remodeled area (where such key facilities are required for the physically handicapped), and the key facilities themselves accessible to the physically handicapped. Without making such paths of travel and key facilities serving the remodeled area accessible and usable by the physically handicapped, we think that portion of the structure which is remodeled would not be functionally usable by the physically handicapped pursuant to Section 4456 and this would, therefore, defeat the legislative purpose in

---

[32] There may be some disagreement as to whether Title 24 went into effect July 1, 1982, or earlier: People Ex Rel. Deukmejian v. CHE, *supra*, stated Title 24 was effective as of 12/31/81, but the legislative history indicated July 1, 1982.

enacting Chapter 7 that is provided for in Section 4450. That purpose, as quoted above, states that public buildings and facilities are to be accessible to and usable by the physically handicapped. It is established that statements of legislative intent of this kind may be given considerable weight by the courts in determining the intent of statutes. (Friends of Mammoth v. Board of Supervisors 8 Cal.3d 247, 256-259) (Emphasis added)

[A full copy of this March 31, 1979, Opinion by the California Office of Legislative Counsel is included in the Appendix, Section IX-D of this book.]

4. FROM 1970 UNTIL THE 1982 ADOPTION OF THE STATE ARCHITECT'S TITLE 24 REGULATIONS, HEALTH & SAFETY CODE §19959 AND THE "ASA" REGULATIONS REQUIRED AN ACCESSIBLE PATH OF TRAVEL TO ANY AREA OF ALTERATION, IN ORDER FOR THIS AREA TO BE MADE "ACCESSIBLE"

As explained in James Donald v. Sacramento Bank (1989) 209 Cal.App.3d 1183, prior to the adoption of the State Architect's Regulations, effective July 1, 1982, Government Code § 4451(d) required that facilities subject to Health & Safety Code § 19955 et seq., "shall conform to the American Standards Association's specifications A117.1/1961." These were known as the "ASA" regulations (but sometimes called "ANSI"). (See § II.B.1.d.(1).(b), *supra*.)

Defendants have on occasion asserted that there were no explicit "path of travel" requirements under the ASA. Any claim, that from 1970 to 1982, Health & Safety Code § 19959 had no "path of travel" requirements simply because the words "path of travel" do not appear in the ASA Regulations, would ignore both case law and the policy and purpose of the statutory scheme.

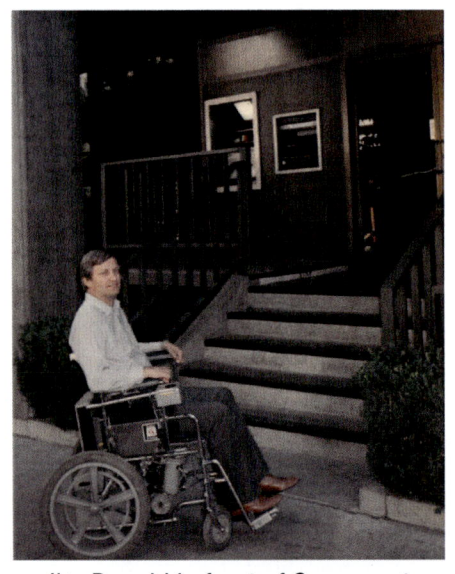

Jim Donald in front of Sacramento Valley Bank ATM stairs

James Donald v. Sacramento Valley Bank (1989) 209 Cal.App.3d 1183, and People ex rel. Deukmejian v. CHE, Inc. (1983) 150 Cal.App.3d 123, both involved enforcement of access requirements under the ASA (for 1975 and 1977 alterations, respectively). The requirement of an accessible path of travel is implicit in the concept of "accessibility." Alterations prior to the January, 1982, effective date of Title 24 of the Administrative Code (the State Architect's Regulations") were governed by Health and Safety Code § 19959 and the "ASA" standards that were in effect until the 1982 adoption of the State Architect's Regulations. As pointed out in James Donald v. Sacramento Valley Bank (1989) 209 Cal.App.3d 1183, the ASA standards were formulated in 1961 and do not spell out any reference to an "automatic teller machine." Yet, Sacramento Valley Bank held that an "ATM" was clearly a "facility" and that it was the purpose of the ASA to provide access to all public facilities. Similarly, while not using the words "path of travel," the court found such a requirement from the provisions for accessible "walkways" under § 4.2.2 of the ASA. Section 4.2.2 stated, "Such walks shall be of a continuing common surface, not interrupted by steps or abrupt changes in level." (Sacramento Valley Bank, *supra*, at 1193 to 1194.)

As noted, an accessible "path of travel" requirement is implicit in the concept of making any area "accessible." Donald v. Sacramento Valley Bank, *supra*, turned on the issue of whether the ASA Regulations required an accessible path of travel from the exterior sidewalk to the location of the Automated Teller Machine added to the Bank's exterior wall (up five stairs) in 1975. The court found the accessible "walkways" requirement of the ASA sufficient for this purpose (209 Cal.App.3d at 1193-1194), rejecting the defendants' allegations that ATM's were not specifically mentioned in the (1961) ASA Regulations. The court found that

> The ASA standards apply to "all buildings and facilities used by the public," and list as their purpose "to make all buildings and facilities used by the public accessible to and functional for the physically handicapped... (ASA Standard A117.1 / 1961 ¶1.2) (Emphasis added)
> Donald v. Sacramento valley Bank, *supra*, 209 Cal.App.3d 1183, at 1194.

5. **PEOPLE EX REL. DEUKMEJIAN V. CHE, INC.** (1983) 150 CAL.APP.3D 123 APPLIED THE ASA STANDARDS, TRACED THE LEGISLATIVE HISTORY, AND OUTLINED IMPORTANT POLICY CONSIDERATIONS FOR STATUTORY CONSTRUCTION

   a. THE CHE CASE SPELLED OUT THE STATUTORY HISTORY OF CALIFORNIA DISABLED ACCESS LAWS AND THE INTERRELATION OF STATUTES AND REGULATIONS FROM 1968 TO 1981

   Case law prior to Donald v. Sacramento Valley Bank, *supra*, required an accessible path of travel under the (pre-Title 24) ASA. In People ex rel. Deukmejian v. CHE, Inc. (1983) 150 Cal.App.3d 123 at 132-133, the court enforced the requirement for proper access through the front door of an "altered" restaurant, under ASA 5.2.1. In that Attorney General prosecution, the court traced the history of the statutory schemes under Government Code § 4450 et seq and Civil Code §54 et seq., noting that the legislature intended to create access for disabled persons and to use the 1961 ASA Standards as "minimum requirements" to insure facilities were "accessible":

   > In 1968, the Legislature enacted two statutory schemes to avoid discriminating against the physically disabled. Government Code

section 4450, et seq. is designed to guarantee access and use of all public buildings. Section 4450 directed the State Architect to adopt and submit proposed building standards for approval. During the interim, Government Code section 4451 required builders [to] adhere to the American Standards Association specifications A117.1-1961. The Legislature created these temporary standards as "minimum requirements to insure that buildings, structures and related facilities covered by this chapter are accessible to, and functionable for, the physically handicapped to, through, and within their doors, *without loss of function, space, or facility where the general public is concerned.*" Gov.Code § 4452, italics added (by the court). ASA specification 5.2.1 provides:

> "At least one primary entrance... shall be useable by individuals in wheelchairs. (All emphasis by the court)

The court then discussed the statutory scheme in the Civil Code, commencing with,

> Section 54, et seq., declaring the physically disabled are entitled to the same right as the able bodied to full and free use of streets, highways, sidewalks, walkways, public buildings, public facilities, and other public places (Civ. Code, § 54), and declaring they were "entitled to full and equal access, as other members of the general public, to accommodations, advantages, facilities, and privileges of... hotels, lodging places, places of public accommodation, amusement or resort, and other places to which the general public is invited..." (Civ.Code, §54.1, subd. (a).)

The court then discussed the passage of Health & Safety Code § 19955 et seq.; the provision of § 19957 for "hardship" exceptions; the provision of § 19958 for local governmental enforcement of access law provisions; and the rules of statutory construction, emphasizing the "primary importance" that we "ascertain the intent of the Legislature so as to effectuate the purpose of the law":

> The questioned provision must be given a reasonable and common sense interpretation consistent with the apparent purpose and intention of the lawmakers, practical rather than technical in nature, which, upon application, results in wise policy rather than mischief or absurdity. [Citations] If possible, significance should be attributed to every word, phrase, sentence and part of an act in pursuance of the legislative purpose, as "the various parts of a statutory enactment must be harmonized by considering the particular clause or section in the context of the statutory framework as a whole." (Moyer v. Workman's Comp. Appeals Bd., 10 Cal.3d at p. 230.)

People ex rel. Deukmejian v. CHE, Inc., *supra*, 150 Cal.App.3d 123, at 132-133.

In a section entitled, <u>The Legal Standard For Accessibility For The Handicapped</u>, the court then traced the California legislative history:

> Our construction of the legislative schemes commences with Civil Code section 54, et seq. which declares, in part, that all physically handicapped are entitled to the same right as the able bodied to full and free use of public facilities and places (§ 54), requiring operators of such facilities to "open its doors on an equal basis to all that can avail themselves of the facilities without violation of other valid laws and regulations." (Marsh v. Edwards Theatres Circuit, Inc., 64 Cal.App.3d 881, 892, 134 Cal.Rptr. 844; Civ.Code, § 54.1, subd. (a).) To give meaning to the public accommodation law prohibiting discrimination against the handicapped, the Legislature enacted Government Code section 4450, et seq. providing for the establishment of standards for buildings constructed with public funds designed to insure accessibility by the handicapped. A year later, the Legislature expanded these requirements to facilities constructed with private funds (§ 19955, et seq.) and, with certain limited exceptions, required conformance with the same standards set forth within Government Code section 4450, et seq. <u>The underlying legislative intent of these statutory schemes is to require affirmative conduct so as to guarantee access to the physically handicapped upon construction of new facilities or with the repair or alteration of existing facilities</u>. (Marsh v. Edwards Theatres Circuit, Inc., *supra*, at p. 888, 134 Cal.Rptr. 844.) The Supreme Court explained in re Marriage of Carney, 24 Cal.3d 725, 738, 157 Cal.Rptr. 383, 598 P.2d 36, these statutory schemes were part of "<u>a growing body of legislation intended to reduce or eliminate the physical impediments</u>" to "<u>their participation in community life</u>." (Emphasis added)
>
> <u>People ex rel. Deukmejian v. CHE, Inc.</u>, *supra*, 150 Cal.App.3d 123, at 133.

The court then described Health & Safety Code § 19956 expressly incorporating the legal standards of Government Code § 4450 et seq.,

> which in turn describes its purpose as assuring the construction of public facilities which are accessible to and useable by the physically handicapped, and establishes the specific standard of compliance as that set forth within the American Standard Associations Specifications A117.1-1961. These latter specifications, like the express purpose of Government Code section 4450 and the language within the exemption in section 19956, were expressly intended to make all buildings and facilities used by the public accessible to and functionable for the physically handicapped. Similar to section 19957, the specifications provide: "[i]n case of the practical difficulty, unnecessary hardship, or extreme differences, administrative authorities may grant exceptions from the literal requirements of this standard or permit the use of other

methods or materials, but only when it is clearly evident that equivalent facilitation and protection are thereby secured." (ASA, spec. I.2, italics added) (Italics added by the court.)

People ex rel. Deukmejian v. CHE, Inc., *supra*, 150 Cal.App.3d 123, at 133-134.

b. CHE FOUND THE 1981 TITLE 24 REGULATIONS "CLARIFIED" THE PRIOR "ASA" REGULATIONS IN SPECIFYING PATH OF TRAVEL REQUIREMENTS

The CHE court went on to explain how the statutory construction should consider this legislative purpose.

> Reading these provisions in harmony, we conclude the latter two statutory schemes regarding access to public buildings and facilities were enacted to provide substance to the full and equal access right of the handicapped, setting forth the legal standard requiring at least one primary entrance be accessible to and useable by the physically handicapped. Where a second primary entrance is necessary in order to satisfy this requirements, it need not be identical in character; however, it must satisfy our construction of the phrase "primary entrance" (*infra*), because the statutory and regulatory law, read as a whole, is designed to guarantee safe access for the physically disabled while permitting them to function as equals to the maximum extent feasible within every aspect of society. Consequently, exception to the literal statutory and regulatory requirements is warranted only when equivalent facilitation and protection are not denied. (ASA, spec.I.2; §19957.) Thus, equality, at minimum, requires access free from difficulties or obstacles (see American Heritage Dictionary (New College Ed.1976) p. 469, col. 2) and potential hazards which would endanger even the most cautious physically handicapped. (Emphasis added)

> People ex rel. Deukmejian v. CHE, Inc., *supra*, 150 Cal.App.3d at 134.

The court went on to construe the phrase "primary entrance," relying in part on regulations promulgated by the State Architect in 1981, in Title 24 (which the court found was effective December 31, 1981). The court explained why it was entitled to rely upon these later (Title 24) regulations of the State Architect even as to the proper meaning to be given to the ASA regulations which were in effect prior to the State Architect's regulations:

> However, there is further guidance in the regulations on handicapped access promulgated by the State Architect in 1981 (effective 12-31-81) within the State Building Code, 24 California Administrative Code, section 2-101, et seq. There, a primary entrance is defined as "any entrance to a facility which has a substantial flow of pedestrian

traffic to any specific major function of the facility." (24 Cal.Admin. Code, § 2-417(k).) We are entitled to rely on this definition because it constitutes a <u>clarifying regulatory amendment</u> to the statutory schemes in controversy which from their enactment incorporated by reference the phrase "primary entrance." For, "[w]hile it is true that as a general rule statutes are not to be given retroactive effect unless the intent of the Legislature cannot be otherwise satisfied (DiGenova v. State Board of Education, 57 Cal.2d 167, 176 [18 Cal.Rptr. 369, 367 P.2d 865]), an exception to the general rule is recognized in a case where the <u>legislative amendment merely clarifies the existing law</u>. (Balen v. Peralta Junior College Dist., 11 Cal.3d 821, 828, fn. 8...) The rationale of this exception is that in such an instance, in essence, no retroactive effect is given to the statute because the true meaning of the statute has been always the same..." [Emphasis added]

<u>People ex rel. Deukmejian v. CHE, Inc.</u>, *supra*, 150 Cal.App.3d 123, at 134-135.

It is similarly clear that the requirement of an accessible path of travel is implicit in the concept of making a particular area "accessible." The spelling out of a path of travel requirement in the State Architect's regulations merely defined and clarified what was already implicit in the accessibility standards of the ASA when read in context of this legislative intent. (See discussion of 1979 Legislative Counsel's Opinion, section I.D.3., *supra*.)

The <u>CHE</u> court went on to "reject" defendants' argument that separate entrances for handicapped and non-handicapped patrons were acceptable, and spelled out further the <u>legislative policy</u> that should be considered by the court in <u>interpreting</u> issues related to handicapped access.

> The prohibition against discrimination of the handicapped within Civil Code section 54, et seq., the enactment of Government Code section 4450, et seq., and section 19955, et seq., and the incorporation by reference of the phrase "primary entrance" within the applicable specifications, reflect a legislative sensitivity to the hardships suffered by those afflicted with a wide range of physical disabilities. They are part of an expanding legislative effort to attain "the commendable goal of total integration of handicapped persons into the mainstream of society...." (In re Marriage of Carney, *supra*, 24 Cal.3d 725, 740, 157 Cal.Rptr. 383, 598 P.2d 36.) The Legislature has declared "[i]t is the policy of this state to encourage and enable disabled persons to participate fully in the social and economic life of the state...." (Gov.Code, § 19230, subd.(a).) These legislative responses are designed to lessen their entire burden, by guaranteeing equal and full access to public buildings, facilities, and accommodations, without

> jeopardizing their safety. We believe the law intended to promote accommodation of the physically handicapped by insuring them access to public restaurants without facing the unnecessary, adverse psychological impact of being separated from regular customer traffic and shunted through secondary entrances.

People ex rel. Deukmejian v. CHE, Inc., *supra*, 150 Cal.App.3d 123, at 135-136.

6. PATH OF TRAVEL REQUIREMENTS UNDER THE 1970-1982 "ASA" STANDARDS (DONALD V. SACRAMENTO VALLEY BANK (1989) 209 CAL. APP. 3rd 1183)

The State Architect's explicit requirements for a path of travel in all of the State Architect's Regulations (1982 to the present) is a recognition that an accessible path of travel is implicit in the concept of making an area accessible, and that a path of travel was also previously required under the ASA standards, and independently under Health & Safety Code § 19959 in terms of making an area "accessible" when an alteration, structural repair or addition was made to that area.

James Donald v. Sacramento Valley Bank (1989) 209 Cal.App.3d 1183, involved the 1975 alteration of a building by the addition of an ATM (Automated Teller Machine) on the building exterior. A wheelchair accessible "path of travel" from the sidewalk to the ATM was triggered by the alteration. Based on the "walks and levels" provisions of ASA 4.2.2, "such walks should be of a continuing common surface, not interrupted by steps or abrupt changes in level". (The ASA regulations controlled until the [July 1, 1982] effective date of the State Architect's Regulations.)

Sacramento Valley Bank, at 1192, held the following:

> Most importantly, Government Code section 4451 required public buildings and related facilities to adhere to existing ASA standards. The statute provided in relevant part: "(c) Except as otherwise provided by law, buildings, structures, sidewalks, curbs and related facilities subject to the provisions of this chapter or Part 5.5. (commencing with Section 19955) of Division 13 of the Health and Safety Code shall conform to the regulations adopted pursuant to Section 4450 which are in effect on the date a building permit is issued therefor... [¶] All buildings, structures and related facilities which are required to conform to the American Standards Association Specifications A117.1-1961 prior to the effective date of the regulations adopted by the State Architect shall continue to conform to the American Standards Association Specifications A117.1-1961...." (Emphasis by the court); Stats.1974, ch. 995, §2, p.2104

The court further found that provisions of Health & Safety Code § 19955 et seq. were applicable "with respect to buildings constructed after July 1, 1970, or to the repair and alteration of existing facilities after that date." (Id. At 1192-1193)

The court in interpreting § 19955 (209 Cal.App.3d 1183, at 1194, footnote 8) noted the following:

> The 1961 ASA standards also specify the specifications apply to all buildings and facilities used by the public. As relevant to this appeal, the 1961 ASA standards provided: "1.1 Scope [¶] 1.1.1 This standard applies to all buildings and facilities used by the public. It applies to temporary or emergency conditions as well as permanent conditions. It does not apply in private residences. [¶] 1.2 Purpose. This standard is intended to make all buildings and facilities used by the public accessible to and functional for the physically handicapped, to, through, and within their doors, without loss of function, space or facility where the general public is concerned." (Emphasis added)

In applying the ASA "walkway" provisions to access from a public sidewalk to an ATM on the outside of the building, the court definitively answered "Yes" to the question of whether a "path of travel" from the exterior of a structure to the remodeled area needed to be accessible to the physically handicapped to the same extent that the remodeled area itself is required to be accessible.

7. "PATH OF TRAVEL" IS EXPLICITLY DEFINED IN THE 1982 STATE ARCHITECT'S REGULATIONS ("TITLE 24") THE 1984 STATE ARCHITECT'S INTERPRETIVE MANUAL, AND THE 1984 AND 1989 REGULATIONS

"Path of travel" was defined in the 1982 State Architect's Regulations (Title 24), (at p.27, of the 1984 State Architect's Interpretive Manual, at § 2-417(c)), and by the State Architect's "interpretation." The regulation states:

> (c) <u>Path of Travel</u>: Path of travel is a passage that may consist of walks and sidewalks, curb ramps, and pedestrian ramps, lobbies and corridors, elevators, other improved areas, or a necessary combination thereof, that provides free and unobstructed access to and egress from a particular area or location, for pedestrians and/or wheelchair users.

The State Architect's interpretation to the "Path of Travel" definition of § 2-417(c) in the 1984 Interpretive Manual includes the following:

> The point of path of travel is that people arriving at the building site have <u>accessibility</u> <u>from the</u> <u>exterior</u> of the building <u>including either the right of way and/or</u> <u>parking lot to</u> <u>the interior portions</u> of the building. This path of travel could include various elements including the entrance, walkways, ramps, etc. necessary to provide a direct accessible route to the interior of the building. <u>All</u> <u>features</u> within the path of travel are to adhere to these regulations. (Emphasis added)

Similar to the language of §19959 Health & Safety Code, the State Architect's Regulations apply the same standards to privately owned public accommodations as earlier regulations applied to publicly funded buildings when "alterations, structural repairs or additions" are made. Per 2-105(b)11B(4), (1984 numbering)

> All existing <u>privately funded</u> public accommodations when alterations, structural repairs or additions are made to such public accommodations as set forth under 11A(5), (6), and (7).
>
> <u>Interpretation</u>:
> Very Important - The requirements for existing privately funded buildings that are to be remodeled are the same as for publicly funded. So you are referred to the publicly funded section to get this information.

[The 1984 Regulations use the number 2-105(b)11A, whereas the 1989 edition lists nearly identical regulations at 110A(b)11A.]

Title 24, § 110A(b)11 (1989), applicable to publicly funded public accommodations, and to privately funded public accommodations (see above), spelled out the need for access for entrance, path of travel and restrooms.

> 11. OSA/AC - Access Compliance, Office of the State Architect General. To assure that barrier-free design is incorporated in all buildings, facilities, site work and other improvements to which this code applies; to assure that these improvements are accessible to and usable by physically disabled persons. Additions, alterations and structural repairs to buildings and facilities shall comply with these provisions for new buildings, except as otherwise provided and specified herein...
>
> > (5) All existing publicly funded buildings and facilities when alterations, structural repairs or additions are made to such buildings or facilities. <u>This requirement shall only apply to area of specific alteration, structural repair or addition and shall not be construed to mean that the entire structure or facility is subject to this code.</u> <u>Compliance shall require</u>:
> >
> > a. That a <u>primary entrance</u> to the building or facility and the <u>primary path of travel</u> to the specific area shall be <u>accessible to and usable by</u> handicapped persons;
> >
> > b. That <u>sanitary facilities</u>, drinking fountains and public telephones <u>serving the remodeled area</u> shall be accessible to and usable by handicapped persons. (Emphasis added)
>
> The accompanying State Architect's "<u>interpretation</u>" states:
> > <u>Existing Buildings</u> - <u>Very Important</u> - This is the section that details the extent to which an existing building must comply if an addition, alteration, or repair is made. Full compliance in an existing building incorporates the following work only:

1) The area of remodel must comply.

2) A path of travel to the remodeled area must comply.

3) Bathrooms, telephones and drinking fountains serving the remodeled area must comply.

These requirements apply to all remodeling jobs <u>regard-less of the valuation of the job</u>. (Emphasis in original.)

The Regulations themselves, using the same language as in Health & Safety Code § 19959, and also requiring an accessible path of travel, show that there has never been anything inconsistent between § 19959's provisions and the path of travel regulations. In fact, without an accessible path of travel, "access" is non-existent.

8. ARNOLD v. UNITED ARTISTS CONFIRMED THE VALIDITY OF THE STATE ARCHITECT'S REGULATIONS AND THE "GREAT WEIGHT" TO BE GIVEN TO THE STATE ARCHITECT'S INTERPRETATIONS

After the State Architect's Regulations went into effect in 1982, some defendants challenged the validity of the State Architect's Regulations (Title 24, now the "State Building Code) and the <u>Interpretations</u> of these regulations by the State Architect's office. The December 7, 1993 Memorandum Opinion and Order by (former Chief) Judge Thelton Henderson, in <u>Arnold v. United Artists</u> (N.D.Cal.), affirmed the validity of the State Architect's Regulations, and held that the State Architect's Interpretive Manual, as "a state agency's interpretation of its own regulations is entitled to great weight." Judge Henderson further held that any of the specific provisions of Title 24 should be interpreted in light of the State Architect's interpretations, and with particular regard to the "accessibility" and "usability" regulations:

"Section 2-102.1(b) of Title 24 provides that the <u>purpose</u> of the state building code disability regulations is" to assure that [facilities] are <u>accessible to, and usable by</u>, physically handicapped persons.
Cal. Code Regs. tit. 24, § 2-102.1(b)
[Emphasis by Judge Henderson]

Order of 12/7/93, <u>Arnold, et al. v. United Artists Theater Circuits, Inc.</u> US District Court, No. C93-0079 TEH, p.12, l.16-18, p.13, l.1.

On the issue of "interpretation," Judge Henderson stated:
Although there is no California case law directly addressing the question of how to interpret Title 24 regulations in this context, there is precedent for the practice of treating the terms of the § 2-102.1(b) purpose section as providing a gloss on the specific regulations contained in § 2-611. See Donald v. Café Royale, Inc., 266 Cal.Rptr. 804, 810, 218 Cal.App.3d 168 (1st Dist. 1990). Plaintiffs also invoke in support of their reading of the regulations the interpretive materials published by the State Architect.

Since November 1986, the Interpretive Manual issued by the State Architect has construed § 2-611(b)1.A as follows:

> It is required that these seating areas be integrated with the general seating arrangements so that people with disabilities can sit with able-bodied friends and family members.
>
> State Architect's Interpretive Manual at § 2-611(b)1.A (2d ed. 1986 & 3d ed. 1989) The parties agree that the State Architect's interpretations do not themselves have the force and effect of law. However, the Office of the State Architect is the agency statutorily charged with fashioning state disability access standards, see Government Code § 4450, and, indeed, it was the State Architect's Office that drafted the Title 24 regulations. Under California administrative law, a state agency's interpretation of its own regulations is entitled to great weight. Ontario Community Foundation, Inc. v. State Board of Equalization, 201 Cal.Rptr. 165, 35 Cal.3d 811, 678 P.2d 378 (Cal. 1984)
>
> Order of 12/7/93, Arnold, et al. v. United Artists Theater Circuits, Inc. US District Court, No. C93-0079 TEH, p.15, l.8-28, p.16, l.1-8.

9. **SEPTEMBER 17, 1992 OPINION OF CALIFORNIA ATTORNEY GENERAL DAN LUNGREN, A STATEWIDE DIRECTIVE TO ALL CALIFORNIA BUILDING OFFICIALS, CONFIRMED THE "PATH OF TRAVEL" REQUIREMENTS**

The opinion of California Attorney General Dan Lungren in his September 17, 1992 Statewide Directive to all California Building Officials, represents the official policy of the Attorney General's office as of that date. In this directive, Attorney General Lungren spelled out the duties of current building inspectors to investigate all complaints about architectural barriers which denied "full and equal" access to disabled persons, and that the state Attorney General's office would limit its direct enforcement to situations involving an abuse of discretion by local officials. The Attorney General's description of some specific access requirements which had not been properly enforced in the past were laid out in an "Appendix," and included, inter alia, (1) "path of travel" requirements; (2) alterations which triggered access requirements; and (3) no "exceptions" being given except where the statutory written criteria for unreasonable hardship findings have been made and recorded. (Opinion included in this Book's Appendix, at section IX-E-1)

The Appendix to the Attorney General's Directive lists important principles of disabled access law and addresses common violations of state disabled access laws and regulations. At page 3, on "Remodeling of Existing Buildings," the A.G. stated:

> A remodel triggers the applicability of disabled access requirements in "pre-code" buildings and facilities. Not only must the specific area of remodel comply with access regulations, but the restrooms, public telephones and

drinking fountains serving the remodeled area and the path of travel to the remodeled area must also be brought into compliance. The "path of travel" includes all elements necessary to provide access to the remodeled area and includes parking, sidewalks, walks, doorways, and a primary entrance. (Regulation § 2-110A(b)11A.) All remodels commenced to bring a facility into compliance with the ADA must also comply with the above state law requirements. (Emphasis added)

10. THE ADA SPECIFIES THAT DISABLED PERSONS ARE ENTITLED TO BOTH ADA AND CALIFORNIA STATE LAW PROTECTIONS, AND TO WHICHEVER STATUTE PROVIDES "GREATER OR EQUAL PROTECTION"

This last sentence of the September 17, 1992 California Attorney General's Opinion, above, requiring compliance with both the ADA and state law requirements, refers to the overlap in California between the ADA and California law. The ADA adds "readily achievable" barrier removal requirements to the California access requirements, which requirements are based on new construction or alterations. The AG notes that remodels done on an ADA "readily achievable" basis must still comply with California's current standards. The ADA itself makes clear that the stronger protections between state or federal law will apply if there is any purported "conflict." See ADA § 501(b), "Relationship to Other Laws":

> Nothing in this section shall be construed to invalidate or limit the remedies, rights and procedures of any Federal law or law of any State or political subdivision on any State or Jurisdiction that provides greater or equal protection for the rights of individuals with disabilities than are afforded by this Act...

(Emphasis added)

11. PATH OF TRAVEL REQUIREMENTS INCLUDE AN ACCESSIBLE, SAFE AND PRIMARY PUBLIC ENTRANCE

   a. "PATH OF TRAVEL" ACCESS THROUGH THE FRONT ENTRANCE, REQUIRING SAFETY FEATURES AT THE FRONT ENTRANCE, ARE TRIGGERED BY ANY ALTERATION INSIDE A RESTAURANT OR OTHER PUBLIC BUILDING

   As an example, in Atwood v. El Torito Restaurants, et al. (Alameda County Superior Court, Action No. 677858-1, a case tried to the court in 1996), the San Leandro El Torito had an access ramp leading to the front door,[33] but safety problems existed: despite major alterations inside the restaurant, requiring access per the 1984 Title 24 regulations, there were no hand railings on the lower part of the ramp; further the "landing" area configuration, because

---

[33] In People ex rel. Deukmejian v. CHE, Inc. (1983) 150 Cal.App.3d 123, *supra* (as discussed in § I.D.5, *supra*), the court spelled out the importance of access through a "primary" building entrance.

of a 6% "side slope" and the "door opening" configuration where the level landing area was too small, posed the possibility that a disabled person approaching the entrance in a wheelchair might get knocked down the front stairs when patrons exiting the restaurant pushed the door open! Alterations <u>anywhere</u> inside a building trigger access through the front (primary) entrance. Code sections required a level landing (§ 2-3303(i)2). "Level" was defined as having no more than a 2% side slope, (§ 2-413(a) of the 1984 State Architect's Regulations.) The requirements as to clearances for the level space at the exit door were described at § 2-3303(i)2A, B and C.

Further, per § 2-3306(d)(3), "Encroachment of Doors," doors <u>in any position</u> shall not reduce the minimum dimension of the landing to less than 42". (Emphasis added) (At the 1996 <u>Atwood v. El Torito</u> trial, plaintiff's expert, Richard Skaff,[34] testified that the actual landing clearance was only 19" rather than 42".) § 2-3306(e) requires handrails the full length of the handicapped ramp; § 2-3306(h) requires wheel guides to keep wheelchairs from going off the edge of a ramp.

b. ALTERATIONS MAY TRIGGER THE NEED TO CORRECT ANY CONTINUING DANGER TO DISABLED PERSONS AT A FRONT ENTRANCE, A LANDING, AND/OR AN ACCESS RAMP

Safety regulations are set up for safety purposes. At the <u>Atwood v. El Torito</u> trial, the testimony and photographs offered in evidence by plaintiff's access expert, Richard Skaff, made clear that the front door could open directly against the body of a person in a wheelchair approaching the front door from the access ramp; that there was insufficient clearance for wheelchair passage when the door opened; and that the <u>side slope</u> of the landing <u>toward the steps</u> was <u>6%</u>, three times the maximum allowed by Title 24. However, it should not take an expert witness to recognize (1) the <u>danger</u> in having a front entrance door open directly into the path of any disabled person (in a wheelchair or using a cane or walker) coming up the access ramp; (2) that there was not sufficient room on the landing for a disabled person to safely maneuver around the open door, with 19" of clearance instead of the required 42" (§ 2-3306(d)); and (3) that the side slope of 6%, 3 times the 2% side slope set by the code, (§ 2-3303(i)2 and § 2-413(A)), added to the dangers for disabled persons. [<u>Atwood v. El Torito Restaurants, et al.</u>, Alameda Cty. Sup. Ct., Action No. 677858-1](Concluded by attorney fees Order, October 7, 1999.)[35]

---

[34] Expert Richard Skaff, himself a disabled wheelchair user, was also the plaintiff and prevailing party in an important, precedent setting 9th Circuit case, <u>Skaff v. Meridien North America Beverly Hills, LLC</u>, 506 F.3d 832 (9th Cir. 2007), represented by attorney Sidney J. Cohen of Oakland. This opinion clarified issues regarding a plaintiff's standing to sue for injunctive relief, and entitlement to attorney fees as "prevailing party" under federal and state law.

[35] The trial court awarded an injunction and a damage award for the plaintiff. Substantial attorney fees were awarded pursuant to plaintiff's post-trial motion, including a 1.5 multiplier enhancement per California Code of Civil Procedure § 1021.5 because of public interest results of the law suit.

c. COMPLIANCE IS GOVERNED BY THE SPECIFIC REQUIREMENTS SPECIFIED IN THE REGULATIONS, NOT BY ANY "EXPERT'S" NOTION OF "ACCESSIBLE AND USEABLE"

Health & Safety Code §§ 19955-19959, and the provisions of Government Code §§ 4450-4456 incorporated therein, set the minimum standards for access. Specific details for minimum legal access were specified since 1982 in the Title 24 Regulations. A defendant may suggest that its facilities' current configuration for access is "sufficient" because a <u>particular</u> disabled person (including one hired as a "consultant!") uses a wheelchair and testifies he was "able" to "use" the facilities. This testimony is <u>irrelevant</u> if code requirements were not met. The code and regulations set "minimum" standards for access, so defendants cannot argue that some lesser standard is "good enough."

Testimony about usability by a particular disabled person is not a substitute for compliance with the specific requirements of Title 24 Regulations. These regulations are set up to accommodate those who have many different forms of mobility disability, including, for example, persons who walk with canes, walkers or prosthetic limbs, or those who use wheelchairs, including the larger, heavier electric powered wheelchairs. They also protect semi-ambulatory persons, including elderly persons who may need properly positioned grab bars to regain their feet after using the toilet. Expert testimony by access consultants such as Marin County based expert Richard Skaff in <u>Atwood v. El Torito</u>, *supra*, or Oakland based expert Peter Margen at the trial in <u>Hankins v. El Torito</u>,

 supra, can explain the practicalities of how various deficiencies could adversely affect the use of specific facilities by disabled persons with different disabilities.[36]

For example, in <u>Martin v. Cavalier Oceanfront Resort, et al</u> (C.D.Cal.) Case No. CV-02-02259 AHM, summary judgment was obtained for plaintiff <u>under California law</u> as to the need to provide access to multiple hotel guest rooms at a 90 guest room San Simeon resort.

Summary judgment for plaintiff was supported largely by the expert declaration of Santa Cruz based access expert Jonathan Adler. (See Summary Judgment Order, November 14, 2003.) Similarly, the work of another leading access expert, Barry

---

[36] It should be kept in mind that California law and the ADA also protect persons with visual or hearing disabilities, and their needs may be very different from those of persons with mobility disabilities. The 2005 U.S. Census Bureau reported 54.2 million Americans had some level of disability, and 35 million, or 12.5% of the population were classified as having a "severe" disability. In <u>George, et al. v. BART</u> (N.D.Cal.) Case No. C00-02206 CW, plaintiffs sought through ten years of litigation to force BART to paint yellow contrast warning stripes at the top of staircases to protect visually disabled persons from falling down unmarked stairs. Following a reversal by the 9th Circuit Court of Appeal (<u>George, et al. v. BART</u>, (9th Cir. 2009) 577 F.3d 1005) overturning plaintiffs' summary judgment order under the ADA, the state law liability issue remained. The case was settled by payment of agreed damages for the plaintiffs, an agreement by BART to provide the injunctive relief sought, and payment of a portion of plaintiff's costs and attorney fees.

Atwood (whose office is in Berkeley), has been instrumental in obtaining access in several hundred disability access lawsuits (in addition to many instances when Mr. Atwood, often as a volunteer and without compensation, investigated access issues and provided advice leading to improved "voluntary" access at numerous public facilities).

The ability of a disabled person to "access" an area does not exist if this person cannot get to the area. A "path of travel" requirement is consistent with Health & Safety Code § 19959, per overwhelming authority, since July 1, 1970. Any interpretation that an area can be "accessible" without an accessible route to the area would be absurd, and would be contrary both to public policy and to the specified purpose of all of the statutes and regulations in this area of law: To maximize the ability of disabled persons to participate in society on an equal and integrated basis.

    d. ARE CROSS-WALKS REQUIRED FOR A SAFE AND "ACCESSIBLE" PATH OF TRAVEL FROM PARKING AREAS TO STORE ENTRANCES?

An issue that has occasionally arisen in litigation involving shopping malls is the necessity for disabled persons to cross a vehicular pathway or street in order to travel from designated "disabled accessible" parking places to and up the curb cut leading to a store entrance. Defendants may contend that there is no direct reference to "crosswalks" in Title 24 or ADAAG regulations. The following analysis, concluding that a marked crosswalk is required by current California and federal law, was supplied by an experienced Berkeley access consultant, Barry Atwood:

> Title 24 Analysis
> An accessible route between the accessible parking spaces and the primary entrance to the facilities on the site is required by Title 24 in Section 1127B.1, which states:
>> " Site development and grading shall be designed to provide access to all entrances and exterior ground floor exits, and access to normal paths of travel, and where necessary to provide access, shall incorporate pedestrian ramps, curb ramps, etc. Access shall be provided within the boundary of the site from public transportation stops, accessible parking spaces, passenger loading zones if provided, and public streets or sidewalks."
>
> An accessible route is defined in section 1102B of Title 24 as "…a continuous unobstructed path connecting all accessible elements and spaces in an accessible building or facility that can be negotiated by a person with a severe disability using

a wheelchair, and that is also safe for and usable by persons with other disabilities."

NOTE: This means that a path of travel that is not safe for a disabled individual to use cannot be used as an accessible route. Crossing a busy vehicular way is an obviously dangerous area for disabled individuals, who are often less visible, are inherently less mobile so they require more time to cross safely and are less agile so they are less able to avoid an accident than an able bodied individual would be.

ADAAG Analysis
An accessible route between the accessible parking spaces and the primary entrance to the facilities on the site is required by ADAAG in Section 4.1.2, which states:

"At least one accessible route complying with 4.3 shall be provided within the boundary of the site from public transportation stops, accessible parking spaces, passenger loading zones if provided, and public streets or sidewalks, to an accessible building entrance."

Section 3.4 of the ADAAG defines an accessible route as "A continuous unobstructed path connecting all accessible elements and spaces of a building or facility. Interior accessible routes may include corridors, floors, ramps, elevators, lifts, and clear floor space at fixtures. Exterior accessible routes may include parking access aisles, curb ramps, crosswalks at vehicular ways, walks, ramps, and lifts.

NOTE: This definition clearly sets forth a complete list of the elements that may be used as a part of a compliant accessible route. If a disabled individual is required to cross a vehicular way that is not clearly marked by a crosswalk, that path of travel is <u>not</u> a compliant accessible route and is, therefore, a clear violation of the code.

Conclusion
Therefore, we believe that requiring a disabled person to cross a vehicular way without providing a marked crosswalk, subjects them to a hazardous condition and that path of travel does not constitute the "accessible route" required by the code.

E. "CONSTRUCTION DIMENSIONAL TOLERANCES" IS NOT A DEFENSE WHEN (A) THERE IS NO SHOWING OF STRUCTURAL IMPRACTICABILITY, OR (B) WHERE REGULATION REQUIRES SPECIFIC MAXIMUM OR MINIMUM

1. STRICT COMPLIANCE WITH ADAAG STANDARDS IS REQUIRED UNDER FEDERAL LAW UNLESS THE "INFEASIBILITY EXCEPTION" APPLIES

A current controversy exists as to the existence and application of the principle of "construction dimensional tolerances." For certain defense experts, this means that if a feature is "technically" out of compliance, but not by "too great" a degree, it doesn't have to be made compliant. In a September 4, 2009, Order by Northern District Judge Sandra Armstrong in <u>CDR v. California Dept. of Transportation</u>, C09-5125, the Court held that the California DOT had a legal duty to upgrade non-compliant curb ramps whenever they modified an adjacent roadway. The Court held that street surfacing was an "alteration" and that <u>strict compliance with ADAAG standards was required</u> where there was no showing that it was structurally impracticable to make the facilities "readily accessible" to disabled persons:

> Defendants' argument ignores that "minor" deviations from the ADAAG do not insulate them from liability unless the infeasibility exception applies. See <u>Ability Ctr. of Greater Toledo v. City of Sandusky</u>, 133 F. Supp. 2d 589, 592 (N.D. Ohio 2001) (finding that "[t]here are no exceptions allowed to [ADAAG] requirements"); see also <u>Long v. Coast Resorts, Inc.</u>, 267 F.3d 918, 923 (9th Cir. 2001) (strict compliance with ADAAG required where there was no showing that it was "structurally impracticable" to make facility "readily accessible" to disabled persons) (citing 42 U.S.C. § 12183(a)(1)).
> In sum, the Court concludes that Defendants have a legal duty to upgrade noncompliant curb ramps when altering an adjacent roadway.

2. **CALIFORNIA TITLE 24 REQUIREMENTS DO NOT ALLOW APPLICATION OF "CONSTRUCTION TOLERANCE" STANDARDS WHERE THE CODE ALREADY STATES A "RANGE" WITH SPECIFIC MINIMUM AND MAXIMUM END POINTS**

While this issue is not without controversy, section 1101B.5 of the 2007 version of Title 24, the California Building Code, states that:

> All dimensions are subject to conventional industry tolerances, except where the requirement is stated with specific minimum and maximum end points.

According to access expert Barry Atwood, who has 25 years of experience in this area, this section is a codification of the standards developed by the Office of Universal Design, Division of the California State Architect. This office is the agency responsible for developing and proposing all accessibility related changes to Title 24, the California Building Code. Item G14 of their 2003 plan-check instrument contained the following:

> The Code provides a range for this dimension. It is recommended that, unless there are compelling reasons not to do so, a dimension in the middle of the
>
> range should be chosen, to provide the contractor with a safety buffer for construction tolerances. (Note: <u>construction tolerances cannot be applied to justify overstepping code required minima and maxima</u>) (Emphasis added)

3. POSSIBLE USE OF "HANDBOOK OF CONSTRUCTION TOLERANCES"

Handbook of Construction Tolerances by David Kent Ballast (John Wiley & Sons, Second Ed. 2007) is an accepted authority on construction tolerances. It compiles and collects "tolerances" from industry publications, for the entire range of building construction. It also contains chapters on measuring compliance and documenting construction tolerances.

Ballast acknowledges throughout the book whenever no accepted tolerance standard exists for a given construction item. In the introduction, Ballast states, "Interestingly, there are still many construction tolerances that do not exist as industry standards. Although many can be derived from combined individual and accumulated tolerances, the various trade associations need to continue work on setting realistic and enforceable standards for both tolerances and uniform measurement protocols. This is especially the case in the areas of accessibility and code compliance." (2nd Ed. 2007 page xv.)

Remember, this Handbook still comprises only one person's opinion, though the author is respected. Neither the U.S. Department of Justice nor the California Department of the State Architect have adopted any construction tolerance standards. However, the Handbook may be useful for challenging any "expert's" stated opinions about a particular tolerance, and for resolving measurement disputes.

4. EXAMPLE: REASONS FOR REQUIRING COMPLIANCE WITH "TECHNICAL" DISABLED PARKING PLACE "SIDE SLOPE" REQUIREMENTS

Business owners sometimes question why a designated "disabled" parking space should have no greater than 2% side slope. However, many "disabled modified" vans have a passenger side exit ramp rather than a lift, and already require the disabled passenger or driver to exit down a significant slope on the ramp itself. According to access consultant Barry Atwood, based on 25 years expertise about disabled accessibility, the addition of several more degrees of slope through excessive "side slope" (or "slope" for rear-exit vans) may cause a disabled wheelchair user to come down the ramp at an excessive speed for safe embarkation or turning (at the bottom of the ramp), and cause a wheelchair user to tip over and risk serious injury. For example, a man exiting on his van ramp, after being forced to park in a parking place with excessive side slope due to lack of proper "accessible" parking, outside a funeral home he was visiting (to make arrangements for a deceased family member), had the footrests of his wheelchair strike the pavement, ejecting him from the chair. He struck his head on a nearby curb and suffered a severe scalp laceration and extended medical treatment. McPhee v. Sunset View Cemetery Ass'n (N.D. Cal.) C95-27288.

F. ACCESSIBLE PUBLIC RESTROOMS ARE GUARANTEED BY LAW FOR "THE PUBLIC, CLIENTS OR EMPLOYEES" BY HEALTH AND SAFETY CODE § 19955 AND TITLE 24 REGULATIONS (§ 2-105(B)11B(2) IN 1984)

   1. HEALTH AND SAFETY CODE §19955 AND TITLE 24 REGULATIONS (§2-105(b)11B(2) IN 1984) REQUIRE ACCESSIBLE SANITARY FACILITIES FOR EMPLOYEES AS WELL AS PATRONS

      When any public accommodations, including dining, entertainment, and theater facilities, don't have accessible public restrooms, many disabled persons are <u>effectively excluded</u> from use of the facilities.

      <u>Accessible</u> restroom facilities are required under law both for members of the public <u>and for employees</u>. This was specified both by Health & Safety Code § 19955 and in the Title 24 Regulations. Since its 1970 inception, Health & Safety Code § 19955(a) has required that,

      > When sanitary facilities are made available for the public, clients, or employees in such accommodations or facilities, they shall be made available for the physically handicapped.

      Likewise, § 2-105(b)11B of the 1984 Title 24 applied the previously adopted requirements for "publicly funded" buildings and facilities to "privately funded" public accommodations or facilities. The <u>text</u> of the regulation, (at p.11 of the 1984 Disabled Access Regulations Interpretive Manual,) specified, "Note: See Health and Safety Code commencing with § 19955." Section 2-105(b)11B(2) then applies access requirements to "Any sanitary facilities which are made available for the public, clients, or employees in such accommodations or facilities." The interpretive note in the Manual, (at p.12), directly below the last section, stated, "Notice that all sanitary facilities made available to the public, clients, or employees must also be made accessible."

      Thus, in a <u>McDonald's</u> restaurant case where there were alterations in the kitchen area, and/or an <u>addition</u> to create a "drive-by window," the drive-by booth should have been accessible and the restroom facilities servicing this booth and "window" must be accessible. Further, any disabled person who purchases food and beverages at this window, then parks their car or van to consume the purchase, is entitled to leave their parked vehicle and use an (accessible) public restroom! <u>Stickney v. McDonald's Corp., et al.</u> (N.D.Cal.)Case No. C99-00558 VRW (settled after court ordered liability by Northern District Chief Judge Vaughn Walker.)

   2. THE PRACTICAL RESULT, WHEN A RESTROOM DOES NOT MEET "TECHNICAL REQUIREMENTS," MAY BE TO TRAP A DISABLED PERSON IN THE RESTROOM

      Sometimes it may seem that an "access" requirement is just a "technical" one. However, the consequences of non-compliance may be a humiliating experience for a disabled wheelchair user, including a public "bodily functions" accident. For example, the requirement of an 18" "strike edge clearance" for exiting doorways (under both Title

24 and the ADA) may seem too technical to require compliance. However, the practical consequence may be that a disabled wheelchair user may be able to "push" his way into the restroom, but be unable to exit, because his may have insufficient room to pull a door <u>toward himself</u> and <u>get past it</u> in order to exit.

If there is insufficient "strike edge" (where the door latches) clearance, a wheelchair user may be trapped inside until he can be rescued. For example, in <u>Lawson v. Shell Oil Co.</u>, Case No. C98-2695 (N.D. Cal. 1998), a disabled wheelchair user was trapped inside a service station restroom for 45 minutes, until another customer entered and was able to assist in rescuing him. Similarly in <u>Jones v. Rosie's</u> (E.D. Cal. 2009) 2:09-CV-00913 WBS/KJM a restaurant patron using a motorized wheelchair was trapped in the restroom and unable to open the door to get out. (In both these cases the plaintiffs were also impeded in turning around to exit because the restrooms lacked the required floor space for a 60" turning radius.)

3. MAXIMUM DOOR OPENING FORCE OF 5 POUNDS MUST BE PROVIDED

If the force needed to open a door is more than 5 lbs. for any door in buildings servicing the public, these doors must be adjusted to 5 lbs or less, or an automatic door opener must be provided. Otherwise disabled persons using a wheelchair, crutches or a walker (for example) may be unable to open the doorway to enter the building or a restroom. An automatic door opener (with disabled designated "paddle" to push) is especially useful when a person unable to open a door due to lost muscle strength, or in a manually pushed wheelchair by an assistant, approaches a door that opens out toward them, or a door that lacks sufficient "strike edge clearance" to open. California Building Code, Title 24, <u>Section 1133(b).2- Doors</u>, requires no more than 5 pounds of force to open.[37]

G. ANY VIOLATION OF THE ADA ALSO VIOLATES CIVIL CODE §§ 54(C) AND 54.1(D) BY SPECIFIC STATUTORY INCORPORATION, UNDER BOTH OF THESE STATUTES

1. CALIFORNIA LAW EFFECTIVELY ADDS "DAMAGES" AS A REMEDY FOR ANY ADA VIOLATION WHICH DAMAGES OR DETERS A DISABLED PERSON

In 1996 the California legislature incorporated violations of the ADA as per se violations of California Civil Code §§ 51, 54, and 54.1. Any violation of the ADA now also constitutes a violation of California law per Civil Code §§ 51(b), 54(c), and 54.1(d). Therefore it's necessary to understand (a) the ADA liabilities bases; and (b) that any complaint that pleads the ADA as part of its legal basis (at least as to injunctive relief), may be removed by defendants to federal court, as can be done with any complaint which relies upon a federal statute. (See Civil Code section 55.56 for

---

[37] This has been emphasized in an article by Richard Skaff, Executive Director of "Designing Accessible Communities," a leading ADA expert, reachable at www.designingaccessiblecommunities.org.

"damages" requirements, as required by SB 1608, effective January 1, 2009.)

2. **THE ADA'S INCORPORATION INTO CALIFORNIA STATUTES DOES NOT CREATE FEDERAL JURISDICTION**

However, the 9th Circuit has held that pleading damages based on proving a violation of the ADA incorporated into §§ 54(c) and 54.1(d) will not by itself be the basis for federal court jurisdiction. Wander v. Kaus (2002) 304 F.3d 856.

Wander held that, where there was no injunctive relief available under the ADA because defendants had provided access (either before or during the lawsuit), and any ADA injunctive relief was therefore "moot," mandatory jurisdiction in the federal court was not created by the damage provisions of §§ 54(c) and 54.1(d) even though they incorporated the standards of the ADA. Plaintiff's federal case was dismissed, presumably to be refiled in California state court within 30 days. 28 USC 1441. A California state court of appeal later followed Wander, noting that the 9th Circuit had held that:

> there is no federal question jurisdiction over a lawsuit for damages brought under California's [DPA] even though the California statute makes a violation of the federal [ADA] a violation of state law... Federal-question jurisdiction is not created merely because a federal law is an element of a state law claim. (Id. at 857.)
> Louie v. BFS Retail and Commercial Operations, LLC., 178 Cal. App. 4th 1544, quoting Wander.

This case also held that an ADA class action implementing a consent decree did not preclude any individual customer's claims for damages under the DPA, where "there was express language in the stipulated judgment withdrawing any issue of damages, and indeed the federal court in Florida relied upon this reservation to lessen the standard for notice to class members." Id. at 1560.

Similarly, a federal case may be "mooted" as to the need for injunctive relief if a business closes and there is no immediate likelihood that another public facility will be opened at the same physical location. Under these circumstances, if the federal court dismisses the case for "mootness," under the ADA, and also exercises its "discretion" to refuse to maintain its supplemental jurisdiction over the remaining California state law cause(s) of action, such dismissal is without prejudice to plaintiff refiling a complaint in state court. The federal statute allows only 30 days to refile the state law causes of action in state court, if the statute of limitations would otherwise have already run. 28 USC 1441.

3. **THE FEDERAL COURT RETAINS DISCRETIONARY JURISDICTION OVER PLAINTIFF'S STATE LAW CLAIMS**

Of course a federal court retains discretionary jurisdiction to continue handling plaintiff's state law damages and attorneys fees claims which the court was handling under 28 USC §1367, under the court's "supplemental jurisdiction" over factually related state law claims. Some courts will continue to handle such a case, to avoid unnecessary waste of judicial resources by forcing the case to "start over" in a State Superior Court. For example, during litigation of Paulick v. Bavarion Lion Vineyard Development, LLC, et al., No C-08-04860 (N.D. Cal.), defendants sought dismissal of plaintiff's state law claims, arguing that the Court should exercise its discretion not to take supplemental jurisdiction over them. The Court denied the motion citing Executive Software v. United States District Court, 24 F.3d 1524, 1556-57 (9th Circuit) that "economy, convenience, fairness and comity" should be considered in an analysis of supplemental jurisdiction. The District Court (Hon. Claudia Wilken) concluded:

> Because the federal and state court claims here derive from a common nucleus of operative facts, it is in the interest of 'economy, convenience, fairness and comity' for plaintiff's state and federal claims to remain in federal court. Accordingly, the court will exercise supplemental jurisdiction under section 1367(c)(3) over plaintiff's state law claims.

Order of March 10, 2009, at p.7. (Judge Wilken was elected Chief Judge in 2012.)

4. SECTION 51(f) CIVIL CODE ALSO INCORPORATES ANY VIOLATION OF THE ADA, ADDING MINIMUM DAMAGES PER VIOLATION REMEDY

Wilson v. Haria, 479 F.Supp.2d 1127 (E.D. Cal. 2007), held that "not readily achievable" was an affirmative defense which was waived when defendant "failed to plead that barrier removal is not readily achievable in its answer." Id. at 1133. The Court also held that encountering one or more "violations" of code on a single visit constituted one "violation" for section 52 Civil Code's minimum damages purposes ($4,000) even if there were multiple "violations" of code encountered on each visit to the business. Accordingly the Court awarded $4,000 statutory minimum damages on summary judgment, for each of plaintiff's 13 visits to the business, a total of $52,000 Id. at 1141. (Note 2012's SB 1186 added certain damages considerations as to multiple visits to the same inaccessible facility to limit unnecessary "stacking." (See appendix K *infra*)

H. REBUTTING DEFENSES ASSERTED BY BUILDING OWNERS AND OPERATORS
1. CALIFORNIA STANDARDS FOR ENFORCING DISABLED ACCESS REQUIREMENTS BY PRIVATE LAWSUIT DO NOT ALLOW "EXCEPTIONS" TO DISABLED ACCESS UNLESS EQUIVALENT FACILITATION IS PROVIDED

The standards for use of a private lawsuit to enforce disabled access statutes by "private" suits for injunctive relief and damages were first set out in James Donald v. Sacramento Valley Bank (1989) 209 Cal.App.3d 1183 (the "automated teller machine" case, originally an unpublished opinion, ordered published by the California Supreme Court), and James Donald v. Café Royale (1990) 218 Cal.App.3d 168. These cases held, inter alia: (1) that failure to provide access past architectural barriers, in violation of building code regulations, was a violation of a disabled person's rights to "full and equal access" under Civil Code §54.1; (2) that no discriminatory "intent" need be proved to show a violation of Civil Code §54.1; and (3) that at least statutory minimum damages must be awarded for a denial of full and equal access to any public facility.

Previous enforcement suits by public agencies, the California Attorney General and the San Francisco City Attorney, had set important precedents. San Francisco v. Grant Co. (1986) 181 Cal.App.3d 1085 held that the granting of a building permit by local building officials does not "estop" government officials or handicapped persons from suing to enforce the law. People Ex Rel Deukmejian v. CHE, Inc. (1983) 150 Cal.App.3d 123 upheld a lawsuit based on Civil Code §54.1 and Health & Safety Code §19955. CHE, *supra*, held that, even if a formal variance (or "exception") from compliance was issued by a building department, such variance may be challenged as an abuse of discretion by the department if the variance was improperly given.

In the CHE case, granting a variance was held to be an abuse of discretion because the building owner failed to provide "equivalent facilitation" as required by Health & Safety Code § 19957 as a condition precedent to granting an "exception." (CHE, 150 Cal.App.3d 123, at 137, 197 Cal.Rptr. 484, at 493). "Equivalent facilitation" means some other effective means for a disabled person to use the premises without difficulties which are not faced by the "able-bodied," i.e., entry through an entrance used by other members of the general public, not entry through a kitchen., the only disabled route in CHE. The Court held that offering the disabled entry only through a kitchen did not provide "full and equal" access. In 1984, § 2-406(c) of Title 24 defined "equivalent facilitation" as "an alternative means of complying with the literal requirements of these standards and specifications that provides access in terms of the purpose of these standards and specifications." (Most basic definitions in Title 24 have remained the same, though numbering has changed, since 1982's inception of the State Architect's Regulations, also known as "the California Building Code.")

Another "condition precedent" for a variance is that the total cost of the alteration project must be under a specified "valuation threshold": in 1982 this was $50,000. Per §105(b)11A(6)), the updated threshold level was $58,725 in 1985; $126,764 for the year 2009. If the total project cost was higher, providing access would not be a "hardship," and a building would be ineligible to apply for an exception. New construction is not eligible for any "hardship" application. Reportedly Squaw Valley was required to spend more than $500,000 to make its "High Camp" facilities accessible after improper $15 million new construction in 1989 at the top of the "TRAM" without accessible restrooms or restaurant entrances, etc. Leiken v. Squaw Valley Ski Corp., Alex Cushing, (E.D. Cal.) Case No. CIV-S-93 505 LKK/GGH. Similarly Heavenly Valley Ski Area was required to install an elevator after spending a reported $20 million to build a new gondola "midmountain" in approximately 2000: the gondola cars were accessible but plaintiff faced 42 stairs down to ground level at the gondola terminus. Christine Burke, a minor, by her Guardian Ad Litem Randy Burke v. Heavenly Valley Limited Partnership, et al., (E.D.Cal.) Case No. CIV-S04-0957 DFL/PAN.

2. NON-ENFORCEMENT OF THE LAW BY BUILDING DEPARTMENTS IS <u>NOT</u> A VALID DEFENSE

   a. ENFORCEMENT BY PRIVATE LAWSUIT OF ISABLED ACCESS REQUIREMENTS IS APPROPRIATE WHEN BUILDING DEPARTMENTS HAVE ISSUED PERMITS WITHOUT ENFORCING STATUTORY ACCESS REQUIREMENTS

   Health and Safety Code §§19955, et seq., were enacted in order to protect the civil rights of people with disabilities. To that end, the Legislature provided for enforcement by any of three entities: the local building departments, the State, and private individuals. The Legislature also provided judicial review because <u>the judiciary has historically proven to be our society's best protector of civil rights</u>. Courts should reject a Defendants' arguments that the "approval" by a local building department is a "defense" to access suits, because, (1) such an interpretation of the statute is contrary to the language of the statute itself; (2) such an interpretation is contrary to existing precedent; and (3) such an interpretation would undermine legislative intent and effectively eliminate judicial review. An official does not have legal authority to authorize an illegal act. (See also Uniform Building Code sections 303(c) and 305(a) discussed *infra* at section 2-e).

   In Leiken v. Squaw Valley Ski Corp., Alex Cushing, (E.D. Cal.) Case No. CIV-S-93 505 LKK/GGH Judge Karlton granted an injunction against the resort's policy of banning wheelchair users from riding cable cars up to the newly constructed $15 million "High Camp" facilities, even though the local "Handicapped Access Appeals Board" had (wrongly) granted a "variance" allowing the new inaccessible 1989 construction, based on its cable car "tram" exclusion policy- allegedly because disabled persons might be "more difficult to rescue" in case of an emergency" (Order of June 29, 1994). (Plaintiff's injunction motion supported by expert declarations showed that this excuse was not valid: disabled persons were no more difficult to "rescue" than injured persons.)

   Health & Safety Code § 19953 provides specific statutory authority for private enforcement actions: "<u>Any person</u> who is aggrieved or potentially aggrieved by a violation of this part, Chapter 7 (commencing with Section 4450) of Division 5 of Title 1 of the Government Code, or Part 5.5 (commencing with Section 19955) of Division 13 of the Health and Safety Code <u>may bring an action to enjoin the violation</u>." Public enforcement is also authorized. Health & Safety Code provision, § 19954 states:[38]

> The district attorney, the city attorney, the county counsel if the district attorney does not bring an action, the Department of Rehabilitation acting through the Attorney General, or the Attorney General may bring an action to enjoin any violation of this part.

For example, <u>San Francisco v. Grant Co.</u> (1986) 181 Cal.App.3d 1085 and <u>People ex rel Deukmejian v. CHE, Inc.</u> (1983) 150 Cal.App.3d 1231, were access cases involving enforcement by the San Francisco City Attorney and the California Attorney General's office. <u>Donald v. Sacramento Valley Bank</u> (1989) 209 Cal. App.3d 1183, and <u>Donald v. Café Royale</u> (1990) 218 Cal.App.3d 168, were both private enforcement actions, but in each of these the California Attorney General's office filed an <u>amicus curiae</u> brief supporting plaintiff's position. In every one of these cases the building department had erroneously "permitted" a construction or alteration without properly requiring access, yet the courts held that defendants still had the duty to provide access, because access was required by statute.

b. ENFORCEMENT OF DISABLED ACCESS REQUIREMENTS IS NOT THE EXCLUSIVE DOMAIN OF THE BUILDING DEPARTMENT

While a building department has enforcement authority pursuant to Health & Safety Code § 19958, the code specifies a dual enforcement responsibility with the other law enforcement personnel of the city, county and state, and by "aggrieved" individuals. Health & Safety Code § 19958.5 states: "The district attorney, the city attorney, the Department of Rehabilitation acting through the Attorney General, or the Attorney General may bring an action to enjoin a violation of this part." Section 19953 allows an injunction to enforce, inter alia, section 5.5 (commencing with § 19955) by <u>any</u> "aggrieved or potentially aggrieved" person.

The public agencies specified in § 19958.5 have encouraged enforcement of access laws through private lawsuits. As noted at p.9 of the amicus curiae brief filed by the California Attorney General, the San Francisco District Attorney, and the San Francisco City Attorney, on behalf of plaintiff James Donald during plaintiff's successful appeal in <u>James Donald v. Café Royale</u> (1990) 218 Cal.App.3d 168,
> It is the experience of the Attorney General's office and the San Francisco City Attorney's and District Attorney's offices that <u>most</u> <u>violations</u> occur

---
[38] Section 19958.5 has almost identical language. See section 2-b, *infra* (next section).

in the same manner as the instant case; i.e., <u>the building department has erroneously granted a permit to a building which in fact does not comply</u> with handicapped access statutes and regulations. Even though the violation was not intentional, the result is the same: the handicapped are denied full and equal use of the premises, ... <u>Therefore it is important that the violation be corrected.</u> (Emphasis added).

The support by the California Attorney General's Office for the encouragement and necessity of private lawsuits was recognized by the Court in <u>Blackwell v. Foley</u>, *supra*, 724 F. Supp. 2d 1068, at 1075-1076:

> Encouraging competent attorneys to handle ADA Title III cases is necessary for effective enforcement: former California Attorney General Dan Lungren, in a 1993 Opinion, held that California building officials could not independently enforce the ADA, and that enforcement was left primarily to private lawsuits. (Attorney General's Opinion, No. 93-203.) Previously California Attorney General John Van de Kamp had supported private enforcement lawsuits, and filed amicus curiae briefs on behalf of the plaintiff in both <u>Donald v. Sacramento Valley Bank</u>, 209 Cal.App.3d 1183, 260 Cal.Rptr. 49 (1989) and <u>Donald v. Café Royale</u>, *supra*, stressing the limited resources of its Civil Rights Division and supporting the need for private lawsuits to enforce disabled access.

c. FAILURE TO COMPLY WITH DISABLED ACCESS STATUTES IS NOT EXCUSED BY "APPROVAL" BY THE BUILDING DEPARTMENT; NEITHER THE BUILDING DEPARTMENT, THE STATE NOR PRIVATE DISABLED PERSONS ARE "ESTOPPED" FROM ENFORCING THE LAW

"Non-enforcement" is not "formal approval." <u>Donald v. Café Royale</u>, *supra*, disapproved the defendant's reliance on a <u>verbal</u> "approval" by a building inspector actually communicated to defendant's representative at the time the work was done. Defense testimony as to the alleged thought processes of any building official, who did not apply the <u>written hardship criteria findings</u> required by § 422(c) of Title 24 (1984 numbering), cannot provide any relevant legal defenses.

<u>San Francisco v. Grant</u> (1986) 181 Cal.App.3d 1085 held that parties other than the building inspector could not be "estopped" from later bringing an action to enforce the regulations, and expressed doubt, due to public policy considerations, whether even the City building department which had approved construction permits could be estopped from enforcing a regulation which was intended for the public welfare. The concurring opinion by Justice Kline specifically noted that estoppel would not be proper even against the City, citing <u>public policy reasons</u>:

> This is not one of the exceptional cases in which the doctrine of equitable estoppel may be applied against a governmental body. In those few cases which hold that a governmental body may be estopped

> by the conduct of its officers, "the facts clearly established that a grave injustice would be done if estoppel were not applied, and it did not appear that use of the doctrine would defeat any strong public policy or result in the direct enforcement of an illegal contract."....
>
> .... Moreover, said laws embody "a strong rule of policy adopted for the benefit of the public." (Strong v. County of Santa Cruz (1975) 15 Cal.3d 720, 725, 125 Cal.Rptr. 896.) Though the belated enforcement of those laws would doubtless work a hardship on appellants, it would not work a "grave injustice." The doctrine of equitable estoppel therefore would have no application in this case even if the elements of estoppel could technically be made out against either or both of the governmental bodies.
> Id at 1093.

As noted, prior issuance by the building department of alteration permits which do not require provision of disabled access directly or by "equivalent facilitation" may be an "abuse of discretion," and allow injunctive relief by lawsuit to require that proper access be provided. San Francisco v. Grant Co. (1986) 181 Cal.App.3d 1085; People Ex Rel. Deukmejian v. CHE, Inc., *supra*, loc cit. A court may reject and overrule a building department's non-enforcement even when an "unreasonable hardship exception" has been granted by a building department's "Handicapped Access Appeals Board." (See Order in U.S. District Court, Eastern District of California, by Judge Lawrence Karlton in Leiken v. Squaw Valley, et al., Case No. Civ-S-93-505 LKK, Order of June 29, 1994.) In the Leiken case the owners of the Squaw Valley ski resort had been allowed to construct a $15 million facility, "High Camp," in 1989, without providing any disabled access to its newly built public facilities, including four new but inaccessible restaurants (built with stairs at each entryway 20 years after enactment of Health & Safety Code § 19955). The "hardship" variance on which Squaw Valley relied in not providing accessible facilities had been granted by the local "handicapped access" appeals board (5-0) on the grounds that the only way to reach these facilities was to ride up the Tram, and that Squaw Valley had adopted a policy - "for safety reasons" - barring all wheelchair users and other "handicapped" persons from using the Tram! The Court held that this policy itself was discriminatory and in violation of ADA Title III and California Civil Code § 54.1. Once the court had held that this policy and the variance which relied on this policy were both invalid, defendants agreed to make the Tram and all facilities at High Camp fully disabled accessible. In 1994 this policy violated the ADA regardless of the cost of providing access. (While cost is a relevant factor in determining what barrier removal is "readily achievable" under the standards of the ADA (see §§ 301(9) and 302(b)(2)(A)(iv) and (v)), cost is not a factor when it is shown that new construction or alterations were carried out without providing the access statutorily required under existing state or federal law, and is not a factor justifying a discriminatory policy.)

d. THERE IS NO CALIFORNIA EVIDENCE CODE § 664 "PRESUMPTION" THAT THE ACCESS LAW WAS PROPERLY ENFORCED BY THE BUILDING DEPARTMENT, ESPECIALLY WHEN ANY VARIANCE IS GIVEN WITHOUT PROVIDING "EQUIVALENT FACILITATION AND PROTECTION" FOR THE DISABLED

Reliance on this statutory "presumption" was rejected by the court in People ex rel. Deukmejian v. CHE, Inc., 150 Cal.App.3d 123, at 137, even in a situation where the building department had issued a written determination that defendants had complied with all access requirements and were also:

> entitled to the grant of an exception under Section 19957. Defendants wrongly claim the Evidence Code section 664 presumption that an official duty has been performed, entitles them to summary judgment.

After reviewing cases discussing the effect of § 664, a presumption affecting the burden of proof (§ 660 California Evidence Code), the court addressed the application to the claim for a handicapped access "exemption" or "exception": "As to the exemption, there are no facts showing [the building official] ever granted one. Moreover, to warrant an exemption, equivalent facilitation and protection must be provided." (The court also found plaintiff had also provided evidence to rebut the effect of any such "presumption." People ex rel. Deukmejian v. CHE, Inc., 150 Cal. App.3d 123, at 138.) [See also section I-H-6-e, *infra*]

Approval or non-enforcement by a local building inspector or department is not a defense.[39] An appellate court which dealt with this issue rejected the notion that non-enforcement of disabled access requirements by a building official constitutes a defense.[40] To claim non-enforcement of the law is a defense in a civil action, would be equivalent to a driver causing an accident by speeding at 90 mph, then defending his action because a traffic policeman didn't stop him. I'm not aware of any reported case which has allowed a defendant to successfully sue a city or its building officials for failure to enforce the law. However, a disabled person might have better results

---

[39] "Good faith" reliance on a public official's permit approval might be relevant if plaintiff made defendant's "intent" an issue, for example by seeking treble or punitive damages.

[40] Keith Kellum, a pioneer in disability civil rights, sued Oakland's Silver Dragon Restaurant in 1976 because the restaurant was constructed, after the 1970 inception of section 19955 Civil Code, with steps at its only entrance. Kellum v. Silver Dragon Restaurant, Ala. Co. Sup. Ct. (1976) The Silver Dragon owners agreed to provide an accessible entrance and settled with plaintiff Kellum, but cross-complained against the City of Oakland for failure to properly enforce the law. In turn the City of Oakland cross-complained against the California Attorney General's and State Department of Rehabilitation. The First District Court of Appeal held that neither the Department of Rehabilitation or the Attorney General had a mandatory duty to make sure that the City enforced laws governing accessibility of public buildings to the handicapped. It left unclear whether the building owners could sue the City for failure to enforce the law. [See "Silver Dragon" related appellate decision, State of California ex rel Dept. Of Rehabilitation, et al v. Superior Court, City of Oakland Real Party in Interest,.137 Cal. App. 3d.

by suing a city under the ADA Title II for failure in its federal duties as a public entity to carry out a "program" of enforcement. [See section II-A, B and C, *infra*]

e. THE UNIFORM BUILDING CODE PROVIDES THAT ISSUANCE OF A PERMIT, APPROVAL OF PLANS, OR SUBSEQUENT APPROVAL AS THE RESULT OF AN INSPECTION, DO <u>NOT</u> CONSTITUTE APPROVALS FOR VIOLATION OF ANY ORDINANCE

Per UBC Section 302(d),

<u>Information on Plans and Specifications</u>. Plans and specifications shall be drawn to scale upon substantial paper or cloth and shall be of sufficient clarity to indicate the location, nature and extent of the work proposed and show in detail that it will conform to the provisions of this code and all relevant laws, ordinances, rules and regulations.

Per Section 303(c),

<u>Validity of Permit</u>. The issuance or granting of a permit or approval of plans, specifications and computations <u>shall not be construed to be a permit for, or an approval of, any violation of any of the provisions of this code</u> or of any other ordinance of the jurisdiction. <u>Permits presuming to give authority to violate or cancel the provisions of this code</u> or other ordinances of the jurisdiction <u>shall</u> not be valid.

The issuance of a permit based on plans, specifications and other data shall not prevent the building official from thereafter requiring the correction of errors in said plans, specifications and other data, or from preventing building operations being carried on thereunder when in violation of this code or of any other ordinances of this jurisdiction. (Emphasis added)

Per Section 305(a),

Approval as the result of an inspection shall <u>not</u> be construed to be an <u>approval of a violation</u> of the provisions of this code or of other ordinances of the jurisdiction. <u>Inspections presuming to give authority to violate or cancel provisions of this code</u> or other ordinances of the jurisdiction <u>shall not be val</u> Id. (Emphasis added)

f. DISABLED PERSONS' RIGHTS CAN'T BE INVALIDATED BY A BUILDING OFFICIAL'S MISTAKE

The rights of disabled persons cannot be adversely precluded forever because a building official makes a mistake in failing to enforce the laws which require provision of access. <u>San Francisco v. Grant Co.</u> (1986) 181 Cal.App.3d 1085. In the past, building officials responsible for requiring a facility to obey the law sometimes did not properly require "equivalent facilitation and protection" when granting a purported "hardship" exception, even though such alternative form of access is required as a specific <u>condition precedent</u> to granting any exception, per Health &

Safety Code § 19957. Failing to require such "equivalent facilitation" would be an <u>abuse of discretion</u> invalidating any hardship exception given without this necessary <u>condition precedent</u> being satisfied. (<u>People ex rel. Deukmejian v. CHE, Inc.</u> (1983) 150 Cal.App.3d 123, at 137.)

3. BUILDING OFFICIALS' PRIOR FAILURE TO REQUIRE ACCESS UPGRADES SHOULD NOT LEAVE A BUILDING IN LESS THAN LEGALLY ACCESSIBLE CONDITION
    a. DEFENDANTS CANNOT PROPERLY OBTAIN A HARDSHIP EXCEPTION WITHOUT COMPLIANCE WITH § 422'S REQUIREMENTS

    During litigation defendant building owners may be shown to have failed to avail themselves of the § 422 "unreasonable hardship" procedure (for a particular alteration project), although evidence may show they well <u>knew about</u> the handicapped access issue. Some defendants' actually choose to <u>refuse</u> to provide handicapped access <u>until after they are actually sued</u>. They cannot then rely on a "hardship" claim unless they meet their burden of proving a <u>retroactive</u> "unreasonable hardship" exception, that somehow shows it "would have been" granted upon proper application to the Building Department. A building official's mistake in non-enforcement of the law when alterations were permitted should never justify non-enforcement by a court.

    There is a particular irony in Defendants trying to justify their conduct on the basis that it was "approved" by a building official. In some cases defendants have attempted to use the testimony of the very person who <u>failed</u> to enforce the law as the justification for their being able to continue, in perpetuity, to maintain conditions discriminating against and dangerous to disabled persons.[40] Code violations may represent a <u>danger</u> to disabled persons as well as a denial of access.[41] We should remember that section 19959 is part of the <u>Health and Safety Code</u>. The Title 24 regulations are for protection of both the civil rights <u>and</u> the <u>safety</u> of disabled persons. The regulations themselves, and numerous court interpretations, indicate the <u>purpose</u> of the regulations' requirements. For example, the requirements for wheel-guides and/or handrails on a ramp are there to protect disabled persons from going off the edge of the ramp. (See § 2-3306, especially § 3306(d)(3) and § 3306(e) and (h)). As stated in <u>CHE</u>, *supra* at 134, "Thus, equality, at minimum, requires access free from difficulties or obstacles [cite omitted] and potential hazards which would endanger even the most cautious physically handicapped."

    Sometimes a relatively "minor" building code violation may result in serious

---

[40]This is particularly pernicious if the former building official witness has been paid by defendant as a "consultant" prior to his testimony!

[41]Thus a disabled person injured due to a code violation may choose to sue under Civil Code section 54.1 rather than on grounds of "negligence." This has the advantages of recovering damages, potential treble damages, and attorney fees under section 54.3, and not requiring proof of wrongful intent or negligence.

personal injuries suffered by a disabled person. In <u>Rosler v. Stanford University</u> (N.D. Cal.) Case No. C03-3579 JF, plaintiff sued after suffering serious personal injuries when she tripped (while walking with a cane) over a bollard (a post holder set into the ground) in the middle of a walkway toward the Stanford Memorial Church, where plaintiff had tickets for a symphony orchestra performance. Had she reached the Church, she would have faced further access problems: four stairs at the entrance and no accessible restrooms. Her lawsuit obtained substantial damages, statutory attorney fees, and a consent decree to remove all access barriers and provide accessible entrance, restroom and parking facilities. (Settlement was at a settlement conference before Chief Magistrate Judge Patricia Trumble.)

b. A BUILDING OFFICIAL MAY NOT GIVE A "RETROACTIVE" HARDSHIP EXCEPTION WITHOUT COMPLYING WITH § 422(c) OF TITLE 24

A building official may not "create" a retroactive hardship exception by testimony that he gave "mental" hardship exceptions without complying with the requirements of § 422(c), Title 24, (1984 Code) that such exceptions be specified according to five (5) enumerated factors and that <u>all findings be in writing</u>.

§ 422(c): <u>Unreasonable Hardship</u>: An unreasonable hardship exists when the enforcing agency finds that compliance with the building standard would make the specific work of the project affected by the building standard <u>unfeasible</u>, based upon an overall evaluation of the following factors:

1. The cost of providing access.
2. The cost of all construction con-templated.
3. The impact of proposed improvements on financial feasibility of the project.
4. <u>The nature of the accessibility which would be gained or</u> <u>lost</u>.
5. The nature of the use of the facility under construction and its availability to handicapped persons.

<u>The details of any finding of unreasonable hardship shall be recorded and entered in the files of the enforcing agency</u>. (Emphasis added)

(Although the numbering system later changed, the essence of Title 24's requirements have remained relatively consistent since being promulgated in 1982.)

c. CASE LAW HAS REJECTED RELIANCE ON BUILDING DEPARTMENT PERMITS WHICH IMPROPERLY ALLOWED ALTERATIONS WITHOUT PROVIDING ACCESS

In virtually every one of the reported cases which upheld enforcement actions by the Attorney General's office or by private disabled litigants relying on construction/ alteration history, the defendants had been <u>allowed</u> by local building departments to alter their premises <u>without</u> being <u>required</u> to provide disabled access. A court should not accept as evidence the "opinion" of the local building inspector who did not require access, as the basis for the court's decision on the law's requirements.

People ex rel. Deukmejian v. CHE, Inc. (1983) 150 Cal.App.3d 123, allowed a court to overrule a building department's decision, even when a formal written application for hardship variance was applied for by defendants and allegedly granted at the time of the construction. Donald v. Sacramento Valley Bank (1989) 209 Cal.App.3d 1183, held that attaching an ATM to a bank in 1975, (seven years before adoption of the first explicit "path of travel" Title 24 regulations in 1982), was an "alteration" which triggered access and a path of travel to the altered facility under the "ASA" regulations in effect from 1970-1982. City & County of San Francisco v. Grant Co. (1986) 181 Cal.App.2d 1085, rejected the building department's "OK" as a defense.

All alterations to any level of a restaurant or other building trigger full and equal access to the altered areas, including an accessible "path of travel" in conformity with code regulations and specifications regarding the configuration of the entrance ramp and landing; proper handrails; proper side slope; proper clear turning radius; and a safe passage through the entrance for physically disabled persons using an entrance ramp. Any significant interior alterations trigger full and equal access to and through the front entrance so that a restaurant is "accessible to and usable by" physically disabled persons. Per sections 19955 and 19959 Health and Safety Code, and related Title 24 regulations, alterations to any portion of a building also triggers the need for accessibility of restrooms that "serve" the area of alteration.[43]

d. ANY LOCAL REGULATIONS WHICH CONFLICT WITH STATE BUILDING CODE REQUIREMENTS ARE INVALID AS PREEMPTED

In California Apartment Ass'n v. City of Fremont, (2002) 97 Cal.App.4th 693, the Court explained:
> In 1970, the Legislature put an end to this practice [local codes] by declaring a statewide interest in uniform building codes and by otherwise expressing an intent to preempt the field of setting building code standards. (See generally Briseno v. City of Santa Ana (1992) 6 Cal.App.4th 1378, 1382- 1383, 8 Cal.Rptr.2d 486.) Since then uniform statewide building standards have been generally specified by the Legislature. (See §17922 [adoption of specific uniform building standards relating to construction dealing with everything from plumbing to fire safety incorporated into state law].) The State Code is a compilation of these building standards and is binding on the state and other public agencies, including private parties and entities. (Id., at p 697; emphasis added)

---

[43] To make such restrooms "accessible," businesses must also ensure that the "path of travel" to the restroom is also wheelchair accessible. In one San Francisco restaurant, alterations on a raised on a raised level of the restroom required not only that the restroom itself be made accessible, but that a path of travel bypassing three stairs also be provided. This was done by installation of an access lift next to the stairs. (Berne v. Garibaldi's)

4. THE COURTS, NOT THE LOCAL BUILDING DEPARTMENT, ARE THE FINAL AUTHORITY FOR ENFORCEMENT OF DISABLED ACCESS UNDER CALIFORNIA AND FEDERAL LAW

The building department has <u>neither</u> the <u>only</u> enforcement authority nor the <u>final</u> enforcement authority. The final authority lies with the court. It is the court that is vested with the judicial function of being the arbiter of what the facts were and what the law is. The court is indeed <u>supposed</u> to "second guess" the local building department's interpretation and application of the law, especially when the protection of rights of disabled persons are at stake, an important California public policy priority.

It is the job of the courts to interpret and apply the law and to protect the rights of disabled persons. They have done so in most cases interpreting access laws: <u>Donald v. Sacramento Valley Bank</u> (1989) 209 Cal.App.3d 1183; <u>Donald v. Café Royale</u> (1990) 218 Cal.App.3d 168; <u>People ex rel Deukmejian v. CHE, Inc.</u> (1983) 150 Cal.App.3d 123; <u>San Francisco v. Grant Co.</u> (1986) 181 Cal.App.3d 1085; <u>Wilshire Financial Towers v. City of Los Angeles</u> (1990) 217 Cal.App.3d 119. Any defendant's insistence that building officials' bureaucratic decisions are uniquely impervious to judicial review would be without merit or precedent.

Finally, as building departments in California are not authorized to enforce any ADA requirements (except to the extent that such requirements have been incorporated into California law), they certainly have no authority to <u>waive</u> or grant exceptions to any ADA requirements. [See Attorney General Daniel E. Lungren's July 14, 1993 Opinion; Attorney General Opinion No 93-203, included here in the Appendix at X-E-2.] Thus even a valid state law exception granted by a building department would not invalidate any otherwise applicable federal ADA requirements.

5. SUCCESSOR OWNER LIABILITY: SUCCEEDING OWNERS AND OPERATORS ARE LIABLE FOR ALTERATIONS BY PRIOR OWNERS WHICH TRIGGERED ACCESS

   a. LACK OF ACCESS IS A PUBLIC <u>NUISANCE</u> WHICH "RUNS WITH THE PROPERTY"; RESPONSIBILITY PASSES TO ANY SUCCESSIVE OWNER

   Once the right to access has accrued to disabled members of the public, it is not lost simply because the building is subsequently sold to a new owner. Without required access being provided, the building constitutes a "non-conforming structure" and is in the nature of a <u>continuing nuisance</u>, (especially to disabled persons), until it is repaired and proper access is provided. (See Northern District Chief Judge Vaughn Walker's opinion in <u>Stickney v. McDonald's</u>, Case No. C99-0558 VRW, confirming liability of successive owners for liability triggered by previous owners' alterations.) <u>Stickney</u>

noted the public policy consideration, that an owner can't end his access obligations by simply selling a building to a new owner; the obligations to provide access pass with the property to the new owners. [See discussion at § 5.b, *infra*.]

What happens when one owner constructs or substantially alters a building triggering access requirements, but then sells the non-compliant building to a new owner? Defendants sometimes argue that a current building owner is not responsible for correcting building code violations created by the previous owners of a restaurant. This would be a rather shocking concept. If so, a building owner could do $100,000 of improvements inside a building - with or without a permit - and then sell the building, and the new owner would have no responsibility to provide access to disabled persons. This is contrary to both public policy and the letter of the law.

Such position ignores case law that failure to provide access at the time of alterations constitutes a public nuisance. (San Francisco v. Grant Co., *supra*, 181 Cal.App.3d at 1088, holding the lack of disabled access constituted a "public nuisance" subject to abatement action; cf. Leslie Salt Company v. San Francisco Bay Conservation And Development Commission, 153 Cal. App. 3d 605, 619-620 (1984), on liability of successor owner to remove nuisance placed by others; see also CEEED, et al. v. California Coastal Zone Conservation Comm., 43 Cal.App.3d 306, 308 (1974).) The responsibility to abate a public nuisance runs with the property, per Civil Code § 3483.

Defendants are responsible for any non-conforming structure when they take over a building, just as they would be for continuing to maintain a sign over the door saying "Whites Only." (See quote from 1967 Report of the National Commission on Architectural Barriers to Rehabilitation of the Handicapped, at § I.A.1. of this book, *supra*.) Sections 51, 54 and 54.1 California Civil Code are civil rights laws, not just building codes.

If a prior owner failed to install legally required fire sprinklers, would a new owner be relieved of the continuing obligation to install the fire sprinklers needed for fire safety protection? The obligation to provide access must always be on the current owner or operator of a business, as they are the only ones who have control of the premises and can provide necessary access improvements. Enforcement actions against the prior owner, for example, could not result in provision of any access for the public. (Of course, if a building is sold after a disabled plaintiff has been denied access and suffered damages, the prior owner may be responsible for the damages suffered by the disabled person at the time of his/her visit, and for the attorneys fees incurred in obtaining these damages. See §54.3 Civil Code.)

Some statutes make this ongoing responsibility explicit. For example, Health & Safety Code § 19952(a), specifies a duty upon current owners and managers: "Any person or public or private firm, organization or corporation who owns or manages places of public amusement and resort... shall provide seating or accommodations to physically disabled persons in a variety of locations within the facility..." (Emphasis added)

In San Francisco v. Grant Co. (1986) 181 Cal.App.3d 1085, 227 Cal.Rptr. 154, the San Francisco Director of Public Works declared the defendants' restaurant a public nuisance for its failure to comply with California Civil Code § 54.1 and Health & Safety Code § 19955 et seq. "Rosebud's," a restaurant and bar, had been remodeled in 1977 and the "city building Department issued a construction permit and conducted site inspections." The city failed to require handicapped access, "due evidently to the building department's mistaken assumption that state handicap access requirements then in effect applied only to completely new construction and not to remodeling." Id. at 1088. As a result of Rosebud's refusal to comply with access requirements, the restaurant was declared a public nuisance by the city. "The city filed the instant action in superior court, seeking to abate the nuisance and compel compliance." San Francisco v. Grant Co., Id.

The basis for a finding of "public nuisance" is that it interferes with use or enjoyment by a significant sector of the community. (Civil Code §3480, 3501). Section 3501 allows remedies against a private nuisance, including "1. A civil action, or 2. Abatement." Civil Code § 3483 requires that "Every successive owner of property who neglects to abate a continuing nuisance upon, or in the use of, such property created by the former owner is liable therefore in the same manner as the one who first created it." This statutory requirement comports with public policy requirements: The current owners and operators of a building and a business are the ones who control the ability to make access changes and improvements.

b. TWO ORDERS BY NORTHERN DISTRICT CHIEF JUDGE VAUGHN WALKER ESTABLISHED THE LIABILITY OF A SUCCESSOR OWNER
Public policy grounds for rejecting the concept that a succeeding owner could not be liable for access alterations by prior owner were offered by Judge Vaughn Walker (N.D.Cal. 1998), in Susan Hodges v. El Torito Restaurants, Inc., et al., No. C-96-2242 VRW (1998 WL 95398, *3-4):

> El Torito argues that it cannot be held liable for the violations of El Caballo - the restaurant that previously occupied the building. While there is surprisingly little case law addressing this issue, the court concludes that El Torito's position cannot be an accurate assessment of the law.

> If courts were to adopt El Torito's position, businesses would be able to circumvent California's various accessibility requirements through sham sales and transfers. Furthermore, businesses that chose not to comply with California's various access-ibility requirements would not lose any resale value in their buildings. Surely, the legislature did not intend to enact such a self-serving law. . . . It is therefore clear that the best way to effectuate the goals of California's accessibility laws is to have current owners of buildings liable for the existing violations. . . . El Torito had the opportunity to address these issues when it purchased the building. Much like the situation with a non-latent defect or a cloud on title. El Torito had constructive knowledge of these violations [Emphasis added]

Judge Walker cited this precedent later in Stickney v. McDonald's, No. C99-0558 VRW, rejecting defendant's "position that it cannot be held liable for the failure of a former owner to make their restaurant accessible." (Id at p.7)

> If plaintiff had to sue a possibly defunct former owner for violations that allegedly first appeared while they first occupied a building, it is unlikely that plaintiffs could obtain money damages. Furthermore, because the former owner no longer has control over the building, plaintiffs could not achieve the ultimate goal of the various laws at issue - an accessible facility. It is therefore clear that the best way to effectuate the goals of California's accessibility laws is to hold the current owners of buildings liable for existing violations. [Emphasis added] Id.

c. ALTERATIONS BY ANY PREVIOUS OWNER AFTER JULY 1, 1970 TRIGGERED A HEALTH & SAFETY CODE ACCESS REQUIREMENT WHICH PASSES WITH OWNERSHIP

The right to access is not lost to disabled persons whenever a building is sold. Defendants may allege that they are not responsible for any alterations which "triggered" an access requirement during the period prior to the current owner's purchase of the business. Health and safety requirements must "run with the property" or the safety of the public would be sacrificed. For example if a prior owner sold a Restaurant in 1990, would the new owners have no responsibility for access triggered by 1985 alterations? Do the new owners of a toxic dump which is leaking into a river have no duty to stop the continuing nuisance which harms the public? Both situations are in nature of a continuing public nuisance.

Records of the sale should be checked. For example, when the El Torito Corporation purchased their San Leandro restaurant as part of a multiple restaurant purchase of the Casa Maria chain, they were put on specific notice by the seller (Host International) of the continuing liability for handicapped access by documents in the Casa Maria sale disclosure. A six page letter from the California Attorney General to Host International, informed Host (and, thereby, later purchaser El Torito) of the access difficulties at the Sacramento Casa Maria, and of the legal requirements for handicapped access. The reason "disclosure" of this issue was required of Host

International, as seller, was because of the legal duty imposed on the buyer to bring all health and safety features up to code, public protection requirements that neither seller nor buyer could "waive."

d. ANALOGIES FROM TOXIC WASTE CASES SUPPORT A CONTINUING DUTY TO PROVIDE ACCESS

In CEED v. California Coastal Zone Conservation Comm'n (1974) 43 Cal.App.3d 306, 318) the court imposed strict liability on land owners for illegal land fill, including the duty of removing the fill placed by former owners. This is particularly applicable to access situations where a prior owner has created an illegal nuisance by building or altering a public facility without providing access. (San Francisco v. Grant Co. (1986) 181 Cal.App.3d 1085)

Leslie Salt Co. v. San Francisco B.C.D.C. (1984) 153 Cal.App.3d 605, 607 discussed the nuisance concept, recognizing that "Under the common law, liability for a public nuisance may result from the failure to act as well as from affirmative conduct." [Emphasis added] (Leslie Salt at 619) This is particularly appropriate in the "access" situation where the lack of access is usually visually apparent to the purchaser at the time of purchase. The availability of public records showing permitted alterations may also put the purchaser on constructive notice. Certainly every purchaser must be "presumed to know the law" that any building built or altered after 1970 must have access provided (Health & Safety Code §§ 19955-19959). The Leslie Salt case held that any "innocence" of a subsequent owner did not matter, as the abatement of a public nuisance is an appropriate place for the application of strict liability for policy reasons:

> "Thus whether the context be civil or criminal, liability and the duty to take affirmative action flow not from the land owner's active responsibility for a condition of his land that causes widespread harm to others or his knowledge of or intent to cause such harm, but rather, and quite simply, from his very possession and control of the land in question. (See Sprecher v. Adamson Companies (1981) 30 Cal.3d 358, 369-70 [178 Cal.Rptr. 783]) This principle that the private right to control land carries with it certain strictly enforceable public responsibilities is, as we have seen, a venerable idea; and it is one that grows progressively more vital in the law as the interdependencies in our society become more apparent and the threats to the integrity of our environment more ominous."
> (Emphasis added)

Similarly, as in the situation of land fill, the lack of disabled access is an ongoing public nuisance which can be remedied only by the current owner of the property.

e. BOTH LANDLORD AND TENANT ARE LIABLE TO THE DISABLED PLAINTIFF, ALTHOUGH THEY MAY ARRANGE INDEMNITY THROUGH LEASE AGREEMENTS

The DOJ Technical Assistance Manual clearly interprets § 12181(a) to mean that any allocation of responsibility under a lease agreement is only effective between the parties, and that landlords and tenants remain "fully liable" for all ADA violations. (TAM § III-1.2000; see, Independent Living Resources v. Oregon Arena Corp., 982 F.Supp. 698, supplemented, 1 F.Supp.2d 1159 (D. Org. 1998), and Botosan v. Fitzhugh, 13 F.Supp.2d 1047 (USDC S.Cal. 1998).)

As stated in Independent Living Resources, *supra*,
> Both the landlord and the tenant are public accommodations and have full responsibility for complying with all ADA title III requirements applicable to that place of public accommodation. The title III regulation permits the landlord and the tenant to allocate responsibility, in the lease, for complying with particular provisions of the regulation. However, any allocation made in a lease or other contract is only effective as between the parties, and both landlord and tenant remain fully liable for compliance with all provisions of the ADA relating to that place of public accommodation. TAM § III-1.2000. (Id., at 767, 768.) [Emphasis added]

Although a landlord and tenant can contractually allocate ADA responsibility between them, such an allocation is not binding on third parties. Accordingly, a tenant could not defend against a Title III suit on the ground that under its lease it was the landlord's duty to accommodate the disabled. Botosan v. Paul McNally Realty, 216 F.3d 827 (9th Cir. 2000).

The Department of Justice's Technical Assistance Manual states that both the owner and the tenant have equal liability for compliance with Title III of the ADA.
> Both the landlord and the tenant are public accommodations and have full responsibility for complying with all ADA title III requirements applicable to that place of public accommodation. The title III regulation permits the landlord and the tenant to allocate responsibility, in the lease, for complying with particular provisions of the regulation. However, any allocation made in a lease or other contract is only effective as between the parties, and both landlord and tenant remain fully liable for compliance with all provisions of the ADA relating to that place of public accommodation. (TAM § III-1.2000, interpreting 28 CFR §36.201(b); italics added.)

In Blackwell v. Foley, 724 F.Supp.2d. 1068 (N.D. Cal 2010), the Court specified that liability of landlord and tenant was joint and several, not only for damages but also for attorney fees, litigation expenses and costs:

All Defendants, landlords and tenants, are jointly and severally liable for Plaintiff's attorney fees, litigation expenses and costs

Regardless of any indemnification agreement among themselves, all Defendants signed the Consent Decree; and all are jointly and severally responsible for Plaintiff's attorney fees. Landlord and tenant have joint and several responsibility to Plaintiff for violation of the ADA. Botosan v. McNally Realty, et al., 216 F.3d 827, 832 (9th Cir.2000), cited by the court in Kosloff v. Washington Square Assoc., 2007 WL 2023497, (N.D.Cal.2007) held that defendants were "joint and severally liable for all compensation to plaintiff under the ADA including federally authorized attorney's fees."

Under both federal and California law, liability among defendants for a successful plaintiff's attorney fees is generally joint and several. Turner v. District of Columbia Bd. of Elections & Ethics, 354 F.3d 890 (D.C.Cir.2004); California Trout, Inc. v. Superior Court, 218 Cal.App.3d 187, 212, 266, 266 Cal.Rptr. 788 CR 788 (1990); Corder v. Gates, 947 F.2d 374, 383 (9th Cir.1991). It has also been held proper for a court to award fees against one defendant for time spent litigating against another. Californians for Responsible Toxics Mgmt. v. Kizer, 211 Cal.App.3d 961, 976, 259 CR 599 (1989)

Blackwell v. Foley, *supra* at 1075.

[On joint and several liability of both landlord and tenant under the ADA, see also section III-G, *infra*]

6. HARDSHIP ETC. "EXCEPTIONS" ARE ONLY VALID WHEN THEY MEET STATUTORY REQUIREMENTS, PROVIDE EQUIVALENT FACILITATION, AND PROVIDE WRITTEN FINDINGS PER TITLE 24 CRITERIA

   a. "HARDSHIP" "EXCEPTIONS" MUST MEET THE REQUIREMENTS OF HEALTH & SAFETY CODE § 19957 AND § 422(c) OF TITLE 24 REGULATIONS [See Also Section 3(b), *supra*.]

   Inequities of possible disproportion between the cost of the alteration and the cost of providing access are provided for by an "exception" process for "unreasonable hardships," per Health and Safety Code § 19957 and § 422(c) of Title 24. (The applicable provisions of law, including Title 24, are those that were in effect at the time of the permitted alterations.) However, several conditions precedent must be shown by building owners seeking such "unreasonable hardship" exception in order to justify an "exception," including the following:

   (1) The "total construction cost of alterations, structural repairs or additions" must "not exceed a valuation threshold" of $58,725 (in 1984, per § 2-105(b)11A(6) of 1984 Title 24 regulations and State Architect's commentary, p.10 of 1984 Interpretive Manual.) If it does exceed this, full accessible features must be provided.[44]

---
[44] The valuation cutoff in 2009 was $126,764.

(2) "Equivalent facilitation and protection" for disabled persons must still be provided even if an exception from the "literal requirements" is granted. Health & Safety Code §19957 "Equivalent facilitation" was defined by §2-406(c) of the 1984 Title 24 Regulations as, an alternative means of complying with the literal requirements of these standards and specifications that provide access in terms of the purpose of these standards and specifications.[45]

To achieve a hardship exception under Title 24 criteria, owners must have complied with the detailed requirements of § 422(c). In litigation, to rely on an alleged "exception," defendants must show that they offered evidence, as to each alteration, relevant to the five criteria required by § 2-422(c), and its requirements for detailed <u>written findings</u>:

§ 2-422(c) Unreasonable Hardship: An unreasonable hardship exists when the enforcing agency finds that compliance with the building standard would make the specific work of the project affected by the building standard unfeasible, based upon an overall evaluation of the following factors:

1. The cost of providing access.
2. The cost of all construction contemplated.
3. The impact of proposed improvements on financial feasibility of the project.
4. The nature of the accessibility which would be gained or lost.
5. The nature of the use of the facility under construction and its availability to handicapped persons.

The details of any finding of unreasonable hardship shall be recorded and entered in the files of the enforcing agency.

b. "ABUSE OF DISCRETION" TO GRANT PERMIT WITHOUT COMPLIANCE
It is an abuse of discretion by building officials if they do not require equivalent facilitation and Title 24 compliance as a condition of granting any "hardship" exception. The courts, not the building departments, must be the final arbiters of the legality of any claim for "hardship exception." (<u>People ex rel Deukmejian v. CHE, Inc.</u> (1983) 150 Cal.App.3d 123, 137) The defendant has the burden of proof on any claimed "exception." [See section I-B-2-f, *supra*]

c. THE POLICY OF THE LAW IS TO BROADLY CONSTRUE REQUIREMENTS FOR DISABLED ACCESS

---

[45] See discussion in CHE, *supra*, at 133 to 134 for discussion of, and definition of, "equivalent facilitation," and application of relevant legal standards in light of public policy considerations requiring maximum "full and equal access" for disabled persons.

The <u>policy</u> of the law, as evidenced by statute and appellate decisions, has been to <u>broadly</u> construe Civil Rights requirements for disabled persons, and <u>narrowly</u> construe claims of "excuse" or "exception" which would justify the denial of access to the disabled. <u>When alterations are made, access is required</u>. Alleged "<u>disproportionality</u>" in cost is protected against by the statutory availability of "hardship" exceptions. (Health & Safety Code § 19957 ; Title 24, § 2-422 (1984 Code)). The <u>burden</u> of <u>applying</u> for an "<u>exception</u>" is on the owner of a building being altered, at the time that a permit is applied for to do the alteration work. Defendants <u>cannot change that</u>, years later.[46] Public policy considerations requiring a broad interpretation of the scope of disabled access and civil rights laws were expressed by Northern District Chief Judge Thelton Henderson in <u>Walker and Adams v. Carnival Cruise Lines, et al.</u> (2000) 107 F.Supp.2d 1135, at 1145-1146, as to enforcement of the ADA; and in <u>Arnold v. United Artists Theater Circuit, Inc., et al.</u> (N.D.Cal., April 15, 1994) 866 F.Supp 433, at 437-438, 439, as to the broad scope of California Civil Code §§ 51 and 54.1, (extending coverage to disabled persons <u>deterred</u> from using known inaccessible facilities.)

d. NO HARDSHIP EXCEPTION WITHOUT EQUIVALENT FACILITATION
<u>San Francisco v. Grant Co.</u> (1986) 181 Cal.App.3d 1085, and <u>People ex rel. Deukmejian v. CHE, Inc.</u> (1983) 150 Cal.App.3d 123, each held that a court may find a building department's actual granting of an "exception" to be <u>invalid</u>: for example when the "exception" was given in response to <u>factual misrepresentations</u> by the building owners; or on a finding that granting an exception was an "abuse of discretion" by the building department, because no "equivalent facilitation" was concurrently required as a <u>condition precedent</u> to granting the exception. (See California Health & Safety Code §19957 and discussion in <u>CHE</u>, *supra*, at p.134-135.).

In 1985, Title 24 § 2-611(d) required that:

> Dining, banquet and bar facilities shall be made accessible to the physically handicapped as provided in this section.

Section 611(d)1 required,
> Access to these facilities shall be provided at primary entrances.

Section 611(d)2 provided,
> Wheelchair access shall be provided to all areas where each type of

---

[46] Defendants have in some instances attempted to seek undocumented hardship exceptions through the justifications of a former building official as to "why" he now "remembers" he interpreted facts and laws in particular ways, all in his mind and without the required written findings of Title 24, § 2-422 (1984 Code). (Donald v. Café Royale (1990) 218 Cal.App.3d 168) There are no "mental" hardship exceptions.

functional activity occurs.

Exception No. 1 to § 611(d) provides that an "unreasonable hardship" exception may be granted, <u>but only</u> "when equivalent facilitation is provided." <u>People ex rel. Deukmejian v. CHE, Inc.</u>, *supra*, at 137, held that granting a variance without the provision of equivalent facilitation would be an <u>abuse of discretion</u>, so that any such variance would be void and could not be raised as a defense. (Health & Safety Code § 19957).

e. A COURT CANNOT "PRESUME" THAT BUILDING INSPECTORS GRANTED HARDSHIP EXCEPTIONS, BECAUSE TITLE 24 REGULATIONS REQUIRE WRITTEN AND RECORDED FINDINGS OF UNREASONABLE HARDSHIP

In an August 8, 2007 order in the Taco Bell class action litigation, <u>Moeller, et al. v. Taco Bell</u> (WL 2301778), Northern District Judge Martin Jenkins, after explaining why the burden of proof to show an "exception" was upon the defendant asserting it, also rejected defendant's argument that the court could "presume" that building inspectors had granted hardship exceptions:

> Alternatively, Defendant asks the Court to presume that the building inspectors granted hardship exemptions, citing E.R. <u>Bringle v. Bd. of Supervisors, 54 Cal.2d 86, 89, 4 Cal.Rptr. 493, 351 P.2d 765 (Cal.1960)</u> (stating that where an authorized board grants a variance it will be presumed that an official duty was performed and that the existence of the necessary facts was found.) However, that presumption does not apply here because Title 24 regulations require "details of any finding of unreasonable hardship shall [to] be recorded and entered in the files of the enforcing agency." See Title 24-1981 § 2-422(c); Title 24-1984 § 2-422(c); Title 24-1987 § 2-422 at 29; Title 24-1989 § 422(c); Title 24-1994 § 422(c); Title 24-1999 § 222-U at 28; Title 24-2001 § 222-U at 22-23. Courts have determined that where an agency must make such findings, and set forth the relevant supportive facts, the presumption does not apply. <u>Broadway, Laguna, Vallejo Ass'n v. Bd. of Permit Appeals, 66 Cal.2d 767, 773, 59 Cal.Rptr. 146, 427 P.2d 810 (Cal.1967)</u> ("The presumption that an agency's rulings rest upon the necessary findings and that such findings are supported by substantial evidence ... does not apply to agencies which must expressly state their findings and must set forth the relevant supportive facts."); see also <u>Bd. of Permit Appeals, 207 Cal.App.3d at 1107, 255 Cal. Rptr. 307</u>. Because Defendant has failed to present any evidence of any hardship findings or determinations, the Court cannot presume any such findings or determinations were made. Absent any evidence supporting the application of any hardship exceptions, the Court is left with Plaintiffs' unrebutted evidence that Defendant's restaurants contained architectural elements that violated Title 24.

Id., at p.19.

See also <u>People ex rel Deukmejian v. CHE, Inc.</u>, 150 Cal.App.3d 123, at 137, rejecting application of any "presumption" under section 664 Cal. Evidence Code, where there was no evidence a "hardship exception" had been granted by the building department, and where "equivalent facilitation and protection," a basic condition for granting a "hardship exception" per section 19957 California Health and Safety code, had not been provided.
[See also Section I-H-2-d, *supra*.]

    f. THE "TWENTY PERCENT RULE," ORIGINATED IN THE APRIL 1994 TITLE 24 REGULATIONS, AND REQUIRES THAT A SUM EQUAL TO TWENTY PERCENT OF <u>TOTAL</u> CONSTRUCTION COSTS IS THE <u>MINIMUM</u> TO BE <u>SPENT ON ACCESS FEATURES</u>, AND <u>ONLY</u> WHEN A "HARDSHIP" IS ESTABLISHED

If a defendant asserts that the court should consider applying the 20% "hardship" standard (first adopted by the April <u>1994</u> State Architect's Regulations) to alterations made in prior years, this standard would be irrelevant as to any <u>pre-1994</u> alterations. Further, unless defendants can show that they spent a minimum of 20% of their total construction costs on access features, they still could not comply with code requirements.[47]

Relevant portions of California's "Building Code," the Title 24 Regulations, were "adopted" (effective April 1, <u>1994</u>), § 3112.A(a). This code section put a specific percentage figure on what would be defined as a "disproportionate" cost of providing "an accessible entrance, path of travel, sanitary facilities" and other access features, "that is, where it exceeds 20% of the cost of the project without these features."

However, this 20% finding would not <u>excuse</u> access, only <u>limit</u> its cost to the 20% level, and require access be provided to at least this degree. The very next sentence of the § 3112A(a) "<u>Exceptions</u>" section states:

> Where the cost of alterations necessary to make these features <u>fully</u> accessible is disproportionate, access shall be provided <u>to the extent that it can be without incurring disproportionate cost.</u> In choosing which accessible items to provide, priority should be given to those elements that will provide the greatest access, in the following order:
>
> A. An accessible entrance
> B. An accessible route to the altered area
> C. At least one accessible restroom for each sex

---

[47] There is also the question of whether any "hardship exception" limited to 20% of alteration costs, can ever be validly granted if there is no "equivalent facilitation" provided, as required by section 19957. Section 19957 Health and Safety code is the "enabling legislation" against which "hardship exceptions" must be measured.

D. Accessible telephones
.....

The obligation to provide access <u>may</u> <u>not be evaded</u> by performing a series of small alterations to the area served by a single path of travel to that area if those alterations could have been performed as a single undertaking. [Emphasis added]

The following definitions are also provided:

1. Title 24 includes within the definition of "<u>facility</u>" a <u>site</u>, <u>complex</u>, or any portion thereof that is built, altered, improved, or developed to serve a particular purpose.

2. Title 24 includes "facilities" and "site work" within the ambit of those areas that are to be accessible and useable by physically disabled persons.

3. Title 24 provisions applicable to sidewalks and facilities (site, complex) require that when alterations, structural repairs, or additions are made to such facilities (site, complex), that sanitary facilities (restrooms) serving the area shall be accessible to people with physical disabilities.

g. NO "RETROACTIVE" HARDSHIP EXCEPTION IS AVAILABLE YEARS AFTER ALTERATIONS HAVE TRIGGERED ACCESS REQUIREMENTS

Defendants may contend that they are entitled to a "retroactive hardship exception." <u>If so</u>, they should have <u>applied</u> for one, but may have never done so. Nor can they do so now unless they provide evidence of evaluation of the five criteria under § 422 of Title 24, <u>as of the time the work was done</u>.

The availability or non-availability of a "retroactive" hardship exception is irrelevant where the evidence shows <u>either</u> (1) defendants have never applied for one; (2) defendants have not met their burden to show the "total construction costs" were under $50,000 (1982 level, or the applicable limit at the later time the work was done); or (3) defendants have not offered evidentiary bases for the five criteria of § 422, Title 24, the "exceptions" criteria, which also requires detailed written findings.

Once alterations have been shown, the <u>burden of proving any "exceptions"</u> to access requirements is on the defendants. For example, any alterations which occurred in 1985 were governed by the 1984 Title 24 Regulations. Per the 1984 regulations, before any "unreasonable hardship" determination may be made using the five specific criteria in § 422, there was a <u>condition precedent</u> which defendants must show: Pursuant to § 2-105(b)11A(6), there is a requirement that defendants show that the "total construction costs of alterations, structural repairs, or additions does not exceed a valuation threshold of $50,000..." (§ 2-105(b)11A(6), at p.10 of the 1984 State Architect's Interpretive Manual)

Further, what equitable showing was there that an "<u>unreasonable</u> hardship" actually existed? If we don't presently have the facts that were needed to justify the claim of "unreasonable hardship" as of the date of the alteration, it is the <u>defendants' burden of proof</u> which is missing.

In this regard, defendants may cite California Attorney General Dan Lungren's Appendix to his September 17, 1992 letters to California Building Officials. (See Appendix, § IX-E-1 of this book.) The Attorney General's reference to the possibility of a building department granting of a retroactive hardship exception "under very limited circumstances," did not cite any code section or authority for such a grant. Former Attorney General Lungren did require, however, that any such claim could be made <u>only</u> if the "owner establishes that under the <u>facts that existed at the time the relevant building plans were approved</u>, an exception <u>would have been granted</u>. Of course <u>each of the five criteria noted above would have to be considered</u>."(Emphasis added) The full statement of the Attorney General was as follows:

> <u>Granting of Retroactive Hardship Exceptions</u> - As a general rule, applications for exceptions <u>must be made prior to construction.</u> If owners were allowed to freely apply for exceptions after construction was completed and deviations were discovered, exceptions would swallow up access requirements. However, retroactive hardship exceptions may be granted post-construction <u>under very limited circumstances</u>. A hardship exception may be granted post-construction where the owner establishes that <u>under the facts that existed at the time the relevant building plans were approved, an exception would have been granted</u>. Of course each of the five criteria noted above would have to be considered. Of critical importance is that the cost of meeting the literal requirements of the access feature at issue is the cost of meeting same <u>at the time of original plan approval</u> and not the cost of meeting the literal requirements at the time of the application for the retroactive hardship exception. [Emphasis added.]
>
> Id., Appendix (of this book) section IX-E-1, at p. 1 of "Appendix" to Attorney General letter of September 17, 1992.

In <u>Atwood v. El Torito</u> (tried to the court, Alameda County Superior Court, Action No. 677858-1), evidence showed that a permit was issued for $20,000 worth of tenant improvements including replacement of a "glu lam beam" in the kitchen on the upper level and alterations to one window, all without providing a properly accessible entrance to the restaurant. (Item 2 in § 422 requires a comparison of "the cost of all construction contemplated.") Further, no "equivalent facilitation" was ever provided, as required for any "exception" per Health & Safety Code § 19957; nor was any information provided as to the other factors involved in § 422. Defendants did not offer the necessary evidence to meet their burden of proof on their claim for a hardship exception. The trial court held that, <u>assuming</u> it could determine that a building department had the power to "retroactively" grant <u>any</u> "hardship" exception, defendants did not show a factual or equitable basis justifying any retroactive hardship exception. The court (former Alameda County Presiding Judge Joseph Carson) held that a purported retroactive hardship exception (allegedly "granted" by the building department <u>during the pendency of the trial</u>!) was invalid as not meeting the necessary statutory criteria. Further, the Building Department could not overrule the court!

h. THERE IS NO SPECIAL "EXCEPTION" FOR "KITCHEN" ALTERATIONS

(1) ALTERATIONS OF EITHER OF TWO LEVELS OF A GIVEN FLOOR REQUIRES THAT THEY BE JOINED BY A RAMP OR LIFT

Exception No. 3 under § 2-611(c)5(d), (1984 Title 24 regulations) refers to § 2-1752. The "commentary" by the Attorney General's manual for 1984 stated:

> Section 2-1752 requires that floors of a given story be of a common level throughout or be connected by ramp or elevator or access lift. Exception 2 under Section 2-1752 states in part: In new and existing dining, banquet, and bar facilities when it is determined that compliance creates an unreasonable hardship, an exception can be granted. However, a minimum 75 percent of the dining, banquet and bar areas shall be of a common level throughout or connected by ramp, elevator, or lift.

In <u>Donald v. Café Royale</u>, *supra*, 218 Cal.App.3d at 174, the court noted, "It was undisputed however, that Café Royale had never made a hardship request, and, in any event, had far less than 75 percent accessibility." Based on <u>Café Royale</u>, any business must provide that "a minimum 75 percent of the dining, banquet and bar area" is "of a common level throughout or connected by ramp, elevator, or lift," in order to apply for such exception. <u>Connecting both levels</u> with a lift or ramp is required when alterations to either level are carried out. In <u>Atwood v. El Torito</u>, *supra*, construction on an (upper) kitchen level, independently required that the upper level comply with Section 2-1752, and that a lift connect the lower level with the upper level. Similarly, liability in <u>Donald v. Café Royale</u>, (1990) 218 Cal.App.3d 168, was found by the appellate court on the basis of § 522(e) (in the 1989 Code), which contained the same requirements as § 2-1752(a) in the 1984 Code.

(2) ALTERATIONS TO A KITCHEN (A "FOOD PREPARATION AREA") SPECIFICALLY TRIGGER ACCESS PER § 611(d)6 OF TITLE 24 (1984 CODE)

There is no "exception" for alterations made to "kitchen areas." This is so that disabled wheelchair users are not precluded from entering kitchens, either as interested patrons or as employees.

In <u>Atwood v. El Torito</u>, *supra*, the evidence was uncontradicted that there had been extensive "structural" modifications, including "glu lam beam" installation, removing walls and adding walls in the kitchen area, a food preparation area. Section 2-611(d)(6) (1984 Code) specifically states that "Access to food preparation areas shall comply with the provisions for entrance doors and doorways, § 2-3303." The State Architect's interpretation to § 611(d)6 states:

> Here we have general access requirements to employee areas that do not include specific work station requirements. Food preparation areas need only comply with entrance doors and doorway regulations. This means that access need not be provided at specific work stations.

Regardless of whether they "work" in the kitchen, a disabled person who applies for a job (for example, as a <u>restaurant manager</u>, a position plaintiff's access expert Richard Skaff testified he used to have), would require <u>entry</u> to the kitchen, as would any <u>patron</u> who wished to talk to the cook, something patrons who are into dining may do when they enjoy the food and wants to compliment the chef and seek the recipe.

(3) KITCHEN FACILITIES ARE NOT EXCEPTED FROM ACCESS REQUIREMENTS; ALTERATIONS IN THE KITCHEN AREA TRIGGER AN ACCESSIBLE PATH OF TRAVEL FROM THE SIDEWALK THROUGH THE FRONT DOOR

In <u>Atwood v. El Torito</u>, *supra*, defendants alleged that even the "glu lam beam" alteration, a major "structural" alteration to the kitchen area, did not trigger access because the kitchen was not used by the public. In fact, § 2-611(c)5(d) does <u>not</u> provide any exception, but rather states that "Dining, banquet and bar facilities shall be accessible to the physically handicapped as provided in this section." The commentary notes that,

> Each type of functional activity must be made accessible. This means that within any given restaurant each activity must be accessible. These activities could include the restaurant area, a banquet area, a bar area, dancing area, whatever. We emphasize again each type of activity must be accessible.

Section 2-611(c)5(d)2 states, "Functional Activity. Wheelchair access shall be provided to all areas where each type of functional activity occurs." This includes the dining area, the banquet area, and the bar area. Arguably this should also include the kitchen area, as to "entrance doors and doorways" (see section (2) hereinabove) and alterations to the kitchen should trigger access to the restrooms serving the kitchen, especially when section 19955 Health and Safety Code requires accessible sanitary facilities for patrons and employees. Further, to get to the kitchen, an accessible entrance is required.

7. IN OPPOSING EFFORTS TO LIMIT ACCESS, PLAINTIFFS SHOULD NOTE THAT PUBLIC POLICY IN CALIFORNIA CALLS FOR A BROAD INTERPRETATION OF PROTECTIONS FOR DISABLED PERSONS

   a. STATUTE AND DECLARATIONS OF POLICY: IN INTERPRETING ACCESS ISSUES, THE COURT SHOULD APPLY THE STRONG PUBLIC POLICY TO MOST FULLY PROTECT THE NEEDS OF PERSONS WITH DISABILITIES

   Defendants may ask the court to interpret access requirements <u>narrowly</u>, despite the strong policy of California law to maximize handicapped access. (See Government Code § 19230), and the recognition by our courts that civil rights statutes and disabled access statutes should be interpreted in a manner which most fully protects the rights and needs of persons with disabilities. (See, inter alia, <u>People Ex rel Deukmejian v. CHE, Inc.</u> (1983) 150 Cal.App.3d 123, 131-135, <u>Donald v. Sacramento Valley Bank</u> (1989) 209 Cal.App.3d 1183, 1191-1193, <u>Donald v. Café Royale</u> (1990) 218 Cal. App.3d 168, 177-180; and <u>Hankins v. El Torito Restaurants, Inc., et al.</u> (1998) 63 Cal. App.4th 510, 520.)

   In <u>CHE</u>, *supra*, at 134, the court noted that, the statutory and regulatory law, read as a whole, is designed to guarantee safe access for the physically disabled while permitting them to function as equals to the maximum extent feasible within every aspect of society. Consequently, exception to the literal statutory and regulatory requirements is warranted only when equivalent facilitation and protection are not denied.

   The "purpose" of the access laws was set out in <u>Donald v. Sacramento Valley Bank</u>, *supra*. Since the 1968 adoption of California Government Code section 4450ff (requiring access for all new governmental construction and all alterations of existing structures),[48] the provisions of the 1961 ASA standards were incorporated into the Government Code and remained the applicable standard until Title 24 was adopted as the "State Architect's Regulations," effective July 1, 1982. Per <u>Sacramento Valley Bank</u>, *supra*:

   The ASA standards apply to "all buildings and facilities used by the

---
[48] In 1970 the requirements of section 4450ff Government Code were extended to all privately-owned commercial buildings by Health and Safety Code sections 19955-19959.

the public accessible to, and functionally for the handicapped." . . . ASA standard A117.1, 1961 ¶2.
Id. at p. 1194.

The full text of the ASA's statement of "purpose" in ¶1.2 is:

<u>Purpose</u>. This standard is intended to make all buildings and facilities used by the public accessible to, and functionally for, the physically handicapped, to, through, and within their doors, without loss of function, space, or facility where the general public is concerned.

A similar purpose was stated since the earliest (1982) version of Title 24:

<u>Purpose</u>
Section 2-101
(a) <u>Standards</u>. To provide minimum standards to safeguard life or limb, health, property, and public welfare and by regulating and controlling the design, construction, quality of materials, use and occupancy, location and maintenance of all buildings and structures within the scope of this code.

(b) <u>Incorporation</u>. To assure that barrier free design facilities, site work, and other developments to which this code applies <u>to assure that they are accessible to, and usable by, physically handicapped persons</u>. (Emphasis added)

When in 1992 the California Legislature amended section 51 Civil Code to add section 51(f) incorporating <u>any</u> violation of the ADA as a violation of the Unruh Civil Rights Act (section 51ff Civil Code), the intent was to <u>strengthen</u> protections for the disabled:

The general intent of the legislation was expressed in an uncodified section: "It is the intent of the Legislature in enacting this act to strengthen California law in areas where it is weaker than the Americans with Disabilities Act of 1990 (Public Law 101-336) and to retain California law when it provides more protection for individuals with disabilities than the Americans with Disabilities Act of 1990." (Stats.1992, ch. 913, § 1, p. 4282.)

<u>Munson v. Del Taco</u> (2009) 46 Cal.4th 661, at 669.

b. THE POLICY OF THE LAW IS TO BROADLY CONSTRUE REQUIREMENTS FOR DISABLED ACCESS
The <u>policy</u> of the law, as evidenced by statute and by appellate decisions, has been to <u>broadly</u> construe Civil Rights requirements for disabled persons, and <u>narrowly</u> construe claims of "excuse" or "exception" which would justify the <u>denial</u> of access to the disabled. <u>When alterations are made, access is required</u>. Alleged

"disproportionality" in cost is protected against by the statutory availability of "hardship" exceptions. (Health & Safety Code § 19957; Title 24, § 2-422 (1984 Code)). The burden of applying for an "exception" is on the owner of a building being altered, at the time an alteration permit is applied for.

For example, at trial in <u>Atwood v. El Torito</u>, Alameda Cty. Sup. Ct., Action No. 677858-1, the court rejected defendants' efforts to establish a defense by their hired witness, a former building official who offered testimony as to "now remembering" that more than ten years earlier, in connection with permitting for relevant "alterations" which triggered access requirements, he had "exercised his discretion" and interpreted facts and laws in a manner which gave defendants a "mental" hardship exception. The court may have been influenced when cross examination revealed that this "factual" witness (not previously identified as a retained "expert" witness) was being paid for his consultation and testimony "time" by defendants. Cross examination also established that this official had made his purported "mental" hardship determination without making any of the written findings required by Title 24, § 422 (1984 Code). Judgment was eventually entered for plaintiff.[49]

c. **CALIFORNIA STATUTES, CASE LAW, AND BUILDING REGULATIONS FOCUS ON MAXIMIZING ACCESS FOR DISABLED PERSONS**

California Government Code § 19230 is a declaration of public policy:

> The Legislature hereby declares that: (a) It is the policy of this state to encourage and enable individuals with a disability to participate fully in the social and economic life of the state and to engage in remunerative employment.

In a 9th Circuit opinion, broadly construing statutes intended to help the disabled, the court in <u>Greater Los Angeles Council on Deafness, Inc. v. Zolin</u> (9th Cir. 1987) 812 F.2d 1103, at 1114, considered the important policy considerations involved when interpreting statutes intended to protect the rights of "handicapped" persons. (See section I-B-1-a, *supra*)

In 1983, in the <u>CHE</u> case, *supra*, a California appellate court recognized these policies, in a case requiring accessible primary entrances (rather than only secondary "entrances," like "through the kitchen," not used by the general public):

> The prohibition against discrimination of the handicapped within Civil Code section 54 et seq., the enactment of Government Code section 4450 et seq., and section 19955 et seq., and the incorporation by reference of the phrase "primary entrance" within applicable specifications, reflect

---

[49] The judgment included the court awarding more than $615,000 attorney fees and costs to plaintiff. Because defendants had continued to fight the case over a seven year period, challenging every court ruling, seeking "reconsideration," then obtaining a purporte "retroactive" hardship declaration from a building official even after the court had ruled against the defendants, this attorney fees award included a 1.5 multiplier enhancement pursuant to Code of Civil Procedure § 1021.5, the public interest attorney fee statute. (Attorney Fee Order, Oct 7, 1999)

a legislative sensitivity to the hardships suffered by those afflicted with a wide range of physical disabilities. They are part of an expanding legislative effort to attain "the commendable goal of total integration of handicapped persons into the mainstream of society..." (in re Marriage of Carney, *supra*, 24 Cal.3d 725, 740.) The Legislature has declared "It is the policy of the state to encourage and enable disabled persons to participate fully in the social and economic life of the state. Gov. Code § 19230 subd. (a). These legislative responses are designed to lessen their entire burden by guaranteeing equal and full access to public buildings, facilities and accommodations without jeopardizing their safety. We believe the law is intended to promote accommodation of the physically handicapped by assuring them access to public restaurants without facing the unnecessary adverse psychological impact of being separated from regular customer traffic and shunted through secondary entrances. (Emphasis added)
People ex rel. Deukmejian v. CHE, Inc. (1983) 150 Cal.App.3d 123, at 135-136).

d. DISABILITY ACCESS LAWS SHOULD BE INTERPRETED SO AS TO "MAXIMIZE INCENTIVES FOR COMPLIANCE"

In his landmark federal court opinion interpreting California law to require an award of damages to all disabled persons deterred from attempting to enter and use a known inaccessible facility, Arnold v. United Artists, *supra*, (former) Chief Judge Thelton Henderson cited Donald v. Café Royale, *supra*, in stressing the importance of this policy:

> California courts have applied a canon of broad construction to civil rights statutes generally, and to § 51 and § 54.1 in particular. Regarding § 51, the Unruh Act, "The [California] Legislature's desire to banish [discrimination] from California's community life has led [the California Supreme Court] to interpret the [Unruh] Act's coverage 'in the broadest sense reasonably possible.' " Isbister v. Boys' Club of Santa Cruz, 40 Cal.3d 72, 75-76, 219 Cal.Rptr. 150, 152, 707 P.2d 212 (1985) (quoting Burks v. Poppy Construction Co., 57 Cal.2d 463, 468, 20 Cal.Rptr. 609, 370 P.2d 313 (1962)). A similar presumption in favor of broad interpretation in order to further the statute's remedial purpose has been applied in § 54.1 cases. See Donald, 266 Cal.Rptr. at 808-11. In particular, California courts have held that the California disability access laws should be interpreted in a fashion that maximizes the incentives for places of public accommodation to comply with the laws' requirements. See Id. (interpreting § 54.1 as not requiring proof of discriminatory intent in order to establish a violation).

Arnold v. United Artist Theaters, (N.D. Cal, 1994) 866 F.Supp 433, at 438.

8. NO EXCEPTION FOR SECOND FLOOR ACCESS UNLESS SPECIFIC STATUTORY

CRITERIA MET

A frequent cause of access complaint occurs when a disabled person who uses a wheelchair is unable to attend a luncheon, banquet, meeting or other event held on the second floor of a restaurant or other public accommodation (often in a "banquet room") where there is no elevator or lift available for access. Some businesses believe they are immune from second floor liability due to provisions of Health & Safety Code § 19956. However, this often is not the case, and reference must be made to the language of § 19956 that was in effect at the time that the building was constructed, or at the time that any second floor "alterations" occurred (as defined by § 19959). Any California state law liability exists in addition to any possible independent liability under the ADA. There is also the possible liability for the entity which scheduled the luncheon or other event in an inaccessible location. (However such entity would usually not have the power to provide injunctive relief. There may also be policy consideration tending against suing an entity which simply rented the space for a specific occasion, perhaps without advance knowledge that the rented space would be inaccessible.)[50]

The 2008 standards of § 19956 are as follows:

> § 19956. Conformity with Government Code provisions; exceptions
>
> All public accommodations constructed in this state shall conform to the provisions of Chapter 7 (commencing with Section 4450) of Division 5 of Title 1 of the Government Code. However, the following types of privately funded multistory buildings do not require accessibility by ramp or elevator above and below the first floor:
>
> (a) Multistoried office buildings, other than the professional office of a health care provider, and passenger vehicle service stations less than three stories high, or less than 3,000 square feet per story.
>
> (b) Any other privately funded multistoried building that is not a shopping center, shopping mall, or the professional office of a health care provider, <u>and that is less than three stories high or less than 3,000 square feet per story</u> <u>if a reasonable portion of all facilities and accommodations normally sought and used by the public in such a building are accessible to and usable by persons with disabilities</u>. (Emphasis added)

---

[50] For example I once represented three disabled wheelchair users who each suffered humiliating bodily functions accidents while attending a banquet sponsored by a major civil liberties organization at a San Francisco "landmark" hotel. Not a single restroom accessible to wheelchair users existed in the entire hotel! Plaintiffs chose to sue only the hotel, and achieved a cooperative but confidential settlement where the hotel agreed to provide accessible restroom facilities and to pay substantial damages to each of the three plaintiffs. Sometimes organizations can be encouraged (or required) to include in their "by laws" that they will only schedule public events in accessible locations.

Thus, for the second floor portions of a restaurant or other public accommodation to be "exempt" from state access requirements when constructed or altered after July 1, 1970, the building must:

(1) be less than three stories high; <u>OR</u>

(2) be less than 3,000 square feet per story; AND

(3) Not be a professional office of a health care provider or shopping center or mall, AND

(4) provide that "<u>a reasonable portion of all facilities and accommodations</u> normally sought and used by the public in such a building are accessible to and usable by persons with disabilities;" [Emphasis added.][20]

For example if the <u>only</u> "banquet facilities" of a restaurant are on the second floor, "a reasonable portion of all facilities and accommodations" are <u>not</u> "accessible." Also, different problems would exist if there <u>were</u> accessible banquet rooms on the first floor, but the entity renting the facility space for an event erroneously scheduled the event on the second floor and a wheelchair user was excluded. There would probably be an ADA violation by either the scheduling entity or renting entity, or they might also be violating Civil Code § 54.1's guarantee of "full and equal access" even if no Health & Safety Code violation existed. (See ADA § 302(b)(1)(A) and its subsections.) (Under the ADA any owner, operator, lessor or lessee of a public accommodation may be liable. See section III, *infra*.)

9. A BUSINESS' <u>POLICY</u> MAY VIOLATE CIVIL CODE § 54.1 EVEN IF THERE ARE NO ILLEGAL ARCHITECTURAL BARRIERS

In <u>Hankins v. El Torito Restaurants, Inc., et al.</u>, 63 Cal.App.4th 510 (1998), where the only public restrooms were on the second floor, the restaurant's <u>policy</u> - of not allowing use of the "employees only" first floor restroom to an amputee on crutches who was <u>unable</u> to climb stairs to the second floor restroom - was found to violate Civil Code § 54.1's "full and equal access" requirement. "We hold that Civil Code § 54.1 et seq. apply to policies as well as structural impediments." (<u>Hankins</u>, *supra*, at 524.) The Court also held that this policy also violated sections 51-52 Civil Code, which provided an <u>alternative</u> basis for damages. The defendants' efforts in <u>Hankins</u> to make excuses for a policy with a discriminatory effect were recently cited- and rejected- in <u>Stevens v. Optimum Health Institute- San Diego</u>, 810 F.Supp.2d 1024 1091 (2011):

> A defendant may not rely upon "an unsubstantiated and totally speculative concern" to justify a discriminatory practice. <u>Hankins v. El Torito Restaurants, Inc.</u>, 63 Cal.App.4th 510, 520, 74 Cal.Rptr.2d 684 (1998) [held] ("[W]e decline to find that an unsubstantiated and totally speculative concern

---

[51] The attorney (plaintiff or defendant) faced with this issue should check to see the precise language of statutes and Title 24 regulations in effect when construction or alterations for a subject building were permitted. Further, public entities should not rent out inaccessible facilities for public events, or face possible ADA Title II violations.

that El Torito would be unable to prevent a patron from surreptitiously sampling food on the way to or from the [employee] rest room justifies denying a handicapped patron access to the only first floor restroom on the premises.")

[See also the portion of the first Walker v. Carnival Cruise Lines, 63 F.Supp 1083 (1999), decision where (N.D. Cal.) Chief Judge Thelton Henderson held that travel agents could be held liable under section 54 Civil Code, as well as Title III of the ADA for a policy violation of mis-representing that a cruise ship state room was "disabled accessible" without investigating whether the state room was actually accessible.][52] [See also the Chabner 9th Circuit holding that insurance rates discrimination violated the Unruh Act [Chabner v. United of Omaha Life Ins. Co., 225 F.3d 1042 (9th Cir. 2000)] even if it did not violate the public accommodation portions of the ADA Title III.

I. INJUNCTIVE RELIEF IS REQUIRED UNDER CALIFORNIA LAW FOR VIOLATIONS OF "FULL AND EQUAL ACCESS"

1. AN ORDER FOR INJUNCTIVE RELIEF IS REQUIRED UNDER CALIFORNIA LAW

Under California law, violations of Health & Safety Code § 19955 et seq. may be enjoined by a private person pursuant to §19953. Further, violations of Civil Code §§ 54 and 54.1's "full and equal access" provisions, due to violations of Title 24 (the State Architect's Regulations) or otherwise, may be enjoined pursuant to Civil Code § 55. (See Donald v. Sacramento Valley Bank, *supra*, 209 Cal.App.3d at 1195). Civil Code § 55 and Health & Safety Code § 19953 each contain a "prevailing party" attorney fees provision. (Attorneys fees can only be applied against a frivolous, fraudulent or bad faith losing plaintiff, if the constitutional prohibitions of the Christiansburg case, *infra*, are applied. See section IV-H, *infra*) Obtaining access will also usually qualify for Code of Civil Procedure § 1021.5 "public interest" achievement as the basis for an attorney fees award. [However, caveat Jankey v. Lee, (California Supreme Court) December 17, 2012, holding that attorney fees can be awarded against a "good faith" disabled plaintiff if defendant is found to be the "prevailing party" under Civil Code section 55. The same threat is there for section 19953 Health and Safety Code which also has a "prevailing party" attorney fees clause.]

For violations of the Unruh Act, section 51 Civil Code, section 52(c) provides for injunctive relief.

2. INJUNCTIVE RELIEF MAY BECOME "MOOT" WHEN A DEFENDANT SUPPLIES ACCESS AFTER A COMPLAINT IS FILED

---

[52] The second portion of this opinion, dealing with the enforceability of Carnival's forum selection requirement, when applied to two quadriplegic plaintiffs who were physically unable to travel to Florida, was reversed by Judge Henderson, on Reconsideration, in a major decision emphasizing ADA public policy considerations. See Walker and Adams v. Carnival Cruise Lines, (N.D. Cal 2000) 107 F.Supp.2nd 1135.

a. THE ISSUES OF INJUNCTIVE RELIEF MAY BECOME "MOOT" FOR INJUNCTIVE RELIEF PURPOSES WHEN DEFENDANTS FINALLY PROVIDE "ACCESS" DURING LITIGATION; IF SO, A PLAINTIFF MAY BECOME A PREVAILING PARTY UNDER CALIFORNIA LAW STANDARDS AND BECOME ENTITLED TO CIVIL RIGHTS ATTORNEY FEES AS A "CATALYST," BUT ONLY IF THE PLAINTIFF MADE A PRE-LITIGATION OFFER TO SETTLE

Defendants sometimes raise the defense that, because they finally install disabled access - often after many months or years of litigation - the issue of injunctive relief has become "moot." Prior to 2001 these access changes - after the lawsuit - could presumptively be attributed to be the result of plaintiff's lawsuit, and used to provide an independent basis for attorney fees, under California's "catalyst" law standards even in Federal Court. This was the standard in the Ninth Circuit and 11 of the 12 federal circuits until 2001, when the U.S. Supreme Court, in Buckhannon Board & Care Home, Inc., et al. v. West Virginia Dept. of Health & Human Services, et al. (2001) 121 S.Ct. 1835, eliminated the catalyst theory under federal law.

However, pursuant to the California Supreme Court ruling in Graham v. DaimlerChrysler Corp. (2004) 34 Cal.4th 553, the "catalyst" theory can still be applied to make plaintiff a prevailing party and entitled to statutory attorney fees under California law for obtaining the public interest results sought by the request for injunctive relief, but only when plaintiff has made "reasonable" pre-litigation efforts to settle before filing the lawsuit. [See § I.K.2, *infra*.] In addition, a plaintiff in California court (or allowed to remain in federal court, in the court's discretion) may still obtain statutory attorney fees under California law per Civil Code § 54.3 as the "prevailing party" if the attorney obtains damages for the plaintiff. Even statutory minimum damages justify statutory fees. Donald v. Café Royale, *supra*.

Multiple district courts have ruled that once injunctive relief has become "moot," either because all injunctive relief sought has been provided - or the place has permanently closed as a public accommodation - the court, in its discretion, may dismiss the case as "moot" and no longer providing the basis for mandatory federal court jurisdiction.[53] However, upon such discretionary dismissal plaintiff then has (by statute) 30 days to file a new action in state court. The federal court action by statute "tolls" the running of the statute of limitations during this 30 day period and during the period that the case was pending in federal court. A plaintiff then obtaining damages in state court, on the basis of work done while the case was in federal court as well as after it was dismissed as "moot" and refiled in state court, may be entitled to reasonable fees for both the federal court and state court work leading to the damages recovery per section 54.3. Even the "ADA" work could be recoverable where plaintiff shows that he may prove ADA liability to show an incorporated violation of California law per sections 52(f), 54(c) or 54.1(d) Civil Code, as alternative bases for damages. (See <u>Kittok</u> *supra*, "Apportionment is not required when the claims for relief are so intertwined that it would be impracticable, if not impossible, to separate the attorneys time into compensable and non compensable units. <u>Bell v. Vista Unified School District</u>, 82 Cal.App.4th 672, at 686-87 . . . Although plaintiff did not 'prevail' on her ADA claim, all time spent on that claim is equally attributable to the state law claims on which she did 'prevail,' since plaintiff prevailed on her DPA claim by first showing there was a violation of the ADA." <u>Kittok v. Leslie's Poolmart, Inc.</u>, (E.D. Cal. 2009) 687 F.Supp. 953, at 963. (Awarding nearly all fees plaintiff sought.)

b. SHOWING A NEED FOR AN ORDER THAT DEFENDANTS "MAINTAIN" ACCESSIBLE FEATURES MAY AVOID A FINDING OF MOOTNESS

(1) <u>Maintenance of Accessible Features</u> Both the ADA and state law require [TBC] to "maintain in operable working condition those features of facilities and equipment that are required to be accessible to and usable by persons with disabilities. 28 CFR § 36.211; Cal. Code Regs. Title 24 (2002) 1101.B.3.
<u>Moeller v. Taco Bell Corp.</u>, C 02-5849 PJH, 2011 WL 4634250 (N.D. Cal. Oct. 5, 2011) –F.Supp.2d–.

As part of a comprehensive Order in a class action case that had already been litigated for seven years, evidence showed that certain access features, once corrected, had not been properly maintained in an accessible condition. Id. at *28:

Here, in effect, TBC asserts that by removing or remediating the barriers at Taco Bell 4518, it has voluntarily ceased the challenged conduct. A request for prospective injunctive relief will be mooted by a defendant's voluntary compliance only if the defendant meets the "formidable burden" of demonstrating that it is "absolutely clear the alleged wrongful behavior could not reasonably be expected to recur." Friends of the Earth, 528 U.S. at 190; see also Adarand Constructors, Inc. v. Slater, 528 U.S. 216, 221, 120 S.Ct. 722, 145 L.Ed.2d 650 (2000); Rosemere Neighborhood Ass'n v. U.S. Envtl. Protection Agency, 581 F.3d 1169, 1173 (9th Cir.2009). That is, TBC has the " 'heavy burden of persua[ding]' the court that the challenged conduct cannot reasonably be expected to start up again." Friends of the Earth, 528 U.S. at 189 (citation omitted); see also Adarand, 528 U.S.

---

[53] Plaintiff might include in his complaint an injunctive relief prayer that defendants must not only provide "accessible" facilities and policies but "maintain" them in an accessible condition (See 28 CFR § 36.211; Cal. Code Regs. Title 24 (2002) 1101.B.3). This, arguably, could be a basis for continuing federal jurisdiction for enforcement, particularly if a policy is at issue. Also, some Courts may exercise their discretion to maintain jurisdiction over the related state law issues, for reasons of judicial economy. Paulick v. Bavarion Lion Vineyard Development, et al. No C-08-04860 (N.D. Cal.) Order of March 10, 2009.

at 222. Plaintiffs assert that in this case, TBC fails to meet this burden.

The court agrees, and finds that a number of factors demonstrate that TBC has not met its burden under the voluntary cessation doctrine. The evidence presented at trial demonstrates that TBC is not currently following its own access policies, and has a history of not doing so; that TBC's policies are vague and contradictory; and that TBC could rescind the policies at any time.

Moeller v. Taco Bell Corp., C 02-5849 PJH, 2011 WL 4634250 (N.D. Cal. Oct. 5, 2011)

c. IN HANKINS v. EL TORITO, THE COURT FOUND THAT ACCESS WAS PROVIDED BECAUSE OF PLAINTIFF'S LETTERS (BUT CAVEAT GRAHAM AS TO "CATALYST" THEORY LIMITATIONS)

In Hankins v. El Torito Restaurants, Inc., et al. (1998) 63 Cal.App.4th 510 the court found defendants had provided physical access improvements in response to the lawsuit, and awarded Code of Civil Procedure §1021.5 public interest attorneys fees. An access ramp to the front entrance (up six stairs), an accessible unisex restroom, and a handicapped lift to access the lower dining area and entire bar area, were installed in October, 1993, two months after the first scheduled trial date, and as a result of plaintiff's counsels' letters and lawsuit. The close timing of defendants finally filing an application for constructing handicapped access improvements in September, 1992, after plaintiff's letters and Complaint in June and August, 1992, certainly gave rise to a "cause and effect" inference. (Because of the pre-litigation notice, the catalyst fees would presumably also been recoverable even under the later Graham v. DaimlerChrysler, *supra*, standards.) This was especially so when defendants offered no El Torito corporate officer to testify as to why El Torito (and its "parent company", defendant Restaurant Enterprises Group) finally added access features, in October of 1993, more than 1 ½ years after the January 26, 1992 ADA "readily achievable" access compliance deadline. Because defendants installed the accessible restroom, front entrance ramp, and access lift, which were major components of plaintiff's request for injunctive relief, plaintiff argued judgment should be entered for plaintiff on the basis that plaintiff was the "catalyst" and that defendants provided the access requested by plaintiff after more than a year of intense litigation.

---

[54] However, in the 2009 decision in Kittok v. Leslie's Poolmart, 687 F.Supp.2d 953, Central District Court Judge Steven Larson seemed to still be following "catalyst"theory, though he also found plaintiff the prevailing party because he obtained $1,000 minimum statutory damages per section 54.3 Civil Code: "A dismissal for mootness does not make the defendant the prevailing party. Molski v. Arciero Wine Group., 164 Cal.App.4th 786, 798 . . . In such circumstances a plaintiff may still be the prevailing party on the dismissal claim "if the lawsuit was the catalyst motivating the defendant to modify its behavior or the plaintiff achieved the primary relief sought." Id., Barrios v. California Interscholastic Federation, 277 Fed.3d 1128, 1137." Id. at p. 961.

After the 2004 Graham decision, before a "catalyst" may be the basis for a California State Law attorney fees award, a court must also find that plaintiff made a reasonable pre-litigation effort to settle. (Graham v. DaimlerChrysler Corp. (2004) 34 Cal.4th 553)[54] (However, plaintiff Hankins also earned statutory attorney fees on the basis of obtaining an $80,000 damage award, pursuant to Civil Code § 52 and/or § 54.3.) After the defendants unsuccessful Hankins appeal, on remand the trial court also awarded CCP § 1021.5 attorney fees and a (1.4) public interest multiplier, for plaintiff's efforts in defending the judgment on appeal, and for establishing important legal principles on appeal. These included establishing the right to obtain Civil Code § 54.3 damages for a violation of policy, by defendants refusal to allow disabled persons who were unable to climb stairs to the public restrooms to use the available first floor "employees only" restroom.[55]

3. WHEN LIFTS ARE INSTALLED THEY SHOULD USUALLY BE INDEPENDENTLY OPERABLE BY DISABLED PERSONS

   a. THE "LOCKED LIFT" ISSUE: THE HANKINS APPELLATE DECISION FAILED TO RESOLVE WHETHER DEFENDANTS MUST UNLOCK THE LIFT

   The requirements for a lift to be independently operable by a disabled person, is mandated by both Civil Code § 54.1 and the provisions of the Americans With Disabilities Act of 1990 which have been incorporated into Civil Code §§ 51, 54(c) and 54.1(d). A court has jurisdiction under Civil Code § 55 to enjoin any continuing violation of Civil Code §§ 54 and 54.1. The Court has jurisdiction per Civil Code section 52(c) to enjoin any violation of section 51.

   In the Hankins case plaintiff's expert, Oakland access consultant Peter Margen (a private consultant and a previous ADA coordinator for the City of Oakland), was qualified by the Court as an expert with regard to the access needs of disabled persons and his observations and measurements at the El Torito Restaurant. Mr. Margen testified that at the time he visited the restaurant after a lift was installed, the lift was key locked. The parties later stipulated that the lift was kept locked, requiring a disabled person who wanted to use it to locate an employee who had a key and was willing to unlock the lift. Plaintiff asserted that this was in violation of federal ADA regulation ADAAG 4.11.3, which required that if platform lifts are used, they "shall facilitate unassisted entry, operation and exit from the lift in

---

[55] Not reflected in the published appellate opinion, but relevant as to favorable judicial attitudes toward encouraging disabled access, the trial court, on remand after the published DCA Opinion, added another $323,715 attorney fees for work plaintiff's lawyers had done in defending the judgement on appeal. This award included a 1.4 "multiplier" enhancement of attorneys fees, in recognition of the public interest importance of the case, and the policy significance of the published opinion.

compliance with 4.11.2." Plaintiff argued this was also in violation of § 5107(a) of the then current (April, 1994) California Title 24 Code, which required "Special Access (Wheelchair) Lifts... to facilitate <u>unassisted entry</u>, operation, and exit from the lift." Such practice also appeared to be a facial violation of the requirement of Civil Code § 54.1 to "full and equal access." The <u>Hankins</u> appellate opinion did not resolve these issues, but remanded them for further determination by the trial court. On remand to the trial court a <u>compromise</u> resolution was reached, allowing defendants to have an employee with a key always available, and to offer a key to any disabled person who wished to "independently" operate the lift to another level of the restaurant.[56]

b. A RAMP IS PREFERABLE TO A LIFT IN MOST SITUATIONS

While defendants may legally choose to install <u>either</u> a ramp or a lift, it is the author's experience that <u>most</u> disabled persons prefer a ramp: a ramp is quicker, never locked, does not require electrical maintenance or repair, and allows a disabled person access without the added time and unwanted attention involved with entering, operating and using a mechanical lift. Practical experience also dictates against use of an <u>outdoor</u> "lift" which be by subjected to rain or snow conditions, if there is room to build an access ramp instead. In <u>Patricia Berne v. City of Oakland</u> C07-0505 MMC (N.D. Cal 2007), a "lift" to a renovated large outdoor <u>bandstand</u> had been constructed with the lift being kept stored in an underground location- for "aesthetic" purposes. Unfortunately, this storage location was <u>below the waterline</u> for the nearby Lake Merrit, and became wet and never functioned. (The solution- substitution of an aesthetically designed curved access ramp- is described hereinbelow in section c.)

c. UNDER SOME CIRCUMSTANCES THE "INDEPENDENT OPERATION" REQUIREMENT MAY BE INAPPLICABLE AS A PRACTICAL MATTER; BUT A RAMP MAY BE A BETTER SOLUTION

Defendants sometimes voice a need to keep a lift locked to avoid vandalism or possible misuse by children playing on it. Some steep lifts may require staff assistance for safety purposes (as on the stair lift accessing a 24 stair route for a stair lift at the "basement level" Champs Sports store in the San Francisco Center shopping mall). (<u>Berne v. Champs Sports, et al.</u>, N.D.Cal., Case No. C07-1509 WHA.)

However, there are always disadvantages to disabled access when a locked lift is used. Independent use by disabled persons is compromised when a lift is kept locked.

---

[56] There may be other circumstances where a compromise on a "self-operable" lift may be appropriate, but only when an employee is immediately available, so plaintiff does not have to wait. A Santa Cruz case involved a locked lift exterior to the Mirimar Restaurant, with a note telling disabled persons to come up to the front desk (up stairs!) to get a key! (See further discussion *infra*, in section c.)

Keys often disappear or are otherwise "unavailable" when needed by a disabled person. However, the lift takes up less space and is sometimes the only practical solution because of available space or logistics.

One clear example of a lift's potential disadvant-ages was the case of <u>Patricia Berne v. City of Oakland</u>, N.D.Cal., Case No. C07-0505 MMC. When the historic bandstand at Oakland's Lake Merritt Park was renovated after the 1989 earthquake damage, a vertical lift was installed to purportedly provide disabled access to the bandstand, which was about five feet above the ground level. But the lift - stored underground and contaminated by Lake Merritt ground water - apparently <u>never</u> operated properly, although it took a lawsuit several years later to solve the problem: Plaintiff Patty Berne, who used a motorized wheelchair, was <u>excluded</u> from participating in her close friend's wedding at the bandstand. Her lawsuit required Oakland to replace the lift with an architecturally designed (and aesthetically pleasing) circular ramp, to the benefit of all concerned. (Consent Decree entered January 29, 2008).
(See Photo next page)

4. SEPARATE ACCESSIBLE MEN'S AND WOMEN'S RESTROOMS MAY BE REQUIRED (UNLESS AN ACCESSIBLE UNISEX RESTROOM IS ALLOWED AS AN "EQUIVALENT FACILITATION" UNDER A "HARDSHIP" EXCEPTION)
Section 511.1(a)(2) of the 1989 Title 24 requirements, (or other code numbers during the relevant alteration's permitting and construction period,) specifically <u>forbids</u> building a <u>unisex restroom</u> for disabled persons <u>when separate men's and women's restrooms are provided for able bodied persons</u>. Per the State Architect's interpretation, p.40 of the 1989 Manual, Providing a unisex toilet for the disabled while providing a men's and women's toilet for the able-bodied promotes the notion that the disabled are neither fish nor fowl.

This of course is not true if both disabled and non-disabled persons are required to use a single unisex accessible restroom. Then all persons are treated equally.

Similarly, the April, 1994 Title 24 Code, p.71, § 3105A.(b)1A repeated the <u>identical</u> prohibition of unisex restroom facilities where separate men's and women's facilities are provided for non-disabled persons as that contained in § 511.1(a)(2) of the 1989 Code. However, as noted hereinbelow, use of a unisex accessible restroom may be permitted as a "readily achievable" access accommodation under the Americans With Disabilities Act of 1990. It may also be allowed under California law as a form of "equivalent facilitation" <u>if</u> a business shows it is eligible for a "hardship exception"

The ramp at the historic bandstand at Oakland's Lake Merritt Park

due to physical constraints making provision of separate men's and women's accessible restrooms physically difficult or impossible. [See Health & Safety Code § 19957 and Title 24 code sections re: "hardship exception" requirements.]

5. PROVISION OF TWO SINGLE ACCOMMODATION UNISEX RESTROOMS, WITH ONLY ONE ACCESSIBLE, MAY WORK AS A PRACTICAL SOLUTION AS "READILY ACHIEVABLE" UNDER THE ADA OR UNDER CALIFORNIA LAW WHERE A "HARDSHIP" EXCEPTION IS GIVEN

In some smaller businesses, including small restaurants, space limitations may make it difficult to make both men's and women's restrooms accessible. Under these circumstances, one alternative may be to make both restrooms single accommodation and "unisex," and make at least one of these restrooms fully accessible, where possible, including proper signage. Alternatively, combining a small women's restroom and a small men's restroom to create one accessible unisex restroom (especially where the two restrooms are located adjacent to each other), may minimize plumbing needs, be easier to accomplish and more "readily achievable." This is permitted under ADA regulations as a "readily achievable" solution and pursuant to a "hardship" finding under California Law (Health & Safety Code § 19957 and under Title 24).

However, caveat claims that the size of the restaurant's clientele may make a single restroom insufficient for the needs of a large restaurant with many patrons. The ADA should preempt any alleged state or local plumbing code requirements. Further, a restaurant or other public facilities having such large clientele should be able to find room for one unisex accessible restroom. Leaving a facility without any accessible public restrooms should almost never be acceptable.

Per California's Title 24, section 1134B.2.2 (2002 text):
> Where it is technically infeasible in the area of alteration to make existing restroom facilities code compliant and to install separate sanitary facilities for each sex, then installation of at least one unisex toilet/bathroom per floor being altered, located in the same area as existing toilet facilities, will be permitted. Such a facility shall meet with the requirements of section 1115B.7.2
>
> (Section 1115B.7.2 lists the specifications for the "structural strength of grab bars, tub and shower seats fasteners and mounting devices.")

6. SPECIAL STANDARDS OF ACCESSIBILITY FOR BUILDINGS WITH HISTORICAL SIGNIFICANCE

Title 24 refers to special standards under the State Historical Building Code:

> HISTORIC PRESERVATION – SPECIAL STANDARDS OF ACCES-SIBILITY FOR BUILDINGS WITH HISTORICAL SIGNIFICANCE

1135B.1 General. Qualified historical buildings shall comply with the State Historical Building Code, Part 8, Title 24, of the California Code of Regulations, as printed in Part 2, Chapter 34, Division II.

Generally an "historical" building is not "relieved" of access obligations when it undergoes alterations; it simply must follow the standards of the referenced state Historical Building Code, which requires access additions to be as consistent as possible with the existing historical <u>exterior</u> designs. For example, in most situations <u>some</u> accessible entrance is required to a building currently having stairs at every entrance, even though the access changes should be as visually consistent as possible with the historical <u>external</u> appearance. Also, the historical designation of a building should not excuse provision of an <u>interior</u> accessible restroom if such restroom would otherwise be required by law. [for discussion of mulitple related issues, including using historical code while analyzing "readily achievable" issues, see <u>Molski v. Foley Estates Vineyard & Winery, LLC</u>, 531 F.3d 1043 (9th Cir. 2008), also an important case on burden of proof and other issues.]

J. DAMAGES: PURSUANT TO CALIFORNIA CIVIL CODE §§ 51 AND 52, OR, ALTERNATIVELY, 54, 54.1 AND 54.3, A DISABLED PERSON IS ENTITLED TO DAMAGES FOR DENIAL OF CIVIL RIGHTS
  1. STATUTORY AND COMPENSATORY DAMAGES ARE AVAILABLE PER CIVIL CODE §§ 52 and 54.3

      a. CIVIL CODE § 54.3 PROVIDES DAMAGES FOR VIOLATIONS OF CIVIL CODE §§ 54 or 54.1
      § 54.3. Violations; liability
      (1) Any person or persons, firm or corporation who denies or interferes with admittance to or enjoyment of the public facilities as specified in Sections 54 and 54.1 or otherwise interferes with the rights of an individual with a disability under Sections 54, 54.1 and 54.2 is liable for each offense for the actual damages and any amount as may be determined by a jury, or the court sitting without a jury, <u>up to a maximum of three times the amount of actual damages</u> but <u>in no case less</u> than one thousand dollars ($1,000), and attorney's fees as may be determined by the court in addition thereto, suffered by any person denied any of the rights provided in Sections 54, 54.1, and 54.2. "Interfere," for purposes of this section, includes, but is not limited to, preventing or causing the prevention of a guide dog, signal dog, or service dog from carrying out its functions in assisting a disabled person.

      (2) Any person who claims to be aggrieved by an alleged unlawful practice in violation of Section 54, 54.1, or 54.2 may also file a verified complaint with the Department of Fair Employment and Housing pursuant to Section 12948 of the Government Code. <u>The remedies in this section are nonexclusive and are in addition to any other remedy provided by law</u>, including, but not limited to, any action for injunctive

or other equitable relief available to the aggrieved party or brought in the name of the people of this state or of the United States.

(3) A person may not be held liable for damages pursuant to both this section and Section 52 for the same act or failure to act.
(Emphasis added)

§ 52(h) defines "actual damages" as including "special damages and general damages."

b. STATUTORY <u>MINIMUM</u> DAMAGES ARE $1,000 PER CIVIL CODE §54.3 VIOLATION, BUT MORE MAY BE APPROPRIATE BASED ON FACTS.
(1) <u>DONALD V. CAFÉ ROYALE</u> (1990) 218 CAL.APP.3D 168

<u>Donald v. Sacramento Valley Bank</u> (1989) 209 Cal.App.3d 1183 (the "ATM" case) established that violation of California Health & Safety Code §§ 19955-19959 could be the basis for a private lawsuit for injunction and damages. <u>Donald v. Café Royale</u> (1990) 218 Cal.App.3d 168, held that any violation of the architectural barriers laws which results in a disabled person being denied "full and equal access" to a public facility, including an ATM or a public restaurant, justifies damages pursuant to Civil Code § 54.3. In the <u>Café Royale</u> case the appellate court did not disturb the trial court's <u>factual</u> "findings" that the plaintiff, an activist disabled attorney, had not <u>in fact</u> suffered <u>any</u> emotional distress or general damages during his brief visit to and decision not to eat at the subject restaurant because of its inaccessible and effectively segregated seating configuration: all public seating was in raised tiers. The restaurant claimed it had one table next to the piano that a disabled person could use. On this basis the appellate court held that plaintiff was entitled to (at least) the $250 <u>minimum</u> statutory damage award per section 54.3, and also could be awarded attorney fees for the trial and appeal. (The $250 damages <u>minimum</u> is now $1,000 per violation, under Civil Code § 54.3.) Alternatively, section 52 allows <u>minimum</u> statutory damages of $4,000 for section 51, architectural barrier violations, but only when liability is based on incorporation of any ADA violation, per section 52(f). That these are <u>minimum</u> damages, not maximum damages, is reflected in the $80,000 damages awarded and upheld on appeal in <u>Hankins v. El Torito Restaurant, Inc.</u>, (1998) 63 Cal App. 4th 510, (a case that did not involve any medical treatment or "special" out of pocket damages.)

(2) <u>BOTOSAN V. MCNALLY REALTY, ET AL.</u> (9TH CIRCUIT) (2000) 216 F.3D 827

In <u>Botosan v. McNally Realty, et al.</u> (2000) 216 F.3d 827, the 9th Circuit held that <u>at least the minimum $1,000 damages</u> per Civil Code § 54.3 were <u>mandatory</u>, where a disabled driver, attempting to visit a real estate office, drove on when he saw there were no disabled parking spaces provided.

(3) <u>BOEMIO V. LOVE'S RESTAURANT</u> (S.D. CAL. 1997), 954 F.SUPP. 204

Compare <u>Boemio v. Love's Restaurant</u> (S.D. Cal. 1997), 954 F.Supp. 204, where the judge held, under <u>contested facts</u>, <u>minimum</u> statutory damages of $1,000 were sufficient. This low damage award was explained under the particular facts of plaintiff's confrontation with restaurant employees.

(4) <u>HANKINS V. EL TORITO RESTAURANTS, INC.</u> (1998) 63 CAL.APP.4TH 510, AWARDED SUBSTANTIALLY MORE DAMAGES THAN THE STATUTORY "MINIMUM"

Pursuant to both Civil Code §§ 51 and 54.3, plaintiff Mark Hankins was awarded $80,000 damages (statutory and compensatory) when he was refused the use of an "employees-only" restroom and forced into the humiliating "last resort" of urinating in the parking lot (see details hereinbelow at § I-"I"-2-b and I-"I"-3). (<u>Hankins v. El Torito</u>, *supra*.) Civil Code § 54.3 should be interpreted on the same standard of damages allowed by Civil Code § 52, allowing recovery of "actual" damages and an additional amount up to three times the amount of actual damages, but in no event less than $1,000, plus statutory attorney fees. (The minimum per Civil Code § 52, for violation of §51, is now $4,000.)[57] (Civil Code §52(h) defines "actual damages" to be "general" and "special" damages.) Defendants should understand that the $1,000 "minimum" is exactly that, a floor level for any proven civil rights violation.

The <u>Hankins</u> trial judge- presiding Judge Walter Harrington in the "conservative" San Mateo Superior Court jurisdiction- may have been affected both by the Plaintiff's testimony about his humilation, and by the restaurant corporation's arrogant insistence that its restaurant manager's "policy" of refusing use of an "employees" restroom to disabled persons who were unable to climb stairs to the only "public" restroom, <u>was "company policy" and justified</u>.

(5) <u>LONBERG V. CITY OF RIVERSIDE</u> (C.D.CAL.) 2007 WL2005177 ("<u>LONBERG II</u>") AWARDED DAMAGES FOR EACH LACKING CURB CUT ENCOUNTERED

In <u>Lonberg II</u>, plaintiff, a quadriplegic wheelchair user, had complained to the city for many years about the lack of curb cuts near his home in Riverside. The trial court had previously held that "Civil Code section 54.3 is applicable to

---

[57] Section 54.3(c) requires plaintiff to elect, prior to or at trial, whether to proceed under section 52 or section 54.3 in seeking damages.

public entities (Lonberg v. City of Riverside, 300 F.Supp.2nd 942, 949 (C.D. Cal 2004) and damages must be awarded regardless of a public entity's motive or intent. Lentini v. California Center, 370 F.3d 837, 847 (9th Cir. 2004).; Donald v. Café Royale, Inc. 218 Cal.App.3d 168, 179-180 (1990)" Id. at p.8. The Court awarded the "statutory minimum" of $1,000 <u>for the lack of each</u> of 181 curb cuts plaintiff encountered which were legally necessary but not provided; it also awarded $5,000 damages for each of the "8 curb ramps, or lack of curb ramps, that plaintiff encountered very near his home" on <u>multiple</u> occasions (over a 10 year period), for a total of $221,000 in statutory damages. Id. at p.*9. The District Court (Hon. Steven Larson, a George W. Bush appointee) noted, "Although plaintiff may not have suffered a physical injury as a result of the City's discrimination, there is no question that he has suffered a very clear harm- both to his dignity and his ability to become a self-reliant member of society." Id.

c. STATUTORY MINIMUM DAMAGES OF $4,000 PER CIVIL CODE § 51 VIOLATION, PER § 52(a)

In <u>Arnold v. United Artists Theater Circuit, Inc., et al.</u> 866 F.Supp 433 (N.D.Cal. 1994) Northern District Chief Judge Thelton Henderson held that a violation of Civil Code §51 based on §51's incorporation of an ADA violation, could be established on the basis of <u>incorporation</u> of an ADA violation, and that under the ADA no wrongful intent was required for violation. (Section 51 was also applied to persons <u>deterred</u> from using a facility due to its known inaccessibility, in another ruling in this case. See section "e", *infra*.)

The current text of Civil Code section 51 reads (as of May, 2011):

(1) This section shall be known, and may be cited, as the Unruh Civil Rights Act.

(2) All persons within the jurisdiction of this state are free and equal, and no matter what their sex, race, color, religion, ancestry, national origin, disability, medical condition, marital status, or sexual orientation are entitled to the full and equal accommodations, advantages, facilities, privileges, or services in all business establishments of every kind whatsoever.

(3) This section shall not be construed to confer any right or privilege on a person that is conditioned or limited by law or that is applicable alike to persons of every sex, color, race, religion, ancestry, national origin, disability, medical condition, marital status, or sexual orientation.

(4) Nothing in this section shall be construed to require any construction, alteration, repair, structural or otherwise, or modification of any

sort whatsoever, beyond that construction, alteration, repair, or modification that is otherwise required by other provisions of law, to any new or existing establishment, facility, building, improvement, or any other structure, nor shall anything in this section be construed to augment, restrict, or alter in any way the authority of the State Architect to require construction, alteration, repair, or modifications that the State Architect otherwise possesses pursuant to other laws.

For purposes of this section:

(1) "Disability" means any mental or physical disability as defined in Sections 12926 and 12926.1 of the Government Code.

(2) "Medical condition" has the same meaning as defined in subdivision (h) of Section 12926 of the Government Code.

(3) "Religion" includes all aspects of religious belief, observance, and practice.

(4) "Sex" has the same meaning as defined in subdivision (p) of Section 12926 of the Government Code.

(5) "Sex, race, color, religion, ancestry, national origin, disability, medical condition, marital status, or sexual orientation" includes a perception that the person has any particular characteristic or characteristics within the listed categories or that the person is associated with a person who has, or is perceived to have, any particular characteristic or characteristics within the listed categories.

(6) "Sexual orientation" has the same meaning as defined in subdivision (q) of Section 12926 of the Government Code.

(7) A violation of the right of any individual under the Americans with Disabilities Act of 1990 (Public Law 101-336) shall also constitute a violation of this section.

The current text of section 52(a) reads:

(a) Whoever denies, aids or incites a denial, or makes any discrimination or distinction contrary to Section 51, 51.5, or 51.6, is liable for each and every offense for the actual damages, and <u>any amount</u> that may be determined by a jury, or a court sitting without a jury, <u>up to a maximum of three times the amount of actual damage but in no case less than four thousand dollars ($4,000)</u>, and any attorney's fees that may be determined by the court in addition thereto, suffered by any person denied the rights provided in Section 51, 51.5, or 51.6.

(Emphasis added)

d. AUTHORITIES WERE SPLIT ON WHETHER DISCRIMINATORY INTENT WAS REQUIRED FOR CIVIL CODE § 51 VIOLATION; THE CALIFORNIA SUPREME COURT IN MUNSON V. DEL TACO FINALLY HELD (7-0) THAT NO "INTENT" WAS REQUIRED TO BE PROVEN

(1) GUNTHER V. LIN (NOW OVERRULED), A STATE COURT DCA OPINION, HAD HELD THAT A PLAINTIFF MUST PROVE DISCRIMINATORY INTENTION FOR A § 51 VIOLATION

In Gunther v. Lin, 50 Cal.Rptr.3d 317 (Cal.Ct.App. 2006) an appellate California court decision had held that, despite federal cases to the contrary, "wrongful intent" was needed for a violation of Civil Code § 51 even when based on an incorporated violation of the ADA (which in turn did not require proof of a defendant's "intent"). Gunther v. Lin, supra, stated it disagreed with the contrary federal District court decision in Arnold v. United Artists, supra, and with the 9th Circuit's decision in Lentini v. California Center for the Arts (9th Cir. 2004) 370 F.3d 837. The Gunther court stated that the California Supreme Court was not bound to follow federal court decisions interpreting issues of California state law, and that a California appellate court was free to decide how the California Supreme Court was likely to rule on a state law interpretation issue.[58]

(2) IN WILSON V. HARIA AND GOGRI CORP. DBA JACK IN THE BOX, ET AL. (E.D.CAL.) JUDGE KARLTON REJECTED GUNTHER

Gunther v. Lin was rejected by certain federal courts, including Judge Lawrence Karlton of the Eastern District of California in Wilson v. Haria and Gogri Corp. dba Jack in the Box, et al. (E.D.Cal.) 479 F.Supp 1127 (Order of March 22, 2007). Judge Karlton re-analyzed the Gunther holding, found that it was not required by previous precedent, and that it was basically wrong, and that the federal courts were not required to follow Gunther as it was not the decision of the highest court in California, the California Supreme Court; instead Judge Karlton followed the Arnold v. United Artists, supra, and Lentini v. California Center for the Arts (9th Cir. 2004) 370 F.3d 837, 9th Circuit precedent, holding that no intentional violation was required.

(3) IN MUNSON (2009) THE CALIFORNIA SUPREME COURT SETTLED THE ISSUE (7-0): NO INTENT IS NEEDED

The 9th Circuit of Appeals certified the issue to the California Supreme Court, which unequivocally decided no wrongful intent was needed for a violation

---

[58] Gunther was overruled by the California Supreme Court in Munson, discussed here infra at (3), and should not be cited or relied upon.

of section 51(f) California Civil Code which was based on an incorporated violation of the ADA. By a 7-0 vote the California Supreme Court agreed with the 9th Circuit's Lentini case, and rejected and overruled Gunther, *supra*. Munson v. Del Taco, Inc., 46 Cal.4th 661 (2009):

> May an Unruh Civil Rights plaintiff relying on subdivision (f) of section 51 obtain damages for denial of full access to a business establishment in violation of the ADA and the Unruh Civil Rights act without proof the denial involved intentional discrimination? We conclude that a plaintiff proceeding under section 51, subdivision (f) may obtain may obtain damages on proof of an ADA access violation without the need to demonstrate additionally that the discrimination was intentional.
> Id. at 670.

e. CIVIL CODE §§ 51, 52 AND 54.1, 54.3 ALLOW DAMAGES BASED ON DETERRENCE

In Arnold v. United Artists Theater Circuit, Inc., et al. (N.D.Cal., April 15, 1994) 866 F.Supp 433, at 439, Chief Judge Thelton Henderson (a highly esteemed[59] Chief Judge for the Northern District of California), discussed the history of California case law, including Donald v. Café Royale, *supra*, and held that statutory damages were available for incidents of deterrence, i.e.., where knowledge of the lack of access for disabled persons at commercial premises (such as a movie theater), had deterred a disabled person from actually attempting on a specific occasion to use the premises. "Failing to recognize deterrence based claims under § 54.3 and § 52 would significantly reduce the incentives for compliance with the disability access requirements of these laws." Id.

> Since California courts have held that the California disability access laws manifest an intent on the part of the legislature that they be interpreted in a manner that maximizes incentives for compliance, see Donald, 266 Cal.Rptr. at 808-11, the Court concludes that application of this canon of construction requires that § 54.1 and § 51, and their respective damages provisions, § 54.3 and § 52, be interpreted as extending to claims based on incidents of deterrence. The Court therefore holds that where a plaintiff can prove that violations of applicable California disability access standards deterred her on a particular occasion from attempting to attend a place of public accommodation, that plaintiff states a claim for relief under California Civil Code § 54.1 and § 51 and, in particular, for damages, under § 54.3 and § 52.

Connie Arnold v. United Artists Theater Circuit, Inc., et al. (N.D.Cal.

---

[59] An excellent documentary film about judge Henderson, "Soul of Justice: Thelton Henderson's American Journey" was produced by Abbey Ginsburg in 2005.

1994) 866 F.Supp. 433, at 439

If a disabled person can prove that violation of an applicable California disability access standard deterred her on a particular occasion from attempting to visit a place of public accommodation, that person has stated a claim for relief, including damages, without the necessity of actually showing up and being denied admission. This <u>Arnold</u> standard of damages for deterrence has been codified in new civil code section 55.56 (b) and (d), discussed hereinbelow in section f.

f. EFFECTIVE JANUARY 1, 2009, CIVIL CODE SECTION 55.56 LIMITS RECOVERY OF DAMAGES TO PERSONS ACTUALLY ENCOUNTERING OR DETERRED BY A CODE VIOLATION, AND INCLUDES THOSE SUFFERING DIFFICULTY, DISCOMFORT OR EMBARRASSMENT AS A RESULT

Enacted as part of 2008's SB1608, a comprehensive revision and clarification of California state law regarding disabled access, the legislative counsel's digest summarized section 55.56 as follows:

> Damages may be recovered for a violation of a <u>construction-related accessibility standard</u> that denied the plaintiff full and equal access only if that violation was <u>personally encountered by</u> the plaintiff on a particular occasion or deterred the plaintiff on a particular occasion. Evidence that the violation was personally encountered by the plaintiff on a particular occasion <u>may</u> include, but is not <u>limited to, evidence that the</u> <u>plaintiff experienced difficulty, discomfort, or embarrassment</u> because of the violation. A plaintiff shows that he or she was <u>deterred on a particular occasion</u> if he or she had actual knowledge of a violation, which deterred the plaintiff from visiting or otherwise using a place of public accommodation <u>that the</u> <u>plaintiff would have made use of but for the</u> <u>violation</u>. (Emphasis added)

The actual <u>text</u> of section 55.56 (per Westlaw) is the following:

> 55.56 (a) Statutory damages under either subdivision (a) of Section 52 or subdivision (a) of Section 54.3 may be recovered in a construction-related accessibility claim against a place of public accommodation only if a violation or violations of one or more construction-related accessibility standards denied the plaintiff full and equal access to the place of public accommodation on a particular occasion.
>
> (b) A plaintiff is denied full and equal access only if the plaintiff personally encountered the violation on a particular occasion, or the plaintiff was deterred from accessing a place of public accommodation on a particular occasion.
>
> (c) A violation personally encountered by a plaintiff may be <u>sufficient to cause a denial of full and equal access if the plaintiff experienced difficulty, discomfort, or embarrassment because of the violation.</u>

(d) A plaintiff demonstrates that he or she was deterred from accessing a place of public accommodation on a particular occasion only if both of the following apply:

(1) The plaintiff had actual knowledge of a violation or violations that prevented or reasonably dissuaded the plaintiff from accessing a place of public accommodation that the plaintiff intended to use on a particular occasion.

(2) The violation or violations would have actually denied the plaintiff full and equal access if the plaintiff had accessed the place of public accommodation on that particular occasion. (Emphasis added)

This California law code applies to claims for <u>damages</u> in both state court and federal court, whereas certain <u>procedural</u> changes in SB1608, such as requiring specific notices to be served with the Complaint, and requiring a temporary stay of California Superior Court proceedings upon request of a defendant who obtains a CASP report before being sued, can not validly control the <u>procedures in federal court</u>: the federal district court's procedures cannot be set by a state legislature because such procedures are governed by the Federal Rules of Civil Procedure (FRCP) and such local rules as each District may adopt. <u>O'Campo v. Chico Mall</u> 758 F.Supp.2d 976, 985 (E.D. Cal. 2011).

The <u>O'Campo</u> Court, *supra*, discussed the recently enacted "Construction-Related Accessibility Standards Act, C. Civ. Code sections 55.51-55.54, and why its procedural "Notice" and Stay" procedures could not control federal court, and were preempted by the ADA:

> The Act is preempted to the extent that it imposes any additional procedural hurdles to a plaintiff bringing a claim under the ADA. The Ninth Circuit has held that, "[F]or federal law to preempt state law, it is not necessary that a federal statute expressly state that it preempts state law. Federal law preempts state law if the state law "actually conflicts" with federal law." <u>Hubbard v. SoBreck, LLC, 554 F.3d 742 (9th Cir.2009)</u> (citing <u>Cal. Fed. Sav. & Loan Ass'n v. Guerra, 479 U.S. 272, 280–81, 107 S.Ct. 683, 93 L.Ed.2d 613 (1987)</u>). Here, the ADA has no provision for mandatory stays and early settlement conferences where a public accommodation has been inspected by a state official and found to be in compliance with federal as well as state law. Any state law requirement that a claim brought under the ADA be subjected to such a procedure, then, clearly conflicts with federal law. Thus, the Act is preempted to the extent it applies to plaintiff's ADA claim.

Id. at 984-985.

g. A "CONSTRUCTION-RELATED ACCESSIBILITY CLAIM" IS NOW DEFINED BY CODE

In the 2009 Munson decision, the California Supreme Court noted the legislature had also defined a "construction-related accessibility claim as part of the SB1608 definitions:

> A "construction-related accessibility claim" includes a public accommodation access claim brought under the Unruh Civil Rights Act or the Disabled Persons Act for violations of a 'construction-related accessibility standard.' (section 55.52, subd. (a)(1). The latter term refers to a state or federal accessibility standard or regulation for making facilities, whether existing or newly constructed, accessible to persons with disabilities and includes the ADA and ADA accessibility guidelines. (section 55.52 subd. (a)(6).

Munson, *supra*, 46 Cal.4th 661, at 678 f.n. 12

Thus "construction-related accessibility claims" include those based on ADA "readily achievable" barrier removal obligations as well as those triggered under federal or state law by new construction or renovation, alteration, structural repair or additions. The Munson court found this legislative history relevant to the "intentionality" issue:

> The 2008 legislature was informed and may be presumed to have been aware that damages under the Unruh Civil Rights Act might be awarded for denial of ADA mandated access without proof of intentional discrimination.

Id. at 678.

2. DAMAGES COMPUTATION CASE PRECEDENTS

a. TALLARICO V. TRANS WORLD AIRLINES

In Tallarico v. Trans World Airlines (8th Cir. 1989) 881 F.2d 566, the federal court affirmed a trial court's assessment of $80,000 compensatory damages when a disabled woman was wrongfully denied access to an air carrier, even though she was able to fly out on another flight the same day.

In Tallarico, *supra*, a 14 year old disabled girl with cerebral palsy was awarded $80,000 emotional distress damages when TWA refused to allow her to board their plane. Evidence was that she cried, became very upset, and got angry. After the incident she became more withdrawn and stated the incident made her feel badly and had hurt her feelings. The Federal Appeals Court found sufficient evidence presented to support the jury's award.

b. HANKINS V. EL TORITO RESTAURANTS

[Discussed *supra* at I-J-b-(4) and *infra* at § I-"I"-3.] In Hankins v. El Torito Restaurants, Inc., et al. (1998) 63 Cal. App.4th 510, an award of $80,000 (emotional distress) statutory damages was affirmed on appeal for a single incident of disability discrimination. Damages were awarded, alternatively, under California Civil Code §§ 52 and 54.3

The damage award, after a court trial without a jury, was based on El Torito's ratified policy of refusing to allow a disabled person to use El Torito's first floor "employee's" restroom, even where his disability prohibited the plaintiff from climbing 18 stairs to reach the "public" men's restroom. Hankins specifically held that Civil Code § 54.1 could be violated by an illegal policy, unrelated to any architectural barrier.

Hankins was later cited in Stevens v. Optimum Health Institute—San Diego, 2011 WL3741055, at *p.14, for the holding that a defendant may not rely upon "an unsubstantiated and totally speculative concern" to justify a discriminatory practice. Hankins v. El Torito Restaurants, Inc., 63 Cal.App.4th 510, 520, 74 Cal.Rptr.2d 684 (1998) ("[W]e decline to find that an unsubstantiated and totally speculative concern that El Torito would be unable to prevent a patron from surreptitiously sampling food on the way to or from the [employee] rest room justifies denying a handicapped patron access to the only first floor restroom on the premises.")

> Another example of a policy discrimination was where a taxi cab company improperly allowed its drivers to charge a higher fare for disabled wheelchair users. (Cf. Riker v. Friendly Cab, et al. (N.D.Cal.) Case No. C07-4616 EDL)(Settled by Consent Decree, Order of Dec. 3, 2008)

c. H'S LORDSHIPS

The seminal H's Lordships Restaurant case (Weissman v. Terranova Industries, Specialty Restaurant Corporation, dba H's Lordships Restaurant, et al., Alameda County Superior Ct. Action No. 636384-4), resulted in a 1989 jury verdict. The jury awarded $35,000 compensatory damages and $250,000 punitive damages against the corporation and $250,000 in punitive damages against the corporation's president, based on applying Civil Code § 3294. The case was tried by legendary public interest attorney Sid Wolinsky, then with DREDF. Plaintiff's expert was Peter Margen, an experienced Oakland access consultant. The jury was outraged to learn that the contractor, carrying out $250,000 in restaurant alterations, had told the corporation president that a disabled ramp was legally required and could be added for $15,000, but the president had refused to install the ramp in order to save the expense!

Today, it is an open question whether Civil Code § 54.3's provision of a potential treble damage remedy precludes seeking "conscious disregard" punitive damages under Civil Code § 3294. Is the treble damage remedy exclusive? Section 54.3 Civil Code includes the language, "The remedies in this section are non-exclusive and are in addition to any other remedy provided by law."

d. THE "PIERCE COLLEGE" CASE

In Marvin Huezo v. Los Angeles Community College District (Los Angeles Pierce College) (C.D.Cal.) Case No. CV04-9772 MMM/JWJx, plaintiff obtained summary judgment after three years of litigation. Plaintiff, a 20 year old college student, had lost both his legs in an automobile accident while acting as a good Samaritan to help a stranger. Returning to college in a wheelchair just two months after losing his legs, Marvin Huezo discovered that many of his classes were now inaccessible to him, as were multiple paths of travel and most parking facilities on the campus. After defendants had tenaciously resisted admitting liability for several years of litigation, while continuing to subject the disabled plaintiff to multiple denials of access on a daily basis, the trial Court granted plaintiff summary judgment on multiple bases for liability. Huezo v. Los Angeles Community College District, 2007 WL 7289347 (C.D.Cal.). The Court also ordered the case to mediation. After negotiations, led by lead attorneys Patricia Barbosa and Jordon Metz of Los Angeles, plaintiff secured a substantial insurance policy limits settlement, for damages, and for attorney fees, litigation expenses and costs incurred to date. When defendants still failed to provide access improvements as previously represented by defendants, plaintiff went back to the Court a year later and secured a permanent injunction from Judge Margaret Morrow of the Central District. The injunction ordered major changes in Pierce College's policies and physical conditions for disabled persons. Huezo v. Los Angeles Community College District (Los Angeles Pierce College), 672 F.Supp.2d 1045 (C.D. 2008). On motion, the trial court also awarded additional attorneys fees to plaintiff for obtaining the permanent injunction. (Docket No. 66, November 17, 2008.)

e. WILSON V. HARIA AND GOGRI CORP. (DBA JACK IN THE BOX) HELD EACH VISIT MAY BE A COMPENSABLE VIOLATION

The Wilson v. Haria, *supra*, trial court awarded the $4,000 minimum statutory damages per Civil Code section 52 for each of plaintiff's visits to the inaccessible facility, although at each visit to the restaurant plaintiff had encountered multiple features which violated his rights, finding "Plaintiff is entitled to $52,000 for defendant's thirteen violations of the Unruh Act." (Id, 479F.Supp. 2d 1127, at 1141.) The Court also held that defendants had <u>waived</u> any "not readily achievable" defense by failing to plead it as an affirmative defense.

3. DAMAGES FOR DISCRIMINATORY POLICY, CIVIL CODE §§ 51 AND 54.1; <u>HANKINS V. EL TORITO</u> (1998) 63 CAL.APP.4TH 510

   a. DAMAGES TO MARK HANKINS FOR DISCRIMINATION AGAINST A DISABLED PERSON PER CIVIL CODE §§ 51 AND 54.1

   Mark Hankins, an amputee using crutches, suffered direct discrimination pursuant to Civil Code § 51, the Unruh Civil Rights Act, and pursuant to § 54.1's "full and equal access" standards: he was denied full and equal accommodations in a business establishment by the refusal by El Torito's management to allow him to use the first floor "employee's" restroom, when he was unable (being on crutches with only one leg) to climb stairs to the second floor "public" men's restroom.

   Civil Code § 52 states that any denial of rights under § 51 requires an award of:
   the actual damages and any amount that may be determined by a jury, or a court sitting without a jury, up to a maximum of three times the amount of actual damage, but in no case less than $1,000, and any attorney's fees that may be determined by the court in addition thereto suffered by any person denied the rights provided in § 51...

   Civil Code § 52(h) defines, "For purposes of this section 'actual damages' means special and general damages. This subdivision is declaratory of existing law." General damages include damages for physical, mental and emotional injuries; and for denial of Civil Rights. Civil Code § 52(b), incorporates any violation of the Americans With Disabilities Act of 1990 as a per se violation of § 52. However, this section was enacted after the <u>Hankins</u> trial, and was not relied upon by the trial judge.

   The <u>Hankins</u> trial court did not choose to invoke the treble damages remedy, but did award $80,000 compensatory damages for violation of civil rights and for emotional distress after the disabled plaintiff was humiliated by being reduced to urinating in a corner of the parking lot after being refused use of an available first floor "employees restroom" (when he couldn't climb the stairs to the second floor "public" men's restrooms on one leg and crutches). This award was affirmed by the appellate court in <u>Hankins v. El Torito Restaurants, et al.</u> (1998) 63 Cal. App.4th 510. (Instead of blaming the restaurant manager for poor judgment, the corporation argued at trial and on appeal that the manager correctly followed the corporation policy!)

   b. PUBLIC POLICY REQUIRES A BROAD INTERPRETATION OF THE UNRUH ACT (CIVIL CODE § 51 ET SEQ.)

The California Supreme Court has taught that the "Legislature's desire to banish [discrimination] from California's community life has led [that] court to interpret the acts' coverage `in the broadest sense possible.'" Isbister v. Boy's Club of Santa Cruz, Inc. 40 Cal.3d 72, 76 (1985) citing Burks v. Poppy Construction Co. 57 Cal.2d 463, 468 (1962)

Sullivan v. Vallejo City Unified School District (E.D. Cal. 1990) 731 F.Supp. 947 at 953

In a case interpreting California Civil Code section 51's application to issues of disabled access rights, the California Supreme Court recently (2009) reaffirmed the need that the Unruh Civil Rights Act (Sections 51 and 52)

> 'must be construed liberally in order to carry out its purpose' to 'create and preserve a nondiscriminatory environment in California business establishments by 'banishing' or 'eradicating' arbitrary, invidious discrimination by such establishments.' (Angelucci v. Century Supper Club (2007) 41 Cal.4th 160, 167, 59 Cal.Rptr.3d 142, 158 P.3d 718.) The Unruh Civil Rights Act 'serves as a preventive measure, without which it is recognized that businesses might fall into discriminatory practices.' (Ibid.)
> Munson v. Del Taco, (2009) 46 Cal.4th 661, 666.

c. A POLICY OF REFUSING USE OF AN AVAILABLE FIRST FLOOR EMPLOYEE'S RESTROOM TO DISABLED PERSONS UNABLE TO CLIMB STAIRS TO THE SECOND FLOOR PUBLIC RESTROOMS WAS HELD TO BE A DIRECT VIOLATION OF THE UNRUH ACT AND RESULTED IN SUBSTANTIAL DAMAGES

Plaintiff Mark Hankins' Civil Code § 51 cause of action was not based on "architectural barriers," but on the manager's refusal - pursuant to company policy - to allow plaintiff to use the employees' restroom. In defense counsel's opening statement he conceded that the refusal to allow Mark Hankins to use the employee's restroom was based on an El Torito policy to refuse to allow any persons to use the employee restroom, even when they were physically unable to climb the 18 stairs to the only "public restrooms" in the building. To claim that El Torito did not discriminate because they also refused use of the employee restroom to able-bodied persons - persons who did not need to use it - is sophistry. This kind of "equality" is reminiscent of the observation by 19th century writer Anatole France: "The Law in its majesty equally forbids both rich and poor to sleep under bridges and beg in the streets." (from The Red Lily)

Defendants never identified the El Torito manager who refused use of the employees' restroom to Mark Hankins, but he was only "following orders" in light of El Torito's admitted policy in refusing to allow Mr. Hankins to use the "employees'" restroom and directing him to go across a large parking lot to (try to) find a restroom at "another restaurant." Mark Hankins had to leave his wife and friends at the restaurant, go on crutches down the six stairs at the restaurant's entrance and across the parking lot. Finally, after finding that the "other" restaurant was closed, he was forced to relieve himself in a corner of the El Torito's parking lot, embarrassed that his 6'8" height and use of crutches made him the unwanted object of public attention.

Mark Hankins testified to his embarrassment and humiliation, and to having recurring thoughts for months about his demeaning experience. His wife, Maria Hankins, testified to observing the effect on her husband, and about his continuing to brood over the event.

In seeking damages from the trial court, Mr. Hankins' attorneys, Sidney J. Cohen and Paul L. Rein, argued that defendants' discrimination "added insult to injury," adding psychological damage to the physical pain and frustrations already caused by Mr. Hankins' disability. Their arguments recognized that there was no "magic way" to place an exact figure on the value our community, as represented by the court, placed on the personal rights and dignity of a disabled person, or on the emotional shock a disabled person could suffer from being denied access and restroom facilities because of physical barriers; then being refused the use of an available restroom; and then being told to go down stairs and leave the building, on crutches, to search for some other business' restroom. Defendants stipulated that Mark Hankins' treatment by the El Torito manager was part of a regular policy, ratified by El Torito and its parent corporation. They attempted to justify this policy on appeal, all the way to requesting a hearing before the California Supreme Court (which was denied).

The trial court may further have determined that this policy was not "coincidental" when it assessed the defendants' general attitude including the parent company's apparent representation in a "Disclosure" SEC "10 K" Statement to shareholders that it effectively intended to continue to resist making its other restaurants accessible, and to appeal any "adverse" decision which might have the effect of requiring access at their other restaurants![60]

d. DISABILITY DISCRIMINATION IS ANALOGOUS TO RACIAL OR SEX DISCRIMINATION AS TO THE DAMAGE CAUSED

---

[60] Although not discussed in the appellate decision, the Hankins Defendants' also maintained an unusual sign at the front entrance of their Restaurant: "PREMISES NOT WHEEL CHAIR EQUIPPED." Defendants' Interrogatory Answer admitted that this sign was intended as a "warning" to disabled persons, and defendants' pleadings alleged that plaintiff Mark Hankins was "contributorily negligent" for "ignoring this warning!" Practitioners should watch for similar evidence of bad intentions when intentionality becomes relevant in contested litigation, on issues such as the appropriateness of treble damages per section 52 or section 54.3 Civil Code. (No treble damages were awarded in Hankins; the $80,000 award was compensatory only.)(No proof of wrongful intent is needed to prove a violation of the ADA even when incorporated into section 51(f) Civil Code. Munsen v. Del Taco, supra.)

Counsel argued that the shock to Mark Hankins as a disabled person was analogous to the shock of an African-American <u>refused</u> the use of public accommodations because of his race. Indeed, subsequent to the <u>Hankins</u> trial, the California Supreme Court held that disability discrimination can be as harmful as racial or sexual discrimination. As recognized by the California Supreme Court in 1998:
> Disability discrimination is indistinguishable in many ways from race and sex discrimination. Specifically, it can "attack the individual's sense of self-worth in much the same fashion as race or sex discrimination."

<u>City of Moorpark v. Sup. Ct.</u> (1998) 18 Cal.4th 1143, 1160

e. DAMAGES EXAMPLE: HANKINS' TESTIMONY REGARDING DEFENDANTS' DIS-CRIMINATORY TREATMENT AND HIS RESULTING ANGER, EMBARRASSMENT, AND PHYSICAL PAIN

Defendants' discriminatory treatment of Mark Hankins on the occasion of his 1991 visit to the Burlingame El Torito restaurant caused embarrassment, anger, and humiliation, as a result of his being required to relieve himself "in the bushes like an animal." Defendants presented no evidence to rebut the events that took place on the occasion of Mr. Hankins' visit or the emotional impact resulting to Mr. Hankins from the discriminatory treatment he suffered.[61]

f. "FULL AND EQUAL ACCESS" REQUIRED

As is sometimes the case in access litigation, the <u>Hankins</u> defendants alleged that, despite barriers, the plaintiff was "able" to access the restaurant and "able" to get up the six stairs on his one leg and on crutches. Under defendants' thesis, if plaintiff had come in a wheelchair but was <u>carried</u> up the stairs, or <u>crawled</u> up the stairs, defendants would assert plaintiff suffered no damages. Plaintiff was not provided "full and equal access." The issue is not whether or not a disabled person was "able" to "get into" the restaurant; the issue is whether he was denied "full and equal access." (Civil Code §54.1) To claim that Mark Hankins was not "denied access" because he was "able" to get up the stairs, with difficulty, using his crutches, is absurd. (Paraplegic rock climber Mark Wellman was "able" to climb the 3,600 foot rock face of El Capitan in Yosemite National Park in ten days on the rock face - using arm strength with a special pulley system, rising six inches at a time, "No more difficult than 7,200 chin-ups!" Neither Mark Wellman, nor any other disabled person, should be subjected to the indignity of crawling up the front stairs to gain entry to the El Torito Restaurant or any other public accommodation.) In 2005 the United States Supreme Court decided <u>Tennessee v. Lane</u> (2004) 541 U.S. 509, 124 S.Ct. 1978. By a 5-4 vote the court found an ADA Title II violation after

---

[61] In addition to the denial of access to the employees' restroom, physical barriers blocked plaintiff's full and equal access past the six front stairs at the restaurant's entrance. Mr. Hankins was on crutches and one leg (due to problems with his prosthetic leg) and in pain when climbing or later descending the stairs. However the Court did not base its liability decision on the construction and alteration history of the restaurant but only on its policy. <u>Hankins v. El Torito</u>, *supra*.

a litigant had to crawl up steps to make a court appearance in an inaccessible state courthouse. In a previous Alameda County Superior Court case, Michael Pachovas v. Berkeley/ Alameda County Action No. 713973-8 (1996), plaintiff, a quadriplegic wheelchair user arrested after a political demonstration, successfully sued Alameda County (and the City of Berkeley) when he was arrested at a political demonstration, taken 30 miles to the County Jail, and then held for seven hours in an inaccessible holding cell at the "Santa Rita" County jail. A few days later he was unable to attend his own court arraignment (with other arrested activists) because the courtroom was on the second floor of a building with no elevator. His lawsuit in Alameda County Superior Court under existing California law, was successful in obtaining a settlement which required Alameda County to construct an elevator to access the second floor courtrooms, and to construct an accessible holding cell at the Alameda County Jail at Santa Rita. The City of Berkeley was required to construct an accessible entrance to (and accessible holding cell at) the Berkeley Police Department; and to end the City of Berkeley's policy of taking disabled persons arrested in Berkeley all the way out to the County Jail at Santa Rita - 30 miles away - because the Berkeley City Jail was not accessible! (Substantial damages were also obtained by settlement and attorney fees were awarded by motion to the Court.)

> Legislation effective January 1, 2009, clarified that a disabled person was denied full and equal access if he personally encountered or was deterred by a barrier which caused plaintiff to experience, inter alia, "difficulty, discomfort or embarrassment because of the violation." Civil Code §§ 55.56 (b) and 55.56 (c).

Finally, the January 7, 2011, 9th Circuit en banc decision in Chapman v. Pier 1 Imports (USA) Inc., 631 F.3d 939 made clear that full and equal access was denied even if a barrier did not "completely preclude the plaintiff from entering or using a facility in any way." Id. at p 947, citing Doran, *supra*, 524 F.3d at 1041, n. 4, (stating that the ADA "does not limit its antidiscrimination mandate to barriers that completely prohibit access"). Rather, the barrier need only interfere with the plaintiff's "full and equal enjoyment" of the facility. 42 U.S.C. § 12182(a). Chapman, *supra*, at p 947.

g. DAMAGES STANDARD: THE COURT SHOULD AWARD GENERAL DAMAGES FOR DEFENDANTS' DISCRIMINATORY TREATMENT AND FOR THE SPECIFIC PAIN AND SUFFERING, ANGER AND HUMILIATION SUFFERED BY A DISABLED PLAINTIFF

In a Civil Rights case damages should be awarded both for the denial of "full and equal access" (per Civil Code § 54.3) and for the specific physical mental and emotional suffering that the particular plaintiff experienced: For example, damages were suffered by plaintiff Mark Hankins when he was refused use of an available first floor "employees'" restroom and was told to relieve himself at another restaurant across the parking lot (which restaurant turned out to be closed). This forced the disabled plaintiff, an amputee on one leg and using crutches, to urinate in "a bush," "angered and humiliated by this experience." Hankins v. El Torito Restaurants, Inc., et al., 63 Cal.App.4th 510 (1998). In Mark Hankins' case, the trial judge, sitting in a court trial, set plaintiff's damages at $80,000 (the same amount that had been set by the federal court in the (8th Circuit) Tallerico case)[62] This award was affirmed on appeal. (The trial court judge was a reputedly "conservative" Presiding Judge in a "conservative" jurisdiction, San Mateo County, Honorable Walter Harrington.)

The amount of damages is within the sound discretion of the trial court. Although it is difficult to make a comparison with the results of other cases which have different facts, they provide some guidance. The appellate courts will affirm a damage assessment which is supported by sufficient evidence. For example, in Bihun v. AT&T (1993) 12 Cal.App.4th 976, *supra*, an appellate court affirmed $1.5 million in compensatory damages and $500,000 punitive damages for the victim of sexual harassment at work. Plaintiff's attorney (in this 1993 case) was awarded attorney fees at $450/hour.

In Tallarico v. Trans World Airlines, *supra*, the federal appellate court affirmed an $80,000 general damages award for the denial of access to an airline flight to a physically disabled 14 year old girl, despite the fact that she was able to take another flight out later the same day.

In two other cases which were settled at Eastern District (Sacramento) court-supervised settlement conferences, two 16 year old minor girls received similar major damages awards in two separate cases where violations were major and known to defendants. In each of these cases there was at least the potential for a treble damage award, and each monetary settlement was entered after settlement of injunctive relief issues, which guaranteed "full and equal access." In Christine Burke, a minor, by her Guardian Ad Litem Randy Burke v. Heavenly Valley Limited Partnership, et al. (E.D.Cal.) Case No. CIV-S04-0957 DFL/PAN, a young woman required to use a wheelchair because of her spina bifida disability, traveled with her family on a recently completed, $20 million gondola, only to encounter 42 stairs as the only way to reach the ground at the terminus. Her family carried her wheelchair down while she painfully sat on each stair and lowered herself down, and later back up the 42 stairs. The young plaintiff achieved injunctive relief, which included installation of an elevator to bypass the stairs, $80,000 damages, and payment of her statutory

---

[62] Tallarico v. Trans World Airlines (8th Cir. 1989) 881 F.2d 566.

attorney fees by defendant.

In a lawsuit against the City of Sacramento for lack of live performance theater wheelchair seating, except at the very back of the Sacramento Community Theater, plaintiff, a 16 year old minor, received Court-approved $50,000 damages plus payment of statutory attorney fees and an agreement by the City to remedy multiple access problems. The remediation included constructing an ingenious "bridge" route to supply four disabled seats and four companion seats in the 6th row of this live performance theater. Alexandra Stoffel, a Minor, v. Sacramento Community Center Theater, (E.D.Cal.) Case No. 2:08-CV-08-1076 JAM/GGH, settled by Consent Decree (2009).[63]

Section 55.56 California Civil Code, effective January 1, 2009, allows damages to a qualified disabled person who personally encountered a barrier or is deterred on a particular occasion, "if the plaintiff experienced difficulty, discomfort or embarrassment because of the violation."

h. PUBLIC POLICY SUPPORTS LIABILITY AGAINST NON-COMPLYING BUSINESSES

In Hankins v. El Torito, et al, *supra*, plaintiff's counsel argued that if defendants succeeded in avoiding their obligation to provide "full and equal" disabled access, this would encourage other major corporations to avoid the costs of improving access, if they thought that they could get away with it. Yet most California businesses have obeyed the law and have spent their money to comply with access requirements when performing alterations, or when they made the required cost analysis per § 301(9) of Title III the Americans With Disabilities Act of 1990 and complied by providing all "readily achievable" access features. Most businesses have not resorted to misrepresentation or deception to avoid providing access. Compliant businesses have a right to see that no "unfair competition" cost advantage goes to businesses that cheat by "saving money" by not providing access.[64]

Plaintiff's Counsel in Hankins argued that a decision which clearly and unequivocally enforced the full requirements for disabled access in California, would set a precedent that could affect access decisions in untold thousands of other corporate analyses for many years to come, and that this would have a widespread and meaningful effect

---

[63] The solution for a complicated and challenging access improvement (6th row disabled seating instead of 34th row in a theater with stairs on every aisle) was designed by access consultant Jonathan Adler of Santa Cruz, California. (See Theater photo at section IX-J, in Appendix to this book, a composite photo from defendants' website.)

[64] Plaintiffs might consider using Business and Professions code section 17200 to attack "unfair business practices" as a cause of action.

on access to public facilities for all disabled persons in California. Hopefully, the trial court's order (awarding $80,000 damages and $403,000 attorneys fees), and the published appellate opinion of the 1st District Court of Appeal in Hankins v. El Torito Restaurants, Inc., et al. (1998) 63 Cal. App.4th 510, may have had such effect.

After remand to the trial court after the published decision, the trial court awarded an additional $323,000 attorney fees for plaintiff successfully defending the appeal, including a 1.4 public interest multiplier "enhancement" because of the important precedents set by the published opinion. These included application of section 54.1 Civil Code's "full and equal access" requirement to a policy violation (denial of use to a disabled of the first floor "employees" restroom when public restroom on second floor) without reference to any violation of construction or alteration regulations. Such a policy violation may also violate the Unruh Civil Rights Act, Civil Code section 51ff.

4. TREBLE DAMAGES POTENTIAL

   a. PER CIVIL CODE §§ 52 AND 54.3
   In the discretion of the court, the "actual" damages for violation of Civil Rights under Civil Code §§ 51 or 54.1 may be trebled pursuant to either Civil Code §§ 52 or 54.3. This should be done where it would serve the public policy purpose of placing special value on the damage that discrimination inflicts, and the recognition of the importance of "full and equal access" to a disabled person. (However, the Hankins court did not award treble damages, stating that it's $80,000 damage award was "compensatory.")

   The $80,000 damages in the Tallarico, *supra*, case[65] were "general" damages under the Air Carrier Access Act. Civil Code §§ 52 and 54.3 allow the trier of fact to treble any "actual" damages (defined per § 52(h) as general and special damages) otherwise awarded. Counsel can in any case with appropriate facts, seek treble damages, for example, to reflect multiple violations of plaintiff's rights. The court or a jury must set appropriate damages in the trier of fact's role as "conscience of the community" to set an example and deter similar violations.
   I am, however, unaware of any published case which has analyzed the standards for treble damages under Civil Code § 54.3. (But no treble damages against a

---

[65] Tellarico v. Transworld Airlines, 181 F.2d 566 was an 8th Circuit 1989 case which may have influenced the Hankins court in setting the same damages level for a single incident ($80,000). Generally discrimination on airlines is not covered by the ADA, although "public interest" result in California may be eligible for an attorney fee award per California Code of Civil Procedure section 1021.5. discrimination that occurs in California may be covered under the Unruh Act. The Air Carrier Access Act, which may not have a statutory attorney fees provision, may federally "preempt" claims relating to "services" on an airline. However a case which achieves a significant "public interest" result in California may be eligible for an attorney fee award per California Code of Civil Procedure section 1021.5.

public entity. Cal. Govt. Code § 818, as "punishing.")

b. WHILE PROVING WRONGFUL INTENT IS NOT NEEDED TO PROVE LIABILITY UNDER CIVIL CODE §§ 54 AND 54.1, EVIDENCE OF "BAD INTENT" MAY SHOW A BASIS FOR TREBLE DAMAGES OR EVEN PUNITIVE DAMAGES IN AN EXTREME CASE; BUT CAVEAT CALIFORNIA SUPREME COURT LIMITATIONS

Proving a defendant's wrongful "intent" is not an element of the Civil Code § 54.1 architectural barriers civil rights violation. (See Donald v. Café Royale, *supra*, and Hankins v. El Torito, *supra*.) However, a defendant's knowing refusal to fix an access problem even after being notified of its legal obligation to do so would seem an appropriate basis for treble damages, per Civil Code § 54.3. Further, under certain extenuated circumstances, such as refusing a known obligation to provide access where a dangerous condition resulted, this could constitute "despicable conduct" in "conscious disregard" for the rights of disabled persons, justifying punitive damages under the standards of Civil Code § 3294. (See holdings of Judge Saundra Armstrong, U.S. District Court, Northern District, in Fisher v. Millennium Bank (Case No. C96-00800 SBA) and of Northern District Chief Judge Thelton Henderson in Presta v. Peninsula Corridor Joint Powers Board, et al. (1998) 16 F. Supp. 2d 1134.) (See also discussion, *infra* at Section II.C.7 as to requirements of "intentional" violation to get damages directly under Title II) However, other courts have held to the contrary, including a later opinion by Judge Armstrong in Freeman v. Alta Bates, No. C04-2019 SBA, Order of October 12, 2004. In Freeman, Judge Armstrong said she was persuaded by later case law that section 3294 Civil Code punitive damages could not be awarded based on a violation of section 54.1 Civil Code, (but could still be recovered if the underlying violation was based on a cause of action for "negligence per se.") 2004 WL 2326369, at p. 6.

The availability of treble damages under either section 52 or 54.3 Civil Code was recognized by the 9th Circuit in reversing certification of a mandatory "class" of disabled persons. The appellate court held that the district court's approval of the class "settlement" failed to provide individual class members notice and the right to "opt out" of the class, with regard to individual damages, including possible treble damages. Molski v. Gleich, 318 F.3d 937, at 950 - 951. (Gleich also cited Koire v. Metro Car Wash 40 Cal.3d 24 (1985) as to the "punitive nature" of treble damages under sections 52 and 54.3: Gleich, *supra*, at 951.)

Similarly, while the California Supreme Court held in Munson v. Del Taco., 46 Cal.4th 661 (2009), that no proof of wrongful intent was necessary to show a violation of section 51(b) Civil Code, based on an incorporated violation of the ADA, proof of malice or conscious disregard may be relevant toward proving treble damages per section 52 Civil Code.

If allowed by the Court, "bad intent" evidence might also be relevant toward a finding of punitive damages per section 3294 Civil Code standards. It is unclear whether the treble damage provision of sections 52 and 54.3 Civil Code preclude seeking section 3294 punitive damages in an appropriately severe case. However punitive damages have recently have recently been limited by the United States Supreme Court, for example in its "Exxon Valdez" decision in Baker v. Exxon Shipping Company 554 U.S. 471. (June 25, 2008). This decision limited punitive damages which a trial court Jury had awarded for Exxon's conduct resulting in the massive "Exxon Valdez" Alaska oil spill. The Supreme Court reduced punitive damages (under Admiralty law) to a 1 to 1 ratio with compensatory damages. Similarly in State Farm v. Campbell, (2003) 538 U.S. 408; 123 S.Ct. 1513, the Supreme Court set out standards which significantly limited the availability and scope of punitive damages, apparently limiting such damages to a single digit multiplier of compensatory damages, in most cases regardless of a defendant's culpability or financial resources. Critics have complained that this lessened the effect that a potential award of large punitive damages could have as a deterrent effect on illegal practices by large and financially powerful corporations.

5. ARE DAILY STATUTORY DAMAGES AVAILABLE?
   a. ARGUMENT FOR DAILY STATUTORY DAMAGES FOR CONTINUING AND KNOWING VIOLATION, PER CIVIL CODE § 54.3

   Defendants' delay in providing access could be measured from the day of a plaintiff's visit or from the date of service of his Complaint, or from prior written notice to defendants. The court could find, in light of defendants' continuing knowing violations, that every day of refusal to take steps to take action to correct the access deficiencies is a separate statutory violation of Civil Code § 54.1, justifying actual damages and minimum damages of $1,000 per violation, per section 54.3, even in the absence of any "actual" damages. (James Donald v. Café Royale, *supra*.) If the court finds that each day without access constitutes a separate violation, the period from the date of first violation to the date Defendants finally provided an accessible restroom, may be significant! A daily penalty would appropriately recognize that there is a time requirement for providing access, and every day that is delayed is one more day that the disabled are denied "full and equal access."
   (See Botosan v. Fitzhugh, discussed *infra*.)

   Caveat: at least one court has criticized a plaintiff's alleged intentional tactics of waiting a year after an incident to file a complaint, and then alleging statutory daily damages for defendants failure to remedy violations they had not been aware of. Molski v. Evergreen Dynasty Co., 9th Cir. 2007) 500 F.3d 1047 at 1060, discussed *infra*, section "e".

b. A 90 DAY COMPLIANCE PERIOD IS SET BY CODE

Per Government Code § 4452, incorporated by reference into Health & Safety Code § 19955, 90 days is set out as the time allowed for compliance, and the word "shall" appears to make this standard mandatory:

> Any unauthorized deviation from such regulations or building standards shall be rectified by full compliance within 90 days of the discovery of the deviation. (Emphasis added)

It can be argued that a business certainly "discovers" it's deviation, at the latest, when it is served with a complaint and summons! Failure to provide access within a reasonable period of time after actual notice might be a factor justifying enhanced damages at trial. Certainly, in negotiating or obtaining a court order for injunctive relief, the statutory "90 days" is at least a guide post for how swiftly compliance should be supplied, although a longer period may be reasonable when major construction changes are needed for access. A "reasonable" time period could be worked out by the parties in settlement negotiations. However until access is finally supplied, a defendant government or business entity will still be denying access to all disabled persons who encounter continuing barriers, and defendants will still be leaving themselves subject to potential lawsuits by other disabled persons who are denied access in the interim.[66] Therefore the earliest possible compliance is in everyone's best interest!

c. BOTOSAN V. FITZHUGH ALLOWED PLEADING DAILY DAMAGES

In Botosan v. Fitzhugh (S.D.Cal.) 13 F.Supp.2d 1047, the court upheld the pleading of plaintiff's complaint seeking "daily damages in the amount of $1000 per day," based on Civil Code §§ 52 and 54.3. Defendant argued plaintiff had only been to defendant's restaurant once. The court held plaintiff had alleged he was "being subjected to discrimination" because "plaintiff cannot return to or make use of the... restaurant... Read in the light most favorable to plaintiff, this means that plaintiff has been deterred from going to the Cojita restaurant on a daily basis. This deterrence alone suffices to lay claim to actual damages." The court quoted the following from Arnold v. United Artists Theatre Circuit, Inc. 866 F.Supp. 433, 439 (N.D.Cal. 1994) in holding the pleading sufficient on a deterrence basis:

> §§ 54.3 and 52... extend to claims based on incidents of deterrence...

---

[66] In Leiken v. Squaw Valley, *supra*, the resort defended liability as to its "High Camp" inaccessible (up several steps) four restaurants (reachable only by the tram), and other facilities on the basis of Sqauw's alleged "safety policy" of refusing access to their tram to any disabled wheelchair users. They started actually enforcing this policy after they were sued, (resulting in four more lawsuits being brought against them) before the Court (Hon. Lawrence K. Karlton) ruled that their policy itself violated both the ADA and section 54.1 California Civil Code. Squaw Valley immediately ceased their policy, and settled the case with an agreement to make all "High Camp" facilities accessible, and to pay damages and attorneys fees. Squaw Valley also made the entry to the (ground level) Tram building accessible, as well as the four restaurants and restrooms at High Camp.

where a plaintiff can prove that violation of applicable California disability access standards deterred [him] on a particular occasion from attempting to attend a place of public accommodation, that plaintiff states a claim for... damages under § 54.3 and § 52.

Botosan, *supra*, at 1051-1052.

Effective January 1, 2009, deterrence was codified as one basis for damages when California adopted section 55.56 Civil Code.

d. DAILY DAMAGES ON A "DETERRENCE" BASIS

In Brenda Pickern v. Best Western Timber Cove Lodge, 2002 WL202442 (E.D. Cal. 2002) The court (Honorable William Shubb) addressed the issue of whether plaintiff can recover damages for each day she was deterred from visited the facility under California law:

> Although the question remains unsettled as a matter of state law, federal courts have not hesitated to rule on this issue. See Arnold v. United Artists, 866 F.Supp. 433, 439 (1994); Botosan v. Fitzhugh, 13 F.Supp.2d 1047 (S.D.Cal. 1998). In fact this court recently found that daily damages could be recovered under the state statutes in question. Loskot v. Lulu's Restaurant, No. CIVS-00-1497 WBS/PAN (E.D.Cal. 2000).

Id. at p. 8.

e. CAVEAT USE OF DAILY DAMAGES CLAIM AS CONDEMNED BY 9TH CIRCUIT IN MOLSKI V. EVERGREEN DYNASTY CORPORATION, BASED ON IMPROPER "LITIGATION STRATEGY"

In Molski v. Evergreen Dynasty Co. (9th Cir. 2007) 500 F.3d 1047,[67] the federal panel criticized plaintiff Molski for, inter alia, seeking:

> damages of not less than $4000 for each day that a facility did not comply with the ADA. Because Molski would often wait to file suit until a full year elapsed since his visit to the defendants' establishments, defendants often faced claims for statutory damages of over one million dollars. While Molski's claim for daily damages might have been legally justified, it was not clearly erroneous for the district court to find that Molski's litigation strategy evidenced an intent to harass businesses into cash settlements.

Id. at 1060.

(In a footnote the court cited several district court decisions which "disagree about whether a plaintiff may seek daily damages under California Civil Code sections 52(a) and 54.3(a).")

6. STATUTORY DAMAGES ON A "PER VISIT" BASIS

In Wilson v. Haria and Gogri Corp. dba Jack in the Box, et al. (E.D.Cal. 2007) 479 F.Supp.2d 1127, Judge Lawrence Karlton rejected any "intentionality" requirement

---

[67] This case was later denied en banc hearing by "a majority of the non-recused active members of the court," with Chief Judge Kozinski, and Judges Berzon, Pregerson, Reinhardt, Hawkins, McKeown, Wardlaw, Fletcher, and Paez dissenting.

for a violation of Civil Code § 51(b), based on an incorporated violation of the ADA per section 51(f), and held that each visit by the disabled plaintiff to a facility which was "inaccessible" in multiple respects, constituted a single violation of Civil Code § 51[68]. Plaintiff was entitled to $4,000 statutory damages, per Civil Code § 52, "per violation." (Id. at 1141.) Although the court held that the statutory damages were $4,000 per violation, it also held that encountering multiple violations during one visit was still only one "violation," at least for minimum statutory damages purposes. Because plaintiff testified to 13 visits, without contradictory evidence, the Court awarded $52,000 damages, as minimum statutory damages.

In Munson v. Del Taco, *supra*, the California Supreme Court noted the restrictions placed on damages claims filed after January 1, 2009, per SB 1608:

> [T]he new legislation . . . restricts the availability of statutory damages under sections 52 and 54.3, permitting their recovery only if an accessibility violation actually denied the plaintiff full and equal access, that is, only if "the plaintiff personally encountered the violation on a particular occasion, or the plaintiff was deterred from accessing a place of public accommodation on a particular occasion (§ 55.56, subd. (b)). It also limits statutory damages to one assessment per occasion of access denial, rather than being based on the number of accessibility standards violated. (Id., subd. (e).)

Munson, *supra*, 46 Cal.4th 661, at 677-678.

In so ruling the California Supreme Court and the California Legislature each came to the same conclusion that Judge Karlton had reached in Wilson v. Haria and Gorgi, *supra*.

7. PUNITIVE DAMAGES - AVAILABILITY AND STANDARDS

   a. LAW: PLAINTIFF MAY BE ENTITLED TO PUNITIVE DAMAGES UNDER THE CRITERIA OF CIVIL CODE § 3294 WHERE OPPRESSION, FRAUD, MALICE OR CONSCIOUS DISREGARD FOR THE RIGHTS OF DISABLED PERSONS HAVE BEEN PROVEN IN ADDITION TO VIOLATIONS OF THE CIVIL RIGHTS ACTS

Defendants may allege that Civil Code § 54.3 does not include punitive damages. They are correct. Section 54.1 does not require any intent for a violation (Donald v. Café Royale (1990) 218 Cal.App.3d 168), and therefore damages awarded for a violation of § 54.1 alone, as described under § 54.3, are limited to actual damages and up to three times actual damages. However, § 54.1 and § 54.3 are for the primary purpose of compensating a disabled person whose rights have been violated, with or without any wrongful intent, and not for the purpose of punishing but for enforcing the law, and encouraging compliance. (Donald v. Café Royale,

---

[68] The California Supreme Court later agreed with the Wilson v. Haria analysis that no intentionality was needed to prove a violation of the Unruh Civil Rights Act (Section 51 and 52 Civil Code) based upon the incorporation of an ADA violation per section 51(f). Munson v. Del Taco, Inc., 46 Cal.4th.661 (2009).

supra, 218 CA.3d 168, at 177-178.)

Civil Code § 3294 has a different purpose. It allows that in any action (except an action arising from contract), where it is proven by clear and convincing evidence that the defendant has been guilty of oppression, fraud or malice, the plaintiff, in addition to the actual damages, may recover damages "for the sake of example and by way of punishing the defendant." The purposes of punitive damages are stated in § 3294 and do not have the purpose of compensation. They have the purpose of punishing, setting an example, and deterring both the defendant and others from similar wrongful conduct. This being the case, when the additional factors of fraud, oppression or malice are shown, the public purposes of § 3294 allow punitive damages for any tort violation. This was the holding, for example, of Kelly v. Yee (1989) 213 Cal.App.3d 336, which distinguished the purposes of another statute which, even though it allowed trebled damages, (for a rent situation violation), still upheld the additional "public purpose" application of Civil Code § 3294.

b. PUNITIVE DAMAGES MAY BE AVAILABLE PURSUANT TO CIVIL CODE § 3294 FOR ACTIONS WHICH WERE EITHER 1) MALICIOUS OR IN CONSCIOUS DISREGARD OF THE RIGHTS OF DISABLED PERSONS, 2) OPPRESSIVE, OR 3) FRAUDULENT

Civil Code § 3294(a) states:

> In an action for the breach of an obligation not arising from contract, where it is proven by clear and convincing evidence that the defendant has been guilty of oppression, fraud or malice, the plaintiff in addition to the actual damages, may recover damages for the sake of example and by way of punishing the defendant.

Section 3294(b) deals with corporate punitive damage obligations based on ratification of the acts of an employee; for example where the actions and policies of defendants' employees are ratified, despite knowledge by defendant of the fraudulent conduct and conscious disregard of the rights of disabled persons committed by their employees.

Section 3294(c) offers the following definitions:
  (1) "Malice" means conduct which is intended by the defendant to cause injury to the plaintiff or despicable conduct which is carried out by the defendant with a willful and conscious disregard of the rights or safety of others.

  (2) "Oppression" means despicable conduct which subjects a person to cruel and unjust hardship in conscious disregard of that person's rights.

(3) "Fraud" means an intentional <u>misrepresentation, deceit, or concealment</u> of a material fact known to the defendant with the intention on the part of the defendant of thereby depriving a person of property or legal rights or otherwise causing injury. (Emphasis added)

The Supreme Court for California has repeatedly stated:
> The purpose of punitive damages is to penalize wrongdoers in a way that will deter them and others from repeating the wrongful conduct in the future.

<u>Wyatt v. Union Mortgage Co.</u> (1972) 24 Cal.3d 773, 790; <u>Neil v. Farmers Insurance Exchange</u> (1978) 21 Cal.3d 910, 928, fn.13

There is extensive legal authority for an award of Civil Code § 3294 punitive damages based on discrimination, where the elements of malice, fraud or oppression exist <u>in addition</u> to the elements necessary to show discrimination under the Unruh Act. See <u>Commodore Homes System, Inc. v. Superior Ct.</u> (1982) 32 Cal.3d 211, 215, 220-221, 185 Cal.Rptr. 270; <u>Monge v. Superior Ct.</u> (1986) 176 Cal.App.3d 503, 222 Cal.Rptr. 64, 67. <u>Commodore Home Systems v. Superior Court</u>, *supra*, held that when a statute recognizes a cause of action for violation of a right, <u>all forms of relief</u> granted to civil litigants generally are available, including punitive damages in appropriate cases, unless a contrary legislative intent appears.

Similarly, <u>Kelly v. Yee</u> (1989) 212 Cal.App.3d 336, held, inter alia, that statutory damages under a San Francisco rent control ordinance, requiring mandatory treble damages, could be awarded at the same time as, and independently of, punitive damages pursuant to Civil Code § 3294. While defendants alleged that the award of treble damages, mandated under § 37.9(f) of the San Francisco Administrative Code, was preempted by Civil Code § 3294 which authorized punitive damages, the court held the that there was <u>no preemption</u>:

> Local legislation is preempted only where it is in conflict with general law. (<u>People Ex Rel Deukmejian v. County of Mendocino</u> (1984) 36 Cal.3d 476, 484) Treble damages under § 37.9(f) of the San Francisco Rent Control Ordinance serve an entirely different legislative objective than punitive damages under Civil Code § 3294. Such damages promote effective enforcement of the ordinance on behalf of low income tenants, while punitive damages usually serve to deter the sort of extreme disregard for the rights of others that "decent citizens should not have to tolerate." (Flyer's Body Shop Profit Sharing Plan v. Ticor Title Ins. Co. (1986) 185 Cal.App.3d 1149, 1154)

<u>Kelly v. Yee</u> 213 Cal.App.3d 336 at 341-2.

Conversely it may be argued that the Civil Code § 54.3 measure of damages is not exclusive, if the facts additionally show "despicable conduct" in "conscious disregard for the rights or safety" of disabled persons, one definition of "malice," per Civil Code § 3294(c)(1). Section 3294(c)(2) defines "oppression" as "despicable conduct that subjects a person to cruel and unjust hardship in conscious disregard of that person's rights."

Since Civil Code § 54.1 can be violated without any wrongful intent, (Donald v. Café Royale, (1990) 218 Cal.App.3d 168), and since even a Civil Rights plaintiff who has suffered no actual damages is entitled to $1,000 minimum statutory damage award (per Civil Code § 54.3) for each violation, even when the trial judge makes a factual finding that the plaintiff suffered no emotional distress, (cf. Donald v. Café Royale, supra), other standards must control when the additional factors of actual or implied fraudulent or malicious intent are proven.

Civil Rights statutes and disabled access statutes are intended to be given a broad interpretation, to maximize the purpose of these laws, and to maximize the integration of disabled persons into all aspects of social and economic life. (See Government Code § 19230). Yet, defendants sometimes urge interpretations which limit the protections for disabled persons. Defendants may attempt to argue that the very statute guaranteeing "full and equal" access sets up a shield to protect callous corporations from the consequences of their deliberate and "conscious disregard" of the rights of physically disabled men, women and children.

Did the Legislature propose that defendants that act with conscious disregard toward disabled persons should be rewarded by being given special status and immunity from Civil Code § 3294 requirements? If the evidence shows "conscious disregard," defendants should be chastised for their intentional decision to avoid and delay providing access for disabled persons.
[See discussion in section I-J-7-e, infra, re: opinions on this issue.]

"Conscious disregard" under Civil Code § 3294 was the basis for a large punitive damage jury verdict in Alameda County Superior Court in 1989. The pioneer and precedent setting case of Julie Weissman v. Terranova Industries, Specialty Restaurant Corporation, dba H's Lordships Restaurant, et al., Case No. 636384-4, was a case tried by the excellent disability rights attorney Sid Wolinsky.[69] Plaintiff, a quadriplegic and wheelchair using student, took her mother and father to dinner, since she knew H's Lordships had recently undergone major remodeling, and therefore she expected the restaurant to be accessible. Instead she had to be <u>carried</u> down stairs to her table, embarrassing her efforts to show her parents her "independence." The trial resulted in a jury award of $36,000 emotional distress damages, $250,000 punitive damages against the corporation, and $250,000 punitive damages against the corporation's president, sued as an individual defendant: the jury found this corporate president had personally refused to provide an access ramp during a major remodel of the restaurant, because of a dispute about the ramp's cost. A contractor testified at trial that he'd personally advised the corporation's president of the legal requirement to provide an interior access ramp during a $250,000 restaurant renovation, and had offered to install a ramp for $15,000; but the president and his corporation had refused to install the ramp because they didn't want to spend more than $10,000!

c. APPELLATE CASES HAVE UPHELD AWARDING OF CIVIL CODE § 3294 PUNITIVE DAMAGES IN CASES WHERE STATUTORY COMPENSATORY DAMAGES WERE AWARDED FOR SEXUAL DISCRIMINATION, RACIAL DISCRIMINATION, AND AGE DISCRIMINATION

Historically, section 3294 Civil Code punitive damages have been awarded in a large variety of contexts. For example, consider the following:

In a sexual harassment/discrimination case, <u>Bihune v. AT&T</u> (1993) 13 Cal. App.4th 976, at 977, punitive damages in the amount of $500,000 (in addition to compensatory damages) were awarded and upheld on appeal pursuant to Civil Code § 3294.

In <u>Roberts v. Ford Aerospace & Communications Corp.</u> (1990) 224 Cal.App.3d 793, an action alleging racial discrimination, $750,000 in punitive damages were awarded and upheld on appeal, in addition to the statutory compensatory damages for racial discrimination based upon Government Code § 12940.

In <u>Cancellier v. Federated Department Stores</u> (9th Cir 1982) 672 F.2d 1312, the 9th Circuit held that California Civil Code § 3294 punitive damages, as well as emotional distress damages, could be awarded in addition to the ADEA award for back pay, lost benefits, and work related damages. The total award of $2.3 million was upheld for age discrimination.

---

[69] Sid Wolinsky and Larry Paradis formed the outstanding public interest law firm, Disability Rights Advocates in 1993. At the time of the (1989) H's Lordships trial, Mr. Wolinsky was chief attorney for DREDF (Disability Rights Education Defense Fund). He and Arlene Mayerson, directing attorney at DREDF (and author of the 4 volume set, ADA Annotated (2003))were also teaching Disability Rights law at Boalt Hall (Berkeley) and several other law schools, and organizing symposiums on disability rights. Sid Wolinsky, Larry Paradis and Arlene Mayerson remain among the most knowledgeable and effective attorneys and teachers in the disability rights field. Their respective offices are in Berkeley. Plaintiff's access consultant expert was Peter Margen, of Walnut Creek.

Discrimination against persons with disabilities, whether the motivation be actual malice or simple aversion toward spending money, is just as reprehensible as discrimination on the basis of sex, race, or age. As stated by the California Supreme Court in <u>City of Moorpark v. Sup. Ct.</u> (1998) 18 Cal.4th 1143, at 1160:
> Disability discrimination is indistinguishable in many ways from race and sex discrimination. Specifically, it can "attack the individual's sense of self-worth in much the same fashion as race or sex discrimination."

Trial courts have the opportunity to affirm this standard and to represent the community's values toward the importance of fair treatment of the disabled in light of California's established public policy.

Courts have used many reference points to assess appropriate punitive damages to carry out the purposes of Civil Code § 3294 to deter fraudulent, malicious or oppressive conduct, and to set an example. (See cases listed in appendix to <u>Devlin v. Kearny Mesa AMC/Jeep/ Renault, Inc.</u> (1984) Cal.App.3d 381.) One percent (1%) of any Company's net worth would send a message that flagrant violation of the rights of disabled persons will not be tolerated in California. However, note that any punitive damages award may not be allowed to exceed the <u>State Farm v. Campbell</u> apparent limit of "single digit multiplier" (of compensatory damages), as set in 2004 by the U.S. Supreme Court. <u>State Farm v. Campbell</u>, 538 US 408 (2003).

In light of the 5-4 opinion by Justice Scalia in <u>Exxon Shipping Co. v. Baker</u> (2008) 554 U.S. 471 (the V<u>aldez</u> Alaskan oil spill case) <u>severely reducing</u> and limiting the punitive damages award to <u>match</u> the amount of compensatory damages (and effectively limiting any deterrent effect on bad conduct that punitive damage awards might otherwise have), plaintiff's attorneys in California may be better off simply seeking statutory treble damages under sections 52 or 54.3 Civil Code (<u>alternative</u> remedies, one of which must be selected between before trial, per section 54.3 (c).)

d. USE OF "90 DAY" COMPLIANCE PROVISION OF GOVERNMENT CODE § 4452 SHOWING TIME IS OF THE ESSENCE

Government Code § 4452 specifically requires that "Any unauthorized deviation from such regulations or building standards <u>shall be rectified</u> by full compliance <u>within 90 days</u> after discovery of the deviation." (Emphasis added) If evidence shows that defendants knew of the access requirements at all times, but still refused to provide access, a strong argument supports finding an intentional tort, as in the Alameda County Superior Court <u>H's Lordship Restaurant</u> trial (1989) award of $500,000 punitive damages, where the corporate owners of "H's Lordships" restaurant in Berkeley refused to install an access ramp. (Weissman v. Terranova Industries, Specialty Restaurant Corporation, dba H's Lordships Restaurant, et al., *supra*.

The "90 day" provision, by its "shall" language, appears to be mandatory. It set one statutory guideline for a "reasonable" deadline for taking action. Defendants' delay, as seen against the 90 day presumptive time limit of Government Code § 4452, may be evidence of "despicable conduct" in "conscious disregard for the rights and safety" of all wheelchair users and mobility disabled persons who are wrongfully denied entry or use of accessible facilities. This should be especially true as to accessible restroom facilities. It does not take an expert to foresee the types of humiliating bodily functions accidents a disabled person may suffer if they cannot enter and use a restroom toilet stall when they need one. It should also be clear to anyone operating a business that disabled wheelchair users will be totally excluded if entry is blocked by one or more stairs, or by a narrow doorway, etc.

e. IN TOM FISHER v. MILLENNIUM BANK HON. SAUNDRA ARMSTRONG OF THE NORTHERN DISTRICT COURT UPHELD A DISABLED PLAINTIFF'S RIGHT TO SEEK CIVIL CODE § 3294 PUNITIVE DAMAGES FOR CONSCIOUS DISREGARD, BUT SEVERAL YEARS LATER THIS COURT HELD PLAINTIFF MAY BE LIMITED TO CIVIL CODE § 54.3 TREBLE DAMAGES

Plaintiff argued a legal right to prove to a jury, that the choice by a bank with substantial assets to refuse to provide a ramp past a single step blocking its entrance, could constitute "conscious disregard" for the rights and safety of disabled persons. Northern District Judge Saundra Armstrong agreed and allowed plaintiff to seek punitive damages per Civil Code § 3294. (Order filed July 3, 1996 in Fisher v. Millennium Bank, et al. (N.D.Cal.) Case No. C96-0800, after which the case settled) However in a later 2004 case, (four years prior to the Munson, *supra*, decision) Judge Armstrong ruled against using section 3294: the Court noted Fisher, but stated "recent cases, however, have cast doubt on this holding." Freeman v. Alta Bates Summit Medical Center 2004 WL 2326369 at p. 4 citing several district court cases holding that a plaintiff could not seek both punitive damages and section 54.3 Civil Code treble damages. Nevertheless, in Freeman Judge Armstrong denied defendant's motion "without prejudice," because plaintiff had sought section 3294 Civil Code punitive damages alternatively on a "negligence per se" cause of action, citing cases holding plaintiff could plead both theories of recovery and then make an election of remedies either before or at trial. Therefore defendant's motion was denied without prejudice as "premature."

f. THE AMOUNT OF PUNITIVE DAMAGES SHOULD BE SET TO DETER FRAUDULENT, OPPRESSIVE, OR MALICIOUS CONDUCT, AND SET AN EXAMPLE FOR OTHERS

In addition to "willful and conscious disregard," "oppression" and "fraud" are alternative bases for punitive damages. Punitive damages exist to teach a lesson and make a public example. Such damages are particularly appropriate where Defendants are arguably guilty of all three offenses. Civil Code § 3294 damages could be imposed <u>in addition to compensatory damages</u> imposed under other statutes, including Civil Rights statutes, as held by <u>Bihun v. AT&T</u> (1993) 13 Cal. App.4th 976, 977, <u>Roberts v. Ford Aerospace & Communications Corp.</u> (1990) 224 Cal.App.3d 793, and <u>Chancellier v. Federated Dept. Stores</u> (9th Cir. 1982) 672 F.2d 1312. These cases upheld punitive damages of $500,000, $750,000, and $2.3 million, respectively, <u>in addition to</u> statutory compensatory damages awarded under three different code sections.

Defendants may argue that Civil Code § 54.3 and the availability of treble damages limits any other remedies. However, § 54.3 itself says:

> "<u>The remedies in this section are non-exclusive and are in addition to any other remedy provided by law</u>, including but not limited to, any action for injunctive or other equitable relief available to the aggrieved party or brought in the name of the people of this state or of the United States." (Emphasis added)

Especially since <u>James Donald v. Café Royale</u> (1990) 218 Cal.App.3d 168, held that Civil Code § 54.3 damages can be awarded <u>without regard to the intent</u> of a defendant, in effect allowing strict liability, there is no evidence that the Legislature intended to <u>shield</u> from Civil Code § 3294 liability <u>those who also discriminate</u> against disabled persons <u>with a specific fraudulent, malicious, or oppressive intent and course of conduct</u>.

g. PLAINTIFFS' ATTORNEYS SHOULD CONSIDER THE POLICIES BEING ENFORCED IN DETERMINING <u>WHETHER</u> TO PLEAD AND SEEK PUNITIVE DAMAGES

My personal feeling is that punitive damages in disability access cases can be used as a threat and tool, in appropriate cases, to encourage provision of access and payment of appropriate damages; but seeking heavy "punitive" damages should <u>not</u> be the primary goal of an access lawsuit. The primary objective should be to educate, persuade, obtain access and obtain compensatory damages for the plaintiff, not to damage or destroy a defendant business. Indeed, the ADA, Title III, does not provide any damages remedy (although damages may be awarded under California law by ADA incorporation into the Unruh Act (Civil Code§ 51(f)), and the Disabled Persons Act (Civil Code §§ 54(c) and 54.1(d)).[70] In any event, obtaining large punitive damages may be difficult. The United States Supreme Court cases has held that punitive damages must, in most cases, have a relationship to the actual compensatory damages awarded, with a ratio normally not exceeding a single digit, i.e., 1:1 to 9:1. State Farm Ins. Co. v. Campbell (2003) 538 U.S. 408.[71]

A 2007 U.S. Supreme Court case also held that the Due Process clause "forbids a state to use a punitive damages award to punish a defendant for injury that it inflicts on non-parties." Phillip Morris v. Williams (127 S.Ct. 1057, 1063). However, Williams also held that a plaintiff may offer evidence of "harm to other victims" to show the "responsibility" of a defendant's conduct in this case (Id. at 1063-1064), in that it shows the conduct "also posed a substantial risk of harm to the general public, and so was particularly reprehensible." (Id. at 1064.) However, as Justice Stevens criticized in his dissent, "This nuance eludes me." (Id. at 1066-1067,)

h. IN STATE FARM v. CAMPBELL AND EXXON THE U.S. SUPREME COURT HAS PLACED LIMITS ON PUNITIVE DAMAGES
In State Farm v. Campbell (2003) 538 U.S. 408, 123 S.Ct. 1513, a 6 - 3 opinion (hereafter also "Campbell"), the Court:
> decline[d] again to impose a bright-line ratio which a punitive damages award cannot exceed. Our jurisprudence and the principles it has now established demonstrate, however, that, in practice, few awards exceeding a single-digit ratio between punitive and compensatory damages, to a significant degree, will satisfy due process.
>
> Id. at 425.

Here the Court found one million dollars in compensatory emotional dstress damages were already substantial, and $145 million additional in punitive damages was excessive. Id. However the Campbell majority left open the possibility that a higher ratio may be upheld under certain circumstances:
> Nonetheless, because there are no rigid benchmarks that a punitive damages award may not surpass, ratios greater than those we have previously upheld may comport with due process where "a particularly egregious act has resulted in only a small amount of economic damages." Ibid.[referring to BMW v. Gore 517 U.S. 559, at 581 (1996)]; See also ibid. (positing that a higher ratio might be necessary where "the injury is hard to detect or the monetary value of noneconomic harm might have been difficult to determine").
>
> Campbell, *supra*, at 425.

In Exxon Shipping Co. v. Baker (2008) 554 U.S. 471, 128 S.Ct. 2605, involving the

---

[70] However, while both the Unruh act (sections 51-52) and Disabled Persons Act (section 54.1 and 54.3) may be pled as causes of action for damages, plaintiff must make an election between them at or prior to trial. Cal. Civ. C. Section 54.3(c) and Denevi v. LGCC, 121 Cal. App. 4th 1211, 1221 (2004).

[71] Campbell, *supra*, stated that the factors for punitive damages are (1) whether the defendant caused physical harm, disregarded the health or safety of others, took advantage of a financially vulnerable plaintiff, acted pursuant to a pattern or practice, or acted with trickery or deceit; (2) whether there is a reasonable relationship between the amount of punitive damages and the plaintiff's harm; (3) the defendant's financial condition, in determining an amount of punitive damages necessary to punish the defendant and discourage future wrongful conduct.

huge damage caused by the Exxon Valdez oil spill, the Supreme Court decimated a $5 billion punitive damage jury award and reduced it to $507.5 million dollars, matching on a 1-1 basis (under admiralty law) the jury's award of $507.5 million in compensatory damages. Justice Souter wrote for the majority in this 5-3 opinion because Justices Scalia and Thomas concurred based on the Campbell precedent, while stating that they still believed the Campbell "holdings were in error." Justice Stevens, Ginsberg, and Breyer dissented. (Alito, recently appointed, took no part).

8. REBUTTING CERTAIN DAMAGES DEFENSES

   a. "PLAINTIFF WAS ABLE TO GET IN." PLAINTIFF WAS DENIED "FULL AND EQUAL ACCESS" PER CIVIL CODE § 54.1 EVEN THOUGH HE WAS "ABLE" TO GET IN TO THE PUBLIC FACILITY; NEW CIVIL CODE SECTION 55.56 CLARIFIES THIS

   The issue is not whether or not a disabled person was "able" to "get into" a restaurant, courtroom, or other public facility; the issue is whether he was denied "full and equal access." (Civil Code § 54.1) For example, to claim that Mark Hankins, the plaintiff in Hankins v. El Torito, *supra*, was not "denied access" because he might have been "able" to climb stairs to a second floor restroom with only one leg and on crutches, is absurd. Paraplegic rock climber Mark Wellman was "able" to climb the 3,600 foot rock face of El Capitan in Yosemite National Park (using only his arm strength on a pulley, 6" at a time, "no more difficult than 7,200 chin-ups"). However, he should not be subjected to crawling up the front stairs to gain entry to any public accommodation. Indeed, in 2004 the Supreme Court narrowly upheld ADA Title II's constitutionality in Tennessee v. Lane (2004) 124 S.Ct. 1978: five of the nine justices agreed that Congress had a right to legislate that crawling up stairs was something that should not be required of a physically disabled person to enter a courthouse!

   Donald v. Café Royale (1990) 218 Cal.App.3d 168, held that plaintiff Donald was entitled to a minimum of $250 (now $1,000) statutory damages as a matter of law, even though the trial judge had made a legally unreviewable factual determination that Mr. Donald, a quadriplegic attorney, who briefly entered the restaurant with his dinner companion, learned that all dining was on a raised and inaccessible level, and then left, had not personally suffered any "actual damages," i.e., any emotional distress. (Are "attorneys" incapable of suffering emotional distress?) Because it held that this was a trial court "factual" finding upon which the Court of Appeals could not grant a new trial on damages, the appellate court instead awarded Mr. Donald the minimum statutory damages (then $250), plus his attorney fees, reversing a trial court judgment for the defendant which was based on the owner's lack of discriminatory "intent."

In <u>Hankins v. El Torito</u>, *supra*, the testimony of Mark Hankins and his wife demonstrated significant emotional distress, frustration and outrage at the humiliation and embarrassment caused by access denial: as a one legged amputee, he had to first struggle up six stairs on crutches just to enter the restaurant, then found he faced climbing 18 stairs to the (second floor) public restroom on crutches; still worse, the restaurant manager also <u>refused</u> to allow him use of the (first floor) "Employees" restroom because of "company policy"! The court's award of $80,000 compensatory statutory damages, awarded <u>alternatively</u> under Civil Code §§ 52 and 54.3, was affirmed on appeal. Id.

As of January 1, 2009, SB 1608 definitions, California Civil Code section 55.56 clarified what a personal denial of "full and equal access" required:

> "section 55.56(c) A violation personally encountered by a plaintiff may be sufficient to cause a denial of full and equal access if the plaintiff <u>experienced difficulty, discomfort or embarrassment</u> because of the violation."
> (Emphasis added)

Thus it is important that plaintiff be able to plead and prove, in order to recover damages, not just an access "violation" but that <u>encountering</u> the violation caused the plaintiff a denial of full and equal access, <u>including but not limited to</u> experiencing "difficulty, discomfort, or embarrassment."

This issue was addressed in 2011 by the 9th Circuit in a 9-2 <u>en banc</u> decision in <u>Chapman v. Pier One Imports (USA) Inc.</u>, 631 F.3d 939, 947 (9th Circuit, 2011): Because the ADAAG establishes the technical standards required for "full and equal enjoyment," if a barrier violating these standards relates to a plaintiff's disability, it will impair the plaintiff's full and equal access, which constitutes "discrimination" under the ADA. That discrimination satisfies the "injury-in-fact" element of Lujan. Further, <u>Chapman</u> made clear that <u>complete exclusion was not necessary</u> in order to show a barrier violated plaintiff's rights:

> Under the ADA, when a disabled person encounters an accessibility barrier violating its provisions, <u>it is not necessary</u> for standing purposes <u>that the barrier completely preclude the plaintiff</u> from entering or from using a facility in any way. See <u>Doran</u>, 524 F.3d at 1041 n. 4 (stating that the ADA "does not limit its antidiscrimination mandate to barriers that completely prohibit access"). Rather, <u>the barrier need only interfere with the plaintiff's "full and equal enjoyment" of the facility</u>. 42 U.S.C. § 12182(a). As we stated in <u>Doran</u>, Once a disabled individual has <u>encountered or become aware of alleged</u>

<u>ADA violations that deter his patronage of or otherwise interfere with his access</u> to a place of public accommodation, he has already suffered an injury in fact traceable to the defendant's conduct and capable of being redressed by the courts, and so he <u>possesses standing</u> under Article III. . .

<u>Chapman v. Pier One Imports (USA), Inc</u>, *supra*, at 947, quoting <u>Doran v. 7-Eleven</u>, Inc 524 F.3d 1034 (9th Cir. 2008) (Emphasis added)

b. IT IS NOT A "DEFENSE" THAT PLAINTIFF HAS PREVIOUSLY SUED OWNERS OF OTHER FACILITIES FOR ACCESS

Defendants will occasionally attack a disabled rights plaintiff because he or she has previously sued other businesses for access violations.[72] They may attack such person as a "professional <u>plaintiff</u>" or infer that the <u>number</u> of prior actions - <u>even if all</u> these <u>were successful</u> - should cast doubt on the validity of the new action.[73]

This often unjustified attack upon the motives of civil rights plaintiffs for daring to complain about "multiple" ADA violations, suggests that there is something wrong about complaining more than once about civil rights violations. Memory has it that Martin Luther King, and other heroes of the Civil Rights Movement complained <u>more than once</u>! If the lawsuits a plaintiff has previously brought under the ADA and/or California civil rights statutes have resulted in major public accommodations being made accessible for use by disabled persons, and each case was legally meritorious, defendants have no basis to complain.[74]

An unjustified attack on ADA plaintiffs based only on speculation about their motives may itself be in derogation of the spirit of ADA § 503 (42 USC 12203)

---

[72] See also Sections I.V.H-J, *infra*, regarding the "<u>Christiansburg</u>" U.S. Supreme Court rule that no attorneys fees can be sought against a losing but good faith civil rights plaintiff. (<u>Christiansburg Garment Co. v. EEOC</u>, 434 U.S. 412, 421, 98 S.Ct. 694, 54 L.Ed.2d 648 (1978) and <u>Fox v. Vice</u>, 131 S.Ct. 2205 (2011))(But caveat <u>Jankey v. Lee</u> decision by the California Supreme Court allowing fees against a "losing" Civil Code section 55 plaintiff.

[73] However, we must recognize that there have apparently been some truly "professional" plaintiffs, who have sued regarding businesses that they have never attempted to patronize, and sued solely for financial profit, without efforts to obtain access as equitable relief. These may be in violation of existing law if they falsely represent any facts or cannot back up their claims of personally visiting - or being deterred from visiting - a specific restaurant or other public facility. Dishonesty should always be condemned by defense counsel and plaintiff's counsel alike. Judges in federal court can invoke FRCP Rule 11 in appropriate cases. Litigants who seek only damages and do not require that any facility out of compliance actually "fix" its access flaws and provide proper access, are failing to properly protect the public interest. Questionable cases and instances of dubious ethics may have a negative public effect and encourage a "backlash" of public opinion. This may harm the cause of maximizing disabled access. [See also section VII, *infra*, "Are there 'abuses' of the ADA?"] See also new limitations in SB 1186 passed by the California legislature in 2012.

[74] However, plaintiffs should be aware that some judges may allow discovery about a plaintiff's prior lawsuits on the grounds that such discovery may lead to admissible evidence on the issue of damages and the level of a plaintiff's "emotional distress." However, such evidence would open a whole new "can of worms" or "range of issues": Does each mention of a "prior case" entitle either party in a current case to re-litigate the merits - and public interest results - of a prior case? One judge has questioned the "standing" of a defendant in a current case to challenge standing based on what the instant plaintiff

(prohibiting retaliation against anyone for bringing or assisting an ADA action) and contrary to Congress' efforts to <u>encourage</u> ADA lawsuits. As held in <u>Walker and Adams v. Carnival Cruise Lines</u> (2000) 107 F.Supp.2d 1135, by the highly respected former Chief Judge of the Northern District of California, Hon. Thelton Henderson:

> The ADA creates the possibility that successful plaintiffs may establish permanent changes in the design and physical configuration of structures to better accommodate the disabled. 42 U.S.C. § 12101(a)(5). The benefits of such changes clearly redound not only to the plaintiffs themselves, but to similarly situated disabled persons, and the entire society at large. As a result, plaintiffs or plaintiff classes who bring suit pursuant to the ADA do so in the role of "private attorneys general" who seek to vindicate "a policy of the highest priority."...
>
> For example, successful ADA plaintiffs confer a tremendous benefit upon our society at large, in addition to the attainment of redress for their personal individual injuries..."

(107 F.Supp.2d 1135 at 1143)

c. THE <u>MOLSKI V. EVERGREEN</u> 9TH CIRCUIT OPINION CRITICIZED ABUSES BUT MADE CLEAR THAT "SERIAL" LAWSUITS MAY APPROPRIATELY BE USED TO OBTAIN ADA ACCESS

In <u>Molski v. Evergreen Dynasty Corp.</u> (9th Cir. 2007) 500 F.3d 1047, the 9th Circuit upheld certain sanctions against an ADA plaintiff and his counsel, finding they had employed certain ethically questionable tactics as part of 400 individual lawsuits by the same plaintiff, including allegedly exaggerated <u>factual</u> claims for damages (for example, claiming to have injured the same shoulder in as many as five different businesses on the same day). Plaintiff's attorney was also sanctioned and subjected to a <u>pre-filing</u> order in the Central District, based on alleged unethical practices, such as advising defendants not to contact an attorney before settling with plaintiff.

However, the 9th Circuit majority opinion also warned against interpreting its mandate too broadly, and <u>upheld the good faith use of "serial" lawsuits under the ADA</u> (500 F.3d 1047, 1061-1062):

> In summary, we reemphasize that the simple fact that a plaintiff has

---

had alleged in other, previous cases. <u>Wilson v. Pier One Imports (US) Inc.</u>, 411 F.Supp 2d 1196 (E.D. Cal. 2006) This issue could be avoided if plaintiff stipulates to only minimum statutory damages (alternatively) $4,000 per section 52 Civil Code, or $1,000 per section 54.3 and waives any claim for emotional distress. See <u>D'Lil v. Ramada Ltd</u>. 2004 WL 3674244 (C.D. Cal). [See also section VII, *infra*] Further, if a defendant were to bring any aspect of a prior case into evidence, the plaintiff should be allowed to introduce other aspects of the same case, including the public interest accomplished and, if appropriate, the monetary recovery for damages and attorney fees. The result of allowing consideration of other cases might be the trial Court having to deal with the litigation results and underlying facts of multiple other cases, instead of just the one before the court.

filed a large number of complaints, standing alone, is not a basis for designating a litigant as "vexatious." De Long, 912 F.2d at 1147; In re Oliver, 682 F.2d 443, 446 (3d Cir.1982). We also emphasize that the textual and factual similarity of a plaintiff's complaints, standing alone, is not a basis for finding a party to be a vexatious litigant. Accessibility barriers can be, and often are, similar in different places of public accommodation, and there is nothing inherently vexatious about using prior complaints as a template. See Wilson, 411 F.Supp.2d at 1196 (stating that uniform instances of misconduct can justify uniform pleadings).

As we discussed above, the ADA does not permit private plaintiffs to seek damages, and limits the relief they may seek to injunctions and attorneys' fees. We recognize that the unavailability of damages reduces or removes the incentive for most disabled persons who are injured by inaccessible places of public accommodation to bring suit under the ADA. See Samuel R. Bagenstos, The Perversity of Limited Civil Rights Remedies: The Case of "Abusive" ADA Litigation, 54 U.C.L.A. L.Rev. 1, 5 (2006). As a result, most ADA suits are brought by a small number of private plaintiffs who view themselves as champions of the disabled. District courts should not condemn such serial litigation as vexatious as a matter of course. See De Long, 912 F.2d at 1148 n. 3. For the ADA to yield its promise of equal access for the disabled, it may indeed be necessary and desirable for committed individuals to bring serial litigation advancing the time when public accommodations will be compliant with the ADA. But as important as this goal is to disabled individuals and to the public, serial litigation can become vexatious when, as here, a large number of nearly-identical complaints contain factual allegations that are contrived, exaggerated, and defy common sense. False or grossly exaggerated claims of injury, especially when made with the intent to coerce settlement, are at odds with our system of justice, and Molski's history of litigation warrants the need for a pre-filing review of his claims.

(Emphasis added)

The Molski finding sanctioning Molski and his attorney was questioned by nine Circuit Judges of the Court of Appeal, including Chief Judge Alex Kozinski, in an opinion dissenting from the denial of "en banc" consideration by "a majority of the non-recused active judges of the court." (See dissenting opinions at 521 F.3rd 1215) These two separate dissenting opinions stressed the "draconian" nature of pre-filing orders, which "infringe the fundamental right to access courts," Id. at 1216, especially as noted in Chief Judge Kozinski's separate dissent at 1221. Chief Judge Kozinski also noted that the district court made certain findings of fact although "it never held an evidentiary hearing." The dissent by Judge Berzon, joined by 8 other 9th Circuit Judges, noted that the majority's apparent concern with "serial access litigation" should recognize "that there are so many violations of the laws that seek to assure access, and so many disabled people are thwarted from participating equally in the activities of everyday life.":

> At bottom, the panel may be uncomfortable with ADA litigation that it suspects is being brought to induce settlement. This concern with serial access litigation is shared by many, rightly or wrongly. But the phenomenon is a creature of our federal and state statutes and cannot justify the issuing of prefiling orders that enjoin meritorious lawsuits. Moreover, while self interest surely drives serial access litigation in part, <u>the reason there can be so many lawsuits about access to public accommodations is that there are so many violations of the laws that seek to assure access, and so many disabled people are thwarted from participating equally in the activities of everyday life.</u> I fear that the panel's opinion may be widely used to restrict critical private enforcement of civil rights laws by other litigants and lawyers. This case should have been heard <u>en banc</u> to prevent that result.
> Id. at 1220. (Emphasis added)

d. THE NUMBER OF PLAINTIFF'S PRIOR SUCCESSFUL LAWSUITS SHOULD NOT BE USED TO QUESTION A DISABLED PERSON'S "CREDIBILITY" OR "STANDING" TO SUE

In <u>D'Lil v. Best Western et al</u>, 538 F.3d 1031 (9th Cir. 2008), the 9th Circuit warned against "the attempted use of past litigation to prevent a litigant from pursuing a valid claim in federal court":

> The attempted use of past litigation to prevent a litigant from pursuing a valid claim in federal court warrants our most careful scrutiny. See, e.g., <u>Outley v. City of New York</u>, 837 F.2d 587, 592 (2d Cir.1988). This is particularly true in the ADA context where, as we recently explained, the law's provision for injunctive relief only "removes the incentive for most disabled persons who are injured by inaccessible places of public accommodation to bring suit.... As a result, most ADA suits are brought by a small number of private plaintiffs who view themselves as champions of the disabled.... For the ADA to yield its promise of equal access for the disabled, it may indeed be necessary and desirable for committed individuals to bring serial litigation advancing the time when public accommodations will be compliant with the ADA." <u>Molski v. Evergreen Dynasty Corp.</u>, 500 F.3d 1047, 1062 (9th Cir.2007) (citing Samuel R. Bagnestos, <u>The Perversity of Limited Civil Rights Remedies: The Case of "Abusive" ADA Litigation</u>, 54 U.C.L.A. L.Rev. 1, 5 (2006)). Accordingly, we must be particularly cautious about affirming credibility determinations that rely on a plaintiff's past ADA litigation.

[See also <u>Molski</u> quote, *supra* at section I-J-8-c]

In <u>Kittok v. Leslie's Poolmart, Inc.</u> 687 F.Supp.2d 953 (C.D. Cal. 2009) the court granted partial summary judgement on <u>one</u> of plaintiff's disability access claims (an accessible parking space with a $1,000 minimum statutory damages claim per Civil Code section 54.3) and then granted $39,057 of plaintiff's $40,169 fee request. In response to defense counsel's personal attacks on plaintiff and her counsel for bringing this and similar suits under the ADA, the court <u>blasted the defense counsel</u> and found nothing wrong with multiple lawsuits "if <u>this</u> case was meritorious":

> Not only are these attacks on the scruples and ethics of plaintiff and her counsel inappropriate in tone, they are wholly unsupported in substance. The Court acknowledges, both in its experience and as noted elsewhere, that there have been instances of abusive and frivolous litigation brought under the ADA and state disability access laws. . . . However, <u>absent a showing that this case was frivolous, abusive, or somehow brought in bad faith</u>, this Court will not disregard the plain statutory text conferring attorneys' fees upon a prevailing DPA plaintiff if she is otherwise entitled to them. . . .
>
> The Court has already determined that this case was not frivolous, as it awarded judgment in plaintiff's favor. See <u>Franklin v. Murphy, 745 F.2d 1221, 1228 (9th Cir.1984)</u>, quoted in <u>In re Thomas, 508 F.3d 1225, 1227 (9th Cir.2007)</u> (a frivolous complaint is one that recites "bare legal conclusions with no suggestion of supporting facts, or postulating events and circumstances of a wholly fanciful kind" or facts that conflict "with facts of which the district court may take judicial notice").
>
> Defendant's attempts to argue that this case was abusive or brought in bad faith also fail. <u>These arguments are representative of a troubling trend in which disability</u> access defendants attack the motives of <u>plaintiffs and their counsel in nearly every</u> case brought to enforce the right to equal access guaranteed by the ADA and California statutes. . . .
>
> If a plaintiff establishes a violation of law which entitles her to damages and fees, the Court will not question her scruples in filing the case in the absence of any real evidence which would call those scruples into question.[FN2] (Emphasis added)
>
> Inasmuch as defendant seems to suggest that plaintiff's meritorious claim is annoying, difficult for business, or otherwise objectionable, that is an argument for the legislature, not the courts. See <u>Angelucci v. Century Supper Club, 41 Cal.4th 160, 179, 59 Cal.Rptr.3d 142, 158 P.3d 718 (2007)</u> ("It is for the Legislature (or the People through the initiative process) to determine whether to alter the statutory elements of proof

---

[FN2] The fact that plaintiff and her counsel have filed multiple similar suits is of little import here if *this* case was meritorious. See <u>Jankey v. Poop Deck, 537</u> F.3d 1122, 1132 (9th Cir.2008) (disapproving of district court's denial of fees in part based on "Plaintiff's counsel's numerous other lawsuits in the Central District of California [as] those cases are not a part of the record here."); <u>D'Lil v. Best Western Encina Lodge & Suites,</u> 538 F.3d 1031, 1040 (9th Cir.2008) ("The attempted use of past litigation to prevent a litigant from pursuing a valid claim in federal court warrants our most careful scrutiny."); <u>Wilson v. Pier 1 Imports (US), Inc.,</u> 411 F.Supp.2d 1196, 1199 (E.D.Cal.2006) (finding record of litigiousness did not establish bad faith on part of plaintiffs).

to afford business establishments protection against abusive private legal actions and settlement tactics."); Molski v. Evergreen Dynasty Corp., 521 F.3d 1215, 1219 (9th Cir.2008) (Berzon, J., dissenting from denial of rehearing en banc) (noting that if "abusive" litigation is permitted under the Unruh Act, "the appropriate fix is legislative, not judicial"). The persistence of plaintiffs in bringing multiple lawsuits alleging unequal access to places of public accommodation does not demonstrate wrongdoing by plaintiffs anymore than it shows a hesitation of businesses to comply with the law. As the Ninth Circuit has noted in the context of ADA litigation, "For the ADA to yield its promise of equal access for the disabled, it may indeed be necessary and desirable for committed individuals to bring serial litigation advancing the time when public accommodations will be compliant with the ADA." Evergreen Dynasty Corp., 500 F.3d 1047, 1062 (9th Cir.2007) (panel op.), citing Samuel R. Bagenstos, The Perversity of Limited Civil Rights Remedies: The Case of 'Abusive' ADA Litigation, 54 U.C.L.A. L.Rev. 1, 5 (2006). (Emphasis added)

Kittok, *supra*, at p. 959.

e. **PLAINTIFF SHOULD RESIST DISCOVERY OF PAST SETTLEMENTS AS IRRELEVANT; OR AT WORST, COULD STIPULATE TO MINIMUM STATUTORY DAMAGES**

Courts should deny defendants' discovery aimed at other lawsuits plaintiff has filed, unless defendant's offers evidence to show a pattern of filing "frivolous" or factually unsupported cases. (cf. Molski v. Evergreen, 500 F.3d 1047.)

However, a plaintiff faced with discovery as to settlements may also avoid the issue by stipulating to claim no "emotional distress" or general damages and limit claim to minimum statutory damages. In D'lil v. Ramada Ltd., 2004 WL 3674244 (C.D. Cal. July 14, 2004) the Court denied defendant's motion to dismiss based on plaintiff's failure to comply with a Court Order compelling discovery on this basis:

> Defendants' motion to dismiss is DENIED. The Court interprets Plaintiff's submitted "stipulation" as a binding assertion that she will seek no more than the statutory minimums for any emotional distress damage claims at trial. Therefore, in light of Plaintiff's willingness to limit her emotional damages claims to the statutory minimums, Defendants have no need for Plaintiff's past settlement recovery amounts. Defendants are not entitled to discover Plaintiff's past settlement recoveries to attack her standing for injunctive relief. Such information has minimal probative value, if any, and requiring Plaintiff to disclose such information would needlessly invade her privacy as well as that of third parties. Additionally, disclosure would have a significant chilling effect on the willingness of Plaintiff and other individuals to protect and enforce their civil rights.
>
> Id. at p.*1. (Emphasis added)

[See also sections I-H-10, *supra*, and III-I, *infra*.]

9. PROTECTIONS FOR DISABLED PERSONS ASSISTED BY SERVICE ANIMALS

   a. MULTIPLE FEDERAL AND CALIFORNIA STATUTES AND REGULATIONS PROHIBIT DISCRIMINATION AGAINST DISABLED PERSONS WITH SERVICE ANIMALS

   Exclusion or discrimination against any disabled person because they are accompanied by a "qualified" service animal is prohibited by California law and the ADA. Certain ADA protections (discussed *infra* at section III-H) are additional to existing California statutes protecting persons with service animals, including section 54.2 (a) Civil Code and section 365.5 Penal Code. Section 54.2 (a) Civil Code guarantees that "Every individual with a disability has the right to be accompanied by a guide dog, signal dog, or service dog, especially trained for the purpose, in any of the places specified in section 54.1." Section 54.1 includes all "places of public accommodation, amusement or resort, and other places to which the public is invited." Section 54.3 provides remedies, including treble damages, for any violation of sections 54.1 or 54.2.

   [See section III-I, *infra*, for ADA regulations by Department of Justice to guide ADA protections for "Service Animals" including 28 CFR 36.302(c)(1)] [Caveat: See 2011 DOJ Regulations about service "dogs" at section 9-d, *infra*]

   b. CALIFORNIA PENAL CODE SECTION 365.5(b) MAKES IT A CRIME TO REFUSE SERVICE TO A DISABLED PERSON AND HIS/HER SERVICE ANIMAL

   California Penal Code § 365.5(b) prohibits denial of access to any disabled person and their service dog:

   > (b) No blind person, deaf person, or disabled person and his or her specially trained guide dog, signal dog, or service dog shall be denied admittance to accommodations, advantages, facilities, medical facilities, including hospitals, clinics, and physicians' offices, telephone facilities, adoption agencies, private schools, hotels, lodging places, places of public accommodation, amusement, or resort, and other places to which the general public is invited within this state because of that guide dog, signal dog, or service dog.

   The criminal nature of the act would be added support for imposition of treble damages per Civil Code §§ 52 or 54.3 (when pled in conjunction with §§ 51 and 54.1) or even imposition of Civil Code § 3294 punitive damages in the appropriate case. However, caveat the claim that treble damages per §§ 52 and 54.3 may be held to be exclusive and preclude a § 3294 claim for punitive damages.

c. CIVIL CODE §§ 54.1 AND 54.2(a) PROTECT THE RIGHTS OF DISABLED PERSONS TO BE ACCOMPANIED BY A SERVICE DOG

Civil Code § 54.1(a)(1) specifies that "Individuals with disabilities shall be entitled to full and equal access" to all public accommodations and facilities.

> (a)(1) Individuals with disabilities shall be entitled to full and equal access, as other members of the general public, to accommodations, advantages, facilities, medical facilities, including hospitals, clinics, and physicians' offices, and privileges of all common carriers, airplanes, motor vehicles, railroad trains, motorbuses, streetcars, boats, or any other public conveyances or modes of transportation (whether private, public, franchised, licensed, contracted, or otherwise provided), telephone facilities, adoption agencies, private schools, hotels, lodging places, places of public accommodation, amusement, or resort, and other places to which the general public is invited, subject only to the conditions and limitations established by law, or state or federal regulation, and applicable alike to all persons.

Civil Code § 54.2(a) specifies that "Every individual with a disability has the right to be accompanied by a guide dog, signal dog or service dog, especially trained for the purpose, in any of the places specified in § 54.1." Section 54.3 specifies damages and attorney fees as remedies.

d. THE ADA, 28 C.F.R. 36.302, AND DOJ REGULATION SECTION 35.136 PROHIBIT EXCLUSION OF SERVICE ANIMALS

28 CFR 36.302(c)(1). The Department of Justice regulation set up to guide enforcement of the ADA specifies:

> (c) Service animals--
> (1) General. Generally, a public accommodation shall modify policies, practices, or procedures to permit the use of a service animal by an individual with a disability.

As of March 11, 2011, the Regulations regarding service dogs were as follows:[75]

§ 35.136 <u>Service animals</u>

> (a) General. Generally, <u>a public entity shall modify its policies, practices, or procedures to permit the use of a service animal by an individual</u> with a disability.
> (b) Exceptions. A public entity may ask an individual with a disability

---

[75] Additional regulations as to "miniature horses" were included in section 35.136(I) are omitted here. The new regulations specifically limit "service animals" to dogs that have been individually trained to do work performing tasks for the benefit of an individual with a disability. Dogs used purely for "emotional support" are not considered service animals, at least under the ADA regulations. However, the regulations permit use of trained miniature horses as alternatives to dogs, subject to certain limitations. These new regulations may have been set to deal with the issue of whether, for example, a "service snake" carried for the "emotional support" of a disabled person, would qualify for the protections of a "service animal."

to remove a service animal from the premises if—
(1) The animal is out of control and the animal's handler does not take effective action to control it; or
(2) The animal is not housebroken.
(c) <u>If an animal is properly excluded</u>. If a public entity properly excludes a service animal under § 35.136(b), it shall give the individual with a disability the opportunity to participate in the service, program, or activity without having the service animal on the premises.
(d) <u>Animal under handler's control</u>. A service animal shall be under the control of its handler. A service animal shall have a harness, leash, or other tether, unless either the handler is unable because of a disability to use a harness, leash, or other tether, or the use of a harness, leash, or other tether would interfere with the service animal's safe, effective performance of work or tasks, in which case the service animal must be otherwise under the handler's control (e.g., voice control, signals, or other effective means).
(e) <u>Care or supervision</u>. A public entity is not responsible for the care or supervision of a service animal.
(f) <u>Inquiries</u>. A public entity shall not ask about the nature or extent of a person's disability, but may make two inquiries to determine whether an animal qualifies as a service animal. <u>A public entity may ask if the animal is required because of a disability and what work or task the animal has been trained to perform. A public entity shall not require documentation</u>, such as proof that the animal has been certified, trained, or licensed as a service animal. Generally, a public entity may not make these inquiries about a service animal when it is readily apparent that an animal is trained to do work or perform tasks for an individual with a disability (e.g., the dog is observed guiding an individual who is blind or has low vision, pulling a person's wheelchair, or providing assistance with stability or balance to an individual with an observable mobility disability).
(g) <u>Access to areas of a public entity</u>. Individuals with disabilities shall be permitted to be accompanied by their service animals <u>in all areas of a public entity's facilities where members of the public, participants in services, programs or activities, or invitees, as relevant, are allowed to go.</u>
(h) <u>Surcharges</u>. A public entity shall not ask or require an individual with a disability to pay a surcharge, even if people accompanied by pets are required to pay fees, or to comply with other requirements generally not applicable to people without pets. If a public entity normally charges individuals for the damage they cause, an individual with a disability may be charged for damage caused by his or her service animal.
(Emphasis added)

e. EXAMPLES OF LITIGATION PROTECTING THE USE OF SERVICE DOGS
These provisions have been used by my office to enforce the rights of disabled

persons in the following factual examples:
(1) A blind man accompanied by a service animal (a dog fully trained by Guide Dogs for the Blind) was twice ordered out of a restaurant (part of a 400 restaurant "fast food" chain) in Southern California by a restaurant manager who alleged, alternatively, that (a) he didn't realize the man was blind, and (b) he didn't know the law and thought he could exclude service dogs from "food" establishments. (Darren K.; (C.D.Cal.) Case No. Confidential by Settlement Agreement) None of the corporate defendant's designated "Persons Most Knowledgeable" or the manager held up well during depositions: According to the policy knowledgeable "PMK," the chain's "policy" for all complaints- even about the manager- was to send the complainant a certificate for a free hotdog, and send a letter to the manager! Settlement included adding a section in the chain's employee handbook outlining the correct way to deal with disabled persons and service dogs!
(2) A bookstore owner ejected a deaf woman with a service dog from his store, because he didn't understand that disability protections for the use of service animals applied to the deaf and physically disabled, not just to blind persons. (Christy v. L&L Bookstore, et al., (N.D.Cal.)
(3) A disabled woman who used a power wheelchair and a service dog was ejected by a security guard from a large office building. Investigation disclosed that all of the public restrooms in the building were also inaccessible to disabled wheelchair users. A lawsuit obtained both damages and injunctive relief requiring a change in policy toward service dogs and provision of multiple accessible public restrooms. (Hodges v. Zimmerman, 1330 Broadway, et al., Alameda County Superior Court. No. 792611-6.)

f. SAMPLE COMPLAINT: SEE APPENDIX, § IX-g

[Darren K. v. XYZ Corp.] A sample complaint of the type used in litigation against businesses which rejected entry to a disabled person assisted by a service dog, is published here at X-I-3. (This sample also contains allegations of physical barriers to access which also affected visually disabled persons, on whose behalf plaintiff Darren K. also had injunctive relief standing.)(Caveat possible danger of seeking injunctive relief under section 55 Civil Code because of the December 17, 2012, Jankey v. Lee decision allowing "reverse" attorney fees against a losing plaintiff.)

10. TWO YEAR STATUTE OF LIMITATIONS

All disability claims for damages should be presumed to have a two year statute limitations, although there is some authority that a three year statute may apply to the DPA (§ 54ff Civil Code) and ADA Title II (governmental entity) as statutory causes of action. (See detailed discussion by Judge Phyllis J. Hamilton in Kemp

v. Regents of the University of California 2010 WL 2889224, at p.*6-7 (N.D. Cal.):

> The ADA does not contain its own limitations period. Pickern v. Holiday Quality Foods, Inc., 293 F.3d 1133, 1137 n. 2 (9th Cir.2002). Where federal statutes do not contain their own limitations periods, federal courts apply the most appropriate or analogous state statute of limitations. See Goodman v. Lukens Steel Co., 482 U.S. 656, 660, 107 S.Ct. 2617, 96 L.Ed.2d 572 (1987); see also Pickern, 293 F.3d at 1137 n. 2.
>
> A number of federal district courts in California have ruled that California's two-year statute of limitations for personal injury actions applies to federal disability claims brought in California. Pickern, 293 F.3d at 1137 n. 2. Some district courts, however, have found the ADA to be more analogous to California's Unruh Civil Rights Act than to a personal injury action. (Citations omitted)

Kemp, *supra*, at *5.

> The Kemp Court noted that neither the ADA, the Unruh Act, or the Disabled Persons Act (DPA) included their own statute of limitations, and there was no known "formal" decision on "which limitation period applies to Unruh Act claims." Id. at *6. Kemp cited Gatto v. County of Sonoma, 98 Cal. App.4th 744 (2002), as holding "that the personal injury statute of limitations should apply to causes of action under provisions that have evolved from common law, but that the three-year statute (Civil Code section 338) should apply to others" Id.
>
> After further analysis the Kemp Court decided "that California's three year statute of limitations for statutory violations should apply to plaintiff's claim under Title II of the ADA." Id. at *7.

O'Campo v. Chico Mall, 758 F.Supp.2d 976 (E.D. Cal, 2010) held plaintiff's complaint did not have to state the dates of his visits in order to avoid a FRCP 12(b)(1) motion to dismiss, based on plaintiff's failure to allege that he had visited the premises "within the statute of limitations." "Plaintiff is not required to plead facts in anticipation of an affirmative defense (citations omitted) . . . Thus plaintiff need not plead the date of his visit , and defendants motion to dismiss for failure to state a claim is denied." Id. at 983.

11. **POINT-OF-SALE MACHINES MAY VIOLATE STATUTORY PROTECTIONS FOR DISABLED USABILITY**

Point-of-sale machines may violate Title 24, the California Building Code. Per section 1117B.7.2.1 "in grocery stores and other retail outlets with point-of sale machines located at individual check stands, machines that are located at the accessible check

stand must be made accessible," and the screen must be positioned so that it is "readily visable to and usable by a person sitting in a wheelchair." CBC section 1117B.7.5. Attorney Russ Handy of San Diego has successfully won point of sale devise cases where the screen was horizontal and located more than 34 inches above the finished floor, per CBC section 1117.B.7.5.3. Russ Handy also argues it is a violation of ADA Title III to fail to remove "readily achievable" barriers, and that such barriers:
> include devices that 'are mounted at a height that makes them inaccessible to people using wheelchairs.' U.S. Department of Justice, Civil Rights Division, the Americans with Disabilities Act: Title III Technical Assistance Manual section 4.4100 (1993)[76]

K. CALIFORNIA STATUTORY ATTORNEY FEES

1. STATUTES OFFERING ATTORNEY FEES

Attorney fees in ADA/California state law access cases are alternatively available under federal and state law, and in both state court and federal court[77].

   a. FEDERAL LAW FEES, PER ADA § 505, TO "PREVAILING PARTY," WITH NO REQUIREMENT FOR ANY "PRE-LITIGATION DEMAND"

Section 505 of the ADA (42 USC 12205) allows the court to award reasonable attorney fees to the prevailing party. (Per "Christiansburg" principle, no attorney fees may be awarded against a "good faith" plaintiff who loses an ADA case. Brown v. Lucky Stores, Inc., et al. (9th Cir. 2001) 246 F.3d 1182, extended this to awards of costs as well, in the 9th Circuit.) "Attorney fees" are defined to include litigation costs.

> Sec. 505. ATTORNEY'S FEES
>
> In any action or administrative proceeding commenced pursuant to this chapter, the court or agency, in its discretion, may allow the prevailing party, other than the United States, a reasonable attorney's fee, including litigation expenses, and costs, and the United States shall be liable for the foregoing the same as a private individual.

Skaff v. Meridien North America Beverly Hills, LLC (9th Cir. 2007) 506 F.3d 832 rejected several frequently claimed defenses, holding that a prevailing party who obtained damages and injunctive relief was entitled to attorney fees despite the lack of a "pre-litigation demand." (thereby rejecting a prior and contrary District Court holding, Doran v. Del Taco, Inc., et al. (C.D.Cal. 2005) 373 F.Supp.2d 1028,

---

[76] Quoted from attorney Russ Handy's successful Summary Judgment Memorandum in Salinas v. Rite Aid, case C10-74995 SYW (Central District, 2010).

[77] See also section IV, *infra*, in this book, "Attorneys Fees under the ADA".

which had been gleefully accepted by the defense bar.) In Skaff the 9th Circuit reiterated the proper standard in its f.n.12:

> Skaff is also a prevailing party under the ADA pursuant to Buckhannon, which held that "court-ordered consent decrees create the 'material alteration of the legal relationship of the parties' necessary to permit an award of attorney's fees." Buckhannon, 532 U.S. at 604 (quoting Tex. State Teachers Ass'n v. Garland Indep. Sch. Dist., 489 U.S. 782, 792-93 (1989)). Likewise, in Barrios v. California Interscholastic Federation, 277 F.3d 1128, 1134 (9th Cir.2002), we held that "[u]nder applicable Ninth Circuit law, a plaintiff 'prevails' when he or she enters into a legally enforceable settlement agreement against the defendant."

Skaff, *supra*, was followed and expanded upon by the 9th Circuit in Jankey v. Poop Deck (2008) 537 F.3d 1122, which held "that a district court may not use a lack of pre-litigation notice as a factor in determining whether to deny as unjust a request for attorney fees under the ADA." Id. at 1131.

b. STATE LAW FEES PER CIVIL CODE §§ 52, 54.3 AND 55; CODE OF CIVIL PROCEDURE § 1021.5; HEALTH & SAFETY CODE § 19953

Attorney fees are available under multiple California state law statutes which should be pled in the complaint: Civil Code § 52 for violation of Civil Code § 51; Civil Code § 54.3 for obtaining damages for violation of Civil Code §§ 54 or 54.1 (c.f. Hankins v. El Torito, *supra*.); Civil Code § 55 for obtaining injunctive relief for violation of §§ 54 or 54.1;[78] Code of Civil Procedure § 1021.5 ("private attorneys general"); Health & Safety Code § 19953 for obtaining an injunction to enforce California Health & Safety Code §§ 19955-19959. [See detailed discussion of Christiansburg at §IV-D. *infra*.]

c. CALIFORNIA PUBLIC POLICY PROVIDES FOR AN AWARD OF ATTORNEY FEES UNDER THE DPA AND UNDER CODE OF CIVIL PROCEDURE SECTION 1021.5

The attorney fee provision of the DPA is reflective of the California "legislature's awareness of the continuous problems of enforcement" of disability access laws. Donald v. Café Royale, Inc., 218 Cal.App.3d 168,

---

[78] Caveat that some courts have held that an award of fees under section 55 Civil Code is "mandatory" rather than "discretionary." However federal appellate cases have also held that where section 55 allegations are based on parallel facts incorporated into 54 (c) or 54(d) due to alleged ADA violations, the ADA preempts any contrary state law. Hubbard v. Sobreck, 554 F.3d 742 (9th Cir. 2009). Further, Harris v. Maricopa Co. Sup. Ct., 631 F.3d 963 (9th Cir., 2011) held a prevailing defendant seeking fees must show that none of his work dealt with "intertwined" ADA and section 55 issues. (See similar holding in Turner v. Ass'n of American Medical Colleges, 193 Cal. App 4th 1047 (2011); discussed *infra*. at section I-K-8 and Fox v. Vice, 131 S.Ct 2205 (2011) discussed *infra* at IV-J. [See also Jankey v. Lee with a new threat of reverse attorney fees if plaintiff loses a section 55 Civil Code claim and defendant is designated prevailing party, discussed *infra*.]

179, 266 Cal.Rptr. 804 (1990). In explicitly providing for the recovery of attorney's fees, even though the DPA does not require a showing of damages, the California legislature explicitly determined that there is a societal value to the vindication of the rights at issue here.

Kittok v. Leslie's Poolmart, Inc. (E.D. Cal. 2009) 687 F.Supp.2d. 953, 960. The Kittok court, *supra*, went on to strike down several other defense arguments.

> Despite defendant's contrary suggestion, there is no general requirement that a plaintiff prevail on all of her claims to recover attorneys' fees, nor that "attorney fees bear a percentage relationship to the ultimate recovery of damages in a civil rights case."
> (Citations Omitted)
> Id.

In Blackwell v. Foley, 724 F.Supp.2d 1068, the Court held as an <u>alternative basis</u> for awarding attorney fees:
> obtaining a result in the public interest per California Code of Civil Procedure § 1021.5; maximizing the rights of disabled persons is designated as an important public interest by Government Code § 19230:
>
>> The Legislature hereby declares that (a) It is the policy of this State to encourage and enable individual with a disability to participate fully in the social and economic life of the State and to engage in remunerative employment.
>> Blackwell v. Foley, 724 F. Supp. 2d 1068, 1074 (N.D. Cal. 2010)

In Coles v. City of Oakland (2007) WL39304 (N.D.Cal.), Judge Thelton Henderson explained why attorney fee compensation was important to encourage public interest litigation:
> [O]ne of the primary purposes of the private attorney general doctrine, as codified in section 1021.5 of the California Code of Civil Procedure, is to encourage private parties to bring suits that enforce strong public policies and benefit the public interest when they would otherwise be economically infeasible. Woodland Hills Residents Ass'n, 23 Cal.3d at 933, 154 Cal.Rptr. 503, 593 P.2d 200. This purpose would "often be frustrated, sometimes nullified, if awards are diluted or dissipated by lengthy, uncompensated proceedings to fix or defend a rightful fee claim." Serrano IV, 32 Cal.3d at 632, 186 Cal.Rptr. 754, 652 P.2d 985.
> Id. at p.10.

d. ADA PLAINTIFFS ARE CARRYING OUT IMPORTANT PUBLIC POLICIES AS "PRIVATE ATTORNEY GENERALS"

"[P]laintiffs or plaintiff classes who bring suit pursuant to the ADA do so in the role of 'private attorneys general' who seek to vindicate 'a policy 'of the highest priority.'" <u>Walker v. Carnival Cruise Lines, et al.</u>, 107 F.Supp.2d 1135, 1143 (N.D.Cal. 2000).

In <u>Serrano v. Unruh</u> (1982) 32 Cal.3d 621, 639, 186 Cal.Rptr. 754, 652 P.2d 985, the Supreme Court indicated "that, absent circumstances rendering the award unjust, fees recoverable under section 1021.5 ordinarily include <u>compensation for all hours reasonably spent</u> ..." <u>It must be remembered that an award of attorneys' fees is not a gift. It is just compensation for expenses actually incurred in vindicating a public right.</u> [Emphasis added.]

<u>Blackwell,v. Foley</u>, (N.D. Cal, 2010) 724 F.Supp. 2d 1068, 1085-1086, citing <u>Sundance v. Municipal Court</u>, (1987) 192 Cal. App. 3d. 168.

The importance of civil rights plaintiffs in carrying out enforcement of congressional policy was emphasized by the U.S. Supreme Court in <u>Fox v. Vice</u>, 131 S. Ct. 2205 (2011), a June, 2011 unanimous opinion which limited the availability of statutory attorney fees against civil rights plaintiffs to defendant's fees and costs which would not have been incurred "but for" the claims determined by the Court to be <u>entirely "frivolous."</u>

e. **PLAINTIFFS ARE ALSO ENFORCING IMPORTANT PUBLIC POLICY UNDER CALIFORNIA LAW.**

The fee-shifting statutes reflect a judgment that civil rights laws will be underenforced unless private lawyers are given financial incentives to bring cases under those laws.

<u>Kittok v. Leslie's Poolmart, Inc.</u>, 687 F. Supp. 2d 953, 959-60 (C.D. Cal. 2009)
But see dangers of reverse attorney fees, against plaintiff, under <u>Jankey v. Lee</u> California Supreme Court decision, December 17, 2012.

f. **PER <u>MORENO</u>, ATTORNEY FEES MUST BE SET AT DISTRICT'S MARKET RATE FOR ATTORNEYS WITH SIMILAR QUALIFICATIONS**

In 2008 the 9th Circuit addressed the practice of Judges in certain districts- in this case the district court judges in the Eastern District of California- of setting a "cap" or "maximum" hourly rate for civil rights attorneys fees, regardless of a particular attorney's expertise or number of years in practice. In <u>Moreno v. City of Sacramento</u> (9th Cir. 2008) 534 F.3d 1106, Chief Judge Alex Kozinski reversed as unfair to plaintiffs' attorneys the setting of an hourly fee award based on a $250/hr <u>cap</u> set by certain Eastern District Judges: "The Court also erred by applying what appears to be a <u>de facto</u> policy of awarding a rate of $250 an hour to civil rights cases." Id. at 1115.

In this case, the district court used the lodestar method to calculate fees. Under this method, a district court must start by determining

how many hours were reasonably expended on the litigation, and then multiply those hours by the prevailing local rate for an attorney of the skill required to perform the litigation. See Blum, 465 U.S. at 895, 104 S.Ct. 1541. The district court may then adjust upward or downward based on a variety of factors. Hensley, 461 U.S. at 434, 103 S.Ct. 1933.
Id. at 1111.

[SEE ALSO SECTION IV-G, *Infra*.]

2. CALIFORNIA "CATALYST" FEES SURVIVE, BUT ONLY WHEN PRE-LITIGATION OFFER TO SETTLE WAS PREVIOUSLY MADE BY PLAINTIFF
   a. GRAHAM V. DAIMLERCHRYSTLER ALLOWED LIMITED "CATALYST THEORY"

   California's "catalyst" theory may avoid Buckhannon limits on ADA attorney fees and may be appropriate in cases where plaintiff had complained and given advance notice (and made a reasonable effort to settle) prior to filing suit. Such notice may also be of assistance to plaintiff tactically in certain cases, by providing a possible basis for treble damages when defendants make no effort to comply even after being given written notice of access deficiencies.

   Another use of advance notice is in the situation where defendants do take action to remove barriers after they're sued, but do not settle the case. They may fail to settle either because they (a) haven't timely completed the access barrier removals requested, or (b) fail to complete providing access and at the same time refuse to settle reasonably for damages and attorney fees. Under the California Supreme Court's Graham v. DaimlerChrysler Corp. (2004) 34 Cal.4th 553 case, and its companion case, Tipton-Whittingham, et al. v. City of Los Angeles (2004) 34 Cal.4th 604, a plaintiff suing under California law may still obtain "catalyst" attorney fees (per section 1021.5 California Civil Code) despite the United States Supreme Court's holding in Buckhannon Board & Care Home, Inc., et al. v. West Virginia Dept. of Health & Human Services, et al. (2001) 121 S.Ct. 1835 that "catalyst" fees cannot be obtained under federal law, provided that plaintiff has made a reasonable pre-litigation effort to settle.

   Since the "catalyst" fees may be recoverable under Code of Civil Procedure § 1021.5 for obtaining a public interest result, (or possibly under Civil Code § 55 for obtaining injunctive relief to protect a disabled person from ongoing disability related discrimination), the focus in any "failure to settle" issue should be solely regarding the efforts to obtain barrier removal as injunctive relief. However, sometimes the defendant will make the mistake of refusing to settle the injunctive relief unless plaintiff also settles his damages and attorney fees at an inadequate level. In this situation it should be clear that plaintiff has made a reasonable pre-litigation effort to settle the injunctive relief issues, i.e., by a pre-litigation demand which gives defendants a reasonable opportunity to settle (See <u>Graham</u>, *supra*). For example, if defendants, <u>after being sued</u>, finally take action to remove the barriers and then say that the injunctive relief is now "moot," (thus potentially depriving the federal court of its jurisdiction under the ADA cause of action), plaintiff can then point out that defendants have now triggered "catalyst" attorney fees for plaintiff <u>provided that a "pre-litigation" effort to settle was made</u>. Then, by the very act of removing all barriers and then telling the trial court that they have removed all barriers and that therefore the injunctive relief is moot, defendants may help prove plaintiff's right to "catalyst" attorney fees in appropriate cases.

Note that there may be short time limits for filing an attorney fees motion, for example after a federal court's decision to dismiss a case based on mootness and the lack of a continuing federal question (30 days from dismissal Order, 28 USC 1441(e)(1)). Plaintiff's fee motion may, by declarations as well as evidence supplied by defendants themselves, <u>show</u> that the <u>pre-litigation efforts</u> plus the lawsuit itself served as a "catalyst" to get defendants to remove the architectural barriers, change their policy, or otherwise stop discriminating against disabled persons. This may allow a statutory award of attorney fees on a "catalyst" - "plaintiff caused defendants to take this action" - legal theory.

Use of this theory may be particularly important when plaintiff has not had sufficient time or opportunity to obtain summary judgment or other judicial ruling which would make the plaintiff the "prevailing party." (Of course, if the plaintiff <u>is</u> a "prevailing party" he will be able to obtain attorney fees under both federal and state law, even under the <u>Buckhannon</u>, *supra*, holding.) See <u>Skaff</u>, *supra*.

Depending on the facts of the case, the ease of obtaining the requested compliance, and other factors, giving advance notice may provide plaintiff with a useful tactical tool in protecting the public interest while protecting the attorney's right to get paid for his or her public interest work.[79]

Does filing a government claim constitute a reasonable pre-litigation offer to settle? A California Government Tort Claim is required for damages under state law, but <u>including a demand for injunctive relief with the government tort claim</u> may be factually relevant if a "catalyst" issue later arises. This is especially relevant when defendant government agencies often simply ignore- or actually deny- <u>all</u> claims made- (perhaps knowing that many "denied" claims are not followed up on by actual lawsuits.)

    b. NO PRELITIGATION NOTICE OR <u>PRE-LITIGATION</u> SETTLEMENT EFFORTS ARE RELEVANT <u>UNLESS</u> PLAINTIFF SEEKS FEES UNDER CCP 1021.5 ON A <u>CATALYST</u> BASIS

In late 2007 the 9th Circuit made clear that the pre-litigation notice requirement only applied to plaintiff's efforts to claim "catalyst" attorney fees in cases where plaintiff was <u>not</u> the "prevailing party" under California law. In <u>Skaff v. Meridien North America Beverly Hills, LLC</u> (9th Cir. 2007) 506 F.3d 832, plaintiff had obtained injunctive relief and damages in the District Court, and so was the "prevailing party" as a matter of law. However, Judge Manuel Real of the Central District refused to award fees because he decided that plaintiff had no "standing." The District Court ruled that plaintiff could not be awarded statutory ADA and California "public interest" fees where plaintiff had not given any pre-filing "notice" or made any pre-filing settlement effort. In <u>Skaff</u>, the 9th Circuit set broad "standing" rules and again <u>rejected any pretrial "settlement effort" requirement</u> <u>for a "prevailing party"</u> who did not rely on a "catalyst" theory: "We also hold that California law did not in this case require Skaff to make a pre-suit attempt to settle in order to seek attorneys' fees under section 1021.5 of the California Code of Civil Procedure." Id. at 846[24]

    c. WRITTEN SETTLEMENT OFFERS <u>MAY</u> BE RELEVANT PER CIVIL CODE SECTION 55.55 [SEE § I-L, *supra*]

---

[79] Prior to the California Supreme Court's decision in <u>Graham v. DaimlerChrysler Corp</u>. (2004) 34 Cal.4th 553, following the U.S. Supreme Court's ruling in <u>Buckhannon</u>, *supra*, the "catalyst" theory in California was represented by <u>Folsom v. Butte County Association of Governments</u> (1982) 32 Cal.3d 668. There the California Supreme Court affirmed orders granting costs and attorney fees to plaintiff and remanded the matter to the trial court with directions to hear and determine the plaintiffs' request for fees on appeal as well. The Court found that plaintiffs' litigation had been "influential" in the defendant's decision to take actions sought by the complaint; that plaintiffs therefore were the successful parties within the meaning of Code of Civil Procedure § 1021.5; and that the plaintiffs were "prevailing parties" despite a partial summary judgment having been granted in defendants' favor. The Court held that in determining the "prevailing party," the Court would look to the "impact of the action, not the manner of its resolution. If the impact has been `enforcement of an important right affecting the public interest' and the consequent conferral of a `significant benefit on the general public or a large class of persons'," a Code of Civil Procedure § 1021.5 award is justified, regardless of whether the case was settled before trial.

    As Congress seems to have reasoned in enacting the Fees Act: "A `prevailing party' should not be penalized for seeking an out of court settlement, thus helping to lessen docket congestion. Similarly after a complaint is filed, a defendant might voluntarily cease the unlawful practice. A court should still award fees even though it might conclude, as a matter of equity, that no formal relief ... is needed." (Emphasis added)

<u>Folsom v. Butte County Association of Governments</u> 32 Cal.3d 668 at 686.

3. RELEVANT AUTHORITY ON FEE ISSUES

   a. PUBLIC POLICY REQUIRES A FEE AWARD INCLUDING COMPENSATION FOR ALL HOURS REASONABLY INCURRED, ESPECIALLY WHEN PLAINTIFF HAS OBTAINED "EXCELLENT RESULTS"

   Defense counsel are usually paid for all of their hourly billings and compensated for all of their advanced costs and out of pocket litigation expenses, either by the named defendant or the defendant's insurance carrier. Plaintiff's counsel's work in obtaining a public interest result on a contingent fee "risk" basis should also be fully compensated.

   "Where plaintiff has obtained 'excellent results,' his or her attorney should recover a fully compensatory fee." Wallace v. Consumers Co-Op of Berkeley, Inc., *supra*, 170 Cal. App. 3d at 850, quoting Hensley v. Eckerhart (1983) 461 U.S. 424, 434-435. If plaintiff has achieved "excellent results," he should point this out to the court.

   In many cases plaintiff will have succeeded in achieving dual objectives of injunctive relief and damages. Even if he had not been "totally" successful, a diminution of plaintiff's fees would not be appropriate if he achieved one or both of these objectives even though he lost on certain alternative theories. In regard to this issue, important principles for consideration in setting attorneys' fees for a public interest oriented plaintiff were set out in Sundance v. Municipal Court (1987) 192 Cal.App.3d 268, 273:

   > The issue posed is whether plaintiffs are entitled to all hours reasonably spent in pursuit of this litigation or whether compensation for legal theories on which the plaintiffs did not prevail should be excluded from the award, even though the litigation was ultimately successful. In the abstract, this would not seem to present much of a problem. In Serrano v. Unruh (1982) 32 Cal.3d 621, 639 [186 Cal. Rptr. 754, 652 P.2d 985], the Supreme Court indicated "that, absent circumstances rendering the award unjust, fees recoverable under section 1021.5 ordinarily include compensation for all hours reasonably spent..." Section 1021.5 itself simply states that awards are to be made to successful parties, with no mention of excluding compensation for the successful parties' unsuccessful legal theories. Moreover, as a practical matter, it is impossible for an attorney to determine before starting work on a potentially meritorious legal theory whether it will or will not be accepted by a court years later following litigation. It must be remembered that an award of attorneys' fees is not a gift. It is just compensation for expenses actually incurred in vindicating a public

---

[80] A dissent in the Skaff case, which decided the case on California law issues as well as the ADA, was by a visiting judge from the Southern District of New York, "sitting by designation." Skaff was handled by attorney Sid Cohen of Oakland.

right. To reduce the attorneys' fees of a successful party because he did not prevail on all his arguments, makes it the attorney, and not the defendant, who pays the cost of enforcing the public right.
(Emphasis added.)

b. THE FEE AWARD MUST BE LARGE ENOUGH TO ENTICE COMPETENT COUNSEL TO UNDERTAKE DIFFICULT PUBLIC INTEREST CASES

In Blackwell v. Foley 724 F.Supp.2nd 1068 (N.D. Cal. 2010) at 1076, the Northern District Court noted:

> The "fundamental objective" of attorney fee statutes is "to encourage suits effectuating a strong [public] policy by awarding substantial attorney's fees ... to those who successfully bring such suits...." Woodland Hills Residents Ass'n., Inc. v. City Council, 23 Cal.3d 917, 933, 154 Cal.Rptr. 503, 593 P.2d 200 (1979). To accomplish this, the award must be large enough "to entice competent counsel to undertake difficult public interest cases." San Bernardino Valley Audubon Society, Inc. v. County of San Bernardino, 155 Cal.App.3d 738, 755, 202 Cal. Rptr. 423 (1984). As the court decided in Woodland Hills:
>> The Doctrine rests upon a recognition that privately initiated lawsuits are often essential to the effectuation of fundamental public policies...and that, without some mechanism authorizing the award of attorney's fees, private actions to enforce such important public policies would as a practical matter frequently be infeasible.
>
> Blackwell v. Foley, *supra*, 724 F.Supp.2nd 1068 (N.D. Cal. 2010) at 1076, quoting from Woodland Hills, *supra*, at 933.

In Kittok v. Leslie's Poolmart Inc., 687 F.Supp.2d 953, at 959 (E.D. Cal, 2009), the Court emphasized that the purpose of the DPA's attorneys fee provisions was to encourage enforcement by private lawsuits:

> Yes, plaintiff's counsel stand to benefit financially from this lawsuit, as do defendant's counsel, who presumably are not representing defendant on a contingency basis. But this does not, in and of itself, call into question the legitimacy of their fee request. "The fee-shifting statutes reflect a judgment that civil rights laws will be underenforced unless private lawyers are given financial incentives to bring cases under those laws." Bagenstos, *supra*, 54 U.C.L.A. L.Rev. at 30. Defense counsel cannot assert these very incentives as a reason to deny the statutorily conferred right they were designed to bring. "That plaintiffs' lawyers want to be paid the 'reasonable' attorneys' fees authorized by statute should provide no basis for objecting to their litigation practices."
>
> . . .Because the Court found that Leslie's "denie[d] or interfere[d] with admittance to or enjoyment" of a public accommodation, the

statute confers a right to fees. The attorney fee provision of the DPA is reflective of the California "legislature's awareness of the continuous problems of enforcement" of disability access laws. Donald v. Café Royale, Inc., 218 Cal.App.3d 168, 179, 266 Cal.Rptr. 804 (1990). In explicitly providing for the recovery of attorney's fees, even though the DPA does not require a showing of damages, the California legislature explicitly determined that there is a societal value to the vindication of the rights at issue here.

Kittok v. Leslie's Poolmart, 687 F.Supp.2d 953, at 959.

c. UNDER CALIFORNIA LAW A MULTIPLIER "ENHANCEMENT" OF THE LODESTAR MAY BE EARNED FOR THE "RISK" OF HANDLING A CIVIL RIGHTS CASE ON A CONTINGENT FEE BASIS

(1) KETCHUM V. MOSES SET THE STANDARD

In Ketchum v. Moses, (2001) 24 Cal.4th 1122, the California Supreme Court reaffirmed its Serrano holding that fee awards should be fully compensatory, including an award, in appropriate cases, of a multiplier enhancement:

> We held in Serrano IV that, absent circumstances rendering the award unjust, an attorney fee award should ordinarily include compensation for all the hours reasonably spent, including those relating solely to the fee... We explained that the purpose behind statutory fee authorizations -- i.e., encouraging attorneys to act as private attorneys general and to vindicate important rights affecting the public interest -- "will often be frustrated, sometimes nullified, if awards are diluted or dissipated by lengthy, uncompensated proceedings to fix or defend a rightful fee claim."
> . . .
> Subsequently, in Press v. Lucky Stores Inc. (1983) 34 Cal. 3d 311, 322... we underscored the importance of the "proper determination and use of the lodestar figure" in calculating awards of statutory attorney fees... We also reiterated that the lodestar figure may be increased by application of a fee enhancement, or reduced as appropriate, after the trial court has considered other factors concerning the lawsuit, including the contingent nature of the fee award. (Ibid.)(Emphasis added)

Ketchum, *supra*, at 1133-1134.

In Ketchum, the California Supreme Court specifically rejected defendants' "windfall" argument and established that an enhancement for "risk" was necessary to "approximate market-level compensation":

> [T]he purpose of a fee enhancement is primarily to compensate the attorney for the prevailing party at a rate reflecting the risk of nonpayment in contingency cases as a class...

> The adjustment to the lodestar figure, e.g., to provide a fee enhancement reflecting the risk that the attorney will not receive payment if the suit does not succeed, <u>constitutes earned compensation; unlike a windfall, it is neither unexpected nor fortuitous</u>. Rather, it is intended to approximate market-level compensation for such services, which typically includes a <u>premium for the risk of nonpayment or delay in payment of attorney fees</u>.
>
> Ketchum, *supra*, at 1138. (Emphasis added.)

In <u>Green v. Dillingham Constr. N.A., Inc.</u>, 101 Cal.App.4th 418 (2002), a California Court of Appeal clarified that, to the extent that prior case law <u>limited</u> risk multiplier <u>to cases that result in great public value or involve complex legal or factual issues</u>, they were no longer good law after <u>Ketchum</u>, which now <u>requires that a risk enhancement</u> be considered in every contingent fee case:

> Under our precedents, the unadorned lodestar reflects the general local hourly rate for a fee-bearing case; it does not include any compensation for contingent risk, extraordinary skill, or any other factors a trial court may consider under Serrano III. The adjustment to the lodestar figure, e.g., <u>to provide a fee enhancement reflecting the risk</u> that the attorney will not receive payment if <u>the suit does not succeed, constitutes earned</u> compensation; <u>unlike a windfall, it is neither</u> unexpected nor fortuitous. Rather, it is intended to approximate market-level compensation for such services, which typically includes a premium for the risk of nonpayment or delay in payment of attorney fees.
>
> <u>Greene v. Dillingham Constr. N.A., Inc.</u>, 101 Cal.App.4th 418, at 427 (2002). (Emphasis added)

In <u>Greene</u>, *supra*, the Court applied the <u>Ketchum v. Moses</u>, *supra*, standards to a trial court attorney fee decision that had been issued before <u>Ketchum</u> was decided. The <u>Greene</u> court affirmed the trial court's award of over one million dollars in attorney fees, but held it was <u>error</u> for the trial court to <u>fail to consider a fee enhancement, based on the case being handled on a contingent risk basis</u>. The Court held that because the California Supreme Court in <u>Ketchum</u> "has reaffirmed that contingent risk is a valid consideration in determining whether to apply a fee enhancement in cases where attorneys fees are authorized by statute, we must remand the matter to the trial court for it to exercise its discretion on whether a fee enhancement is merited for this case for contingent risk." Id. at 428 - 429. However the Court made clear that "on remand Greene bears the burden of proving that a fee enhancement is warranted," Id., citing <u>Ketchum</u>, *supra*, 24 Cal.4th at p 1138, and that "the trial court is properly guided by the considerations set forth in Ketchum, Weeks, and Flannery."[81] Id.

(2) SOME EXAMPLES OF REASONS FOR "RISK" MULTIPLIER AWARD

The following are several "multiplier" attorney fee awards received by our office, along with each court's rationale for the multipliers:

> In Michael Pachovas v. County of Alameda and City of Berkeley, Case No. 713973-8, plaintiff, a quadriplegic had obtained significant injunctive relief (in addition to recovering his own damages): an accessible jail cell (room) at the Berkeley City Jail, accessible holding cell at Santa Rita Jail, an end to Berkeley Police policy of taking all disabled persons 25 miles to Santa Rita (because Berkeley City jails were all inaccessible); and installation of an elevator to access the second floor courtrooms at the Berkeley Municipal Court. Superior Court Judge Jacqueline Taber awarded all plaintiff's attorneys fees and costs, and added a 1.4 multiplier, finding that:
>
>> The Plaintiff's attorney is highly specialized in a narrow, complicated area of law, the defendant [City of Berkeley] fought plaintiff not only energetically and consistently but, until very recently, maintained no liability whatsoever, putting plaintiff's investment of time and money at great and total risk. Plaintiff, furthermore, had advanced costs out of pocket in the amount of $10,214 with a risk of losing those as well as his time invested. And finally, and probably most importantly, Plaintiff would have been without the practical ability to enforce important rights under California and Federal law were it not for the attorneys such as plaintiff's attorney who was willing to risk so much.
>
> Id. Order of August , 1996, p. 1-2. (Alameda County Superior Court).

> Similarly in Atwood v. El Torito Restaurants, Inc., Restaurant Enterprises Group, Inc., Alameda Superior Court, No. 677858-1, the Honorable Joseph J. Carson awarded an attorney fee multiplier of 1.5, finding inter alia, that the case had extended over a number of years, including trial and multiple motions; that "the facts of the case required specific knowledge" of the applicable codes and regulations; and that:
>
>> few attorneys would have accepted the continued representation

---

[81] Query whether the "risk" of reverse attorney fees to a prevailing defendant under Civil Code section 55 (see Jankey v. Lee, *supra*, December 17, 2012) can now be an additional risk factor for a prevailing plaintiff seking an enhancement of fees?

of plaintiff when confronted with numerous pretrial motions and litigation that extended over a number of years. [Plaintiff's attorney] has demonstrated that he has special skills and experience in the field of civil rights involving handicap access; and an important public service was provided handicap citizens by the prosecution of this case. A popular restaurant was made fully-accessible to citizens in wheelchairs and the dangerous condition of the front landing was corrected.

Id. Order of Oct. 7, 1999.

In Hankins v. El Torito, *supra*, on remand after being affirmed by the Court Appeal, the trial Court awarded additional fees for plaintiff's appellate work, including a 1.4 multiplier because of the policy precedents set by the appellate decision's publication.

d. WHERE ATTORNEY FEES HAVE BEEN DELAYED, THE COURT MAY AWARD FEES AT HIGHER, CURRENT RATES

Plaintiff may request that attorney fee rates be set at current rates for litigation that has spanned a number of years. Per the leading text on attorney fees in California, California Attorney Fee Awards, 2nd Edition (CEB) by Richard Pearl, at § 12.30, Current or Historic Rates.

> To compensate for the length of time the successful party's attorney has had to wait to receive fees (i.e., for the lost use of the funds and for the effects of inflation), the court may either based the award on "historical rates," with an appropriate adjustment in the nature of prejudgment interest, or it may simply award fees at higher current rates as rough compensation for the delay. Missouri v. Jenkins (1989) 491 US 274, 284, 105 L Ed 2d 229, 240, 109 S.Ct. 2463; Pennsylvania v. Delaware Valley Citizens' Council for Clean Air (Delaware Valley II) (1987) 483 US 711, 97 L Ed 2d 585 109 S Ct 3078; Lanni v. New Jersey (3d Cir 2001) 259 F3d 146; Bell v. Clackamas County (9th Cir 2003) 341 F3d 858, 868 (reversing fee award because district court based rate on outdated award); In re Washington Pub. Power Supply Sys. Litig. (9th Cir 1994) 19 F3rd 1291, 1305; Gates v. Deukmejian (9th Cir 1992) 987 F2d 1392; Davis v. City & County of San Francisco (9thCir 1992) 976 F2d 1536, 1548.

As noted, this method was approved by the United States Supreme Court in Missouri v. Jenkins (1989) 491 U.S. 274, 284, which was cited by the District Court in Blackwell v. Foley 724 F.Supp.2nd 1068 (N.D. Cal. 2010) at 1078, in finding "Plaintiff's counsel are entitled to receive their current hourly rates as compensation for the delay in payment."

e. DEFENDANTS' ATTORNEYS' HOURS SPENT ARE <u>NOT</u> A PROPER CRITERIA FOR MEASURING THE REASONABLENESS OF PLAINTIFF'S ATTORNEYS' HOURS

In <u>Chabner v. United Of Omaha Life Insurance Co.</u>, 1999 WL 33227443 (N.D.Cal.) C95-0447 MHP (Opinion of October 12, 1999), (at p.5, l.5-17) Judge Marilyn Hall Patel rejected defendants' efforts to compare plaintiff's fees practices with those of defendants:

> [T]he court notes a flawed premise upon which defendant repeatedly relies in its opposition to plaintiff's proposed lodestar. Defendant uses its own counsel's practices as a benchmark for evaluating the conduct of plaintiff's attorneys. The comparisons defendant draws are inapposite. Seyfarth, Shaw... and Disability Rights Advocates (DRA) each has its own unique organizational chart. The pyramidal staffing pattern of a commercial insurance defense firm contrasts with the flatter, looser structure of a small nonprofit law center. <u>Defendant ignores the crucial differences between prosecuting and defending a case. These include the burden of proof, the relative difficulty of obtaining access to essential information</u>, and the chance that a given case may have greater precedential value for one side than the other. [citation] <u>Finally, defendant lost this case, so defendant's approach does not recommend a model for conducting litigation.</u> [Emphasis added]

The practice of certain defense attorneys of attacking a plaintiff's attorneys' requested rates or timekeeping methods solely on the basis of the defense attorneys' own personal opinion, has recently been questioned by Judge Patel in <u>Blackwell</u>, *supra*:

> Defense counsel Mr. Tcheng, <u>with no particular expertise beyond his own Bar card</u>, attempts to analyze the time sheets of Plaintiff's counsel, objecting to certain percentages of time as excessively spent on certain tasks. As the court did in <u>Chabner</u>, this Court rejects this uninformed second-guessing and finds, following a review of Plaintiff's attorneys' time records, that the hours expended by Plaintiff's attorneys were reasonable.
>
> <u>Blackwell v. Foley</u> 724 F.Supp.2nd 1068 (N.D. Cal. 2010) at 1078. (Emphasis added)

f. PLAINTIFF'S ATTORNEY IS ENTITLED TO COMPENSATION FOR ALL HOURS REASONABLY SPENT, AND MAY ESTABLISH THOSE HOURS BY VERIFIED TIME STATEMENTS

"[A]bsent circumstances rendering the award unjust, fees recoverable ... ordinarily include compensation for all hours reasonably spent, including those necessary to establish and defend the fee claim." Ketchum v. Moses (2001) 24 Cal.4th 1122, at 1141, quoting Serrano v. Unruh (Serrano IV) (1982) 32 Cal.3d 621, 638.

As noted by Judge Thelton Henderson in Coles v. City of Oakland, 2007 WL 39304 (N.D.Cal), at p.8: "Because attorneys are officers of the Court, verified time statements of an attorney seeking fees are 'entitled to credence in the absence of a clear indication the records are erroneous.'"

4. THE AMOUNT OF DAMAGES RECOVERED CANNOT SERVE AS A CAP OR LIMITATION ON THE AMOUNT OF FEES AWARDED, ESPECIALLY IN SITUATIONS IN WHICH DEFENDANTS' RESISTANCE DRIVES UP THE AMOUNT OF A PLAINTIFF'S FEES

a. NO CAP OR LIMITATION ON AMOUNT OF FEES

Because the primary purpose of private attorney general fee statutes is to encourage the enforcement of important statutory rights -- rights that often do not involve large damages but provide significant nonpecuniary benefits -- the amount of damages recovered cannot serve as a cap or limitation on the amount of fees to be awarded under these statutes. (See e.g., City of Riverside v. Rivera (1986) 477 U.S. 561, 574, affirming a fee award of $245,000 where Plaintiffs obtained no injunctive or declaratory relief and only $33,350 in damages; Serrano v. Unruh ("Serrano IV") (1982) 32 Cal.3d 621, 639 n. 29; Camacho v. Schaefer; (1987) 193 Cal.App.3d 718, 724; Drouin v. Fleetwood Enterprises (1985) 162 Cal.App.3d 486, 493; Quesada v. Thomason (9th Cir. 1988) 850 F.2d 537, 540, reversing private attorney general fee award as inadequate where trial Court reduced fee because of low damage award; purpose of fee statutes is to enable Plaintiffs to secure competent attorneys even where damages are small; Bonnette v. Health and Welfare Agency (9th Cir. 1983) 704 F.2d 1465, 1473 affirming fee award of $100,000 where Plaintiffs recovered only $20,000 in damages; United States Football League v. National Football League (2d Cir. 1989) 887 F.2d 408, upholding fee award of more than $5,000,000 in an antitrust action where Plaintiff recovered only $1 in damages (trebled to $3) "Because of the importance of the policy of encouraging private parties to bring anti-trust actions, recovery of their reasonable attorney's fees must be sustained regardless of the amount of damages awarded."; James Donald v. Cafe Royale (1990) 218 Cal.App.3d 168, awarding attorney fees under

Civil Code Section 54.3 even though the disabled Plaintiff himself was an attorney who suffered no emotional distress or actual damages and in which the Appellate Court awarded only $250 statutory minimum damages (in 1990; current section 54.3 minimum is $1,000 "per violation").

> If fees were limited by the amount of damages, no matter how meritorious the clients' claims might be, attorneys simply would not take these cases. This would be contrary to legislative determinations that statutory attorney fees should encourage attorneys to represent disabled persons. Moreover, courts have recognized that limiting fee awards by the amount of damages recovered would be especially inappropriate where the amount of fees was driven up by the defendants' resistance to the lawsuit. (Cf. Lipsett v. Blanco, 975 F.2d 934, at 939 (1st Cir.1992).) The fact that Defendants battled over the terms of the Consent Decree is, if anything, an indication that they didn't consider the terms to be "minimal." Access for people with disabilities is not "minimal"; a facility is either accessible or it isn't. Defendant's restaurant was inaccessible prior to Plaintiff's lawsuit and it was accessible afterwards. End of story.
>
> Blackwell v. Foley, 724 F.Supp.2nd 1068 (N.D. Cal. 2010), at 1077.

In Hankins v. El Torito Restaurants, (1998) 63 Cal. App. 4th 510, the trial judge set compensatory statutory damages at $80,000 for a single incident. The trial court also awarded $403,000 attorney fees for plaintiff's Superior Court representation. When defendants' appealed (unsuccessfully), to both the Court of Appeals and the California Supreme Court, on remand the trial Court added $323,000 attorney fees for plaintiff's appellate court representation, defending plaintiff's judgment. The court included a 1.4 multiplier "enhancement" because of the important policy holdings set by the published appellate decision. (Order of April 20, 1999)

In Moreno, *supra*, the 9th Circuit disapproved the Eastern District Courts' imposition of an arbitrary "cap" of $250/hr for all disability rights attorneys, and required setting each attorney's rate based on "market rate" factors. Id. 534 F.3d at 1115.

b. DEFENDANTS' CONDUCT DRIVING UP FEES

Moreover, the Courts recognize that limiting fee awards by the amount of damages recovered would be especially inappropriate where the amount of fees was driven up by the Defendants' resistance to the lawsuit. In Stokus v. Marsh (1990) 217 Cal.App.3d 647 the Court of Appeal upheld a $75,000 fee award in an unlawful detainer action involving only $6,166 in damages. The Court explained:

> "Plaintiff's counsel were met at every step with learned, energetic,

imaginative, concentrated and extensive opposition by extremely able counsel who specialize in housing matters. Defendants...put up the stoutest resistance...." (217 Cal.App.3d at 657.)

See also Camacho v. Schaefer, *supra*, 193 Cal.App.3d at 724 ("while...appellant had a legal right to take the positions he did, ...[he] could not then complain when his litigation posture generated additional legal expenses for respondents.") As recognized by the California Supreme Court: "[A party] cannot litigate tenaciously and then be heard to complain about the time necessarily spent by the Plaintiff in response." Serrano v. Unruh (1982) 32 Cal.3d 621, 638.

> Per Lipsett v. Blanco (US Court of Appeals, 1st Dist.) 975 F.2d 934, at 939: This case was bitterly contested. Appellants mounted a Stalingrad defense, resisting Lipsett at every turn and forcing her to win her hard earned victory from rock to rock and from tree to tree. Since a litigant's staffing needs often vary in direct proportion to the ferocity of her adversaries handling of the case, this factor weighs heavily in the balance. The record reflects that the court below carefully considered the parties' importunings in light of the relevant policies and precedents, concluding that the staffing, though abundant, was "reasonable and necessary given the nature of the case."

Several pages later the Lipsett court again referred to the defendants' intransigence in explaining why it was sometimes proper for the attorney's fee award (in a case that had only damages as an objective, and not injunctive relief), for the attorney's fees to exceed the damage award for the plaintiff:

> In the ordinary course of events, one would not expect a fee award to outpace a substantial award of money damages. In this instance, the discrepancy is explained largely by what we have referred to as the "Stalingrad." While this hard-nosed approach to litigation may be viewed as effective trench warfare, it must be pointed out that such tactics have a significant downside. The defendants suffer the adverse effects of that downside here. There is a corollary to the duty to defend to the utmost - the duty to take care to resolve litigation on terms that are, overall, the most favorable to a lawyer's client. Although tension exists between the two duties, they apply concurrently. When attorneys blindly pursue the former, their chosen course of action may sometimes prove to be at the expense of the latter. Lipsett, *supra*, at 941 (Emphasis added).

Some defendants' intransigence and unfair attacks on plaintiffs attorneys were highlighted by the Court in Kittok v. Leslie's Poolmart, Inc., (E.D. Cal. 2009) 687 F.Supp.2d 953, at 957:

> Unrelated to any specific objection, defendant begins its opposition with an indignant screed against litigation brought

under the ADA and other disability access laws, both in general and particularly focusing on litigation brought by plaintiff and her counsel. Defendant describes ADA lawsuits as " 'shakedown schemes' for attorney's fees," and opines that "California, in particular, has been a magnet for unscrupulous plaintiffs and counsel due to the availability of hefty monetary damages under state law." Opp'n at 1. Additionally, <u>defendant states that "plaintiff and her counsel have followed the typical ADA scheme pattern to a tee," pointing out previous cases filed by plaintiff.</u>

. . .

Defendant's attempts to argue that this case was abusive or brought in bad faith also fail. <u>These arguments are representative of a troubling trend in which disability access defendants attack the motives of plaintiffs and their counsel in nearly every case brought to enforce the right to equal access guaranteed by the ADA and California statutes.</u>

. . .

If a plaintiff establishes a violation of law which entitles her to damages and fees, the Court will not question her scruples in filing the case in the absence of any real evidence which would call those scruples into question.[FN2]

Not only are these attacks on the scruples and ethics of plaintiff and her counsel inappropriate in tone, they are wholly unsupported in substance.

Id. at 957-958. (Emphasis added)

c. PLAINTIFF IS ENTITLED TO FEES FOR ENFORCING COMPLIANCE WITH AN INJUNCTION OR CONSENT DECREE

<u>The Supreme Court has held that all activities to defend a consent decree and safeguard its results are fully compensable as prevailing party attorney fees. Pennsylvania v. Delaware Valley</u> (1986) 478 U.S. 546, a suit under the Clean Air Act, involved a prevailing party attorney fee provision similar to the ADA's. Because Pennsylvania failed to keep its consent decree promises, the Supreme Court upheld plaintiff's grant of "enforcement" attorney fees:

> <u>Protection of the full scope of relief afforded by the consent decree was thus crucial to safeguard the interests asserted by Delaware Valley; and enforcement of the decree...</u> involved the type of work which is properly <u>compensable as a cost of litigation</u> under §304... <u>[M]easures necessary to enforce the remedy ordered by the District Court cannot be divorced from the matters upon which Delaware Valley prevailed in securing the consent decree.</u>

(Penn., *supra*, at 558-559)

The Ninth Circuit has held similarly in Keith v. Volpe (9th Cir. 1987) 833 F.2d 850. In Keith, brought under 42 U.S.C. § 1988, the court stated:

> As in Garrity, the district court here "was entitled to believe that relief [for the plaintiffs under the consent decree] would occur more speedily and reliably" if the Center engaged in these monitoring activities, and the post-judgment monitoring by the Center was, therefore, "a necessary aspect of plaintiffs' 'prevailing' in the case." [citation] Interpreting the notion of "prevailing party" in a practical, not formal, manner, we conclude that the plaintiffs satisfied the prevailing party requirement of 42 U.S.C. §1988.
>
> Keith, *supra*, at 857

Keith also held that a contempt finding is not a prerequisite to an award of attorney fees for enforcement proceedings under a prevailing party statute. (Id.) NAACP v. San Francisco Unified School Dist. (9th Cir. 2002) 284 F.3d 1163 held:

> It is settled law in this circuit that a district court has discretion to award fees to a prevailing party in consent decree litigation for work reasonably spent to monitor and enforce compliance with the decree, even as to matters in which it did not prevail.
>
> (NAACP, *supra*, at 1166, emphasis added.)

In a well-reasoned opinion in Burt v. County of Contra Costa (in which fees were sought as "prevailing party" fees under the Civil Rights Act of 1964 for enforcing a 25 year old consent decree), Northern District Magistrate Judge Joseph Spero upheld attorney fees for work enforcing a consent decree:

> There is no suggestion in Buckhannon that the Court intended to overturn its prior precedent on this issue. To the contrary, the distinction drawn by the Court in Buckhannon between private settlements and consent decrees, and, in particular, the reference to the "judicial approval and oversight" of the latter, implicitly affirms the reasoning of Pennsylvania v. Delaware Valley [citation]. Therefore, this Court concludes that the cases holding that a prevailing party may be awarded fees for reasonable monitoring of a court-approved consent decree - with or without subsequent judicial intervention - remain good law. (Burt, 2001 WL 1135433, at p. 9)

Perry v. O'Donnell (9th Cir. 1985) 759 F.2d 702, involved enforcement of a settlement in a case with no attorney fees provision for the underlying claims. In that case, one party filed contempt proceedings to enforce a settlement, and several months after the contempt proceedings, made a request for attorney fees. The court held that such fees could be granted, despite the passage of time:

> Olson maintains that attorneys' fees must be <u>awarded when the contempt order is entered</u> or when the fine for contempt is imposed. This argument is without merit. ... In the absence of a specific statutory or local rule time restriction, a <u>fee request "is timely if filed within a reasonable period after the entry of judgment and if it does not unfairly surprise or prejudice the affected party."</u>

<u>Perry</u>, *supra*, at 704)

<u>Applying this body of law to an attorney fees motion in a Northern District ADA case, Mannick v. Kaiser Foundation Health Plan, Inc.</u> (N.D.Cal.), (Order of September 28, 2007), Judge Phyllis Hamilton observed:

> Code of Civil Procedure section 1021.5 authorizes the court to award fees to a successful party in an action that has resulted in the enforcement of an important right affecting the public interest if three conditions exist - a "significant benefit" has been conferred on the general public or a large class of persons; the necessity and financial burden of private enforcement are such as to make the award appropriate; and such fees should not be paid out of the recovery, if any. Cal. Civ. P. Code section 1021.5.
>
> A plaintiff confers a significant benefit on the general public when he/she continues with efforts to obtain the defendant's compliance with a stipulated injunction. A party "may be considered a successful party within the meaning of section 1021.5 if that party's efforts had the effect of ensuring compliance with the trial court's order." <u>Vasquez v. State of California</u>, 154 Cal. App. 4th 406, 419 (2007) (quoting <u>Nat'l Parks & Conservation Ass'n v. County of Riverside</u>, 81 Cal. App. 4th 234,242 (2002)).
>
> Here, plaintiff's efforts have resulted in ensuring Kaiser's compliance with the consent decree, and that work has all occurred post-offer. Thus, plaintiff is entitled to fees for the consent decree compliance work.

<u>Mannick v. Kaiser Foundation Health Plan, Inc.</u>, 2007 WL 2892647 at p.*12.

d. NO EFFORTS ARE "DUPLICATIVE" WHEN THEY ARE REASONABLY MADE TOWARD A COMMON GOAL OR TASK

<u>In Moreno v. City of Sacramento</u> (9th Cir., 2008) 534 F.3d 1106, the court warned against labeling work as "duplicative" because multiple attorneys worked on different portions of a project, or performed "duplication" which was "necessary duplication," "inherent in the process of litigating over time":

> <u>It must also be kept in mind that lawyers are not likely to spend unnecessary time on contingency fee cases in the hope of inflating</u>

> their fees. The payoff is too <u>uncertain, as to both the result and the amount of the fee. It would therefore be the highly atypical civil rights case where plaintiff's lawyer engages in churning. By</u> and large, the court should defer to the winning lawyer's professional judgment <u>as to how much time he was required to spend on the case; after all, he won, and</u> might not have, had he been more of a slacker.

<u>Moreno</u>, *supra*, at 1112.

But the burden of producing a sufficiently cogent explanation can mostly be placed on the shoulders of the losing parties, who not only have the incentive, but also the knowledge of the case to point out such things as excessive or duplicative billing practices. If opposing counsel cannot come up with specific reasons for reducing the fee request that the district court finds persuasive, it should normally grant the award in full, or with no more than a haircut.

<u>Moreno</u>, *supra*, at 1116. The court defined the presumptive "haircut" as 10% or less. Id. at 1112.

e. PLAINTIFF'S ATTORNEYS ARE ENTITLED TO SPEND THE TIME REASONABLY NECESSARY TO AFFORD PLAINTIFF "QUALITY REPRESENTATION"

<u>In Blackwell v. Foley</u>, *supra*, Judge Marilyn Hall Patel quoted from Judge Thelton Henderson's Order in <u>Chavez v. Chevy's</u> (C01-4322 TEH, N.D. Cal. March 27, 2003, in response to a similar argument of "excessive time" being spent:

> 'Defendants would have the Court penalize Mr. Rein for litigating the case in a manner that afforded plaintiff quality representation, and the Court will not do so.' (Order at p. 4, 1.1-3) Judge Henderson also rejected defense challenges in that case which were similar to those in this case: that plaintiff's counsel charged for clerical tasks-'It is lead counsel's responsibility to oversee his staff and ensure that critical, even if mundane steps are completed properly.' (Id. at 1.14-15) Likewise Judge Henderson rejected criticism of 'excessive meetings' between co-counsel, finding 'they were within the scope of work reasonably to be expected in litigation of this nature and magnitude.' (Id. at 1.21-22). Regarding criticism of 'excessive' time being billed, the court 'finds that the time billed in this case is perfectly reasonable, and that spending much less time likely would have jeopardized the quality of counsel's representation.' (Id. at p. 5, 1.1-3)

<u>Blackwell v. Foley</u>, 724 F. Supp. 2d 1068, 1079 (N.D. Cal. 2010), adopting the recommendations of Magistrate Judge James Larson's opinion.

f. DEFENDANTS' CHALLENGES TO PLAINTIFF'S STAFFING DECISIONS AND "BILLING JUDGMENT" WERE REJECTED BY JUDGE PATEL IN <u>CHABNER V. UNITED OF OMAHA LIFE INS. CO.</u>, 1999 WL 33227443 (N.D.CAL. 1999) AND <u>BLACKWELL V. FOLEY</u>, *Supra*, AND BY JUDGE THELTON HENDERSON IN <u>CHAVEZ V. CHEVY'S</u>, C01-4322 TEH (N.D.CAL. 2003)

Defense counsel may fault plaintiff's counsel for billing attorney fees for tasks that "could" have been done by either a lower-priced attorney or someone else on the staff, and assert that plaintiff's attorneys should charge lower fees for certain tasks. This "staffing decision" defense was rejected by Judge Patel in <u>Chabner v. United Of Omaha Life Insurance Co.</u>, 1999 WL 33227443 (N.D.Cal. October 12, 1999). As noted by Judge Patel in <u>Blackwell v. Foley</u>, *supra*, at p. 1080, such a defendants' position would also be contra to 9th Circuit precedent: "<u>Davis v. City & County of San Francisco</u>, 1976 F.2d 1536, 1548 (9th Cir. 1992), rejecting contention that court must award different fees for different tasks; <u>Gates v. Roland</u>, 39 F.3d 1439, 1451 (9th Cir. 1994) (same)." Id. A contrary holding in <u>Macdougal v. Catalyst Night Club</u>, 58 F.Supp 2d 1101 (N.D. Cal. 1999) was <u>rejected</u> by the <u>Blackwell</u> Court, citing 9th Circuit precedents, because the <u>MacDougal</u> holding was "inapposite to an ADA access case. Attorneys in these cases do not vary their hourly fees according to task-these are hourly statutory fees to be paid by the defendant." Id. at 1080.

5. IF DEFENDANT "MOOTS" A FEDERAL COURT ADA ACTION BY FULL ACCESS COMPLIANCE OR BY CLOSING THE SUBJECT FACILITY, FORCING PLAINTIFF TO REFILE THE ACTION IN STATE COURT TO OBTAIN DAMAGES AND FEES, PLAINTIFF'S ATTORNEY FEES, LITIGATION EXPENSES, AND COSTS INCURRED IN THE U.S. DISTRICT COURT ACTION SHOULD BE RECOVERABLE IN THE STATE COURT ACTION

It is well settled that a trial court may, in its discretion, determine that time reasonably expended on an action includes time spent on other separate but closely related proceedings (see, e.g., <u>L.T. Wallace v. Consumers Cooperative of Berkeley</u> (1985)170 Cal.App.3rd, 836, 849; 216 Cal.Rptr 649, 658, and cases cited therein; <u>Children's Hospital and Medical Center, et. al. v. Diana Bonta, as Director</u> (2002) 97 Cal.App.4th 740, 779, 780)118 Cal.Rptr.2nd, 629, 659-660 and cases cited therein. As unequivocally stated in <u>Children's Hospital</u>, *supra*:

> "...California case law clearly provides a trial court discretion to award a fee that compensates work performed in a collateral action that may not have been absolutely necessary to the action in which fees are awarded but was nonetheless closely related to the action in which fees are sought and useful to its resolution....". (97 Cal.App.4th 779-780; 118 Cal. Rptr.2nd at 659)
>
> . . .
>
> "<u>The principles articulated in the cases just discussed allow a trial court discretion</u> to award fees in circumstances such as those presented in this

case. The ancillary judicial proceedings with which we are here concerned related very directly to the issues presented in the action in which fees were awarded, and respondent prevailed in those proceedings. While the federal proceedings may not have been a necessary precondition of the superior court action, they materially contributed to the resolution of the constitutional issues presented to that court." (97 Cal. App. 4th at 781; 118 Cal. Rptr. 2nd at 660)

Moreover, the Court in Children's Hospital pointed out that the trial court may determine that time reasonably expended on an action includes time spent on other separate but closely related proceedings even if the plaintiff did not prevail in the separate proceeding (97 Cal.App.4th, at 780-781; 118 Cal.Rptr.2d, at 660).

All the work performed in the District Court action should be compensable in the state court action, especially where all the facts in the predecessor District Court action and the State Court action are identical, and all of the elements of proof and legal issues are identical. Because the injunctive relief issues and damages issues in both the predecessor District Court Action and the State Court action require that Plaintiff prove that Defendants are in violation of State disabled access statutes and regulations and/or the ADA as incorporated by reference therein, all the facts and law developed in the District Court action are applicable to and have been and/or will be used in the State Court action. For example, any motion for summary judgment to be made in the State Court case could include all the moving papers filed in the predecessor District Court action if, for example, defendants closed the facility in order to moot the District Court action and avoid a summary judgment decision by the federal Court. Likewise, if the case proceeded to trial, virtually all of the pretrial and trial preparation in the District Court action, such as documentary evidence, voir dire, jury instructions, trial brief, etc., could be used in the State Court action. Further, rulings previously made in the District Court action would be res judicata in the subsequent State Court action. For example, if the District Court had made the factual determination that providing access was "readily achievable" for injunctive relief purposes, defendants' liability for damages under Civil Code sections 52(b), 54(c), or 54.1(d) may have already been established.

Thus the District Court proceedings will usually relate directly to the issues presented in the State Court action and/or will materially contribute to the resolution of the issues present in that action. If so, all the attorney fees reasonably incurred in the District Court action should be recoverable when and if Plaintiff is determined to be the "prevailing party" in State Court. (See also Kittok, *supra*, 687 F.Supp.2nd 953, at 958.)

6. **PLAINTIFF'S ATTORNEY FEES SHOULD BE SET AT "MARKET" RATES, AND AT CURRENT RATES TO OFFSET DELAY IN PAYMENT**

   <u>Plaintiff's attorneys are entitled to be compensated at rates that reflect the reasonable market value of their services in the community.</u> (Serrano v. Unruh, (1982) 32 Cal.3d at 643) Plaintiff's attorneys' rates here are based on what attorneys with comparable skill and experience charge.

   > Affidavits of the plaintiff['s] attorneys and other attorneys regarding prevailing fees in the community and rate determinations in other cases, particularly those setting a rate for the plaintiff['s] attorneys are satisfactory evidence of the prevailing market rate. <u>United Steelworkers of America v. Phelps Dodge Corp.</u> (9th Cir. 1990) 407 F.2d 403, 407

In Moreno v. City of Sacramento, 534 F.3d 1106 (9th Cir. 2008), the Court <u>rejected any "cap" on a civil rights plaintiff's attorney's hourly rate, and reiterated the rule of using the "prevailing local market rate"</u>:

> In making the award, the district court must strike a balance between granting sufficient fees to attract qualified counsel to civil rights cases, (citations omitted), and avoiding a windfall to counsel, (citations omitted). The way to do so is to compensate counsel at the prevailing rate in the community for similar work; no more, no less.

> Id. at 1111.

> In using the "lodestar method to calculate fees," the Court held, a district court must start by determining how many hours were reasonably expended on the litigation, and then multiply those hours by the prevailing local rate for an attorney of the skill required to perform the litigation. See Blum, 465 U.S. at 895, 104 S.Ct. 1541.

> Id.

<u>The Moreno</u> court also reiterated "certain factors" in calculating "the hourly rate for successful civil rights attorneys" to include "the novelty and difficulty of the issues, the skill required to try the case, whether or not the fee is contingent, the experience held by counsel, and the fee awards in similar cases. (Citations omitted)"

Id. at 1114.

Rates awarded to attorneys of comparable experience are highly determinable in setting Lodestar rates. (<u>Margolin v. Regional Planning Comm'n</u> (1982) 134 Cal.App.3d 99, 1000)

In a sexual harassment case, <u>Bihune v. AT&T (1993)</u> 13 Cal.App.4th 976, 977, the court upheld a rate of $450/hr., for work done prior to 1992 (now 20 years ago):

> The trial court determined that a $450 hourly rate was a reasonable fee for Mr Grassini's services based on his "knowledge, skill, experience and reputation." In setting the hourly fee the court was entitled to consider "fees customarily charged by that attorney and others in the community for similar work." Ackerman v. Western Electric Co., Inc. (9th Cir. 1988) 860 F.2d 1514, 1520. We find the amount set by the trial court, albeit at the 'high end" is not "off the scale" in light of the record.

Under the Lodestar method, plaintiff's attorneys are entitled to be compensated for "all hours reasonably spent on the matter." Serrano IV, *supra*, 32 Cal.3d at 763; Sundance v. Municipal Court (1987) 192 Cal. App.3d 268, 273-274. An attorney's sworn testimony that, in fact, it took the time claimed "...is evidence of considerable weight on the issue of the time required..." Perkins v. Mobile Housing Bd. (11th Cir. 1988) 847 F.2d 735, 738. To deny compensation, "it must appear that the time claimed is obviously and convincingly excessive under the circumstances." Ibid. Plaintiff is also entitled to current, rather than "historical" market rates, to compensate for the delay in payment:

> Furthermore, Plaintiff's counsel are entitled to receive their current hourly rates as compensation for the delay in payment. Missouri v. Jenkins, 491 U.S. 274, 109 S.Ct. 2463, 105 L.Ed.2d 229 (1989) ("an appropriate adjustment for delay in payment-whether by the application of current rather than historic hourly rates or otherwiseis within the contemplation of the statute.") (internal citation omitted) In that case, the fees were paid several years after services were rendered and the Court found that receiving fees years later that were calculated on the hourly rates in effect at the time the services were rendered would not be equivalent to receiving fees paid reasonably promptly as the legal services were performed, as would be the case with private billings. Defense counsel probably has not waited until now to be paid, but received their fees as they went along, from 2008 to the present.
> Blackwell v. Foley, *supra*, at p. 1078.

7. NO FEES ARE AWARDED TO "PREVAILING PARTY" DEFENDANTS AGAINST A "GOOD FAITH" CIVIL RIGHTS PLAINTIFF, EVEN UNDER CALIFORNIA LAW: HUBBARD V. SOBRECK, LLC (9th CIRCUIT, 2009) 554 F.3d 742 [BUT CAVEAT JANKEY V. LEE, *Infra*, AT SECTION I-K-10]

The Sobreck 9th Circuit opinion held, as a matter of federal law, that:

> A violation of the federal ADA constitutes a violation of CDPA. See, e.g., Cal. Civ. Code §§ 54(c), 54.1(d), 54.2(b). Therefore, to the extent that California's Section 55 mandates the imposition of fees on a losing plaintiff who brought both a nonfrivolous ADA action and a parallel action under Section 55, an award of attorney's fees under Section 55 would

> be inconsistent with the ADA, which would bar imposition of fees on the plaintiff. In such a case, the proof required to show a violation of the CDPA and of the ADA is identical. In that circumstance, it is impossible to distinguish the fees necessary to defend against the CDPA claim from those expended in defense against the ADA claim, so that a grant of fees on the California cause of action is necessarily a grant of fees as to the ADA claim. As federal law does not allow the grant of fees to defendants for non-frivolous ADA actions, we must conclude that <u>preemption principles preclude the imposition of fees on a plaintiff for bringing nonfrivolous claims under state law that parallel claims also filed pursuant to the federal law</u>. See <u>Cal. Fed. Sav., 479 U.S. at 280-81, 107 S.Ct. 683</u>.
>
> <u>Sobreck</u>, *supra*, 554 F. 3d 742, 745. (Emphasis added)

In early 2010 one California Court of Appeal purported to "disagree" with the 9th Circuit's <u>Sobreck</u> holding, even though <u>Sobreck</u> was decided on the basis of a federal law issue. Although that case was <u>depublished</u> and designated "not for citation" by the California Supreme Court, which also granted a hearing, but <u>affirmed</u>![82]

Neither attorney fees nor costs may be assessed, under the ADA, against a losing but "good faith" civil rights plaintiff. <u>Brown v. Lucky Stores</u> (9th Cir. 2001) 246 F.3d 1182, citing <u>Christiansburg Garment Co. v. E.E.O.C.</u> (1978) 434 U.S. 412, held that even "costs" cannot be awarded - even to a prevailing defendant - against a civil rights plaintiff unless the case was frivolous or brought in bad faith. The unanimous <u>Christiansburg</u> Supreme Court noted "policy considerations" (at 418-419):

> [T]here are at least two strong equitable considerations counseling an attorney's fee award to a prevailing Title VII plaintiff that are wholly absent in the case of a prevailing Title VII defendant. First,... the plaintiff is the chosen instrument of Congress to vindicate "a policy that Congress considered of the highest priority."... Second, when a district court awards counsel fees to a prevailing plaintiff, it is awarding them against a violator of federal law... "[T]hese policy considerations... are not present in the case of a prevailing defendant."

As held in <u>Brown</u>, *supra*, at 1190, "Because § 12205 makes fees and costs parallel, we hold that the Christiansburg test also applies to an award of costs to a prevailing defendant under the ADA." <u>Summers v. Techert and Sons, Inc.</u>, 127 F.3d 1150, 1154 (9th Cir. 1997) adopted the Title VII standard in <u>Christianburg Garment Co.</u>, *supra*, for the defendants to recover attorney fees under the ADA, i.e. only for "frivolous" plaintiffs' lawsuits.

---

[82] Therefore the California Court of Appeal decision is not precedent, cannot be cited, and will not be cited here! However the California Supreme Court in <u>Jankey v. Lee</u> (December 12, 2012) adopted the same position and allowed attorney fees under section 55 Civil Code to a "prevailing" defendant, even against a "good faith" plaintiff! See section I-K-10, *infra*, and I-K-12 for possible alterative approaches for plaintiff's attorneys. <u>Oliver</u>, *supra*, followed <u>Sobreck</u> and said federal district courts were required to follow the 9th Circuit's decision. (See discussion in "Introduction," section 4.F [p.16])

8. IN THE 2011 <u>TURNER</u> DECISION, A CALIFORNIA APPELLATE COURT HELD THAT NO ATTORNEY FEES COULD BE AWARDED TO A PREVAILING DEFENDANT UNDER CIVIL CODE SECTION 55 BECAUSE THIS WOULD CONFLICT WITH PUBLIC POLICY SET BY THE LEGISLATURE IN SECTIONS 52 AND 54.3, WHEN HOURS WORKED WERE INTERTWINED

In <u>Turner v. Ass'n of Am. Med. Colleges</u>, 193 Cal. App. 4th 1047 (2011), the First District Court of Appeal held that a "prevailing defendant" could not seek an award of attorney fees pursuant to Civil Code § 55 when defendants' hours on § 55 issues "were inextricably intertwined with the hours incurred in defending claims under sections 52 and 54.3." Id. at p.1054.

> When the Legislature enacted the unilateral, "prevailing plaintiff" fee-shifting provisions in sections 52 and 54.3, it created an exception to section 55 by implication, prohibiting a fee award to a prevailing defendant for the same hours devoted to defending claims under sections 52 and 54.3.

Id. at p.1054.

In <u>Turner</u>, the court noted the Legislature's "conscious decision" to award attorney fees under sections 52 and 54.3 "only to prevailing plaintiffs," because:
> if prevailing defendants were able to obtain fees for attorney hours spent defending claims under the Unruh Act and <u>section 54.3</u>., it would undermine the purpose of the unilateral fee provisions - to encourage enforcement of the statutes without fear of an adverse fee award in the event the enforcement action fails.

Id. at p.1060.

<u>Turner</u> also cited <u>Covenant Mutual Ins. Co. v. Young</u> (1986) 179 Cal.App.3d 318, 324, as to the public purpose of "unilateral fee shifting provisions" [for prevailing plaintiffs only] "as a deliberate stratagem for advancing some public purpose, usually by encouraging more effective enforcement of some important public policy." Id, at p.1060. "[A] fee award to a prevailing defendant in that context 'obviously would frustrate the legislative intent to allow more injured people to seek redress and to encourage improved enforcement of public policy.'" Id, at p.1060, quoting <u>Covenant</u> at 325-326. Further,
> a fee award to a prevailing defendant on a claim with a unilateral fee-shifting provision would "discourage the meritorious as well as the frivolous lawsuit and thereby defeat the legislative goal of encouraging the redress of grievances and enhancing the enforcement of public policy."

Id. at p.1060, quoting Covenant at p. 328.

After discussing the imposition of fees against a good faith but losing plaintiff under Civil Code § 55 in <u>Molski v. Arciero Wine Group</u> (2008) 164 Cal.App.4th 786, the <u>Turner</u> court distinguished <u>Molski</u> where, the plaintiff apparently did not argue that sections 52 and 54.3 prevail over section 55 and the court did not address the conflict between the various fee provisions. Here, the fact that plaintiffs could have elected to forgo injunctive relief under section 55, and thus avoided the risk of any conflicting statutory directives on fee shifting, does not justify, as matter of public policy, a section 55 fee award to a prevailing defendant that concedes it did not incur even one extra hour of attorney fees defending the section 55 claim. <u>To award fees under section 55 would frustrate the purposes of the unilateral fee-shifting provisions in sections 52 and 54.3</u>, and in this case impose a crushing fee award on civil rights plaintiffs who did not even seek damages from defendant. <u>Moreover, such an award would also undermine enforcement of section 55, which benefits all disabled persons, by discouraging future plaintiffs from including claims for injunctive relief under section 55, even where inclusion of the claim would not increase the burden of the litigation</u>. It is reasonable to conclude the Legislature intended to discourage the filing of meritless lawsuits under section 55, but there is no reason to believe the Legislature intended to discourage requests for injunctive relief under section 55 that add nothing to the defendant's litigation burden.

Id. at p.1071. (Emphasis added) [Unfortunately the California Supreme Court in <u>Jankey v. Lee</u>, *supra*, seemingly ignored these policy concerns. See § 10, herein below.

9. [SEE ALSO SECTION IV-J *Infra* RE U.S. SUPREME COURT'S <u>FOX V. VICE</u> (2011) DECISION]

10. <u>JANKEY V. LEE</u>, (2012) 55 Cal 4th 1038 (CAL. DEC. 17, 2012) - NEW DECISION UPHOLDING "REVERSE" ATTORNEY FEES AND POSSIBLY CHILLING DISABLED RIGHTS LITIGATION

    On December 17, 2012, the California Supreme Court gave illegally inaccessible California businesses an early Christmas present by erasing 40 years of progressive legislation and threatening any disabled person who sought Civil Code § 55 injunctive relief to remove barriers under California law with the possibility that - if they <u>lost</u> their civil rights case - they would have to pay for the offending business's attorney fees and costs. In <u>Jankey v. Lee</u>, *supra*, the California Supreme Court declared that it "disagreed" with the 9th Circuit's contrary position in <u>Hubbard v. Sobreck, LLC</u>, 554 F.3d 742 (9th Cir. 2009): If a disabled person dared to seek injunctive relief under California Civil Code § 55 to require an inaccessible business to remove barriers to access and <u>lost</u> the case, <u>even if the lawsuit was brought in good faith and with legal justification</u>, the disabled person would be <u>subject to paying the defendant business's attorney fees and costs</u> in defending the case <u>against providing access</u>!

    In a unanimous 7-0 opinion the <u>Jankey</u> Court effectively held that if the disabled plaintiff had sought only to collect <u>personal damages</u> under Civil Code §§ 54.1 and 54.3, they would not face this threat; but that if plaintiff dared to also seek an injunction to require access for all disabled persons, i.e., an injunction in the public interest, Civil Code § 55 mandated an award of attorney fees and costs to the "prevailing" defendant. For good measure they added that the plaintiff would also have to pay for defendants' attorney fees and costs for the appeal itself for seeking to enforce the legislative scheme first initiated in 1970 - seeking to make all of California's public accommodations accessible for disabled persons.

The immediate effect of this decision will probably be to intimidate many civil rights attorneys from handling disabled rights cases under California law seeking to create a more accessible society for wheelchair users and other disabled persons. Other attorneys, unwilling to be intimidated but hesitant to risk an award of attorney fees against their disabled and often low-income clients, may use Business and Professions Code § 17200 in place of Civil Code § 55, by alleging that maintaining an illegally inaccessible business is a form of unfair competition.

But what is next? Will the courts also interpret the "prevailing party" attorney fees language of Health and Safety Code § 19953 to also threaten defense attorney fees if a disabled person seeks only injunctive relief to enforce the California Building Code against businesses that are newly constructed or remodeled ("altered") without providing access? Will California be brought back down to the level of protection in most other states by allowing only ADA § 308 injunctive relief? California had been 20 years ahead of the 1990 ADA in passing legislation (effective 1970) to protect the rights of disabled persons to "full and equal access." (See Donald v. Café Royale, 218 Cal.App.3d 168 (1990); Donald v. Sacramento Valley Bank, 209 Cal.App.3d 1183 (1989); and People ex rel. Deukmejian v. CHE, Inc., 150 Cal.App.3d 123 (1983))

Combined with the newly legislated (2012) enactment of SB 1186, 40 pages of new statutes designed to make it more difficult for disabled persons to bring access actions, including requiring (effective January 1, 2013), that all access complaints by disabled persons be "verified" - a requirement not found in any other civil rights statutes protecting against discrimination based on race, religion, gender, national origin, or any other protected class of person - disabled persons are being told it is no longer California's proud public policy to encourage disabled rights lawsuits. Previously it was clear that,
> The fee shifting statutes reflect a judgment that civil rights laws will be unenforced unless private lawyers are given financial incentives to bring cases under those laws.
> Kittock v. Leslie's Poolmart 687 F.Supp 2d 953, at 959 (E.D. Cal. 2009).

Interpretations of California law in Jankey v. Lee, *supra*, and new pleading and notice hurdles set up by the California Legislature in SB 1186, are directly contrary to basic California public policy as set out many years ago in California Government Code § 19230:

> The Legislature hereby declares that: (a) It is the policy of this state to encourage and enable individuals with a disability to participate fully in the social and economic life of the state and to engage in remunerative employment.

Should this now be amended to add, "If individuals with a disability seek to enforce California public policy and lose, they must face the prospect of disastrous bankruptcy?"

Whether the federal courts will honor new California law requirements for federal court complaints remains to be seen. (See O'Campo, *supra*, as possibly relevant on this issue), May 10, 2013 opinion, Oliver, supra, held federal district courts were required to follow the 9th Circuit's decision. (See discussion in "Introduction," section 4.F [p.16])

11. **THE SAME PUBLIC POLICIES PROTECTED BY THE CHRISTIANSBURG DOCTRINE SHOULD APPLY TO CALIFORNIA LAW CIVIL RIGHTS ACTIONS**

In Edwards v. Princess Cruise Lines, Ltd., 471 F.Supp.2d 1032 (2007), Magistrate Judge Bernard Zimmerman denied attorney fees to a defendant who had been awarded summary judgment under the ADA and Civil Code § 55. After finding that it was not clear whether defendants had in fact "prevailed" on the merits, and that there was "no evidence that passenger filed her ADA or CDPA claims in bad faith or with no reasonable bases in law of fact." Id at 1034.

The Court further stated,

> Defendant's position is also inconsistent with the policy objectives that support attorney's fee awards in civil rights cases. As the Supreme Court has explained, differing standards for awarding attorney's fees to prevailing plaintiffs and prevailing defendants are appropriate to advance "the important policy objectives of the Civil Rights Statutes, and the intent of Congress to achieve such objectives through the use of plaintiffs as private attorney[s] general." Fogerty v. Fantasy, Inc., 510 U.S. 517, 523, 114 S.Ct. 1023, 127 L.Ed.2d 455 (1994) . . .. Though the Supreme Court was speaking of federal civil rights statutes, defendants have advanced no good reason why the policy underlying California civil rights laws should be different.

> Id. at 1034-1035.

12. **"CAVEAT" - POSSIBLE TACTIC TO AVOID NEED TO PLEAD CIVIL CODE § 55, IN LIGHT OF JANKEY V. LEE**

When in doubt, a plaintiff's attorney may be safer to skip seeking injunctive relief under Civil Code § 55 or Health & Safety Code § 19953 - which both have "prevailing party" state law attorney fees provisions - and instead,

(1) seek injunctive relief in federal court under the Americans with Disabilities Act of 1990 (ADA), which does not have "reverse" attorney fees so long as the complaint is not frivolous or fraudulent;

(2) seek injunctive relief under Business & Professions Code §§ 17200 et seq., for any "unfair business practice," including violation of the ADA or other discriminatory practice (See <u>Californians for Disability Rights v. Mervyn's LLC</u>, 165 Cal 4th 571 (2008); and,

(3) seek damages and "plaintiff only" attorney fees under Civil Code § 54.3 for any violation of Civil Code §§ 54 or 54.1, including any violation of the ADA as an incorporated violation of Civil Code §§ 54(c) and 54.1(d).

If kicked out of federal court because of "mootness" or lack of "readily achievable" status, plaintiff would still have the <u>option</u> to refile in state court and seek the same damage remedies, and injunctive relief pursuant to Business & Professions Code §§ 17200 et seq., including injunction and damages based on the construction and alteration history. And an ADA § 303 violation may still be found for any triggering alterations in the last 20 years!

L. EFFECT OF SB 1608 AND NEW CALIFORNIA CIVIL CODE § SECTION 55.55: WRITTEN SETTLEMENT OFFERS ARE NOW RELEVANT

Civil Code § 55.55 was added (effective January 1, 2009) as part of SB 1608, and allows consideration of written settlement communications between the parties by a court considering a statutory attorney fees motion with respect to any "construction-related" accessibility claim:

> 55.55. Notwithstanding subdivision (f) of Section 55.54, in determining an award of reasonable attorney's fees and recoverable costs with respect to any construction-related accessibility claim, the <u>court may consider</u>, along with other relevant information, <u>written settlement offers made and rejected by the parties</u>. Nothing in this section affects or modifies the inadmissibility of evidence regarding offers of compromise pursuant to Section 1152 of the Evidence Code, including but not limited to, inadmissibility to prove injury or damage.
>
> (Emphasis added)

This section applies only to "written" settlement offers and may be a double edged sword: plaintiffs can also show that defendants caused prolonged litigation and larger attorney fees on both sides by the failure of defendants to respond to plaintiff's written settlement proposals.

How this section will interact with existing state and federal statutes making settlement discussions inadmissible remains to be seen. Would use of written settlement offers made during Northern District General Order 56 mediation procedures possibly violate the confidentiality of mediation procedures under General Order 56? The legal implications of making disabled persons the only civil rights litigants subject to having their fees affected by a court's interpretations of their settlement negotiations will probably be an issue in litigation. Further, in light of reference to California "Evidence Code 1152," this provision may apply only in California State Court, not Federal Court, as seems clearly the case for most <u>procedural</u> provisions of SB 1608.[83] (Can the California Legislature direct procedural changes for the Federal Court?) On the other hand, statutory attorney fees for state law violations is itself a legislative creation. (See sections 52, 54.3, and 55 California Civil Code.)

M. STATUTE OF LIMITATIONS: IN CALIFORNIA THE "SOL" IS NOW TWO YEARS FROM THE DATE WHEN PLAINTIFF SUFFERED INJURY, UNLESS A GOVERNMENT TORT CLAIM IS INVOLVED

1. TWO YEAR STATUTE OF LIMITATIONS FROM DENIAL OF ACCESS/INJURY
   It is black letter law that a plaintiff's statute of limitations cannot arise until he is injured. The general rule is that a limitations period begins to run "when the plaintiff knows or has reason to know of the injury which is the basis of the action." (<u>Trotter v. International Longshoremen's & Warehousemen's Union</u>, 704 F.2d 1141, 1143 (9th Cir. 1983).) Failure to provide access upon an alteration is a continuing nuisance (<u>San Francisco v. Grant Co.</u>, 181 Cal.App.3d 1085 (1986)) and is a continuing violation of law until rectified. California's personal injury statute of limitations is two years from the date of damaging incident.

2. IF A GOVERNMENT ENTITY MAY BE INVOLVED, PLAINTIFF MUST MEET SIX MONTH CALIFORNIA DEADLINE FOR FILING A GOVERNMENT CLAIM TO OBTAIN STATE LAW DAMAGES, AND MUST FILE LAWSUIT WITHIN SIX MONTHS OF CLAIM DENIAL
   [See also section 3, hereinafter]

   Per California Government Code section 911.2(a):

   A claim relating to a cause of action for death or for injury to person or to personal property or growing crops shall be presented as provided in Article 2 (commencing with Section 915) not later than six months after the accrual of the cause of action. A claim relating to any other cause of action shall be presented as provided in Article 2 (commencing with Section 915) not later than one year after the accrual of the cause of action.

   (<u>See Government Code sections 910ff for other time requirements</u> including time to

---

[83] However the SB 1608's definition of "Full and Equal Access" violations, per Civil Code section 55.56, seem clearly related to defining and clarifying state law as to damages, and should be properly considered as such in both federal and state courts. Re: procedural v. substantive laws and applications in federal Court, see also <u>O'campo v. Chico Mall</u>, 758 F. Supp. 2d 996 (E.D. Cal. 2010) and section I-N, *infra*.

file complaint after claim is formally denied by the entity, or denied "by law" <u>after 45 days pass</u> from claim, without response to the claims unless defendant later files a formal denial which may set a new 6 month period running.) [See also section 3, *infra* and the caveat at FN 82 hereinbelow as to procedures existing for "late claims" applications to the Court]

3. NO STATE LAW GOVERNMENT CLAIM IS REQUIRED TO OBTAIN DAMAGES DIRECTLY UNDER ADA TITLE II, BUT PROBABLY IS REQUIRED IF PLAINTIFF SEEKS TO USE AN INCORPORATED "ADA" VIOLATION AS THE BASIS FOR VIOLATION OF SECTION 51(f), 54(c), OR 54.1(d) CALIFORNIA CIVIL CODE AND SEEKS STATE LAW DAMAGES

Per <u>Munson v. Del Taco</u>, Inc. 46 Cal. 4th 661 (2009), a violation of Civil Code sections 51(f), 54(e) or 54.1(d) can be established by any violation of the ADA, and without the need for proof of any "wrongful intent" to discriminate. However, to preserve the right to seek state law "tort" damages under California laws) it is necessary to comply with the California Government Code's tort claim statute, including a "<u>6 month SOL</u>" for a government tort claim.[28] Further, to prove a violation of Title II seeking damages, the Courts have required proof of "intentional" discrimination as determined by the "deliberate indifference" standard. <u>Duvall v. County of Kitsap</u>, 260 F.3d 1124, 1138. Deliberate indifference requires both knowledge that harm to a federally protected right is substantially likely, and a failure to act upon that likelihood. Id at 1139. [See section II-C-7, *infra*.]

N. SB 1186 (2012) MADE MAJOR CHANGES IN CALIFORNIA DISABILITY RIGHTS LAWS

1. CAVEAT: NEW LEGISLATION EFFECTIVE IMMEDIATELY (AT LEAST FOR STATE COURT ACTIONS)

On September 19, 2012, Governor Jerry Brown signed into law detailed new legal requirements for filing and proving disability access complaints based on a public building's construction and alteration history. Sections 24 and 25 of the statute made findings that a "very small number of plaintiffs' attorneys have been abusing the right of petition under sections 52 and 54.3 of the Civil Code." The legislation prohibited demand letters seeking money rather than seeking removal of barriers. They also imposed various service notice and complaint filing requirements for attorneys in actions based on the construction and alteration history of public accommodations.

Certain <u>procedural</u> requirements of these laws may be invalid when applied to federal court actions under the "Erie" doctrine as taught in law school based on <u>Erie R. Co. V. Tompkins</u>, 304 U.S. 64, 585 S. Ct. 817 (1938), (which distinguishes "procedural" requirements from substantive requirements). <u>O'Campo v. Chico Mall, LP</u>, 758 F. Supp. 2d 976 (E.D. Cal. 2010). However, attorneys practicing in this field must make themselves thoroughly aware of these newly legislated requirements. This is especially true since the statutes include a requirement that violation of certain standards will be considered the basis for discipline by the California State Bar! (See Civil Code sections 55.3, 55.31, 55.32.).

It remains to be seen whether these legislative changes will result in reducing "abuses" of California disability access laws, or will simply result in many attorneys deciding they will no longer represent disabled persons in civil rights cases where liability is based on California law requirements for failing to provide proper access when triggered by new construction or later alteration of a public facility.

The complete text of these new laws is included at the end of this book as "Appendix K." A summary is provided hereinbelow from the California Legislative Counsel:

2. LEGISLATIVE COUNSEL'S DIGEST OF SB 1186

The following is the Legislative Counsel's Digest, as a summary of the new laws enacted by

SB 1186:

SB 1186, Steinberg. Disability access.

(I) Existing law requires an attorney to provide a written advisory to a building owner or tenant with each demand for money or complaint for any construction-related accessibility claim, as specified. A violation of this requirement may subject the attorney to disciplinary action. This bill would, instead, require an attorney to provide a written advisory with each demand letter or complaint, as defined, sent to or served upon a defendant or potential defendant for any construction-related accessibility claim, as specified. The bill would require the Judicial Council to update the form that may be used by attorneys to comply with this requirement on or before July 1, 2013. The bill would require an allegation of a construction-related accessibility claim in a demand letter or complaint to state facts sufficient to allow a reasonable person to identify the basis for the claim. The bill would require any complaint alleging a construction-related accessibility claim to be verified by the plaintiff, and would make any complaint filed without verification subject to a motion to strike. The bill would prohibit a demand letter from including a request or demand for money or an offer or agreement to accept money. The bill also would prohibit an attorney, or other person acting at the direction of an attorney, from issuing a demand for money to a building owner or tenant, or an agent or employee of a building owner or tenant, on the basis of one or more construction-related accessibility violations, as specified. The bill would require an attorney to include his or her State Bar license number in a demand letter, and to submit copies of the demand letter to the California Commission on Disability Access and, until January 1, 2016, to the State Bar. The bill also would require, until Janumy 1, 2016, an attorney to submit a copy of a complaint to the commission. The bill would provide that a violation of these requirements may subject the attorney to disciplinary action, as specified. This bill would require the commission to review and report on the demand letters and complaints it receives until January 1, 2016. The bill also would require the State Bar, commencing July 31, 2013, and annually each July 31 thereafter, to report specified information to the Legislature regarding the demand letters that it receives.

(2) Existing law provides, upon being served with a summons and complaint asserting a construction-related accessibility claim, a qualified defendant, as defined, may file a request for a court stay and early evaluation conference in the proceedings, as specified. Existing law requires the Judicial Council to prepare and post on its Internet Web site instructions and a form for a qualified defendant to use to file an application for stay and early evaluation conference pursuant to this provision. This bill would permit other defendants to file a request for a court stay and early evaluation conference pursuant to this provision, including (A) a defendant, until January 1, 2018, whose site's new construction or improvement on or after January 1, 2008, and before January 1, 2016, was approved pursuant to the local building permit and inspection process,

(3) a defendant whose site's new construction or improvement was approved by a local public building department inspector who is a certified access specialist, and (C) a defendant who is a small business, as described. The bill would require the Judicial Council to prepare and post a form for filing an application for stay and early evaluation conference for use by qualified defendants and these additional defendants, and any additional forms appropriate to implement these provisions, as specified. The bill also would authorize a defendant who does not qualify for an early evaluation conference pursuant to these provisions, or who forgoes those provisions, to request a mandatory evaluation conference, as specified. The bill would authorize a plaintiff to make that request if the defendant does not make that request. (3) Existing law provides statutory damages in a construction-related accessibility claim against a place of public accommodation if a violation of construction-related accessibility standards denied the plaintiff full and equal access to that site on a particular occasion. A plaintiff is denied full and equal access only if, on a particular occasion, the plaintiff personally encountered the violation or was deterred from accessing the site. These statutory damages are in the amount of actual damages and any additional amount determined by a jury or the court up to a maximum of 3 times the amount of actual damages but not less than $4,000, or, for certain violations, $1,000. This bill would require the court, in assessing liability in any action alleging multiple claims for the same construction-related accessibility violation on different particular occasions, to consider the reasonableness of the plaintiff's conduct in light

of the plaintiff's obligation, if any, to mitigate damages. The bill would reduce a defendant's minimum liability for statutory damages in a construction-related accessibility claim against a place of public accommodation to $1,000 for each offense if the defendant has corrected all construction-related violations that are the basis of the claim within 60 days of being served with the complaint and other specified conditions apply, and would reduce that minimum liability to $2,000 for each offense if the defendant has corrected all construction-related violations that are the basis of the claim within 30 days of being served with the complaint and the defendant is a small business, as specified. The bill would require the Department of General Services to make a biannual adjustment to financial criteria defining a small business for these purposes, and to post those adjusted amounts on its Internet Web site.

(4) Existing law requires the State Architect to develop and submit for approval and adoption building standards for making buildings, structures, sidewalks, curbs, and related facilities accessible to, and usable by, persons with disabilities, as specified. Existing law provides for the inspection of places of public accommodation by certified access specialists to determine if the sites meet all applicable construction-related accessibility standards, and the provision of specified certificates and reports regarding those inspections. Existing law regulates the hiring of real property. This bill would require a commercial property owner to state on a lease form or rental agreement executed on or after July 1, 2013, if the property being leased or rented has undergone inspection by a certified access specialist.

(5) The federal Americans with Disabilities Act of 1990 and the California Building Standards Code require that specified buildings, structures, and facilities be accessible to, and usable by, persons with disabilities. Existing law establishes in the Depat1ment of General Services, the Division of the State Architect with responsibilities relating to architectural services, state buildings, and disability access. Existing law requires the State Architect to establish a certified access specialist program for voluntary certification by the state of any person who meets specified criteria as a certified access specialist. Existing law authorizes the State Architect to require applicants for certification and renewal of certification under the certified access specialist program to pay specified fees, including an application fee, a course fee, and an examination fee, at a level sufficient to meet the costs of administering the program, for deposit into the Certified Access Specialist Fund. In administering the certified access specialist program, this bill would require the State Architect to periodically review its schedule of fees for certification under the program to ensure that the fees are not excessive. The bill would prohibit the State Architect from charging a California licensed architect, landscape architect, civil engineer, or structural

engineer, an application fee for certification that exceeds $250. This bill would impose, on and after January 1, 2013, and until December 31, 2018, an additional state fee of $1 on any applicant for a local business license or equivalent instrument or permit, or renewal thereof, for purposes of increasing disability access and compliance with construction-related accessibility requirements and developing educational resources for businesses to facilitate compliance with federal and state disability laws, as specified. The bill would divide those moneys for the state between the local entity that collected the moneys and the Division of the State Architect, pursuant to specified percentages. The bill would create a continuously appropriated fund, the Disability Access and Education Revolving Fund, for the deposit of funds to be transfened to the Division of the State Architect, thereby making an appropriation. The bill would make an appropriation by authorizing local government entities to retain 70% of the fees imposed. By adding to the duties of a local entity, this bill would impose a state-mandated local program.

(6) Existing law establishes the California Commission on Disability Access for purposes of developing recommendations to enable persons with disabilities to exercise their right to full and equal access to public facilities and facilitating business compliance with the laws and regulations to avoid unnecessary litigation. Existing law sets forth the powers and duties of the commission, as specified. Existing law requires the commission to study and make reports to the Legislature regarding disability access laws and compliance, as specified. Existing law requires the commission to act as an information center on the status of compliance with disability access laws, to publish a biennial report, and to coordinate with other state agencies and local building departments to ensure the uniformity of information provided to the public on disability access.

This bill would revise and recast those duties and powers, as specified, and eliminate the biennial reporting requirement. The bill would instead provide that a priority of the commission shall be the development and dissemination of educational materials and information to promote and facilitate disability access compliance, including a requirement that the commission work with the Division of the State Architect and the Department of Rehabilitation to develop educational materials for use by businesses. The bill would require the commission to post specified information on its Internet Web site, including, but not limited to, educational materials and information that will assist business owners. The bill would require the commission to report to the Legislature on its implementation by a specified date. The bill would require the commission to compile data with respect to any demand letter or complaint sent to the commission and post that information on its Internet Web site.

(7) Existing law, the California Building Standards Law, requires a

state agency responsible for the adoption of building standards to submit its standards to the California Building Standards Commission for review and approval, subject to specified procedures and a triennial code adoption cycle. Existing law requires the commission to codify and publish approved standards in the California Building Code, as set forth in Title 24 of the California Code of Regulations. Existing law provides that building standards become effective 180 days after its publication, as specified.

This bill would provide, for the purpose of an alleged violation of a construction-related accessibility standard, that upon publication of the 2013 California Building Standards Code, but prior to its effective date, as specified, compliance with the building standards for disabled accessibility in the 2013 California Building Standards Code is authorized as an alternative method of compliance.

(8) The California Constitution requires the state to reimburse local agencies and school districts for certain costs mandated by the state. Statutory provisions establish procedures for making that reimbursement. This bill would provide that, if the Commission on State Mandates
determines that the bill contains costs mandated by the state, reimbursement for those costs shall be made pursuant to these statutory provisions.

(9) This bill would declare that it is to take effect immediately as an urgency statute. Appropriation: yes.

3. COMMENTARY ON PASSAGE OF SB 1168

These statutory changes sponsored by California State Senator Darryl Steinberg, a Democrat, joined by Senator Dutton, a Republican, were passed (after hearings in the summer of 2012), by the California legislature despite opposition from many disability rights advocates, with the Chamber of Commerce and other "business" groups pushing the legislation and some former champions of disabled rights- including CAOC, the Consumer Attorneys of California- taking "no position" and thereby allowing this legislation to pass.

It remains to be seen how some of this legislation will be interpreted by the Courts or accepted by the federal courts as to complaints filed in federal district court, where jurisdiction is based on alleged parallel violations of the ADA. With regard to similarly motivated legislation just 4 years ago (SB 1608), certain state procedural, notice and "stay" requirements have been ruled inapplicable to federal court because of ADA preemption and federal court jurisdiction over its own procedures. See O'Campo v. Chico Mall, LP, 758 F. Supp. 2d 976 (E.D. Cal. 2010). On the other hand, damages are controlled by California law, even though sections 51(f), 54(c) and 54(d) of the California Civil Code incorporate any violation of the ADA as a violation of California law as well, allowing damages to be sought under sections 52 and 54.3 of the Civil Code.

Only time will tell as to the validity of some of these measures, and their effect upon lawsuits seeking to enforce the civil rights of physically disabled persons in California.

II. GOVERNMENTAL ENTITIES - OBTAINING ACCESS TO PUBLIC BUILDINGS UNDER CALIFORNIA LAW AND ADA TITLE II[84]*

  A. CALIFORNIA LAW ACCESS REQUIREMENTS APPLY TO ALL GOVERNMENTAL CONSTRUCTION AND ALTERATIONS SINCE 1968

   1. GOVERNMENT CODE §§ 4450 ET SEQ. APPLY TO ALL GOVERNMENTAL CONSTRUCTION AND ALTERATIONS, STRUCTURAL REPAIRS AND ADDITIONS TO EXISTING BUILDINGS SINCE NOVEMBER 1968

   An early appellate decision laying out the "legislative scheme" for "handicapped access statutes and regulations" was James Donald v. Sacramento Valley Bank (1989) 209 Cal.App.3d 1183. Although that case also spelled out the later incorporation of government code section 4450ff standards into section 19955-59 Health and Safety Code, for application to privately financed buildings, it started by explaining the standards applicable to "public buildings constructed with public funds:

   > The principal statutory scheme regarding access to and use of public facilities by disabled persons is found in Government Code sections 4450 through 4458. Those sections direct the state architect to adopt as minimum standards of accessibility regulations concerning handicap access to buildings and related facilities. (Gov. Code, §§ 4450, 4452.) As relevant to this appeal, section 4450 provided in 1975: "4450. It is the purpose of this chapter to insure that all buildings, structures, sidewalks, curbs, and related facilities, constructed in this state by the use of state, county, or municipal funds, or the funds of any political subdivision of the state shall be accessible to and usable by, the physically handicapped. The State Architect shall adopt by regulation standards for making buildings, structures, and related facilities accessible to and usable by the physically handicapped.

   Id. at 1191.

   The statute required the state architect to adopt by regulation standards to ensure this result. Per the 1968 version of section 4451, until the state architect adopted such standards, "existing ASA standards" would apply and "all buildings, structures, and related facilities" must "conform to the American Standards Association specifications A117.1-1961." Id. at 1192. [See section IX, *infra*, Appendix C-1 for the 1961 ASA

---

[85] This section is not fully developed, as to the full scope of Title II, but focuses on physical access for government buildings and services, (see especially Huezo v. Los Angeles Community College District, 672 F.Supp.2d 1045 re: community college access requirements). [For general overview, see "Title II of the Americans with Disabilities Act and Section 504 of the Rehabilitation Act: Making Programs, Services and Activities Accessible to All," a comprehensive 2003 article by attorney Larry Paradis of Disability Rights Advocates, a Berkeley based public interest law firm. (Stanford Public Policy Review, Vol. 14.2 (2003) p 389-415).

regulations so adopted.] These were trade standards- ASA or "ANSI" regulations- which were adopted into law until the July 1, 1982, effective date of the State Architects Regulations (also known as "Title 24" or the California Building Code).

2. PUBLIC POLICY REQUIRES ACCESS, INCLUDING AN ACCESSIBLE PATH OF TRAVEL TO THE AREA OF ALTERATION, WHENEVER ALTERATIONS ARE MADE

Since "handicapped access" legislation was first passed into law as to governmental facilities (1968) and privately owned public facilities (1970), California has protected the rights of "full and equal access" for disabled persons, including wheelchair users and others with mobility limitations. Government Code section19230(a) sets California policy: "It is the policy of the state to encourage and enable disabled persons to participate fully in the social and economic life of this state." In re Marriage of Carney, 24 Cal.3d 725, 740 (1979) quoted this statute in further finding that "Both the state and federal governments now pursue the commendable goal of total integration of handicapped persons into the mainstream of society." Donald v. Café Royale, Inc., 218 Cal.App.3d 168, 173 (1990), further supported this important public policy: "The various legislative pronouncements of our state's policy leave no doubt that the purpose of section 54 et seq. ... is to reduce or eliminate the physical impediments to participation in community life by the physically handicapped."
(Emphasis added)

ASA Provision 1.2, entitled "Purpose," stated in part that "This standard is intended to make all buildings and facilities...accessible to and functional for the physically handicapped to, through and within their doors." (Emphasis added). (A copy of the 1961 "ASA" regulations is included in Appendix section IX-C). Consistent with that purpose, making any area of a public facility "accessible" has always required provision of an accessible "path of travel" in any public facility, from the "outside" public walkways. The "path of travel" concept recognizes that in order to make an area inside a building "accessible to," "useable by" and "functional for" disabled members of the public, these persons must be able to travel to the "accessible" area from the adjoining public property.

ASA Sections 4.1 ("Site Development"), 4.2 ("Walkway"), 5.2.1
  ("Doors") and 5.6 ("Toilets") are also relevant. For illustrative purposes, provision 5.6 states that "It is essential that an appropriate number of toilet rooms. . . be made accessible to and useable by the physically handicapped." How can this be achieved unless there is an accessible path of travel to the toilet rooms from the area of alteration? How can the area of alteration itself be "accessible" unless there is an accessible path of travel from the walkways and parking lots outside of a building or facility to the area of alteration?

Government Code sections 4450-4456 (adopted in 1968) have the same accessibility requirements for government buildings, upon alteration, as those of Health & Safety Code sections 19955 - 19959, adopted two years later (as of July 1, 1970) for privately owned public facilities, because Health & Safety Code section 19955 et seq. <u>adopts and incorporates</u> the requirements of Government Code sections 4450 et seq.

Since the very <u>purpose</u> of all access codes, starting with the earliest 1961 American Standards Association (ASA) Regulations, per § 1.2, was to make public buildings "accessible to, through and within their doors," any "interpretation" of regulations and codes must be consistent with this purpose. A detailed policy discussion, as to "ascertaining the intent of the Legislature so as to effectuate the law" and applying that policy to the interpretations of "handicapped access" law is found in <u>Donald v. Sacramento Valley Bank</u>, (1989) 209 Cal. App. 3d 1183, at 1191-1192.

A section entitled, <u>"The Legal Standard For Accessibility For The Handicapped</u>," People ex rel. Deukmejian v. CHE, Inc., (1983) 150 Cal.App.3d 123, at 133, outlined the California legislative history:

> Our construction of the legislative schemes commences with Civil Code section 54, et seq. which declares, in part, that all physically handicapped are entitled to the same right as the able bodied to full and free use of public facilities and places (§ 54), requiring operators of such facilities to "open its doors on an equal basis to all that can avail themselves of the facilities without violation of other valid laws and regulations." (Marsh v. Edwards Theatres Circuit, Inc., 64 Cal.App.3d 881, 892, 134 Cal. Rptr. 844; Civ.Code, § 54.1, subd. (a).) To give meaning to the public accommodation law prohibiting discrimination against the handicapped, the Legislature enacted Government Code section 4450, et seq. providing for the establishment of standards for buildings constructed with public funds designed to insure accessibility by the handicapped. A year later, the Legislature expanded these requirements to facilities constructed with private funds (§ 19955, et seq.) and, with certain limited exceptions, required conformance with the same standards set forth within Government Code section 4450, et seq. <u>The underlying legislative intent of these statutory schemes is to require affirmative conduct so as to guarantee access to the physically handicapped upon construction of new facilities or with the repair or alteration of existing facilities.</u> (<u>Marsh v. Edwards Theatres Circuit, Inc.</u>, *supra*, at p. 888, 134 Cal.Rptr. 844.) The Supreme Court explained in re Marriage of Carney, 24 Cal.3d 725, 738, 157 Cal.Rptr. 383, 598 P.2d 36, these statutory schemes were part of "<u>a growing body of legislation intended to reduce or eliminate the physical impediments</u>" to "<u>their participation in community life</u>." (Emphasis added)

The CHE court emphasized the <u>legislative policy</u> that should be considered in <u>interpreting</u> any issues related to handicapped access:

The prohibition against discrimination of the handicapped within Civil Code section 54, et seq., the enactment of Government Code section 4450, et seq., and section 19955, et seq., and the incorporation by reference of the phrase "primary entrance" within the applicable specifications, reflect a legislative sensitivity to the hardships suffered by those afflicted with a wide range of physical disabilities. They are part of an expanding legislative effort to attain "the commendable goal of total integration of handicapped persons into the mainstream of society...." (In re Marriage of Carney, *supra*, 24 Cal.3d 725, 740, 157 Cal.Rptr. 383, 598 P.2d 36.) The Legislature has declared "[i]t is the policy of this state to encourage and enable disabled persons to participate fully in the social and economic life of the state...." (Gov.Code, § 19230, subd.(a).) These legislative responses are designed to lessen their entire burden, by guaranteeing equal and full access to public buildings, facilities, and accommodations, without jeopardizing their safety.

CHE, Inc., *supra*, at 135-136.

3. ALL CONSTRUCTION AND ALTERATIONS TRIGGER ACCESS REQUIREMENTS

Per the original and subsequent versions of California Government Code section 4450ff, all new construction after November 3, 1968- including construction still underway on that date- were required to be accessible per sections 4450 and 4451, and to apply the ASA regulations from 1968 to the July 1, 1982, adoption of the State Architect's Regulations, Title 24 of the Administrative Code. (Title 24 is also known as the State Building Code.) Effective 1971, Government Code section 4456 also required access upon any "alteration, structural repairs, or additions."

For example, a "community" theater or other government building constructed in 1979 would have been subject to the requirements of the Government Code sections 4450ff, which then incorporated for detailed regulations the requirements of the (1961) ASA/ANSI A 117.1 regulation standards. Any such construction or alterations were also directly in violation of section 54 civil code, which applied to all "public places."[86] "Policy" violations may also be relied upon under both state and federal law. (See, for example, discussion of Pachovas v. County of Alameda, City of Berkeley at section I-J-3-B involving both police policy and physical accessibility of a courthouse and jails.

4. FOR ALTERATIONS AFTER JULY 1, 1982, "PATH OF TRAVEL" IS EXPLICITLY DEFINED IN THE 1982 STATE ARCHITECT'S REGULATIONS ("TITLE 24") AND THE 1984 STATE ARCHITECT'S INTERPRETIVE MANUAL

"Path of travel" was defined in the 1982 State Architect's Regulations (Title 24); (at

---

[86] Marsh v. Edwards Theaters, (1976) 64 Cal.App.3d 881, a case of dubious precedential value today, held that a private theater constructed in 1968 did not deny access per sections 54 and 54.1 California Civil Code because no regulations were yet specified. The ASA regulations were incorporated into Health and Safety Code section 19955 - 19959 effective July 1, 1970.

p.27 of the 1984 State Architect's Interpretive Manual, at § 2-417(c)); and by the State Architect's "interpretation." Regulation 2-417(c) states:

> (c) <u>Path of Travel</u>: Path of travel is a passage that may consist of walks and sidewalks, curb ramps, and pedestrian ramps, lobbies and corridors, elevators, other improved areas, or a necessary combination thereof, that provides free and unobstructed access to and egress from a particular area or location, for pedestrians and/or wheelchair users.

The State Architect's interpretation to the "Path of Travel" definition of § 2-417(c) in the 1984 Interpretive Manual includes the following:

> The point of path of travel is that people arriving at the building site have <u>accessibility from the exterior</u> of the building <u>including either the right of way and/or parking lot to the interior portions of the building</u>. This path of travel could include various elements including the entrance, <u>walkways, ramps, etc. necessary to provide a direct accessible route to the interior of the building.</u> <u>All features</u> within the path of travel are to adhere to these regulations. (Emphasis added)

Which Title 24 regulations apply, depends on the date of each alteration and the then applicable Government Code and Title 24 or ASA requirements. Government Code section 4456 enacted in 1971, is entitled "Alteration of existing building or facilities:"

> After the effective date of this section, any building or facility which would have been subject to this chapter but for the fact it was constructed prior to November 13, 1968, shall comply with the provisions of this chapter <u>when alterations, structural repairs or additions are made to such building or facility</u>. This requirement shall only apply to the area of specific alteration, structural repair or addition and shall not be construed to mean that the entire structure or facility is subject to this chapter. (Emphasis added)

Making an area of alteration "accessible" includes creating an accessible <u>entrance</u> to the facility; an accessible <u>path of travel</u> to the "altered" area; and "accessible <u>sanitary facilities, drinking fountains, and public telephones serving the remodeled area</u>. . ." For example, the 2002 Title 24 Regulations on "Accessibility for Existing Buildings" spelled out the requirements for the types of access triggered by "renovation, structural repair, alterations and additions to existing buildings":

> SECTION 1134B – ACCESSIBILITY FOR EXISTING BUILDINGS
>
> 1134B.1 Scope. The provisions of this division apply to renovation, structural repair, alteration and additions to existing buildings, including those identified as historic buildings. This division identifies minimum standards for removing architectural barriers, and providing and maintaining accessibility to existing buildings and their related facilities.
>
> 1134B.2 General. All existing buildings and facilities, <u>when alterations, structural</u>

<u>repairs or additions are made to such buildings or facilities</u>, shall comply with all provisions of Division I, New Buildings, except as modified by this division. These requirements shall apply only to the area of specific alteration, structural repair or addition and shall include those areas listed below:

> 1134B.2.1 A primary entrance to the building or facility and the primary path of travel to the specific area of alteration, structural repair or addition, and sanitary facilities, drinking fountains, signs and public telephones serving the area. (Emphasis added)
>
> (Similar provisions, though numbered differently, appear in the Title 24 regulations for 1984 - to the present.)

5. FROM 1970 UNTIL THE 1982 ADOPTION OF THE STATE ARCHITECT'S TITLE 24 REGULATIONS, GOVERNMENT CODE § 4450 ET SEQ., HEALTH & SAFETY CODE §19959 AND THE "ASA" REGULATIONS ALL REQUIRED AN ACCESSIBLE PATH OF TRAVEL TO ANY AREA OF ALTERATION, IN ORDER FOR THAT AREA TO BE MADE "ACCESSIBLE"

As explained in <u>Donald v. Sacramento Valley Bank</u>, *supra*, 1192-1194, prior to the adoption of the State Architect's Regulations (effective July 1, 1982), Government Code section 4451(d) required that facilities subject to Government Code sections 4450 et seq. or Health & Safety Code sections 19955 et seq., "shall conform to the American Standards Associations specifications A117.1/1961" (also known as the "ASA" or American National Standards Institute "ANSI" regulations).

The State Architect's <u>explicit</u> requirement for an accessible path of travel in all of the State Architect's Regulations (1982 to the present) is a recognition that an accessible path of travel (POT) to the area of alteration is implicit in the concept of making an area "accessible," and that a path of travel was also previously required under the ASA standards. An accessible POT was also required under Government Code section 4456 and Health & Safety Code section 19959 in terms of making an area "accessible" when an alteration, structural repair or addition was made to that area.

<u>Donald v. Sacramento Valley Bank</u>, *supra*, involved the 1975 alteration of a building by the addition of an ATM on the building's exterior, up several stairs. A wheelchair accessible "path of travel" from the exterior sidewalk to the ATM was triggered by the alteration. Based on the "walks and levels" provisions of ASA 4.2.2, "such walks should be of a continuing common surface, not interrupted by steps or abrupt changes in level." Thus, for example, an uninterrupted POT is required to any theater's box seats added in 1975. The ASA regulations set the standard until July 1, 1982, the effective date of the State Architect's Regulations.

<u>Sacramento Valley Bank</u>, *supra*, at 1192, held the following:

Most importantly, Government Code section 4451 required public buildings and related facilities to adhere to existing ASA standards. The statute provided in relevant part: "(c) Except as otherwise provided by law, buildings, structures, sidewalks, curbs and related facilities subject to the provisions of this chapter or Part 5.5. (commencing with Section 19955) of Division 13 of the Health and Safety Code shall conform to the regulations adopted pursuant to Section 4450 which are in effect on the date a building permit is issued therefor... [¶] All buildings, structures and related facilities which are required to conform to the American Standards Association Specifications A117.1-1961 prior to the effective date of the regulations adopted by the State Architect shall continue to conform to the American Standards Association Specifications A117.1-1961...." (Emphasis by the court); Stats.1974, ch. 995, §2, p.2104

The court found that,

> The ASA standards apply to "all buildings and facilities used by the public," and list as their purpose "to make all buildings and facilities used by the public accessible to and functional for the physically handicapped. . . (ASA Standard A117.1 / 1961 ¶1.2) (Emphasis added)

Donald v. Sacramento Valley Bank, *supra*, 209 Cal.App.3d 1183, at 1194.

The court further found that provisions of Health & Safety Code sections 19955 et seq. were applicable "with respect to buildings constructed after July 1, 1970, or to the repair and alteration of existing facilities after that date." (Id. At 1192-1193.)

The court in interpreting section 19955 (209 Cal.App.3d 1183, at 1194, footnote 8) noted the following:

> The 1961 ASA standards also specify the specifications apply to all buildings and facilities used by the public. As relevant to this appeal, the 1961 ASA standards provided: "1.1 Scope [¶] 1.1.1 This standard applies to all buildings and facilities used by the public. It applies to temporary or emergency conditions as well as permanent conditions. It does not apply in private residences. [¶] 1.2 Purpose. This standard is intended to make all buildings and facilities used by the public accessible to and functional for the physically handicapped, to, through, and within their doors, without loss of function, space or facility where the general public is concerned." (Emphasis added)

In applying the ASA "walkway" provisions to access from a public sidewalk to an ATM on the outside of the building, the court definitively answered "Yes" to the question of whether a "path of travel" (from the exterior of a structure to the remodeled area) needed to be accessible to the physically "handicapped" to the same extent that the remodeled area itself is required to be accessible.

Sacramento Valley Bank, *supra*, and People ex rel. Deukmejian v. CHE, Inc., *supra*, both involved enforcement of access requirements under the ASA (for 1975 and 1976 alterations, respectively). As pointed out in Sacramento Valley Bank, *supra*, the ASA standards were formulated in 1961 and did not make any reference to an "automatic teller machine" - or many other specific types of "facilities." Yet, the Court held that it was the <u>intention</u> of the ASA, as adopted by the Legislature, to provide access to all public facilities. (See "Purpose," ASA § 1.2).

An area cannot be considered "accessible" under the ASA unless it can be reached by an accessible route. Sacramento Valley Bank and "CHE", both applied access requirements under the ASA, and showed why an "accessible" "path of travel" was an implicit requirement to make an area "accessible to and usable by" disabled persons. While there is no use of the phrase "path of travel" in the ASA, there are analogous requirements in the ASA that all <u>walkways</u> be accessible, as held in <u>Sacramento Valley Bank</u>. The court found a "path of travel" requirement implicit from the provisions for accessible "walkways" under § 4.2.2 of the ASA. Section 4.2.2 stated, "Such walks shall be of a continuing common surface, not interrupted by steps or abrupt changes in level." (Sacramento Valley Bank, *supra*, at 1193 to 1194.)

CHE established that building owners and operators are obligated under the statutes and regulations in effect during 1970-1982 to provide access to any public facility constructed or altered during this period. In CHE the court specifically found a requirement for proper access through the front door of an "altered" second story restaurant under California Statutes and the ASA/ANSI requirements. A secondary entrance through the kitchen could not be justified as a form of the "equivalent facilitation" required as a condition of any "hardship exception" allowed under Health & Safety Code section 19957. (CHE at p.134.) The court explained why public policy required such an interpretation, to avoid second class treatment and segregation from able-bodied patrons:

> Because we find the required primary entrance must necessarily be burdened by a substantial flow of pedestrian traffic, a public restaurant entrance used by no patrons other than the physically handicapped cannot realistically be a "primary entrance."
> CHE at 135.

Similarly, seating all disabled wheelchair users at the very back of a <u>live</u> performance theater owned and operated by a government entity may treat them as segregated, second class citizens. (Ironically for a <u>movie</u> theater, especially a "stadium seating" theater, it is seating in the first row that is the worst!)

6. CHE FOUND THE 1981 TITLE 24 REGULATIONS "CLARIFIED" THE PRIOR "ASA" REGULATIONS IN SPECIFYING PATH OF TRAVEL REQUIREMENTS

The ASA requirements for an accessible path of travel, in light of public policy and the purpose of the statutes involved, were established by the court's interpretation in People ex rel Deukmejian v. CHE, *supra*. The CHE court treated Title 24, the successor to the ASA, as a "legislative amendment" which "merely clarified the existing law." Title 24's explicit requirement for an "accessible" path of travel was held to be an implicit access requirements of Health & Safety Code section 19959 even under the previous "ASA" regulations.

The CHE court explained how the statutory construction should consider this legislative purpose:

> Reading these provisions in harmony, we conclude the latter two statutory schemes regarding access to public buildings and facilities were enacted to provide substance to the full and equal access right of the handicapped, setting forth the legal standard requiring at least one primary entrance be accessible to and useable by the physically handicapped. Where a second primary entrance is necessary in order to satisfy this requirements, it need not be identical in character; however, it must satisfy our construction of the phrase "primary entrance" (*infra*), because the statutory and regulatory law, read as a whole, is designed to guarantee safe access for the physically disabled while permitting them to function as equals to the maximum extent feasible within every aspect of society. Consequently, exception to the literal statutory and regulatory requirements is warranted only when equivalent facilitation and protection are not denied. (ASA, spec.I.2; §19957.) Thus, equality, at minimum, requires access free from difficulties or obstacles (see American Heritage Dictionary (New College Ed.1976) p. 469, col. 2) and potential hazards which would endanger even the most cautious physically handicapped. (Emphasis added)

People ex rel. Deukmejian v. CHE, Inc., *supra*, 150 Cal.App.3d at 134.

The court went on to construe the phrase "primary entrance," relying in part on regulations promulgated by the State Architect in 1981, in Title 24. The court explained why it was entitled to rely upon these later (Title 24) regulations of the State Architect even as to interpreting the ASA regulations which were in effect prior to the State Architect's regulations:

> However, there is further guidance in the regulations on handicapped access promulgated by the State Architect in 1981 (effective 12-31-81) within the State Building Code, 24 California Administrative Code, section 2-101, et seq. There, a primary entrance is defined as "any entrance to a facility which has a substantial flow of pedestrian traffic to any specific major function of the facility." (24 Cal.Admin.Code, § 2-417(k).) We are entitled to rely on this definition because it constitutes a clarifying regulatory amendment to the statutory schemes in controversy which from their enactment incorporated by reference the phrase "primary entrance." For, "[w]hile it is true that as a general rule statutes are not to be given retroactive effect unless the intent

of the Legislature cannot be otherwise satisfied (DiGenova v. State Board of Education, 57 Cal.2d 167, 176 18), an exception to the general rule is recognized in a case where the legislative amendment merely clarifies the existing law. (Balen v. Peralta Junior College Dist., 11 Cal.3d 821, 828, fn. 8...) The rationale of this exception is that in such an instance, in essence, no retroactive effect is given to the statute because the true meaning of the statute has been always the same..."

People ex rel. Deukmejian v. CHE, Inc., *supra*, at 134-135.
(Emphasis added.)

It is clear that the requirement for an accessible path of travel is implicit in the concept of making an area "accessible." The spelling out of a path of travel requirement in the State Architect's regulations merely defined and clarified what was already implicit in the accessibility standards of the ASA, when read in the context of legislative intent.

7. A 1979 CALIFORNIA LEGISLATIVE COUNSEL'S OPINION RECOGNIZED THAT AN ACCESSIBLE PATH OF TRAVEL TO AN AREA WAS IMPLICITLY REQUIRED IN ORDER FOR THIS AREA TO BE CONSIDERED "ACCESSIBLE" UNDER THE ASA STANDARDS AND UNDER THE STATE ARCHITECT'S (TITLE 24) REGULATIONS THEN BEING FORMULATED

"Path of travel" requirements have always been a basic component for making any area "accessible" to disabled persons. A March 31, 1979, California Office of Legislative Counsel's Opinion recommended that the "path of travel" concept be spelled out in the pending State Architect's Regulations (then in the planning stages, but not issued and effective until July 1, 1982, as Title 24, Part 2), and concluded that such path of travel requirements were already implicitly required under Government Code section 4456 for any alterations after 1972.

Such a "path of travel" requirement was implicit in the concept of "accessibility," and consistent with the stated "purpose" of Government Code section 4450, which is to ensure that "public buildings are to be accessible to and usable by the physically handicapped." The 1979 Legislative Counsel's opinion explained why an accessible path of travel was a necessary component of usability for an accessible location:

> It is our opinion that the specific limitation in Section 4456, which requires only the providing of accessibility to, and usability by, the physically handicapped to that portion of the public building or facility constructed prior to November 13, 1968, which is altered, repaired or added after March 4, 1972, does not exempt the administrative authority of the building or facility from also making a path of travel from the exterior of the structure to the remodeled area, a path of travel from any key facilities serving the area to the remodeled area (where such key facilities are required for the physically handicapped), and the key facilities themselves accessible to the physically handicapped. Without making such paths of travel and key facilities serving the remodeled area accessible and usable by the

physically handicapped, we think that portion of the structure which is remodeled would not be functionally usable by the physically handicapped pursuant to Section 4456 and this would, therefore, defeat the legislative purpose in enacting Chapter 7 that is provided for in Section 4450. That purpose, as quoted above, states that public buildings and facilities are to be accessible to and usable by the physically handicapped. It is established that statements of legislative intent of this kind may be given considerable weight by the courts in determining the intent of statutes. (Friends of Mammoth v. Board of Supervisors 8 Cal.3d 247, 256-259)

The Legislative Counsel concluded, as to the period prior to the 1982 adoption of the State Architect's Regulations,

> Thus it is our opinion that when a public building or facility that was constructed prior to November 13, 1968 is structurally remodeled after March 4, 1972, Section 4456 [Gov't Code] requires that a path of travel from the exterior of the structure to the remodeled area, a path of travel from any key facilities serving the remodeled area of the structure to the remodeled area, (where such key facilities are required for the physically handicapped), and the key facilities themselves be accessible to the physically handicapped to the same extent that the remodeled area of the structure is to be so accessible.

[A full copy of this March 31, 1979, Opinion by the California Office of Legislative Counsel is attached as Section IX, Appendix D to this book.]

8. GOVERNMENT CODE SECTION 11135, ESTABLISHED IN 1977, ALSO REQUIRES "FULL AND EQUAL ACCESS"

California Government code section 11135 has required since 1977, that "no person" in certain listed categories, including disability,

> "be unlawfully denied full and equal access to the benefits of, or be unlawfully subjected to discrimination under, any program or activity that is conducted, operated, or administered by the state or by any state agency, is funded directly by the state, or receives any financial assistance from the state. Notwithstanding Section 11000, this section applies to the California State University.

Section 11135(a) government code (in present wording)

Section 11135(b) specifically incorporates the ADA's section 202's standards:

> With respect to discrimination on the basis of disability, programs and activities subject to subdivision (a) shall meet the protections and prohibitions contained in Section 202 of the Americans with Disabilities Act of 1990 (42 U.S.C. Sec. 12132), and the federal rules and regulations adopted in implementation thereof, except that if the laws of this state prescribe stronger protections and prohibitions, the programs and activities subject to subdivision (a) shall be subject to the stronger protections and prohibitions. (Emphasis added)

9. CAVEAT: SIX MONTH GOVERNMENT CLAIM REQUIRED FOR DAMAGES UNDER CALIFORNIA LAW

Damages for governmental action or failure to act resulting in denial of civil rights should be treated as a "personal injury" claim for purposes of time limits to file a government tort claim. This is generally "not later than 6 months after the accrual of the cause of action." § 911.2 California Government Code. Although there are certain procedures for seeking to file a "late" claim, when plaintiff's attorney can allege and prove a legal excuse, the claim must be "presented as provided in Article 2 (commencing with section 915). Id.

[See also section I-M-2, *supra*, Such procedures are not discussed in this book.]

B. SECTION 504 OF THE REHABILITATION ACT OF 1973, THE FEDERAL PREDECESSOR TO THE ADA, REQUIRED REMOVAL OF BARRIERS AND PROVISION OF ACCESS FOR ALL RECIPIENTS OF FEDERAL FINANCIAL ASSISTANCE

Section 504 of the Rehabilitation Act (as amended in 1992) provides that "No otherwise qualified individual with a disability... shall, solely by reason of his or her disability, be excluded from the participation in, be denied the benefits of, or be subjected to discrimination under any program or activity receiving Federal financial assistance." 29 USC § 794(a). Thus a "private" program or activity may still be subject to section 504, if they have accepted federal funding, as have, for example, many large "private" schools and universities.

"The legislative history of the ADA indicates that Congress intended judicial interpretation of the Rehabilitation Act be incorporated by reference when interpreting the ADA." Huezo v. Los Angeles Community College District (Los Angeles Pierce College), 672 F.Supp.2d 1045 (2008), quoting Collings v. Longview Fibre Co., 63 F.3d 828, 832 n. 3 (9th Cir.1995).

C. ADA TITLE II COVERS ALL GOODS AND SERVICES, PROGRAMS AND ACTIVITIES OF STATE AND LOCAL GOVERNMENT AGENCIES

1. TITLE II COVERS BOTH BUILDINGS AND SERVICES (BUT THIS BOOK WILL FOCUS ON BUILDINGS, AND SERVICES PROVIDED BY ACCESSIBLE BUILDINGS)

Any defendant which is a governmental public entity is subject to Title II of the Americans with Disabilities Act of 1990 as well as Section 504 of the Rehabilitation Act of 1973, discussed *supra*. In 1990 the ADA mandated that "no qualified individual with a disability shall, by reason of such disability, be excluded from participation in or be denied the benefits of the services, programs, or activities of a public entity, or be subjected to discrimination by any such entity." 42 U.S.C. 12132; 42 U.S.C. 12111. Therefore programmatic access under federal law does not depend upon when the facility was constructed or altered. Regardless of the facility's construction and alteration history, compliance with Title II of the ADA requires compliance with the ADA Accessibility Guidelines (ADAAG) regulations <u>currently in effect</u>.[87]

"Public entities" include any state or local government and any of its departments, agencies or other instrumentalities. Title II applies to all activities of state or local governments whether or not they receive federal funds. The Title III "readily achievable" standards are not applicable to public entities, which must comply with ADA Title II.

To establish a violation of Title II of the ADA, a plaintiff must show that, "(1) he is a qualified individual with a disability; (2) he was excluded from participation in or otherwise discriminated against with regard to a public entity's services, programs or activities; and (3) such exclusion or discrimination was by reason of [his] disability." <u>Lovell v. Chandler</u>, 303 F.3rd 1039, 1052 (9th Cir. 2002); <u>Huezo v. Los Angeles Community College District (Los Angeles Pierce College)</u>, 672 F.Supp.2d 1045, 1049.

Regulations spelling out certain Title II ADA access requirements are set forth in 28 C.F.R. §§ 35.149-151. Section 35.149 sets forth a general prohibition against discrimination; § 35.150 governs the accessibility of existing facilities; and § 35.151 governs the accessibility of new construction and alterations. Section 35.150 requires that a public entity "operate each service, program, or activity so that the service, program, or activity, when viewed in its entirety, is readily accessible to and usable by individuals with disabilities." 28 C.F.R. § 35.150(a) (Emphasis added)

> Title II, Subtitle A- Prohibition Against Discrimination and Other Generally Applicable Provisions:
> Section 201 Definition.
>
> As used in this subchapter:
> (1) Public entity
> The term "public entity" means--
>
> (A) any State or local government;
> (B) any department, agency, special purpose district, or other instru-mentality of a State or States or local government; and
> (C) the National Railroad Passenger Corporation, and any commuter authority (as defined in section 24102(4) of Title 49).
> (2) Qualified individual with a disability
>
> The term "qualified individual with a disability" means an individual with a

---

[87] An excellent article describing the ADA Title II requirements and those of section 504 of the Rehabilitation Act of 1973, was published by DRA Executive Director Larry Paradis in a 2003 article. Be aware of possible statutory and case law changes and developments since the 2003 publication of this article.

disability who, with or without reasonable modifications to rules, policies, or practices, the removal of architectural, communication, or transportation barriers, or the provision of auxiliary aids and services, meets the essential eligibility requirements for the receipt of services or the participation in programs or activities provided by a public entity.

Section 202 Discrimination.
Subject to the provisions of this subchapter, no qualified individual with a disability shall, by reason of such disability, be excluded from participation in or be denied the benefits of the services, programs, or activities of a public entity, or be subjected to discrimination by any such entity.

Section 203 Enforcement.
The remedies, procedures, and rights set forth in section 794a of Title 29 shall be the remedies, procedures, and rights this subchapter provides to any person alleging discrimination on the basis of disability in violation of section 12132 of this title.

Section 204 Regulation.
(a) In general
Not later than 1 year after July 26, 1990, the Attorney General shall promulgate regulations in an accessible format that implement this part. Such regulations shall not include any matter within the scope of the authority of the Secretary of Transportation under section 12143, 12149, or 12164 of this title.

(b) Relationship to other regulations
Except for "program accessibility, existing facilities", and "communications", regulations under subsection (a) of this section shall be consistent with this chapter and with the coordination regulations under part 41 of title 28, Code of Federal Regulations (as promulgated by the Department of Health, Education, and Welfare on January 13, 1978), applicable to recipients of Federal financial assistance under section 794 of Title 29. With respect to "program accessibility, existing facilities", and "communications", such regulations shall be consistent with regulations and analysis as in part 39 of title 28 of the Code of Federal Regulations, applicable to federally conducted activities under such section 794 of Title 29.

(c) Standards
Regulations under subsection (a) of this section shall include standards applicable to facilities and vehicles covered by this part, other than facilities, stations, rail passenger cars, and vehicles covered by part B of this subchapter. Such standards shall be consistent with the minimum guidelines and requirements issued by the Architectural and Transportation Barriers Compliance Board in accordance with section 12204(a) of this title.
42 U.S.C.A. §§ 12131-12134 (West)

[This book does not cover "Subtitle B- Actions Applicable to Public Transportation Provided By Public Entities Considered Discriminatory"]

Per an <u>early edition</u> of the DOJ's Publication, <u>Title II Highlights</u>, <u>Title II put certain requirements on State and Local governments</u>. They:

"May not refuse to allow a person with a disability to participate in a service, program, or activity simply because the person has a disability."

"Must provide programs and services in an integrated setting, unless separate or different measures are necessary to ensure equal opportunity."

"Must eliminate unnecessary eligibility standards or rules that deny individuals with disabilities an equal opportunity to enjoy their services, programs or activities unless 'necessary' for the provisions of the service, program or activity."

"Are required to make reasonable modifications in policies, practices, and procedures that deny equal access to individuals with disabilities, unless a fundamental alteration in the program would result."

"Must furnish auxiliary aids and services when necessary to ensure effective communication, unless an undue burden or fundamental alteration would result."

"May provide special benefits, beyond those required by the regulation, to individuals with disabilities."

"May not place special charges on individuals with disabilities to cover the costs of measures necessary to ensure nondiscriminatory treatment, such as making modifications required to provide program accessibility or providing qualified interpreters."

"Shall operate their programs so that, when viewed in their entirety, they are readily accessible to and usable by individuals with disabilities."

This same DOJ publication identified "Qualified Individuals with Disabilities":

An "individual with a disability" is a person who --

Has a physical or mental impairment that substantially limits a "major life activity", or

Has a record of such an impairment, or

Is regarded as having such an impairment.

"Major life activities" include functions such as caring for oneself, performing manual tasks, walking, seeing, hearing, speaking, breathing, learning, and working.

"Qualified" individuals.

A "qualified" individual with a disability is one who meets the essential eligibility requirements for the program or activity offered by a public entity. In a section on "Program Access," the DOJ advised, "The ADA does not require retrofitting of existing buildings to eliminate barriers." However it notes that it may require such changes, if necessary, to provide "programmatic" access, where that access cannot be provided in some other way.

In a section entitled "Integrated Programs," the DOJ advised:

"Integration of individuals with disabilities into the mainstream of society is fundamental to the purposes of the Americans with Disabilities Act. Public entities may not provide services or benefits to individuals with disabilities through programs that are separate or different, unless the separate programs are necessary to ensure that the benefits and services are equally effective.

Even when separate programs are permitted, an individual with a disability still has the right to choose to participate in the regular program.

For example, it would not be a violation for a city to offer recreational programs specially designed for children with mobility impairments, but it would be a violation if the city refused to allow children with disabilities to participate in its other recreational programs.

State and local governments may not require an individual with a disability to accept a special accommodation or benefit if the individual chooses not to accept it."

2. INJUNCTIVE RELIEF IS AVAILABLE TO OBTAIN ACCESSIBLE COURTHOUSES, VETERANS BUILDINGS, LIBRARIES, PUBLIC COLLEGES AND UNIVERSITIES, AND ALL OTHER GOVERNMENTAL BUILDINGS, AND TO "MAINTAIN" ACCESSIBLE FEATURES

    Regarding Title II obligations, "One form of prohibited discrimination is the exclusion from a public entity's services, programs, or activities because of the inaccessibility of the entity's facili[ties]." Barden v. City of Sacramento, 292 F.3d 1073, 1075 (9th Circuit, 2002)

In Lonberg II, 2007 WL 2005177 at *8 the Court applied the Barden, *supra*, standards to grant a preliminary injunction and find damages for multiple curb cuts not provided by the City of Riverside:

By ordering the City to bring all of the curb ramps and sidewalk segments ... in[to] full compliance with the federal and state standards, the Court is promoting the Congressional objective of eliminating physical obstacles and preventing discrimination against disabled persons. Further, the repeated and significant difficulty Plaintiff encounters when attempting to use the non-compliant streets and sidewalks is a real and immediate threat of substantial and irreparable harm and it is exactly the type of discrimination that the ADA seeks to prevent. Barden v. City of Sacramento, 292 F.3d 1073, 1075-1077 (9th Cir.2002). The Court finds that the public interest would be greatly served by the issuance of an injunction requiring the City to comply with the ADA and California's disability access laws. Indeed, when passing the ADA Congress found that " '[t]he employment, transportation, and public accommodation sections of ... [the ADA] would be meaningless if people who use wheelchairs were not afforded the opportunity to travel on and between the streets." ' Kinney v. Yerusalim, 9 F.3d 1067, 1071 (3rd Cir.1993)

The above statement was as quoted in Judge Margaret M. Morrow's September 9, 2008 "Order Granting Plaintiff's Motion for Permanent Injunction" in Huezo v. Los Angeles Community College District (Los Angeles Pierce College) 672 F.Supp.2d 1045, 1064 (E.D. Cal, 2008).) However, a permanent injunction requiring the City of Riverside to "implement a transition plan," as described by 28 C.F.R. § 35.150(d) was reversed by the 9th Circuit in Lonberg v. Riverside 571 F.3d 846 (2009), which held there was no individual right to enforce this provision and require a public entity to adopt a transition plan. (Judge Morrow made a similar holding in Huezo, *supra*.) The lack of a transition plan might, however, be of evidentiary value in helping to prove Title II "intentional" discrimination as the basis for a Title II damages award.

A more difficult issue faces disabled plaintiffs who are arrested and "detained" in an inaccessible jail but released from custody without future likelihood of being arrested again. Do they have to prove they are likely to be arrested again and returned to face the same inaccessible conditions in the same jail in order to have Title II "standing"? Or do the statutes (federal and/or state) confer enforcement standing on anyone who has suffered disability discrimination, as a matter of public policy? For some statutes, the language of the statute itself may control. (See also section II-C-8-d, "JAILS" *infra*.)

Title II regulations also require that a public Accommodation "maintain" accessible features:
> In the DOJ's interpretation—which is entitled to deference—this regulation recognizes that it is not sufficient to provide features such as accessible routes, elevators, or ramps, if those features are not maintained in a manner that enables individuals with disabilities to use them. See Guidance on ADA Regulation on Nondiscrimination on the Basis of Disability by Public Accommodations and in Commercial Facilities. originally published on July 26, 1991, 28 C.F.R. Pt. 36, App. C (Mar. 15, 2011). While isolated or temporary obstructions are not prohibited, allowing obstructions to persist

or "[f]ailure ... to ensure that accessible routes are properly maintained and free of obstructions ... would also violate this part." Id. The 2002 version of Title 24 contained language similar to 28 C.F.R. § 36.211(a). See Cal. Code Regs. tit. 24 (2002) § 1101B.3.1.

Moeller v. Taco Bell Corp., 816 F. Supp. 2d 831, 858 (N.D. Cal. 2011).

3. AFFIRMATIVE STEPS BY THE GOVERNMENT ENTITY ARE REQUIRED TO AVOID DISCRIMINATION

An entity, such as a college, cannot simply place on disabled students the burden of requesting accommodation and identifying barriers, i.e., by requiring them to personally request accommodation to overcome barriers that exist. A defendant's failure to take affirmative steps to ensure that its programs and facilities were operated so that they were readily accessible to disabled persons is discriminatory within the meaning of the ADA and the Rehabilitation Act. See Putnam v. Oakland Unified School District, No. C93-3772 CW, 1995 WL 873734 (N.D.Cal., June 9, 1995); Huezo v. Los Angeles Community College District (Los Angeles Pierce College), 672 F.Supp.2d 1045 (2008).

Also see Bacon v. City of Richmond, 386 F.Supp.2d 700, 708 (E.D.Va. 2005) ("The law does not require... that Plaintiffs request some specific form of accommodation as a prerequisite to a valid ADA claim... The ADA requires that any program or activity held at a school be made accessible to the handicapped. The burden is not on the disabled to create accommodation solutions, but on those that provide services or facilities which hinder their participation").

In Huezo v. Los Angeles Community College District (Los Angeles Pierce College), 672 F.Supp.2d 1045 (2008), the Court granted plaintiff's motion for a permanent injunction, citing the requirements of ADA Title II and the regulations applicable to a publically operated college:

> As noted in the court's order granting Huezo's motion for partial summary judgment, the access requirements of the ADA are set forth in 28 C.F.R. §§ 35.149-.151. Section 35.149 sets forth a general prohibition against discrimination; § 35.150 governs the accessibility of existing facilities; and § 35.151 governs the accessibility of new construction and alterations. Section 35.150 requires that a public entity "operate each service, program, or activity so that the service, program, or activity, when viewed in its entirety, is readily accessible to and usable by individuals with disabilities." 28 C.F.R. § 35.150(a) (emphasis added). In deciding the motion for partial summary judgment, the court found that Huezo had established that he did not have the "high degree of convenient accessibility" to Pierce College campus facilities to which he is entitled under the ADA, given the difficulties he had encountered in obtaining accessible workstations and parking, and entering inaccessible classrooms.

The court also noted that Huezo had proffered undisputed evidence that he had had to personally request accommodation to overcome barriers that exist on the Pierce College campus. The court found that the District had improperly placed the burden of requesting accommodation and identifying on disabled students. It determined that the District's failure to take affirmative steps to ensure that its programs and facilities were operated so that they were readily accessible to disabled persons was discriminatory within the meaning of the ADA and the Rehabilitation Act. See Putnam v. Oakland Unified Sch. Dist., No. C-93-3772CW, 1995 WL 873734, *10 (N.D.Cal. June 9, 1995). As the Putnam court stated:

> "Defendants ... mistakenly argue that the regulations do not require entities to take any action to address architectural barriers creating the potential for denial of access, but instead allow entities to deal with problems when they 'actually arise,' either by then removing the barrier or by alternative means. However, the regulations impose upon schools the affirmative duty continuously 'to operate each program ... so that the program ..., when viewed in its entirety, is readily accessible to handicapped persons.'
>
> . . .
>
> "Although the regulations do not require removal of all architectural barriers to achieve such ready accessibility, they do require prompt implementation of a plan making all programs readily accessible. The approach of taking no action to render programs accessible until a student or parent identifies an accessibility problem does not make a program 'readily' accessible. Rather, this approach imposes the discriminatory requirement that a disabled student ascertain which barriers deny her access and brave possible disapproval to point them out and request that they be remedied. Furthermore, it imposes the further discrimination of forcing the student to wait for the barriers to be remedied, and in the meantime either be excluded or be subjected to the perils attendant to the barriers. Finally, Defendants' approach also has the discriminatory effect of discouraging students from entering or staying in the inaccessible school system, or from attempting to participate in classes and other programs located in inaccessible facilities." Id. At 1061-1062 (Emphasis added)

The Court noted the impropriety of requiring students to complain:
> The District concedes that to receive an accommodation of any kind-including basic services such as accessible furniture and transportation to otherwise inaccessible parts of campus-each disabled student must fill out certain forms prior to the beginning of each semester.-By continuing to require disabled students to request accommodation in this manner, the District has failed to operate its facilities and services in a non-discriminatory manner.[FN88] Cf. Bacon, 386 F.Supp.2d at 708; Putnam, 1995 WL 873734 at *10.

Id. at 1062-1063.

In FN 88 the court noted:

> Citing several opinions of the Office of Civil Rights, the District argues that at the college level, the student must request accommodation. (Def.'s Opp. at 12). The court, however, has determined that the ADA and Rehabilitation Act place an affirmative duty on the public entity to operate its services, programs, or activities in a non-discriminatory manner. (February 27, 2007 Order at 22-29). It has concluded that by requiring disabled students to point out barriers to access and seek accommodations, the District has violated the ADA and § 504 of the Rehabilitation Act by excluding Huezo from participation in and denying him the benefits of its services, programs, and activities, or otherwise discriminating against him on the basis of his disability.

Id. at 1063.

The court concluded that the District Court could not place the burden of complaining upon the students:

> In sum, the court concludes that the District's programmatic response to the pervasive lack of curb cuts, accessible paths of travel, and accessible desks and workstations does not meet the § 35.150's requirement that a public entity "operate each service, program, or activity so that the service, program, or activity, when viewed in its entirety, is readily accessible to and usable by individuals with disabilities." 28 C.F.R. § 35.150(a) (emphasis added). This is particularly true given that the District continues to place the burden on disabled students to identify barriers-e.g., lack of accessible workstations, inaccessible paths of travel-and request accommodation. Furthermore, Huezo has demonstrated that he will continue to take classes at Pierce College and continue to suffer irreparable injury due to the numerous access barriers he encounters as a result of the District's policies and procedures.

Id.

As a remedy, the court granted a permanent injunction:

> Because he has shown a likelihood that he will suffer irreparable injury and the inadequacy of remedies at law, the court grants Huezo's request for interim modifications to the District's policies and procedures. The court hereby enjoins the District to provide accessible desks, workstations, and other equipment with priority signage in all classrooms in use during a given semester; to hire an ADA access expert approved by plaintiff responsible for overseeing the placement of accessible desks, tables, and other workstations in all classrooms in use; to cease charging disabled students for parking permits to use the teachers' parking lots and keys to the library elevator; to provide regularly scheduled shuttle service for disabled students; to update the Special Services Student Handbook to reflect these changes; and to

publicize the existence and availability of the handbook as a resource for disabled students.
Id. at 1063-1064.

4. TRANSPORTATION SERVICES ARE ALSO COVERED BY TITLE II, BUT WILL NOT BE COVERED IN THIS BOOK

ADA Title II also covers transportation services. Some of the laws covering governmental transportation services may be found at 42 USC sections 12141 - 12165, and will not be discussed in this book. (I have little experience in this area) Under the ADA, Title II, Subtitle B, "Actions Applicable to Public Transportation," see ADA sections 221-246, [42 USC 12141 - 12166]

5. ANY VIOLATION OF THE ADA, INCLUDING TITLE II, IS INCORPORATED AS A VIOLATION OF CALIFORNIA LAW, PER. CIVIL CODE §§ 51(f), 54(c) AND 54.1(d)

Although damages may be obtained directly under Title II if "intentional" discrimination is proven (see section II-C-7, *infra*), amendments to Civil Code sections 54(c) and 54.1(d) may allow damages recovery from governmental defendants upon proof of an incorporated ADA violation. (Section 51(f) which also incorporates the ADA, probably does not apply to governmental agencies, unless they are a "business.") However any claim of damages directly under California law will presumably require compliance with California's Government Tort claim provisions [See Gov. Code sections 910 ff]

6. NO CALIFORNIA LAW "GOVERNMENT CLAIM" IS NEEDED TO BRING A TITLE II ACTION, BUT TITLE II DAMAGES ARE LIMITED TO "INTENTIONAL" DISCRIMINATION WHEREAS SECTION 54.3 CIVIL CODE DAMAGES FOR VIOLATIONS OF SECTIONS 54 AND 54.1 PROBABLY ARE NOT SO LIMITED

See Donald v. Café Royale, *supra*, re: no "intent" required.

7. DAMAGES: ADA TITLE II REQUIRES "INTENTIONAL" DISCRIMINATION FOR RECOVERY OF DAMAGES

   a. PROOF OF CONDUCT IN "CONSCIOUS DISREGARD" OF OR "DELIBERATE INDIFFERENCE" TO DISABILITY RIGHTS

   Section 203 [42 USC 12133] "Enforcement" incorporates the remedies and procedures and rights that this title provides to any person alleging discrimination on the basis of disability in violation of section 202.

   The ADA also required governmental entities, no later than January 26, 1992, to perform a self-evaluation and implement a "Transition Plan" to remove architectural barriers and/or alter their programs, services and activities to provide access to persons with disabilities. When a defendant's Transition Plan enumerates many accessibility violations at the facility and these have not been rectified after being discovered, defendant's knowing maintenance of inaccessible public facilities may evidence the "deliberate indifference" necessary to prove Title II damages under federal law evidencing an "intentional" violation. 42 USC 12131.

This ADA transition plan and other documents obtainable from government defendants through discovery may demonstrate a defendant's awareness of its access barriers, and that continued denial of access was evidence of "deliberate indifference" to its discriminatory effect upon disabled persons. However <u>failure to adopt a "transition plan"</u> is not <u>itself</u> something an individual can remedy by an injunction. <u>Lonberg v. Riverside</u> 571. F.3d 846 (9th Circuit 2009).

In the 9th Circuit, "deliberate indifference" to the rights and safety of disabled persons is a form of "intentional discrimination" which may justify an award of damages under ADA Title II. <u>Duvall v. County of Kitsap</u> (9th Cir. 2001) 260 F.3d 1124. For example, when a theater owned and operated by a governmental entity was constructed during the period 1968 - 1974, it may have had an obligation to comply with the ASA requirements for disabled seating, which applied to all construction not completed prior to November 13, 1968. California Government Code section 4450ff. Thereafter, when complaints were brought to the entity's attention that its lack of disabled seating anywhere in the theater (except <u>behind</u> the last row) was having a discriminatory effect on a young woman wheelchair user, and offered only designated disabled seating which was <u>not</u> accessible, the City faced a <u>possible</u> award of Title II damages. Such was the situation leading to a settlement during litigation about the Sacramento Community Theater in 2009. <u>Stoffel, a Minor, v. Sacramento Community Center Theater</u>, (E.D.Cal.) Case No. 2:08-CV-08-1076 JAM/GGH. (Settlement also included installation of a new entry door system and path of travel allowing seating four disabled persons and four companions in the 6th row instead of only the 34th row.) (See photo, Appendix J, *infra*).

If plaintiff additionally proves not only "deliberate indifference" but "conscious disregard" for the rights and/or safety of disabled persons, arguably a defendant government agency violating section 54(c) could also be held subject to treble damages pers section 54.3 civil code. [But caveat issues of the propriety and legality of allowing treble damages against a governmental entity; see Government Code section 818.]
For construction or alterations between November 13, 1968, and the adoption of Title 24 (the State Architect's Regulations) effective July 1, 1982, the "ASA" or ANSI A117.1 standards applied. They were incorporated into government code sections 4450, 4451, and 4452 for this period until the State Architect's Title 24 Regulations went into effect in 1982.

The Title 24 standards for disabled seating have changed in numerical designation but have been largely unchanged since 1982. Per current California Code of Regulations, Title 24, section 1104B.3.5, "Placement of Wheelchair Locations," wheelchairs and companion seating must be provided at a range of prices and at a range of locations, "so as to provide persons with disabilities a <u>choice of . . . line of sight comparable to those for members of the general public</u>." (Emphasis added) [See evolving "line of sight cases," *infra*, at section III-K]

b. LIABILITY FOR INJUNCTIVE RELIEF UNDER TITLE II DOES NOT REQUIRE "INTENTIONAL" DISCRIMINATION, WHERE A GOVERNMENT POLICY HAS A DISPARATE IMPACT ON DISABLED PERSONS

Plaintiff does not have to prove "intentional" discrimination to prove a violation of ADA Title II in order to obtain injunctive relief. <u>Crowder v. Kitigawa, Chairman Hawaiian Bd. of Control</u>, 81 F.3d 1480 (9th Cir. 1996) In <u>Crowder</u>, *supra*, a 60 day quarantine "equally" applied as to <u>all</u> dogs entering the state, and treating service dogs on the same basis as "pets," would have had a devastating effect upon blind and disabled persons who relied upon and had great need for guide dogs and service animals.[88]

c. NO PUNITIVE DAMAGES AGAINST A GOVERNMENT AGENCY (GOV. CODE § 818)

Government code section 818, "Exemplary Damages" reads:

> Notwithstanding any other provisional law, a public entity is not liable for damages awarded under section 3294 of the Civil Code or other damages imposed primarily for the sake of example and by way of punishing the defendant

8. PUBLIC ENTITIES COVERED BY TITLE II: COURTHOUSES, COLLEGES, JAILS, PUBLIC PARKING LOTS AND PUBLIC PROPERTY RENTED TO PRIVATE TITLE III ENTITIES.

a. COURTHOUSE CASES AND <u>TENNESSEE V. LANE</u>

In a case representing the foremost challenge to date to the constitutionality of Title II of the ADA, the United States Supreme Court decided <u>Tennessee v. Lane</u> in a 5-4 decision 124 S. Ct. 1978 (2004), upholding Title II at least <u>as to courthouse liability</u>. The Court held that Title II of the ADA, as applied to cases implicating the fundamental right of access to the courts, constituted a valid exercise of Congress'

---

[88] Similarly, no wrongful intent is needed to show a violation of Title III of the ADA, <u>Helen L. V. Didario</u>, 46 F.3d 325, 335 (3rd Cir. 1995) or to show a violation of section 51(f) California Civil Code, based on an incorporated violation of the ADA. <u>Munson v. Del Taco, Inc.</u>, 46 Cal.4th 661 (2009) Also no "intentionality" is needed for a violation of Civil Code section 54.1 <u>Donald v. Café Royale</u>, 218 Cal.App.3d 168 (1990), *supra*.

enforcement power under the 14th amendment to the United States Constitution. Paraplegic wheelchair user George Lane had to crawl up two flights of stairs to get to a courtroom to answer criminal charges:

> When Lane returned to the courthouse for a hearing, he refused to <u>crawl</u> again or to be carried by officers to the courtroom; he consequently was arrested and jailed for failure to appear.

Id. at 1983.

Rather than detail the opinion and dissent, I find it <u>incredible</u> that four members of the U.S. Supreme Court could argue in their dissent that Congress could not enforce the Due Process Clause of the 14th Amendment, to hold that all citizens- including the disabled- had a right to enter a courtroom and participate in their own hearing. Fortunately in California we did not have to depend on the federal ADA to require accessible courthouses:

section 54 Civil Code and section 4450ff Government Code already required this for all courthouses constructed or physically altered after November 3, 1968, in California. State Court and Federal Court lawsuits, some under California law, successfully obtained access to multiple County Courthouses in Alameda County, Sonoma County, Amador County, and elsewhere in California. The late Jim Donald, acting as attorney and plaintiff, reportedly obtained access to entrances and courtrooms in Napa County, including accessible judge's benches! [89]

b. COLLEGES

Individual lawsuits have successfully obtained greatly improved access at many universities and colleges in California, including the Stanford University (<u>old</u>) football stadium, Stanford's Maples Pavilion basketball stadium; the Stanford Memorial Church (site of public orchestra performances); Wheeler Hall (the largest lecture hall on campus), Zellerback Hall and other facilities at the University of California Berkeley; Fresno City College; Los Madano College; Laney College; Berkeley City College; College of Marin; Chabot College; Los Angeles Pierce College (<u>Huezo v. Los Angles Community College District</u>); Sonoma State College and several others, in addition to access obtained through negotiation and "voluntary" access improvements.

c. PUBLIC PROPERTY RENTED TO PRIVATE PUBLIC ACCOMMODATIONS

---

[89] A $250,000 accessible entrance ramp was obtained for the Alameda County Courthouse, 1225 Oak street, Oakland by the filing of a government claim followed by negotiations with Alameda County Officials, informally supervised by then presiding Judge Joseph Carson and accomplished voluntarily with a waiver of any claim for damages or attorney fees. State Court lawsuits succeeded in improving access at six other Alameda County Courthouses, including "Berkeley I" and "Berkeley III", the Hayward Superior Courthouse, Wiley Manual Courthouse, and Alan E. Broussard Courthouse, including entrances, public restrooms, and courtroom entrances, all more than 10 years before <u>Tennessee v. Lane</u>, *supra*.

(1) "BARNES AND NOBLE" AT JACK LONDON SQUARE

If a city owns property, or the land on which a commercial building is built, the city may be responsible under either Title II or Title III. A lawsuit against tenant Barnes and Noble Books and landlord City of Oakland resulted in a consent decree improving interior and exterior building access and parking facility accessibility at Oakland's Jack London Square. Taylor v. Barnes and Noble, et al, Settlement Decree and Order, February 23, 2011. (Because Barnes and Noble vacated the City of Oakland premises after the lawsuit was filed, injunctive relief was only against the city, which owned the former book store premises and the Jack London Square exterior plaza, paths of travel, and underground parking lot. The City agreed to make all accessible)

(2) CITY LIABLE AS OWNER, OPERATOR, LESSOR, OR LESSEE

If a public entity has one of these relationships to the property of a business with architectural barriers to access, should the public entity be jointly liable for the business's denial of access, as well as for the City's own paths of travel and parking? Cleveland v. Isabella's at Wharfside, Inc., et al, (N.D. Cal. 2010) Settlement Agreement and Order, December 22, 2010. (City owned wharf and was master lessor to the restaurant and owned and operated two parking lots serving all businesses on the Monterey Fisherman's Wharf. The Court's ruling on plaintiff's (contested) attorneys fee motion held the City and restaurant jointly and severally responsible for plaintiff's attorney fees.) Cleveland v. Isabella's at Wharfside, Inc., (N.D.Cal.) Case No. C09-02376 RMW, Order of March 14, 2012

d. JAILS

In Armstrong v. Schwarzenegger 622 F.3d 1058 (9th Cir., 2010), the 9th Circuit reaffirmed that the State of California "defendants are responsible for providing reasonable accommodations to the disabled prisoners and parolees that they house in county jails." Id at 1063. The appellate court affirmed the validity of a regulation implementing Title II of the ADA, 28 CFR § 35.30(b)(1): "a public entity, in providing any aid, benefit, or service, may not, directly or through contractual, licensing, or other arrangements, discriminate against individuals with disabilities." Id. at 1065

This 2010 opinion reiterated that "the ADA entitles inmates to receive the "benefits" of the incarcerating institution's programs and services without facing discrimination on account of a disability. See Armstrong, 124 F.3d at 1023." Id. at 1067-1068.

The Armstrong court rejected defendant's position that incarcerated persons are not entitled to the benefits of ADA Title II's protections:

> This contention is foreclosed by our precedent and that of the Supreme Court. Although we have noted that "incarceration itself is hardly a 'program' or 'activity' to which a disabled person might wish access," we have made clear that the ADA entitles inmates to receive the "benefits" of the incarcerating institution's programs and services without facing discrimination on account of a disability. See Armstrong, 124 F.3d at 1023. The Supreme Court has also rejected defendants' position, saying, "We disagree" with the contention "that state prisons do not provide prisoners with 'benefits' of 'programs, services, or activities' as those terms are ordinarily understood.... Modern prisons provide inmates with many recreational 'activities,' medical 'services,' and educational and vocational 'programs,' all of which at least theoretically 'benefit' the prisoners." Yeskey, 524 at 210.
>
> Here, plaintiffs do not complain that they have been denied incarceration on account of their disabilities. Instead, they contend that, on account of their disabilities, they have been denied benefits provided to other incarcerated persons or required by due process. The State's contracts and arrangements with the counties are not simply to incarcerate parolees and prisoners, but to provide such individuals with various positive opportunities, from educational and treatment programs, to opportunities to contest their incarceration, to the fundamentals of life, such as sustenance, the use of toilet and bathing facilities, and elementary mobility and communication. The restrictions imposed by incarceration mean that all of these positive opportunities must be provided or allowed to individuals incarcerated pursuant to state contracts and arrangements to the same extent that they are provided to all other detainees and prisoners. Accordingly, such state-county arrangements include "benefits" of programs or services provided to class members by defendants through their contracts and other arrangements with the counties, and come under the purview of the ADA and its regulations. [Emphasis added.]
>
> Id. at 1068.

This opinion is especially important as the use of privately owned "for-profit" prisons is growing, with many obvious risks to prisoners' welfare when the state attempts to "delegate" its responsibilities to private entities.

The Armstrong court also rejected the assertion by defendant state entity that plaintiff should have sued the entities the prisons had contracted with:

> It is elementary that a plaintiff may sue a party who is liable for his injury and that a defendant cannot avoid liability, or the remedy for that liability, by demonstrating that plaintiff could have sued another party as well.

Id. at 1072.

A public entity defendant cannot point to other possible defendants in order to "shirk their obligations under the ADA." Id. at 1072.

9. TITLE II REGULATIONS ESTABLISH THAT DEFENDANT PUBLIC ENTITIES HAVE THE BURDEN OF PROVING THE EXISTENCE OF ANY AFFIRMATIVE DEFENSES

In its decision granting plaintiff, disabled student Martin Huezo, partial summary judgment on his Title II claims (at Pierce College) in Marvin Huezo v. Los Angeles Community College, Case No. CV 04-9772 (C.D. Cal., Order of March 2, 2007), the Court noted plaintiff's expert's opinion and defendant's failure to prove its affirmative defenses:

> [Expert] Margen offers the undisputed opinion that "the majority if not all of the access barriers identified in [his] report could be brought into compliance with the Americans with Disabilities Act Accessibility Guidelines . . . without significantly altering the nature of the programs, services, and activities provided by Defendant at Pierce Community College.". . . Defendant, moreover, has not argued that correcting the physical barriers identified in the report "would result in undue financial and administrative burdens." See 28 C.F.R. § 35.150(a)(3) (establishing this as an affirmative defense to actions asserting violations of Title II and stating that the public entity has "the burden of proving" the existence of an undue financial or administrative burden).
> Id. at 28, fn.65.

The Huezo summary judgment order also held that defendant had the burden to show it had taken affirmative steps to remove barriers, not simply respond when a disabled person complained:

> Defendant's failure to take affirmative steps to ensure that its programs and facilities are operated in a manner that is readily accessible to disabled persons is, as Huezo correctly argues, discriminatory within the meaning of the ADA and the Rehabilitation Act. See Putman v. Oakland Unified Sch. Dist., No. C-93-3772CW, 1995 WL 873734 [(N.D. Cal. June 9, 1995)] at *10. As the Putman court stated:
>> Defendants . . . mistakenly argue that the regulations do not require entities to take any action to address architectural barriers creating the potential for denial of access, but instead allow entities to deal with problems when they "actually arise," either by then removing the barrier or by alternative means. However, the regulations impose upon schools the affirmative duty continuously "to operate each program . . . so that the program . . . when viewed in its entirety, is readily accessible to handicapped persons."
>
> Huezo, supra, at 27.

The Huezo court also cited Bacon v. City of Richmond, 386 F. Supp.2d 700, 708 (E.D. Va. 2005):

> ("The law does not require . . . that Plaintiffs[] request some specific form of accommodation as a prerequisite to a valid ADA claim. . . . The ADA requires that any program or activity held at a school be made accessible to the handicap[ped]. The burden is not on the disabled to create accommodation solutions, but on those that provide services or facilities which hinder their participation").
>
> Huezo, *supra*, at 28.

The Huezo court concluded that the entry of partial summary judgment for Huezo on his ADA and Rehabilitation Act claims was warranted by "Huezo's undisputed evidence that he had to ask for accommodations, and the lack of any evidence that defendant took affirmative steps to make its programs and facilities readily accessible, in combination. . . ." Id. at 28-29.

10. ATTORNEY FEES, LITIGATION EXPENSES, AND COSTS ARE AVAILABLE PER ADA SECTION 505

Attorney fees, litigation expenses, and costs are available to a prevailing plaintiff under section 505 ADA. Such "litigation expenses" may include the costs of expert witnesses and consultants. (See section 36.505 of Attorney General Regulations) Attorney fees and costs may also be awarded on a "public interest" basis per section 1021.5 California Code of Civil Procedure.[90]

Under California law, a government entity, may also face liability for any violation of section 54 Civil Code. Section 54(a) states:

> Individuals with disabilities or medical conditions have the same right as the general public to the full and free use of the streets, highways, sidewalks, walkways, public buildings, medical facilities, including hospitals, clinics, and physicians' offices, public facilities, and other public places.

Any violation of section 54 requires an award of damages and attorneys fees (per § 54.3) and/or an injunction and attorneys fees (per § 55).

[For a fuller discussion of ADA section 505, Attorney Fees, see section IV, Attorney Fees Under the ADA, *infra*]

---

[90] A potential attorney fee enhancement of as much as 2.0 is available under California State law, even in a federal court proceeding. Crommie v. State of California, et al., 840 F. Supp. 719 (1994); Mangold; Crommie v. California Public Utilities Comm'n et al., 67 F.3d 1470 (9th Cir. 1995). A multiplier based on contingency "risk" factors may also be awarded under California law. Ketchum v. Moses, 24 Cal.4th 1122 (2001).

III. ADA TITLE III STANDARDS AND INTERRELATION WITH CALIFORNIA LAW

A. ADA "ACCESS" REQUIREMENTS ADD TO EXISTING LIABILITY BASES UNDER CALIFORNIA LAW

1. BOTH NEW CONSTRUCTION AND ALTERATION AND "READILY ACHIEVABLE" ACCESS REQUIREMENTS UNDER THE ADA PROVIDE SEPARATE BASES FOR INJUNCTIVE RELIEF AND ATTORNEY FEES

   In all states, including California, access is also required by Title III (Public Accommodations) of the Americans With Disabilities Act of 1990. ADA section 303 covers new construction and alteration. Section 302(b)(2)(A)(iv) (discussed *infra*), requires that all "barrier" removal" steps be taken that are "readily achievable" to achieve handicap access. Any disabled person has standing to sue for injunctive relief under the ADA, having suffered a personal denial of access or having been "deterred" by knowledge of such lack of access. Suit may be filed by,

   > any person... who has reasonable grounds for believing that such person is about to be subject to discrimination in violation of Section 303. Nothing in this section shall require a person with a disability to engage in a futile gesture if such person has actual notice that a person or organization covered by this title does not intend to comply with its provisions.

   (§308(a)1)

   Effective January 26, 1993, (30 months from the ADA's enactment) ADA section 303 [42 USC 12183] defined as "discrimination", "as applied to public accommodations and commercial facilities" "a failure to design and construct facilities for first occupancy . . . that are readily accessible to and usable by individuals with disabilities. . ." Section 303 also established requirements for "alteration" defining as "discrimination",

   > a failure to make alterations in such a manner that, to the maximum extent feasible, the altered portions of the facility are readily accessible to and usable by individuals with disabilities, including individuals who use wheelchairs.[91]

   Section 303 is important nationwide, because it states that new construction or alterations after January 26, 1993 also trigger access. However this is less important in California where construction or where alterations have <u>already</u> required access under Health & Safety Code §§ 19955-19959, since July 1, 1970. (See § I-B-1 and 2, *supra*.)

   Most important in California is the ADA Title III "readily achievable" standard of § 301(9) and 302(b)(2)(A)(iv) and § 301(9), setting out "readily achievable" standards

---

[91] Section 303 (b) contains an "elevator" exception, which itself excludes several important categories from the "exception": Subsection (a) of this section shall not be construed to require the installation of an elevator for facilities that are less than three stories or have less than 3,000 square feet per story mall, or the professional office of a health care provider or unless the Attorney General determines that a particular category of such facilities requires the installation of elevators based on the usage of such facilities. (Emphasis added)

[42 USC 12181 and 12182] and "that failure to remove architectural barriers ... where such removal is readily achievable" constitutes section 302 (a) "discrimination." This adds the "readily achievable" basis for barrier removal requirements even if there has been no construction or alteration since July 1, 1970.

In Munson v. Del Taco the California Supreme Court explained the "readily achievable" standard of the ADA, while explaining the purpose of the amendment to the Unruh Act incorporating any violation of the ADA as a violation of section 51(f) California Civil Code, allowing damages without proof of any wrongful "intent." First the Court defined "readily achievable":

> The term 'readily achievable' means easily accomplishable and able to be carried out without much difficulty or expense." (42 U.S.C. § 12181(9).) Pursuant to the ADA's provision for issuance of regulations (42 U.S.C. § 12186(b)), the federal government has issued ADA Accessibility Guidelines that set forth standards of design and construction to ensure the disabled access to public accommodations (28 C.F.R. § 36, appen. A (2008)).

Munson v. Del Taco, *supra*, 46 Cal.4th. 661, at 670 (f.n. 6).

In Munson, *supra*, the California Supreme Court applied its public policy analysis to find that no "intentionality" element was needed to prove a violation of the ADA or of its incorporation into California Civil Code section51(f):

> May an Unruh Civil Rights Act plaintiff relying on subdivision (f) of section 51 obtain damages for denial of full access to a business establishment in violation of the ADA and the Unruh Civil Rights Act without proof the denial involved intentional discrimination? We conclude that a plaintiff proceeding under section 51, subdivision (f) may obtain statutory damages on proof of an ADA access violation without the need to demonstrate additionally that the discrimination was intentional.
> Munson, *supra*, 46 Cal.4th at 670.[92]

The Injunctive Relief remedy is available directly under the ADA. Injunctive Relief for violation of section 302(b)(2)(a)(iv) "shall include an order to alter facilities to make such facilities readily accessible to and useable by individuals with disabilities to the extent required by this title." (§ 308(a)(2)) In Arnold v. United Artists (N.D.Cal. 1994) 866 F.Supp. 433, Northern District Chief Judge Thelton Henderson held that a disabled person deterred from using a public accommodation had both standing to sue for injunctive relief and a right to at least statutory minimum damages.[90]

2. EXPLANATION OF ADA, ITS PURPOSES, ITS SUPREMACY OVER ANY STATE

---

[92] Munson was a particularly important interpretation of California disability access law as it was an unanimous (7-0) decision of the California Supreme Court written by Justice Kathryn Werdeger.

[93] See the December 17, 2012, Jankey v. Song Koo Lee, 290 P.3d 187 (Cal. 2012) decision, *supra*. Seeking Title III injunctive relief may allow omission of any potential dangers from attorneys fees against a good faith plaintiff under section 55 Civil Code.

REQUIREMENTS; NO PREEMPTION OF STATE LAW REMEDIES

In the landmark "Chapman" case (2011) the 9th Circuit reiterated the ADA's purpose; it's application to both intentional and unintentional "discrimination" against the disabled; and the standards requiring "readily achievable" barrier removal in existing buildings:

> The ADA was enacted "to provide clear, strong, consistent, enforceable standards addressing discrimination against individuals with disabilities." 42 U.S.C. § 12101(b)(2). Its passage was premised on Congress's finding that discrimination against the disabled is "most often the product, not of invidious animus, but rather of thoughtlessness and indifference," of "benign neglect," and of "apathetic attitudes rather than affirmative animus." Alexander v. Choate, 469 U.S. 287, 295–96, 105 S.Ct. 712, 83 L.Ed.2d 661 (1985). The concept of "discrimination" under the ADA does not extend only to obviously exclusionary conduct—such as a sign stating that persons with disabilities are unwelcome or an obstacle course leading to a store's entrance. Rather, the ADA proscribes more subtle forms of discrimination—such as difficult-to-navigate restrooms and hard-to-open doors—that interfere with disabled individuals' "full and equal enjoyment" of places of public accommodation. 42 U.S.C. § 12182(a); see also PGA Tour, Inc. v. Martin, 532 U.S. 661, 674–75, 121 S.Ct. 1879, 149 L.Ed.2d 904 (2001); Alexander, 469 U.S. at 295, 105 S.Ct. 712 (noting Congress's conclusion that "we can no longer tolerate the invisibility of the handicapped in America" (quoting 118 Cong. Rec. 525–26 (1972))).
>
> As defined by the ADA, unlawful "discrimination" occurs when features of an accommodation subject an individual or class of individuals on the basis of a disability or disabilities of such individual or class, directly, or through contractual, licensing, or other arrangements, to a denial of the opportunity of the individual or class to participate in or benefit from the goods, services, facilities, privileges, advantages, or accommodations of an entity.
>
> 42 U.S.C. § 12182(b)(1)(A)(i). In the context of existing facilities, discrimination includes "a failure to remove architectural barriers ... where such removal is readily achievable." Id. § 12182(b)(2)(A)(iv). In the case of newly constructed facilities, compliance with the ADA's antidiscrimination mandate requires that facilities be "readily accessible to and usable by individuals with disabilities." Id. § 12183(a)(1).
>
> Chapman v. Pier 1 Imports (U.S.) Inc., 631 F.3d 939, 944-45 (9th Cir. 2011)

Congress passed the Americans With Disabilities Act of 1990, 42 USC 12101 et seq., effective July 26, 1990, in order to set national standards to assist in eliminating discrimination against individuals with disabilities. Title III of the ADA, 42 USC 12181 et seq., deals with requirements for public accommodations and services operated by private entities. It should be noted that although this law is national in scope, Congress made clear in § 501(b), (42 USC 12201), that there is no pre-emption of any state laws:

(b) Relationship to Other Laws

Nothing in this act shall be construed to invalidate or limit the remedies, rights and procedures of any federal law or law of any state or political subdivision of any state or jurisdiction that provides greater or equal protection for the rights of individuals with disabilities than are afforded by this act.

Section 302(a) states the general rule prohibiting discrimination by public accommodations:

No individual shall be discriminated against on the basis of disability in the full and equal enjoyment of the goods, services, facilities, privileges, advantages or accommodations of any place of public accommodation by any person who owns, leases (or leases to) or operates a place of public accommodation.

Section 302(b)(2)(a) defines different forms of discrimination which are prohibited by the ADA, which include, with relation to a duty to remove architectural barriers, subsections (iv) and (v). Thus,

for purposes of subsection (a), discrimination includes... (iv) a failure to remove architectural barriers... in existing facilities ... where such removal is readily achievable; and (v) where an entity can demonstrate that the removal of a barrier under clause (iv) is not readily achievable, a failure to make such goods, services, facilities, privileges, advantages or accommodations available through alternative methods if such methods are readily achievable. (Emphasis added)

3. ENFORCEMENT OF TITLE III IS PRIMARILY BY PRIVATE LAWSUITS; ADA PLAINTIFFS ACT AS PRIVATE ATTORNEYS GENERAL

   a. AS ADA COMPROMISE, PRIMARY ENFORCEMENT IS BY PRIVATE LAWSUIT

   As one of the compromises involved in Congress passing and then President George H.W. Bush (George the First) signing the ADA into law in 1990, enforcement of Title III, the public accommodations section, is almost entirely by private lawsuits. (While enforcement has varied with other priorities of each federal administration, at best U.S. Department of Justice enforcement has generally not involved individual plaintiff cases, or enforcement of the "readily achievable" standard, at least not in California.) Although the U.S. Department of Justice has jurisdiction to enforce the ADA, there are no administrative agencies or federal "building inspectors," and no costly "bureaucracy" to enforce the law, an economic factor that was probably attractive to "conservatives" in 1990. Passage of the ADA in 1990 was a compromise in this respect: attorney fees were made awardable per § 505 to a prevailing disabled plaintiff, to encourage private attorneys to handle enforcement actions, rather than putting in place a potentially expensive bureaucracy to enforce this law.

In 1993 a California Attorney General's opinion made clear that the California Attorney General and local California building inspectors would not directly enforce Title III, but that Congress had left enforcement to the United States Department of Justice and to private lawsuits. (Ops. No. 93-203.) This opinion, by conservative Republican Attorney General Dan Lungren, may be cited to show the essential importance of enforcement by private lawsuits. The resulting importance of private lawsuits to enforce the ADA was recognized in an opinion by Northern District (former) Chief Judge Marilyn Hall Patel in 2010:[94]

> Encouraging competent attorneys to handle ADA Title III cases is necessary for effective enforcement: former California Attorney General Dan Lungren, in a 1993 Opinion, held that California building officials could not independently enforce the ADA, and that enforcement was left primarily to private lawsuits. (Attorney General's Opinion, No. 93-203.) Previously California Attorney General John Van de Kamp had supported private enforcement lawsuits, and filed amicus curiae briefs on behalf of the plaintiff in both Donald v. Sacramento Valley Bank, 209 Cal.App.3d 1183, 260 Cal.Rptr. 49 (1989) and Donald v. Café Royale, *supra*, stressing the limited resources of its Civil Rights Division and supporting the need for private lawsuits to enforce disabled access. Despite efforts made over the last 30 years to encourage attorneys to handle California law disability rights cases which seek public interest injunctive relief (and, since 1990, ADA cases), relatively few competent private attorneys have been willing to do so. Instead, much press attention has been paid to the few attorneys who may have "abused" use of the "ADA" statutes.

Blackwell v. Foley, 724 F.Supp 2d 1068 (N.D.Cal., 2010), at p 1075-1076.

b. PUBLIC POLICY TO ENCOURAGE PRIVATE ATTORNEY GENERAL ACTIONS
The importance of encouraging ADA Title III cases, and recognition that ADA plaintiffs carry out important roles as private attorneys general, was underscored by Northern District Chief Judge Thelton Henderson in Walker and Adams, et al. v. Carnival Cruise Lines, et al. (N.D.Cal. 2000) 107 F.Supp.2d 1135, 1140[95]:

> There can be no question that the Americans With Disabilities Act,

---

[94] Judge Patel's opinion adopted the "Report and Recommendation" of Magistrate Judge James Larsen, a former Chief Magistrate for the Northern District.

[95] The Walker case, handled by the Rein Law Office, resulted in fully accessible features being required on the Carnival "Holiday" cruise ship, as well as payment by defendants of $50,000 in damages and substantial attorney fees, litigation expenses and costs. The two day settlement conference was supervised by Northern District Mag. Judge Joseph Spero, who presided in a Miami, Florida, federal courtroom in conjunction with concurrent settlement of a separate Florida based class action involving 14 other Carnival cruise ships. (Action on Florida class action was stayed pending resolution of legal issues in the previously filed California individual action. "The tail wagged the dog.") This case was won by plaintiffs on the basis rulings by the Northern District Court of applying the ADA to a foreign flag cruise ship some four years before the United States Supreme Court upheld the validity of such an action in 2005. (Spector v. Norwegian Cruise Line LTD 125 S.Ct. 2169)

passed in 1990, established as law the nation's interest in eradicating the bigotry and barriers faced by individuals with disabilities... In fact, the ADA states its first goal as being "to provide a clear and comprehensive national mandate for the elimination of discrimination against individuals with disabilities." See 42 U.S.C. §12102(b)(1) (1990). The ADA creates the possibility that successful plaintiffs may establish permanent changes in the design and physical configuration of structures to better accommodate the disabled. 42 U.S.C. §12101(a)(5). The benefits of such changes clearly redound not only to the plaintiffs themselves, but to similarly situated disabled persons, and the entire society at large. As a result, plaintiffs or plaintiff classes who bring suit pursuant to the ADA do so in the role of "private attorneys general" who seek to vindicate "a policy of the highest priority." (See Christiansburg Garment Co. v. EEOC, 434 U.S. 412, 417, 98 S.Ct. 694, 698)

For example, successful ADA plaintiffs confer a tremendous benefit upon our society at large, in addition to the attainment of redress for their personal individual injuries. Successful ADA plaintiffs, like plaintiffs under Title VII, are entitled to 42 U.S.C. section 1988's fee shifting provision... As the Eleventh Circuit recently has explained, "in Title VII cases as well as cases under the ADA, the enforcement of civil rights statutes by plaintiffs as private attorneys general is an important part of the underlying policy behind the law. Such a policy ensures an incentive for 'impecunious' plaintiffs who can ill afford to litigate their claims against defendants with more resources..." (Emphasis added)

The United States Department of Justice has also supported the necessity of private lawsuits to enforce the ADA:

Private plaintiffs play an important role in enforcing the ADA, particularly in the area of public accommodations, which includes a large number of entities. See 42 U.S.C. 12188{a)(l). The United States could not investigate every place of public accommodation in the country to determine if it is in compliance with the ADA. Effective enforcement of Title III, therefore, depends upon a combination of suits by the United States and litigation by individuals with disabilities who are aware of and .encounter violations in their local communities. The United States therefore has an interest in ensuring that the standing of private plaintiffs to sue under Title III is not unduly restricted. {From DOJ amicus brief in Chapman v. Pier 1.)

4. ANY VIOLATION OF THE ADA ALSO VIOLATES CIVIL CODE §§ 51(f), 54(c) AND 54.1 (d) AND EARNS DAMAGES PER §§ 52 AND 54.3

The ADA was passed by Congress without any damages provision for denial of civil rights under Title III, the only enforcement incentive being the attorney fees provisions.

(See § 505.) However, in the 1990's California amended its civil rights statutes to add Civil Code §§ 51(f), 54(c) and 54.1(d). These sections <u>allow damages under state law</u> per California Civil Code §§ 52 and 54.3 for any violations of the ADA, although the ADA Title III itself does not include a damage remedy. The Legislature determined that it would <u>adopt</u> any violation of ADA standards as also constituting a denial of "full and equal access" under California Law, when a disabled person was affected by the ADA violation. (See also Civil Code § 55, which provides for injunctive relief). As opponents of the ADA have pointed out, California's unique position of allowing damages under state law for ADA violations, combined with having its own disabled access statutes since 1970, have resulted in more ADA lawsuits being filed in California than anywhere else in the country.

In <u>Munson v. Del Taco, Inc.</u>, 46 Cal.4th 661 (2009) the California Supreme Court held that section 51(f) could be violated by <u>unintentional</u> as well as intentional violations of the ADA, requiring thereby an award of at least a minimum of $4,000 damages per violation, per section 52 Civil Code.

5. CAVEAT REMOVAL TO FEDERAL COURT: PLEADING AN ADA VIOLATION IN STATE COURT COMPLAINT MAY RESULT IN REMOVAL TO FEDERAL COURT

If plaintiff includes an ADA cause of action in a state court Complaint, defendants will have the <u>option</u> to remove the case to federal court. See 28 USC § 1441. Per section 1441(a):

> Except as otherwise expressly provided by Act of Congress, any civil action brought in a State court <u>of which the district courts of the United States have</u> <u>original jurisdiction</u>, may be removed by the defendant or the defendants, to the district court of the United States for the district and division embracing the place where such action is pending. For purposes of removal under this chapter, the citizenship of defendants sued under fictitious names shall be disregarded.

(Emphasis added)

Plaintiffs should be aware that a <u>federal</u> jury verdict must be unanimous. If a plaintiff wishes to avoid federal court jurisdiction, and the subject facilities were clearly constructed or altered in relevant parts after July 1, 1970, the ADA causes of action could be omitted, and the complaint could rely entirely on state court liability. Any construction after July 1, 1970, or alteration after 1971, without concurrent provision of disabled access, was in violation of California Health & Safety Code §§ 19955-19959, and will constitute a violation of Civil Code §§ 54 and 54.1, allowing damages and attorney fees per Civil Code § 54.3, and injunctive relief and attorney fees per Health & Safety Code § 19953 or Civil Code § 55. However, if in state court plaintiffs now risk "reverse" attorney fees under Jankey v. Song Koo Lee, 55 Cal. 4th 1038 (2012) if a defendant prevails under Civil Code section 55, it may be more prudent to seek injunctive relief in Federal Court under the ADA.

a. MAY BE TACTICAL CHOICE WITH MANY FACTORS TO CONSIDER

If the plaintiff's attorney is more comfortable in state court and has no need to use the "readily achievable" standards of Title III, the ADA cause of action might be omitted.[96] For example, in Californians for Disability Rights v. Mervyn's LLC (2008) 165 Cal.App.4th 571, the 1st District Court of Appeal reversed a trial court judgment for defendant, finding a single count cause of action for violation of California Business and Profession Code section 17200 was sufficient to allow proof of a violation of California Civil Rights Statutes which incorporated any violation of ADA standards even though the ADA had not been pled as a separate cause of action:

> CDR brings this case under California's unfair competition law, which defines unfair competition to include any unlawful business act or practice. (Bus. & Prof.Code, § 17200 (§ 17200).) "By proscribing 'any unlawful' business practice, 'section 17200 "borrows" violations of other laws and treats them as unlawful practices' that the unfair competition law makes independently actionable." (Cel-Tech Communications, Inc. v. Los Angeles Cellular Telephone Co. (1999) 20 Cal.4th 163, 180, 83 Cal.Rptr.2d 548, 973 P.2d 527.) CDR claims Mervyn's has unlawfully failed to provide disabled customers with full and equal access to its retail department stores, in violation of state law under California's Unruh Civil Rights Act (the Unruh Act) (Civ.Code, § 51 et seq.) and the Disabled Persons Act (the DPA) (Civ.Code, § 54 et seq.), which incorporate protection standards of the federal Americans with Disabilities Act ("ADA," 42 U.S.C. § 12101 et seq.). To determine if Mervyn's business practice is unlawful, we must first review an array of disability civil rights law.
> Id. at 582-583.

The appellate court then began an extensive analysis of both the ADA and California statutes incorporating the ADA, ultimately finding for the plaintiff: although the Court found that Mervyn's had produced "substantial evidence that removal of architectural barriers would result in a significant loss of sales, and thus removal is not readily achievable" (id. at 594), it reversed the judgment for

---

[96] However there may be tactical and practical reasons for a plaintiff to litigate in federal Court. Note special procedural requirements for state court cases, per SB 1608, effective January 1, 2009, including notices to defendants required for any prelitigation demand for money, and for service with complaint in any state court case. These procedural requirements have been held inapplicable to an action filed in federal Court. O'Campo v. Chico Mall, (E.D. Cal, 2010) 758 F.Supp. 2d 976. Also the General Order 56 procedures in the Northern District of California have reportedly been successful in assisting in earlier settlement of Title II and Title III ADA cases, for the benefit in most cases for all parties involved. Forty pages of new law were added at the end of 2012 by SB 1186. (See Appendix K, *infra*.)

defendant Mervyn's because there was "insufficient evidence that Mervyn's made its facilities available <u>through alternate methods</u>." (Emphasis added) (Id. at 598) [42 USC 12182(b)(2)(A)(v)].

    b.   TIME LIMITS FOR REMOVAL IN ACCORDANCE WITH SECTIONS 1141, 1146 AND 1369

        The removal of an action under this subsection shall be made in accordance with section 1446 of this title, except that a notice of removal may also be filed before trial of the action in State court within 30 days after the date on which the defendant first becomes a party to an action under section 1369 in a United States district court that arises from the same accident as the action in State court, or at a later time with leave of the district court.
        28 USC 1441 (e)(1).

However section 1441(e)(2) allows the district court which "has made a liability decision requiring further proceedings as to damages" to remand the damages issue to state court, "unless the court finds that, for the convenience of parties and witnesses and in the interest of justice, the action should be retained for the determination of damages."
28 USC 1441(e)(2).

6.   SUPPLEMENTAL JURISDICTION OVER STATE LAW CLAIMS; PLAINTIFF MUST RE-FILE IN STATE COURT WITHIN 30 DAYS OF ANY "DISCRETIONARY" DISMISSAL

The federal Court handling an ADA claim has discretionary "supplemental jurisdiction" over related state law claims. Per section 1367 [28 USCA § 1367] with certain specified exceptions, in any civil action of which the district courts have original jurisdiction, the district courts shall have supplemental jurisdiction over all other claims that are so related to claims in the action within such original jurisdiction that they form part of the same case or controversy under Article III of the United States Constitution. Such supplemental jurisdiction shall include claims that involve the joinder or intervention of additional parties.

Section 1367(c) provides the standards under which the federal court can exercise its discretion to accept or decline supplemental jurisdiction:

    The district courts may decline to exercise supplemental jurisdiction over a claim under subsection (a) if--
        (1) the claim raises a novel or complex issue of State law,
        (2) the claim substantially predominates over the claim or claims over which the district court has original jurisdiction,
        (3) the district court has dismissed all claims over which it has original jurisdiction, or

(4) in exceptional circumstances, there are other compelling reasons for declining jurisdiction.

Commentary: Although most defendants prefer federal courts, sometimes they are eager to settle or get dismissed the federal claims, so that defendants can ask the court to dismiss the supplemental jurisdiction state law claims (in the Court's discretion) and force plaintiff to re-file these claims in the local county superior court. Plaintiff may prefer not do to this if he ends up in a small county with more politically sensitive judges, or travel concerns, etc.[97]

Section 1367(d) protects the plaintiff by tolling statute of limitations and allowing refiling of dismissed state law claims in state court within 30 days after dismissal:

> The period of limitations for any claim asserted under subsection (a), and for any other claim in the same action that is voluntarily dismissed at the same time as or after the dismissal of the claim under subsection (a), shall be tolled while the claim is pending and for a period of 30 days after it is dismissed unless State law provides for a longer tolling period.

B. "READILY ACHIEVABLE" BURDEN OF PROOF
   1. DEFENDANTS HAVE THE BURDEN OF PROOF TO SHOW "NOT READILY ACHIEVABLE"

   a. BURDEN OF PRODUCTION AND BURDEN OF PROOF TO SHOW "NOT READILY ACHIEVABLE" ARE BOTH UPON DEFENDANTS IN THE 9th CIRCUIT

   The burden of proof to show that "removing" architectural barriers to access is "<u>not</u> readily achievable" is placed by the ADA statute and federal precedent <u>upon the defendants</u>.

   Section 302 of Title III, <u>Prohibition of Discrimination by Public Accommodations</u>, states,
   > (a) GENERAL RULE - No individual shall be discriminated against on the basis of disability in the full and equal enjoyment of the goods, services, facilities, privileges, advantages or accommodations of any place of public accommodation by any person who owns, leases (or leases to) or operates a place

---

[97] Plaintiff's should caveat settling ADA injunctive relief claims, even by a consent decree, and then having defendants ask the court to dismiss the remaining state law claims and force plaintiff to start over again in state court. However, any liability findings or admissions in federal court should remain res judicata subsequent in State Court proceedings. Also federal Court has discretion to retain "supplemental jurisdiction over related state law claims (See <u>Paulick v. Bavarian Lion Vineyard</u> Dev., LLC, C 08-04860 CW, 2009 WL 691123 (N.D. Cal. Mar. 10, 2009) and 28 USC 1367(d): "Because the federal and state claims here derive from a common nucleus of operative facts, it is in the interest of "economy, convenience, fairness and comity" for Plaintiff's state and federal claims to remain in federal court. Accordingly, the Court will exercise supplemental jurisdiction under § 1367(c)(3) over Plaintiff's state law claims." Id. at *7.

of public accommodation.

Section 302(b)(2)(A) defines

> (A) DISCRIMINATION - For purposes of subsection (a), discrimination includes -
>> (iii) a failure to take such steps as may be necessary to ensure that no individual with a disability is excluded, denied services, segregated or otherwise treated differently than other individuals because of the absence of auxiliary aids and services, <u>unless the entity can demonstrate</u> that taking such steps would fundamentally alter the nature of the good, service, facility, privilege, advantage, or accommodation being offered or would result in an undue burden;
>>
>> (iv) a failure to remove architectural barriers, and communications barriers that are structural in nature, in existing facilities... where such removal is readily achievable; and
>>
>> (v) <u>where an entity can demonstrate that the removal of a barrier under clause (iv) is not readily achievable</u>, a failure to make such goods, services, facilities, privileges, advantages or accommodations available through alternative methods if such methods are readily achievable. (Emphasis added)

"Readily Achievable is defined in ADA section 301(9):
(9) Readily achievable

The term "readily achievable" means easily accomplishable and able to be carried out without much difficulty or expense. In determining whether an action is readily achievable, factors to be considered include--

(A) the nature and cost of the action needed under this chapter;

(B) the overall financial resources of the facility or facilities involved in the action; the number of persons employed at such facility; the effect on expenses and resources, or the impact otherwise of such action upon the operation of the facility;

(C) the overall financial resources of the covered entity; the overall size of the business of a covered entity with respect to the number of its employees; the number, type, and location of its facilities; and

> (D) the type of operation or operations of the covered entity, including the composition, structure, and functions of the workforce of such entity; the geographic separateness, administrative or fiscal relationship of the facility or facilities in question to the covered entity.

These sections seem to make clear that it is the subject <u>entity</u> defendant - the business that is claiming that accommodating a disabled person is <u>not</u> readily achievable - which must "<u>demonstrate</u> that the removal of a barrier under clause (iv) is not readily achievable." Claims that removal of barriers is "not readily achievable" are affirmative defenses that shift the burden of proof to defendants. (<u>Parr v. L&L Drive Inn, et al.</u> (D.Hawaii 2000) 96 F.Supp 2d 1065, 1085; <u>Wilson v. Haria et al</u>, 479 F.Supp.2nd 1127., Especially FN 7.)

However, some courts have put the burden on plaintiff of coming forward with evidence of an "easily accomplishable" barrier removal plan or method before putting upon defendants the burden to demonstrate that providing access is "not readily achievable."

In the Tenth Circuit, for example, <u>Colorado Cross Disability Coalition v. Hermanson Family Limited Partnership</u> (2001) 264 F.3d 999, put the "initial burden of production" upon <u>plaintiff</u>
> <u>to present evidence</u> that a suggested method of barrier removal <u>is readily achievable,</u> i.e., can be accomplished easily and without much difficulty or expense. If Plaintiff satisfies this burden, Defendant then has the opportunity to rebut that showing. <u>Defendant bears the ultimate</u> <u>burden of persuasion</u> regarding its affirmative defense that a suggested method of barrier removal is not readily achievable.
>
> Id. at 1005-1006. (Emphasis added)

Although much of the opinion stresses reasons why the "burden of persuasion" is upon the defendant to prove "the affirmative defense that barrier removal is not readily achievable" (<u>id.</u> at 1006), the Tenth Circuit still ended up by placing the "initial burden" on plaintiff:

> Plaintiff must initially introduce evidence tending to establish that the proposed method of architectural barrier removal is "readily achievable," i.e., "easily accomplishable and able to be carried out without much difficulty or expense" under the particular circumstances. 42 U.S.C. § 12181(9). Only if Plaintiff satisfies this initial

burden does the burden of persuasion shift to Defendant to prove that the requested barrier removal method is not readily achievable.

Id. at 1007.

Ultimately, the Colorado Cross Disability decision ruled against the plaintiff, because "[p]laintiff's expert testimony failed to demonstrate that under the particular circumstances installing a ramp would be readily achievable." Id. at 1009. Even the dissent seemed to agree the initial evidence should come from the plaintiff, although disagreeing with the majority's findings in this particular case:

> I find it unreasonable to require ADA Title III plaintiffs to anticipate and counter any and all potential objections as part of their prima facie case. Placing too high a burden on ADA plaintiffs risks ignoring Congressional intent and gutting the ADA's private right of action. If plaintiffs must all but present the court with a pre-approved construction contract for a sum certain which includes detailed plans, impact statements, engineering studies, and permits to meet their threshold burden, virtually no plaintiff could afford to bring an architectural barrier removal claim under 42 U.S.C. § 2182(b)(2)(A)(iv). Plaintiffs should present some evidence as to cost and feasibility that recognizes and addresses these considerations but should not be required to have final, detailed answers as to any of them.

Id. at 1010-1011 (footnotes omitted).

Subsequently the Ninth Circuit has rejected Colorado Cross Disability's standard, holding that the burden of production regarding the "readily achievable" solution of an exterior ramp should be placed on the defendant. In Molski v. Foley Estates Vineyard (2008) 531 F.3d 1043, 1048, the Ninth Circuit rejected the Tenth Circuit's conclusion in Colorado Cross and found that ADAAG § 4.1.7 "counsels in favor of placing the burden of production on the defendant."[98] Id., n.5. They interpreted this in conjunction with 28 C.F.R. § 36.304 which includes a provision that, if compliance with certain regulations "would not be readily achievable, "a public accommodation may take other readily achievable measures to remove the barriers that do not fully comply with the specified requirements. 28 C.F.R. § 36.304(d)

---

[98] Section 4.1.7 sets out the procedure for requesting alternative requirements for alleged "historical buildings": "[I]f the entity undertaking the alterations believes that compliance with the requirements . . . would threaten or destroy the historic significance of the building . . . the entity should consult with the State Historic Preservation Officer" and seek alternative requirements in § 4.1.7(3)

(2)." Id. at 1047.

In so holding, and <u>citing and agreeing with the dissent by Judge Lucero in Colorado Cross</u>, quoted hereinabove, the Ninth Circuit reasoned,

> We do not require an ADA plaintiff to undertake heroic measures. Congress relies on private actors, i.e., disabled individuals, to enforce the ADA by filing lawsuits. Thus plaintiffs should not be deterred from filing meritorious claims by an inappropriate allocation of the burden of production.
>
> We find that the language of § 4.1.7, the access to information, and the congressional intent behind the ADA support placing the burden of production on the defendant. Thus, we reverse and remand for the district court to assign the burden of production to the defendant on the issue of whether barrier removal would threaten the historical significance of the building.

<u>Molski v. Foley Estates</u>, *supra*, at 1049.

The court explained the policy basis for its ruling in this "historic" preservation defense case:

> By placing the burden of production on the defendant, we place the burden on the party with the best access to information regarding the historical significance of the building. The defendant sought the historical designation in this case. Thus, the defendant possesses the best understanding of the circumstances under which that designation might be threatened. The defendant is also in the best position to discuss the matter with the Santa Barbara County Historic Landmarks Advisory Commission and to request an opinion on proposed methods of barrier removal. As a result, the defendant is in a better position to introduce, as part of its affirmative defense, detailed evidence and expert testimony concerning whether the historic significance of a structure would be threatened or destroyed by the proposed barrier removal plan.

Id. at 1048.

The court concluded, "We find that the language of § 4.1.7, the access to information, and the congressional intent behind the ADA support placing the burden of production on the defendant." Id.

However one 2008 California Court of Appeal placed the burden of production on plaintiff, apparently before the 9th Circuit's <u>Molski v. Foley Estates</u>, *supra*, opinion, citing <u>Colorado Cross</u>, *supra*, instead of the 9th Circuit's <u>Foley Estates</u> case:

> In action alleging disability discrimination with respect to architectural barriers in public accommodations that are 'existing facilities' under Americans with Disabilities Act (ADA), initial burden is on plaintiff to introduce evidence tending to show that proposed method of removal of architectural barrier is readily achievable, and if the plaintiff meets its burden of production, then defendant must counter with evidence of its own and carries the ultimate burden of persuasion on its defense that removal is not readily achievable.

> <u>Californians for Disability Rights v. Mervyn's, LLC</u>, July 29, 2008, 165 Cal.App.4th 571, 592[99]

> Regarding "readily achievable," the <u>Mervyn's</u> case went on to say, at 592,
>> The defendant bears the ultimate burden of proving that removal of an architectural barrier is not readily achievable, as an affirmative defense. <u>(Colorado Cross Disability Coalition v. Hermanson Family Ltd. Partnership I (Hermanson) (10th Cir.2001) 264 F.3d 999, 1002-1003.)</u> Every federal court that has considered the matter has put "the initial burden on the plaintiff to introduce evidence tending to show that the proposed method of removal of an existing architectural barrier is readily achievable." <u>(MacClymonds v. IMI Investments, Inc., *supra*, 2007 WL 1306803 at p. 5</u> [collecting cases]). If the plaintiff meets its burden of production, then the defendant must counter with evidence of its own and "carries the ultimate burden of persuasion on its defense that removal is not readily achievable...." (Ibid.)

> Also at 592 in <u>Mervyn's</u>, quoting, <u>Massachusetts v. E*Trade Access, Inc. (D.Mass.2006) 464 F.Supp.2d 52, 61.</u>),
>> "Practically speaking, there may often be an information imbalance between a plaintiff and a defendant, with the defendant possessing the additional experience and knowledge gained from owning and operating the facility containing the architectural ... barrier. Nevertheless, a plaintiff should at a minimum provide a general plan and discuss its feasibility, bearing in mind both structural concerns and estimated costs." (Ibid.)

> Continuing in <u>Mervyn's</u>, at 593:

---
[99] However the <u>Mervyn's</u> appellate court declined plaintiff's favor even under the <u>Colorado Cross</u> standard. See III-B-3, *infra*

has introduced prima facie evidence tending to show that removal of an existing architectural barrier is readily achievable, a plaintiff should not be expected to address industry and operational concerns best known by the retailer. Plaintiff made a specific proposal to remove the architectural barrier caused by narrow merchandise pathways by, among other things, rotating merchandise tables, contracting display racks, and removing display rack extensions. Plaintiff should not be required to provide a plan so specific that it fully accommodates industry techniques for highlighting merchandise and Mervyn's specific presentation practices.

In the Northern District of California, at least one recent opinion applied the Molski v. Foley Estates analysis in holding that,

> defendants must bear the initial burden of production as well as the ultimate burden of persuasion in establishing that remediation is not readily achievable. Further, defendants must carry their burden with respect to each identified barrier to access in the facility.
> Rodriguez v. Barrita, Inc., C 09-04057 RS, 2012 WL 3538014 (N.D. Cal. Mar. 1, 2012), on reconsideration in part, C 09-04057 RS, 2012 WL 2308069 (N.D. Cal. June 18, 2012).

b. **PRECEDENTIAL ANALOGOUS CIVIL RIGHTS CASE LAW SUPPORTS SHIFTING THE BURDEN OF PROOF TO DEFENDANTS**

These statutory requirements are consistent with federal Civil Rights standards in employment cases, such as Corning Glass Workers v. Brennan 417 US 188, 41 L.Ed.2d 1, 94 Sup.Ct. 223, holding that the application for an exception under the Fair Labor Standards Act is a matter of affirmative defense upon which the employer has the burden of proof. (41 L.Ed.2d 1, at 11)

Similarly, in Equal Employment Opportunities Comm. v. Whitin Mach. (4thCir. 1980) 635 F.2d 1095, at p.1097, it was held that while the burden of establishing a prima facie violation (of the Equal Pay Act) was upon the plaintiff,

> Once there is a showing of unequal pay for equal work, the burden of proof shifts to the employer since the facts underlying the wage differential are usually within his unique knowledge. Corning Glass Works v. Brennan 417 US 188, 94 Sup.Ct. 2223, 41 L.Ed.2d 1, (1974). It is clear from the evidence presented at trial... that the burden was properly that of the company to raise any justification for the disparity in pay. (Emphasis added)

Under the ADA, once an individual has shown that architectural barriers have excluded him from services or facilities because of his disability, the defendant must "demonstrate" that "removal of the barrier" "is not readily achievable."[100] The facts as to the defendant's resources under § 301(9), defining the financial standards to determine what is "readily achievable," are "usually within [defendants'] unique knowledge."

c. WILSON V. HARIA AND GOGRI CORP. DBA JACK IN THE BOX, ET AL. (2007) HELD THAT THE BURDEN OF PROOF WAS UPON DEFENDANTS, AND THAT THEY WAIVED THIS DEFENSE BY NOT PLEADING "NOT READILY ACHIEVABLE" AS AN AFFIRMATIVE DEFENSE

In Wilson v. Haria and Gogri Corp. dba Jack in the Box 479 F.Supp.2d 1127 (E.D. Cal., 2007), Judge Lawrence Karlton reviewed prior case law and held that "not readily achievable" was an affirmative defense which was waived unless pled by defendant in its answer, noting also the "burden shifting framework" set up by the 10th Circuit in the Colorado Cross Disability case. At FN7, Judge Karlton held:
The Ninth Circuit has yet to rule on this issue, but courts are generally in agreement that whether barrier removal is readily achievable is an affirmative defense. See Colorado Cross Disability Coalition v. Hermanson Family Ltd. P'ship, 264 F.3d 999, 1002-03 (10th Cir.2001); Gathright-Dietrich v. Atlanta Landmarks, Inc., 452 F.3d 1269, 1274 (11th Cir.2006). See also Lentini v. Calif. Ctr. for the Arts, 370 F.3d 837 (9th Cir.2004) (holding that whether an accommodation "fundamentally alters" a service or facility is an affirmative defense).

In Colorado Cross, the Tenth Circuit established a burden-shifting framework in which the plaintiff bears in the initial burden of production but the defendant bears the ultimate burden of persuasion. 264 F.3d at 1002-03. The plaintiff must first suggest a method of barrier removal and proffer evidence that the method meets the statutory definition of readily achievable. Id. Thereafter, the burden shifts to the defendants to rebut that showing and prove that the suggested method is not readily achievable. Id. Here, defendant has failed to plead that barrier removal is not readily achievable in its answer. Accordingly, the defense is waived. Enlow v. Salem-Keizer Yellow Cab Co., Inc., 389 F.3d 802, 819 (9th Cir.2004). While plaintiff has not come forward with any evidence regarding barrier removal, he need not do so where such evidence would be unnecessary, given defendant's waiver. In contrast, the Colorado Cross court noted that the defendant in that case had properly pled that barrier removal was not readily achievable as an affirmative defense. Id., n. 3.

d. PLAINTIFF'S POSITION: DEFENDANTS HAVE THE BURDEN OF PROVING THAT EACH AND EVERY ACCESS FEATURE WAS NOT READILY ACHIEVABLE

Defendants have the burden of proving, for each alleged ADA violation, that provision of each access feature is not readily achievable. Defendants will not meet

---

[100] See ADA sections 302(b)(2)(A)(iv) and (v) [42 USC 12182 (b)(2)(A)(iv) and (v)]

their burden unless they offer witnesses to show that they made a cost analysis and considered whether removal of each barrier to access (i.e., a toilet stall without grab bars or of improper size, a restroom without fully accessible features, stairs on a path of travel, etc.), was "readily achievable," based on the financial standards set out by § 301(9):

> (9) READILY ACHIEVABLE. - The term "readily achievable means easily accomplishable and able to be carried out without much difficulty or expense. In determining whether an action is readily achievable, factors to be considered include-
>
> (A) the nature and cost of the action needed under this Act;
> (B) the overall financial resources of the facility or facilities involved in the action; the number of persons employed at such facility; the effect on expenses and resources, or the impact otherwise upon the operation of the facility;
> (C) the overall financial resources of the covered entity; the overall size of the business of a covered entity with respect to the number of its employees; the number, type, and location of its facilities; and
> (D) the type of operation or operations of the covered entity, including the composition, structure, and functions of the workforce of such entity; the geographic separateness, administrative or fiscal relationship of the facility or facilities in question to the covered entity. (Emphasis added)
>
> These standards were specified, discussed, and approved by the 9th Circuit in Botosan v. McNally Realty (9th Cir. 2000) 216 F.3d 27, *supra*.

The burden of proof to show access barrier removal is readily achievable is on the defendants. Wilson v. Haria, *supra*. Molski v. Foley Estates Vineyard, 531 F.3d 1043 (9th Cir. 2008).

e. IS BURDEN ON DEFENDANT SET BY STATUTE TO "DEMONSTRATE" BARRIER REMOVAL IS "NOT READILY ACHIEVABLE"?

Query- why is this even an issue? The text of the ADA itself puts the burden on defendant to "demonstrate that removal of a barrier . . . is not readily achievable." (Emphasis added). Per section 42 USC 12182, section 302(b)(2)(A)(v) states that discrimination exists, "where an entity can demonstrate that the removal of a barrier under clause (iv) is not readily achievable, a failure to make such goods, services, facilities, privileges, advantages, or accommodations available through alternative methods if such methods are readily achievable."

(Emphasis Added)

2. "READILY ACHIEVABLE" STATUTORY STANDARDS INCLUDE COMPARISON OF ACCESS COSTS WITH ALL RESOURCES, INCLUDING THOSE OF ANY PARENT COMPANY

   a. PINNOCK UPHELD THE ADA'S CONSTITUTIONALITY AND SET CERTAIN STANDARDS

   "Readily achievable" for purposes of the ADA is a primarily financial concept which compares the cost of removing each barrier complained of against the overall financial resources of the "entity," and the financial resources of any parent company involved. 28 CFR section 36.104 defines "readily achievable" and includes consideration of the resources of "any parent corporation or entity."

   "Readily achievable" under the ADA is a factual question which must specifically consider (among other factors), the "financial resources of the covered entity." What is "easily accomplishable and able to be carried out without much difficulty, or expense" is very different, for example, for a "mom and pop" grocery store than for a billion dollar corporation.

   "Readily achievable" standards are defined in § 301(9) of the ADA and in Regulation 36.104, Definitions, at p.III-34 of the ADA Handbook. (Americans with Disabilities Handbook published by the Equal Employment Opportunity Commission and the United States Dept. of Justice, Oct. 1991, No. EEOC-BK-19). Page III-35 describes "readily achievable" standards under § 301(9) of the ADA, specifically in regard to the definition that "readily achievable" requires consideration of "the overall financial resources of any parent corporation or entity." The commentary states,

   > The list of factors included in the definition is derived from §301(9) of the ADA. It reflects the Congressional intention that a wide range of factors be considered in determining whether an action is readily achievable. It also takes into account that many local facilities are owned or operated by parent corporations or entities that conduct operations at many different sites. This section makes clear that, in some instances, resources beyond those of the local facility where the barrier must be removed, may be relevant in determining whether an action is readily achievable. One must also evaluate the degree to which any parent entity has resources that may be allocated to the local facility."

   Pinnock v. Int'l House of Pancake, Majid Zahedi, et al. (1993) 844 F.Supp 574, upheld the constitutionality of Title III against various constitutional challenges, in a decision by Judge John Rhoades of the Southern District of California. At p.581:

1. Readily Achievable Barrier Removal

Title III requires existing places of public accommodation to remove architectural barriers to access, where such removal is "readily achievable." 42 U.S.C. § 12182(b)(2)(A)(iv) (Supp. II 1990). The term is defined in the statute as "easily accomplishable and able to be carried out without much difficulty or expense." 42 U.S.C. § 12181(9) (Supp. II 1990). The statute enumerates four factors to consider when determining whether a modification is readily achievable, and the legislative history lists examples of the types of changes Congress believes are readily achievable. These include specific examples for small stores and restaurants such as rearranging tables and chairs and installing small ramps and grab bars in restrooms. See U.S. Mem. in Support of Cross Mot. for Sum. J. at n.27 (citing 42 U.S.C. § 12181(9) (Supp. II 1990)).

In addition, the federal regulation further elucidates the term "readily achievable" by adding other factors. <u>These include the overall financial resources of the parent corporation and safety requirements. 28 C.F.R. § 36.104, at 460-61 (1991)</u>. The regulation lists 21 examples of barrier removal likely to be "readily achievable" in many circumstances, such as installing ramps and repositioning shelves and telephones. See Id. § 36.304(b), at 466, & app. B, at 576-77.
(Emphasis added)

Finally, the preamble to the regulation provides further explanation and notes that use of a more specific standard would contravene the goals of the ADA:
> the Department has declined to establish in the final rule any kind of numerical formula for determining whether an action is readily achievable. It would be difficult to devise a specific ceiling on compliance costs that would take into account the vast diversity of enterprises covered by the ADA's public accommodation requirements and the economic situation that any particular entity would find itself in at any moment.

(Id. at § 36.104, app. B, at 577.)

<u>Pinnock</u> also defines the terms: "alternatives to barrier removal;" "reasonable modifications of policies and procedures;" "most integrated setting appropriate;" "undue burden;" and "full and equal enjoyment and opportunity to participate." (Id. at p.582-583)

Defendants' obligations for barrier removal to comply with ADA Title III barrier removal had a <u>deadline</u> of January 26, 1992, following <u>an 18 month grace period</u> after the ADA's passage:
> The ADA provided an eighteen month notice period in which businesses could comply with the Act's requirements and no liability was imposed prior to the end of that period. See 42 U.S.C. § 12181 note (Supp. II

1990) Small businesses were given an even lengthier notice period. Id. Pinnock's complaint was not filed until September 9, 1992, nearly two years after the ADA was passed on July 26, 1990. Id. at 584.

Thus, a defendant must show not only the "overall financial resources of the site or sites involved;" per the specific requirements of § 301(9)(c) of the ADA, they must also show the "<u>overall financial resources</u> of the covered entity." This is emphasized by the following quote from the Technical Assistance Manual, III-4.4200, "Readily Achievable Barrier Removal", at p.30,

> If the public accommodation is a facility that is owned or operated by a parent entity that conducts operations at many different cites, the public accommodation must consider the <u>resources of both the local facility and the parent entity</u> to determine if removal of a particular barrier is "readily achievable." The administrative and fiscal relationship between the local facility and the parent entity must also be considered in evaluating what resources are available for any particular act of barrier removal. (Emphasis in original.)

Only the defendant business itself can supply the records and information which are relevant to each of the criteria listed in § 301(9). Therefore it is appropriate to place the burden of proof under the ADA's "readily achievable" standards upon the objecting defendant.

b. DISCOVERY MAY BE NEEDED TO COMPARE THE COSTS OF PROVIDING ACCESS AGAINST THE "OVERALL FINANCIAL RESOURCES" OF EACH DEFENDANT

In this regard, the financial resources of the defendants must be compared to the cost of putting in <u>each</u> of the access features at issue. For example, a restaurant may need <u>both</u> (1) a ramp to allow access over steps at the front entrance; and (2) installation of grab bars and widening of a toilet stall to create an accessible restroom. Defendants cannot lump together all access costs to claim that no feature is individually "readily achievable." Further, because the standard is the "overall financial resources" of both the local entities and any parent company, all such resources must be considered, not merely, for example, the resources of one local <u>franchisee</u>, i.e. of one local Jack in the Box or McDonald's. (See <u>Botosan v. McNally Realty</u>, *supra*.)

On discovery I once challenged a bank's claim that putting in a ramp (which they "estimated" would cost $50,000) was "not readily achievable." (When they later installed the ramp it only cost them $25,000!) However, plaintiff's interrogatories asked for the financial resources of the bank and of any "parent company" of the bank. When we received answers to our interrogatories, it turned out that the parent company was the "National Bank of Paris," and the resources of the parent company were over $200 billion. I said, "I bet you can afford a ramp!" and they decided to agree. (Fisher v. Bank of the West, (N.D. Cal.) C92-4356 FMS).

It is difficult to imagine that any bank in California can successfully claim that entry ramps or ATM accessibility is "not readily achievable." Under California law all ATMs already must be accessible. James Donald v. Sacramento Valley Bank (1989) 209 Cal.App.3d 1183, already required this under existing California law, recognizing that all ATMs in California had apparently been installed after the 1970 effective date of Health & Safety Code §§ 19955-19959, and constituted "alterations" triggering provision of access per § 19959. As to the "readily achievable" requirement of the ADA, it should be remembered that, when asked why he had made a practice of robbing banks, famed 1930s bank robber Willie Sutton responded "That's where they keep the money!"

c. CAVEAT DEFENSES BASED ON ALLEGED "MOM AND POP STORE" FINANCIAL FACTORS WHICH MAKE BARRIER REMOVAL MORE DIFFICULT

Some defendants have argued that the "not very expensive" standard can be considered in a vacuum, i.e. that a ramp costing "$50,000" is "expensive" regardless of the financial resources of the business which needs a ramp to access steps at its entrance. But the statute itself (section 301(a) ADA) sets out the specific factors to consider. For example, for a bank owned by a mulitnational corporation, such as Wells Fargo or Bank of America, a $50,000 ramp is "not very expensive," especially in light of the readily achievable standard requiring consideration of defendants' "overall financial resources" over the last twenty years. (See section 42 USC 12181(9)(B) / section 301(a) ADA) These are not the proverbial "mom and pop" businesses.

d. BOTOSAN V. MCNALLY REALTY SET THE 9ᵀᴴ CIRCUIT STANDARD FOR THE "NOT READILY ACHIEVABLE" DEFENSE

The cost of an accessible unisex restroom may be in the $10,000 to $20,000 price range. Whatever the cost, under the "readily achievable" standards of Title III, § 301(9) of the ADA and the barrier removal requirements of § 302(b)(2)(a)(iv), defendants' have an absolute duty to remove barriers and provide access unless they can sustain the burden of proving that such barrier removal is not "readily achievable." Further, under "(v) where an entity can demonstrate that the removal of a barrier under clause (iv) is not readily achievable, a failure to make such goods, services, facilities, privileges, advantages or accommodations available through alternative methods, if such methods are readily achievable," constitutes a violation. (Emphasis added). The duty to "demonstrate" a lack of the presumptively "readily achievable" ability to remove architectural barriers makes clear that the burden of proof of this affirmative defense is upon defendant. (C.f. Botosan v. McNally Realty, et al. (2000) 216 F.3d 827, 836.

Case law makes plain that in order to prevail on a defendant's affirmative defense that provision of access is "not readily achievable," each defendant must consider evidence of its "overall financial resources" since 1990, when the obligation to evaluate barriers for removal went into effect. (Cf. standards in Botosan v. McNally Realty, et al. (2000) 216 F.3d 827, at 836.) In this regard, because the standards of ADA § 301(9) require a comparison of the cost of each item of access with the "overall financial resources" of all owners, operators, lessors and lessees, this justifies discovery of the financial assets and other financial information of every defendant, whether an individual or business entity. This applies not only to a comparison of the cost for installing an elevator or a lift for access to the restaurant, but also to the costs of removal of each other barrier to access, whether it be widening a restroom door, widening a toilet stall, providing signage, mounting safety grab bars, and so forth.

Per the analysis in Wilson v. Haria and Gogri Corp, (E.D. Cal 2007) 479 F.Supp. 2d 1127, 1133: (1) "not readily achievable" is an affirmative defense, waived if not plead as an affirmative defense in the Answer; and (2) under the "burden shifting analysis" adopted by the 10th Circuit in the Colorado-Cross case, *supra*, and Disability Coalition v. Hermanson Family, Ltd Parternship, 264 F.3d 999, at 1002-03 (10th Cir, 2001), "defendant bears the ultimate burden of persuasion." In the 9th Circuit, such a defendant also bears the initial "burden of production."(Cf. Molski v. Foley Estates, 531 F.3d 1043 (9th Cir. 2008)).

e. PARENT COMPANY'S OVERALL FINANCIAL RESOURCES ARE RELEVANT AND DISCOVERABLE

The Chief Judge for the Northern District, Hon. Marilyn Hall Patel, issued an opinion, after referencing the same four factors specified in 42 U.S.C. § 12181(9) [ADA § 301(9)], allowing consideration of "parent company" overall financial resources. In its Order of October 28, 1999, the court in Lieber v. Macy's West, Inc., 80 F.Supp.2d 1065 (N.D. Cal. 1999) held:

> The ADA defines "readily achievable" as "easily accomplishable and able to be carried out without much difficulty or expense." 42 U.S.C. § 12181(9). The ADA sets forth the following factors, among others, in deciding whether an action is to be considered readily achievable: (i) the nature and cost of the action; (ii) the overall financial resources of the facility involved and the effect on expenses and resources, or the impact otherwise of such action upon the operation of the facility; (iii) the overall financial resources of the covered entity, including the number of its employees; and (iv) the type of operation of the covered

entity. 42 U.S.C. § 12181(9). The Title III regulations specify that if applicable the <u>overall financial resources of any parent corporation or entity should also be considered. 28 C.F.R. § 36.104 (definition of "readily achievable"</u>).

> ... The ADA statute makes clear that the readily achievable barrier removal obligation must consider the "overall financial resources," "effect on expenses and resources," and the "effect on operations" of the facilities involved in the action. 42 U.S.C. § 12181(9), ("Definitions"). (Emphasis added)
> (<u>Macy's</u>, *supra*, at 1078)(Emphasis added)

The <u>Mervyn's</u>, *supra*, court cited <u>Macy's</u> while emphasizing that a claim of not "readily achievable" must deal with both parent company financial and operational factors:

> However, the regulations further provide that "[t]he rearrangement of temporary or movable structures, such as furniture, equipment, and display racks is not readily achievable to the extent that it results in a 'significant loss of selling or serving space.' " (<u>28 C.F.R. § 36.304(f)</u> (2007).) At least one court has held that the " 'significant loss of selling space' " standard is "only meaningful to the extent that it affects operations." (<u>Lieber v. Macy's West, Inc.</u>, *supra*, 80 F.Supp.2d at p. 1078.) "The ADA statute makes clear that the readily achievable barrier removal obligation must consider the 'overall financial resources,' 'effect on expenses and resources,' and the 'effect on operations' of the facilities involved in the action." (<u>Ibid.</u>) In calculating the financial resources of a facility, the DOJ states that the resources of both the local facility and parent entity must be considered. (ADA Manual, § 4.4200, p. 32.) In practice, this has meant consideration of the financial resources of both the immediate corporate entity owner and its parent corporation. (See <u>Guzman v. Denny's Inc. (S.D.Ohio 1999) 40 F.Supp.2d 930, 932, 936</u> [inaccessible rest room at a single Denny's restaurant; court considered resources of Denny's and its parent corporation].)

In <u>Guzman v. Denny's Inc.</u>, 40 F.Supp.2d 930 (S.D. Ohio 1999), the Court emphasized that, even for a corporation such as large as <u>Denny's Inc.</u>, the financial resources of any "parent" corporation also had to be considered when a defendant alleged any barrier removal would be "not readily achievable":

> Plaintiff directs the Court to consider all of the factors the ADA provides for determining if an architectural barrier is readily achievable. Plaintiff argues that Defendant failed to consider the financial resources of the parent entity when it concluded that the proposed renovations would not be readily achievable. The Department of Justice has recommended that if "the public accommodation is a facility that is owned or operated by a parent entity that conducts operations at many different sites, the public accommodations must consider the resources of both the local facility and the parent entity to determine if removal of the particular barrier is 'readily achievable.' " The Americans with Disabilities Act:

Title III Technical Assistance Manual, § III-4.4200 at p. 30 (1992).

> Plaintiff presents credible evidence that from which a reasonable jury could conclude that Denny's and its parent corporation, Flagstar Corporation, have sufficient financial resources to make the accessibility modifications. According to the Form 10-K filed with the Securities Exchange Commission by Flagstar Companies, Inc. for the fiscal year ending December 31, 1995 Denny's is the "largest full-service family restaurant chain in the United States in terms of both the number of units and total revenues." Moreover, the Form 10-K states that Flagstar operates three other restaurant chains and is one of the largest restaurant companies in the United States. This evidence raises a genuine issue of material fact regarding the financial ability of Defendant to renovate the restroom facilities.

Id. at 935-936.

f. ADAAG SECTION 4.1.7 (ADA ACCESSIBILITY GUIDELINES) SETS THE STANDARD FOR EVALUATING "READILY ACHIEVABLE"

Molski v. Foley Estates Vineyard 531 F.3d 1043, (9th Cir. 2008), discusses the standards for "readily achievable" and ADAAG guidelines, and says that the standards of the Americans With Disabilities Act Accessibility Guidelines for buildings and facilities, 28 CFR § 36 App. A § 4.1.7 ("ADAAG § 4.1.7" or "§ 4.1.7") should be used to evaluate whether an accessible ramp would be readily achievable. The burden of production and burden of proof on the "not readily achievable" defense were both held to be upon defendants, rejecting the contrary 10th Circuit standards from Colorado Cross Disability Coalition v. Hermanson Family Limited, 264 F.3d 999 (10th Cir., 2001).

3. EVEN IF BARRIER REMOVAL IS "NOT READILY ACHIEVABLE," A BUSINESS MAY BE LIABLE FOR FAILING TO MAKE FACILITIES AVAILABLE THROUGH ALTERNATIVE MEANS

In Mervyn's, *supra*, although the Court of Appeals held that removal of barriers (narrow aisles for clothing displays) was "not readily achievable," it reversed the trial court's judgment in favor of defendant because "there is insufficient evidence that Mervyn's made its facilities available through alternative methods." Californians for Disability Rights v. Mervyn's LLC, (2008) 165 Cal.App.4th 571, at 598-599. The court relied on ADA section 302(b)(2)(A)(v) [42 USC § 12182(b)(2)(A)(v)]:

> A retailer's obligation to provide access to the disabled is not limited to the readily achievable removal of physical barriers. Where removal of physical barriers is not readily achievable, a retailer must adopt alternative methods for providing full and equal access to its goods and services. (42 U.S.C. § 12182(b)(2)(A)(v).) The ADA expressly provides: "[W]here an entity can demonstrate that the removal of a barrier ... is not readily achievable,

a failure to make such goods, services, facilities, privileges, advantages, or accommodations available through alternative methods" is actionable discrimination, "if such methods are readily achievable." (Ibid.)

The appellate court also found Mervyn's could not satisfy this obligation by "access to Mervyn's new remodeled stores." Id. at 600. "Nothing in the ADA suggests that a corporate chain of department stores satisfies its obligation to make existing facilities accessible (to the extent readily achievable) by constructing new and geographically distant facilities that are accessible." Id.

The Mervyn's appellate Court found Mervyn's had violated the ADA, and thereby also violated multiple California statutes:

> Mervyn's failure to provide access by alternative methods constitutes a violation of the ADA, and thus a violation of both the Unruh Act and the DPA. (42 U.S.C. § 12182(b)(2)(A)(v); Civ.Code, §§ 51, subd. (f), 54, subd. (c).) Mervyn's violation of federal and state law is also a violation of the unfair competition law, which defines unfair competition to include any unlawful business act or practice. (§ 17200)

Id. at 600-601. A cause of action plead only under section 17200 California Business and Professions Code seems a very roundabout way to invoke ADA standards, and was probably used by plaintiffs in this action to avoid directly pleading an "ADA" violation and "risking" probable removal to federal court, if they preferred to litigate in state court.[101] However, Jankey v. Song Koo Lee, 55 Cal. 4th 1038 (2012), leaves a threat of "reverse" attorney fees if plaintiff relies on Civil Code section 55 for injunctive relief, and loses, and the Court determines that the defendant is the "prevailing party." Perhaps use of Business and Professions Code section 17200 combined with seeking Code of Civil Procedure section 1021.5 attorney fees may be an alternative. The ADA cause of action itself does not involve the risk of "reverse" attorney fees. (See ADA section 505 and attendant DOJ regulations.)

In Walker v. Carnival Cruise Line, 63 F. Supp. 2d 1083 (1999), Judge Thelton Henderson held that the ADA did apply to a travel agency's failure to provide accurate information about a cruise ship's accessibility. This court's later opinion, on rehearing, Walker v. Carnival Cruise Lines, 107 F. Supp. 2d 1135, reversed the earlier invocation of a "forum selection" clause but did not effect the earlier opinion on travel agency liability.

4. A BUSINESSES' POLICY MAY ALSO VIOLATE ADA TITLE III IN SETTING INSURANCE RATES OR NOT PROVIDING ACCURATE TRAVEL AGENCY

---

[101] Some practitioners are more comfortable in state court, are more familiar with state court procedures, and in the rare event an access case must be decided by a jury, prefer state court three quarters jury mandate, whereas a unanimous jury is required in federal court. Also federal court judges in certain areas, appointed for life, are known to be somewhat hostile to ADA cases. However, Oliver v. In-n-Out Burgers, supra, following Sobreck, supra, may encourage filing in federal court to avoid the Jankey fees threat.

INFORMATION

A discriminatory insurance rating policy was found to violate the ADA Title III in the Chabner v. United Omaha Life Ins. Co. district court attorney fee Order:

> Nondiscriminatory access to insurance for disabled persons is important because it provides a non-employment-based route to health care and investment. Plaintiff's success also has ramifications beyond the insurance context. Chabner has been cited with approval in its holding that Title III of the ADA applies to more than barriers to physical access. See, e.g., Walker v. Carnival Cruise Lines, No. 98-2926, 1999 WL 692341, at *9 (N.D.Cal. Aug. 3, 1999) (citing Chabner v. United of Omaha Life Insurance Co., 994 F.Supp. 1185 (N.D.Cal.1998) in finding that Title III may require travel agents to provide accurate information regarding disabled accessibility of accommodations).

Chabner v. United Omaha Life Ins. Co. (N.D. Cal.) 1999 WL 33227443.

However the 9th Circuit rejected the ADA portion of the District Court's Summary Judgment Order (Chabner v. United of Omaha Life Ins. Co., 994 F. Supp. 1185 (N.D. Cal 1998)), holding that insurance rate discrimination did not violate the ADA. It nevertheless affirmed the District Court's summary judgment Order for Plaintiff, holding that insurance rate discrimination did violate California's Unruh Act (Civil Code section 51) and "Unfair Competition Law" (Business and Professions Code section 17200). Chabner v. United of Omaha Life Ins. Co., 225 F.3d 1042 (9th Cir., 2000).

(See also Hankins v. El Torito, *supra* re: a policy of refusing a disabled patron's use of a first floor "Employees Only" restroom violated both California Civil Code sections 51 and 54 in a pre-ADA case, where the only "public" restroom was up a flight of stairs.)

5. EXAMPLES AND PRIORITIES IN DOJ REGULATIONS: 28 CFR § 36.304 "REMOVAL OF BARRIERS"

§ 36.304 Removal of barriers.
(a) General. A public accommodation shall remove architectural barriers in existing facilities, including communication barriers that are structural in nature, where such removal is readily achievable, i.e., easily accomplishable and able to be carried out without much difficulty or expense.

(b) Examples. Examples of steps to remove barriers include, but are not limited to, the following actions--
(1) Installing ramps;

(2) Making curb cuts in sidewalks and entrances;

(3) Repositioning shelves;

(4) Rearranging tables, chairs, vending machines, display racks, and other furniture;

(5) Repositioning telephones;

(6) Adding raised markings on elevator control buttons;

(7) Installing flashing alarm lights;

(8) Widening doors;

(9) Installing offset hinges to widen doorways;

(10) Eliminating a turnstile or providing an alternative accessible path;

(11) Installing accessible door hardware;

(12) Installing grab bars in toilet stalls;

(13) Rearranging toilet partitions to increase maneuvering space;

(14) Insulating lavatory pipes under sinks to prevent burns;

(15) Installing a raised toilet seat;

(16) Installing a full-length bathroom mirror;

(17) Repositioning the paper towel dispenser in a bathroom;

(18) Creating designated accessible parking spaces;

(19) Installing an accessible paper cup dispenser at an existing inaccessible water fountain;

(20) Removing high pile, low density carpeting; or

(21) Installing vehicle hand controls.

   (c) Priorities. A public accommodation is urged to take measures to comply with the barrier removal requirements of this section in accordance with the following order of priorities.

   (1) First, a public accommodation should take measures to provide access to a place of public accommodation from public sidewalks, parking, or public transportation. These measures include, for

example, installing an entrance ramp, widening entrances, and providing accessible parking spaces.

(2) Second, a public accommodation should take measures to provide access to those areas of a place of public accommodation where goods and services are made available to the public. These measures include, for example, adjusting the layout of display racks, rearranging tables, providing Brailled and raised character signage, widening doors, providing visual alarms, and installing ramps.

(3) Third, a public accommodation should take measures to provide access to restroom facilities. These measures include, for example, removal of obstructing furniture or vending machines, widening of doors, installation of ramps, providing accessible signage, widening of toilet stalls, and installation of grab bars.

(4) Fourth, a public accommodation should take any other measures necessary to provide access to the goods, services, facilities, privileges, advantages, or accommodations of a place of public accommodation.

28 C.F.R. § 36.304

C. SECTION 503 PROHIBITS ACTIONS WHICH RETALIATE AGAINST OR PUNISH A PLAINTIFF OR HIS LEGAL REPRESENTATIVES FOR ENFORCING THE ADA

1. SECTIONS 503 (a) AND (b) PROHIBIT BOTH RETALIATION AND HARASSMENT

Counsel should watch for direct or subtle efforts to <u>discourage</u> use of a facility by disabled persons; efforts to intimidate disabled persons from bringing lawsuits; and efforts to retaliate against plaintiffs who have actually made ADA claims or file ADA lawsuits. Section 503 of the ADA, is entitled, "prohibition against retaliation and coercion."
Section 503(a) Retaliation

> No person shall discriminate against any individual because such individual has opposed any act or practice made unlawful by this chapter or because such individual made a charge, testified, assisted, or participated in any manner in an investigation, proceeding, or hearing under this chapter.
> § 503(b) makes it:
> unlawful to coerce, intimidate, threaten or interfere with any individual in the exercise or enjoyment of, or on account of his or her having exercised or enjoyed.... any right granted or protected by this act. (42 USC §12203 (b)).

Section 503(c) specifies the remedies of "section 308 of this act shall be available to aggrieved persons for violations of subsection (a) and (b) with respect to ... title III. Section 308(a)(1) specifies that the remedies of:

> section 204(a) of the Civil Rights Act of 1964 142 USC 2000a-3(a) are the remedies to any person who is being subjected to discrimination in violation of this title or who as reasonable grounds for believing that such person is about to be subjected to discrimination in violation of section 303.

However, it would appear incorporation of any violation of the ADA as a violation of Civil Code 51(f) would allow damages per section 52. [See section III-C-2, *infra*.]

Section 503 is also one of the few "disability rights" statutes which gives potential "standing" to sue to a person who is not themselves disabled.[102] Section 503(a)'s protections include those who "made a charge, testified, assisted or participated in any manner in an investigation, proceeding, or hearing under this act." Section 503(b) protections extend to those who have "aided or encouraged any other individual in the exercise or enjoyment of any right granted or protected by this act."

As a factual backdrop to Hankins v. El Torito, *supra*, defendants posted a sign outside their inaccessible restaurant, "Premises Not Wheelchair Equipped." Particularly coupled with defendants' stated intention to use the sign as a "warning"(per defendants' own interrogatory answers), the "Premises Not Wheel Chair Equipped" sign was arguably a direct violation of sections 51 and 54.1 Civil Code and the ADA. (Defendants argued plaintiff was "comparatively negligent" for ignoring the sign!) This 1992 lawsuit was brought in state court under state law, and did not rely upon the recently enacted ADA, (although the ADA was to be considered on remand to the trial court on a remaining issue regarding whether defendants could keep locked the "lift" that was finally installed, with the manager retaining the key). (The retaliation issue, an evidence matter, was not addressed by the appellate court's opinion.)

Although this offensive sign's removal by defendants during litigation rendered an injunction for its removal "moot," its removal was one of the successful results of that lawsuit. Similarly, attacks upon a plaintiff in one lawsuit because he or she has previously filed other lawsuits under the ADA or has otherwise complained of the lack of access at other public facilities, may constitute improper violations of the letter and intent of ADA § 503 (which prohibits "retaliation" or "intimidation" against a disabled person on the basis he has brought an ADA enforcement action).

---

[102] In Atwood v. El Torito, for example, the disabled wheelchair using plaintiff was able to recover damages as well as injunctive relief under sections 54.1 and 54.3 Civil Code, when he and his wife were forced to dine by themselves as all other restaurant seating was up stairs. However the Court held the wife had no personal "standing" to sue.

But caveat the actions taken by plaintiff and his lawyer in Molski v. Evergreen Dynasty Corp., 500 F.3d 1047 (9th Cir. 2007). Attorney and plaintiff were heavily criticized by the 9th Circuit, for a pattern of alleged factual misrepresentations to the Court, while generally affirming the right of a "serial" plaintiff to bring multiple lawsuits if they encounter violations at multiple public accommodations.

2. DAMAGES ARE AVAILABLE FOR EITHER HARASSMENT OR RETALIATION

In Wilson v. Murillo 163 Cal.App.4th 1124 (2008) the California 1st District Court of Appeal held that any violation of ADA section 503's "retaliation" provision could be the basis of a cause of action for damages and injunctive relief under California's Civil Code sections 51(c) and 54.1(d). Per footnote 6 at p 1131, "[B]y incorporating the ADA, both the Unruh Act and the Disabled Persons Act prohibit retaliation or interference against any individual who exercises his or her rights under the ADA."

This important decision (won by attorneys Tom Frankovich and Jennifer Steneberg of San Francisco) established that section 503 could be the basis for damages in a non-employment situation. In Wilson, *supra*, defendant restaurant owner harassed a disabled wheelchair user customer who had previously sent letters to her demanding that she provide extensive access improvements. Defendant restaurant owner "Murillo ultimately spent in excess of $130,000 in bringing the restaurant into compliance with applicable law." Id. at 1129. However the appellate court held plaintiff raised a triable issue of fact that his rights under section 503 had been violated, when the evidence showed that, when plaintiff and another wheelchair user returned to the restaurant for lunch, Murillo told them they were not welcome, held up a sign that said, "We reserve the right to refuse service to anyone," ordered them to leave the premises, and called the police to the scene and asked them (unsuccessfully) to remove plaintiff and his companion from the restaurant. (Restaurant employees also repeatedly photographed them, taunted them, and one made "an offensive gesture with his middle finger." (Id. at 1130)). Presiding Justice Ruvalo reversed the trial court's granting summary judgment (and reversed the trial court's award of attorney fees and costs against plaintiff for more than $50,000!)

The appellate court held that, "Section 503(b) directly forbids coercion, intimidation, threats and interference with the exercise of protected rights under the ADA." Id. at 1133. We should distinguish retaliation in public access cases from employment cases. Alvarado v. Cajun Operating Company, 588 F.3d 1261 (9th Circuit, 2009) the panel held that compensatory and punitive damages are not available when based solely on an ADA Title I retaliation claim against an employer.

3. BURDEN OF PROOF STANDARD

Wilson v. Murrillo, *supra*, also established that the burden-shifting analysis used in landmark employment discrimination cases such as McDonnell Douglas Corp. v. Green (1973) would apply:

> Once the plaintiff proves a prima facia case, courts apply the same burden-shifting analysis to retaliation claims as is employed in other discrimination cases. (Citations) ... After a prima facia case of retaliation is established, the burden is on defendant to establish a legitimate reason for the adverse action, which plaintiff may rebut by producing credible evidence of pretext. McDonnell Douglas, *supra*, at pp. 802-805.

Id. at 1134.

However, the Wilson Court did not incorporate other employment law standards sought by defendants, finding them inappropriate, instead following an 11th Circuit case, Shotz v. City of Plantation Fla. (11th Cir. 2003), which held that "an ADA plaintiff must demonstrate that a reasonable person in his position would view the ... action in question as adverse," and that "while conduct must be material to be adverse in this context, it need not be traumatic [citation]. If we set the bar too high, we run the risk of chilling legitimate opposition to unlawful and discriminatory practices, and 'could stifle [a person's] willingness to file charges of discrimination.'" Wilson, *supra*, at 1136.

Adopting and applying the Shotz standards, the Court held that Wilson's negative subjective reaction must also be "objectively reasonable, analyzing his claim of retaliation on a fact specific basis to determine whether a reasonable person in Wilson's position would believe that the conduct allegedly taken against him was materially adverse." Id. The Court held evidence offered by Wilson clearly met this standard.

4. DOJ REGULATIONS PROTECT AGAINST RETALIATION

In Wilson v. Murillo *supra*, the court said its holding was reenforced by the Justice Department's "administrative guidance" at section 3.600 of the DOJ's 1993 edition of the ADA Title III Technical Assistance Manual which stated that, "[i]ndividuals who exercise their rights under the ADA, or assist others in exercising their rights, are protected from retaliation." The Court then cited one illustrative example which was "particularly relevant: A restaurant may not refuse to serve a customer because he or she has filed an ADA complaint against the restaurant or against another public accommodation." Id. at 1138.

Alternatively, the Court found separate violations of both sections 503(a) [42USC

12203(a) and 503(b) 42 USC 12203(b), "prohibiting harassment against those who are simply exercising their ADA rights" Id. 1138-1139. The Court cited the DOJ's Code of Federal Regulations, Part 36.206 (28 CFR §36.206, 2007), which gave as an example of a violation, "(2) Threatening, intimidating, or interfering with an individual with a disability seeking to obtain or use the goods, services, facilities, privileges, advantages or accommodations of a public accommodation." (Id. at 1139)

5. DISCOVERY AIMED AT QUESTIONING PRIOR SUCCESSFUL ADA LAWSUITS BY A PLAINTIFF MAY ITSELF VIOLATE SECTION 503

No disabled person should be required to divulge in discovery the details of every other ADA lawsuit ever brought, as the "price" for prosecuting an action to enforce the ADA. To order plaintiff to be subjected to this intrusion based solely on having filed more than one ADA action. and being accused thereby of being a "professional plaintiff," would be unfair and a miscarriage of justice.

This may be an appropriate situation to enforce a rule necessary to protect the enforcement of the ADA, and supported by § 503's prohibition against retaliation: that no disabled person who files a "meritorious" ADA lawsuit should have to later face questioning about that suit as the "price" for filing any other ADA action.

Plaintiff may ask the Court to rule, as a matter of policy per §503, that the fact of plaintiff filing - and winning - other ADA lawsuits will not be admissible at trial. If so, efforts to discover evidence of plaintiff filing and winning other meritorious ADA lawsuits cannot "lead" to admissible evidence, and motions to compel such disclosures should be denied.

There is another practical reason to prohibit in effect relitigation of ADA lawsuits: Aside from the constitutional and § 503 issues, if evidence of other lawsuits were introduced at all, plaintiff would have the right to disclose all other relevant facts about the lawsuits, their objectives and results. The expenditure of time to deal fairly with the full merits of multiple previous separate meritorious suits under the ADA would be phenomenal! And a waste of the Court's time and resources.

D. PUBLIC POLICY IS TO PROTECT THE RIGHTS OF DISABLED PERSONS TO ENFORCE THE ADA, AND ENCOURAGE "PRIVATE ATTORNEY GENERAL" ACTIONS

In Bernard Walker and Christina Adams v. Carnival Cruise Lines (2000) 107 F.Supp.2d 1135, (also discussed infra at § V-F, re: encouraging ADA lawsuits as private attorney generals), the court found an exception to the U.S. Supreme Court's "forum selection" decisions in Shute v. Carnival Cruise Lines, Inc., 1991

499 U.S. 585. The Walker court (Hon. Thelton Henderson) held that requiring two disabled quadriplegics - who could not travel to Florida - to litigate their California based ADA suit only in Florida, would effectively deny them their ADA rights:

> Enforcing the forum selection clause here would actually serve to undermine society's strong interest in rooting out discrimination and ensuring that the disabled members of our society may equally partake in social intercourse, because to do so would erode a clearly enunciated federal policy of the highest order. It would be perverse to enforce this forum selection clause where, as a result, plaintiffs effectively would be prohibited from seeking redress, as a direct consequence of the very disabilities that give rise to this suit. See e.g., Crowder v. Kitigawa, 81 F.3d 1480, 1483 (9th Cir. 1995) (discussing effective preclusion of disabled individuals based upon their disability pursuant to facially neutral regulation).
> Strict interpretation and blind enforcement of the forum selection clause here at issue would do nothing less than re-victimize these plaintiffs.

The Court concluded that,
> For the foregoing reasons, this Court finds that enforcement of the forum selection clause here at issue would be fundamentally unfair to these plaintiffs as enforcement would deprive them of their day in court due to their physical and economic disabilities. Moreover, enforcement, under these circumstances, would contravene the strong national policy underlying the ADA, that as private attorneys general, civil rights plaintiffs should not be deterred from bringing good faith claims to vindicate their rights. Venue is proper and will lie in the Northern District of California.

Id. at 1142-1143.

E. "STANDING" TO BRING A TITLE III ADA ACTION FOR INJUNCTIVE RELIEF REQUIRES HAVING ENCOUNTERED AT LEAST ONE BARRIER TO ACCESS OR HAVING BEEN DETERRED FROM DOING SO, AND AN INTENT TO USE THE FACILITIES AFTER ACCESS HAS BEEN SUPPLIED

1. PROVING "STANDING" FOR A TITLE III ADA ACTION IN FEDERAL COURT: TITLE III, § 308(a) OF THE ADA SPECIFICALLY GRANTS PLAINTIFF STANDING, TO SEEK INJUNCTIVE RELIEF FOR CONTINUING ARCHITECTURAL BARRIERS WHICH DENY ACCESS TO PERSONS WITH DISABILITIES

ADA 308(A) / 42 USC 12188 reads:
(a) IN GENERAL
(1) AVAILABILITY OF REMEDIES AND PROCEDURES
The remedies and procedures set forth in section 2000a-3(a) of this title are the remedies and procedures this subchapter provides to any person who is being subjected to discrimination on the basis of disability in violation of this subchapter or who has reasonable grounds for believing

> that such person is about to be subjected to discrimination in violation of section 12183 of this title. Nothing in this section shall require a person with a disability to engage in a futile gesture if such person has actual notice that a person or organization covered by this subchapter does not intend to comply with its provisions.
>
> (2) INJUNCTIVE RELIEF
> In the case of violations of sections 12182(b)(2)(A)(iv) and section 12183(a) of this title, injunctive relief shall include an order to alter facilities to make such facilities readily accessible to and usable by individuals with disabilities to the extent required by this subchapter. Where appropriate, injunctive relief shall also include requiring the provision of an auxiliary aid or service, modification of a policy, or provision of alternative methods, to the extent required by this subchapter.
>
> 42 USC 12188.

However, plaintiffs may need to allege - and even prove by testimony- that, as of the date they filed a complaint, they had the intent to <u>return</u> to the facility <u>once it was made accessible</u>.

Any remaining questions about "standing" to seek injunctive relief in federal court under the ADA should finally have been settled by the 9th Circuit's 9-2 <u>en banc</u> decision in <u>Chapman v. Pier 1 Imports</u>, 631 F3d 939 (9th Cir. 2011), which "clarified" the issue:

> We now clarify that when an ADA plaintiff has suffered an injury-in-fact by encountering a barrier that deprives him of full and equal enjoyment of the facility due to his particular disability, he has standing to sue for injunctive relief as to that barrier and other barriers related to his disability, even if he is not deterred from returning to the public accommodation at issue. First, we hold that an ADA plaintiff can establish standing to sue for injunctive relief either by demonstrating deterrence, or by demonstrating injury-in-fact coupled with an intent to return to a noncompliant facility. Second, we hold that an ADA plaintiff who establishes standing as to encountered barriers may also sue for injunctive relief as to unencountered barriers related to his disability. Here, however, Chapman has failed to allege and prove the required elements of Article III standing to support his claim for injunctive relief under the ADA. Specifically, he has not alleged or proven that he personally suffered discrimination as defined by the ADA as to encountered barriers on account of his disability.
>
> <u>Chapman v. Pier 1 Imports</u>, 631 F3d 939 (9th Cir. 2011), at 944.[103]

Per the <u>Chapman</u>, *supra*, quote (hereinabove), deterrence due to knowledge of a

---

[103] On remand, the District Court allowed Chapman to file a first amended complaint, and eventually entered summary judgment in favor of the <u>Chapman</u> plaintiff. <u>Chapman v. Pier 1 Imports, Inc.</u>, CIV. S-04-1339, 2011 WL 1047430 (E.D. Cal. Mar. 18, 2011)

discriminatory inaccessible condition continues to be <u>one</u> of several possible bases for standing. Members of a class of disabled persons who were <u>deterred</u> from attending inaccessible theaters were granted ADA standing to sue by Judge Thelton Henderson's landmark decision in <u>Connie Arnold, et al v. United Artists</u>, 866 F.Supp 433 (N.D. 1994).

2. PUBLIC POLICY REQUIRES A BROAD INTERPRETATION OF "STANDING": AS A MATTER OF PUBLIC POLICY CONGRESS SPECIFICALLY WROTE INTO THE AMERICANS WITH DISABILITIES ACT OF 1990 A BROAD RIGHT OF "STANDING" FOR ANY DISABLED PERSON WHO KNEW THAT HE WOULD BE DISADVANTAGED BY VISITING AN INACCESSIBLE PUBLIC FACILITY, AND TO ALLOW HIM TO BRING A LEGAL ACTION TO OBTAIN ADA COMPLIANT ACCESS WITHOUT GOING THROUGH THE "FUTILE ACT" OF ACTUALLY VISITING THE FACILITY

From the language of the ADA itself it is clear that the public policy purpose of the ADA is to maximize disabled access to public facilities. Even without specific statutory authority, a disabled person should not have to personally visit a <u>known</u> inaccessible facility to forseeably be discriminated against. To make its intent clear, Congress passed and the President signed into law a specific broad standing right, embodied in § 308(a). However, since any violation of the ADA is automatically a violation of §§ 54(c), and 54.1(d), does learning of an inaccessible facility give a right to damages even if a disabled person does not actually go there?

This issue appears to have been established (or "clarified") by (effective 1/1/09) California Civil Code section 55.56, which specifies the necessity of a plaintiff to have personally encountered and been denied "full and equal" access on a specific occasion, <u>or been deterred from visiting on a specific occasion</u>, in order to obtain damages on the basis of violation of a "construction related accessibility standard." The statute specifically "does not alter the applicable law for awarding injunctive or other equitable relief for ... violations of ... construction related accessibility standards."

For example, successful suits obtained damages and injunctive relief at several public facilities when disabled persons were excluded from <u>scheduled office dinner parties</u>, because they were held on the second floor, with no elevator. (<u>White v. TGI Fridays, et al.</u> (N.D.Cal.) Case No. Case No. C02-1062 JCS; <u>Fischl v. Big Horn Grill, et al.</u> (N.D.Cal.) Case No. C02-01347 JCS; <u>Madison v. Pedro's, et al.</u> (N.D.Cal.) Case No. C04-03936 JF) [See also <u>Arnold v. United Artist</u> (N.D.Cal. 1994) 866 F.Supp. 433, on standing based on deterrence, and Civil Code §§ 54(c) and 54.1(d) on damages based on an incorporated ADA violation.]

3. CONGRESSIONAL INTENT IS CLEAR IN SECTION 308(A)(1) OF THE ADA THAT STANDING TO SUE TO REQUIRE READILY ACHIEVABLE ACCESS TO A

PUBLIC FACILITY IS GRANTED TO ANY DISABLED PERSON WITHOUT THE "FUTILE GESTURE" OF VISITING A FACILITY KNOWN TO BE INACCESSIBLE

Section 308(a)(1) of Title III of the Americans With Disabilities Act of 1990 (42 USC 12188), states that its remedies are available,

> To any person who is being subjected to discrimination on the basis of disability in violation of this title, or who has reasonable grounds for believing that such person is about to be subjected to discrimination in violation of section 303. (Emphasis added)

The term "in violation of this title" refers to Title III of the ADA. The fact that this section goes on in the disjunctive to also grant standing under § 303, ("or who has reasonable grounds for believing that such person is about to be subjected to discrimination in violation of section 303,") does not negate that the remedies are available to one who is already "being subjected to discrimination on the basis of disability in violation of this title." The next sentence in § 308(a)(1) applies to both of these situations:

> Nothing in this section shall require a person with a disability to engage in a futile gesture if such person has actual notice that a person or organization covered by this title does not intend to comply with its provisions.

The Congressional intent is further made clear by the next paragraph, § 308(a)(2), Injunctive Relief:

> In the case of violations of sections 302(b)(2)(A)(iv) and section 303(a), injunctive relief shall include an order to alter facilities to make such facilities readily accessible to and usable by individuals with disabilities to the extent required by this title.

Section 302(b)(2)(A)(iv) is the section defining discrimination as, "(iv) A failure to remove architectural barriers and communication barriers that are structural in nature in existing facilities... where such removal is readily achievable.

Congress set it up so that any disabled person with actual notice that a public facility did not provide legally required access would have standing to sue for an injunction to require that "readily achievable" access changes be made.[104]

4. PUBLIC POLICY SUPPORTS BROAD VIEW OF CONSTITUTIONAL STANDARDS; PRIVATE ENFORCEMENT IS THE PRIMARY METHOD OF OBTAINING ADA COMPLIANCE

In evaluating whether a civil rights litigant has satisfied these requirements, "The Supreme Court has instructed us to take a broad view of constitutional standing in Civil Rights cases," especially where, as under the ADA, private enforcement suits

---

[104] "Standing" under the ADA to sue for injunctive relief may be different from the standards for awarding California law damages. Since January 1, 2009, Civil Code section 55.56ff defines the necessity for personal interference with access or actual deterrence, and on a specific occasion, as the basis for seeking a damage award. [See section 55.56ff]

"are the primary method of obtaining compliance with the Act." (Doran v. 7-Eleven, 524 F.3d 1034, 1039-40, (9th Cir., 2008)(quoted and followed in Chapman, *supra*, 631 F.3d 939 at 946.

This view is reenforced by the July 15, 1993 opinion by then California Attorney General Daniel Lungren which discussed enforcement requirements of the ADA and concluded, "we conclude that ... the primary responsibility for enforcement of the ADA access requirements through legal action rests with private litigants and the United States Attorney General." [See appendix IX-E-2 at p. 8]

Enforcement of the ADA depends on private lawsuits with plaintiffs as "private attorneys general."

> In Title VII cases as well as cases under the ADA, the enforcement of civil rights statutes by plaintiffs as private attorneys general is an important part of the underlying policy behind the law. Such a policy ensures an incentive for "impecunious" plaintiffs who can ill afford to litigate their claims against defendants with more resources and thus justifies the differential treatment of prevailing plaintiffs and prevailing defendants....
> Bruce v. City of Gainesville, 177 F 3d 949, 951-952

> Walker and Adams v. Carnival Cruise Lines, (N.D. Cal. 2000) 107 F.Supp.2nd 1135, at 1043.

5. §36.501 OF THE ADAAG REGULATIONS ALSO SPECIFIES THAT STANDING WITHOUT A "FUTILE GESTURE" VISIT IS AVAILABLE FOR ANY VIOLATION OF TITLE III, NOT SIMPLY §303 CASES

> Section 36.501 of the ADAAG Regulations for "private suit" provides
> (a) General. Any person who is being subjected to discrimination on the basis of disability in violation of the Act or this part or who has reasonable grounds for believing that such person is about to be subjected to discrimination in violation of Section 303 of the Act or subpart D or this part may institute a civil action for preventative relief, including an application for a permanent or temporary injunction, restraining order, or other order.... Nothing in this section shall require a person with a disability to engage in a futile gesture if the person has actual notice that a person or organization covered by Title III of the Act or this part does not intend to comply with its provisions. (Emphasis added)

While it is true that § 303 violations are one form of violation for which the "no futile gesture" broad standing rule has been adopted, there is no indication that this broad "standing" policy is limited to "§ 303 cases" (anticipated new construction). The same policy principles apply, and the regulations specify that § 36.501 applies to both sections 308(a)(1) and 308(a)(2) cases, architectural barriers removal cases. At Federal

Register, Vol. 56, No. 144, Friday, July 26, 1991, Rules and Regulations, p.35589,
> Section 36.501 describes the procedures for private suits by individuals and the judicial remedies available. In addition to the language in Section 308(a)(1) of the Act, § 36.501(a) of the part includes the language from Section 204(a) of the Civil Rights Act of 1964 [42 USC 2000a-3(a)] which is incorporated by reference in the ADA....
>
> ... To avoid unnecessary suits, this section requires that the individual bringing the suit have "reasonable grounds" for believing that a violation is about to occur, but does not require the individual to engage in a futile gesture if he or she has notice that a person or organization covered by Title III of the Act does not intend to comply with its provisions.

The next section specifies that these provisions apply to <u>both</u> situations: Failure to remove architectural barriers in <u>existing facilities</u> or new construction or alterations:
> Section 36.501(b) restates the provisions of section 308(a)(2) of the Act, which states that <u>injunctive relief for the failure to remove architectural barriers in existing facilities</u> or the failure to make new construction and alterations accessible "shall include" an order to alter these facilities to make them readily accessible to and usable by person with disabilities to the extent required by title III. (Emphasis added)

The statute clearly calls for broad "standing" rights and encouragement for any disabled person who knows that he or she can't enter a public facility to be able to bring an action for relief without having to go through the "futile gesture" of <u>revisiting</u> a known inaccessible public restaurant. In California this is also consistent with the public policy rules of broadly construing civil rights statutes and broadly construing disabled access statutes in light of the strong California public policy of maximizing the integration of the disabled into California society, etc. (See, i.e., Government Code § 19230)

> As noted § 308(a) states:
>
>> Nothing in this section shall require a person with a disability to engage in a futile gesture if such person has actual notice that a person or organization covered by this title does not intend to comply with its provisions.

This "standing" provision is essential in regard to removing architectural barriers under the ADA. Otherwise, a person in a wheelchair, with knowledge that a major facility was inaccessible would have to visit the facility in order <u>not</u> to be able to use it - the very type of "futile gesture" precluded by § 308(a)(1).

Section 308(a)(1) even allows standing for any disabled person to sue if he or she has reasonable cause to believe a building that is currently being constructed will not comply with requirements of § 303. Certainly a disabled person who has already visited a facility and personally found its features denied him access has standing to complain that the remedying of such conditions, though readily achievable, was not done by January 26, 1992.

Connie Arnold v. United Artists, (N.D. Cal 1994) 866 F.Supp. 433 held that standing for members of a class was properly based on disabled persons deterred from attending United Artist theaters by knowledge of these theaters' inaccessibility. The Court held that "deterrence" was a valid basis for damages as well as injunctive relief under both Civil Code sections 51 and 54.1. In coming to this conclusion, the Court (the very respected Hon. Thelton Henderson, Chief Judge for the Northern District) made certain policy determinations that were relevant to later arguments about the place of "deterrence" in disability access litigation. After discussing analogous issues in U.S. Supreme Court employment and race based public accommodations cases, the Arnold Court observed:

> Similar policy considerations militate strongly in favor of recognizing deterrence claims under the California disability access laws. Otherwise, the most egregious violators would largely escape liability for damages under the laws since, where it is well-known that a particular establishment has no adequate accommodations for disabled persons, few disabled would-be patrons would make the futile and probably humiliating gesture of showing up and asking to be accommodated. Indeed, unlike most employment cases where the deterring conduct is largely subjective and is subject to differing interpretations, the existence of, for instance, an architectural disability access barrier is an objectively ascertainable fact and therefore is even more likely to have a deterring effect.
> Id. at 438.

The Court further recognized that:
> Failing to recognize deterrence-based damage claims under § 54.3 and § 52 would significantly reduce the incentives for compliance with the disability access requirements of these laws. Since California courts have held that the California disability access laws manifest an intent on the part of the legislature that they be interpreted in a manner that maximizes incentives for compliance, see Donald, 266 Cal.Rptr. at 808-11, the Court concludes that application of this canon of construction requires that § 54.1 and § 51, and their respective damages provisions, § 54.3 and § 52, be interpreted as extending to claims based on incidents of deterrence.
> Id. at 439.

By the January 1, 2009 addition of Civil Code section 55.56 the California Legislature made clear that "deterrence" was a basis for statutory damages under California law with certain conditions:

> (d) A plaintiff demonstrates that he or she was deterred from accessing a

place of public accommodation <u>on a particular occasion</u> only if both of the following apply:

(1) The plaintiff had actual knowledge of a violation or violations that prevented or reasonably dissuaded the plaintiff from accessing a place of public accommodation that the plaintiff intended to use on a particular occasion.

(2) The violation or violations <u>would have actually denied the plaintiff full and equal access</u>[105] if the plaintiff had accessed the place of public accommodation on that particular occasion.
(Emphasis Added)

In enacting § 308(a) allowing <u>any</u> disabled person with knowledge that a public facility was inaccessible after January 26, 1992 to challenge this inaccessibility by lawsuit without engaging in the "futile gesture" of attempting to visit the facility that he <u>already knew was inaccessible</u> Congress was clear as to its intention and effect.

Note: the <u>Chapman</u> en banc decision 631 F.3d 939 (9th Cir. 2011) held one alternative way to assert "standing" was "by demonstrating deterrence." [See § III-E-1, *supra*]

6. TACTICS: THE STRONGER CASE MAY STILL REQUIRE A PERSONAL VISIT ATTEMPT TO ASSURE DAMAGES PER CIVIL CODE SECTION 55.56

If the plaintiff expects damages beyond the statutory minimum, an attempt to actually visit and "try" to obtain access is desirable, although damages are also available on a deterrence basis. Per SB 1608, Civil Code § 55.56, specifies a requirement that a person claiming damages based on construction / alteration of premises under California law, has to show a "violation was personally encountered by the plaintiff on a particular occasion or deterred the plaintiff on a particular occasion." Section 55.56 (a) - (e) spells out these requirements in detail. Section 55.56 (f) specifies there is no change in the existing law regarding injunctive relief standing:

This section does not alter the applicable law for the awarding of injunctive or other equitable relief for a violation or violations of one or more construction related accessibility standards, nor alter any legal obligation of a party to mitigate damages.

7. SKAFF V. MERIDIEN NORTH AMERICA BEVERLY HILLS, LLC (9TH CIR. 2007) CLARIFIED FEDERAL "STANDING" STANDARDS REGARDING SEEKING INJUNCTIVE RELIEF AND STATUTORY PREVAILING PARTY ATTORNEY FEES

<u>Skaff v. Meridien North America Beverly Hills, LLC</u>, 506 F.3d 832 (9th Cir. 2007), rejected several frequently claimed defenses, holding that a prevailing party who obtained damages and injunctive relief was entitled to attorney fees despite the lack of

---

[105] Section 55.56(c) defines denial of full and equal access to include that the plaintiff "experienced difficulty, discomfort, or embarrassment because of the violation."

a "pre-litigation demand." The 9th Circuit rejected the prior and contrary District Court holding of <u>Doran v. Del Taco, Inc. Et al.</u> 373 F.Supp.2d. 1028 (C.D. 2005) (which itself was also reversed by the 9th Circuit, at 524 F.3d. 1034, discussed *infra*.) The <u>Skaff</u> court reiterated the proper prevailing party standard in its f.n. 12:

> Skaff is also a prevailing party under the ADA pursuant to <u>Buckhannon,</u> which held that "court-ordered consent decrees create the 'material alteration of the legal relationship of the parties' necessary to permit an award of attorney's fees." <u>Buckhannon</u>, 532 U.S. at 604, 121 S.Ct. 1835 (quoting Tex. <u>State Teachers Ass'n v. Garland Indep. Sch. Dist.</u>, 489 U.S. 782, 792-93, 109 S.Ct. 1486, 103 L.Ed.2d 866 (1989)). Likewise, in <u>Barrios v. California Interscholastic Federation, 277 F</u>.3d 1128, 1134 (9th Cir.2002), we held that "[u]nder applicable Ninth Circuit law, a plaintiff 'prevails' when he or she enters into a legally enforceable settlement agreement against the defendant."

Id. at 844, f.n. 12.

8. A BROAD STANDING HOLDING WAS ISSUED BY THE 9TH CIRCUIT, IN <u>DORAN V. 7-ELEVEN, INC.</u> (2008) GIVING STANDING TO REQUIRE REMEDIATION OF ALL BARRIERS TO ACCESS FOR PERSONS WITH PLAINTIFF'S DISABILITIES

   In <u>Doran v. 7-Eleven,</u> 534 F.3d 1034 (2005), the 9th Circuit clarified the "standing" issue, giving broad standing for injunctive relief:
   > An ADA plaintiff who has encountered or has personal knowledge of at least one barrier related to his or her disability when he or she files a complaint, and who has been deterred from attempting to gain access to the public accommodation because of that barrier, has suffered an injury in fact for the purpose of Article III. <u>Pickern</u>, 293 F.3d at 1138. An ADA plaintiff who has Article III standing as a result of at least one barrier at a place of public accommodation <u>may, in one suit, permissibly challenge all barriers in that public accommodation that are related to his or her specific disability</u>. Steger, 228 F.3d at 894.

   <u>Doran</u>, *supra*, at 1041. (Emphasis added)

   The court specified that such plaintiff had standing to sue for injunctive relief for "all barriers... related to his specific disability, <u>including those identified in his expert's site inspection</u>." Id. [Emphasis added] This should avoid the past situation where defendants sometimes have attempted to limit the scope of plaintiff's "standing" and his expert's site inspection to the specific barriers identified in plaintiff's complaint, or even to those barriers specifically encountered by the plaintiff himself.[106] As the Court explained, public policy supported broad standing, even as to barriers first determined during discovery, <u>so that all barriers to access could be addressed in one lawsuit</u>:

> The relevant section of the ADA provides that "discriminat[ion] ... on the basis of disability" includes "a failure to remove architectural barriers ... where such removal is readily achievable." 42 U.S.C. § 12182. While 7-Eleven did remove some of the architectural barriers at the North Harbor location about which Doran had complained, others remained in place that would have interfered with his access as a wheelchair user, as evidenced by the site inspections of Doran's expert. Thus the discrimination against Doran, and the corresponding Article III injury of deterrence from visiting the store, continued even after the violations he initially listed were corrected. Although he is aware of this fact because his expert had an opportunity to inspect the location, many disabled individuals will not have this chance and so, under the district court's view, would have uncertainty about whether the list of access barriers they perchance encountered or learned about before being deterred is exhaustive or whether other, potentially dangerous obstacles to a person with their disability remain in place, only to be encountered when the disabled persons return to the site after the "successful" conclusion of their suit. Such uncertainty is itself an actual, concrete and particularized injury under the deterrence framework of standing articulated in <u>Pickern</u>, for when a disabled individual knows that a facility is noncompliant with the ADA in at least some respects but does not know the full extent of the noncompliance, he or she is likely to be deterred from returning to that facility, even if some of the violations are corrected, until he or she can get more information about the extent of the violations. This presents a real and concrete burden for a disabled person, especially when unknown violations may pose safety hazards to that individual.
>
> . . .
>
> Given that an ADA plaintiff has standing because of deterrence from returning in the face of uncertainty, it is prudent to eliminate that uncertainty through the judicial device of discovery, thus allowing the plaintiff to obtain by formal means the information about the scope of the defendant's violations that he may have been unable to safely ascertain himself because of those same violations. This course is consistent with Constitutional requirements, for we have been instructed to take a broad view of Article III standing in civil rights cases where private rights of action are the primary means of enforcing the statute. See <u>Trafficante</u>, 409 U.S. at 209, 93 S.Ct. 364. Indeed, the enforcement scheme of Title III of the ADA would be severely undermined if we were to adopt the piecemeal approach to standing advocated by 7-Eleven. The statute provides that where an individual, like Doran, has suffered discrimination in the form of a refusal to remove architectural barriers, he may seek injunctive relief including "an order to alter facilities to make such facilities readily accessible ... and usable." 42 U.S.C. § 12188(a)(2). Such injunctive relief could not be crafted,

---

[106] The dissent filed in both the <u>Skaff</u> and <u>Doran</u> cases, *supra*, was by a District Court judge from the Southern District of New York, Hon. Kevin Thomas Duffy, sitting by designation.

however, if the parties had not been allowed to determine through discovery precisely what barriers prevented the facility in question from being "readily accessible to and usable by" Doran. <u>We therefore hold that where a disabled person has Article III standing to bring a claim for injunctive relief under the ADA because of at least one alleged statutory violation of which he or she has knowledge and which deters access to, or full use and enjoyment of, a place of public accommodation, he or she may conduct discovery to determine what, if any, other barriers affecting his or her disability existed at the time he or she brought the claim.</u> This list of barriers would then in total constitute the factual underpinnings of a single legal injury, namely, the failure to remove architectural barriers in violation of the ADA, which failure actually harmed the disabled person by deterring that disabled person from visiting a facility that otherwise would have been visited at a definite future time, yielding Article III standing. See <u>Pickern</u>, 293 F.3d at 1138. (Emphasis added)

<u>Doran v. 7-Eleven</u>, *supra*, 524 F.3d 1034, at 1043-1044. In the Northern District the General Order 56 required cooperative site inspection may disclose such barriers without the need for formal discovery. (But caveat <u>Oliver v Ralph's</u> 654 F.3d 903 requiring Plaintiff to move to amend his complaint to give defendents "Fair notice" of additional barriers.)

9. THE 9TH CIRCUIT REAFFIRMED <u>DORAN V. 7-ELEVEN</u>'S BROAD "STANDING" STANDARDS IN <u>WILSON V. KAYO OIL CO.</u> AND IN THE "<u>EN BANC</u>" <u>CHAPMAN</u> DECISION (2011)

In its 2009 decision in <u>Wilson v. Kayo Oil Co.</u>, the 9th Circuit reaffirmed the broad standing standards of <u>Doran v. 7-Eleven</u>, *supra*:

"Standing is a question of law that we review de novo." Salmon Spawning & Recovery Alliance v. Gutierrez, 545 F.3d 1220, 1224 (9th Cir. 2008). "Allegations that a plaintiff has visited a public accommodation on a prior occasion and is currently deterred from visiting that accommodation by accessibility barriers establish that a plaintiff's injury is actual or imminent." Doran v. 7-Eleven, 524 F.3d 1034, 1041 (9th Cir. 2008). Here, Wilson makes these minimal allegations, and therefore survives a facial attack on standing. See Id. at 1041.

<u>Wilson v. Kayo Oil Co.</u>, (2009, 9th Circuit) 563 F.3d 979, 980.

The Court in <u>O'Campo v. Chico Mall, LP,</u> 758 F.Supp. 2d 976 (E.D. Cal. 2010) presented a simplified definition of "standing":

Thus, in order to demonstrate standing, plaintiff merely needs to allege that he has encountered or has knowledge of barriers at a place of public accommodation and that he intends to return to the public accommodation in the future.

Id. at 982.

<u>Chapman v. Pier 1 Imports</u>, 631 F.3d 939 (9th Cir. 2010) included an extended discussion

to "clarify" the broad standing principles of the ADA:

> We now clarify that when an ADA plaintiff has suffered an injury-in-fact by encountering a barrier that deprives him of full and equal enjoyment of the facility due to his particular disability, he has standing to sue for injunctive relief as to that barrier and other barriers related to his disability, even if he is not deterred from returning to the public accommodation at issue. First, we hold that an ADA plaintiff can establish standing to sue for injunctive relief either by demonstrating deterrence, or by demonstrating injury-in-fact coupled with an intent to return to a noncompliant facility. Second, we hold that an ADA plaintiff who establishes standing as to encountered barriers may also sue for injunctive relief as to unencountered barriers related to his disability.
>
> Chapman v. Pier 1 Imports (U.S.) Inc., 631 F.3d 939, 944 (9th Cir. 2011)

In Chapman the United States Department of Justice filed an amicus brief supporting a broad interpretation of standing so that the ADA could be properly enforced by private lawsuits. [See quote at section III-A-3-b, *supra*.]

10. A DISABLED PERSON HAS STANDING TO COMPLAIN ABOUT DENIAL OF "COMPANION SEATING" IN A THEATER OR SPORTS ARENA

    Although only a disabled person has standing to seek injunctive relief or damages under the ADA, a disabled person also has standing to complain about the exclusion of a "companion."[107] In Fortyune v. American Multi-Cinema, Inc., 364 F.3d 1075 (9th Cir. 2004), the Court held that a quadriplegic wheelchair user could state a cause of action where a movie theater refused to make a "non-companion" move from a "companion seat" adjoining a space reserved for wheelchair use, so that the plaintiff's wife could sit next to him: the presence of a companion was held to be a "condition precedent" to the disabled patron's enjoyment of the theater's services and facilities, and of his rights under the ADA. Asking the other patron to move to other seating was held to be a reasonable modification in policy.

F. THERE IS NO "EXHAUSTION OF ADMINISTRATIVE REMEDY" OR PRE-FILING "NOTICE" REQUIREMENT UNDER TITLE III OF THE ADA

1. IN BOTOSAN V. MCNALLY REALTY THE 9TH CIRCUIT HELD THERE WAS NO "NOTICE" REQUIREMENT

    The defense of a "failure to file an administrative claim" was rejected in the 9th Circuit in the 2000 case of Botosan v. McNally Realty (9th Cir. 2000) 216 F.3d 827.[108]

---

[107] Persons retaliated against for assisting or encouraging a disabled person in asserting their ADA rights have standing to complain and seek injunctive relief per section 503(a) and (b) [42 U.S.C. 12203] Per sections 51(f), 54(c) and 54.1(d) California Civil Code, any violation of the ADA may also be the basis for damages under sections 52 and 54.3.

Moreover, the Department of Justice took the position (filing an amicus brief in another case) that there is no notice requirement for Title III actions, and notice in California is a futile gesture by reason of the fact that the state Attorney General does not prosecute cases where a complainant is represented by counsel.

An excellent article was written by the late Professor Adam Milani, "Make My 90 Days: Should Plaintiff Be Required to Provide Notice to Defendants Before Filing Suit Under Title III of the Americans with Disabilities Act?" Wisconsin Law Review Vol. 2001, No. 1. (This article was written before Botosan, *supra*, was decided by the 9th Circuit.)

2. IN SKAFF V. MERIDIEN NORTH AMERICA BEVERLY HILLS, LLC, THE 9TH CIRCUIT HELD THERE IS NO PRE-SUIT NOTICE REQUIREMENT

   In Skaff V. Meridien North America Beverly Hills, LLC (9th Cir. 2007) 506 F.3d 832 at 846, the 9th Circuit held that,

   > the ADA requires neither that plaintiffs give defendants pre-suit notice that they intend to sue, nor that plaintiffs give defendants an opportunity to cure the alleged violation or violations before filing suit as a pre-requisite to recovering attorneys' fees.[109]

   (Botosan v. McNally Realty, et al. (9th Cir. 2000) 216 F.3d 827 had previously held there is no pre-suit requirement to notify any state or local agency as a prerequisite to filing a private lawsuit under the ADA.)

3. DEFENDANTS' FAILURE TO PLEAD THE "NOTICE" ISSUE UNDER § 2000a-3(c) MAY WAIVE THIS DEFENSE

   Although the factual basis of this "defense" (of not pleading "notice" and "exhaustion of administrative remedies") is evident from the face of the complaint, if a defendant fails to plead in its answer any such affirmative defense, and fails to plead any defense based on the specific code section, 42 U.S.C. § 2000a-3(c), the defendant may have waived these "defenses." (FRCP Rule 8(c); Wyshak v. City National Bank, 607 F.2d 824, 827 (D. Ariz. 1979) (Under Rule 8(c), a pleading must give fair notice of the defense).) On the other hand, defendants might continue to plead this defense to avoid

---

[108] Of the approximately twenty-five (25) courts which dealt with this issue prior to Botosan v. McNally Realty, twenty-one (21) held that Congress did not require any administrative notice or procedures to be "exhausted." Two of the "minority" courts holding otherwise later reversed their position. No court – except Snyder v. San Diego Flowers, 21 F.Supp.2d 1207; (S.D. Cal. 1998), in dicta - found any requirement to provide notice to the defendant. Further, the only "remedy" applied by even the "minority" courts was a sixty (60) day suspension of the proceedings while plaintiff made the requisite communication to government authorities. No court suggested dismissal of an action based on lack of pre-litigation notice, and none is required. (See discussion of Skaff, *supra*, and in section 2, hereinbelow.

[109] Plaintiff's attorney in the Skaff case was sole practitioner Sidney J. Cohen of Oakland. Sid was also successful co-counsel at trial and on appeal in Hankins v. El Torito, *supra*.

waiver and in hopes that either (1) the 9th Circuit will change its ruling; or (2) that a Congressional amendment to the ADA may add new requirements; or (3) that the U.S. Supreme Court might issue a ruling contrary to the 9th Circuit in Skaff.

4. PLAINTIFF COULD VOLUNTARILY PROVIDE WRITTEN NOTICE TO THE CALIFORNIA OR UNITED STATES ATTORNEY GENERAL'S OFFICES OR LOCAL OFFICIALS

Despite the lack of any "administrative remedy" or notice requirement, plaintiff could choose to write to the California or United States Attorney General, advising the Chief of the Civil Rights Division of the public issues of the lawsuit, and inviting the Attorney General's participation. (This is clearly no longer a requirement after Botosan v. McNally, *supra*, and the November 1, 2007 decision in Skaff V. Meridien North America Beverly Hills, LLC 506 F.3d 832 (9th Cir. 2007).

However an attorney handling an important public interest case might consider asking the attorney general office, or the local district attorney, city attorney,[110] or an advocacy group such as DRA, DREDF, or Disability Rights California for assistance or co-counseling in the appropriate case.[111]

5. THE CODE SECTION THAT DEFENDANTS USED TO RELY UPON, 42 USC § 2000a-3(c), IS NOT INCORPORATED INTO THE AMERICANS WITH DISABILITIES ACT OF 1990 (ADA)

Section 308(a)(1) of the ADA (42 USC 12188) provides:

> (1) AVAILABILITY OF REMEDIES AND PROCEDURES. —— The remedies and procedures set forth in section 204(a) of the Civil Rights Act of 1964 (42 U.S.C. 2000a-3(a)) are the remedies and procedures this title provides to any person who is being subjected to discrimination on the basis of disability in violation of this title or who has reasonable grounds for believing that such person is about to be subjected to discrimination in violation of section 303. Nothing in this section shall require a person with a disability to engage in a futile gesture if such person has actual notice that a person or organization covered by this title does not intend to comply with its provisions. (Emphasis added)

Thus only section 204(a) (subsection (a) of §2000a-3) is incorporated into the ADA; there is no incorporation of the subsection 3(c)), the notification section dealing with notification of matters in "Title II" actions. Therefore the issue of state and local enforcement proceedings is not included as part of the ADA.

Even under the specific language of § 2000a-3(c), the act alleged must be "prohibited

---

[110] See Civil Code section 55.1 and Health and Safety Code section 19958.

[111] [For possible legal resources, see Appendix F, *infra*.]

by this title [42 USCS §§ 2000a-2000a-6]." "This title" refers to Title II of the Civil Rights Act of 1964 dealing with racial discrimination, and requires notice to local and state enforcement authorities when there are state laws prohibiting these practices. There is no reference to the ADA or to disability discrimination in Title II.

Further, § 2000a-3(c) deals only when there is "a state or local law prohibiting such act or practice, and establishing or authorizing a state or local authority to grant or seek relief from such practice...However: (1) there is no provision directly under California law which allows a complaint for barrier removal on a "readily achievable" basis pursuant to § 301(9) of the ADA, alleged in this case; and (2) there is no authority in California for any state or local agency to enforce the ADA, although there is specific authority to enforce California's laws per section 55.1 Civil Code and section 19958 Health and Safety Code, inter alia. California Attorney General Dan Lungren issued an official opinion (July 14, 1993) which specifically stated that the California Attorney General's office and local building officials in California do not have the authority to enforce the "readily achievable" provisions of the ADA, and that enforcement is left to the U.S. Attorney General and to private litigants. [See Appendix IX-E-2. Opinion No. 93-203.]

Attorneys should also be aware that California Civil Code § 54(c), and 54.1(d) incorporate ADA violations and may be enforced by the District Attorney, the City Attorney, the Department of Rehabilitation or the California Attorney General who each "may bring an action to enjoin any violation of section 54 or 54.1." Civil Code section 55.1.

6. SEVERAL "PRE-BOTOSAN" DISTRICT COURTS IN CALIFORNIA REJECTED ANY NOTICE REQUIREMENT IN WELL-REASONED OPINIONS

Prior to Botosan, *supra*, multiple California federal court decisions were rejected any notice requirement, finding that § 2000a-3(c) was not incorporated into § 308(a)(1) of the ADA. For example, the May 4, 1999 opinion of Judge William B. Shubb of the Eastern District of California, in Heard v. Vagabond Inns, Inc., Case No. CIV-S-98-2085 WBS, and the August 9, 1999 opinion of Judge Thomas Whelan of the Southern District of California in Dennis Sharp v. Waterfront Restaurants, 1999 U.S. Dist. LEXIS 15376, gave well-reasoned decisions. In Heard Judge Shubb held that:

> This court adopts the majority view which finds the clear statutory language to indicate no exhaustion requirement. The Department of Justice's regulations do not support a conclusion that the language of 42 U.S.C. §12188(a) is ambiguous. First 28 C.F.R. §36.501 incorporates

the language of subsection 2000a-3(c) without incorporating any other subsections of 2000a-3. Second, the attorney's fee provision of 28 C.F.R. §36.505 does not imply the ADA's inclusion of subsection 2000a-3(b), because the ADA itself explicitly allows for attorney's fees in 42 U.S.C. §12205.

But most importantly, the language of the statute is clear and unambiguous. 42 U.S.C. §12188(a) incorporates subsection 2000a-3(a) specifically. It makes no mention of the other subsections. Likewise, subsection 2000a-3(a) does not mention subsection (c) and can be applied independently of subsection (c). Finally, subsection 2000a-3(c) itself limits its application to cases of alleged acts or practices prohibited by the public accommodations provision of Title VII. Had Congress desired subsection 2000a-3(c) to apply to the ADA, it certainly could [have] written or amended the statutes explicitly to do so.

Most of the cases dealing with this issue were analyzed by Judge Shubb in the Heard case:
> Only a handful of courts have addressed the applicability of subsection 2000a-3(c) to Title III of the ADA. The majority view is that subsection 2000a-3(c) does not apply, because Congress unambiguously specified that the remedies and procedures set forth in subsection 2000a-3. [Citations omitted.] Applying the rule of statutory construction "expressio unis est exclusio alterius," these courts reasoned that to read 42 U.S.C. §12188(a) as incorporating all of section 2000a-3, including the administrative exhaustion requirement of subsection (c), "is to impermissibly render superfluous the explicit textual reference to §2000a-3(a)." [Citation omitted.] (Id. at pp. 3-4.)

Judge Whelan in the Sharp case, *supra*, concluded:
> In this case, Congress' decision to draft ADA §308(a)(1) to selectively incorporate subsection (a) of §2000e-3 suggests that it did not intend to incorporate any other subsection of §2000e-3, including the administrative notification requirements contained in subsection (c). Had Congress intended to require administrative notification under Title III of the ADA, it could have (1) drafted ADA §3-8(a)(1) to specifically incorporate subsection (c) (or all) of §2000e-3, (2) repeated the language of subsection (c) within ADA §308, or (3) enacted a separate statute governing administrative notification. See Proffer v. Columbia Tower, No. 98-CV-1404 K (AJB) at 5 (S.D.Cal. Mar.3, 1999) ("In effect, defendants' interpretation of the ADA would render Congress' explicit reference to §2000e-3(a) superfluous."). The selective incorporation of §2000e-3(a), the ADA's conspicuous silence on the issue of administrative notification, and the overall comprehensiveness of the ADA's statutory scheme all suggest that Congress had no intention of requiring plaintiffs to notify any state agency before commencing private actions under Title III.

Sharp also found that the statute
> ... merely obviates the need for a disabled person to "engage in a futile gesture" if the disabled person has actual notice that the defendant will not comply with the ADA. The statute codifies and makes applicable to

private Title III ADA actions the "futile gesture" doctrine developed by the Supreme Court in International Brotherhood of Teamsters v. United States 431 U.S. 324, 97 S.Ct. 1843, 52 L.Ed.2d 396 (1977). ("International Brotherhood") In International Brotherhood, the Supreme Court held that a plaintiff can bring a Title VII action for employment discrimination even if he or she has not specifically sought employment with the defendant:

> If an employer should announce his policy of discrimination by a sign reading "Whites Only" on the hiring-office door, his victims would not be limited to the few who ignored the sign and subjected themselves to personal rebuffs... When a person's desire for a job is not translated into a formal application solely because of his unwillingness to engage in a futile gesture he is... a victim of discrimination... Id at 365-66, 97 S.Ct. at 1870. (Sharp, *supra*, at *11-12.)

The analogy to a "Whites Only" sign is particularly applicable to architectural barriers discrimination prohibited by ADA Title III. Forty six years ago the 1967 "Report of the National Commission on Architectural Barriers to Rehabilitation of the Handicapped" concluded:

> As clearly as "NO IRISH ALLOWED" and "WHITE ONLY" the stairways, narrow doors and sidewalk curbs of our society indicate to handicapped persons their exclusion from the centers of our social life.

7. COURTS SHOULD GIVE CONSIDERABLE WEIGHT TO THE ADMINISTRATIVE DETERMINATION BY THE DEPARTMENT OF JUSTICE THAT THE NOTICE REQUIREMENTS OF §2000a-3(c) DO NOT APPLY TO TITLE III ACTIONS UNDER THE ADA

The U.S. Department of Justice made the administrative determination that the notice requirements of § 2000a-3(c) do not apply to Title III actions under the ADA. In an amicus brief filed in Colorado Cross-Disability Coalition v. Nine West Group, Inc., USDC for the Dist. of Colorado, No. 96-WY-2492-AJ, the Department of Justice successfully convinced the court to reverse its position from an earlier case and find § 2000a-3(c) inapplicable to Title III.

8. DEFENDANTS CANNOT SHOW ANY PREJUDICE FROM LACK OF PRIOR NOTICE TO AN APPROPRIATE LOCAL AUTHORITY

While some "pre-Botosan" district Courts discussed the possible "value" of prior notice, no notice to a defendant is required. Even under § 2000a-§ 3(c) notice (from the Civil Rights Act of 1964) would only be required to the government agency, not to the defendant directly

Congress did indeed intentionally "create an incentive for attorneys to seek statutory fees" when it enacted § 505's attorney fee provisions as the only incentive for ADA lawsuits, as the ADA itself provides no monetary damages remedy. [See section IV, *infra*.]

In Skaff v. Meridien North America Beverly Hills, LLC (9th Cir. 2007) 506 F.3d 832, the 9th Circuit hopefully laid to rest any basis for the "no notice" defense. At p.14, "[W]e hold that the ADA does not require, either explicitly or by reference to another statute, that a plaintiff give notice of intention to sue before filing suit as a prerequisite to the recovery of attorneys' fees and costs."Id. at 845.

G. BOTH LANDLORD AND TENANT OF A BUSINESS PROPERTY REMAIN JOINTLY RESPONSIBLE TO A DISABLED PLAINTIFF REGARDLESS OF ANY INDEMNITY AGREEMENTS

42 USC § 12182(a) states that "any person who owns, leases (or leases to), or operates a place of public accommodation," is subject to the non-discrimination provisions of Title III of the ADA. The DOJ regulation CFR § 36.201(b) provides that both the landlord and the tenant are public accommodations under Title III and have full responsibility for complying with all provisions of Title III in the place of public accommodation. The only circumstance when a contract or lease between tenant and landlord may be relevant is in the allocation of responsibility for the corrections of the access deficiencies and who will pay the costs of the corrections per indemnity between defendants. The lease agreement will not affect the joint liability of both landlord and tenant to the plaintiff.

The DOJ Technical Assistance Manual clearly interprets § 12181(a) to mean that any allocation of responsibility under a lease agreement is only effective between the parties, and that landlords and tenants remain "fully liable" for all ADA violations. (TAM § III-1.2000; see, Independent Living Resources v. Oregon Arena Corp., 982 F.Supp. 698, supplemented, 1 F.Supp.2d 1159 (D. Org. 1998), and Botosan v. Fitzhugh, 13 F.Supp.2d 1047 (USDC S.Cal. 1998).)

> As stated in Independent Living Resources, *supra*,
> Both the landlord and the tenant are public accommodations and have full responsibility for complying with all ADA title III requirements applicable to that place of public accommodation. The title III regulation permits the landlord and the tenant to allocate responsibility, in the lease, for complying with particular provisions of the regulation. However, any allocation made in a lease or other contract is only effective as between the parties, and both landlord and tenant remain fully liable for compliance with all provisions of the ADA relating to that place of public accommodation. TAM § III-1.2000. (Id., at 767, 768.) [Emphasis added]
>
> Although a landlord and tenant can contractually allocate ADA responsibility between them, such an allocation is not binding on third parties. Accordingly, a tenant could not defend against a Title III suit on the ground that under its lease it was the landlord's duty to accommodate the disabled. Botosan v. Paul McNally Realty, 216 F.3d 827 (9th Cir. 2000).

H. LIABILITY OF LANDLORD AND TENANT FOR PLAINTIFF'S ATTORNEY FEES IS ALSO "JOINT AND SEVERAL"

Liability for attorney fees is a "joint and several" obligation of all liable defendants. Under both California and federal law, liability among defendants for a successful plaintiff's attorney fees is generally joint and several. Turner v. District of Columbia Bd. of Elections & Ethics,354 F.3d 890 (DC Cir. 2004); California Trout, Inc. v. Superior Court 218 CA3d 187, 212, 266 CR 788 (1990); Corder v. Gates, 947 F2d 374, 383 (9th Cir. 1991). It has also been specifically held proper for a court to award fees against one defendant for time litigating against another. Californians for Responsible Toxics Mgmt. v. Kizer, 211 CA3d 961, 976, 259 CR 599 (1989).

In Botosan v. McNally Realty, et al., *supra*, the 9th Circuit noted that the landlord and tenant had joint and several liability under Title III, and that,
> any allocation made in a lease or the contract is only effective as between the parties, and both landlord and tenant remain fully liable for compliance with all provisions of the ADA relating to that place of public accommodation.

Botosan v. McNally Realty, et al., 216 F.3d 827, 832 (9th Cir. 2000).

This case and this provision were cited by the Northern District Court in Kosloff v. Washington Square Assoc. 2007 WL2023497, in holding that defendants were "joint and severally liable for all compensation to plaintiff under the ADA including federally authorized attorney's fees." Kosloff, *supra*, was cited and followed by (former Chief) Judge Marilyn Hall Patel in Blackwell v. Foley, 724 F.Supp.2d 1068 (N.D. Cal, 2010) at 1075:

> **All Defendants, landlords and tenants, are jointly and severally liable for Plaintiff's attorney fees, litigation expenses and costs.**[112]
>
> Regardless of any indemnification agreement among themselves, all Defendants signed the Consent Decree; and all are jointly and severally responsible for Plaintiff's attorney fees. Landlord and tenant have joint and several responsibility to Plaintiff for violation of the ADA. Botosan v. McNally Realty, et al., 216 F.3d 827, 832 (9th Cir.2000), cited by the court in Kosloff v. Washington Square Assoc., 2007 WL 2023497, (N.D.Cal.2007) held that defendants were "joint and severally liable for all compensation to plaintiff under the ADA including federally authorized attorney's fees."
>
> Under both federal and California law, liability among defendants for a successful plaintiff's attorney fees is generally joint and several. Turner v. District of Columbia Bd. of Elections & Ethics, 354 F.3d 890 (D.C.Cir.2004); California Trout, Inc. v. Superior Court, 218 Cal.App.3d 187, 212, 266, 266 Cal. Rptr. 788 CR 788 (1990); Corder v. Gates, 947 F.2d 374, 383 (9th Cir.1991).

---

[112] Boldface in the Original

It has also been held proper for a court to award fees against one defendant for time spent litigating against another. Californians for Responsible Toxics Mgmt. v. Kizer, 211 Cal.App.3d 961, 976, 259 CR 599 (1989).

I. SERVICE ANIMALS HAVE SPECIFIC ADA PROTECTIONS

28 CFR 36.302(c)(1) The Department of Justice regulations set up to guide enforcement of the ADA specifies:

(c) Service animals--

(1) General. Generally, a public accommodation shall modify policies, practices, or procedures to permit the use of a service animal by an individual with a disability.

California Penal Code section 365.5(b) states,
No blind person, deaf person, or disabled person and his or her specially trained guide dog, signal dog, or service dog shall be denied admittance to accommodations, advantages, facilities, medical facilities, including hospitals, clinics, and physicians' offices, telephone facilities, adoption agencies, private schools, hotels, lodging places, places of public accommodation, amusement, or resort, and other places to which the general public is invited within this state because of that guide dog, signal dog, or service dog.

Violation of this requirement, or otherwise denying "full and equal access" to a blind or otherwise physically disabled person on the basis that they are accompanied by a qualified service animal, can be pled as the basis for a violation of California Civil Code section 52 (the Unruh Civil Rights Act) and of sections 54 and 54.1, California Civil Code, the Disabled Persons Act. If the circumstances justify, such denial may also be the basis for seeking treble damages under sections 52 and 54.3 Civil Code. Other statutes may also apply. (These examples are not meant to be exhaustive.) For example a policy of denying access for service animals may also violate ADA section 302(b)(2)(A)(ii): "failure to make reasonable modifications in policies, practices, or procedures when such modifications are necessary to afford such goods, services, facilities, privileges, advantages or accommodations to individuals with disabilities."

In Crowder v. Kitigawa, 81 F.3d 1480 (9th Cir. 1996), a facially "neutral" Hawaii state statute requiring a sixty day quarantine of all dogs brought into the State was held to have a discriminatory and disparate effect upon disabled persons when applied to a blind person's "service animal" (or seeing-eye dog). (Crowder also held that no "discriminatory intent" was needed for a violation of the ADA.)

[See Appendix, *infra*, § IX-G, for sample Complaint example, under California law and ADA Title III, in case where a service dog is excluded from a public accommodation.] [See also section I.J.9, *supra*, "Protections for Disabled Persons Assisted by Service Animals, including 2011 DOJ Regulations at section 35.136, "Service Animals"]

J. THE FEDERAL COURT SHOULD MAINTAIN SUPPLEMENTAL JURISDICTION WHERE STATE LAW CLAIMS ARE BASED ON THE SAME FACTS AS THE ADA CLAIM

In <u>O'Campo v. Chico Mall, LP</u>, 785 F.Supp. 2d 976 (E.D. Cal. 2010) the Court denied defendant's request that the Court sever and dismiss plaintiff's state law claims "and decline supplemental jurisdiction . . ." Id. at 985 (E.D. Cal. 2010). The Court noted,

> In this case, the federal and state claims turn on virtually identical facts and similar theories of liability. It appears to the court to be an inappropriate use of judicial resources to have the federal courts and the state courts simultaneously resolve cases with virtually identical facts. Consequently, the court shall exercise supplemental jurisdiction over the state law claims.

Id. (See also <u>Paulick v. Bavarian Lion Vineyard Dev., LLC</u>, C 08-04860 CW, 2009 WL 691123 (N.D. Cal. Mar. 10, 2009), also retaining federal court discretionary jurisdiction to avoid a waste of judicial resources.

K. THEATER "LINE OF SIGHT" CASES:
FEDERAL AND CALIFORNIA REQUIREMENTS

Theater seating requirements for disabled wheelchair users may be different for movie theaters versus "live" theaters: In movie theaters viewers can often have good viewing from seats at the rear of the theater, if properly located, with space for companion seating, etc. However, the front rows of most movie theaters are the worst seating in the house, particularly for "stadium style" seating, where people in the first few rows must crane their necks to see the screen at all, often a blur at close range. By contrast, most patrons of live performance theaters <u>want to be as close to the performers on stage as possible</u>, to see their faces, expressions and subtle movements. A seat at the rear of the theater is vastly inferior and is seen by disabled wheelchair users as analogous to the "back of the bus" in racial segregation situations from the 1950's and 1960's.

In actions involving "too close" front row seating for disabled persons in movie theaters, the date of construction has proven critical under federal law. A major class action under the ADA granting injunctive relief for nearly 2,000 theaters nationwide was reversed by the 9th Circuit in 2008 as overbroad, because the Court found that some defendants' due process rights were violated because defendants were not told the rules of building stadium style seating theaters until 1998, the date when the federal Department of Justice filed an amicus brief that advocated that ADAAG Regulations require comparable viewing angles. <u>U.S. v. AMC Entertainment, Inc</u>., 549 F.3d 760, 767 (2008). However, the injunction holding remained valid for theaters constructed in the 9th Circuit, where the "comparable viewing angles" issue had been decided by the 2003 decision in <u>Oregon Paralyzed Veterans of America v. Regal Cinemas, Inc.</u>, 339 F.3Rd 1126, 1133 (9th Cir. 2003), which found for the disabled plaintiffs:

In the theaters at issue in this case, wheelchair-bound movie theater patrons must sit in seats that are objectively uncomfortable, requiring them to crane their necks and twist their bodies in order to see the screen, while non-disabled patrons have a wide range of comfortable viewing locations from which to choose. We find it simply inconceivable that this arrangement could constitute "full and equal enjoyment" of movie theater services by disabled patrons. Yet, in rejecting DOJ's interpretation, this is precisely what the district court in this case held: No matter where in the theater the seats are, and no matter how sharp the viewing angle, so long as there is no physical object standing between the disabled patron and the screen, DOJ is not free to interpret its own regulation as requiring anything more.

We hold that DOJ's interpretation of "lines of sight comparable to those for members of the general public" in § 4.33.3 to require a viewing angle for wheelchair seating within the range of angles offered to the general public in the stadium-style seats is valid and entitled to deference. Accordingly, the judgment of the district court is reversed, and the case is remanded with instructions to enter summary judgment in favor of the plaintiffs on their ADA claim.

Id.

Alternatively, line of sight requirements of California law under Title 24 have been clear since 1989: the State Architect's interpretation of Title 24 regulations defined "a wheelchair seating space [as] a level area which is provided for persons confined to wheelchairs so that they can sit safely, comfortably, and view the presentation" and required "that these seating areas be integrated with general seating arrangements so that people with disabilities can sit with their able-bodied friends or family members." [Emphasis added.] (Title 24, section 611(b)(1)(A)(2), 1989.)

Each individual case will depend on when access-triggering construction and alterations occurred (since 1972, pursuant to Health & Safety Code § 19959 as to California law, and § 303 of the ADA after 1993). An alternative issue could be whether barrier removal is "readily achievable" under the ADA §§ 301(9) and 302(b)(2)(A)(iv). A consent decree and order which settled a relevant stadium seating "line of sight" case, Overbo and Brown-Booker v. Loews California Theatres, Inc., dba AMC Loews Metreon 16 IMAX, C07-5368 MHP, Docket No. 56 (N.D.Cal.), as to injunctive relief, is included, *infra*, in Appendix IX-I. In the San Francisco "Metreon" theater complex, most disabled seating in 16 stadium style seating theaters was located in the first row, instead of being dispersed throughout each theater. Plaintiffs alleged that defendants had violated California laws and Title-24 regulations by constructing a theater complex that did not disperse its wheelchair seating "so as to provide persons with disabilities a choice of ... line of sight comparable to those for members of the general public." [Emphasis added.] (Title 24, 1104B.3.5, "Placement of Wheelchair Locations.")

A separate California law basis for liability may be the failure of defendants to offer disabled persons seating in a "variety of locations." California Health & Safety Code § 19952(a), which applies to all facilities "for which a building permit or a building plan for new construction has been issued on or after January 1, 1985," (§ 19952(c)), requires such a "variety of locations":

> § 19952. Seating or accommodations in various locations within facility; removable seats; application; construction (a) Any person, or public or private firm, organization, or corporation, who owns or manages places of public amusement and resort including theaters, concert halls, and stadiums shall provide seating or accommodations for physically disabled persons in a variety of locations within the facility, to the extent that this variety can be provided while meeting fire and panic safety requirements of the State Fire Marshal, so as to provide these persons a choice of admission prices otherwise available to members of the general public.

An issue of some contention arises when plaintiffs request, on a "readily achievable" basis for privately owned theaters and on a Title II (government building and services) basis, changes at "live performance" theaters, where disabled seating is relegated to the last row. In spite of some difficult construction issues, alternate seating near the front was obtained by separate lawsuits against the three largest "live" theaters in San Francisco (the Orpheum, Golden Gate and Curran Theaters). It was also ordered at several publicly owned municipal theaters, including the Sacramento Community Center Theater (Stoffel v. City of Sacramento, (E.D. Cal. 2009) Consent Decree Order of November 24, 2009), and the Berkeley Community Theater (Rodriguez v. Live Nation, Berkeley Unified School District). Consent Decree Order of September 2, 2010. (N.D. Cal 2010)

IV. ATTORNEY FEES UNDER THE ADA
[SEE ALSO SECTIONS I - K, *Supra*, UNDER "CALIFORNIA STATUTORY ATTORNEY FEES"]

A. PREVAILING PARTY STANDARD RE: ATTORNEY FEES, LITIGATION EXPENSES AND COSTS TO A PREVAILING PLAINTIFF

1. ADA ATTORNEYS FEES, LITIGATION EXPENSES AND COSTS MAY BE AWARDED PER SECTION 505 [42 USC 12205]
Section 505 Attorneys Fees:

> In any action or administrative proceeding commenced pursuant to this chapter, the court or agency, in its discretion, may allow the prevailing party, other than the United States, a reasonable attorney's fee, including litigation expenses, and costs, and the United States shall be liable for the foregoing the same as a private individual.

> The Department of Justice Regulations: Title III [28 C.F.R. §36.505] repeat the identical language of ADA section 505. ADA § 505 of the allows recovery of costs and "litigation expenses," including expert witness expenses. (See DOJ Analysis, 28 CFR Pt. 36, App.B, §36.505, "Litigation expenses include items such as expert witness fees, travel expenses, etc.") Expert witness fees were also awarded per § 505 of the ADA in Chabner v. United of Omaha Life Ins. Co., U.S.D.C., C95-0447 MHP.

> [See also D'Lil v. Best Western, 538 F.3d 1031 (2008); Blackwell v. Foley, (N.D. Cal., 2010) 724 F.Supp 2d 1068, 1084-1085.

In February, 2008, the California Supreme Court reversed prior case law authority and held that there was no right for a plaintiff prevailing under California Code of Civil Procedure § 1021.5 to collect expert witness fees as part of his statutory attorney fees. (Olson v. Automobile Club of Southern California (2008) 42 Cal.4th 1142) However, such fees remain specifically recoverable under § 505 of the ADA [42 USC 12205]. Regulations enacted to implement § 505 have explicitly defined "litigation expenses" to include expert witness fees. [28 C.F.R. § 36.305. See also Judiciary Committee Report at 73.]

2. PREVAILING PARTY PLAINTIFF IS ENTITLED TO STATUTORY ATTORNEY FEES, WITHOUT ANY PRE-LITIGATION DEMAND, IF HE OBTAINED A COURT ENFORCEABLE SETTLEMENT AGREEMENT
A 2007 9th Circuit opinion (Skaff v. Meridien North America Beverly Hills, LLC, 506 F.3d 832 (9th Cir. 2007)), rejected several frequently claimed defenses, holding that a prevailing party who obtained damages and injunctive relief was entitled to

attorney fees despite the lack of a "pre-litigation demand," thereby rejecting the prior and contrary District Court holding of Doran v. Del Taco, Inc., et al. (C.D.Cal. 2005) 373 F.Supp.2d 1028 (which itself was reversed by the 9th Circuit at 524 F.3d 1034, discussed *infra*.). The Skaff court reiterated the proper standard in its f.n.12:

> Skaff is also a prevailing party under the ADA pursuant to Buckhannon, which held that "court-ordered consent decrees create the 'material alteration of the legal relationship of the parties' necessary to permit an award of attorney's fees." Buckhannon, 532 U.S. at 604 (quoting Tex. State Teachers Ass'n v. Garland Indep. Sch. Dist., 489 U.S. 782, 792-93 (1989)). Likewise, in Barrios v. California Interscholastic Federation, 277 F.3d 1128, 1134 (9th Cir.2002), we held that "[u]nder applicable Ninth Circuit law, a plaintiff 'prevails' when he or she enters into a legally enforceable settlement agreement against the defendant."

Id. at 844.

Skaff, *supra*, also held attorneys fees could not be denied because plaintiff had not given defendants "pre-suit notice that they intended to sue" or "an opportunity to cure the alleged violation ... before filing suit." Skaff at 846.

Barrios v. California Interscholastic Federation, et al. (9th Cir. 2002) 277 F. 3d 1128, an ADA case, reaffirmed plaintiff's right to full attorney fees after entering a federal court settlement for damages and injunctive relief. Barrios was followed in Richard S. v. Dept. of Developmental Services (9th Cir. 2003) 317 F.3d 1080, specifically holding that a court enforceable settlement agreement providing either payment of damages or enforceable injunctive relief satisfied requirements of Buckhannon Board & Care Home, Inc., et al. v. West Virginia Dept. of Health & Human Services, et al. (2001) 121 S.Ct. 1835. (See also Skaff v. Meridien North America Beverly Hills, LLC 506 F.3d 832 (9th Cir. 2007), to same effect, holding a plaintiff who obtained a court-enforceable settlement was, a prevailing party under the ADA pursuant to Buckhannon, which held that "court-ordered consent decrees create the 'material alteration of the legal relationship of the parties' necessary to permit an award of attorney's fees." Buckhannon, 532 U.S. at 604)"

Plaintiff is the prevailing party when he succeeds in obtaining major objectives of his lawsuit, including either or both (a) damages under California law; and/or (b) injunctive relief to make the public accommodation disabled accessible.

As outlined in an ADA Title III access case attorney fees decision by the Ninth Circuit (Fischer v. SJB-P.D., Inc., et al. (9th Cir. 2000) 214 F.3d 1115) and reaffirmed in Barrios, *supra*, the test is "Whether the plaintiff has obtained an enforceable judgment or settlement that requires the defendant to do something he otherwise would not have to do." (Id. at p.1118, emphasis added) In Fischer, an agreement to provide a "statement describing its policy of non-discrimination toward people with disabilities" (Id.) was held sufficient, even though no damages were paid. At p.1118, the court described the "prevailing party" test:

> Under the test articulated in Farrar v. Hobby, 506 U.S. 103, 111-12, "a plaintiff 'prevails' when actual relief on the merits of his claim materially alters the legal relationship between the parties by modifying the defendant's behavior in a way that directly benefits the plaintiff." The Court explained that "a material alteration of the legal relationship occurs [when] the plaintiff becomes entitled to enforce a judgment, consent decree, or settlement against the defendant. Id. at 113

B. GRAHAM V. DAIMLER-CHRYSLER PRESERVED "CATALYST" ATTORNEY FEES UNDER CALIFORNIA LAW, BUT ONLY UNDER NEW REQUIREMENT FOR A PRE-LITIGATION EFFORT TO SETTLE; NO PRE-LITIGATION EFFORT IS NEEDED WHEN PLAINTIFF IS THE PREVAILING PARTY

Although no pre-litigation demand is required for a prevailing plaintiff to earn attorneys fees under the ADA or under California law, in order to obtain "Catalyst" fees under section 1021.5 California Code of Civil Procedure, a pre-litigation demand is now required, per the California Supreme Court.

Graham v. DaimlerChrysler Corp. (2004) 34 Cal.4th 553 held that a plaintiffs could still earn "catalyst" attorney fees under California law, including Code of Civil Procedure § 1021.5, if they could show that they made a reasonable effort to settle before filing suit, and their lawsuit was the catalyst to cause the defendant to change its position (i.e., provide some of the relief sought), even if they did so before plaintiff obtained a "court enforceable" order. However, it did not require any pre-litigation efforts as a prerequisite for statutory attorney fees in any case in which the plaintiff was a "prevailing party." Skaff, *supra*, had been the prevailing party by obtaining a court ordered consent decree requiring provision of access, but the trial court erroneously held that he had additional obligations -including pretrial notice - which were not found in the statute. Skaff was sent back to the trial court by the 9th Circuit to obtain an attorney fees award.

Several previous cases held that there was no pre-litigation notice requirement as a prerequisite to filing an ADA Title III public accommodations lawsuit. (Botosan v. McNally Realty, et al. (9th Cir. 2000) 216 F.3d 827 and a majority of previous District Court opinions in California). One judge, who decided notice was still required as a condition for plaintiff to be awarded attorney fees, was reversed on this issue by the 9th Circuit in the Skaff case, *supra*.

However, the United States Supreme Court has held that no "Catalyst" fees can be awarded directly under federal law. In Buckhannon v. West Virginia Dept. of Health, (2001) 121 S.Ct 1835, the Court rejected the federal "Catalyst" theory (which had been accepted in 11 of the 12 federal circuits!) and instead held that a "material alteration of the legal relationship of the parties" was necessary to permit an award of attorneys fees. Buckhannon, *supra*, 121 S.Ct. 1835, 531 U.S. at 604.

C. PUBLIC POLICY CALLS FOR <u>ENCOURAGING</u> TITLE III ADA LAWSUITS

1. ADA TITLE III ENFORCEMENT IN CALIFORNIA BY PRIVATE LAWSUITS
   In 1993, the California Attorney General, Dan Lungren, issued an opinion that the ADA may be enforced <u>only</u> by the U.S. Department of Justice <u>and by private lawsuits</u>. (Opinion No. 93-203, July 14, 1993.) [See § IX (Appendix) E-2, *infra*.] Congress intended prosecution by private lawsuits to enforce ADA Title III. Only disabled persons have standing to sue. Rather than spend taxpayers' money by setting up a bureaucratic agency to enforce Title III access laws, Congress left enforcement (other than by the U.S. Department of Justice) to private lawsuits. Congress chose to use the right to recover attorney fees, litigation expenses and costs as the incentive for attorneys to be willing to handle such cases without having to opbtain fees from the (often low income) disabled plaintiffs. Without private lawsuits, public accommodations which still did not provide accessible facilities, would be able to continue to do so in perpetuity. The contingent fee basis for an attorneys fee - statutory in civil rights cases (and on a percentage basis in personal injury lawsuits) remains the "poor man's key to the courthouse." Otherwise only those persons rich enough to pay lawyers on an hourly basis could afford the cost of hiring competent counsel.

   Similarly, under California law, a building inspector's <u>failure</u> to properly enforce the law has been the background for many of the reported cases which required provision of access (San Francisco v. Grant Co., *supra*; People ex rel. Deukmejian v. CHE, Inc.(1983) 150 Cal.App.3d 123; Donald v. Cafe Royale (1990) 218 Cal.App.3d 168, *supra*; Donald v. Sacramento Valley Bank (1989) 209 Cal.App.3d 1183). Disabled persons would forever be unable to use inaccessible public facilities unless <u>someone</u> with "standing" was willing to risk bringing a lawsuit.[113]

2. ENTITLEMENT TO REASONABLE ATTORNEY FEES EVEN WHEN DAMAGES AWARDED ARE MINIMAL
   In Donald v. Cafe Royale, *supra*, the trial court refused to award damages to a disabled plaintiff (who was himself an attorney), the court "finding" <u>factually</u> that plaintiff had suffered <u>no</u> emotional distress. (Apparently the trial court believed that disabled persons

---

[113] For that reason, "good faith" civil rights plaintiffs -including disabled persons suing under the ADA- should not face the threat of attorney fees or costs being awarded against them.

who are attorneys don't suffer emotional distress when they face discrimination!) The appellate court, inter alia, reversed the legal rulings of the trial court, but rather than order a new trial on damages, ordered an award for plaintiff of statutory minimum damages, per Civil Code § 54.3 (because the appellate court was forced to accept the trial court's factual findings that plaintiff suffered no emotional distress) and awarded plaintiff statutory attorney fees per Civil Code § 54.3.

"Standing to sue" in federal court is not dependant upon the right to recover damages, especially as ADA Title III does not include a damages remedy. (See Skaff v. Meridien, *supra*.)

While Congress did not provide a damages remedy for violation of Title III of the ADA, it did provide for recovery of statutory attorney fees, litigation expenses and costs: without damages, there would be no incentive for disabled persons to bring a suit if they also had to pay for their own lawyer! A defendant's cost of paying plaintiff's attorney fees in an ADA action was Congress' economic incentive for a business to promptly provide access. (See ADA § 505, and related DOJ Regulations.)

3. **ADA PLAINTIFFS ARE ENFORCING THE PUBLIC INTEREST, SEEKING TO VINDICATE A POLICY OF THE "HIGHEST PRIORITY"**
   Civil rights lawyers should be aware that they may face personal attacks as attorneys for disabled plaintiffs, and attacks on their right to seek attorney fees. These are efforts to discourage attorneys from handling ADA actions and, if aggravated enough, may violate the spirit and letter of § 503's prohibition against retaliation. Relevant here is Chief Judge Thelton Henderson's policy statement in Walker v. Carnival, (N.D. Cal.), where Judge Henderson emphasized that plaintiffs
   > who bring suit pursuant to the ADA do so in the role of "private attorneys general" who seek to vindicate "a policy 'of the highest priority'."... [S]uccessful ADA plaintiffs confer a tremendous benefit upon our society at large, in addition to the attainment of redress for their personal individual injuries...

   Walker, *supra*,107 F.Supp. 2d 1135, 1143)

The lessons of the racial civil rights movement in the United States, and the legal as well as physical attacks on civil rights lawyers and activists - particularly those in Southern states during the 1950s, 1960s and 1970s - should be a reminder that those who oppose equal rights for minorities have historically attacked the motivations of those who have used the courts to enforce civil rights.

In Kittok v. Leslie's Pool Mart, Inc., (E.D. Cal.) 687 F.Supp. 2d 953, at 960, the Court noted that the California legislature had also chosen private lawsuits and the prospect

of plaintiff's attorneys earning statutory fees as the <u>best way to enforce</u> disabled rights:
> The attorney fee provision of the DPA is reflective of the California "legislature's awareness of the continuous problems of enforcement" of disability access laws. <u>Donald v. Café Royale, Inc.</u>, 218 Cal.App.3d 168, 179, 266 Cal.Rptr. 804 (1990). In explicitly providing for the recovery of attorney's fees, even though the DPA does not require a showing of damages, the California legislature explicitly determined that there is a societal value to the vindication of the rights at issue here.

The recent <u>Fox v. Vice</u> unanimous U.S. Supreme Court case, 131 S.Ct. 2205 (2011), while largely concerned with delineating a "but for" test, (that a court could award fees <u>against</u> a civil rights plaintiff <u>only</u> for work necessitated solely to contest frivolous claims) also reiterated that a plaintiff need not be victorious on every claim in order to earn fees for "time his attorney reasonably spent in achieving the favorable outcome":
> [W]e have made clear that plaintiffs may receive fees under § 1988 even if they are not victorious on every claim. <u>A civil rights plaintiff who obtains meaningful relief has corrected a violation of federal law and, in so doing, has vindicated Congress's statutory purposes</u>. That "result is what matters," we explained in Hensley v. Eckerhart, 461 U.S. 424, 435, 103 S.Ct. 1933, 76 L.Ed.2d 40 (1983): <u>A court should compensate the plaintiff for the time his attorney reasonably spent in achieving the favorable outcome, even if "the plaintiff failed to prevail on every contention."</u> Ibid. The fee award, of course, should not reimburse the plaintiff for work performed on claims that bore no relation to the grant of relief: Such work "cannot be deemed to have been expended in pursuit of the ultimate result achieved." Ibid. (internal quotation marks omitted). But the presence of these unsuccessful claims does not immunize a defendant against paying for the attorney's fees that the plaintiff reasonably incurred in remedying a breach of his civil rights.

Fox v. Vice, 131 S. Ct. 2205, 2214, 180 L. Ed. 2d 45 (2011)(Emphasis added)

4. ADA § 503 PROTECTS BOTH DISABLED PERSONS AND THEIR REPRESENTATIVES AGAINST RETALIATION OR INTIMIDATION

Section 503 of the ADA (42 USC § 12203) prohibits retaliation, interference, coercion and intimidation against disabled litigants and against their lawyers, or others who have "aided or encouraged" their exercise of their ADA rights.

SEC. 503. PROHIBITION AGAINST RETALIATION AND COERCION

(a) RETALIATION. - No person shall discriminate against an individual because such individual has opposed any act or practice made unlawful by this Act or because such individual made a charge, testified, assisted, or participated in any manner in an investigation, proceeding, or hearing under this Act.

(b) INTERFERENCE, COERCION, OR INTIMIDATION. - It shall be unlawful to coerce, intimidate, threaten, or interfere with any individual in the exercise or enjoyment of, or on account of his or her having exercised or enjoyed, or on account of his or her having aided or encouraged any other individual in the exercise or enjoyment of, any right granted or protected by this Act.

(c) REMEDIES AND PROCEDURES - The remedies and procedures available under sections 107, 203 and 308 of the Act shall be available to aggrieved persons for violations of subsections (a) and (b), with respect to title I, title II and title II, respectively.

Especially since ADA § 505 and the D.O.J. Regulations implementing this statute make clear that attorney fees can not be recovered against a "good faith" ADA plaintiff (i.e., in the absence of a plaintiff's fraudulent or frivolous action), and specifically incorporate the "Christiansburg" principles [DOJ Regulation 28 CFR 36.305, and Christiansburg Garment Co. v. EEOC, 434 U.S. 412, 417, 98 S.Ct. 694, 698], any threat to seek attorney fees against a "good faith" plaintiff may itself be a violation of § 503.

Lawyers should be careful in negotiating settlements not to agree to confidentiality terms which may prohibit telling other civil rights lawyers the results of previous litigation, or prohibit assisting or encouraging other disabled persons in potential ADA litigation against a defendant's other inaccessible properties. [See also section III-C-5, *supra*, re: discovery as a possible section 503 violation.]

D. ADA TITLE III PLAINTIFFS ARE ACTING AS "PRIVATE ATTORNEYS GENERAL" IN THE PUBLIC INTEREST

Particularly when a defendant makes an attack upon a plaintiff for bringing an action, plaintiff should respond by citing § 503, and also emphasize the role that plaintiff is taking in seeking injunctive relief as a "private attorney general." The public interest will suffer if disabled persons willing to be private attorneys general are needlessly and unfairly subjected to personal abuse and harassment in violation of their rights. In a seminal case involving cruise ship acess, Walker and Adams v. Carnival Cruise Lines, et al. (2000) 107 F.Supp.2d 1135, former Chief Judge Thelton Henderson of the Northern District explained why disabled persons who file lawsuits under the ADA are acting in the public interest enforcing Congressional policy, and confer a "tremendous benefit upon society":

This Court is persuaded that enforcing defendants' forum selection clause, under the circumstances presented here, would contravene the strong national policy of eradicating disability discrimination and promoting full and equal access to the legal system for civil rights plaintiffs. There can be no question that the Americans With Disabilities Act, passed in 1990, established as law the nation's interest in eradicating the bigotry and barriers faced by individuals with disabilities. 42 U.S.C. § 12102 et. seq. (hereafter "ADA"). In fact, the ADA states its first goal as being "to provide a clear and comprehensive national mandate for the elimination of discrimination against individuals with disabilities." See 42 U.S.C. §12101(b)(1)(1999). The ADA creates the possibility that successful plaintiffs may establish permanent changes in the design and physical configuration of structures to better accommodate the disabled. 42 U.S.C. § 12101(a)(5). The benefits of such changes clearly redound not only to the plaintiffs themselves, but to similarly situated disabled persons, and the entire society at large. As a result, plaintiffs or plaintiff classes who bring suit pursuant to the ADA do so in the role of "private attorneys general" who seek to vindicate "a policy 'of the highest priority'." See Christiansburg Garment Co. v. EEOC, 434 U.S. 412, 417, 98 S.Ct. 694, 698. See also Bruce v. City Of Gainesville, Ga., 177 F.3d 949, 951 (11th Cir. 1999) (discussing ADA plaintiffs as private attorneys general); Rosenberg v. Merrill Lynch, Pierce, Fenner & Smith, Inc., 170 F.3d 1, 11 (1st Cir. 1999).

For example, successful ADA plaintiffs confer a tremendous benefit upon our society at large, in addition to the attainment of redress for their personal individual injuries, successful ADA plaintiffs, like plaintiffs under Title VII, are entitled to 42 U.S.C. section 1988's fee shifting provision. See 42 U.S.C. §1988. As the Eleventh Circuit recently has explained,

"[i]n Title VII cases as well as cases under the ADA, the enforcement of civil rights statutes by plaintiffs as private attorneys general is an important part of the underlying policy behind the law. Such a policy ensures an incentive for 'impecunious' plaintiffs, who can ill afford to litigate their claims against defendants with more resources ...
Bruce v. City of Gainesville, Ga., 177 F.3d 949, 951 (11th Cir. 1999) (citing Fogerty v. Fantasy Inc., 510 U.S. 517, 524, 114 S.Ct. 1023, 127 L.Ed.2d 455 (1994) as "declining to apply Christiansburg to cases under the Copyright Act because unlike the civil rights context, both the plaintiffs and defendants can 'run the gamut from corporate behemoths to starving artists.'").

Because the promotion of equal treatment and equal access is a value of paramount importance, it is appropriate for courts to use a more piercing scrutiny when considering the enforcement of a forum selection clause in a civil rights law suit. This Court is not the first to follow such a proposition.

In RedBull Assoc. v. Best Western, Inc., plaintiff Red Bull hotel chain asserted that the Best Western Inc. had canceled its affiliation with the chain based upon the race of many of Red Bull's tenants. RedBull Assoc. v. Best Western, Inc., 686 F.Supp. 447 (S.D.N.Y. May 17, 1988), affd' 862 F.2d 963, 967 (2d Cir. 1988). The district court refused to enforce an otherwise valid, exclusive forum selection clause and transfer the case to Arizona based in large part upon the "plaintiffs' role as 'private attorneys general' carrying out important community civil rights imperatives." RedBull, 862 F.2d at 965. The Second Circuit affirmed the district court's refusal to enforce the clause as it would frustrate enforcement of a civil rights statute, specifically Title VII. The Second Circuit explained that
> [The district court] correctly followed a strong federal public policy favoring enforcement of the civil rights laws so important to the

advancement of modern society and concluded that implementation of the forum selection clause would frustrate that purpose. While individuals are free to regulate their purely private disputes by means of contractual choice of forum, we cannot adopt a per se rule that gives these private arrangements dispositive effect where the civil rights laws are concerned ... [t]he existence of a forum selection clause cannot preclude the district court's inquiry into the public policy ramifications of transfer decisions.

Walker, *supra*, 107 F.Supp.2d 1135, 1143, citing Red Bull, 862 F.2d at 967.

Finding that enforcement of the cruise ship contract's forum selection clause might preclude two quadriplegic disabled ADA plaintiffs from being able (to travel to Florida) to attend their own trial, the Court held that this might "do nothing less than re-victimize these plaintiffs" (Id, at 1145, emphasis in original), and kept the case in federal court in San Francisco. After rulings by the Court rejected several defense motions to dismiss, (including the allegation that the "readily achievable" language of the ADA did not apply to cruise ships, especially foreign flag cruise ships) the parties reached a settlement by which the "Holiday" cruise ship was made fully accessible by defendants. Settlement in a "companion" class action - filed by attorney Matthew Dietz in Florida after Walker was filed in California but stayed by the Florida federal court pending litigation of related issues in Walker - resulted in Carnival's agreement to improve access on fourteen other Carnival cruise ships which docked in American ports.

E. "LAWYERS MUST EAT" - ENFORCEMENT OF CIVIL RIGHTS DEPENDS ON ADEQUATE ATTORNEY FEES AWARDS

In a classic statement of the practical necessity for adequate attorney fees awards if the Congressional wish for private enforcement of civil rights statutes is to be met, 9th Circuit Chief Judge Alex Kozinski recently issued an opinion stressing the importance of adequate attorney fee awards:

Lawyers must eat, so they generally won't take cases without a reasonable prospect of getting paid. Congress thus recognized that private enforcement of civil rights legislation relies on the availability of fee awards: "If private citizens are to be able to assert their civil rights, and if those who violate the Nation['s] fundamental laws are not to proceed with impunity, then citizens must have the opportunity to recover what it costs them to vindicate these rights in court." S.Rep. No. 94-1011, at 2 (1976), as reprinted in 1976 U.S.C.C.A.N. 5908, 5910. FN1

Moreno v. City of Sacramento (9th Cir. 2008) 534 F.3d 1106, at 1111. (Emphasis added)

Footnote 1 reemphasized the importance of a fee award:

FN1 Congress emphasized the importance of attorneys' fees in cases seeking injunctive relief, where there is no monetary light at the end of the litigation tunnel: "If successful plaintiffs were routinely forced to bear their own attorneys' fees, few aggrieved parties would be in a position to advance the public interest by invoking the injunctive powers of the Federal courts." S.Rep. No. 94-1011, at 3 (1976), as reprinted in 1976 U.S.C.C.A.N. 5908, 5910.

This opinion also warned against various excuses for reducing a plaintiff's fee award, and the necessity for the court to explain its reasoning:

> When the district court makes its award, it must explain how it came up with the amount. The explanation need not be elaborate, but it must be comprehensible. As Hensley described it, the explanation must be "concise but clear." 461 U.S. at 437, 103 S.Ct. 1933 (emphasis added). Where the difference between the lawyer's request and the court's award is relatively small, a somewhat cursory explanation will suffice. But where the disparity is larger, a more specific articulation of the court's reasoning is expected. See Bogan v. City of Boston, 489 F.3d 417, 430 (1st Cir.2007). We review the legal principles underlying the fee award de novo. Ferland v. Conrad Credit Corp., 244 F.3d 1145, 1148 (9th Cir.2001).

> Id., at 1111-1112.

The Moreno court also explained why courts should normally defer to the winning lawyer's professional judgment as to what work was "necessary" to spend on winning the case:

> It must also be kept in mind that lawyers are not likely to spend unnecessary time on contingency fee cases in the hope of inflating their fees. The payoff is too uncertain, as to both the result and the amount of the fee. It would therefore be the highly atypical civil rights case where plaintiff's lawyer engages in churning. By and large, the court should defer to the winning lawyer's professional judgment as to how much time he was required to spend on the case; after all, he won, and might not have, had he been more of a slacker.

> Id., at 1112. (Emphasis added)

As to reducing fees because of possible "duplicative work when several attorneys work together on one case, Moreno noted some duplication may be necessary and reasonable and should be compensated:

> One certainly expects some degree of duplication as an inherent part of the process. There is no reason why the lawyer should perform this necessary work for free.

> Id. at 1112. (Emphasis added.)

The burden is upon defendants to show any "unreasonable" use of plaintiff's attorney's time:

Defendants complain that such time was spent unreasonably, but they fail to identify any specific time entries representing work that was unnecessary to respond to Defendants' strong and comprehensive opposition to Plaintiffs' fee request. Defendants cannot be allowed to "litigate tenaciously and then be heard to complain about the time necessarily spent by the plaintiff in response." Serrano IV, 32 Cal.3d at 638, 186 Cal.Rptr. 754, 652 P.2d 985 (citations omitted).

Coles v. City of Oakland, 2007 WL 39304 (N.D. Cal.) At p.*11.

F. FEES MUST BE SET AT MARKET RATES USING "MORALES" FACTORS: PLAINTIFF'S ATTORNEY FEE RATES MUST BE BASED ON THE ATTORNEYS' EDUCATION, EXPERIENCE AND LEGAL SKILLS

As recently summarized in Blackwell v. Foley, *supra*, 724 F.Supp. 2d 1068, at 1081:
In determining plaintiff's counsel's reasonable hourly rate, the Court must take into account the following factors:

1) the time and labor required, (2) the novelty and difficulty of the questions involved, (3) the skill requisite to perform the legal service properly, (4) the preclusion of other employment by the attorney due to acceptance of the case, (5) the customary fee, (6) whether the fee is fixed or contingent, (7) time limitations imposed by the client or the circumstances, (8) the amount involved and the results obtained, (9) the experience, reputation, and ability of the attorneys, (10) the "undesirability" of the case, (11) the nature and length of the professional relationship with the client, and (12) awards in similar cases.

Morales v. City of San Rafael 96 F.3d 359, (9th Cir.1996), citing Kerr v. Screen Guild Extras, Inc., 526 F.2d 67, 70 (9th Cir.1975) cert. denied, 425 U.S. 951, 96 S.Ct. 1726, 48 L.Ed.2d 195 (1976).

As stated by the Court in Lindy Bros. Builders v. American Radiator (3rd Cir. 1976) 540 F.2d 102, at 117:

As a first principle, the court must recognize that a consideration of "quality" inheres in the "lodestar" award: counsel who possess or who are reputed to possess more experience, knowledge and legal talent generally command hourly rates superior to those who are less endowed.

Id.

Moreno, *supra*, also held rates must be set at prevailing market rates with no artificial "cap" set by local practice. Moreno reaffirmed the Hensley factors in setting rates:"

The hourly rate for successful civil rights attorneys is to be calculated by considering certain factors, including the novelty and difficulty of the issues, the skill required to try the case, whether or not the fee is contingent, the experience held by counsel and fee awards in similar cases. See Hensley, 461 U.S. at 430 n. 3, 103 S.Ct. 1933 (citing Johnson v. Georgia Highway Express, Inc., 488 F.2d 714 (5th Cir.1974)).

Moreno, at 1114.

Even before the 2008 Moreno decision, *supra*, at least one 9th Circuit case had questioned whether the 1975 Kerr factors were still the essential considerations in the Ninth Circuit, as noted in Yahoo!, Inc. v. Net Games, Inc., 329 F.Supp.2d 1179, 1182 (N.D.Cal. 2004):

> Before the lodestar method was developed, the Ninth Circuit applied the twelve-factor test set forth in Kerr v. Screen Guild Extras, Inc., 526 F.2d 67, 70 (9th Cir.1975), to determine attorney fee awards in fee-shifting cases. The lodestar method greatly simplified this analysis by limiting the court's consideration to two factors: the reasonableness of the number of hours and the reasonableness of the hourly rate. In sifting through the remains of the Kerr factors, courts have determined that at least five of the Kerr factors have been deemed "subsumed in the initial lodestar calculation." Morales v. City of San Rafael, 96 F.3d 359, 363–64 (9th Cir.1996). These factors include "(1) the novelty and complexity of the issues, (2) the special skill and experience of counsel, (3) the quality of representation, * * * (4) the results obtained, and (5) the contingent nature of the fee agreement." Id. at 364 n. 9 (internal quotation and citations omitted; alteration in original). Although the subsumed Kerr factors might be helpful in analyzing reasonableness under the lodestar method, the analysis must now focus on what constitutes a reasonable attorney fee in light of case law subsequent to Kerr. See Fischer v. SJB–PD, Inc., 214 F.3d 1115, 1119 n. 3 (9th Cir.2000). (Emphasis added.)

Therefore, the Court's analysis should focus on whether Plaintiff's attorneys' hourly rates are reasonable under current standards, and whether the hours claimed are reasonable.[114]

G. A COURT SHOULD NOT "SECOND GUESS" PLAINTIFF'S "STAFFING DECISIONS"
While it is appropriate to consider the skill required to perform a task, Hensley, 461 U.S. at 430 n. 3, 103 S.Ct. 1933, the district court may not set the fee based on speculation as to how other firms would have staffed the case. . . . Modeling law firm economics drifts far afield of the Hensley calculus and the statutory goal of sufficiently compensating counsel in order to attract qualified attorneys to do civil rights work. . . . The court may permissibly look to the hourly rates charged by comparable attorneys for similar work, <u>but may not attempt to impose its own judgment regarding the best way to operate a law firm, nor to determine if different staffing decisions might have led to different fee requests</u>. The difficulty and skill level of the work performed, and the result achieved-<u>not whether it would have been cheaper to delegate the work to other attorneys</u>-must drive the district court's decision. (Emphasis added)
Moreno v. City of Sacramento, 534 F.3d 1106 (9th Cir. 2008), at 1114-1115.

---

[114] Among recent decisions setting ADA attorney fees in the Northern District (in a difficult prison rights case) based on the number of years in practice, see Armstrong v. Brown 2011 WL 3443922 (Order of August 8, 2011).

H. NO ATTORNEY FEES CAN BE AWARDED AGAINST A "GOOD FAITH" CIVIL RIGHTS PLAINTIFF (CHRISTIANSBURG RULE) [AT LEAST UNDER FEDERAL LAW]

1. CHRISTIANSBURG RULE IS INCORPORATED INTO § 505 OF THE ADA
   The attorney's fee provision of the ADA allows the court to award a prevailing private party "a reasonable attorney's fee, including litigation expenses, and costs." 42 U.S.C. § 12205 (emphasis added). Attorney's fees under § 12205 should be awarded to a prevailing defendant only if "'the plaintiff's action was frivolous, unreasonable, or without foundation.'" Summers v. A. Teichert & Son, Inc., 127 F.3d 1150, 1154 (9th Cir.1997) (quoting Christiansburg Garment Co. v. EEOC, 434 U.S. 412, 421, 98 S.Ct. 694, 54 L.Ed.2d 648 (1978))

   Brown v. Lucky Stores, Inc. (2001) 246 F.3d 1182, 1190

In the landmark case of Christiansburg Garment Co. v. Equal Employment Opportunity Comm. (1978) 434 U.S. 412, 98 S.Ct. 694, 1978 U.S. Lexis 148, the United States Supreme Court explained the public policy reasons why a prevailing defendant should not be awarded attorney fees against a losing civil rights plaintiff, unless the court finds that plaintiff's "claim was frivolous, unreasonable or groundless, or that the plaintiff continued to litigate after it clearly became so." (Id. at 422)

In so ruling, the court emphasized that,
... there are at least two strong equitable considerations counseling an attorney's fee award to a prevailing Title VII plaintiff that are wholly absent in the case of a prevailing Title VII defendant.

First, ... the plaintiff is the chosen instrument of Congress to vindicate "a policy that Congress considered of the highest priority."... Second, when a district court awards counsel fees to a prevailing plaintiff, it is awarding them against a violator of federal law. ... "[T]hese policy considerations which support the award of fees to a prevailing plaintiff are not present in the case of a prevailing defendant."
Id. at 418-419.

In setting out its rule that fees would only be awarded against a plaintiff whose claim was "frivolous, unreasonable or groundless," as well as brought "in bad faith," the court warned against applying "hindsight logic" against a plaintiff who "did not ultimately prevail," as "this kind of hindsight logic could discourage all but the most airtight claims, for seldom can a prospective plaintiff be sure of ultimate success." (Id. at 422.)

Because of the importance of this issue, and the public policy not to discourage legitimate civil rights lawsuits by the threat of an adverse attorney fees award, the reasoning behind the Christiansburg court's holding is worth repeating here:

... In sum, a district court may in its discretion award attorney's fees to a prevailing defendant in a Title VII case upon a finding that the plaintiff's action was frivolous, unreasonable, or without foundation, even though not brought in subjective bad faith.

In applying these criteria, it is important that a district court <u>resist the understandable</u> <u>temptation to engage in post hoc reasoning by concluding that, because a plaintiff did not ultimately prevail, his action must have been unreasonable or without foundation. This kind of hindsight logic could discourage all but the most airtight claims, for seldom can a prospective plaintiff be sure of ultimate success.</u> No matter how honest one's belief that he has been the victim of discrimination, no matter how meritorious one's claim may appear at the outset, the course of litigation is rarely predictable. Decisive facts may not emerge until discovery or trial. The law may change or clarify in the midst of litigation. Even when the law or the facts appear questionable or unfavorable at the outset, a party may have an entirely reasonable ground for bringing suit. That § 706 (k) allows fee awards only to prevailing private plaintiffs should assure that this statutory provision will not in itself operate as an incentive to the bringing of claims that have little chance of success. <u>To take the further step of assessing attorney's fees</u> against plaintiffs simply because they do not finally prevail would substantially add <u>to the risks inhering in most litigation and would undercut the efforts of Congress</u> to promote the vigorous enforcement of the provisions of Title VII. Hence, a plaintiff should not be assessed his opponent's attorney's fees unless a court finds that his <u>claim was frivolous, unreasonable, or groundless, or that the plaintiff continued to</u> litigate after it clearly became so. And, needless to say, if a plaintiff is found to have brought or continued such a claim in bad faith, there will be an even stronger basis for charging him with the attorney's fees incurred by the defense.

Id. at 421-422. (Emphasis added)

2. RULE ALSO APPLIES TO LITIGATION EXPENSES AND COSTS IN 9TH CIRCUIT (<u>BROWN V. LUCKY STORES</u>)

In <u>Brown v. Lucky Stores, Inc.</u> (9th Cir. 2001) 246 F.3d 1182, at 1190, the court held that, "Because § 12205 makes fees and costs parallel, we hold that the <u>Christiansburg</u> test also applies to an award of costs to a prevailing defendant under the ADA." Thus neither attorney fees nor costs can be awarded against a "good faith" ADA plaintiff. (The same principles should apply to any civil rights "good faith" action under state law, but this is less clearly affirmed to date.) In <u>Jankey v. Lee</u>, *supra*, the California Supreme Court upheld attorney fees under California Civil Code section 55 against a good faith plaintiff. Further challenges of this ruling are expected. [See <u>Fox v. Vice</u>, *infra*, section IV-J a 2011 unanimous U.S. Supreme Court Decision]

3. THE DEPARTMENT OF JUSTICE SECTION-BY-SECTION ANALYSIS: TITLE III [28 C.F.R. PT. 36, APP. B, §36.505] CLARIFIES THAT "LITIGATION EXPENSES" INCLUDE EXPERT WITNESS FEES AND TRAVEL EXPENSES, AND THAT PLAINTIFFS ARE PROTECTED BY THE "CHRISTIANBURG" STANDARDS

In § 505 of the ADA and in the Department of Justice Regulations: Title III [28 CFR §36.505] both Congress and the Department of Justice have specified the recovery of attorney fees to the "prevailing party" in an ADA action. However, in the Department of Justice section-by-section analysis: Title III [28 CFR pt 36, App. B, §36.505] the D.O.J. specified that such fees:

> will be assessed against a plaintiff only under the standard set forth in Christiansburg Garment Company v. EEOC, (1978) 434 US 412: Section 36.505 states that courts are authorized to award attorney fees, including litigation expenses and costs, as provided in section 505 of the Act. Litigation expenses include items such as expert witness fees, travel expenses, etc. The Judiciary Committee Report specifies that such items are included under the rubric of "attorney's fees" and not "costs" so that such expenses will be assessed against a plaintiff only under the standard set forth in Christiansburg Garment Company v. Equal Employment Opportunity Commission, 434 US 412, 98 S. Ct. 694, 54 L.Ed. 2d 648 (1978) (Judiciary report at 73.)

In an excellent four volume set, The ADA Annotated (2003) by Professor Arlene Mayerson of DREDF, Berkeley, (who has taught at law schools including Boalt and Stantford) the "Commentary" to this regulation explains its scope and purpose:

> The Judiciary Report clarifies that the term "litigation expenses" was included in this provision to respond to rulings by the Supreme Court, such as Crawford Fitting Co. v. J. T. Gibbons, which required that items such as expert fees, travel expenses, etc. be expressly included if intended to be covered under an attorney's fee provision. Because litigation expenses are included under the rubric of "attorney's fees" and not costs, such expenses can only be assessed against a plaintiff under the strict standards set forth in Christanburg Garment Co. v. EEOC, which requires that plaintiff's claim be "frivolous, unreasonable, or groundless."

> Moreover, the amendment to Section 706(k) of Title VII of the 1964 Civil Rights Act explicitly refers to expert fees as part of a reasonable attorney's fee award. Since Title I of the ADA explicitly incorporates section 706 of Title VII, the attorney's fee provision of the 1991 Civil Rights act applies to Title I of the ADA. (Footnotes omitted)

> Id. at § 6:117.

4. A DEFENDANT'S DEMAND FOR ATTORNEY FEES AGAINST A DISABLED PLAINTIFF MAY CONSTITUTE A THREAT WHICH VIOLATES § 503(b) OF THE ADA

ADA § 503 sets a clear policy that physically disabled persons may not be retaliated against or intimidated on the basis that they have brought ADA claims. Congressional policy requires that ADA plaintiffs are to be <u>encouraged</u>, not discouraged. Section 503 states as follows:

> (a) RETALIATION. - No person shall discriminate against an individual because such individual has opposed any act or practice made unlawful by this Act or because such individual made a charge, testified, assisted, or participated in any manner in an investigation, proceeding, or hearing under this Act.

> (b) INTERFERENCE, COERCION, OR INTIMIDATION. - It shall be unlawful to coerce, intimidate, threaten, or interfere with any individual in the exercise or enjoyment of, or on account of his or her having exercised or enjoyed, or on account of his or her having aided or encouraged any other individual in the exercise or enjoyment of, any right granted or protected by this Act.

Some defendants have attacked disabled persons who file more than one ADA lawsuit as "professional plaintiffs" despite their having suffered, for example, experiencing a humiliating incident occurring because of a restaurant's inaccessible restrooms. The California Supreme Court recognized that:

> Disability discrimination is indistinguishable in many ways from race and sex discrimination. Specifically, it can "attack the individual's sense of self-worth in much the same fashion as race or sex discrimination."

<u>City of Moorpark v. Sup. Ct.</u> (1998) 18 Cal.4th 1143, 1160.)

In <u>Bruce v. City of Gainesville</u> (11th Circ. 1999) 177 F 3d 949, the Appellate Court applied the <u>Christiansburg</u> principle to reverse an award of attorneys fees against as ADA plaintiff, noting at FN. 2, that a prevailing plaintiff is obtaining fees against a violator of federal law, <u>a factor not present as to a defendant</u>. Most essentially a plaintiff is awarded fees, per <u>Christiansburg</u>, as "the chosen instrument of Congress to vindicate 'a policy that Congress considered of the highest priority'." <u>Christiansburg</u>, 439 US at 418. [115]

> "The ADA's legislative history indicates that Congress intended that the standards set forth in Christiansburg would apply to cases brought under the ADA. The House Report cites <u>Christiansburg</u> in finding that, "it is intended that the term 'prevailing party' be interpreted consistently with other civil rights laws. Plaintiffs should not be assessed opponents' attorneys' fees unless a court finds the plaintiff's claim is 'frivolous, unreasonable, or groundless. [Citations omitted] Finally, we note that <u>Christiansburg's</u> rationale applies squarely in ADA cases. <u>In Title VII cases as well as cases under the ADA, the enforcement of civil rights statutes by plaintiffs as private attorneys general is</u>

---

[115] See also Hubbard v. Sobreck, discussed *infra* at section IV-C-6.

an important part of the underlying policy behind the law. Such a policy ensures an incentive for "impecunious" plaintiffs who can ill afford to litigate their claims against defendants with more resources and thus justifies the differential treatment of prevailing plaintiffs and prevailing defendants.... [I]n determining whether a suit is frivolous, "a district court must focus on whether the case is so lacking in arguable merit as to be groundless or without foundation rather than whether the claim was ultimately successful." [Emphasis added]

Bruce v. City of Gainesville, *supra*, at 951-952.

5. THERE IS NO EXCEPTION TO THE CHRISTIANSBURG RULE SIMPLY BECAUSE ONE ADA PLAINTIFF HAS FILED MULTIPLE PREVIOUS LAWSUITS, SO LONG AS THE INSTANT LAWSUIT IS NOT "FRIVOLOUS"

It may often be unnecessary to respond to a defendants' demand to be awarded attorney fees against a disabled civil rights plaintiff as it should be clear that they will not be a prevailing party in the litigation.

However, defendants have on occasion tried to intimidate a disabled plaintiff by threatening to seek attorney fees against a disabled plaintiff, in the event plaintiff does not prevail. Some defense counsel have asked the Court to create an "exception" to Christiansburg because a plaintiff has previously (successfully) sued other inaccessible facilities and obtained disabled access ADA compliance, ending ongoing discrimination against disabled persons. To our knowledge there is no legal authority in support of this novel and insidious suggestion. Would Martin Luther King have had less standing to complain when he was denied service at a lunch counter in Alabama because he had previously complained about segregated lunch counters at other restaurants? Congressman John Lewis of Alabama, author of "Walking With the Wind" (an autobiography focusing on the history of the civil rights movement), established himself as a civil rights hero in the 1960s, repeatedly challenging established segregation to the point of being arrested more than 40 times for civil rights activities.

Congress clearly intended to make ADA suits easy to file and available to anyone with standing to bring them. Particularly as no damage remedy is provided by Title III of the ADA, there are should be no limits on how often a particular disabled person may be a plaintiff seeking to make businesses remove barriers and comply with the ADA.

Defendants may attempt to prejudice the Court by describing the disabled plaintiff as a "professional plaintiff," and asserting that anyone who successfully files a "number" of ADA actions should therefore face the threat of attorney fees. Since there is no legal significance to this fact, their only purpose is to ask the Court to be hostile to this plaintiff because of his previous ADA enforcement actions.

In <u>Wilson v. Murillo</u> 163 Cal.App.4th 1124 (2008), at 1128, the Court noted in a footnote, in response to defendant labeling Wilson as a "serial litigant," that the fact Wilson had filed numerous ADA access lawsuits was "immaterial" to the Court's resolution of the case, citing with approval a previous federal court decision involving the same plaintiff:

> "Wilson does not dispute that he has filed many ADA access lawsuits. <u>Numerosity alone</u>, however, <u>is insufficient to show that his lawsuits are frivolous or harassing</u>. One court has examined the contents of Wilson's filings and has made an express finding that his ADA claims are not frivolous and that he is not a vexatious litigant. "From all that appears, the <u>number of lawsuits</u> [Wilson] has filed does not reflect that he is a vexatious litigant; rather, it <u>appears to reflect the failure of the defendants to comply with the law</u>." (<u>Wilson v. Pier 1 Imports (US), Inc</u>. (E.D.Cal.2006) 411 F.Supp.2d 1196, 1200.)"

<u>Wilson v. Murillo</u>, 163 Cal. App.4th 1124 (2008) (Emphasis added).

Defendants cannot assert that any of a plaintiff's <u>prior</u> access lawsuits have been "frivolous, fraudulent or meritless" if all prior suits have been successful, i.e., have resulted in obtaining disabled accessible public facilities!

It was held that awarding attorney fees <u>against</u> an ADA plaintiff was inappropriate even where summary judgment was granted against plaintiff. <u>Summers v. Teichert & Son, Inc.</u>, 127 F.3d 1150, 1154 (9th Cir. 1999)) held that, under <u>Christiansburg</u>, <u>no fees</u> should be awarded:

> Attorney's fees should be granted to a defendant in a civil rights action only "upon a finding that the plaintiff's action was frivolous, unreasonable, or without foundation." <u>Christiansburg Garment Co. v. EEOC</u>, 434 U.S. 412, 421, 54 L.Ed.2d 648, 98 S.Ct. 694 (1978). Given that standard, we believe that a grant of attorney's fees would be inappropriate in this case.

For a defendant to seek attorney fees <u>against</u> a civil rights plaintiff in a clearly meritorious action not only ignores the <u>Christiansburg</u> principles, but violates the spirit of § 503(b) as an effort to intimidate plaintiff and punish him for enforcing the ADA. Courts should discourage such threats, which are contrary to both the spirit and letter of the ADA.

[See section 6, *infra*, re: <u>Hubbard v. Sobreck</u> holding extending the <u>Christianburg</u> rule to section 55 Civil Code actions based on state law "parallel" claims to those under the

ADA.] [See also 2011 decision by 9th Circuit in Harris v. Maricopa County Superior Court 631 F.3d 963 (9th Cir. 2011)] Caveat the December 17, 2012, decision by the California Supreme Court in Jankey v. Song Koo Lee, 55 Cal. 4th 1038 (2012) "disagreeing" with Sobreck, *supra*, and allowing section 55 Civil Code attorneys fees to a "prevailing" defendant, even against a "good faith" but losing plaintiff at least in state court. Does this interpretation of Section 55 and federal policy mean that the federal courts will follow State Court's decision? Sobreck relied on the preemptive effect of federal statutes when conflicting with state law statutes. Can a State Court simply "disagree" with the 9th Circuit's interpretation of federal law? § 55, a state statute, but is it procedural rather than substantive? Hopefully not too many attorneys will leave this field in frustration. However, the first district court to decide this issue followed Sobreck. Oliver v. In-n-Out Burgers.

6. IN MOLSKI V. EVERGREEN DYNASTY CORP. (9TH CIR. 2007) THE 9TH CIRCUIT SPECIFIED THAT EVEN "SERIAL PLAINTIFFS" MAY BE JUSTIFIED

   The majority of the en banc 9th Circuit judges allowed the trial court in Molski v. Evergreen Dynasty Corp., (9th Circuit 2007) 500 F.3d 1047, *supra*, to sanction the plaintiff and plaintiff's attorney for certain questionable allegations (i.e., filing complaints claiming the same physical injury to plaintiff's shoulder at three different facilities on the same day). (The dissent by Chief Judge Kozinski pointed out that even this "finding" was made by the trial Court without benefit of any evidentiary hearing). However, even the majority opinion stressed that it was not condemning the filing of multiple ADA cases by any single plaintiff, so long as the facts alleged in each case were true; this was contrary to the factual findings against plaintiff. Molski, whom the District Court had found (by "looking at the allegations of hundreds of lawsuits.") had made "baseless and exaggerated claims for injuries [which] exceeded any legitimacy and were made for the purpose of coercing settlement." (Id. at 1061)

   > In summary, we reemphasize that the simple fact that a plaintiff has filed a large number of complaints, standing alone, is not a basis for designating a litigant as "vexatious".... We also emphasize that the textual and factual similarity of a plaintiff's complaints, standing alone, is not a basis for finding a party to be a vexatious litigant. Accessibility barriers can be, and often are, similar in different places of public accommodation, and there is nothing inherently vexatious about using prior complaints as a template. See Wilson, 411 F.Supp.2d at 1196 (stating that uniform instances of misconduct can justify uniform pleadings)....
   >
   > [M]ost ADA suits are brought by a small number of private plaintiffs who view themselves as champions of the disabled. District courts should not condemn such serial litigation as vexatious as a matter of course... For the ADA to yield its promise of equal access for the disabled, it may indeed be necessary and desirable for committed individuals to bring serial litigation

advancing the time when public accommodations will be compliant with the ADA.

Molski, (panel decision) (2007), *supra* at 1061-1062. (Emphasis added.)[116]

7. IN HUBBARD V. SOBRECK (2009), THE 9th CIRCUIT EXTENDED THE CHRISTIANBURG PRINCIPLES TO DENY CALIFORNIA CIVIL CODE § 55 ATTORNEYS' FEES TO A PREVAILING DEFENDANT AGAINST A "GOOD FAITH" DISABLED PLAINTIFF; [BUT CAVEAT JANKEY V. LEE, WHERE THE CALIFORNIA SUPREME COURT "DISAGREED"]

In Hubbard v. Sobreck, LLC, 554 F3d 742 (9th Circuit 2009), the 9th Circuit held that where section 55 Civil Code liability was based on an incorporation of the ADA into the "CDPA" (California Disabled Persons Act, sections 54(c) and 54.1(d), it was improper to award any of defendant's attorney fees against a "good faith" plaintiff. This was because the ADA, and its protections for disabled plaintiffs pursuant to Christianburg principles preempted California laws:

> We hold that to the extent that section 55 does authorize the award of fees to a prevailing defendant on non-frivolous ADA claims, there is a conflict and the ADA preempts section 55 of the CDPA."

Accordingly the order awarding attorney fees to defendant was reversed. Hubbard v. Sobreck, LLC, 554 F3d 742 (9th Circuit 2009).

However on December 17, 2012, the California Supreme Court issued Jankey v. Lee which allowed "prevailing" defendants to get section 55 attorney fees against a "good faith" plaintiff. (See section I-K-10, and IV-H-5, *supra*).[117]

I. IN 2011 HARRIS REITERATED THE CHRISTIANBURG PRINCIPLES, HOLDING NO FEES AGAINST PLAINTIFF EXCEPT FOR "FRIVOLOUS" CLAIMS, AND ONLY FOR WORK "ATTRIBUTABLE EXCLUSIVELY TO PLAINTIFF'S FRIVOLOUS CLAIMS"

In Harris v. Maricopa County Superior Court, 631 F.3d 963 (9th Cir. 2011), the Court in a detailed opinion made clear that the Christianburg policy required protection of a plaintiff against paying any of defendant's attorney fees except for any specific defendant's work "attributable exclusively to plaintiff's frivolous claims":

> Our laws encourage individuals to seek relief for violations of their civil rights, and allow a defendant to recover fees and costs from a plaintiff in a

---

[116] There were major dissenting opinions by Judge Berzon and Kozinski, who argued that the sanctions against Molski and his attorneys was not justified. (These dissents were to en banc majority decision denying rehearing. Molski v. Evergreen, 521 F.3d 1215 (9th Circuit. 2008)(The citations are confusing, and the reader should check out both opinions and dissents!)

[117] On May 10, 2013 a federal district court ruled that federal courts will continue to follow Sobreck, *supra*. (See section F of Introduction, p. 16, re: Oliver v. In-n-Out Burgers.)

civil rights case only "in exceptional circumstances" in which the plaintiff's claims are "frivolous, unreasonable or without foundation." See Barry v. Fowler, 902 F.2d 770, 773 (9th Cir.1990) (internal quotation marks, citation omitted); Christiansburg Garment Co. v. EEOC, 434 U.S. 412, 422, 98 S.Ct. 694, 54 L.Ed.2d 648 (1978). Moreover, only fees "attributable exclusively to plaintiff's frivolous claims," are recoverable by a defendant. See Tutor-Saliba Corp. v. City of Hailey, 452 F.3d 1055, 1064 (9th Cir. 2006)
Id. at *1.

J. IN FOX V. VICE THE UNITED STATES SUPREME COURT DETERMINED THAT A PREVAILING DEFENDANT COULD ONLY RECOVER FEES FOR COSTS DEFENDANT WOULD NOT HAVE INCURRED BUT FOR ANY FRIVOLOUS CLAIMS BY A CIVIL RIGHTS PLAINTIFF

In Fox v. Vice, 131 S.Ct. 2205 (2011), a unanimous Supreme Court came to a similar conclusion that the 9th Circuit had reached in Harris v. Maricopa Co, *supra*, earlier in 2011: that because of the different policies governing a prevailing plaintiff in a civil rights case, compared to a prevailing defendant, a defendant could only recover fees if a plaintiff had forced it to defend against frivolous claims, and such fees had to be solely attributable to work that would not have been done but for the frivolous claims. In an opinion authored by Justice Kagan, in a case involving "both frivolous and non-frivolous claims,"

> a court may grant reasonable fees to the defendant in this circumstance, but only for costs that the defendant would not have incurred but for the frivolous claims.

Id. at 2211.

In so holding, the Court differentiated the very different standards for plaintiffs than defendants, based on congressional policy:

The statute involved here, 42 U.S.C. § 1988, allows the award of "a reasonable attorney's fee" to "the prevailing party" in various kinds of civil rights cases, including suits brought under § 1983. Most of our decisions addressing this provision have concerned the grant of fees to prevailing plaintiffs. When a plaintiff succeeds in remedying a civil rights violation, we have stated, he serves "as a 'private attorney general,' vindicating a policy that Congress considered of the highest priority." Newman v. Piggie Park Enterprises, Inc., 390 U.S. 400, 402, 88 S.Ct. 964, 19 L.Ed.2d 1263 (1968) (per curiam). He therefore "should ordinarily recover an attorney's fee" from the defendant—the party whose misconduct created the need for legal action. Christiansburg Garment Co. v. EEOC, 434 U.S. 412, 416, 98 S.Ct. 694, 54 L.Ed.2d 648 (1978) (internal quotation marks omitted). Fee shifting in such a case at once reimburses a plaintiff for "what it cos[t][him] to vindicate [civil] rights," Riverside v. Rivera, 477 U.S. 561, 577–578, 106 S.Ct. 2686, 91 L.Ed.2d 466 (1986) (internal quotation marks omitted), and holds to account "a violator of federal law," Christiansburg, 434 U.S., at 418, 98 S.Ct. 694.
Id. at 2213.

By contrast, the Court cited the "Christianburg" principles, recognizing a defendant was not carrying out congressional policy, but was entitled to protect itself against frivolous claims:

> In Christiansburg, we held that § 1988 also authorizes a fee award to a prevailing defendant, but under a different standard reflecting the "quite different equitable considerations" at stake. Id., at 419, 98 S.Ct. 694. In enacting § 1988, we stated, Congress sought "to protect defendants from burdensome litigation having no legal or factual basis." Id., at 420, 98 S.Ct. 694. Accordingly, § 1988 authorizes a district court to award attorney's fees to a defendant "upon a finding that the plaintiff's action was frivolous, unreasonable, or without foundation." Id., at 421, 98 S.Ct. 694; see also Kentucky v. Graham, 473 U.S. 159, 165, n. 9, 105 S.Ct. 3099, 87 L.Ed.2d 114 (1985).
>
> Id.

In determining fees, the trial court is granted great discretion, but must apply the correct standard:

> But the trial court must apply the correct standard, and the appeals court must make sure that has occurred. See Perdue v. Kenny A., 559 U.S. ——, ——, 130 S.Ct. 1662, 1676, 176 L.Ed.2d 494 (2010) ("Determining a 'reasonable attorney's fee' is a matter that is committed to the sound discretion of a trial judge, ... but the judge's discretion is not unlimited"); Cf. Koon v. United States, 518 U.S. 81, 100, 116 S.Ct. 2035, 135 L.Ed.2d 392 (1996) ("A district court by definition abuses its discretion when it makes an error of law"). That means the trial court must determine whether the fees requested would not have accrued but for the frivolous claim. And the appeals court must determine whether the trial court asked and answered that question, rather than some other. A trial court has wide discretion when, but only when, it calls the game by the right rules.

Id. at 2216-2217 (Emphasis added)

Because the trial court had used the wrong standard, the Supreme Court reversed and remanded:
> On this record, we must return the case to the lower courts. See, e.g., Perdue, 559 U.S., at —— – ——, 130 S.Ct., at 1675–1677; Pennsylvania v. Delaware Valley Citizens' Council for Clean Air, 478 U.S. 546, 566–568, 106 S.Ct. 3088, 92 L.Ed.2d 439 (1986); Hensley, 461 U.S., at 438–440, 103 S.Ct. 1933. In a suit of this kind, involving both frivolous and non-frivolous claims, a defendant may recover the reasonable attorney's fees he expended solely because of the frivolous allegations. And that is all. Consistent with the policy underlying § 1988, the defendant may not receive compensation for any fees that he would have paid in the absence of the frivolous claims. We therefore vacate the judgment of the Court of Appeals and remand the case for further proceedings consistent with this opinion.

Id. at 2217-2218.

K. LANDLORD AND TENANT MAY BE JOINTLY AND SEVERALLY LIABLE FOR A PREVAILING PLAINTIFF'S ATTORNEY FEES

As previously noted in sections I-G-5-e and III-H, both landlord and tenant have joint and several liability under Title III and "any allocation made in a lease or the contract is only effective as between the parties, and both landlord and tenant remain fully liable for all compliance with all provisions of the ADA related to that place of public accommodation." Botosan v. McNally Realty, 216 F.3d 827 (9th Cir. 2000). Botosan was cited by the Northern District Court in Kosloff v. Washington Sq. Assoc. 2007 WL 2023497, holding that defendants were "jointly and severally liable for all compensation to plaintiff under the ADA including federally authorized attorney's fees."

[See Also Section I-H-5-e *supra*, and see Blackwell v. Foley, (N.D. Cal. 2010) 724 F.Supp. 2d 1068, 1075 for same holding]

L. ATTORNEY LICENSED IN ANY STATE CAN PRACTICE IN FEDERAL COURTS OF OTHER STATES

The Sixth Circuit Court of Appeals has held that state law cannot prohibit an attorney from practicing in a federal court in that state so long as he was licensed to practice law in another state and was admitted to the federal District Court bar in the state in question. (In re: Desilets (6th Cir. 2002) 291 F.3rd 925.)

V. PRACTICAL APPROACHES: NOTICE, COOPERATION & SETTLEMENT

A. INTRODUCTION: CONSIDER EARLY COMMUNICATION WITH DEFENDANTS

In many cases the <u>primary</u> purpose for a disabled person in seeking the assistance of an attorney may be to obtain access improvements at a public accommodation. For example, while disabled persons in California can obtain damages under California State law, Title III of the ADA only offers injunctive relief- to require barrier removal and improved access- but does not directly provide damages. For this reason, plaintiffs' attorneys should seek the best way to rapidly achieve access, consistent with the specific rights and objectives of the particular plaintiff. (But see new limitations on letter writing in SB1186, passed in October, 2012, as reprinted in Appendix IX-K *infra*. See <u>inter alia</u> new § 55.32 Civil Code.)

Some disabled persons who have standing to sue as a plaintiff may prefer and approve their attorney first sending a letter requesting compliance, prior to initiating litigation.[118] Others, particularly if they have already suffered a humiliating experience compensable in damages, may prefer to file a lawsuit first, before making efforts to "negotiate" compliance. It has been the experience of many plaintiff's attorneys that it is difficult to seek to obtain damages in settlement <u>after</u> pre-litigation efforts to negotiate attainment of access.

"SB 1608" was enacted in 2008 by the California legislature, effective January 1, 2009. It set up special procedures to be followed in California courts when a lawsuit was filed for disabled access damages based on a construction or alteration based claim for liability. It was passed unanimously by a bipartisan legislative effort to improve prospects for early settlement and thus address some concerns by business and avert a possible expensive "initiative war." It contains detailed "notice" requirements for <u>state court</u> cases and a procedure for requiring the Court to issue a "stay" and carry out certain settlement procedures, if the business had access properly evaluated <u>before</u> being sued. These notices are probably <u>not</u> required in federal cases, as the statute is limited to "Superior Court judges and commissioners."

It should also be clear that the California legislature cannot set up <u>procedural</u> requirements for federal courts. In <u>O'Campo v. Chico Mall, LP</u> 750 F. Supp 976 (E.D. Cal. 2010), Judge Lawrence K. Karlton, as a matter of apparent first impression, held that the ADA preempted California's Construction-Related Accessibility Standards Compliance Act to the extent it applied to ADA claims, citing <u>Hubbard v. Sobreck, LLC</u>, 554 F.3d 742 (9th Cir. 2009). Accordingly the Court applied the "Erie" Doctrine (<u>Erie Railroad Co. v. Tomkins</u>) and held that a federal court would not apply state procedural law requiring a stay of proceedings and an early evaluation conference, and denied defendants' motion seeking such stay, per California Civil Code sections 55.51- 55.54.

---

[118] However, caveat the limitations on letter writing, effective January 1, 2103, due to requirements of SB 1186.

As to the Construction Related Accessibility Standards Act (which was enacted as part of SB 1608 in 2008 effective January 1, 2009), O'Campo, *supra*, held that "the Act is preempted to the extent that it imposes any additional procedural hurdles to a plaintiff bringing a claim under the ADA." Id. at *7. "Accordingly this federal Court cannot order a plaintiff to engage in an early evaluation conference." Id. The Court also held, "the Act is preempted to the extent that it imposes any additional procedural hurdles to a plaintiff bringing a claim under the ADA." Id.

However, <u>attorneys who file disabled access cases in state court must be aware of and comply with the notice provisions and other new procedural requirements</u>. These include service upon defendants of certain notices, <u>which will not be detailed here</u>. See complete text of SB 1186 in Appendix K, *infra*.

B. PROMPTLY INFORM DEFENDANTS OF THE VALUE OF AN EARLY SETTLEMENT

Consistent with the wishes of the client, there may be advantages in plaintiff's attorney notifying defendants at an early stage of plaintiff's objectives in the lawsuit. This could be done, for example, by service of an appropriate letter when the complaint and summons, etc., are served. (Under California state law legislation (SB 1608 and SB 1186), certain "notice" information will have to be served with the lawsuit, at least with state court complaints.) A letter spelling out the lawsuit's objectives (and labeled "privileged for settlement purposes") may invite a cooperative approach during the litigation and encourage defendants to explore a cooperative settlement at an early stage. However in cases of serious access denial now 40 years after California access laws, and 20 years after the ADA, defendants may comply more rapidly after being sued!

C. PROTECT THE PUBLIC INTEREST AS PRIME OBJECTIVE

For many years I have been encouraging attorneys in California to handle lawsuits for access on behalf of disabled persons to advance the public interest while earning statutory attorney fees. My first such article, "Wheelchair Access Litigation," was published in the Fall, 1982 edition of <u>Forum</u> magazine, a publication of the California Trial Lawyers Association ("CTLA" later renamed "Consumer Attorneys of California" or CAOC). I outlined how access could often be obtained under California law, (prior to enactment of the ADA in 1990). Unfortunately, <u>some</u> lawyers appear to have sought damages and attorney fees without regard to obtaining improved access or other public service objectives. If barriers to access remain at a defendant's facilities, it does disservice to disabled members of the public for lawyers to seek to settle damages and attorneys fees <u>without</u> insisting that the barriers to access be removed as a condition precedent to any settlement.

D. CONGRESS' ATTORNEY FEE PROVISIONS ARE A MESSAGE TO NON-COMPLYING BUSINESSES, AND SUPPORT THE PURPOSES OF THE ADA

In enacting the Americans With Disabilities Act of 1990, the United States Congress made specific findings per 42 USC § 12101 regarding physically disabled persons, determining that laws were needed to more fully protect "some 43,000,000 Americans [with] one or more physical or mental disabilities;" and that "historically, society has tended to isolate and segregate individuals with disabilities;" that "such forms of discrimination against individuals with disabilities continue to be a serious and pervasive social problem." Congress stated that "the Nation's proper goals regarding individuals with disabilities are to assure equality of opportunity, full participation, independent living, and economic self-sufficiency for such individuals;" and that "the continuing existence of unfair and unnecessary discrimination and prejudice denies people with disabilities the opportunity to compete on an equal basis and to pursue those opportunities for which our free society is justifiably famous..." Based on later census data, <u>the number of disabled persons</u> protected by the Americans with Disabilities Act of 1990, Public Law 101-336, is <u>now in excess of fifty million Americans</u>.

Congress stated multiple purposes in enacting the Americans with Disabilities Act of 1990. Per 42 USC § 12101(b),
It is the purpose of this Act

(1) to provide a clear and comprehensive national mandate for the elimination of discrimination against individuals with disabilities;

(2) to provide clear, strong, consistent, enforceable standards addressing discrimination against individuals with disabilities;

(3) to ensure that the Federal Government plays a central role in enforcing the standards established in this Act on behalf of individuals with disabilities; and

(4) to invoke the sweep of congressional authority, including the power to enforce the fourteenth amendment and to regulate commerce, in order to address the major areas of discrimination faced day-to-day by people with disabilities.

E. **PLAINTIFF'S ATTORNEYS SHOULD CARRY OUT EARLY INVESTIGATION, RESEARCH AND PREPARATION SO THAT THEY ONLY FILE MERITORIOUS AND "GOOD FAITH" CASES**

It is in the public interest and the disabled plaintiff's best interests - as well, ultimately, in the best interests of a defendant commercial business - if the plaintiff's representatives carry out a thorough investigation of the premises, and research all available public records, <u>before</u> filing a lawsuit. Such records may disclose all owners, operators, lessors and lessees to assist the lawyer in determining which are necessary and appropriate defendants in a case. For example, suing a tenant business without including the lessor and owner of a Title

III public accommodation may omit a party necessary for proper injunctive relief.

Public records of building departments and/or planning departments of the local city and/or county agency involved in authorizing construction and alteration projects may disclose sufficient construction and/or alteration projects to ensure liability under ADA § 303 and California Health & Safety Code §§ 19955-19959. (Section 19959, since 1972, and California's Title 24 - the California Building Code - since 1982, both require provision of access upon any "alterations, structural repairs or additions.)

Proper preparation will not only assist in plaintiff winning the case, but will ensure - in the unlikely event that plaintiff is not ultimately determined to be the "prevailing party" - that plaintiff can show that the lawsuit was brought "in good faith" and was not "frivolous" or "fraudulent" or otherwise place the plaintiff at risk for an award to defendants of fees or costs, per the Christiansberg principles. (Christiansburg Garment Co. v. EEOC, 434 U.S. 412, 417, 98 S.Ct. 694, 698) Such preparation is also desirable to show that plaintiff's counsel complied with FRCP Rule 11 in finding good cause to bring a lawsuit. [See section IV, *supra*, and Fox v. Vice, (2011) 131 S.Ct. 2205]

F. "SEND ME A LETTER, THE SOONER THE BETTER" - WHILE NO ADVANCE NOTICE IS LEGALLY REQUIRED UNDER FEDERAL OR CALIFORNIA LAW, THERE MAY BE TACTICAL OR PRACTICAL REASONS FOR DOING SO

   1. WHILE NO ADVANCE NOTICE IS REQUIRED, THERE MAY BE TACTICAL OR PRACTICAL REASONS TO DO SO IN A PARTICULAR CASE
      No letter or other pre-filing "notice" advising a business that it is out of access compliance is legally required prior to filing a lawsuit against the business to obtain access. In Skaff v. Meridien North America Beverly Hills, LLC (9th Cir. 2007) 506 F.3d 832, the 9th Circuit unequivocally stated:
      > [W]e hold that the ADA requires neither that plaintiffs give defendants pre-suit notice that they intend to sue, nor that plaintiffs give defendants an opportunity to cure the alleged violation or violations before filing suit as a pre-requisite to recovering attorneys' fees.

      Id. at 846.

      Yet in some situations, after full discussion with the client, a plaintiff's attorney may choose to send a letter and attempt a pre-litigation settlement to obtain accessible facilities - with or without any demand for damages and/or attorney fees - if this is consistent with the client's goals and expectations. (But caveat limitations on "demand" letter writing set forth in SB1186, in Appendix-K, *infra*.) This may, as a practical matter, be sufficient to obtain compliance when the access sought is truly "easily accomplished." If access is not supplied, the notice may be relevant for seeking "catalyst" attorney fees if a lawsuit is later still necessary, but defendant provides access after being sued but before there is a judicial determination of liability. [See section V-F-5, *infra*.] [See also "reporting" and notice with complaint service requirements of SB 1186, effective January 1, 2013., per new sections § 55.3, 55.31, 55.32 etc.]

However, if a business promptly complies when a notice is sent, it may be more difficult to then seek damages for the discrimination already suffered by the disabled person. There will no longer be federal jurisdiction based on ADA Title III, as Title III addresses only injunctive relief- not damages- as a remedy. These and other factors should be explained to and understood by any (potential) disabled plaintiff, in determining how to proceed.

2. DISCUSSING GOALS AND TACTICAL ALTERNATIVES WITH CLIENT

An attorney representing a disabled person facing access barriers should discuss goals and tactical alternatives with his client. Sometimes a client will wish for personal reasons to attempt a cooperative settlement. In such case, the attorney may agree to send a letter, but with the understanding that if the defendants do not cooperatively comply a lawsuit will follow. This should be carefully considered with the client and possibly memorialized in a written agreement. Then, depending on the cooperation or lack of it from the defendant who was notified, the client may authorize a lawsuit or may decide to waive damages in return for prompt compliance. [Again, be aware of new requirements of SB 1186, *infra*, Appendix K.]

Sometimes the item complained about can be rapidly corrected without construction or permit required. For example, if the main problem at the business is the lack of an accessible path of travel through the business - for example, a restaurant whose tables or hallway chairs block a path of travel to a restroom - this can be corrected by moving furniture without any structural changes to walls or other none moveable objects; or, similarly, where there is a complaint simply about the lack of a proper grab bar - where one is provided but two are required - and there is evidence that the business intended to comply but did not do so fully or properly. Other minor problems, such as the location of a toilet paper dispenser or other inconvenient but easily remedied problems, might also be addressed by a letter, (But caveat <u>new restrictions on letter writing</u> contained in SB1186, *infra*, Appendix 15).

However, if the particular "minor" access deficiency is simply part of a number of "minor" problems which together create an unusable facility for a disabled person, it may be more appropriate to take direct legal action. We have often found that problems and misunderstandings may occur when a business corrects the problem but the client still expects to obtain damages. If this is the disabled plaintiff's objective, a lawsuit from the beginning may be the appropriate tactical choice.

3. **REJECT LEGISLATIVE EFFORTS TO REQUIRE MANDATORY 90 DAY NOTICE**
Even attorneys who choose to send a letter of notification to some or all defendants should join in resisting state or federal efforts to water down the effectiveness of disabled rights lawsuits, by requiring any form of advance notice. Such an effort was urged upon Congress in 2000 by actor/producer Clint Eastwood, who supported the purported "ADA Notification Act" - which it's disabled opponents characterized as the "ADA Nullification Act" - sponsored by (now "former") Congressman Mark Foley of Florida. No civil rights plaintiff besides disabled persons would be required to give such "advance notice" to a potential defendant who had already violated a plaintiff's civil rights, before they could file suit to obtain damages for the discrimination they had already suffered - and for an injunction to stop it from happening again. (Congressman Foley's rapid resignation from Congress (while under investigation by Congress for alleged improper communications with Congressional "Page" boys) makes it unlikely that any proposed legislation will still be referred to as the "Foley Bill.")

Regarding the "notice" issue, an August 4, 2003 letter opinion by the California Attorney General observed that legislation requiring advance notice and an opportunity to "correct" violations before litigation had been "soundly defeated in both the legislature and in Congress. The disabled community, which strongly opposes this legislation, believes that a 'wait period' is inappropriate given the fact that state and federal access laws have been in effect for a long time." [See Apendix IX-E-3, August 4, 2003 California Attorney General Letter Opinion]

4. **HAVE DEFENDANTS ALREADY BEEN PUT ON NOTICE OR ARE THEY PART OF A LARGER COMPANY THAT HAS PREVIOUSLY BEEN PUT ON NOTICE?**
In certain cases the Rein office has handled, we've discovered that months or years previously a letter giving notice that facilities were out of compliance with access laws had already been sent to one or more of the owners and operators of an inaccessible public facility. (We have written to hundreds of businesses to advise them their premises were out of compliance with access requirements, and requesting voluntary removal of barriers, without any claim for damages or attorney fees.) These prior notices and complaints may be valuable in proving that a particular defendant knew it was denying access but continued to do so. Although wrongful intent is not an element in proving liability under Civil Code §§ 54 and 54.1 (James Donald v. Cafe Royale (1990) 218 Cal.App.3d 168; Mark Hankins v. El Torito Restaurants, Inc. (1998) 63 Cal. App.4th 510), proof of actual wrongful intent may be helpful in proving one basis for an award of treble damages under Civil Code § 54.3. (An award under Civil Code §§ 51-52 does not require proof of wrongful intent. The California state court appellate decision in Gunther v. Lin (Cal.Ct.App. 2006) 50 Cal.Rptr.3d 317 has now been overruled by the California Supreme Court in Munson v. Del Taco, *supra*).

5. TACTICAL USE OF ADVANCE NOTICE

   a. USING ADVANCE NOTICE AS A POSSIBLE BASIS FOR TREBLE DAMAGES UNDER CALIFORNIA CIVIL CODE SECTIONS 52 AND 54.3

   In the <u>Rosler v. Stanford University</u>, (N.D.Cal.) No. C03-03579 JF, the threat of treble damages was a factor which, we believe, contributed toward an excellent settlement in the unusual case where the plaintiff had suffered serious personal injuries as the result of one aspect of her denial of legally required access. (<u>Rosler</u> was a trip-and-fall case where the plaintiff, disabled and using a cane, tripped over an unprotected "bollard" post holder in the direct path of travel to premises.)[119] Most ADA cases do not involve major physical personal injuries. However, even non-injury disability rights discrimination cases have the potential for treble damages per Civil Code § 54.3. This potential might be advanced if a plaintiff voluntarily sent a pre-litigation notice to the owner of the inaccessible business to demand provision of access, and the owner, despite "actual notice," declined to take any remedial action. This could arguably evidence "conscious disregard" for the rights and/or safety of disabled persons, one proper basis for § 54.3 treble damages (although I am unaware of any precedential cases setting treble damage standards under § 54.3 Civil Code). Of course, most cases involving serious personal injury should be promptly filed.

   Certain plaintiff's attorneys and their clients have been criticized where the attorneys have allegedly filed ADA suits for "trivial" access irregularities (such as a proverbial "towel rack being mounted an inch too high"). However, new statutes per SB1608 (2008 and SB1186 require specific pleading of how an alleged defect caused "difficulty, discomfort or embarrassment" in order to qualify for California law damages.) Other attorneys have allegedly "set up" cases on a mass production basis, "sending" the same disabled persons to several hundred places, etc. Some actions have been the subject of court orders finding litigant and attorney to be "vexatious litigants," and have spurred a political backlash against cases asserting access rights for disabled persons. (Cf. <u>Molski v. Mandarin Touch Restaurant</u> (C.D. Cal.) Case No. CV04-0450 ER, orders of 12/9/04 and 3/8/05, affirmed in part by the 9th Circuit in <u>Molski v. Evergreen Dynasty Corp.</u> (9th Cir. 2007) 500 F.3d 1047.) As part of the backlash, demands have been made by certain business interests that the laws be changed to require advance notice before any ADA or California law lawsuit could be filed.

---

[119] There were also four stairs at the entrance to the facility, no accessible restroom and no proper disabled parking. All deficiencies were corrected pursuant to a consent decree settlement which included substantial personal injury damages and payment of statutory attorney fees.

There certainly has been some misuse of the ADA, and the right wing has done its best to portray such cases as the "typical" ADA case, just as the right wing and tort reformers cite evidence of faked auto crash cases in Southern California as accurately representing how "most" plaintiff's cases are engineered.

Citing examples of businesses wrongly sued over trivialities that they allegedly "would have instantly corrected if only [they] had been asked," certain legislators including former Congressman Mark Foley of Florida and his posterboy, Clint Eastwood, have demanded the ADA be amended to require that businesses be given 90 days advance written notice, preferably by Certified Mail, prior to filing any ADA lawsuit. Federal and state proposed legislation would require such notice as a pre-condition for filing suit, even when a disabled person has already suffered a civil rights violation (and even a "bodily functions" accident, trying to get their wheelchair into a non-compliant restroom.) Of course such a "notice" requirement would single out disabled persons from other categories of persons discriminated against, who were required to give advance notice to the "discriminator" before they could file their civil rights lawsuit.[120]

Ironically, Clint Eastwood admitted during the September, 2000 San Jose federal jury trial of zum Brunnen v. Mission Ranch, Clint Eastwood, et al. (N.D. Cal.) Case No. C97-20668 JW, that the disabled plaintiff had actually sent him such a notice by Certified Mail, and that Eastwood refused to accept it, and had mailed it back to her "rejected." (He also testified at trial that he never accepts Certified Mail!) Further, despite such complaints, and multi-million dollar remodeling, he failed to provide an access ramp to the resort's office, proper accessible parking, proper disabled restrooms, or accessible guest rooms at his 35 guest room resort and restaurant, until after he was sued. As a further irony, Eastwood left the ranks of the "tort reformers" when he sued his own insurance company for rejecting coverage, and recovered $500,000 (by settlement) from Cal Farm Insurance, representing his alleged "costs of defense" in the "Mission Ranch" case.

But I have a novel twist on the notice issue: Plaintiffs' attorneys might consider, in cases where there are major access defects, sending an advance notice letter and perhaps insisting that defendants agree within 30 days that needed access will be provided within an additional 60 days.[121] Maybe they'll "fix" things and provide access; if so, your client will probably be ecstatic. But if they don't, or if

---

[120] Since Congressman Foley's fall from grace as a result of the Congressional "page boy" scandal in late 2006, resulting in Rep. Foley's resignation from Congress, it is unlikely that any future rendition of this bill will retain the name of the "Foley" bill.

[121] But caveat new California Legislation requirements of SB 1186 as to letters!

there is evidence that they have had prior complaints but failed to remove barriers, this could be the basis for seeking treble damages per Civil Code § 54.3, on a "conscious disregard" standard. [Gov't Code § 4452 has set the standard since 1968 that "Any unauthorized deviation from such regulations or building standards shall be rectified by full compliance within 90 days <u>after discovery of the deviation</u>." [Emphasis added]]

I am not aware of any published case interpreting "treble damages" standards for disability rights violations, although they are statutorily available under both Civil Code § 52 (for a violation of the Unruh Act, discrimination on the basis of "sex, race, color religion, ancestry, national origin, disability or medical condition" under § 51), and under § 54.3, part of California's Disabled Persons Act (for violation of § 54 or § 54.1's right to "full and equal access").[122] While no "notice" is required by law - and none should be, as such a requirement would weaken disabled rights enforcement and give incentive to businesses to withhold the expense of providing access until given such notice - giving notice might provide plaintiff with a tactical advantage: a plaintiff could then argue that (especially since businesses have pushed so hard to demand that they be given notice), when businesses <u>are</u> given advance notice and they still refuse to provide access, this shows "conscious disregard" of a known danger to disabled persons and justifies <u>treble damages</u>. Such damages are "available" now under statute, but are seldom awarded. This suggests one possible way to maximize plaintiff's damages recovery.

b. ADVANCE NOTICE ALSO USEFUL FOR POSSIBLE "CATALYST" ATTORNEY FEES UNDER CALIFORNIA LAW

Another use of advance notice - in addition to it providing a possible basis for treble damages when defendants make no effort to comply - is in the situation where defendants do take action to remove barriers after they're sued, but do not settle the case. They may fail to settle either because they (a) haven't timely completed the access barrier removals requested, or (b) fail to complete providing access and at the same time refuse to settle reasonably for damages and attorney fees. Under the California Supreme Court's <u>Graham v. DaimlerChrysler Corp.</u> (2004) 34 Cal.4th 553 case, and its companion case, <u>Tipton-Whittingham, et al. v. City of Los Angeles</u> (2004) 34 Cal.4th 604, a plaintiff suing under California law may still obtain "catalyst" attorney fees despite the United States Supreme Court's holding in <u>Buckhannon Board & Care Home, Inc., et al. v. West Virginia Dept. of Health & Human Services, et al.</u> (2001) 121 S.Ct. 1835 that "catalyst" fees <u>cannot</u> be obtained <u>under federal law</u>. The new catalyst rule, however, requires that plaintiff has made <u>a reasonable pre-litigation effort to settle.</u>

---

[122] In <u>Molski v. Gleich</u>, 318 F.3d 937 (9th Cir. 2003) the appellate Court reversed a mandatory class certification by the trial court, in part because the Consent Decree failed to protect the rights of individual class members to opt out of the class and seek treble damages under sections 52 and 54.3 Civil Code.

Since the "catalyst" fees may be recoverable either under Code of Civil Procedure § 1021.5 for obtaining a public interest result, or possibly under Civil Code § 55 for obtaining injunctive relief to protect a disabled person from ongoing disability related discrimination, the focal issue where "failure to settle" is alleged will be solely regarding the requested injunctive relief. However, sometimes the defendant will make the mistake of refusing to settle the injunctive relief unless plaintiff also settles his damages and attorney fees at an inadequate level. In this situation it should be clear that plaintiff has made a reasonable pre-litigation effort to settle the injunctive relief issues, i.e., by a pre-litigation demand which gives defendants a reasonable opportunity to settle. If defendants, after being sued, finally take action to remove the barriers and then say that the injunctive relief is "moot," for example (thus depriving the federal court of its jurisdiction under the ADA cause of action), plaintiff can then point out that defendants have now triggered "catalyst" attorney fees for plaintiff. Thus, if plaintiff has made a pre-litigation effort to settle, defendants may help prove plaintiff's right to "catalyst" attorney fees by the very act of removing all barriers and then telling the trial court that they have removed all barriers and that therefore the injunctive relief is moot.

Note that there may be short time limits for filing an attorney fees motion, for example after a federal court's decision to dismiss a case based on mootness and the lack of a continuing federal question. Plaintiff's fee motion may, by declarations as well as evidence supplied by defendants themselves, show that the pre-litigation efforts and the lawsuit itself served as a "catalyst" to get defendants to remove the architectural barriers, change their policy, or otherwise stop discriminating against the disabled person. This may allow a statutory award of attorney fees on a "catalyst" - "plaintiff caused defendants to take this action" - legal theory.

Use of this theory may be particularly important when plaintiff does not have sufficient time or opportunity to obtain summary judgment or other judicial ruling which makes the plaintiff the "prevailing party." Of course, if the plaintiff is a "prevailing party" he will be able to obtain attorney fees under both federal and state law, even under the Buckhannon, *supra*, holding. See especially Skaff v. Meridien North America Beverly Hills, LLC (9th Cir. 2007) WL 3197038, for this specific ruling, where plaintiff obtained a court-enforceable settlement agreement, following Barrios v. California Interscholastic Federation (9th Cir. 2002) 277 F. 3d 1128, 1134, that "plaintiff 'prevails' when he or she enters into a legally enforceable settlement agreement against the defendant." If so, no "pre-litigation" demand is needed.

Depending on the facts of the case, the ease of obtaining the requested compliance, and other factors, giving advance notice may provide plaintiff with a useful tactical tool in protecting the public interest while protecting the attorney's right to get paid for his or her public interest work.

c. IS FILING A GOVERNMENT CLAIM A "REASONABLE PRE-LITIGATION OFFER TO SETTLE"?

While a government claim's main function in California has been as a prerequisite for suing for damages under California law against a governmental agency, this government claim may certainly be considered as a "reasonable pre-litigation" offer to settle if it clearly specifies the barriers to access which are the basis for the damage claim. Details of the requirements for earning "catalyst" fees will be developed through litigation and court decisions following Graham v. DaimlerChrysler Corp. (2004) 34 Cal.4th 553, *supra*. But it may be difficult for a government entity to ignore completely government claims in access cases, and then later argue that plaintiff did not make an effort to settle pre-litigation. Our experience has been that there is rarely an effort by government entities to settle after being served with a government claim.

d. NEITHER ADVANCE NOTICE NOR SETTLEMENT EFFORTS ARE NEEDED UNDER CODE OF CIVIL PROCEDURE § 1021.5 OR THE ADA FOR ATTORNEY FEES TO PLAINTIFF AS PREVAILING PARTY

In Skaff v. Meridien North America Beverly Hills, LLC, 506 F.3d 832 (9th Cir. 2007) the 9th Circuit made clear that the "pre-litigation notice" requirements of Graham v. DaimlerChrysler Corp. (2004) 34 Cal.4th 553, applied only when plaintiff sought fees on a "catalyst" basis, and had no application when plaintiff was a prevailing party (by judgment or court-enforceable settlement agreement). Id. at 843-844. "Because Skaff did not make use of the catalyst theory, California law did not require him to make a reasonable attempt to settle before filing suit." Id.

G. IN LITIGATION, APPROACH DEFENDANT EARLY RE: SETTLEMENT

1. SEEK "WIN-WIN" EARLY SETTLEMENT

It is in the interests of all parties, as well as the public interest, if an early agreement on provision of access can avoid the necessity of discovery, full litigation, and necessary attorney fees.[123] Once defendants agree to provide access, negotiation can proceed as to appropriate damages for the plaintiff. Negotiation of statutory attorney fees, litigation expenses and costs should come last, only after agreement on injunctive relief, followed by agreement on damages. If this procedural order is followed, the attorneys fees necessitated by a discovery battle may be avoided. The parties can either negotiate attorneys fees, expenses, and costs or agree that the plaintiff can ask the Court to determine them by motion.

---

[123] However a formal inspection by plaintiff's access expert, either per General Order 56 in the Northern District of California, or per discovery under FRCP Rule 34, may be necessary in order to advise defendant of the nature of all access violations. Plaintiff has standing to include these claims for injunctive relief, per Doran v. 7-Eleven, Inc., *supra*, as reconfirmed by the January 7, 2011, en banc decision by the 9th Circuit in Chapman v. Pier 1 Imports, (9th Cir., 2011) 631 F.3d 939.

2. IN THE NORTHERN DISTRICT OF CALIFORNIA, GENERAL ORDER 56 REQUIRES EARLY DISCLOSURES, COOPERATIVE SITE INSPECTION AND MEDIATION PROCEDURES

General Order 56 in the Northern District of California, in effect since June 21, 2005 encourages early settlement by requiring disclosure of relevant information, mandating an early site inspection by attorneys and experts, and requiring settlement discussions and mediation before either party is allowed formal discovery, motions, or trial. [Copy of General Order 56, May 29, 2012 update, at Appendix H, *infra*, last revision to date]

3. ASK EARLY COOPERATIVE, SITE INSPECTION

When defendants recognize that they are probably liable under California law to provide the requested access, meeting at the site to explore and discuss alternatives to providing access for the primary items is often in the best interests of all parties. This is now required in all Title III access lawsuits in the federal courts in the Northern District of California by General Order 56, established in 2005 by Chief Judge Vaughn R. Walker. (See May 29, 2012 updated General Order 56 in Appendix H) Assuming that most defense counsel, as well as most plaintiff's counsel, will have the best interests of their clients in mind, and don't need to run up large attorney fees through discovery, interrogatories and depositions before approaching settlement, General Order 56 will often lead to full exchanges of information, an agreement on access, and an ADR Unit-supervised mediation, all intended to lead to early settlement. All of the General Order 56 requirements must be followed before the parties are allowed to move into formal discovery, dispositive motions, and pretrial preparation.

4. IF POSSIBLE, PLAINTIFF SHOULD CONSULT A QUALIFIED EXPERT BEFORE FILING A LAWSUIT, AND SHARE THE EXPERT'S PRELIMINARY CONCLUSIONS WITH DEFENDANTS DURING AN EARLY STAGE OF LITIGATION

If plaintiff is going to use an expert to help prove his case, why not get the benefit of the expert's "preliminary" opinion before deciding to file a lawsuit? Reliance on a qualified expert will help a plaintiff's disability lawyer to determine which claims are most meritorious and which, if any, will be more difficult to prove. Consultation with an expert is also one way an attorney may insure that he or she can prove that a lawsuit was brought "in good faith," and thus insulate both attorney and client from the threat of a defendant seeking statutory attorney fees under ADA § 505 or Civil Code § 55 in the event that plaintiff should lose the case. Protection for "good faith" civil rights plaintiffs was recognized by the Supreme Court in setting the constitutional attorney fees standards, the "Christiansberg" principles. (See Christiansburg Garment Co. v. EEOC, 434 U.S. 412, 417, 98 S.Ct. 694, 698. [See section IV-H-J, *supra*, re: possible attorney fees for a prevailing defendant being severely limited. But see Jankey v. Song Koo Lee, 55 Cal. 4th 1038 (2012), for contrary California Supreme Court authority.

Neither fees nor costs can be awarded against a losing plaintiff under ADA § 505 [42 USC § 12205] unless "the plaintiff's action was frivolous, unreasonable or without foundation." And see Hubbard v. Sobreck, 554 F.3d 742 (9th Cir. 2009) applying same principles to section 55 Civil Code, where cause of action was based on incorporation of the ADA, but see Jankey v. Lee, *supra*, to the contrary. [See Section IV-A-I, *supra*, re: recovery of expert consultant fees by plaintiffs]

While it is often helpful toward settlement for plaintiff to share his or her expert's report (and label it "privileged for settlement purposes only" and "draft report") some defendants may seek to use the report as a checklist, remove all barriers (generally a good thing!) but then ask the Court to dismiss the ADA cause of action because injunctive relief is now "moot" and argue plaintiff has lost federal court standing! (This is generally not a good thing for the plaintiff, as the court may exercise its discretion to dismiss the state law causes of action and require plaintiff to re-file the complaint in the appropriate county Superior Court and effectively start over! However, there are certain advantages in State Court, including the need for only a 9-3 jury verdict- rather than a unanimous jury, if defendant insists on a jury trial.)

If plaintiff is suspicious of a defendant's motives, he may prefer to make a list of demands without sharing the expert report itself, or insist on a stipulation that defendant will not attempt to "moot out" the federal claim. Plaintiff may wish to evaluate a defendant's actual needs and "good faith" objectives before deciding to share the report itself (before the necessary "expert disclosures," whenever scheduled by the Court) and thereby effectively waiving an otherwise assertable "work product" privilege. (Such report, if shared, should be labeled "draft only" and "privileged for settlement".)

5. INSIST ON PROVISION OF PROPER ACCESS AS A CONDITION OF ANY SETTLEMENT OF FINANCIAL ISSUES (DAMAGES AND FEES)
   One of the drawbacks of a "small claims" action for damages (up to the $7,500 small claims court's monetary jurisdictional limit), is that "equitable relief," i.e., an injunction, is not available in small claims court. But a non-complying business might agree to provide access in return for a waiver of damages, or do so voluntarily to avoid being sued again by others.

This author's strong feeling is that plaintiffs and their attorneys should never be "bought off," i.e., should never agree to accept payment of damages and/or attorney fees conditioned on not insisting on provision of access. It is frustrating for a plaintiff to discover, for example, that an inaccessible defendant restaurant was sued several years earlier by someone else but had "settled" the case by paying money to the first plaintiff

<u>without</u> agreeing to provide the necessary access- thereby leaving the inaccessible premises as a trap for other disabled persons! If access is not provided as part of the resolution of a lawsuit, the next disabled person who seeks to use the premises will also be denied access, and the public interest in maximizing access will not be satisfied.[124]

Reportedly certain plaintiff's and their attorneys sue <u>only</u> for damages and attorney fees in state court, and avoid federal court jurisdiction by <u>not</u> seeking injunctive relief under Title III of the ADA. Thus they may be "bought off," leaving the public accommodation in the same inaccessible condition it was before the suit. Such lawsuits do little to further the public interest, and may cause a public sentiment "backlash" which hurts the interests of disabled persons in the public perception.

SB 1186, effective January 1, 2013, includes a prohibition against attorneys sending a pre-litigation demand letter seeking money without provision of access.

H. RESIST "CONFIDENTIALITY" AS A CONDITION OF SETTLEMENT

1. RESIST CONFIDENTIALITY

Defendants will sometimes demand some form of "confidentiality" as a condition for a cooperative settlement. This author personally believes that confidentiality as a principle is inherently adverse to the public interest in having an informed public, and that confidentiality should be resisted <u>unless</u> such agreement is <u>essential</u> to obtaining some major benefit to the public interest or to your individual client.

While publicizing the financial results of a lawsuit may sometimes be counter-productive to the legitimate interests of the client, there can be little value in hiding the injunctive relief aspects of a successful lawsuit, and it may set a positive example. A court ordered injunction or consent decree will of course not be "confidential."
It is a rare case where a defendant will refuse an otherwise mutually valuable settlement unless the plaintiff agrees to confidentiality. Continued public litigation will usually cause <u>more</u> negative publicity for a defendant than settling the case. Further, should plaintiff <u>prove liability</u> by summary judgment, a motion for injunctive relief, or a trial judgment, defendant will no longer have any control over the resulting negative publicity. Settlement may allow a defendant to enter into a consent decree which allows defendant to continue to <u>deny liability</u> <u>while agreeing to provide full access:</u> these are standard provisions for many cooperative consent decrees.

2. PLAINTIFF DOES NOT HAVE TO AGREE! IF DEFENDANT FIGHTS <u>INSTEAD</u> JUST BECAUSE PLAINTIFF WON'T SIGN A CONFIDENTIALITY

---

[124] Perhaps the subsequent plaintiff should seek treble damages, using the prior lawsuit to show obvious "knowing" violations, as well as seeking the necessary injunctive relief!

AGREEMENT, THE ULTIMATE PUBLICITY MAY BE COUNTERPRODUCTIVE TO DEFENDANT

Sometimes its worth calling a defense counsel's bluff and refusing to agree to any confidentiality as a "condition" of settlement. If defendant is <u>really</u> concerned about keeping a low image, extended litigation, depositions and trial may pose more of a threat for public exposure than a cooperative settlement. [125]

3. CONFIDENTIALITY IS USUALLY AGAINST PUBLIC POLICY AND IN SOME CIRCUMSTANCES MAY BE UNETHICAL

The public's need to protect itself against dangerous products has been illustrated by findings of dangerous toys and other products, defective cars (including those with exploding gas tanks), dangerous medications and other prescribed and over the counter drugs, etc. Secret settlements have helped to hide information about these dangers, and blocked warnings which might have saved other consumers from serious injury or death.

In the ADA field, "confidential" settlements may keep plaintiff's attorneys from sharing relevant information, legal theories, or litigation techniques with other disability rights attorneys. While this is exactly what some business defendants want, it does not help disabled members of the public when confidentiality clauses in settlement agreements block sharing of information.

In a 2010 article, "When Secret Settlements Are Unethical . . . And Bad For Your Practice," attorneys Patrick A. Melone (of Washington, D.C.) and John Bauer (of Hartford, Connecticut) advised lawyers that ethical standards, including two specific provisions of the Model Rules of Professional Conduct (Rules 3.4(f) and 5.6(b)) should preclude,

> secrecy provisions that prohibit voluntary disclosures of relevant evidence to other litigants, or prohibit further disclosure of the allegations made in publicly filed court documents
>
> Id. at p.1

The article warns that,

> Secret settlements undermine the proper functioning of the adversary system by concealing evidence that may be crucial to other parties' claims. For example, for decades lawyers for archdioceses routinely settled sexual abuse cases with gag orders that prevented other victims from learning that their abusers were serial offenders whose misdeeds were already known to church authorities. Settlements that prohibit any mention of the allegations raised in a lawsuit also interfere with the public's ability to find the lawyer best qualified to handle a particular case, by making it impossible for

---

[125] On the other hand, confidentiality as to damages amounts paid to a plaintiff may not affect the public interest, and may be a subject that the plaintiff has no desire to publicize. The client must be consulted on this issue. Many disabled persons feel they are more vulnerable to robbery than other persons, and may prefer to keep the monetary amounts of their settlement confidential. Even if there is no "confidentiality" agreement, plaintiff and his attorney may not wish to affirmatively publicize the financial components of a settlement, though they may wish to use the settlement's precedent in negotiating settlement in other cases.

plaintiffs' lawyers to inform prospective clients of the identities of the defendants they have litigated against and what those cases were all about.

The authors of this article state that
> Rule 3.4(f) of the Model Rules prohibits a lawyer from requesting any person, other than a lawyer's own client or the client's relatives or employees, to refrain from voluntarily providing relevant information to another party.[126]

This article also cites Model Rule 5.6(b):
> This rule, which has been adopted, with some variations, in every U.S. jurisdiction, prohibits lawyers from participating in any settlement agreement that restricts a lawyer's right to practice.
> Id. at p.3-4.

This article should be read in full by any attorney faced with the "confidentiality request" issue. Ultimately, the article concludes, at p.8,
> Plaintiff's attorneys need to "just say no" when unethical provisions are proposed for settlement agreements. The public, and the legal profession, will be better off for it.

4. DISABLED PERSONS AND THEIR ATTORNEYS SHOULD PRESERVE THEIR RIGHTS OF FREE SPEECH

My law firm has been extremely reluctant to agree to any "confidentiality" as a condition of settlement, because we felt that confidentiality was often against the public interest. In <u>Jorgensen v. Denny's, Inc., Flagstar Corp.</u> (filed 1994) Alameda County Superior Ct. Action No. 745658-9, Denny's may have <u>misused</u> a confidentiality agreement. Plaintiff reluctantly agreed, at the urging of an excellent and respected judge, to enter into a confidentiality agreement as a required condition of settlement, finally agreeing because of the major public interest results of such settlement: a single "individual plaintiff's lawsuit" was being used to obtain a court enforceable agreement that <u>232</u> "company owned" Denny's restaurants would be <u>made fully accessible</u> for disabled persons within the following three years. However, thereafter, while plaintiff was blocked by the confidentiality clause from publicizing the agreement, Denny's reportedly used the agreement to discourage other disabled persons and their attorneys who threatened or brought suit about any of the subject 232 Denny's, using the "confidential" agreement to argue that Denny's (and its parent company, Flagstar Corp.) had "already" been sued and settled issues as to all of their premises, and that <u>therefore the other lawsuits were unnecessary and without merit!</u>

After a lawsuit against Stanford University involving the Stanford Memorial Church

---

[126] The authors also note, however, that, "California is the only remaining state whose ethics code is not based on the Model Rules, but a proposal to adopt many of the provisions of the Model Rules, including Rule 3.4(f) has been endorsed by the California State Bar and is awaiting judicial approval." Id. at p.4, fn 8.

- a symphony concert venue - was (we thought) fully settled at a court-supervised settlement conference, Stanford refused to complete the settlement unless plaintiff and her attorneys agreed to partial confidentiality: a "no press conference" and "no press release" addendum to the written agreement. Because of the needs of the severely injured plaintiff to the large damage settlement negotiated as part of the agreement, as well as personal preference not to "publicize" settlements, plaintiff and her attorneys agreed. However, several years later, and after two more necessary (and successful) lawsuits against Stanford for access violations at the ("old") Stanford Football Stadium and Stanford's Maples Pavilion (basketball stadium), plaintiff's attorney had the satisfaction of telling the stories of all three cases (without discussing the financial settlement amounts) in an article entitled "Beating Up Stanford" (with reference to an unrelated article by the same title concerning a 1916 boxing match between arch rivals Cal and Stanford).[127]

5. **PLAINTIFFS SHOULD RESIST CONFIDENTIALITY BEING A CONDITION OF SETTLEMENT**

The author's personal feelings as to a plaintiff agreeing to confidentiality as a condition of settlement is (under most circumstances): Don't agree to it! If you have a strong case, there's no reason for the settlement to be confidential. On the other hand, I personally believe there's no need to adversely publicize or intentionally embarrass a defendant that has cooperated and agreed to remove all barriers.

Certainly the injunctive relief could not be confidential, especially when putting the settlement on the record as a court enforceable consent decree or otherwise court-enforceable settlement agreement.[128] This should be a matter of public record. This may also be of some advantage to a defendant that, if later sued by someone else, can point to the consent decree as already guaranteeing that access will be provided according to an agreed reasonable time table. (This is not necessarily a valid defense to being sued by someone else before remedial action is taken. Damages to the plaintiff have already occurred. However it may be relevant to the entities involved in plaintiff seeking injunctive relief.)

Possible Compromise - Sometimes when defendants are adamant about at least partial confidentiality, and express valid concerns, plaintiff might agree that the amount of money paid by the defendants will be confidential, with certain exceptions that

---

[127] When asked if he was "offended" by this teasing of Stanford by a "rival" Cal graduate, the following statement was made by one of California's best trial lawyers, a respected lawyers leader - and proud Stanford graduate: "Paul, Stanford is one of the greatest universities in the world! There is no excuse for it not being fully accessible to the disabled!"

[128] To be Court enforceable by the same court- rather than requiring a new action for "breach of contract"- the settlement agreement and court enforceability must be approved and ordered by the Court. The parties can't by agreement impose jurisdiction on the Court, unless the Court agrees and signs such an order.

allow the plaintiff's attorney to use the settlement amounts in negotiations with other defendants in a confidential setting, i.e., as part of a settlement conference statement (which is lodged and not filed) or mediation statement, or in settlement discussions at a settlement conference or mediation. This compromise may satisfy defendants who are concerned that publicity about their having entered into a monetary settlement may encourage others to sue the same business, or other establishments owned by the same defendants.

Also, monetary confidentiality is not an evil from a "public interest" viewpoint: ordinarily the amount of monetary settlement, both as to damages and attorney fees, is unrelated to the public interest goals of maximizing access at each public facility. On the other hand, setting an example that denial of access may lead to an expensive lawsuit, may influence other businesses to "voluntarily" comply, for example sharing information about the Hankins v. El Torito damages and attorney fees award and affirmation on appeal. Even adverse complaints about the fact that some disabled persons have sued multiple businesses for access may encourage other businesses to voluntarily provide access improvements ("barrier removal"). This would thereby not only further the public interest but also save defendants who have voluntarily complied from the expenses of being sued by other disabled persons who have "encountered barriers." (See Doran v. 7-Eleven, *supra* and Chapman, *supra*).

I. SETTLEMENT PROCEDURES: GENERAL ORDER 56 IN NORTHERN DISTRICT OF CALIFORNIA AND ITS MEDIATION PROGRAM

As of June 21, 2005, and as last amended May 29, 2012, the "G.O. 56" program in the Northern District of California was issued and amended by U.S.N.D. Chief Judge Vaughn R. Walker, General Order 56 now applies to all ADA Title II and Title III cases filed in Northern District Federal Court. The Court, pursuant to FRCP Rule 16, set out special procedures to encourage early settlement in ADA "access" cases, including an early exchange of information (disclosures); an early cooperative site inspection by attorneys and experts of the subject property; an initial "stay" on "all other discovery and proceedings;" a requirement for all attorneys, parties, and if the parties so elect, experts, to "meet in person and confer" and "discuss all claimed premises violations;" and communications as to which "claimed violation" defendants are willing to remediate (G.O. 56, No. 4) "If defendant claims any proposed remediation is not readily achievable, defendant shall specify the factual basis for this claim." In light of case law on "readily achievable standards," presumably defendant must explain why such remediation cannot physically be done, or why it would be "very expensive," including a comparison of the cost of each proposed item of barrier removal, and the financial factors included in ADA §302 (6)(2)(A)(iv), including, but not limited to the "overall financial resources" of each "owner, operator, lessor or lessee." (See Botosan v. McNally Real Estate, (9th Circuit, 2000) 216 Fed. 3d 827)

(See also <u>Molski v. Foley Estates Vineyard</u> 531 F.3d 1043 (2008) for burden of production and burden of proof upon defendants as 9th Circuit standard.)

Thereafter, <u>if</u> the parties "reach a tentative agreement on remediation, plaintiff shall forthwith provide defendant with a statement of damages, if any, claimed under California law, and of costs and attorney's fees incurred to date, and make a demand for settlement of the case in its entirety." (G.O. 56, No.4) Such "tentative agreement on remediation" must include an agreement for a timetable as to each item of remediation; otherwise an agreement on "items" to remediate would be useless. The <u>timetable</u> is generally a crucial item for agreement.

Plaintiff's attorneys should caveat General Order 56 procedures which seem to suggest that a "tentative agreement" requires them to make a demand for damages and attorney fees. Sometimes this will work. Other times the "tentative agreement" may not include all of the necessary terms, and, i.e., after defendants agree that they'll remove certain barriers, they may (a) not agree to do it in a timely fashion, or (b) insist that settlement must be subject to confidentiality or some other unacceptable term. Therefore, the safest thing is to <u>insist that all terms of the "tentative agreement" be put into writing</u> before there is any negotiation of damages or disclosure of fees.

If the parties do not reach settlement of all items in issue - remediation, damages, and fees, and an agreed timetable for each, and do so "within 45 days from the joint site inspection," a procedure is set for filing a "Notice of Need for Mediation" by the plaintiff, and the matter is referred to the ADR Department of the Federal Court for assignment to a mediator and the scheduling of an early mediation "as soon as possible." Most Northern District mediations are scheduled for a federal courtroom at the San Francisco Federal Court, 16th Floor, though some are set by the "non-staff" mediators- a volunteer panel of attorneys and retired judges- for their offices.

If the case does not resolve at mediation, plaintiff must file a "Motion for Administrative Relief pursuant to LR 7-11 requesting a Case Management conference." (G.O. 56, No. 7) Any party who wishes to be relieved of any requirement of G.O. 56 "may file a Motion for Administrative Relief pursuant to LR 7-11."

Our personal experience has been the success of G.O. 56 to reach relatively early resolution of many cases before the necessity of parties entering into full discovery. Three experienced mediators who administer the ADR Office of the Northern District handle many mediations themselves. Mediators who do not have any experience with ADA cases are less likely to achieve satisfactory results- to the detriment of all parties involved.

[See Appendix H, *infra*, for text of G.O. 56 as amended May 29, 2012.]

Because the ADA itself establishes its purpose to ensure Federal Government enforcement of its standards protecting the rights of individuals with disabilities, a "tentative agreement on remediation" should include an insistance that enforcement be guaranteed by a consent decree and order issued by the federal Court. Per 42 USC 12101, ADA section 2 (b):

It is the purpose of this chapter--

(1) to provide a clear and comprehensive national mandate for the elimination of discrimination against individuals with disabilities;

(2) to provide clear, strong, consistent, enforceable standards addressing discrimination against individuals with disabilities;

(3) to ensure that the Federal Government plays a central role in enforcing the standards established in this chapter on behalf of individuals with disabilities; and

(4) to invoke the sweep of congressional authority, including the power to enforce the fourteenth amendment and to regulate commerce, in order to address the major areas of discrimination faced day-to-day by people with disabilities.

VI. OTHER REMEDIES FOR DISABILITY DISCRIMINATION
A. SMALL CLAIMS COURT

Particularly in smaller cases or cases involving single incidents or minor problems, disabled persons should be informed of their right and option to bring a small claims action without a lawyer. California Civil Code §52.2, added to the Code in 1999, specifies "an action pursuant to section 52 or 54.3, which requests damages of $7,500 or less may be brought in small claims court." Disabled persons should argue <u>each</u> incident of violation, i.e. <u>each time</u> they don't have proper disabled parking or restroom, requires a minimum damage award of $4,000 per section 52 or alternatively $1,000 per section 54.3. Copies of all relevant statutes and case law relied upon should be supplied to the judge at the small claims hearing.

Small Claims Court allows a disabled person who has been denied rights under § 51 or § 54 of Civil Code to sue for damages. As to sections 54 and 54.1, such violation may be based on the construction or alteration history (after July 1, 1970 – see §§ 19955-59 Health & Safety Code). It may also be on an ADA "readily achievable" basis, as any ADA violation is incorporated as a violation of § 51(f), § 54(c) and § 54.1(d) Civil Code.

This allows a disabled person to litigate without a lawyer, and thereby get the immediate attention of a business owner. To protect the public interest, it is recommended that plaintiff insist that the barriers complained of be removed on an early but reasonable schedule, as a condition of any settlement, even though <u>injunctive relief is not available as a small claims court remedy</u>.

A copy of the statutes and relevant case law, for submission to the court, would be helpful. Small Claims Court is often presided over by lawyers serving as "<u>pro</u> <u>tem</u>" judges, and they and other "regular" judges may not be familiar with relevant law. As is the case for lawyers, <u>pro</u> <u>per</u> litigants would be wise to educate the judges, preferably with copies of relevant cases or a small legal brief.

<u>Minimum</u> damages are $1,000 "per violation" pursuant to § 54.3 Civil Code (see <u>Donald v. Café Royale</u> (1990) 218 Cal.App.3d 168) and $4,000 per violation per § 52. The California Supreme Court in 2009 held that no proof of "intentional discrimination" is needed to prove a § 51(f) violation when the violation is based on an incorporated violation of the ADA. <u>Munson v. Del Taco</u> (2009) 46 Cal.4th 661. No "intent" is needed to prove a violation of sections 54 or 54.1; see <u>Donald v. Café Royale</u>, *supra*.

While the statute (Civil Code § 54.3) specifies "minimum" damages, there is no "maximum" damages for physical injury or emotional distress. For example, in <u>Hankins v. El Torito</u>

Restaurants, Inc., et al. (1998) 63 Cal.App.4th 510, the appellate court upheld a trial judge's award of $80,000 damages alternatively under Civil Code § 54.3 and Civil Code § 52, in a case with no "special" damages or medical treatment, where a restaurant not only had no disabled accessible public restrooms, but refused to allow a disabled man to use an available "employees only" restroom. However, the current statutory maximum in any small claims action is $7,500.

Civil Code § 52.2 allows a pro per disabled plaintiff to bring an action for damages in small claims court, pursuant to either §§ 52 or 54.3, but there does not appear to be jurisdiction to seek injunctive relief: "An action pursuant to sections 52 or 54.3 may be brought in any court of competent jurisdiction," and this is specified to include small claims court, so long as the jurisdictional limit (now $7,500) is not exceeded.

§ 52.2. Court of competent jurisdiction; defined; actions
An action pursuant to Section 52 or 54.3 may be brought in any court of competent jurisdiction. A "court of competent jurisdiction" shall include small claims court if the amount of the damages sought in the action does not exceed the jurisdictional limits stated in Sections 116.220 and 116.221 of the Code of Civil Procedure.

Disadvantages:
1. No injunctive relief is available in small claims court: A plaintiff cannot compel a defendant business owner or operator to remove an architectural barrier or cease a discriminatory policy. (But they can sue for damages each time their rights are violated.)
2. The small claims judges may be "pro tem" judges, lawyers sitting as temporary judges. They may or may not know anything about this area of law. To ensure success, a litigant should prepare a legal brief on all relevant points of law - just as a lawyer should in Superior Court or federal court. Educate the judge!
3. As any violation of the ADA is also a violation of section 51(f) Civil Code; minimum damages per section 52 are $4,000 per violation. A business owner sued successfully for damages per section 51 may well decide to "voluntarily" provide access rather than facing the possibility of a successful small claims action, or a series of actions.

B. CLASS ACTIONS
   1. INTRODUCTION / DISCLAIMER
   I am not an authority on class actions, but I have participated in several successful injunctive relief class actions under the leadership of attorneys Sid Wolinsky and Larry Paradis of Disability Rights Advocates (DRA), an excellent public interest law firm in Berkeley, California. (These cases expanded the individual actions I filed into class actions, which achieved, for example, major access improvements at more than 1400 Jack in the Box restaurants.) However, it seems appropriate to mention some of the advantages - and pitfalls of using the "class action" remedy.

2. A CLASS ACTION COULD BE BROUGHT UNDER THE ADA FOR INJUNCTIVE RELIEF AND ATTORNEY FEES ONLY WITHOUT A CLAIM FOR DAMAGES EXCEPT AS TO THE NAMED PLAINTIFF

If a "damages" claim regarding members of an "injunctive relief" class is omitted, there may be no threat of preclusion of the rights of individual plaintiffs to sue for damages they personally incurred, and thus no need for "actual" notice to members of the class. (See examples, *infra*, section 4 herein below.) For example, a class action might seek to obtain access at a chain of restaurants, service stations or transportation stations, and set up a reasonable detailed timetable for compliance. If court approved, with a certified class, this might protect the business chain from multiple individual ADA lawsuits for injunctive relief, without affecting the rights of individual disabled persons to claim any personal damages under California law. (But see section 5, *infra*, as to the dangers of a "purported" class action which protects neither the class nor the public interest.)

3. UNDER THE ADA, CLASS ACTIONS ARE LIMITED TO INJUNCTIVE RELIEF AND ATTORNEY FEES

Because there are no individual damages available as a remedy under Title III of the ADA (except as an ADA violation is incorporated into California Civil Code §§ 51(f), 54(c) and 54.1(d)), a class action for injunctive relief should not cut off individual damage rights of disabled persons who may all be normally part of a class. (See Molski v. Gleich, *infra* at VI-B-5-c) However, if damages are sought for all members of the class under California law, class members should be allowed to "opt out" of the class, in order to be allowed to prove their own individual damages (including treble damages) if they believe their personal damages may exceed the damages obtainable in the class action for individual class members. For example, each disabled person who is deterred from using restaurants in a particular chain (because of knowledge that many of these restaurants are inaccessible) may be eligible for an award of statutory minimum damages as part of the class action. However, any disabled person should be able to "opt out" of the class and prove their individual damages actually suffered. For example, a person suffering a bodily functions accident as the result of denial of accessible restroom facilities may be entitled to substantial personal damages. Their damages recovery should not be limited to the damages available to other "class members" who were simply "deterred" on one or more occasions.[129]

4. EXAMPLES OF "CLASS" ACTIONS HANDLED IN CONJUNCTION WITH "DRA," WHICH OBTAINED MAJOR INJUNCTIVE RELIEF AT MULTIPLE BUSINESSES, BUT LEFT DAMAGES ISSUES TO INDIVIDUAL PLAINTIFFS

---

[129] Re: the possibility of damages to class members who were deterred from using theaters because of their inaccessibility, see Arnold v. United Artists Theater Circuit Inc., et al (N.D. Cal. 1994) 866 F.Supp 433, an opinion by (former) Chief Judge Thelton Henderon.

a. 232 DENNY'S RESTAURANTS (JORGENSEN V. DENNY'S INC., FLAGSTAR CORPORATION) (ALAMEDA COUNTY SUPERIOR COURT, 1994)

In this state court action, plaintiff (the late and courageous Concetta Jorgensen) sued one Denny's restaurant and its parent company, Flagstar. Several prior lawsuits had accomplished ADA barrier removal at individual restaurants, but did not apparently motivate defendants to spend the money to voluntarily make their other restaurants accessible. I associated disability class action expert, attorney, Sid Wolinsky, and requested that the court expand the Jorgensen lawsuit into a class action (with plaintiff Concetta Jorgensen's consent.) Instead, defendants suggested, (and the court recommended) that in "settlement" of our individual plaintiff's case, defendants agree to make all 232 "company owned" Denny's fully accessible to disabled persons within 3 years. Defendants also paid compensatory damages to the individual plaintiff. On a contested motion for attorneys fees, the Alameda County Superior Court judge, Hon. Ken Kawaichi, awarded a 1.6 "enhancement" of fees because of the important public interest results of our lawsuit, pursuant to California Code of Civil Procedure section 1021.5.

b. 1,400 JACK IN THE BOX RESTAURANTS (JORGENSEN V. JACK IN THE BOX) FOODMAKER, INC.

In Concetta Jorgensen v. Jack in the Box Restaurants, Foodmaker, Inc., N.D. Cal. Case No. C95-406 SAW, an "individual plaintiff" Northern District federal court case was expanded into an injunctive relief class action after I associated as (lead) co-counsel attorneys Larry Paradis and Sid Wolinsky of DRA. (An extremely competent attorney and access expert, Larry Paradis, sat down with defendants and worked out detailed plans for over 100 different designs involved in the more than 1400 Jack in the Box restaurants, to make each fully accessible, including accessible parking, entryways, seating, and restrooms.) The settlement included all company owned Jack-in-the-Box restaurants, and a company "request" that all "franchise" holders also agree to remove all barriers, or each would be added as a defendant to our lawsuit. Due to the excellent class action work of the DRA attorneys, all Jack in the Box restaurants were required to be made accessible per ADA standards, without taking away the right of any individual disabled person to bring their own damages action if they felt they had suffered damages compensable under California law.

c. 150 BP SERVICE STATIONS (HODGES V. BP OIL)

Sue Hodges, a disabled wheelchair user and a respected disabled rights activist, brought an individual action against a single B.P. Oil gas station and its owners and operators. This lawsuit was expanded to a class action requiring that 150 service stations to be made accessible as to parking, entryways, restrooms, etc. Sue Hodges v. B.P. Exploration and Oil, Tosco Corp., Case No., C95-022115 (N.D. Cal. 1995)

d. ALL CALIFORNIA GREYHOUND BUS STATIONS (IMPERIALE, POTTER V. GREYHOUND)

This action, brought by plaintiffs Paul Imperiale and Steve Potter, resulted in Greyhound's agreement to make <u>all</u> of its California bus stations accessible. <u>Imperiale, et al v. Greyhound Lines, Inc</u>. Case No. C94-04435 SAW (N.D. Cal. 1995).

5. <u>CAVEAT</u> CLASS ACTION EFFECT ON EXISTING OR SUBSEQUENT INDIVIDUAL ACTIONS

   a. INDIVIDUAL ACTIONS MAY BE PUT ON HOLD WITH STAY ON DISCOVERY (<u>TACO BELL</u> EXAMPLE)

   One individual action involving denial of access to a Taco Bell under ADA standards is still on "hold" after 6 years while a "related" class action drags on. However it is the class action which will obtain major public interest results, and by the end of 2011 had obtained several major rulings in favor of the class.

   Sometimes relating a case to a pending ADA class action case may result in major delays in obtaining any injunctive relief or damages for an individual plaintiff, where his liability claims are actually or effectively limited to proving "readily achievable" liability under the ADA. Such individual actions are likely to have all action "stayed" until the resolution of the class action. (The major class action against Taco Bell involved the "readily achievable" status for barrier removal at hundreds of restaurants.)

   b. WATCH FOR PHONY "CLASS ACTION" SETTLEMENTS THAT ATTEMPT TO INSULATE DEFENDANTS FROM OTHER LAWSUITS BUT DO NOT PROTECT THE PUBLIC INTEREST OR THE RIGHTS OF INDIVIDUAL DISABLED PLAINTIFFS.

   <u>Molski v. Gleich</u> (9th Cir. 2003) 318 F.3d 937) invalidated a purported class action "settlement" because it didn't really benefit or protect the members of the "class". The 9th Circuit rejected the class settlement approved by the District Court, because it unfairly cut off the damage rights for the individuals comprising the class, excepting out only those persons who suffered "physical" injuries but denying all class members any statutory damages or treble damages, even for those who proved physical injuries caused by illegal access barriers. The injunctive relief terms of the settlement were not specifically challenged by the 9th Circuit, but it gave defendants six years to make "readily achievable" access improvements, with no real standards or practical supervision on enforcement along the way, during these six years. It also allowed defendant ARCO, with regard to "approximately 1200 gas stations and minimarts in the State of California" (Id. at 942) to <u>decline</u> to complete "accessibility enhancements,"

if it is "Structurally Impracticable, Technically Infeasible or Virtually Impossible; or if completion of such Enhancement would involve a Significant Risk or Loss of Selling or Serving Space," or if it would violate a federal, state, or local law.

Id. at 943. (This sure left of a lot of discretion to the oil company!) Under the class "settlement" approved by the District Court:
> the class members lost their rights to pursue any claims (excepting those for physical injury); the class representative received monetary relief of $5,000; and the class counsel was paid $50,000.

Id. at 953. The 9th Circuit concluded:
> In sum, the class members received nothing; the named plaintiff and class counsel received compensation for his injury and their time; and the defendant escaped paying any punitive or almost any compensatory damages. Id. ("[A]ll the settlement does for ... [the absent class members] is cut them off at the knees."). This outcome is particularly problematic because only a minimal amount of discovery occurred in this case, and <u>the primary components of the agreement were reached prior to filing of the class action.</u>

Molski v. Gleich, *supra*, 318 F.3d at 954. (Emphasis added)

The Molski v. Gleich opinion reversing the class certification and the settlement agreement also held:
> Because the consent decree released almost all of the absent class members' claims with little or no compensation, the settlement agreement was unfair and did not adequately protect the interests of the absent class members.

Id. at 955.

As a final reason for reversal, the Court noted:

> Moreover, we are concerned about the possible collusiveness between the named plaintiff, class counsel, and defendants. The record shows that the named plaintiff and defendants reached an agreement regarding the primary components of the consent decree within four months. Although this fact does not amount to collusiveness *per se* as argued by Appellants, it indicates that the named plaintiff and class counsel "failed to prosecute or defend the action with due diligence and reasonable prudence." [Citations omitted.]

Id. at 955-56.[130]

---

[130] The plaintiff, Jarek Molski, was also the subject of a number of 9th Circuit and District Court opinions, including Molski v. Evergreen Dynasty Corp. (9th Cir. 2007) 500 F.3d.1047, which upheld sanctions against Molski and his attorney, as confirmed by a divided en banc decision by the 9th Circuit, with strong dissents by Chief Judge Alex Kozinski and eight other circuit judges, at 521 F.3d 1215.

When there is a class action against a particular defendant which is limited to injunctive relief, and does not purport to limit individual actions for damages, res judicata principles do not bar an individual litigant's right to seek damages under California's DPA (§§ 54.1 and 54.3 Civil Code). (The individual's claim for damages was based on multiple visits to a number of automotive retail and service centers where the counter-tops were too high for a wheelchair user to use. Louie v. BFS Retail and Commercial Operations, LLC, 178 Cal.App.4th 1544 (2009)). The class action had been in Florida federal court, settled with a national class action Consent Decree for injunctive relief only. The federal court had authorized no notice to class members precisely "because no damages were sought and the court was certifying the class under Federal Rules of Civil Procedure, Rule 23(b)(2) . . . which allows a class action without notice to class members" when certain prerequisites were met. Id. at 1550.

C. PUBLICIZING THE VIOLATION MAY HAVE POSITIVE EFFECT

Sometimes direct action may motivate a business to comply with the law. Direct picketing of discriminating businesses was used successfully with regard to the Civil Rights movement of the 1960s, from those walking picket lines regarding San Francisco "Auto Row" businesses to lunch counter sit-ins and "Freedom Rider" buses in the deep South.

In 2008 certain Bay Area demonstrations were held regarding a large San Francisco theater complex, the Metreon 16 screen theater, which showed a movie regarding disabled rights advocates ("The Music Within") at a theater with "stadium seating" which relegated disabled wheelchair users to "front row only" seating, the least desirable location in the movie theater.[131] Certain picketing of an "industry" building in Sacramento by wheelchair users may have contributed to the dropping of a threatened anti-disabled access ballot initiative in early 2006.

---

[131] However a lawsuit was necessary in order to win a Consent Decree settlement. Overbo and Brown-Booker v. Loews California Theatres, Inc., et al (N.D. Cal. 2008) C07-05368 MHP. Consent Decree Order of February 2, 2010. (See Appendix D), The lawsuit, an individual action by plaintiffs Jana Overbo and Nikki Brown-Booker, obtained improved access seating locations in a sixteen theater complex, including an IMAX, substantial damages for the two plaintiffs, and other access improvements for the theaters and entry into the building, etc. Substantial attorney fees, litigation expenses, and costs, per ADA section 505 and California statute, were awarded per motion to the Court. (Order of September 7, 2010)

VII. ARE THERE "ABUSES" OF THE ADA? WE CAN PROTECT "GOOD FAITH" BUSINESSES WITHOUT WEAKENING THE ADA OR CALIFORNIA'S LAWS PROTECTING THE DISABLED

A. INTRODUCTION: IS "SERIAL" ADA LITIGATION "ABUSIVE"? OR ARE ATTORNEY FEE AWARDS CONGRESS' INCENTIVE TO <u>ENCOURAGE</u> ENFORCEMENT OF THE ADA?

In 2006, before the appellate courts addressed the issues of possible "abuses" of the ADA, and the related issues of "serial" litigation and "vexatious litigants" a relevant article was published in the UCLA Law Review: "The Perversity of Limited Civil Rights Remedies: the Case of 'Abusive' ADA Litigation," by Samuel R. Bagenstos, a professor of law at Washington University School of Law. Professor Bagenstos observed that the ADA controversy should be seen as part of a larger picture: enforcement of civil rights laws by private litigation. He concludes his article:

> The controversy over serial ADA litigation highlights the continuing ambivalence about Civil Rights law as a profit making enterprise. But the legal system must get past that ambivalence if civil rights laws are to be enforced. The private, profit making bar has been essential to civil rights enforcement.

Id. at p. 25.

Bagenstos discusses the necessity of private attorneys' litigation:

> Because the government does not fully enforce the ADA, private enforcement is essential. But in the private bar, 'most civil rights litigation is not brought by institutional litigators or by large firms engaging in pro bono activity' but by individual lawyers who are trying to make a living. Accordingly, enforcement largely depends on lawyers who need to earn income on their cases to keep their practices viable. As in other areas of public interest litigation, Congress sought to provide an incentive for enforcement of the ADA's public accommodations provisions by giving prevailing party plaintiffs the right to recover attorneys' fees. But the incentives to bring ADA accessibility cases are still likely to be too weak to lead to full enforcement.

Id. at p. 8.

As 9th Circuit Chief Judge Alex Kozinsky noted in <u>Moreno v. City of Sacramento:</u>

> Lawyers must eat, so they generally won't take cases without a reasonable prospect of getting paid. Congress thus recognized that private enforcement of civil rights legislation relies on the availability of fee awards: "If private citizens are to be able to assert their civil

rights, and if those who violate the Nation['s] fundamental laws are not to proceed with impunity, then citizens must have the opportunity to recover what it costs them to vindicate these rights in court." S.Rep. No. 94-1011, at 2 (1976), as reprinted in 1976 U.S.C.C.A.N. 5908, 5910.FN1.

Moreno v. City of Sacramento (9th Cir. 2008) 534 F.3d 1106, at 1111.
In Molski v. Evergreen Dynasty Corp. (9th Cir. 2007) 500 F.3d 1047 the 9th Circuit panel, upheld sanctioning Molski and his attorney for specific factual exaggerations and a dishonest and unethical course of conduct - including writing to unrepresented defendants and advising them not to seek legal advice of an attorney - but specifically upholding use of "serial litigation" as a possibly necessary tool to enforce the ADA and achieve an accessible society. [See also § V.D.5., *supra*] The entire 9th Circuit (all 26 judges sitting en bank) reconsidered Molski, and the majority upheld the decision requiring prefiling application for all Central District filings by attorney Tom Frankovich and disabled plaintiff Jared Molski. Molski v. Evergreen Dynasty Corp., (9th Cir. 2008) 521 F.3d 1215. However, an unusual coalition of "conservative" Chief Judge Alex Kozinski and eight of the more moderate and "liberal" judges on the panel (Judges Berzon, Pregerson, Reinhardt, Hawkins, McKueown, Wardlaw, W. Fletcher and Paez) filed strong dissents, urging that a pre-filing limitation on civil rights cases was the wrong remedy and drastically affected the rights of all of attorney Frankovich's disabled clients, possibly having a chilling effect on legitimate ADA lawsuits. The dissent of Judge Kozinski also noted that the trial court made its factual findings without benefit of any evidentiary hearing. Id. at p. 1216 - 1222.

Yet even the 9th Circuit panel decision upholding the pre-filing orders against plaintiff Molski and attorney Frankovich sought to warn against district courts condemning "serial litigation as vexatious as a matter of course." In Molski v. Everygreen Dynasty Corp., et al, *supra*, 500 F.3d 1047, this 9th Circuit panel cautioned against interpreting its decision as a criticism of any plaintiff for simply filing multiple complaints:
> In summary, we reemphasize that the simple fact that a plaintiff has filed a large number of complaints, standing alone, is not a basis for designating a litigant as "vexatious." De Long, 912 F.2d at 1147; In re Oliver, 682 F.2d 443, 446 (3d Cir.1982). We also emphasize that the textual and factual similarity of a plaintiff's complaints, standing alone, is not a basis for finding a party to be a vexatious litigant. Accessibility barriers can be, and often are, similar in different places of public accommodation, and there is nothing inherently vexatious about using prior complaints as a template. See Wilson, 411 F.Supp.2d at 1196 (stating that uniform instances of misconduct can justify uniform pleadings).

As we discussed above, the ADA does not permit private plaintiffs to seek damages, and limits the relief they may seek to injunctions and attorneys' fees. We recognize that the unavailability of damages reduces or removes the incentive for most disabled persons who are injured by inaccessible places of public accommodation to bring suit under the ADA. See Samuel R. Bagenstos, The Perversity of Limited Civil Rights Remedies: The Case of "Abusive" ADA Litigation, 54 U.C.L.A. L.Rev. 1, 5 (2006). As a result, most ADA suits are brought by a small number of private plaintiffs who view themselves as champions of the disabled. District courts should not condemn such serial litigation as vexatious as a matter of course. See De Long, 912 F.2d at 1148 n. 3. For the ADA to yield its promise of equal access for the disabled, it may indeed be necessary and desirable for committed individuals to bring serial litigation advancing the time when public accommodations will be compliant with the ADA. But as important as this goal is to disabled individuals and to the public, serial litigation can become vexatious when, as here, a large number of nearly-identical complaints contain factual allegations that are contrived, exaggerated, and defy common sense. (Emphasis added)

Id. at 1061-1062.[132]

In Antoninetti v. Chipotle Mexican Grill, 9th Cir., 2010, 643 F.3d 1165, the 9th Circuit criticized the District Court's use of plaintiff's history of suing "over 20 business entities" as a factor against his credibility:

Courts must tread carefully before construing a Disability Act plaintiff's history of litigation against him. As we have noted more than once, "[f]or the [Disabilities Act] to yield its promise of equal access for the disabled, it may indeed be necessary and desirable for committed individuals to bring serial litigation advancing the time when public accommodations will be compliant with the [Disabilities Act]." D'Lil v. Best W. Encina Lodge & Suites, 538 F.3d 1031, 1040 (9th Cir.2008) (quoting Molski v. Evergreen Dynasty Corp., 500 F.3d 1047, 1062 (9th Cir.2007) (citing Samuel R. Bagnestos, The Perversity of Limited Civil Rights Remedies: The Case of "Abusive" ADA Litigation, 54 UCLA L.Rev. 1, 5 (2006). We must therefore be "particularly cautious" regarding "credibility determinations that rely on a plaintiff's past [Disabilities Act] litigation."

Id. at 1075.

In Kittok v. Leslie's Pool Mart, Inc., (E.D. Cal), 687 F.Supp. 2d. 953, at 959-960, the Court explicitly recognized that the attorney fee incentive of the ADA were intended by Congress to encourage attorneys to handle civil rights cases for disabled persons, even when multiple lawsuits resulted:

The persistence of plaintiffs in bringing multiple lawsuits alleging unequal access to places of public accommodation does not demonstrate wrongdoing by plaintiffs anymore than it shows a hesitation of businesses to comply with the law. As the Ninth Circuit has noted in the context of ADA litigation,

---

[132] The Court went on to find the district court had not "abused its discretion in declaring Molski a vexatious litigant and imposing a pre-filing order against him." Id. at 1062.

> "For the ADA to yield its promise of equal access for the disabled, it may indeed be necessary and desirable for committed individuals to bring serial litigation advancing the time when public accommodations will be compliant with the ADA." Evergreen Dynasty Corp., 500 F.3d 1047, 1062 (9th Cir.2007) (panel op.), citing Samuel R. Bagenstos, The Perversity of Limited Civil Rights Remedies: The Case of 'Abusive' ADA Litigation, 54 U.C.L.A. L.Rev. 1, 5 (2006).
>
> . . .
>
> Yes, plaintiff's counsel stand to benefit financially from this lawsuit, as do defendant's counsel, who presumably are not representing defendant on a contingency basis. But this does not, in and of itself, call into question the legitimacy of their fee request. "The fee-shifting statutes reflect a judgment that civil rights laws will be underenforced unless private lawyers are given financial incentives to bring cases under those laws." Bagenstos, *supra*, 54 U.C.L.A. L.Rev. at 30. Defense counsel cannot assert these very incentives as a reason to deny the statutorily conferred right they were designed to bring. "That plaintiffs' lawyers want to be paid the 'reasonable' attorneys' fees authorized by statute should provide no basis for objecting to their litigation practices." Id.

Id. at 960.

Similarly, the Kittok Court found similar public policy reasons to enforce the similar attorney fees provisions of California Law:

> Because the Court found that Leslie's "denie[d] or interfere[d] with admittance to or enjoyment" of a public accommodation, the statute confers a right to fees. The attorney fee provision of the DPA is reflective of the California "legislature's awareness of the continuous problems of enforcement" of disability access laws. Donald v. Café Royale, Inc., 218 Cal.App.3d 168, 179, 266 Cal.Rptr. 804 (1990). In explicitly providing for the recovery of attorney's fees, even though the DPA does not require a showing of damages, the California legislature explicitly determined that there is a societal value to the vindication of the rights at issue here.

Id. at 960.

B. ANYONE WHO COMMITS FRAUD UNDER THE GUISE OF THE ADA OR OTHERWISE SHOULD BE PUNISHED FOR THE FRAUDULENT CONDUCT, UNDER CURRENTLY AVAILABLE LEGAL REMEDIES; NO AMENDMENTS TO WEAKEN THE ADA ARE NECESSARY

Apparently those who complain about "frivolous" lawsuits or those involving "de minimus" violations are not aware of the currently available remedies for a wrongfully sued business. (See Skaff v. Meridien North America Beverly Hills, LLC (9th Cir. 2007) 506 F.3d 832, for lengthy discussion of meaning of "de minimis.")[133] However, existing law allows an award

---

[133] The application by the Court of the "de minimis" concept to one aspect of plaintiff's complaint - being unable to shower overnight while a hotel guest paying for an "accessible" hotel room should not be labeled "de minimis" because it only caused a denial of "full and equal access" for a "few hours" - seems factually questionable. However the Court found many other aspects of plaintiff's assertions to be valid.

of attorney fees against a plaintiff who brings a frivolous or fraudulent lawsuit, so long as such a fee award does not penalize a losing but "good faith" civil rights plaintiff, per the "Christiansburg" standards.[134] (See Brown v. Lucky Stores, Inc., et al. (9th Cir. 2001) 246 F.3d 1182, extending the Christianburg principles to deny an order of costs against a losing but good faith plaintiff.) Statutes which can be used by prevailing defendants, where plaintiff has not sued in good faith, include ADA § 505 and California Civil Code §§ 54.3 and 55.

However, Section 55 Civil Code <u>cannot</u> be used to award attorney fees against a "good faith" plaintiff, as held by the 9th Circuit in Hubbard v. Sobreck, *supra*, overruling certain State Court cases holding to the contrary. Hubbard v. Sobreck, *supra*, relied on the Christianburg principles, and held the ADA preempted this issue by section 505 and regulations specifically adopting the Christianburg rationale, insofar as sections 55(c) and 54.1(d) incorporated any violation of the ADA into California law, and was the basis for section 55's injunctive relief. [But caveat Jankey v. Lee, *supra*, to the contrary.]

In Skaff, *supra*, the Court noted that the district Court already "has at its disposal appropriate tools to protect its own and the public's interest, in that if allegations are unfounded, sanctions can be awarded or pre-filing orders can be imposed." Id. at 845. However the 9th Circuit also reminded businesses not to complain if they are in actuality out of compliance: "Conversely, if damage allegations are founded on true facts, then a party should not be faulted for seeking damages and the attorney fees the ADA expressly permits the party to pursue." Id.

C. EFFORTS TO WEAKEN DISABILITY LAWS BY PROVIDING A NINETY (90) DAY NOTICE REQUIREMENT WOULD DESTROY ENFORCEABILITY OF THE ADA AND RELATED CALIFORNIA LAWS

1. REQUIRING ADVANCE NOTICE WOULD DESTROY INCENTIVE FOR BUSINESSES TO PROVIDE ACCESS, AND ALLOW THEM TO DELAY DOING SO UNTIL FORMAL COMPLAINTS ARE RECEIVED

    The attorney fees provisions of the ADA, § 505, and related fee provisions of California state laws (See Civil Code §§ 52, 54.3 and 55; Code of Civil Procedure § 1021.5; Health & Safety Code § 19953), are intended to encourage attorneys to handle these cases by providing a statutory attorney fees remedy. The threat of being subject to such fees is a current incentive to businesses to comply with their access law obligations. If businesses knew in advance that they had a "grace period" and could deny access in perpetuity to disabled persons, and only had to comply with the existing law that

---

[134] In Fox v. Vice, 131 S. Ct. 2205 (2011) a 2011 Supreme Court Case clearly held the principles of Christiansburg Garment Co. v. Equal Employment Opportunity Comm'n, 434 U.S. 412, 98 S. Ct. 694, 54 L. Ed. 2d 648 (1978) applicable to any prevailing party defense efforts to obtain fees against a civil rights plaintiff. See section IV-J, *supra*.

they were violating after they had received a "90 day" written notice, <u>all incentive for "voluntary" compliance would disappear.</u> In Skaff v. Meridien North America Beverly Hills LLC (9th Cir. November 1, 2007) 506 F.3d 832, 844-845, the 9th Circuit explicitly rejected the concept that any advance notice requirement exists under the ADA, or can be considered as a prerequisite or factor relevant to an award of attorney fees: "We hold that the ADA does not require, either explicitly or by reference to another statute, that a plaintiff give notice of intention to sue before filing a suit as a prerequisite to the recovery of attorneys' fees and costs." Id. at 845. [See also § VI.E.3, *supra*.]

2. THE CALIFORNIA ATTORNEY GENERAL ADDRESSED THIS ISSUE IN A 2003 LETTER OPINION WHICH FOUND NO REASON TO REQUIRE ADVANCE "NOTICE" BEFORE A LAWSUIT

The California Attorney General's Office established is position on the "frivolous lawsuit" issue in an official August 4, 2003, letter issued by Chief Deputy Attorney General Steve Coony on behalf of Attorney General Bill Lockyer (included here in Appendix X-E-3). In response to claims that "frivolous" lawsuits for "minor violations" of the ADA had been filed, the Attorney General's letter (to the Los Angeles City Attorney's Office) made a number of relevant observations:

> Specifically, no complainant has asserted or provided evidence that the access violations which are the subject of any civil action filed against them or their clients do not exist. Moreover, while some of these complainants contend that the access violations for which they have been sued are "minor," whether such violations are in fact minor is debatable. While a violation may be minor in the eye of a business owner, the violation may not be minor to a person with a disability. . . .
>
> . . .
>
> We are very mindful of the difficulties that small businesses may face in bringing their buildings and facilities into compliance with state and federal access laws and regulations. Nevertheless, we cannot ignore the fact that the ADA has been in effect for 12 years, and state laws requiring privately funded accommodations to be fully accessible to persons with disabilities have been in existence for over 30 years. Unfortunately, non-compliance with state and federal access laws and their implementing regulations continues to be a pervasive and persistent problem in California and throughout the country. Compliance with our access laws and regulations is not optional. The best way to avoid litigation is to take proactive steps to comply with these laws and regulations.

The Attorney General's letter also responded to complaints "that business owners are not given notice of access violations and the opportunity to cure these violations before a lawsuit is filed":

> However, in recent years both state and federal legislation that would have required plaintiffs to notify business owners of the existence of access

violations at their facilities and to give them a specified time period to correct these violations prior to filing a lawsuit were soundly defeated in the Legislature and Congress. The disability community, which strongly opposed this legislation, believes that a "wait period" is inappropriate, given the fact that state and federal access laws have been in effect for a long time.

The Attorney General's letter concluded:
The Attorney General is strongly committed to the enforcement of our access laws and is supportive of those who pursue private enforcement actions in a lawful manner. However, we will consider taking action against those who pursue actions in an unlawful manner. If you are aware of any such cases, please feel free to bring them to our attention.

D. SOME COURTS HAVE CREATED THEIR OWN REMEDIES TO PUNISH WHAT THEY FOUND TO BE UNETHICAL OR "ABUSIVE" CONDUCT

1. MOLSKI 9th CIRCUIT DECISIONS/ORDERS

In Molski v. Mandarin Touch Restaurant (C.D.Cal., Case No. CV04-0450 ER), Judge Edward Rafeedie found that plaintiff Molski had filed more than 400 lawsuits; that many were without merit; and issued an order finding that Mr. Molski "is a vexatious litigant" and that Mr. Molski will not be permitted to file any new lawsuits without obtaining leave of court. The Court also pointed out the existence of possible FRCP Rule 11 sanctions against Molski's attorney. Thus (regardless of the "correctness" of this Court's order against Mr. Molski), this Court's ruling makes clear the availability of existing remedies, without the need for legislative action to weaken the Unruh Act or other California civil rights laws.

As noted in Footnote 9 of a recent 9th Circuit case which protected the rights of disabled persons to obtain statutory attorney fees in meritorious cases, Skaff v. Meridien North America Beverly Hills, LLC (9th Cir. 2007) 506 F.3d 832, remedies already exist for abuses:

If it develops that discovery shows that a party did not have a good-faith basis for the general factual allegations made in a complaint, then that party will be subject to sanctions under the normal standards. See Molski v. Evergreen Dynasty Corp., No. 05-56452, 2007 WL 2458547 at *14 and n. 8 (9th Cir. Aug. 31, 2007) (per curiam). Moreover, if there is a persistent pattern of unfounded allegations, in an appropriate case a litigant or his or her counsel may be subjected to the rigors of a pre-filing order. See id.

Molski was modified by the 9th Circuit in denying en banc hearing [(9th Cir. 2007) 521 F.3d 1215], but certain sanctions were left in place. There were major dissents joined by nine Circuit Judges, who felt there was insufficient evidence to justify imposing a pre-litigation "leave of court" requirement before Molski or his attorney could file any new "ADA" actions in the Central District. (A state bar proceeding against the attorney reportedly ended with his exoneration of all State Bar accusations.)

2. THESE CASES ARE EVIDENCE THAT THE COURTS ALREADY HAVE REMEDIES FOR "ABUSES;" THERE'S NO NEED TO WEAKEN CIVIL RIGHTS LAWS IN ORDER TO DETER "MISUSE"

Both federal and state laws already have "prevailing party" attorney fees provisions. While these can only be awarded against a civil rights plaintiff in circumstances where the action was not brought in good faith (see Brown v. Lucky Stores, Inc., et al. (9th Cir. 2001) 246 F.3d 1182), this shows that there are already remedies for the "abusive" and "bad faith" actions that critics claim are already prevalent.

(See also standards of Hubbard v. Sobreck, 554 F.3d 742 (9th Cir. 2009), where the 9th Circuit reaffirmed that a winning defendant could not seek attorneys fees against a losing plaintiff under Civil Code section 55, for seeking injunctive relief based on an incorporated violation of the ADA per violation alleged under sections 54(c) or (54.1(d), unless the Christianburg standards were violated, i.e. the lawsuit was "frivolous, fraudulent, or without any merit.") (See also the 2011 9th Circuit opinion by Judge Stephen Reinhardt in Harris v. Maricopa County Superior Court (9th Cir. Ariz.) 2011 WL 16704 spelling out standards for finding aspects of a lawsuit to be truly "frivolous" but limiting "prevailing" defendants to a heavy burden of proof, that any fees or costs claimed were incurred solely to defendant against the "frivolous" portions of a lawsuit.)[Caveat the December 17, 2012, California Supreme Court holding in Jankey v. Lee, *supra*, that section 55 Civil Code attorney fees could be available to a prevailing defendant even against a "good faith" plaintiff.]

There is no reason that we should pass new laws to "protect" businesses that are actually in violation of the ADA and California civil rights laws and which are, in fact, discriminating against physically disabled persons.

FRCP Rule 11 sanctions in federal court and CCP § 128.5 sanctions in state court are available to punish "frivolous" lawsuits. Litigants who file multiple lawsuits which are found to be frivolous may be sanctioned and limited under existing laws. As to some proposed legislation, there is no need to single out disabled persons for a unique limitation on their civil rights. Further, most forms of proposed limitation could also be extended to other civil rights protections, a "slippery slope" which merits the support of disabled persons by all persons and organizations who value the protection of civil rights.

As noted by Congresswoman Maxine Waters during the Congressional committee hearings in May 2000 (during which Clint Eastwood and Rep. Tom Foley (R - Florida) attempted to impose limits on the ADA), there are multiple existing ways to discipline any attorneys who do not act legally or ethically, including Court sanctions and State Bar sanctions. As Rep. Waters stated, we should not cut back on important civil rights protections for physically disabled persons for the purpose of disciplining lawyers.

E. JUDGE KARLTON'S DECISION IN WILSON V. PIER 1 IMPORTS (2006), HELD THAT DEFENDANTS DON'T HAVE STANDING TO COMPLAIN ABOUT WHAT PLAINTIFF MAY HAVE DONE IN OTHER CASES, ESPECIALLY WHEN DEFENDANTS WERE NOT "BLAMELESS" AS TO ADA VIOLATIONS

Prior to the Ninth Circuit's final order in Molski v. Evergreen, *supra*, Judge Karlton addressed the sometimes popular defense tactic of attacking any plaintiff who had filed multiple cases by accusing the plaintiff of being a "vexatious litigant" and seeking a "pre-filing order," as done by Judge Rafeedie in the Central District in Molski v. Mandarin Touch Restaurant (C.D. Cal. 2004) 347 F. Supp.2d 860. Judge Karlton's opinion rested on an issue apparently not raised in other similar litigation: the standing of a defendant in one case to challenge a plaintiff's lawsuit on the basis of that plaintiff's alleged conduct in other litigation:

> [D]efendants, like any litigant, must possess traditional standing. In this context, that means that in order to bring the motion the defendants must be subject to the injury complained of, vexatious litigation. Put differently, their righteous indignation must be bottomed on their own blameless conduct, and that they are the subject to a frivolous lawsuit because they, in fact, have not violated the ADA. They have failed to demonstrate compliance with the statute.

Wilson v. Pier 1 Imports (E.D. Cal. Jan. 27, 2006), 411 F.Supp.2d 1196, 1199.

As to the propriety of attacking plaintiff because he had filed 85 ADA lawsuits, and considering plaintiff's detailed evidence offered to support the validity of at least 43 of these lawsuits, the Court concluded:

> From all that appears, the number of lawsuits plaintiff has filed does not reflect that he is a vexatious litigant; rather, it appears to reflect the failure of the defendants to comply with the law. Accordingly, the court cannot find that plaintiff has filed frivolous ADA lawsuits.

Id. at 1200.

Similarly, the Court found no basis to find plaintiff's attorney, Lynn Hubbard, a "vexatious litigant" because he had filed "approximately 1,030 lawsuits in the past four years," noting "mere litigiousness is insufficient: DeLong, 912 F.2d at 1147." While finding that a number of "Hubbard's complaints are virtually identical," the court continued, "It is unclear to this court, however, why uniform instances of misconduct do not justify uniform pleadings."

Id. at 1201.

The court concluded, "Based on the evidence presented, defendants have not shown that Hubbard is a vexatious litigant. Indeed, they have left the court with the distinct fear that the motion is frivolous."
Id.

F. FILING A LARGE NUMBER OF LAWSUITS DOES NOT, BY ITSELF, SHOW THE LAWSUITS ARE "FRIVOLOUS" OR "VEXATIOUS"

In Wilson v. Murillo 163 Cal.App.4th 1124 (2008), at 1128, the Court noted in a footnote, in response to defendant labeling Wilson as a "serial litigant," that the fact Wilson had filed numerous ADA access lawsuits was "immaterial" to the Court's resolution of the case, citing with approval a previous federal court decision involving the same plaintiff:

> "Wilson does not dispute that he has filed many ADA access lawsuits. Numerosity alone, however, is insufficient to show that his lawsuits are frivolous or harassing. One court has examined the contents of Wilson's filings and has made an express finding that his ADA claims are not frivolous and that he is not a vexatious litigant. "From all that appears, the number of lawsuits [Wilson] has filed does not reflect that he is a vexatious litigant; rather, it appears to reflect the failure of the defendants to comply with the law." (Wilson v. Pier I Imports (US), Inc. (E.D.Cal.2006) 411 F.Supp.2d 1196, 1200.)"

Wilson v. Murillo, *supra* at 1128.

[See also quote from Antoninetti v. Chipotle Mexican Grill, Court, *supra*, at section VII-A of this book.]

G. FILING MULTIPLE ADA LAWSUITS IS NOT VEXATIOUS, NOR IS USE OF BOILERPLATE COMPLAINTS, SO LONG AS THE ALLEGATIONS IN EACH ARE SUPPORTED BY THE FACTS

A similar attempt to have a plaintiff declared a "vexatious litigant" because he had filed 219 lawsuits was also rejected in Doran v. Vicorp Restaurants, Inc. (C.D. Cal. 2005) 407 F.Supp.2d 1115, another action in which both plaintiff Doran and his attorney, Lynn Hubbard, were attacked. In this case the court also found that a party represented by counsel ordinarily is incapable of being declared a vexatious litigant. The court, however, need not resolve the issue because – even if a represented party can be vexatious – the Court finds that Doran is not.
Id. at 1118.

The court found that,
> Doran's litigiousness has produced results which conform to the spirit of the ADA and its private attorney general enforcement provision. Any dissent regarding that provision is properly addressed to, and resolved by, Congress rather than the courts.

Id. at 1120.

As to use of "boilerplate" complaints, the court found "nothing inherently wrong with boilerplate complaints – provided that counsel has conducted the appropriate inquiry under Rule 11" and noted that "the California Judicial Council has adopted form complaints in a number of areas to assist both counsel and pro se litigants." Id. at 1120, n.5. Similarly the Court in Wilson v. Pier 1 Imports, *supra*, ruled that evidence an ADA attorney had filed 1030 lawsuits alleging "boiler plate" violations of the ADA and had settled 99.8% of those suits before trial, did not show he had filed any suits in bad faith. "A settlement rate no more indicates a plaintiff's lack of confidence than it does a defendant's." Id. at 1201.

H. DO DEFENDANTS IN ONE CASE HAVE "STANDING" TO COMPLAIN ABOUT PLAINTIFF'S FILING OF OTHER LAWSUITS?

In Wilson v. Pier 1 Imports (E.D. Cal. 2006) 411 F.Supp 2d 1196, Judge Karlton held that defendants in one case could not complain about the plaintiff's conduct in filing other lawsuits, especially when defendants could not show that they were "blameless", i.e., that they had not violated the ADA:

> [Defendant's] righteous indignation must be bottomed on their own blameless conduct, and that they are the subject to a frivolous lawsuit because they, in fact, have not violated the ADA.

Id. at 1199.

Similarly the Court in Kittok, *supra*, noted that:

> The fact that plaintiff and her counsel have filed multiple similar suits is of little import here if this case was meritorious. See Jankey v. Poop Deck, 537 F.3d 1122, 1132 (9th Cir.2008) (disapproving of district court's denial of fees in part based on "Plaintiff's counsel's numerous other lawsuits in the Central District of California [as] those cases are not a part of the record here.")

Id. at 958.

I. ADA SECTION 503 MAY PROHIBIT ATTACKS ON DISABLED PLAINTIFFS WHO HAVE FILED PRIOR ADA LAW SUITS
[SEE SECTIONS I-J-8-b, III-C, AND IV-C-4, *Supra*]

J. SB 1608 (effective 1/1/09) CHANGED CALIFORNIA STATUTES TO GIVE PROCEDURAL ASSISTANCE TO "GOOD FAITH" BUSINESSES IN STATE COURT PROCEEDINGS [See also II.k., *supra*.]

SB 1608 gave businesses the opportunity to "do the right thing" by hiring "certified access consultants" to evaluate their premises, and gave certain procedural advantages to businesses which obtained an "expert's" access report followed by the expert's advice, but got sued for access violations anyway. Such changes included the right (at least in state court proceedings as to procedural requirements) to have a Superior Court Judge put a stay on discovery and order an early settlement conference, if a defendant alleged it had hired a CASp certified access consultant and obtained a report and was following the report, <u>before</u> it was sued. New civil code sections include provisions for plaintiff to advise defendants of certain rights when serving a state law complaint (see sections 55.51 - 55.54 however). Such <u>procedural</u> requirements adopted by the California State legislature should only be required for state court procedures, not federal court. (See <u>O'Campo v. Chico Mall</u>, 758 F.Supp 2d 976 (E.D. Cal. 2010).

Other changes defined damages obtainable for denial of "full and equal access" by "deterrence." (§55.56 Civil Code)

K. TRUE DISABLED ADVOCATES SHOULD JOIN IN CRITICIZING UNETHICAL CONDUCT BY PLAINTIFFS AS WELL AS BY DEFENDANTS.

Allegations have come to my attention that certain disabled persons and their attorneys have undertaken "serial" litigation in state court, but instead of seeking barrier removal they have filed multiple lawsuits seeking <u>only</u> damages and attorney fees. Such actions, which seek only money from defendants and do <u>not</u> require improved access by seeking injunctive relief, are of questionable ethical value and may cause a negative public reaction or motivate negative legislative action. However, ironically, the recent California Supreme Court <u>Jankey v. Lee</u>, *supra*, decision may <u>discourage</u> actions seeking injunctive relief under Civil Code section 55 because of the threat of "prevailing" defendants being awarded attorney fees against a "good faith" plainitff!

L. A POSSIBLE CHECKLIST OF ISSUES TO HELP DETERMINE WHETHER AN ATTORNEY'S ACTION IN BRINGING A LAWSUIT OR MAKING A DEMAND UPON A BUSINESS IS "ABUSIVE"

Here is a partial checklist (in the writer's opinion) to identify violations that justify legitimate lawsuits no matter what is said about the "motivation" of the person bringing them:

1. Is there in fact a significant denial of access to the entrance, paths of travel to services, or restrooms of a business facility? (See Civil Code § 55.56 definitions, discussed hereinbelow, per amendments effective January 1, 2009)
2. If so, the defendants have no one but themselves to blame, because anyone who visited them in a wheelchair was in fact denied "full and equal access." The issues of the amount of damages and the reasonableness of attorney fees incurred can be addressed by the parties (in negotiation) or by the court.
3. Similarly there are certain things that do <u>not</u> seem proper in any case:
    (A) A letter from an attorney to a business owner asking them to pay damages or attorney fees in exchange for <u>not</u> being required to put in access.
    (B) A letter from an attorney to a business owner asking them <u>not</u> to contact or

retain their own attorney, but to deal with the letter sender directly.

(C) A letter from an attorney to a business owner asking him not to contact his insurance company (which might provide insurance coverage and an attorney for the defense), but suggesting that the business owner should, instead, deal with plaintiff's attorney directly.

(D) Threats demanding that a business owner pay any amount of money in return for the sender not to send disabled persons to one or more locations in order to create lawsuits.

(E) Any action involving alleged violations of Title III (for which injunctive relief and attorney fees is the remedy) offering not to insist on compliance in return for payment of money to the disabled plaintiff and/or his attorney.

(F) Deliberately filing a lawsuit about a public accommodation which has only de minimis violations, violations which do not effect the usability of the facility for patrons who use a wheelchair, i.e., the proverbial 1/8 of an inch too high towel hanger. These cases probably don't exist, but since some business representatives claim they do, we can safely add them to our list).

Commentary

Ninth Circuit case law has already defined a "de minimis" violation as being inadequate by itself to cause a violation, so the fact that something is "de minimis" is already a defense. Skaff v. Meridien North America Beverly Hills, LLC, 506 F.3d 832 (9th Cir. 2007). However, the example held by the Skaff court to be "de minimis" is possibly a poor example under current statutory definitions of what constitutes a "denial" of access: e.g., going overnight in a hotel room without a useable bath or shower may be a major "discomfort," and Civil Code § 55.56 now defines a denial of "full and equal access" as including causing "difficulty, discomfort or embarrassment." After the January 1, 2009 adoption by the legislature of the standards of Civil Code § 55.56, being denied an accessible shower when needed, overnight, would seem to fall within the Civil Code § 55.56 (b) and (c) definitions:

(b) A plaintiff is denied full and equal access only if the plaintiff personally encountered the violation on a particular occasion, or the plaintiff was deterred from accessing a place of public accommodation on a particular occasion.

(c) A violation personally encountered by a plaintiff may be sufficient to cause a denial of full and equal access if the plaintiff experienced difficulty, discomfort, or embarrassment because of the violation. (Emphasis Added)

Certainly, per Kittok, supra, and Wilson, supra an otherwise proper lawsuit cannot have its legitimacy questioned by questioning the "motivations" of a plaintiff to receive statutory damages, or his attorney to seek fees for the enforcement of the policy of the United States Congress or the California Legislature.

VIII. CONCLUSION

A. OPPOSING DISABLED ACCESS: MONEY, PREJUDICE AND IGNORANCE

According to United States Census,[135] 51.2 million Americans live with some level of disability. Of these, 1.8 million are blind, 2.7 million use wheelchairs, and 9.1 million use an ambulatory aid such as a cane, crutches or walker. This is a significant portion of our populace, and growing daily as people live longer and the "Baby Boomer" generation approaches retirement. In California, both California civil rights laws and the Americans with Disabilities Act of 1990 ("ADA") provide the basis for private lawsuits to enforce the access rights of persons with disabilities. Yet, 20 years after passage of the ADA, many public accommodations are still not fully accessible to persons with mobility or visual disabilities.

Most people cheer the courage of disabled persons who strive to carry on full public lives despite physical limitations. Most people support maximizing public access for those whose physical disabilities require accommodation. However, there are others – often financially motivated – who oppose expansion of disabled access rights. They oppose expanding disabled rights because this may cost money. For <u>some</u> businesses, money trumps human rights.

Even though disabled access costs money, most businesses will benefit from architectural renovations that improve access. Businesses that fear the cost of installing a ramp, widening a door, or installing an accessible toilet because this "costs money" will still reap back benefits from increased patronage by disabled persons and their companions, friends and relatives who will go out to dinner or the theater or other public places with disabled persons. The crocodile tears shed by business interests about the high costs of the ADA should be balanced by the satisfaction of attracting new paying customers.

For those for whom the prospect of new business is <u>not</u> sufficient, other major reasons to provide access are: (1) it is the right thing to do, and (2) disabled access has been required since 1970 by law in California, and violating the law can prove expensive. Private lawsuits may enforce the law and require defendants to pay fees to their own attorneys and to plaintiffs' attorneys, if the disabled plaintiff prevails.

There is another opponent to access that we must reluctantly recognize: the continued existence of <u>actual prejudice</u>. There are those who <u>dislike</u> social encounters with disabled persons because of that old demon, simple prejudice. Prejudice has not disappeared from our society. Racial prejudice has not disappeared from our society, even though our laws fully support freedom of social opportunity and freedom to enter all public accommodations

---

[135] Americans with Disabilities, 2002 report at http://www.census.gov/Press-Release/www/Releases/archives/agingpopulation/006809.html.

and not be held back by racial, religious or gender discrimination. Most people support social equality, but recognize that discrimination and prejudice still exist.

Prejudice also exists against the physically disabled. Like other prejudices, this prejudice has significantly lessened in recent years but there are still those among us who suffer the personality defect of prejudice against other human beings. Some discrimination suffered by disabled persons is a product of this "actual prejudice." As was recognized in hearings leading up to passage of the ADA in 1990:

> [O]ur society is still infected by the ancient, now almost subconscious assumption that people with disabilities are less than fully human and therefore are not fully eligible for the opportunities, services, and support systems which are available to other people as a matter of right. The result is massive, society wide discrimination.[136]

Fortunately (or unfortunately), most discrimination against disabled persons is due to "carelessness" rather than viciousness; to neglect rather than hatred; to ignorance rather than intentionality. At least that's what I'd like to believe.

Lawsuits to remove architectural barrier discrimination that blocks access to disabled persons can succeed without the need to prove bad intentions on the part of owners or operators. Donald v. Café Royale, 218 Cal.App.3d 168 (1990) (no intent needed re Cal. Civ. Code § 54.1); Crowder v. Kitigawa, Chairman Hawaiian Bd. of Control, 81 F.3d 1480 (9th Cir. 1996) (no proof of intent needed under the ADA); Munson v. Del Taco, Inc., 46 Cal.4th 661 (2009) (no intent needed under Civ. Code § 51(f)). This allows focus on removal of barriers as the priority, not "punishment" of businesses. Disabled rights attorneys may earn statutory attorney fees without the need to prove "actual" damages or a defendant's bad intent. Statutory minimum damages of $4,000 may be proven for each Unruh Act violation (Wilson v. Haria and Gogri Corp. dba Jack in the Box, et al., 479 F.Supp.2d 1127 (2007)) without proving wrongful intent (Munson v. Del Taco, Inc., supra)).

"Wrongful intent" would become relevant only to prove oppression, fraud, "malice" or "conscious disregard" to justify punitive damages (Civ. Code § 3294) or treble damages (Civ. Code § 52 or 54.3). Section 3294(c) defines these types of conduct:

(1) "Malice" means conduct which is intended by the defendant to cause injury to the plaintiff or despicable conduct which is carried on by the defendant with a willful and conscious disregard of the rights or safety of others.

(2) "Oppression" means despicable conduct that subjects a person to cruel and unjust hardship in conscious disregard of that person's rights.

---

[136] S.Rep. No. 101-116, at 8-9 (1989) as quoted by attorney Lawrence Paradis in his comprehensive 2003 article in the Stanford Law and Policy Review, "Title II of the Americans with Disabilities Act and Section 504 of the Rehabilitation Act: Making Programs, Services and Activities Accessible to All"

(3) "Fraud" means an intentional misrepresentation, deceit, or concealment of a material fact known to the defendant with the intention on the part of the defendant of thereby depriving a person of property or legal rights or otherwise causing injury.

A fraud might occur if a business obtains a building department "variance" from disabled access requirements as a result of misrepresentations that it intends to construct accessible facilities, then does not, resulting in exclusion of disabled persons. "Malice" might be shown by "conscious disregard" for disabled persons by maintaining inaccessible public facilities for many years, despite complaints by the disabled and despite knowledge that the disabled could not use the premises because of architectural barrier inaccessibility. This wrongful intent may be the basis for seeking treble damages under Civil Code § 52 or 54.3, or, in an especially egregious situation, punitive damages pursuant to Civil Code § 3294. (The issue of whether the specific treble damages provisions of sections 52 or 54.3 preclude seeking § 3294 "punitive damages" has not been conclusively decided.)

But the primary purpose of "access lawsuits" should remain removal of all barriers to disabled access. ADA Title III does not directly offer damages as an incentive, only injunctive relief and attorney fees; however, damages can be obtained under state law. Plaintiffs' lawyers should join with defendants in opposing any suits that seek damages or fees without also seeking removal of barriers that still block "full and equal" access for the disabled in our society. (But the December 17, 2012, California Supreme Court decision in Jankey v. Song Koo Lee, *supra* may be an incentive to rely on the ADA or Business and Professions Code section 17200 to obtain injunctive relief rather than risking "reverse" attorney fees to prevailing defendants under California Civil Code section 55.)

B. THE NEW ATTACK ON DISABLED RIGHTS

In late 2012 the California legislature and California Supreme Court have hit the disabled community with a one-two punch which may discourage many disabled persons from using the courts to enforce California laws which have protected disabled access rights for hte past 40 years. They have also made it much more difficult for plaintiff's lawyers to represent the disabled.

Under political pressure in the 2012 election year, the legislature made findings that a "very few" disabled persons and their lawyers were abusing the access laws and bringing "too many" civil rights actions for disabled persons. Supposedly the "evil" that the new SB 1186 legislation was enacted to counter was that some lawyers were sending letters or bringing lawsuits seeking only statutory minimum damages ($4,000 statutory minimum for any violation of Civil Code §§ 51 et seq.), and for statutory attorney fees. 40 pages of new laws intended to make bringing actions for damages more difficult were included in SB

1186, including prohibitions on pre-litigation monetary demand letters and requirements for including various notices of defendants' rights and tactical alternatives, with the service of any Complaint. Strangely, SB 1186 was sponsored by State Senate President Pro Tem Darryl Steinberg, a Democrat and formerly a staunch defender of disability rights. He did so as co-sponsor with Republican Senator Dutton, under pressure from various Chambers of Commerce and from U.S. Senator Diane Feinstein, who threatened federal legislation to weaken the ADA if the California Legislature did not take action. SB 1186 was passed effective in part on October 23, 2012, and in part on January 1, 2013. Lawyers who "violate" such new requirements as having to file verified complaints - a requirement for the disabled not imposed upon any other category of persons discriminated against - and including specified "rights" notices to defendants with service of any complaint based in any part on a businesses' illegal construction history, now face having their complaint stricken and being referred for disciplinary action by the State Bar.

If the purpose of the new law was to encourage suits for injunctive relief rather than just for damages, a subsequent decision by the California Supreme Court ensured just the opposite result was likely: On December 17, 2012, a date that may live in infamy for the rights of disabled persons, a unanimous California Supreme Court voted to interpret that the attorney fees provisions of Civil Code § 55- the primary code used to seek injunctive relief to gain access under California law- were entirely reciprocal, even against the most good faith disabled plaintiff. Jankey v. Song Koo Lee, 55 Cal. 4th 1038 (2012). If the plaintiff sought injunctive relief in the public interest under § 55 and lost, he or she now faces a mandatory requirement to pay the "prevailing party" defendant all of its attorney fees and costs. If, on the other hand, the lawsuit seeks only damages for the same violation, under Civil Code § 54.3 by proving a denial of "full and equal access" under Civil Code § 54.1, statutory damages are available only to a prevailing plaintiff. Thus the result will be to encourage lawsuits seeking only damages, and discourage public interest lawsuits seeking barrier removal under California State law, directly opposite to the major purported objective of the recent SB 1186 legislation.

In deciding Jankey, *supra*, the California Supreme Court rejected the 9th Circuit's 2009 contrary decision in Hubbard v. Sobreck, LLC, 554 F.3d 742 (9th Cir. 2009), which found that the ADA preempted such a result when Civil Code § 55 injunctive relief was paralleling enforcement of the ADA incorporated as a violation of §§ 54(c) and 54.1(d) of the Civil Code. The 9th Circuit's holding was based on its interpretations of federal law - that the ADA preempted state law and protected against fees being awarded against a "good faith" civil rights plaintiff to avoid a "chilling" effect on the ability and motivation of lawyers to prosecute civil rights cases and enforce the policy of Congress (Cf. Christiansburg Garment Co. v. Equal Employment Opportunity Comm., 434 U.S. 412 (1978). Instead, the

California Supreme Court purported to interpret only the California statute, Civil Code § 55, and "disagreed" with the Hubbard Court's finding that allowing § 55 to result in attorney fees against a good faith plaintiff caused a necessary entanglement with the objectives of the Americans with Disabilities Act.

The result in the Jankey case (where a California Superior Court had granted summary judgment that it was "not readily achievable" for a business to ramp one 7" step that blocked wheelchair users from entering the business), was to uphold a $118,458 trial Court attorney fees award against the disabled plaintiff; then they added to this burden plaintiff's responsibility for all of defendants' attorney fees on appeal. (The Court found plaintiff had waived appeal of the summary judgment finding, and waived raising the U.S. Supreme Court holding in Fox v. Vice 131 S.Ct. 2205 (2011), that fees could be awarded in an ADA case only for portions of the work not connected in any way to ADA issues, and only for portions of the case which were "frivolous" or "fraudulent" under principles of Christiansburg Garment Co. v. Equal Employment Opportunity Comm., 434 U.S. 412 (1978) principle. As Christianburg pointed out, a civil rights plaintiff was seeking to enforce Congressional policy, but a defendant business was not. Apparently the California Supreme Court did not consider the policy concerns of Christianburg, that such attorney fees threat would "chill" civil rights actions, as applying to California civil rights statutes.

Disabled persons are often low income or impecunious, and as a group have the highest unemployment rate of any discernable class of persons in California and America. How can California lawyers represent disabled persons in "good faith" lawsuits seeking to obtain access to businesses which have been subject to state law access requirements for the last 40 years, if losing the case will mean driving the disabled into bankruptcy?

Of course there is still the possibility of seeking injunctive relief solely under the ADA. However, this would effectively require all suits to be brought in federal court, or state court filings will be removed by defendants to federal court, based on "federal question" jurisdiction. If the case is originally filed in state court, "artful pleading" using such vehicles as Business and Professions Code §§ 17200 et seq. for injunctive relief, combined with a Code of Civil Procedure § 1021.5 request for public interest attorney fees, may still seek to enforce the public interest goals without subjecting good faith disabled plaintiffs to the draconian threat of facing a huge defense attorney fees award if they lose. However the net result of SB 1186 and the Jankey "reverse attorney fees" decision will, as a practical matter, discourage many legitimate disability rights lawsuits from even being filed.

It has been said that the measure of a society is how it treats its weakest and most vulnerable citizens. The recent laws and decisions attacking the rights of physically disabled persons are a sad chapter in the history of Civil Rights in California.

C. PROVIDING ACCESS CAN BE A "WIN-WIN" SITUATION

The ADA was enacted as a compromise legislation, approved and signed by a Republican President, George H. Bush in 1990, and based on the premise that it would

(1) provide an opportunity for disabled persons to force access in government facilities (Title II), and in privately owned public accommodations (Title III);

(2) encourage lawyers to handle public interest cases and injunctive relief to improve access by providing these lawyers the opportunity to earn statutory attorney fees, litigation expenses and costs (see ADA § 505);

(3) save money for the government and taxpayers by <u>not</u> setting up a nationwide enforcement bureaucracy but instead relying on private lawsuits for enforcement; and

(4) Not provide a damages remedy under Title III and limit damages under Title II to instances of "intentional" discrimination. (California's legislature later provided a damages remedy by incorporating ADA violations as also constituting violations of California law [Civil Code §§ 51(b), 54(c) and 54.1(d)).

While there has been some controversy regarding specific compliance "issues," both California law and the ADA have significantly improved public access in many ways. Hopefully this book has shared information and insights useful to attorneys and disabled persons in California; to businesses interested in complying with disability access requirements; and to defense attorneys advising or representing business clients or otherwise involved in disability rights cases.

Fortunately it can be a "win-win" situation: The more access barriers removed, the more businesses that disabled persons (and their companions) can patronize and spend their money in. Voluntary compliance will result in less need for litigation and less need for paying attorney fees to plaintiff attorneys and defense lawyers. Most disabled rights attorneys are working for the day when our society is fully accessible to persons with disabilities, and litigation will no longer be necessary. But until that day comes, disabled access litigation should remain an essential tool in the fight to achieve an "accessible" society.

IX. APPENDIX (Table of Contents)

   A. LEADING CASES LIST

   1. People ex rel. Deukmejian v. CHE, Inc.
      (1983) 150 Cal.App.3d 123

   2. Donald v. Sacramento Valley Bank
      (1989) 209 Cal.App.3d 1183

   3. Donald v. Café Royale (1990) 218 Cal.App.3d 168

   4. Hankins v. El Torito Restaurants, Inc., et al.
      (1998) 63 Cal. App.4th 510

   5. Walker and Adams v. Carnival Cruise Lines, et al.
      (2000) 107 F.Supp.2d 1135

   6. Skaff v. Meridien North America Beverly Hills, LLC,
      506 F.3d 832 (9th Cir. 2007).

   7. Blackwell v. Foley, 724 F.Supp.2d 1068 (N.D. Cal, 2010)

   B. CALIFORNIA GOVT. CODE § 4450 AND 4451, EFFECTIVE 11/13/68 APPLIED TO NEW CONSTRUCTION AND ALTERATION INCLUDING "BUILDINGS AND FACILITIES UNDER CONSTRUCTION" AT THAT TIME

   C. ASA REGULATIONS (EFFECTIVE NOV. 13, 1968 TO 1/1/1982 PER GOVERNMENT CODE §§ 4450 AND 4451 (1968) AND CALIFORNIA HEALTH & SAFETY CODE § 19956 (1970))

   D. OFFICE OF LEGISLATIVE COUNSEL, OPINION OF MARCH 31, 1979 RE: PATHS OF TRAVEL REQUIREMENTS UNDER ASA REGULATIONS

   E. ATTORNEY GENERAL'S OPINIONS
   1. September 17, 1992 statewide directive to California Building Officials (See § II.D.9)(With supervising deputy attorney general Louis Verdugo, Jr's Authentication Declaration)

   2. Attorney General Opinion No 93-203, the 1993 opinion that ADA enforced only by the DOJ and by private lawsuits (No. 93-203)

   3. August 4, 2003 opinion letter by chief Deputy Attorney General Steve Coony on behalf of California Attorney General Bill Lockyer (re: No "Advance Notice laws" needed, etc!)

F. RESOURCES FOR DISABLED PERSONS
   1. Disability Rights Organizations
      Center for Independent Living
      Ed Roberts Campus, 3075 Adeline, <u>Suite 100</u>
      Berkeley CA 94703 (510/841-4776)

      DREDF (Disability Rights Education Defense Fund)
      Ed Roberts Campus, 3075 Adeline, Suite 210,
      Berkeley CA 94703 (510/644-2525)

      DRA (Disability Rights Advocates)
      2001 Center St., 3rd Fl.
      Berkeley, CA 94704-1204 (510/665-8644)

      WID (World Institute on Disability)
      Ed Roberts Campus, 3075 Adeline, Suite 280,
      Berkeley CA 94703 (510/763-4100)

      Through the Looking Glass (Promotes Services for Parents of Disabled Children)
      Ed Roberts Campus, 3075 Adeline, Suite 120
      Berkeley CA 94703   (510/848-1112)

      Disability Rights California (formerly Protection and Advocacy, Inc.)
      1330 Broadway Suite 5001
      Oakland 94612
      (800/776-5746)(510/267-1200)

      Disability Rights Legal Center
      1441 West Olympic Boulevard
      Los Angeles, CA 90015-3903
      (213) 736-1031

      http://www.disabilityrightslegalcenter.org

   2. Government agencies

      U.S. Department of Justice
      Civil Rights Division
      950 Pennsylvania Avenue, N.W.
      Office of the Assistant Attorney General, Main
      Washington, D.C. 20530

      http://www.justice.gov/crt/
      California Atty General's Office
      Attorney General's Office
      California Department of Justice
      Attn: Public Inquiry Unit
      P.O. Box 944255
      Sacramento, CA 94244-2550

http://oag.ca.gov/
California Department of Rehabilitation
P.O. Box 944222
Sacramento, CA 94244-2220
All District Attorneys and City Attorneys (per Civil Code section 55.1)

3. Texts and treatises

   <u>California Attorney Fees. 2nd Ed.</u> By Richard Pearl, published by Continuing Education of the Bar (CEB) 2011

   <u>Americans with Disabilities Act Annotated</u> (4 volumes) by Arlene Mayerson.

G. Complaint Sample- for Federal Court

   Title III and California law: Service dog exclusion (plus physical barriers affecting blind plaintiff)

H. General Order 56, for the Northern District of California [May 29, 2012 version]

I. Consent Decree Sample, <u>Overbo and Brown-Booker v. Loews California</u> Theaters

J. SACRAMENTO COMMUNITY THEATER COMPOSITE PHOTO (by Access expert Jonathon Adler)

K. TEXT OF SENATE BILL NO. 1186 (2012)

APPENDIX

APPENDIX B

CHAPTER 261

An act to add Chapter 7 (commencing with Section 4450) to Division 5 of Title 1 of the Government Code, relating to public buildings.

[Approved by Governor June 6, 1968 Filed with Secretary of State June 6, 1968.]

The people of the State of California do enact as follows:

SECTION 1. Chapter 7 (commencing with Section 4450) is added to Division 5 of Title 1 of the Government Code, to read:

CHAPTER 7. ACCESS TO PUBLIC BUILDINGS BY PHYSICALLY HANDICAPPED PERSONS

4450. It is the purpose of this chapter to insure that buildings and facilities, constructed in the state by the use of state, county, or municipal funds, or the funds of any political subdivision of the state, adhere to the American Standards Association Specifications A 117.1-1961 for making buildings and facilities accessible to, and usable by, the physically handicapped.

4451. Except as otherwise provided in this section, this chapter shall apply to all buildings and facilities intended for use by the public, which have any reasonable availability to, or usage by, physically handicapped persons, including the University of California, the California State Colleges, and the various junior college districts, which are constructed in whole or in part by the use of state, county, or municipal funds, or the funds of any political subdivision of the state. If an elementary, high school, or unified school district provides special buildings and facilities for the physically handicapped, the other buildings and facilities of such district shall be exempt from this chapter, except that at least one floor of all new elementary, high school, or unified school district buildings, and places of public assembly therein, such as those used for public meetings, will meet the American Standards Association Specifications A 117.1-1961. All such buildings and facilities constructed in this state after the effective date of this chapter from any of these funds or any combination thereof shall conform to each of the standards and specifications as prescribed in American Standards Association Specifications A 117.1-1961, except Sections 2.3, 2.4, 5.11, 5.12, and Figure 1 as related to Section 5.4.1.

These standards and specifications shall be adhered to in those buildings and facilities under construction on the effective date of this chapter, unless the authority responsible for the construction shall determine that the construction has reached a state where compliance is impractical. This chapter shall apply to temporary or emergency construction as well as permanent buildings.

In cases of practical difficulty, unnecessary hardship, or extreme differences, administrative authorities as designated under Section 4453 may grant exceptions from the literal requirements of this standard or permit the use of other methods or materials, but only when it is clearly evident that equivalent facilitation and protection are thereby secured.

4452. It is the intent of the Legislature that American Standards Association Specifications A 117.1-1961 shall be used as minimum standards to insure that buildings and facilities covered by this chapter are accessible to, and functional for, the physically handicapped to, through, and within their doors, without loss of function, space, or facility where the general public is concerned.

Any unauthorized deviation from these specifications shall be rectified by full compliance within 90 days after discovery of the deviation.

4453. The responsibility for enforcement of this chapter shall be as follows:

(a) Where state funds are utilized, by the Director of the Department of General Services.

(b) Where funds of counties, municipalities, or other political subdivisions are utilized, by the governing bodies thereof.

APPENDIX C

ASA
Reg. U. S. Pat. Off.
A117.1-1961

UDC 725/728:
362.6:614.8

American Standard Specifications for

Making Buildings and Facilities Accessible to, and Usable by, the Physically Handicapped

Sponsors

National Society for Crippled Children and Adults

The President's Committee on Employment of the Physically Handicapped

Approved October 31, 1961

AMERICAN STANDARDS ASSOCIATION
INCORPORATED

American Standards

The standard in this booklet is one of over 2000 standards approved to date by the American Standards Association, Incorporated.

The ASA provides the machinery for creating voluntary standards. It serves to eliminate duplication of standards activities and to weld conflicting standards into single, nationally accepted standards under the designation "American Standard."

Each standard represents general agreement among maker, seller, and user groups as to the best current practice with regard to some specific problem. Thus the completed standards cut across the whole fabric of production, distribution, and consumption of goods and services. Manufacturers, consumers, technical organizations, and governmental agencies — all substantially interested and affected groups — are represented on the committees which develop and regularly revise American Standards. The completed standards are used widely by industry and commerce and often by municipal, state, and federal governments.

The ASA, under whose auspices this work is being done, is the American clearinghouse for standards activity on the national level. Founded in 1918, it is a federation of more than 100 trade associations, technical societies, professional groups, and consumer organizations. Some 2200 companies are affiliated with the ASA as company members.

ASA is the United States member of the International Organization for Standardization (ISO). Through this channel American industry makes its position felt on the international level. American Standards are on file in the libraries of the national standards bodies of more than 40 countries.

For a free list of all American Standards or information about membership in the ASA write:

AMERICAN STANDARDS ASSOCIATION
INCORPORATED
10 EAST 40th STREET
NEW YORK 16, NEW YORK

American Standard

Registered United States Patent Office

An American Standard implies a consensus of those substantially concerned with its scope and provisions. The consensus principle extends to the initiation of work under the procedure of the Association, to the method of work to be followed, and to the final approval of the standard.

An American Standard is intended as a guide to aid the manufacturer, the consumer, and the general public. The existence of an American Standard does not in any respect preclude any party who has approved of the standard from manufacturing, selling, or using products, processes, or procedures not conforming to the standard.

An American Standard defines a product, process, or procedure with reference to one or more of the following: nomenclature, composition, construction, dimensions, tolerances, safety, operating characteristics, performance, quality, rating, certification, testing, and the service for which designed.

American Standards are subject to periodic review. They are reaffirmed or revised to meet changing economic conditions and technological progress. Users of American Standards are cautioned to secure the latest editions.

Producers of goods made in conformity with an American Standard are encouraged to state on their own responsibility in advertising, promotion material, or on tags or labels, that the goods are produced in conformity with particular American Standards. The inclusion in such advertising and promotion media, or on tags or labels, of information concerning the characteristics covered by the standard to define its scope is also encouraged.

Published by

National Society for Crippled Children and Adults, Inc.
2023 West Ogden Avenue, Chicago 12, Illinois

with the permission of

American Standards Association, Inc.
10 East 40th Street, New York 16, N. Y.

Copyright 1961 by American Standards Association, Incorporated
Universal Decimal Classification 725/728:362.6:614.8
Printed in U.S.A.

Foreword

(This Foreword is not a part of American Standard Specifications for Making Buildings and Facilities Accessible to, and Usable by, the Physically Handicapped, A117.1-1961.)

Approximately one out of seven people in our nation has a permanent physical disability. This segment of our population represents human resources of inestimable value and is of great economic significance to the entire nation.

The most common design and construction of buildings and facilities cause problems for the physically handicapped that lessen the social and economic gains now evident in the rehabilitation of these individuals. These architectural barriers make it very difficult to project the physically handicapped into normal situations of education, recreation, and employment.

In May, 1959, the ASA, acting on the request of The President's Committee on Employment of the Physically Handicapped, called a general conference of those groups vitally interested in the problem. This conference recommended the initiation of a project, and this recommendation was subsequently approved by the Construction Standards Board. The President's Committee on Employment of the Physically Handicapped and the National Society for Crippled Children and Adults were designated as co-sponsors, and the latter agreed to assume the secretariat.

This standard supplements other American Standards relating to various aspects of buildings and facilities. Its specifications, which are the result of extended and careful consideration of available knowledge and experience on this subject, are intended to present minimum requirements. They are recommended for use in the construction of all buildings and facilities and for adoption and enforcement by administrative authorities, so that those individuals with permanent physical disabilities might pursue their interests and aspirations, develop their talents, and exercise their skills.

The ASA Sectional Committee on Facilities in Public Buildings for Persons with Physical Handicaps, A117, which developed this standard, had the following personnel at the time of approval.

LEON CHATELAIN, JR, *Chairman*   T. J. NUGENT, *Secretary*

Organization Represented	*Name of Representative*
AFL-CIO	WALTER MASON
American Foundation for the Blind	ARTHUR VOORHEES
American Hospital Association	MARGARET E. PETERS
American Hotel Association	JAKE FASSETT
American Institute of Architects	CLINTON H. COWGILL
	F. CUTHBERT SALMON
	CHRISTINE F. SALMON (*Alt*)
American Municipal Association	BARNET LIEBERMAN
	LEO GOLDSTEIN (*Alt*)
American Occupational Therapy Association	MARJORIE FISH
American Physical Therapy Association	LUCY BLAIR
American Society of Landscape Architects	CAMPBELL E. MILLER
The American Society of Mechanical Engineers	JOSEPH W. DEGEN
American Society of Safety Engineers	THOMAS J. BERK
American Vocational Association	CHARLES W. SYLVESTER, M.D.
Associated General Contractors of America	WILLIAM F. LOTZ
	BURT L. KNOWLES (*Alt*)
Association of Casualty and Surety Companies	ROBERT HAGOPIAN
	JAMES C. ROUMAS (*Alt*)
Construction Specifications Institute	EDWIN A. WEED
	CLEMONS J. POIESZ (*Alt*)
Federal Housing Administration	WILLIAM J. O'CONNOR
General Services Administration	J. ROWLAND SNYDER
Industrial Home for the Blind	HERBERT RUSALEM, M.D.
	HAROLD RICHTERMAN (*Alt*)
Industrial Medical Association	KENNETH G. PEACOCK, M.D.
Indoor Sports Clubs, Inc	ARVELLA M. SANDER
Institute for the Crippled and Disabled	ROBERT MCAFEE
	WALTER S. NEFF, M.D. (*Alt*)

Organization Represented	Name of Representative
National Bureau of Standards	(Representation vacant)
National Congress of Organizations for the Physically Handicapped	ELMER JOSEPHS
National Council of Churches	REV. FRANCIS F. FISHER
National Council of Schoolhouse Construction	JOHN L. CAMERON
	E. J. BRAUN (Alt)
National Elevator Manufacturing Industry	D. J. MATHESON
National Paraplegia Foundation	EUGENE AURYANSEN
National Rehabilitation Association	EDWARD STILES
National Safety Council	ROBERT L. JENKINS
National Society for Crippled Children and Adults	LEON CHATELAIN, JR
	JOHN B. KEMP
	D. W. ROBERTS, M.D.
	JAYNE SHOVER
	THERON H. BUTTERWORTH (Alt)
Paralyzed Veterans of America, Inc	ROBERT P. MEIER
	ROBERT CLASSON (Alt)
Paraplegics Manufacturing Company	DWIGHT D. GUILFOIL, JR
	HARRY BENDSTEN (Alt)
Plumbing Fixture Manufacturers Association	RUSSELL W. SMITH
The President's Committee on Employment of the Physically Handicapped	K. VERNON BANTA
	MAJOR GENERAL MELVIN J. MAAS, USMCR (ret)
Society of Industrial Realtors	FRANK D. GARIBALDI
Telephone Group	J. M. STANDRING, JR
United Cerebral Palsy Associations, Inc	HARRY LYONS
U. S. Conference of Mayors	HARRY R. BETTERS
U. S. Department of Health, Education and Welfare	
Bureau of State Services	HOWARD SPENCE
Children's Bureau	CLARA M. ARRINGTON
	GEORGIA PERKINS, M.D. (Alt)
Division of Accident Prevention	EUGENE L. LEHR
Division of Hospital and Medical Facilities	AUGUST F. HOENACK
	PETER N. JENSEN (Alt)
Office of Education	ROMAINE P. MACKIE
Office of Vocational Rehabilitation	PHILIP KLIEGER, M.D.
U. S. Department of Labor	
Bureau of Employment Security	HENDRICK D. MUGAAS
	MELVIN R. BERGSTROM (Alt)
Bureau of Labor Standards	SHELDON W. HOMAN
	WILLIAM G. GRIFFIN (Alt)
U. S. Veterans Administration	H. D. YORK
University of Illinois Rehabilitation Center	T. J. NUGENT

The personnel of the steering committee is as follows:

K. VERNON BANTA   PHILIP A. KLIEGER
LEON CHATELAIN, JR   T. J. NUGENT
CLINTON H. COWGILL   JAYNE SHOVER
H. DWIGHT YORK

Contents

Section	Page
1. Scope and Purpose	6
1.1 Scope	6
1.2 Purpose	6
2. Definitions	6
2.1 Non-ambulatory Disabilities	6
2.2 Semi-ambulatory Disabilities	6
2.3 Sight Disabilities	6
2.4 Hearing Disabilities	6
2.5 Disabilities of Incoordination	6
2.6 Aging	6
2.7 Standard	6
2.8 Fixed Turning Radius, Wheel to Wheel	6
2.9 Fixed Turning Radius, Front Structure to Rear Structure	6
2.10 Involved (Involvement)	6
2.11 Ramps, Ramps with Gradients	6
2.12 Walk, Walks	6
2.13 Appropriate Number	7
3. General Principles and Considerations	7
3.1 Wheelchair Specifications	7
3.2 The Functioning of a Wheelchair	7
3.3 The Adult Individual Functioning in a Wheelchair	7
3.4 The Individual Functioning on Crutches	7
4. Site Development	7
4.1 Grading	7
4.2 Walks	8
4.3 Parking Lots	8
5. Buildings	8
5.1 Ramps with Gradients	8
5.2 Entrances	9
5.3 Doors and Doorways	9
5.4 Stairs	9
5.5 Floors	9
5.6 Toilet Rooms	10
5.7 Water Fountains	10
5.8 Public Telephones	10
5.9 Elevators	10
5.10 Controls	10
5.11 Identification	11
5.12 Warning Signals	11
5.13 Hazards	11
Figures	
Fig. 1 Steps	9
Fig. 2 Knurled Door Handles and Knobs	11

American Standard Specifications for Making Buildings and Facilities Accessible to, and Usable by, the Physically Handicapped

1. Scope and Purpose

1.1 Scope

1.1.1 This standard applies to all buildings and facilities used by the public. It applies to temporary or emergency conditions as well as permanent conditions. It does not apply to private residences.

1.1.2 This standard is concerned with non-ambulatory disabilities, semi-ambulatory disabilities, sight disabilities, hearing disabilities, disabilities of incoordination, and aging.[1]

1.2 Purpose. This standard is intended to make all buildings and facilities used by the public accessible to, and functional for, the physically handicapped, to, through, and within their doors, without loss of function, space, or facility where the general public is concerned. It supplements existing American Standards, and reflects great concern for safety of life and limb. In cases of practical difficulty, unnecessary hardship, or extreme differences, administrative authorities may grant exceptions from the literal requirements of this standard or permit the use of other methods or materials, but only when it is clearly evident that equivalent facilitation and protection are thereby secured.

2. Definitions

2.1 Non-ambulatory Disabilities. Impairments that, regardless of cause or manifestation, for all practical purposes, confine individuals to wheelchairs.

2.2 Semi-ambulatory Disabilities. Impairments that cause individuals to walk with difficulty or insecurity. Individuals using braces or crutches, amputees, arthritics, spastics, and those with pulmonary and cardiac ills may be semi-ambulatory.

2.3 Sight Disabilities. Total blindness or impairments affecting sight to the extent that the individual functioning in public areas is insecure or exposed to danger.

2.4 Hearing Disabilities. Deafness or hearing handicaps that might make an individual insecure in public areas because he is unable to communicate or hear warning signals.

---
[1] See definitions in Section 2.

2.5 Disabilities of Incoordination. Faulty coordination or palsy from brain, spinal, or peripheral nerve injury.

2.6 Aging. Those manifestations of the aging processes that significantly reduce mobility, flexibility, coordination, and perceptiveness but are not accounted for in the aforementioned categories.

2.7 Standard. When this term appears in small letters and is not preceded by the word "American," it is descriptive and does not refer to an American Standard approved by ASA; for example, a "standard" wheelchair is one characterized as standard by the manufacturers.

2.8 Fixed Turning Radius, Wheel to Wheel. The tracking of the caster wheels and large wheels of a wheelchair when pivoting on a spot.

2.9 Fixed Turning Radius, Front Structure to Rear Structure. The turning radius of a wheelchair, left front-foot platform to right rear wheel, or right front-foot platform to left rear wheel, when pivoting on a spot.

2.10 Involved (Involvement). A portion or portions of the human anatomy or physiology, or both, that have a loss or impairment of normal function as a result of genesis, trauma, disease, inflammation, or degeneration.

2.11 Ramps, Ramps with Gradients. Because the term "ramp" has a multitude of meanings and uses, its use in this text is clearly defined as ramps with gradients (or ramps with slopes) that deviate from what would otherwise be considered the normal level. An exterior ramp, as distinguished from a "walk," would be considered an appendage to a building leading to a level above or below existing ground level. As such, a ramp shall meet certain requirements similar to those imposed upon stairs.

2.12 Walk, Walks. Because the terms "walk" and "walks" have a multitude of meanings and uses, their use in this text is clearly defined as a predetermined, prepared-surface, exterior pathway leading to or from a building or facility, or from one exterior area to another, placed on the existing ground level

6

and not deviating from the level of the existing ground immediately adjacent.

2.13 Appropriate Number. As used in this text, appropriate number means the number of a specific item that would be necessary, in accord with the purpose and function of a building or facility, to accommodate individuals with specific disabilities in proportion to the anticipated number of individuals with disabilities who would use a particular building or facility.

EXAMPLE: Although these specifications shall apply to all buildings and facilities used by the public, the numerical need for a specific item would differ, for example, between a major transportation terminal, where many individuals with diverse disabilities would be continually coming and going, an office building or factory, where varying numbers of individuals with disabilities of varying manifestations (in many instances, very large numbers) might be employed or have reason for frequent visits, a school or church, where the number of individuals may be fixed and activities more definitive, and the many other buildings and facilities dedicated to specific functions and purposes.

NOTE: Disabilities are specific and where the individual has been properly evaluated and properly oriented and where architectural barriers have been eliminated, a specific disability does not constitute a handicap. It should be emphasized that more and more of those physically disabled are becoming *participants*, rather than spectators, in the fullest meaning of the word.

3. General Principles and Considerations

3.1 Wheelchair Specifications. The collapsible-model wheelchair of tubular metal construction with plastic upholstery for back and seat is most commonly used. The standard model of all manufacturers falls within the following limits, which were used as the basis of consideration:

(1) Length: 42 inches
(2) Width, when open: 25 inches
(3) Height of seat from floor: 19½ inches
(4) Height of armrest from floor: 29 inches
(5) Height of pusher handles (rear) from floor: 36 inches
(6) Width, when collapsed: 11 inches

3.2 The Functioning of a Wheelchair

3.2.1 The fixed turning radius of a standard wheelchair, wheel to wheel, is 18 inches. The fixed turning radius, front structure to rear structure, is 31.5 inches.

3.2.2 The average turning space required (180 and 360 degrees) is 60 x 60 inches.

NOTE: Actually, a turning space that is longer than it is wide, specifically, 63 x 56 inches, is more workable and desirable. In an area with two open ends, such as might be the case in a corridor, a minimum of 54 inches between two walls would permit a 360-degree turn.

3.2.3 A minimum width of 60 inches is required for two individuals in wheelchairs to pass each other.

3.3 The Adult Individual Functioning in a Wheelchair[2]

3.3.1 The average unilateral vertical reach is 60 inches and ranges from 54 inches to 78 inches.

3.3.2 The average horizontal working (table) reach is 30.8 inches and ranges from 28.5 inches to 33.2 inches.

3.3.3 The bilateral horizontal reach, both arms extended to each side, shoulder high, ranges from 54 inches to 71 inches and averages 64.5 inches.

3.3.4 An individual reaching diagonally, as would be required in using a wall-mounted dial telephone or towel dispenser, would make the average reach (on the wall) 48 inches from the floor.

3.4 The Individual Functioning on Crutches[3]

3.4.1 On the average, individuals 5 feet 6 inches tall require an average of 31 inches between crutch tips in the normally accepted gaits.[4]

3.4.2 On the average, individuals 6 feet 0 inches tall require an average of 32.5 inches between crutch tips in the normally accepted gaits.[4]

4. Site Development[5]

4.1 Grading. The grading of ground, even contrary to existing topography, so that it attains a level with a normal entrance will make a facility accessible to individuals with physical disabilities.

---

[2] Extremely small, large, strong, or weak and involved individuals could fall outside the ranges in 3.3.1, 3.3.2, 3.3.3, and their reach could differ from the figure given in 3.3.4. However, these reaches were determined using a large number of individuals who were functionally trained, with a wide range in individual size and involvement.

[3] Most individuals ambulating on braces or crutches, or both, or on canes are able to manipulate within the specifications prescribed for wheelchairs, although doors present quite a problem at times. However, attention is called to the fact that a crutch tip extending laterally from an individual is not obvious to others in heavily trafficked areas, certainly not as obvious or protective as a wheelchair and is, therefore, a source of vulnerability.

[4] Some cerebral palsied individuals, and some severe arthritics, would be extreme exceptions to 3.4.1 and 3.4.2.

[5] Site development is the most effective means to resolve the problems created by topography, definitive architectural designs or concepts, water table, existing streets, and atypical problems, singularly or collectively, so that aggress, ingress, and egress to buildings by physically disabled can be facilitated while preserving the desired design and effect of the architecture.

4.2 Walks

4.2.1 Public walks should be at least 48 inches wide and should have a gradient not greater than 5 percent.[6]

4.2.2 Such walks shall be of a continuing common surface, not interrupted by steps or abrupt changes in level.

4.2.3 Wherever walks cross other walks, driveways, or parking lots they should blend to a common level.[7]

NOTE: 4.1 and 4.2, separately or collectively, are greatly aided by terracing, retaining walls, and winding walks allowing for more gradual incline, thereby making almost any building accessible to individuals with permanent physical disabilities, while contributing to its esthetic qualities.

4.2.4 A walk shall have a level platform at the top which is at least 5 feet by 5 feet, if a door swings out onto the platform or toward the walk. This platform shall extend at least 1 foot beyond each side of the doorway.

4.2.5 A walk shall have a level platform at least 3 feet deep and 5 feet wide, if the door does not swing onto the platform or toward the walk. This platform shall extend at least 1 foot beyond each side of the doorway.

4.3 Parking Lots

4.3.1 Spaces that are accessible and approximate to the facility should be set aside and identified for use by individuals with physical disabilities.

4.3.2 A parking space open on one side, allowing room for individuals in wheelchairs or individuals on braces and crutches to get in and out of an automobile onto a level surface, suitable for wheeling and walking, is adequate.

4.3.3 Parking spaces for individuals with physical disabilities when placed between two conventional diagonal or head-on parking spaces should be 12 feet wide.

4.3.4 Care in planning should be exercised so that individuals in wheelchairs and individuals using braces and crutches are not compelled to wheel or walk behind parked cars.

4.3.5 Consideration should be given the distribution of spaces for use by the disabled in accordance with the frequency and persistency of parking needs.

4.3.6 Walks shall be in conformity with 4.2.

5. Buildings

5.1 Ramps with Gradients. Where ramps with gradients are necessary or desired, they shall conform to the following specifications:

5.1.1 A ramp shall not have a slope greater than 1 foot rise in 12 feet, or 8.33 percent, or 4 degrees 50 minutes.

5.1.2 A ramp shall have handrails on at least one side, and preferably two sides, that are 32 inches in height, measured from the surface of the ramp, that are smooth, that extend 1 foot beyond the top and bottom of the ramp, and that otherwise conform with American Standard Safety Code for Floor and Wall Openings, Railings, and Toe Boards, A12-1932.

NOTE 1: Where codes specify handrails to be of heights other than 32 inches, it is recommended that two sets of handrails be installed to serve all people. Where major traffic is predominantly children, particularly physically disabled children, extra care should be exercised in the placement of handrails, in accordance with the nature of the facility and the age group or groups being serviced.

NOTE 2: Care should be taken that the extension of the handrail is not in itself a hazard. The extension may be made on the side of a continuing wall.

5.1.3 A ramp shall have a surface that is nonslip.

5.1.4 A ramp shall have a level platform at the top which is at least 5 feet by 5 feet, if a door swings out onto the platform or toward the ramp. This platform shall extend at least 1 foot beyond each side of the doorway.

5.1.5 A ramp shall have a level platform at least 3 feet deep and 5 feet wide, if the door does not swing onto the platform or toward the ramp. This platform shall extend at least 1 foot beyond each side of the doorway.

5.1.6 Each ramp shall have at least 6 feet of straight clearance at the bottom.

5.1.7 Ramps shall have level platforms at 30-foot intervals for purposes of rest and safety and shall have level platforms wherever they turn.

---

[6] It is essential that the gradient of walks and driveways be less than that prescribed for ramps, since walks would be void of handrails and curbs and would be considerably longer and more vulnerable to the elements. Walks of near maximum grade and considerable length should have level areas at intervals for purposes of rest and safety. Walks or driveways should have a nonslip surface.

[7] This specification does not require the elimination of curbs, which, particularly if they occur at regular intersections, are a distinct safety feature for all of the handicapped, particularly the blind. The preferred method of meeting the specification is to have the walk incline to the level of the street. However, at principal intersections, it is vitally important that the curb run parallel to the street, up to the point where the walk is inclined, at which point the curb would turn in and gradually meet the level of the walk at its highest point. A less preferred method would be to gradually bring the surface of the driveway or street to the level of the walk. The disadvantage of this method is that a blind person would not know when he has left the protection of a walk and entered the hazards of a street or driveway.

ACCESSIBLE TO, AND USABLE BY, THE PHYSICALLY HANDICAPPED

5.2 Entrances

5.2.1 At least one primary entrance to each building shall be usable by individuals in wheelchairs.

NOTE: Because entrances also serve as exits, some being particularly important in case of an emergency, and because the proximity of such exits to all parts of buildings and facilities, in accordance with their design and function, is essential (see 112 and 2000 through 2031 of American Standard Building Exits Code, A9.1-1953) it is preferable that all or most entrances (exits) should be accessible to, and usable by, individuals in wheelchairs and individuals with other forms of physical disability herein applicable.

5.2.2 At least one entrance usable by individuals in wheelchairs shall be on a level that would make the elevators accessible.

5.3 Doors and Doorways

5.3.1 Doors shall have a clear opening of no less than 32 inches when open and shall be operable by a single effort.

NOTE 1: Two-leaf doors are not usable by those with disabilities defined in 2.1, 2.2, and 2.5 unless they operate by a single effort, or unless one of the two leaves meets the requirement of 5.3.1.

NOTE 2: It is recommended that all doors have kick plates extending from the bottom of the door to at least 16 inches from the floor, or be made of a material and finish that would safely withstand the abuse they might receive from canes, crutches, wheelchair foot-platforms, or wheelchair wheels.

5.3.2 The floor on the inside and outside of each doorway shall be level for a distance of 5 feet from the door in the direction the door swings and shall extend 1 foot beyond each side of the door.

5.3.3 Sharp inclines and abrupt changes in level shall be avoided at doorsills. As much as possible, thresholds shall be flush with the floor.

NOTE 1: Care should be taken in the selection, placement, and setting of door closers so that they do not prevent the use of doors by the physically disabled. Time-delay door closers are recommended.

NOTE 2: Automatic doors that otherwise conform to 5.3.1, 5.3.2, and 5.3.3 are very satisfactory.

NOTE 3: These specifications apply both to exterior and interior doors and doorways.

5.4 Stairs

Stairs shall conform to American Standard A9.1-1953, with the following additional considerations:

5.4.1 Steps in stairs that might require use by those with disabilities defined in 2.2 and 2.5 or by the aged shall not have abrupt (square) nosing. (See Fig. 1.)

NOTE: Individuals with restrictions in the knee, ankle, or hip, with artificial legs, long leg braces, or comparable conditions cannot, without great difficulty and hazard, use steps with nosing as illustrated in Fig. 1a, but can safely and with minimum difficulty use steps with nosing as illustrated in Fig. 1b.

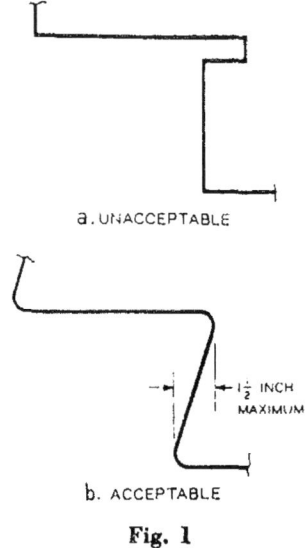

a. UNACCEPTABLE

$1\frac{1}{2}$ INCH MAXIMUM

b. ACCEPTABLE

Fig. 1
Steps

5.4.2 Stairs shall have handrails 32 inches high as measured from the tread at the face of the riser.

NOTE: Where codes specify handrails to be at heights other than 32 inches, it is recommended that two sets of handrails be installed to serve all people. Where traffic is predominantly children, particularly physically disabled children, extra care should be exercised in the placement of handrails in accordance with the nature of the facility and the age group or groups being serviced. Dual handrails may be necessary.

5.4.3 Stairs shall have at least one handrail that extends at least 18 inches beyond the top step and beyond the bottom step.

NOTE: Care should be taken that the extension of the handrails is not in itself a hazard. The extension may be made on the side of a continuing wall.

5.4.4 Steps should, wherever possible, and in conformation with existing step formulas, have risers that do not exceed 7 inches.

5.5 Floors

5.5.1 Floors shall have a surface that is nonslip.

5.5.2 Floors on a given story shall be of a common level throughout or be connected by a ramp in accord with 5.1.1 through 5.1.6, inclusive.

EXAMPLE 1: There shall not be a difference between the level of the floor of a corridor and the level of the floor of the toilet rooms.

EXAMPLE 2: There should not be a difference between the level of the floor of a corridor and the level of a meeting room, dining room, or any other room, unless proper ramps are provided.

5.6 Toilet Rooms. It is essential that an appropriate number[a] of toilet rooms, in accordance with the nature and use of a specific building or facility, be made accessible to, and usable by, the physically handicapped.

5.6.1 Toilet rooms shall have space to allow traffic of individuals in wheelchairs, in accordance with 3.1, 3.2, and 3.3.

5.6.2 Toilet rooms shall have at least one toilet stall that—

(1) Is 3 feet wide
(2) Is at least 4 feet 8 inches, preferably 5 feet, deep
(3) Has a door (where doors are used) that is 32 inches wide and swings out
(4) Has handrails on each side, 33 inches high and parallel to the floor, 1½ inches in outside diameter, with 1½ inches clearance between rail and wall, and fastened securely at ends and center
(5) Has a water closet with the seat 20 inches from the floor

NOTE: The design and mounting of the water closet is of considerable importance. A wall-mounted water closet with a narrow understructure that recedes sharply is most desirable. If a floor-mounted water closet must be used, it should not have a front that is wide and perpendicular to the floor at the front of the seat. The bowl should be shallow at the front of the seat and turn backward more than downward to allow the individual in a wheelchair to get close to the water closet with the seat of the wheelchair.

5.6.3 Toilet rooms shall have lavatories with narrow aprons, which when mounted at standard height are usable by individuals in wheelchairs; or shall have lavatories mounted higher, when particular designs demand, so that they are usable by individuals in wheelchairs.

NOTE: It is important that drain pipes and hot-water pipes under a lavatory be covered or insulated so that a wheelchair individual without sensation will not burn himself.

5.6.4 Some mirrors and shelves shall be provided above lavatories at a height as low as possible and no higher than 40 inches above the floor, measured from the top of the shelf and the bottom of the mirror.

5.6.5 Toilet rooms for men shall have wall-mounted urinals with the opening of the basin 19 inches from the floor, or shall have floor-mounted urinals that are on level with the main floor of the toilet room.

5.6.6 Toilet rooms shall have an appropriate number[a] of towel racks, towel dispensers, and other dispensers and disposal units mounted no higher than 40 inches from the floor.

5.7 Water Fountains. An appropriate number[a] of water fountains or other water-dispensing means shall be accessible to, and usable by, the physically disabled.

5.7.1 Water fountains or coolers shall have up-front spouts and controls.

5.7.2 Water fountains or coolers shall be hand-operated or hand- and foot-operated. (See also American Standard Specifications for Drinking Fountains, Z4.2-1942.)

NOTE 1: Conventional floor-mounted water coolers can be serviceable to individuals in wheelchairs if a small fountain is mounted on the side of the cooler 30 inches above the floor.

NOTE 2: Wall-mounted, hand-operated coolers of the latest design, manufactured by many companies, can serve the able-bodied and the physically disabled equally well when the cooler is mounted with the basin 36 inches from the floor.

NOTE 3: Fully recessed water fountains are not recommended.

NOTE 4: Water fountains should not be set into an alcove unless the alcove is wider than a wheelchair. (See 3.1.)

5.8 Public Telephones. An appropriate number[a] of public telephones should be made accessible to, and usable by, the physically disabled.

NOTE: The conventional public telephone booth is not usable by most physically disabled individuals. There are many ways in which public telephones can be made accessible and usable. It is recommended that architects and builders confer with the telephone company in the planning of the building or facility.

5.8.1 Such telephones should be placed so that the dial and the handset can be reached by individuals in wheelchairs, in accordance with 3.3.

5.8.2 An appropriate number[a] of public telephones should be equipped for those with hearing disabilities and so identified with instructions for use.

NOTE: Such telephones can be used by everyone.

5.9 Elevators. In a multiple-story building, elevators are essential to the successful functioning of physically disabled individuals. They shall conform to the following requirements:

5.9.1 Elevators shall be accessible to, and usable by, the physically disabled on the level that they use to enter the building, and at all levels normally used by the general public.

5.9.2 Elevators shall allow for traffic by wheelchairs, in accordance with 3.1, 3.2, 3.3 and 5.3.

5.10 Controls. Switches and controls for light, heat, ventilation, windows, draperies, fire alarms, and all similar controls of frequent or essential use, shall be placed within the reach of individuals in wheelchairs. (See 3.3.)

[a] See 2.13.

ACCESSIBLE TO, AND USABLE BY, THE PHYSICALLY HANDICAPPED

5.11 Identification. Appropriate identification of specific facilities within a building used by the public is particularly essential to the blind.

5.11.1 Raised letters or numbers shall be used to identify rooms or offices.

5.11.2 Such identification should be placed on the wall, to the right or left of the door, at a height between 4 feet 6 inches and 5 feet 6 inches, measured from the floor, and preferably at 5 feet.

5.11.3 Doors that are not intended for normal use, and that might prove dangerous if a blind person were to exit or enter by them, should be made quickly identifiable to the touch by knurling the door handle or knob. (See Fig. 2.)

EXAMPLE: Such doors might lead to loading platforms, boiler rooms, stages, fire escapes, etc.

5.12 Warning Signals

5.12.1 Audible warning signals shall be accompanied by simultaneous visual signals for the benefit of those with hearing disabilities.

5.12.2 Visual signals shall be accompanied by simultaneous audible signals for the benefit of the blind.

5.13 Hazards. Every effort shall be exercised to obviate hazards to individuals with physical disabilities.

5.13.1 Access panels or manholes in floors, walks, and walls can be extremely hazardous, particularly when in use, and should be avoided.

5.13.2 When manholes or access panels are open and in use, or when an open excavation exists on a site, particularly when it is approximate to normal pedestrian traffic, barricades shall be placed on all open sides, at least 8 feet from the hazard, and warning devices shall be installed in accord with 5.12.2.

5.13.3 Low-hanging door closers that remain within the opening of a doorway when the door is open, or that protrude hazardously into regular corridors or traffic ways when the door is closed, shall be avoided.

5.13.4 Low-hanging signs, ceiling lights, and similar objects or signs and fixtures that protrude into regular corridors or traffic ways shall be avoided. A minimum height of 7 feet, measured from the floor, is recommended.

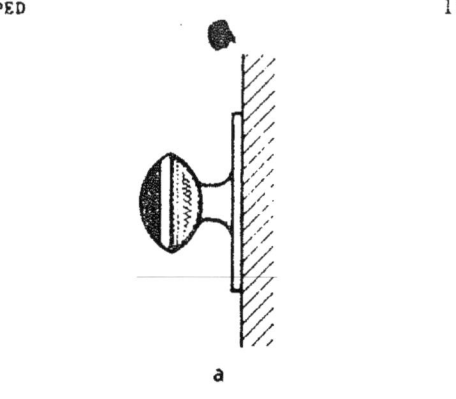

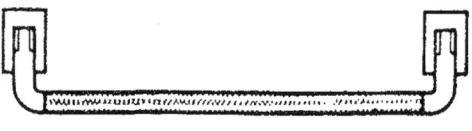

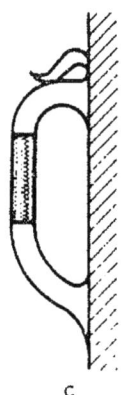

Fig. 2
Knurled Door Handles and Knobs

5.13.5 Lighting on ramps shall be in accord with 1201, 1202, 1203, and 1204 of American Standard A9.1-1953.

5.13.6 Exit signs shall be in accord with 1205 of American Standard A9.1-1953, except as modified by 5.11 of this standard.

APPENDIX D

STATE OF CALIFORNIA

OFFICE OF LEGISLATIVE COUNSEL

Sacramento, California
MAR 3 1 1979

Honorable Leo T. McCarthy
Assembly Chamber

        Physically Handicapped Persons:
        Access to Remodeled Public and
        Private Buildings - #3375

Dear Mr. McCarthy:

QUESTION

When a public building or facility that was constructed prior to November 13, 1968, is structurally remodeled, does Section 4456 of the Government Code require that a path of travel from the exterior of the structure to the remodeled area, a path of travel from any key facilities serving the remodeled area of the structure to the remodeled area (where such key facilities are required for the physically handicapped), and the key facilities themselves, be accessible to the physically handicapped to the same extent that the remodeled area of the structure is required to be accessible by the physically handicapped? Is the State Architect authorized to adopt regulations to this end and, if so, may the State Architect, when he adopts such regulations,* permit minor alterations without regard to making such paths of travel and key facilities serving the remodeled area accessible and usable by the physically handicapped?

---

*   It is our understanding that such regulations have not yet been adopted. Until such time as they are adopted, Section 4451 of the Government Code requires generally that publicly funded buildings and facilities and places of public accommodation conform to the American Standards Association Specifications

Honorable Leo T. McCarthy - p. 2 - #3375

OPINION

When a public building or facility that was constructed prior to November 13, 1968, is structurally remodeled after March 4, 1972, Section 4456 of the Government Code requires that a path of travel from the exterior of the structure to the remodeled area, a path of travel from any key facilities serving the remodeled area of the structure to the remodeled area, (where such key facilities are required for the physically handicapped), and the key facilities themselves be accessible to the physically handicapped to the same extent that the remodeled areas of the structure are to be accessible by the physically handicapped. Such requirements would not be applicable if the building or facility is not reasonably available to or used by the physically handicapped.

The State Architect has the authority to adopt regulations implementing these provisions and may permit minor alterations without regard to such access or usability requirements if such regulations meet certain minimum standards

ANALYSIS

Chapter 7 (commencing with Section 4450) of Division 5 of Title 1 of the Government Code** generally requires all buildings and facilities constructed in this state with public funds to be accessible to, and usable by, the physically handicapped. Responsibility for enforcing these requirements is placed upon the Department of General Services and local governing bodies (Sec. 4453). Section 4450 in Chapter 7 provides, in part, as follows:

> "4450. It is the purpose of this chapter to insure that all buildings, structures, sidewalks, curbs, and related facilities, constructed in this state by the use of state, county or municipal funds, or the funds of any political subdivision of the state shall be accessible to and usable by, the physically handicapped. The State Architect shall adopt by regulation standards for making buildings, structures, sidewalks, curbs, and related facilities accessible to and usable by the physically handicapped. The regulations shall impose as a minimum the standards for buildings and structures as are contained in pertinent

---

** Hereinafter referred to as Chapter 7. All section references are to the Government Code, except as otherwise specified.

Honorable Leo T. McCarthy - p. 3 - #3375

provisions of the latest edition of the
Uniform Building Code, as adopted by the
International Conference of Building
Officials, and shall contain such additional standards relating to buildings,
structures, sidewalks, curbs, and other
related facilities as the State Architect
determines are necessary to assure access
and usability for the physically handicapped.
. . ."

It should be noted that the provisions of Chapter 7 not only affect the accessibility and usability of publicly funded buildings and facilities by the physically handicapped pursuant to that chapter but also the accessibility and usability of public accommodations and facilities by the physically handicapped. Part 5.5 (commencing with Section 19955) of Division 13 of the Health and Safety Code provides for the accessibility by the physically handicapped of "public accommodation or facilities," as defined by Section 19955 of the Health and Safety Code. The Health and Safety Code provisions are substantially similar to the provisions of Chapter 7, and Section 4451 provides that the public accommodations and facilities subject to the accessibility and usability requirements of such provisions of the Health and Safety Code are required to conform to the regulations adopted by the State Architect pursuant to Section 4450 which are in effect on the date a building permit is issued for such public accommodation or facility.

Section 4451, in addition, provides some limited exceptions to the general rule that all newly constructed, publicly funded buildings and facilities be accessible to, and usable by, the physically handicapped. There are two such exceptions in the section. One is when the public building or facility will not be reasonably available to, or used by, the physically handicapped. The second permits the administrative authority of the public building or facility to grant an exception to the requirements of Chapter 7 when it is clearly evident that equivalent facilitation and protection is provided for.

Of concern here, Section 4456 of Chapter 7 provides for the alteration of existing public buildings and facilities to provide access to the physically handicapped, and it reads as follows:

Honorable Leo T. McCarthy - p. 4 - #3375

"4456. After the effective date of this section, any building or facility which would have been subject to this chapter but for the fact it was constructed prior to November 13, 1968, shall comply with the provisions of this chapter when alterations, structural repairs or additions are made to such building or facility. This requirement shall only apply to the area of specific alteration, structural repair or addition and shall not be construed to mean that the entire structure or facility is subject to this chapter."

Section 4456 was added by Chapter 1458 of the Statutes of 1971 which became effective March 4, 1972. Thus, Section 4456 clearly requires that when a publicly funded building or facility constructed prior to November 13, 1968, is altered, repaired, or added to after March 4, 1972, that portion of the building or facility that is remodeled, repaired, or added is required to be made accessible to, and usable by, the physically handicapped to the same extent that other newly constructed, publicly funded buildings and facilities are required to be so accessible and usable pursuant to the provisions of Chapter 7. The question arises whether the specific limitation in Section 4456, requiring only the providing of accessibility and usability to the physically handicapped to that portion of the building or facility which is altered, repaired, or added after March 4, 1972, was intended to exempt the administrative authority of the structure from also being required to make a path of travel from the exterior of the structure to the remodeled area, a path of travel from any key facilities serving the remodeled area to the remodeled area (where such key facilities are required for the physically handicapped), and the key facilities themselves accessible by the physically handicapped.

It is an established rule of statutory construction that statutes be given a fair and reasonable interpretation, with due regard for the language used and for the apparent purpose sought to be accomplished (Cedars of Lebanon Hosp. v. County of L.A., 35 Cal. 2d 729, 735). It is also a fundamental rule of statutory construction that the language of a statute be given a reasonable and commonsense construction in accordance with the apparent purpose and intention of the Legislature and that a statute should be construed with a view to promoting rather than to defeating its general purpose and the policy behind it (City of Costa Mesa v. McKenzie, 30 Cal. App. 3d 763, 769, 770).

Applying the above rules of statutory construction, it is our opinion that the specific limitation in Section 4456, which requires only the providing of accessibility to, and usability by, the physically handicapped to that portion of the public building or facility constructed prior to November 13, 1968, which is altered, repaired, or added after March 4, 1972, does not exempt the administrative authority of the building or facility from also making a path of travel from the exterior of the structure to the remodeled area, a path of travel from any key facilities serving the area to the remodeled area (where such key facilities are required for the physically handicapped), and the key facilities themselves accessible by the physically handicapped. Without making such paths of travel and key facilities serving the remodeled area accessible and usable by the physically handicapped, we think that that portion of the structure which is remodeled would not be functionally usable by the physically handicapped pursuant to Section 4456 and this would, therefore, defeat the legislative purpose in enacting Chapter 7 that is provided for in Section 4450. That purpose, as quoted above, states that public buildings and facilities are to be accessible to and usable by the physically handicapped. It is established that statements of legislative intent of this kind may be given considerable weight by the courts in determining the intent of statutes (Friends of Mammoth v. Board of Supervisors, 8 Cal. 3d 247, 256-259).

Thus, it is our opinion that when a public building or facility that was constructed prior to November 13, 1968, is structurally remodeled after March 4, 1972, Section 4456 requires that a path of travel from the exterior of the structure to the remodeled area, a path of travel from any key facilities serving the remodeled area of the structure to the remodeled area (where such key facilities are required for the physically handicapped), and the key facilities themselves be accessible to the physically handicapped to the same extent that the remodeled area of the structure is to be so accessible. Such requirements would not be applicable if the building or facility is not reasonably available to, or used by, the physically handicapped.

Honorable Leo T. McCarthy - p. 6 - #3375

Section 4450 requires the State Architect to adopt regulations to implement the provisions of Chapter 7. Thus, it is also our opinion that the State Architect has the authority to adopt regulations which require that when a public building or facility that was constructed prior to November 13, 1968, is structurally remodeled after March 4, 1972, the administrative authority of the building or facility shall not only provide accessibility to the physically handicapped to that portion of the building or facility which is remodeled but, in addition, shall provide such accessibility to the physically handicapped along a path of travel from the exterior of the structure to the remodeled area, along a path of travel from any key facilities serving the remodeled area to the remodeled area (where such key facilities are required for the physically handicapped), and in the key facilities themselves.

There remains the question of whether the State Architect may permit minor alterations without regard to making such paths of travel and facilities accessible and usable by the physically handicapped.

Section 4450 requires that the State Architect's regulations meet a minimum standard established by the Uniform Building Code and contain such additional standards as the State Architect determines are necessary.

We think it clear that some minimal alterations of buildings and facilities may be made without regard to the physically handicapped, since to conclude otherwise would mean that any alteration, no matter how minimal and no matter how unrelated to use of the building by the physically handicapped, would result in required alterations for the physically handicapped. We think this would be an unreasonable result and not consistent with the intent of Chapter 7.

Thus, as a general proposition, we think that whether or not alteration of a building or facility requires additional alterations for the physically handicapped would depend upon the nature of the alterations in the particular case, and the State Architect, as part of his general authority to adopt regulations,

Honorable Leo T. McCarthy - p. 7 - #3375

could adopt reasonable regulations as to minimal alterations which can be made without regard to access and usability by the physically handicapped. Of course, such regulations would have to meet the standards of the Uniform Building Code.

                               Very truly yours,

                               Bion M. Gregory
                               Legislative Counsel

                               By
                               James W. Heinzer
                               Deputy Legislative Counsel

JWH:maj

(APPENDIX E-1)

State of California

Office of the Attorney General
Daniel E. Lungren
Attorney General

September 17, 1992

TO: LOCAL BUILDING OFFICIALS

RE: <u>Enforcement of California Disabled Access Standards</u>

On February 21, 1992, I had the pleasure of presenting the keynote address at the Seventh Annual Barrier-Free-Design Conference at Los Angeles, California. At that time, I announced that my office would be implementing a new enforcement strategy for state disabled access laws and regulations. That strategy is focused on ensuring that local building departments, the first line of enforcement authority under state disabled access laws, meet their enforcement responsibilities. This letter is intended to further advise local building officials of my intent to carry out this enforcement strategy, to point out some specific enforcement problems that seem to recur, and to offer some suggestions on how you can improve disabled access enforcement within your jurisdiction.

Under the administrations of prior Attorneys General, when a complaint was received that alleged a particular facility or building was being maintained in violation of state disabled access regulations, this office would investigate the complaint and proceed against the owner to gain compliance. Consistent with the Legislature's mandate of over 20 years ago that local building departments be the primary enforcers of state access requirements, we are now requiring that each complainant first lodge his or her disabled access complaint with the appropriate local building department. We expect every local building department to have a complaint procedure and to investigate disabled access complaints within a reasonable period of time.

1515 K Street • Suite 600 • Sacramento, California 95814

Only after a local building department has completed its investigation of a disabled access complaint and has announced its intended resolution, and upon a request of the complainant would we review the local agency's action for any abuse of discretion. If we were to find such an abuse of discretion, we would ask the local building department to reconsider its decision, and, if it fails to do so, I would be prepared to take legal action to cure that abuse of discretion. Let me make it clear that I do not intend to do any Monday-morning quarterbacking. I only intend to take issue with clear abuses.

Another area for potential legal action by this office concerns local building departments' responsibilities under Government Code section 4452. That section requires commencement of action to correct deviations from state disabled access regulations within 90 days of confirmation of the existence of such deviations. I believe that a reasonable construction of this 90-day requirement is that a final resolution be reached with respect to the confirmed violations within 90 days of confirmation of the violations. A final resolution means that the violations have been corrected, a binding agreement has been reached with the owner to complete any construction necessary to correct the violations within a reasonable time, or the local building department has instituted legal action to compel the owner to correct the violations.[1] Again, with respect to any agreement reached between an owner and a local building department, this office will, upon request, review any such agreement for an abuse of discretion and will take legal action, if necessary, to correct any abuse of discretion.

In order to assist you in evaluating your building department's disabled access enforcement program and/or performance, I have attached an appendix that addresses some common misconceptions about and common violations of state disabled access laws and regulations. I hope that you will find these examples helpful.

Through this office's disabled access enforcement work, we have found that deviations from disabled access requirements are often the result of a lack of adequate resources to carefully check plans, the inadequate training of personnel, and adherence to a philosophy that relaxes enforcement of state disabled access standards. You may want to evaluate your programs to determine whether these areas need to be addressed.

---

1. This construction takes into account that not all construction projects that might be necessary to correct certain disabled access regulations can, in the real world, be completed (and the access violations corrected), within 90 days of confirmation.

Local Building Officials
Page 3
September 17, 1992

California was a pioneer in disabled access. Our laws predate the ADA by over 20 years. I am not asking local building departments to do anything that has not been required of them for over 20 years. What has been the long-standing public policy of this state is now national policy through the ADA. Please join me in a renewed commitment to strong and vigorous enforcement of state disabled access laws and regulations. By ensuring that persons with disabilities have full and equal access to public facilities and privately-funded public accommodations we benefit the State of California by tapping the talents of persons with disabilities, talent that unfortunately has not been utilized to the fullest extent possible. Creating a barrier-free California not only is the right thing to do, but it is in the economic interest of the state to accomplish this goal.

Sincerely,

DANIEL E. LUNGREN
Attorney General

Attachment

APPENDIX

- Unreasonable Hardship Exceptions - While exceptions to the literal requirements of disabled access regulations may be granted by a local building department,[1] that does not mean that a building department is empowered to grant such exceptions under any criteria that it wishes to adopt. Exceptions are truly "exceptions" and can only be granted under the conditions imposed by applicable laws and regulations. One of these conditions is that if the literal requirements of access cannot be met, some sort of access that amounts to "equivalent facilitation" must still be provided. In other words, an "exception" cannot be granted where access is completely denied. In reaching a decision on an application for an exception, the local governing body is required to consider and to make findings on each of the five criteria set forth in regulation section 2-422.[2] Furthermore, the local governing body is required to record and enter the details of these findings in its files.

- Granting Of Retroactive Hardship Exceptions - As a general rule, applications for exceptions must be made prior to construction. If owners were allowed to freely apply for exceptions after construction was completed and deviations were discovered, exceptions would swallow up access requirements. However, retroactive hardship exceptions may be granted post-construction under very limited circumstances. A hardship exception may be granted post-construction where the owner establishes that under the facts that existed at the time the relevant building plans were approved, an exception would have been granted. Of course, each of the five criteria noted above would have to be considered. Of critical importance is that the cost of meeting the literal requirements of the access feature at issue is the cost of meeting same at the time of original plan approval and not the cost of meeting the literal requirements at the time of the application for the retroactive hardship exception.

- Accessibility Of New Restrooms And Public Telephones - Often new buildings are constructed with some but not all restrooms and public telephones being accessible. State access regulations require *all* such restrooms and telephones to be made accessible. Particular attention should be given to the specific mounting heights for fixtures in these restrooms. (Regulation §§2-522, and 2-1501 to 2-1508.) Minor deviations from things like paper towel dispenser mounting height requirements can

---

1. Government Code section 4451(f) and Health & Safety Code section 19957.

2. Regulation section references are to the California Administrative Code, title 24.

1

create major health and safety problems. Furthermore, too often the telephone requirements pertaining to the provision of receivers that generate a magnetic field in receiver caps and volume control to assist the hearing impaired are not enforced. (Regulation §2-522(d)8.)

- <u>Accessibility Of Entrances And Exits</u> - In new construction all entrances <u>and</u> exits are required to be accessible. The same is true for entrances and exits added in remodeling projects. (Regulation §§2-3301, 2-3304 and 2-3325(a).)

- <u>Parking Structure Vertical Clearance Height</u> - State regulations require an 8'2" (not 6'6") vertical clearance height for parking structures. This vertical height clearance requirement applies not only to the entrance of the structure but also applies to the path of travel from the entrance to any and all disabled parking spaces that are required to be provided in that structure. Non-complying parking structures have been discovered often and it is difficult to correct deviations after construction. (Regulation §2-7102(g).)

- <u>Parking Spaces</u> - Very often disabled parking spaces are properly marked on the pavement but required reflectorized signage is not provided. (Regulation §2-7102(f).) Also, disabled spaces are lined up next to each other in a manner that requires a disabled person to go behind a parked vehicle other than his or her own. This is unlawful. (Regulation §2-7102(d).)

- <u>Door Pull Force</u> - Often, both interior and exterior doors exceed the maximum force required to open such doors. This minor requirement, if not followed, creates major access problems. (Regulation §2-3304(i.2).)

- <u>Accessibility Of Employee Side of Work Stations In Selected Facilities</u> - The employee side of work stations in sales facilities, checkstands and ticket booths must be made accessible. (Regulation §§2-611(c.2) and 2-712(b.3.B.).)

- <u>Elevators</u> - Elevators are often overlooked. Too often correct placement and color contrasting for braille symbols and audible signals indicating the direction of travel are ignored. (Regulation §2-5103(d).)

- <u>Curb Ramps</u> - Contrary to the view of some, cities and counties are not free to design their own slope or cross slope requirements for curb ramps. The only lawful requirements are those contained at regulation sections 2-3325 and 2-7103, unless a site specific exception is granted.

- <u>Stairways</u> - It is all too common to find deviations

2

from the requirements that both sides of stairways have handrails (regulation section 2-3306(j.1)) and that color contrasting stripping be provided for the visually impaired (regulation section 2-3306(r)).

- Signaling Devices - Strobe signaling devices that are required for the hearing impaired are often omitted where audible alarms are provided. (Regulation §2-7203.)

- Strike Edge Clearance - Many buildings and facilities, including hotel and motel rooms, lack the proper strike edge clearance on the pull side of doors, making the rooms inside those doors unusable and inaccessible to disabled persons. Contrary to apparent popular belief, the strike edge clearance requirements apply to all hotel and motel rooms, not just those that are designated handicapped accessible. (Regulation §2-3304(i.2C.)

- Parks And Playgrounds - Parks and playgrounds also seem to be ignored or overlooked with respect to disabled access. Particular attention should be given to paths of travel leading to and from activity areas in these facilities. (Regulation §2-1107; see also Public Resources Code §§5410-5411.)

- Changes In Levels On A Given Story - Despite the clear requirement that floors (levels) of a given story be connected by ramp, lift or elevator, it is common to find facilities that do not meet this requirement. It is common to find this violation in restaurants. (Regulation §2-522(d).)

- Remodeling Of Existing Buildings - A remodel triggers the applicability of disabled access requirements in "pre-code" buildings and facilities. Not only must the specific area of remodel comply with access regulations, but the restrooms, public telephones and drinking fountains serving the remodeled area and the path of travel to the remodeled area must also be brought into compliance. The "path of travel" includes all elements necessary to provide access to the remodeled area and includes parking, sidewalks, walks, doorways, and a primary entrance. (Regulation §2-110A(b)11A.) All remodels commenced to bring a facility into compliance with the ADA must also comply with the above state law requirements.

- Seating In Auditoriums, Assembly Halls, Theaters, And Stadiums - Deviations from the requirement that disabled seating in these facilities be integrated or provided in a variety of locations throughout the facility so that disabled persons have the same choice of seating as the general public are common. (Regulation §§2-611(b) and (c).)

- Swimming Pools - Pools must be equipped with assisting devices to aid disabled persons in gaining entry into

3

the pool. (Regulation §2-611(c).)

- <u>Religious Facilities</u> - These facilities must also meet general and specific access requirements. (Regulation §2-611(e).)

- <u>Sales Facilities-Checkstands</u> - Often sales facilities fail to properly sign their accessible checkstands. (Regulation §2-712(b.3.C.).)

LAW OFFICES OF PAUL L. REIN
PAUL L. REIN, ESQ.
200 Lakeside Dr., Suite A
Oakland, CA 94612
(510) 832-5001

Attorney for Plaintiff
CONCETTA JORGENSEN

SUPERIOR COURT FOR THE STATE OF CALIFORNIA,
COUNTY OF CONTRA COSTA

CONCETTA JORGENSEN,

    Plaintiff,

v.

SIZZLER RESTAURANTS INTERNATIONAL, INC. and DOES 1 through 50, Inclusive,

    Defendants.
_____/

ACTION NO. C92 00737

DECLARATION OF LOUIS VERDUGO, JR., SUPERVISING DEPUTY ATTORNEY GENERAL, IN SUPPORT OF PLAINTIFF'S OPPOSITION TO DEFENDANT'S MOTION FOR SUMMARY JUDGMENT OR, IN THE ALTERNATIVE, FOR SUMMARY ADJUDICATION OF ISSUES

Hearing

Date: January 19, 1993
Time: 9 AM
Dept: 5

#c1pl/lvdec.osj

DECLARATION OF LOUIS VERDUGO, JR.

I, LOUIS VERDUGO, Jr., am the Supervising Deputy Attorney General of the Civil Rights Enforcement Unit of the Office of the Attorney General of the State of California. Among my duties is the enforcement of California anti-discrimination laws, including those laws enacted for the protection of physically handicapped persons.

Attached to this declaration as Exhibit A are copies of a letter and an appendix that were sent out on or about September 17, 1992, by California Attorney General Daniel E. Lungren to building department officials throughout California. A list of such officials was provided to the Attorney General's Office by the Office of the State Architect of the State of California. This letter and its appendix, which the letter refers to and which was sent out with each letter, represents the official position of the Attorney General of the State of California with respect to the matters covered therein.

I declare under penalty of perjury that the above facts are true to my personal knowledge, and that this declaration is executed at Los Angeles, California on December 30, 1992.

_____
LOUIS VERDUGO, JR.

(APPENDIX E-2)

JUL 15 1993

TO BE PUBLISHED IN THE OFFICIAL REPORTS

OFFICE OF THE ATTORNEY GENERAL
State of California

DANIEL E. LUNGREN
Attorney General

OPINION : No. 93-203
:
of :
: JULY 14, 1993
DANIEL E. LUNGREN :
Attorney General :
:
GREGORY L. GONOT :
Deputy Attorney General :

THE HONORABLE TOM HAYDEN, MEMBER OF THE CALIFORNIA SENATE, has requested an opinion on the following questions:

1. Are local building departments responsible for enforcing the access requirements of the Americans with Disabilities Act incorporated into California law by chapter 913 of the Statutes of 1992?

2. If not, are local building departments authorized to elect to enforce the federal requirements incorporated into California law?

3. If so, are local building departments immune from liability for enforcing these state building requirements?

4. Is the California Attorney General responsible for enforcing the federal access requirements or civil rights provisions incorporated into California law by chapter 913 of the Statutes of 1992?

1.

93-203

CONCLUSIONS

1. Local building departments are not responsible for enforcing the access requirements of the Americans with Disabilities Act; however, they are required to enforce state and local building codes which have incorporated the federal requirements.

2. Local building departments are not authorized to elect to enforce the federal access requirements; however, they are required to enforce state and local building codes which have incorporated the federal requirements.

3. Local building departments are generally immune from financial liability for enforcing state building requirements.

4. The California Attorney General may bring a civil rights action to enforce state access requirements in certain circumstances; the responsibility for bringing actions to secure compliance with federal access requirements rests with private parties and the United States Attorney General.

ANALYSIS

In analyzing the roles of local building departments and the California Attorney General in enforcing the requirements for accessibility by disabled persons to places of public accommodation and commercial facilities, we preliminarily examine two legislative schemes. The first is a federal law, and the second is a state statute.

A. The Americans With Disabilities Act

The Americans With Disabilities Act of 1990 (Pub.L. No. 101-336; 42 U.S.C. § 12101, et seq.; hereafter "ADA")[1] was enacted by Congress as a civil rights statute to deal with discrimination against individuals with disabilities in the areas of employment (Title I), public services (Title II), and in the construction or alteration of places of public accommodation and commercial facilities (Title III). Unlawful discrimination occurs under Title III when a private party designs and constructs a new public accommodation or commercial facility, or alters an existing one, and fails to make the facility "readily accessible to and useable by individuals with disabilities." (§ 303.)[2] Title III is

---

[1] All unidentified section references hereafter are to the ADA.

[2] Discrimination may also occur through a failure to remove structural barriers when such removal is "readily achievable" or a failure to utilize readily achievable alternative methods if removal of the barriers cannot be readily achieved. (§ 302(b)(2)(A)(iv), (v).)

implemented by regulations issued by the United States Attorney General (§ 306(b)), and the standards included in the regulations are required to be consistent with the minimum guidelines and requirements promulgated by the Architectural and Transportation Barriers Compliance Board (§ 306(c)).

Enforcement of Title III access requirements occurs by means of (1) private suits by individuals who have been subjected to discrimination, or who have reasonable grounds for believing that they are about to be subjected to discrimination (§ 308(a)), and (2) suits commenced by the United States Attorney General when there is reasonable cause to believe that there is a pattern or practice of discrimination, or an individual act of discrimination that raises an issue of general public importance (§ 308(b)).

The United States Attorney General may, upon application of a state or local government, certify that a state law or local building code meets or exceeds the minimum requirements of the ADA for the accessibility and useability of facilities covered by Title III. (§ 308(b)(1)(A)(ii).)[3] Such certification provides rebuttable evidence that the ADA requirements are met or exceeded by the state or local code in an enforcement proceeding under section 308.

B. Chapter 913 of the Statutes of 1992

Chapter 913 of the Statutes of 1992 was enacted by the Legislature "to strengthen California law in areas where it is weaker than the Americans with Disabilities Act of 1990 . . . , and to retain California law when it provides more protection for individuals with disabilities than the Americans with Disabilities Act of 1990." (Stats. 1992, Ch. 913, § 1.) The areas addressed by the state legislation include employment, transportation, public accommodations, state and local government services, and telecommunications.

One of the basic changes in California law effected by chapter 913 was the adoption of the ADA's broad definition of "disability"[4] where that term is used in the Unruh Civil Rights Act (Civil Code, § 51) and various other anti-discrimination and equal rights statutes. (See, e.g., Bus. & Prof. Code, § 126.5; Civil Code, §§ 51.5, 51.8, 52, 53,

---

[3] Modifications to the California Building Standards Code (title 24, Cal. Code of Regs.) have been prepared by the State Architect to bring the code into conformity with the requirements of the ADA. The revisions were approved by the California Building Standards Commission on March 5, 1993, and will become effective 180 days after publication. The code, as revised, may then be submitted to the United States Attorney General for certification.

[4] "Disability" is defined in the ADA (§ 3) and chapter 913 (see, e.g., Bus. & Prof. Code, § 126.5; Civil Code, § 54) to mean any of the following with respect to an individual: (1) a physical or mental impairment that substantially limits one or more of the major life activities of the individual, (2) a record of such an impairment, or (3) being regarded as having such an impairment.

54, 54.1-54.3.) Chapter 913 also added a provision to Civil Code section 51 declaring a violation of the ADA to be a violation of the Unruh Civil Rights Act. However, Chapter 913 left unaffected the following proviso of the Unruh Civil Rights Act which is also contained in other anti-discrimination statutes (Civil Code, §§ 51, 51.5, 51.8, 52):

> "Nothing in this section shall be construed to require any construction, alteration, repair, structural or otherwise, or modification of any sort whatsoever to any new or existing establishment, facility, building, improvement, or any other structure, or to augment, restrict, or alter in any way the authority of the State Architect to require construction, alteration, repair, or modifications that the State Architect otherwise possesses pursuant to other provisions of the law."

Similarly, chapter 913 retained the following proviso in Civil Code section 54.1, subdivision (b), which concerns full and equal access to all housing accommodations:

> "Nothing in this subdivision shall require any person renting, leasing, or providing for compensation real property to modify his or her property in any way or provide a higher degree of care for an individual with a disability than for an individual who is not disabled."

Chapter 913 amended one statute specifically governing building construction. Government Code section 4450 ensures "that all buildings, structures, sidewalks, curbs, and related facilities, constructed in this state by the use of state, county, or municipal funds, or the funds of any political subdivision of the state shall be accessible to and useable by individuals with disabilities." Under this statute the State Architect has adopted regulations and building standards necessary to assure access to and useability of public buildings by individuals with disabilities. The same regulations are made applicable by Health and Safety Code sections 19955 and 19956 to public accommodations or facilities constructed with private funds. Chapter 913 added the directive with respect to these statutes that "In no case shall the State Architect's regulations and building standards prescribe a lesser standard of accessibility or useability than provided by regulations of the Federal Architectural and Transportation Barriers Compliance Board adopted to implement the Americans With Disabilities Act of 1990." (Gov. Code, § 4450, subd. (b).)[5]

Having briefly reviewed both the ADA and chapter 913 as they relate to each other in the context of accessibility requirements imposed at the time of building construction or alteration, we turn to the roles of local building departments and the California Attorney General in enforcing the two legislative schemes.

---

[5] Chapter 913 added the same requirement to Government Code section 19952. Under this section, the owner or manager of a place of public amusement and resort must provide seating or accommodations for physically disabled persons in a variety of locations within the facility at the time of its construction.

C. The Role of Local Building Departments in Enforcing Access Requirements Under the ADA and Chapter 913

The enforcement of state laws that require places of public accommodation and commercial facilities to be made accessible to and useable by individuals with disabilities is the responsibility of local building departments. (Health & Saf. Code, § 19958.) Building standards to ensure such accessibility and useability have been adopted by the State Architect and approved by the State Building Standards Commission. (Health & Saf. Code, § 18938; Gov. Code, § 4450.) These standards have recently been revised to bring the California Building Standards Code (hereafter "CBSC") into conformity with the access requirements of the ADA.[6] While the ADA access requirements have not been incorporated per se into California law, the CBSC's recent revision ensures that the "readily accessible" standard of the ADA will be met when there is construction or alteration of a place of public accommodation or a commercial facility.

Neither chapter 913 nor the ADA has changed the access enforcement responsibilities of local building departments. They continue to be charged only with enforcement of those access requirements which appear as part of the CBSC or local building codes. The ADA does not provide for the enforcement of federal law by local building officials. (See § 308; U.S. Dept. of Justice, Technical Assistance Manual for Implementation of Title III of the ADA, § III-8.1000.) This is true even when the officials are enforcing a state or local code certified by the United States Attorney General. (*Id.*, at § III-9.1000.) The ADA's enforcement mechanism is the traditional case-by-case method of civil rights enforcement which depends on the filing of complaints rather than a system of government inspection. (*Id.*, at § III-9.2000.)

Chapter 913 uses certain features of the ADA to broaden and strengthen California's anti-discrimination and equal rights statutes, but it does not alter the pre-existing statutory structure for ensuring accessibility and useability in the construction or alteration of places of public accommodation and commercial facilities. It does not mandate local building officials to enforce the federal access requirements, nor could it; rather, it directs the State Architect to adopt those ADA requirements which prescribe a greater degree of accessibility and useability than that provided by existing state law while preserving state standards which exceed the level of accessibility and useability afforded by the ADA. Enforcement of state anti-discrimination and civil rights statutes modified by chapter 913 continues to occur as described in the specified statutes.

---

[6] This administrative process was begun in response to the need to obtain certification of the CBSC from the United States Attorney General under the ADA's provisions and was underway when chapter 913 was enacted.

When local building officials review construction activity that might constitute a violation of a state anti-discrimination or civil rights statute, their role is to enforce the terms of the state and local building regulations. They may not elect to assume greater or different enforcement powers than those specifically or necessarily implied under California law. (See *Ferdig v. State Personnel Board* (1969) 71 Cal.2d 96, 103-104 ["Administrative agencies have only the power conferred on them by statute and an act in excess of those powers is void"].)

Chapter 913 does not contain a provision which could be viewed as an implied grant of authority to interpret, apply, or directly enforce ADA accessibility requirements. If a building as proposed or in the process of being constructed contains certain features that are "not up to code" from an accessibility standpoint, a construction permit may be denied and construction halted; but the "code" utilized by local building officials in this regard continues to be the CBSC as revised, and the local building code, if any.[7]

We therefore conclude that local building departments are not responsible for enforcing the access requirements of the ADA; however, they are required to enforce state and local building codes which have incorporated the federal requirements. Local building departments are not authorized to elect to enforce the federal access standards apart from the CBSC and local codes. These conclusions render moot the question as to whether chapter 913, in conjunction with the ADA, affects the traditional immunity from financial liability granted to local building officials who are engaged in the performance of their official duties. (See, e.g., Gov. Code, §§ 820.2, 820.4, 821.2; Cal. Code Regs., tit. 24, § 202, subd. (f).)

D. The Role of the California Attorney General in Enforcing Access Requirements Under the ADA and Chapter 913

As previously noted, the United States Attorney General is responsible for the enforcement of Title III of the ADA and may, under specified circumstances, commence a civil action in United States district court to secure the rights which Title III guarantees to individuals with disabilities. The California Attorney General has no role in directly enforcing the provisions of the ADA, but chapter 913 provides that violations of the ADA constitute violations of the Unruh Civil Rights Act (Civ. Code, § 51). Civil Code section 52, subdivision (c), which applies to the rights secured by Civil Code section 51, provides as follows:

---

[7] Until such time as the revised accessibility-related provisions of the CBSC have been certified by the United States Attorney General, private parties who design and construct places of public accommodation and commercial facilities must look to the ADA in order to have reasonable assurance that they are not engaging in a form of discrimination thereunder.

"Whenever there is reasonable cause to believe that any person or group of persons is engaged in conduct of resistance to the full enjoyment of any of the rights hereby secured, and that conduct is of that nature and is intended to deny the full exercise of the rights herein described, the Attorney General, any district attorney or city attorney, or any person aggrieved by the conduct may bring a civil action in the appropriate court by filing with it a complaint. The complaint shall contain the following:

"(1) The signature of the officer, or, in his or her absence, the individual acting on behalf of the officer, or the signature of the person aggrieved.

"(2) The facts pertaining to the conduct.

"(3) A request for preventive relief, including an application for a permanent or temporary injunction, restraining order, or other order against the person or persons responsible for the conduct, as the complainant deems necessary to insure the full enjoyment of the rights herein described."

Thus, if an act of discrimination as specified under Title III of the ADA (for example, failure to remove architectural barriers when such removal is readily achievable) has occurred, the violation is part of a conduct of resistance to the civil rights of disabled persons, and such conduct is intended to deny disabled persons the full exercise of their civil rights, the California Attorney General (or a district attorney or city attorney) is authorized to bring a civil action against the person or group of persons engaged in the discriminatory conduct. While the complaint is to include a request for preventative relief, because of the proviso contained in subdivision (g) of Civil Code section 52,[a] the relief may not include an order requiring "any construction, alteration, repair, structural or otherwise, or modifications of any sort whatsoever to any new or existing establishment, factory, building, improvement, or any other structure." Consequently, such an action would be limited primarily to securing prospective relief.

The same constraints, however, do not exist when the ADA violation is the subject of a civil action filed by the United States Attorney General in federal court. The United States Attorney General may proceed when there is either a pattern or practice of discrimination (§ 308(b)(1)(B)(i)) or an individual act of discrimination which raises an issue of general public importance (§ 308(b)(1)(B)(ii)). Moreover, the United States Attorney General may, without a finding of intentional discrimination, obtain civil penalties

---

[a] This proviso is also contained in the Unruh Civil Rights Act.

and injunctive relief, including an order to alter facilities to make them readily accessible to and useable by individuals with disabilities. (§ 308(b)(2).)[9]

In light of the foregoing, we conclude that the ability of the California Attorney General to enforce the ADA access requirements through the Unruh Civil Rights Act and related statutes, as modified by chapter 913, is narrowly limited by California law;[10] the primary responsibility for enforcement of the ADA access requirements through legal action rests with private litigants and the United States Attorney General.[11]

* * * * *

---

[9] Under either the ADA or the Unruh Civil Rights Act, a person who has been subjected to discrimination may bring an action against the discriminating party. (See § 308(a)(1), (2); Civ. Code, § 52, subds. (a), (g).) The California Attorney General may intervene in a private action which seeks relief from the denial of the equal protection of the laws under the Fourteenth Amendment to the United States Constitution on account of a person's disability if the case is of general public importance. (Civ. Code, § 52, subd. (d).)

[10] Of course, the California Attorney General has broad general authority to enforce the laws of the state. (See Cal. Const., art. V, § 13; *D'Amico v. Board of Medical Examiners* (1974) 11 Cal.3d 1, 14-15; *People ex rel. Lynch v. Superior Court* (1970) 1 Cal.3d 910, 912, fn. 1.)

[11] To the extent that state access standards exceed those of the ADA, federal enforcement action would not be available.

(APPENDIX E-3)

STATE OF CALIFORNIA
OFFICE OF THE ATTORNEY GENERAL
BILL LOCKYER
ATTORNEY GENERAL

STEVE COONY
Chief Deputy Attorney General
Administration & Policy

August 4, 2003

Don Kass, Esq.
Supervising Deputy City Attorney
Consumer Protection Section
Los Angeles City Attorney's Office
200 North Main Street
Los Angeles, CA 90012-4131

Re: California Bowling Proprietor's Complaint Concerning Filings of Frivolous Lawsuits

Dear Mr. Kass:

Thank you for your letter of July 11, 2003. With your letter, you provide a copy of a complaint you have received from the owner of a bowling alley, Mr. Gene Giegoldt. Mr. Giegoldt alleges that hundreds of "Trevor type" lawsuits have been filed throughout the state for minor violations of the Americans With Disabilities Act (ADA) and that many of these lawsuits target bowling alleys.

Attorney General Lockyer has taken legal action against the Trevor Law Group and its principals and other law firms and attorneys who he determined were engaged in the filing of Business and Professions Code section 17200 actions in bad faith and in violation of the Rules of Professional Responsibility of the State Bar of California. A copy of that complaint is enclosed for your information. Since filing such actions, we have received several complaints from property owners, defense attorneys and business organizations that make allegations similar to those that have been made by Mr. Giegoldt.

To date, however, no one has presented us with a situation involving state and federal access laws that is similar to the Trevor Law Group matter. Specifically, no complainant has asserted or provided evidence that the access violations which are the subject of any civil action filed against them or their clients do not exist. Moreover, while some of these complainants contend that the access violations for which they have been sued are "minor," whether such violations are in fact minor is debatable. While a violation may be minor in the eye of a business

1300 I STREET • SUITE 1730 • SACRAMENTO, CALIFORNIA • 95814 • 916-324-5435 • FAX 916-327-7154 • SCOONY@HDCDOJNET.STATE.CA.US

Don Kass, Esq.
August 4, 2003
Page 2

owner, the violation may not be minor to a person with a disability. Additionally, none of these complainants provided any evidence that there was a lack of a real plaintiff or that the attorney filing the lawsuit failed to conduct an investigation of the facts before filing a civil action. The complaint you have shared with us appears to be similar to other complaints we have received.

We are very mindful of the difficulties that small businesses may face in bringing their buildings and facilities into compliance with state and federal access laws and regulations. Nevertheless, we also cannot ignore the fact that the ADA has been in effect for 12 years, and state laws requiring privately funded public accommodations to be fully accessible to persons with disabilities have been in existence for over 30 years. Unfortunately, non-compliance with state and federal access laws and their implementing regulations continues to be a pervasive and persistent problem in California and throughout the country. Compliance with our access laws and regulations is not optional. The best way to avoid litigation is to take proactive steps to comply with these laws and regulations.

Mr. Giegoldt also complains that business owners are not given notice of access violations and the opportunity to cure those violations before a lawsuit is filed. His concern in this regard is understandable. However, in recent years both state and federal legislation that would have required plaintiffs to notify business owners of the existence of access violations at their facilities and to give them a specified time period to correct those violations prior to filing a lawsuit were soundly defeated in the Legislature and in Congress. The disability community, which strongly opposed this legislation, believes that a "wait period" is inappropriate given the fact that state and federal access laws have been in effect for a long time.

Attorney General Bill Lockyer has made it a priority to address the problem of non-compliance with state access laws and regulations. In 2002, he issued letters to all local building officials and to all city attorneys, district attorneys and county counsel, urging them to step up their enforcement of state access laws and regulations. For your information, copies of those letters are enclosed. Additionally, the Attorney General has sponsored legislation this year, SB 262, which would authorize the Attorney General, city attorneys, district attorneys and county counsel to seek civil penalties against privately funded public accommodations who do not bring their buildings and facilities into compliance with state access laws and regulations.

The Attorney General is strongly committed to the enforcement of our access laws and is supportive of those who pursue private enforcement actions in a lawful manner. However, he will consider taking action against those who pursue actions in an unlawful manner. If you are aware of any such cases, please feel free to bring them to our attention.

Don Kass, Esq.
August 4, 2003
Page 3

If you would like to discuss this issue further, please feel free to contact Senior Assistant Attorney General Louis Verdugo. Louis heads our Civil Rights Enforcement Section and can be reached at (213) 897-2177.

                              Sincerely,

                              STEVE COONY
                              Chief Deputy Attorney General
                              Administration and Policy

Enclosures
cc: Gene T. Giegoldt

(APPENDIX G)

PAUL L. REIN, Esq. (SBN 43053)
LAW OFFICES OF PAUL L. REIN
200 Lakeside Dr., Suite A
Oakland, CA 94612
(510) 832-5001

Attorneys for Plaintiff
DARREN K.

UNITED STATES DISTRICT COURT
CENTRAL DISTRICT OF CALIFORNIA

Darren K.,

    Plaintiff,

v.

XYZ RESTAURANTS, et al.,

    Defendants.

CASE NO. _____
Civil Rights

COMPLAINT FOR PRELIMINARY AND PERMANENT INJUNCTIVE RELIEF AND DAMAGES: DENIAL OF CIVIL RIGHTS AND PUBLIC FACILITIES TO PHYSICALLY DISABLED PERSONS, (CALIFORNIA CIVIL CODE § 51, § 52, § 54, § 54.1, § 55); INJUNCTIVE RELIEF PER TITLE III OF THE AMERICANS WITH DISABILITIES ACT OF 1990

DEMAND FOR JURY TRIAL

Plaintiff Darren K. complains of defendants XYZ RESTAURANTS and DOES 1-20, inclusive, and alleges as follows:

1. This lawsuit seeks injunctive relief and damages on behalf of a disabled blind man who was refused service at an XYZ Restaurant because he was accompanied by his guide dog, in violation of the Americans With Disabilities Act of 1990 ("ADA") and of California's civil rights laws.

INTRODUCTION

2. Plaintiff Darren K. is a physically disabled person who is visually disabled, and has been blind since the age of four. Defendant XYZ RESTAURANTS own, operate, lease and/or are lessors of an XYZ Restaurant, a

public accommodation located in the City of _____, _____ County, California. On information and belief, defendant ROE, as property owner, shares responsibility for architectural barriers to access for physically disabled persons at the subject property, but is not responsible for the policies of the XYZ RESTAURANTS or the conduct of XYZ's agents and employees, including defendant James DOE 1. Plaintiff Darren K. is an 18-year-old senior at ABC High School who, despite his disability, strives to lead a full and active social life, plays the drums in his high school band, and seeks to be independent and have full and equal access to all public facilities.

3. On or about January 1, 20__, plaintiff went to the XYZ Restaurant at [address and city], California, to have a meal with two friends. While plaintiff was patronizing the restaurant, defendants and their restaurant manager blatantly, and in violation of the rights of plaintiff as a disabled person, ordered plaintiff and his service dog to leave the restaurant. Defendants enforced a policy that willfully and with full understanding of its discriminatory effects excluded plaintiff from access to the XYZ Restaurant on the basis of his physical disability and his need for accompaniment by and assistance from his service animal, a properly trained and identified Guide Dog for the Blind. Defendants took their actions despite actual knowledge that Civil Code § 54.2(a) guaranteed that: "Every individual with a disability has the right to be accompanied by a guide dog, signal dog or service dog, especially trained for the purpose, in any of the places specified in § 54.1, which includes all "places of public accommodation, amusement or resort, and other places to which the public is invited...." A public restaurant is such a place.

4. This Complaint is brought as the result of defendants' intentional violation of the anti-discrimination provisions of the Americans With Disabilities Act of 1990, the California Unruh Act, the Disabled Persons Act, and a provision of the California Penal Code. As a result of defendants' illegal acts,

plaintiff suffered damages, and seeks an injunction to enjoin these defendants and this business establishment from continuing their discriminatory policies and practices, which are prohibited by law, or to cease all business operations until such time as they provide full and equal access to persons with disabilities, including plaintiff Darren K.

JURISDICTION AND VENUE

5. This Court has jurisdiction of this action pursuant to 28 USC § 1331 for violations of the Americans With Disabilities Act of 1990, 42 USC §§ 12101 et seq. Pursuant to supplemental jurisdiction, attendant and related causes of action, arising from the same facts, are also brought under California law, including but not limited to violations of California Civil Code §§ 51, 52, 54, 54.1, and 54.2.

6. Venue is proper in this Court pursuant to 28 USC § 1391(b) and is founded on the fact that the real property that is the subject of this action is located in this District and that plaintiff's causes of action arose in this District.

7. This case should be assigned to the [_____] intradistrict as the real property which is the subject of this action is located in the [_____] intradistrict and plaintiff's causes of action arose in the [_____] intradistrict.

PARTIES

8. Defendants are the owners, operators, lessors, and/or lessees of the XYZ RESTAURANT located at [address and city], California (hereinafter "XYZ" or "Restaurant"). Defendants maintain a "business establishment" and "public accommodation or facility" subject to the requirements of California Civil Code §§ 51, 52, 54.1 and 54.2 et seq.

9. Plaintiff Darren K. is a "person with a disability" or

"physically handicapped person." (Hereinafter, the words "physically handicapped" and "physically disabled" are used interchangeably as these words have similar or identical common usage and legal meaning, but the legislative scheme in Part 5.5 Health & Safety Code uses the term "physically handicapped persons," and the Unruh Rights Act, and Disabled Rights Acts, Civil Code §§ 51, 52, 54.1, 54, 54.2 and 54.3 and other statutory measures refer to the protection of the rights of "individuals with disabilities.") Plaintiff Darren K. is physically disabled due to visual impairment: plaintiff is totally blind. As a person with a disability, he is specifically authorized by California law and the Americans With Disabilities Act of 1990 to be accompanied into any public accommodation by a service animal. (See Cal. Civ. Code § 54.2 and 28 CFR §36.302.) California Civil Code § 54.1 states:

> (a)(1) Individuals with disabilities shall be entitled to full and equal access, as other members of the general public, to accommodations, advantages, facilities, medical facilities, including hospitals, clinics, and physicians' offices, and privileges of all common carriers, airplanes, motor vehicles, railroad trains, motorbuses, streetcars, boats, or any other public conveyances or modes of transportation (whether private, public, franchised, licensed, contracted, or otherwise provided), telephone facilities, adoption agencies, private schools, hotels, lodging places, places of public accommodation, amusement, or resort, and other places to which the general public is invited, subject only to the conditions and limitations established by law, or state or federal regulation, and applicable alike to all persons.

Further, California Civil Code § 54.2(a) specifies that: "Every individual with a disability has the right to be accompanied by a guide dog, signal dog or service dog, especially trained for the purpose in any of the places specified in § 54.1."

10. Plaintiff is informed and believes that each of the named defendants herein, including defendants XYZ [and corporate owners and other defendants], inclusive, are and were the owners, operators, lessors and/or lessees of the subject restaurant and/or personally have participated in the pattern and practice of discrimination and exclusion of plaintiff Darren K. (Hereinafter, a reference to "XYZ" or "defendants" will be a reference to all defendants.)

Plaintiff is informed and believes that each of the defendants herein is the employer, agent, ostensible agent, alter ego, master, servant, trustor, trustee, employer, employee, representative, franchiser, franchisee, lessor, lessee, joint venturer, parent, subsidiary, affiliate, related entity, partner, and/or associate, or such similar capacity, of each of the other defendants, and was at all times acting and performing, or failing to act or perform, within the course and scope of such similar aforementioned capacities, and with the authorization, consent, permission or ratification of each of the other defendants, and is personally responsible in some manner for the acts and omissions of the other defendants in proximately causing the violations and damages complained of herein, and have participated, directed, and have ostensibly and/or directly approved or ratified each of the acts or omissions of each other defendant, as herein described. Plaintiff will seek leave to amend this complaint when the true names, capacities, connections, and responsibilities of defendants [XYZ, etc.] and DOES 1-20, inclusive, are ascertained. References to "defendants," unless otherwise specified, shall be deemed to refer to all defendants and each of them.

STATEMENT OF FACTS

11. On or about January 1, 20__, plaintiff Darren K. went to the XYZ in [_____], California, to have lunch with two friends. At the time of his visit plaintiff was accompanied by his service dog, "Lambert," who had been trained and certified as a "service animal" by "Guide Dogs for the Blind," a public non-profit group that trains dogs for use by blind persons. Plaintiff carries identification from Guide Dogs for the Blind identifying his dog as a service animal. Plaintiff's guide dog also wears a special leather harness with a yellow sign with the words "DO NOT PET ME I'M WORKING," to inform the general public that he is not a "pet." Attached and incorporated into this Complaint as **Exhibit 1** is a recent photograph of plaintiff and his guide dog,

Lambert. Lambert is wearing the same harness and sign he wore when he and plaintiff were twice ordered out of the XYZ Restaurant on January 1, 20__.

12. After entering the XYZ Restaurant and using the restroom, but before he could order his food, plaintiff was confronted by a man, later identified as defendant James DOE 1, who repeatedly told plaintiff that he was not allowed to have his guide dog with him in the restaurant, and that he should take his guide dog and leave the restaurant. When plaintiff and his friends advised defendant DOE 1 that it was illegal to exclude a guide dog, defendant DOE 1 replied that he "knew" it was illegal, "but this is a fast food establishment," and that plaintiff and his dog would have to leave, stating, "You can't have that dog in here." Plaintiff, agitated and embarrassed at being ordered to leave the restaurant, asked to speak with the manager. Defendant DOE 1 advised that <u>he was the manager</u> and again demanded that plaintiff and his guide dog leave the restaurant. Under orders from defendants, plaintiff, upset, told his friends, "Let's go outside," and left the restaurant.

13. Outside the restaurant plaintiff called the local police to attempt to get assistance, but was unable to obtain immediate help from the police. After conferring with his friends, who were Explorer Scouts who had received training from the police, and who knew that denying admittance to a public accommodation to a blind person and his specially trained guide dog was a crime, a violation of Penal Code § 365.5, plaintiff again entered the restaurant with his guide dog and attempted to place an order for his food. However, he was again confronted by defendant DOE 1, who said, "I know you called the cops, so what do you want before I kick you out again?" Plaintiff again attempted to communicate with defendant DOE 1 and again offered written proof of his guide dog's status as a service animal and plaintiff's right to bring his guide dog inside any public accommodation, including a restaurant. Plaintiff attempted to present defendant DOE 1 with his certificate from Guide Dogs for

Defendant DOE 1 told Darren K. that the restaurant "owner" was "DOE 2," but that DOE 2 was "out of town." Defendant DOE 1 promised Darren K. to present his complaint and phone number to the owner; but no one ever called Darren K. s back, and no one ever contacted Darren K., or explained why he had been "kicked out" of the XYZ Restaurant.

16. Following the previously described incidents, and the phone call from plaintiff's father Darren K. to defendant DOE 1 at the subject XYZ, on or about January 2, 20__, Darren K. telephoned the corporate offices of defendant DEF, the owner and operator of the subject XYZ Restaurant and of several hundred other restaurants. During Darren K.'s phone call, he complained about the treatment of his blind son, plaintiff Darren K., and about the attitude of defendant's employee, defendant DOE 1. Darren K. complained about manager defendant DOE 1's conduct and the apparent policy of defendants to continue discriminating against disabled persons who patronized while accompanied by service animals, and put defendants on notice of plaintiff's complaint. Defendants' representative promised to pass on the complaint to defendants' "upper management."

17. However, the response of defendants was to ratify the actions of its manager, DOE 1: The only response by defendants to Darren K.'s phone call about the treatment of his blind son was to send Darren K. an apparent form letter dated January 7, 20__ (copy attached and incorporated herein as **Exhibit 4**). This letter, over the signature of ROE 1, Vice President of Operations for defendants, was addressed to Darren K., thanked *him* "for taking the time to let us know about your visit to our restaurant," and asked him to "[p]lease accept the enclosed coupon with our compliments." The "coupon" offered "a free hot dog or sandwich of your choice including condiments, tomato and cheese; a medium soft drink; and a regular size fries. Compliments of **XYZ**." [Emphasis in original.] The letter and the coupon were both signed by "ROE 1, Vice President

of Operations" for defendants. This letter illustrated the insensitive and disdainful nature of defendants' response to plaintiff's complaint about disability discrimination, and is relevant to plaintiff's claim for treble and/or punitive damages.

18. Based on a preliminary investigation by plaintiff's representatives after the subject incident of January 1, 20__, the physical property owned and operated by defendants and each of them was also constructed and maintained in an inaccessible condition for use by physically disabled persons with regard to a number of features that may adversely affect plaintiff, as a disabled and blind person, when he may attempt to return to the restaurant, including but not limited to the lack of proper accessible parking and paths of travel, lack of proper handrails on the entrance path of travel, and other items, according to proof. The restaurant also does not offer Braille menus for its visually disabled patrons, including plaintiff.

FIRST CAUSE OF ACTION:
DAMAGES AND INJUNCTIVE RELIEF FOR DENIAL OF FULL AND EQUAL ACCESS TO PUBLIC FACILITIES AT A RETAIL ESTABLISHMENT
(Cal. Civil Code §§ 54, 54.1, 54.2)

19. Plaintiff repleads and incorporates by reference, as if fully set forth again herein, the allegations contained in Paragraphs 1 through 18 of this Complaint, and incorporates them herein as if separately repled.

20. On information and belief, should plaintiff be allowed by defendants to return to and patronize the premises at the subject XYZ Restaurant, he will also face certain architectural barriers to access for blind persons, caused by defendants' failure to comply with California's Title 24, the State Building Code, including but not limited to improperly configured disabled parking, path of travel from parking to entrance, and the lack of proper handrails on the entry ramp to the restaurant from its parking lot, plus additional barriers, according to

proof. On information and belief, such barriers were constructed and maintained in violation of California Health & Safety Code §§ 19955-19959. Additionally, XYZ does not offer its visually disabled customers the use of a Braille menu, and should be required to provide such menu upon request to any customers who cannot read the posted menu and prices because of their visual disability.

21. Due to defendants' decision to knowingly and willfully exclude plaintiff from their public accommodation and deny plaintiff entrance into their place of business, plaintiff has faced the continuing discrimination of being barred from entering this public accommodation and place of business based upon defendants' illegal exclusion of plaintiff as a disabled person because of his legally protected use of his service dog. Since his exclusion on January 1, 20__, plaintiff has continued to suffer denial of access to this business, and fears violence and/or other unpleasant and discriminatory treatment should he attempt to return to this business until he receives the protection of this Court's injunctive relief, and has continued to suffer discrimination on a daily basis since the date of his visit, all to his statutory damages pursuant to California Civil Code §§ 54.1, 54.2, and 54.3. On information and belief each day upon which plaintiff has continued to be denied access constitutes a separate violation of Civil Code §§ 54.1, 54.2, and 54.3.

22. As a result of the denial of equal access to the facilities of defendants' business, due to defendants' specifically discriminatory exclusionary policy, plaintiff Darren K. suffered a violation of his civil rights and suffered discomfort and injury, mental and emotional shock, emotional distress, embarrassment and humiliation, and statutory violations, all to his damages as hereinafter stated. Defendants' actions and omissions, along with the implementation of defendants' discriminatory policy of denying access to disabled persons who are accompanied by service animals, constitute discrimination against plaintiff on the sole basis that he is a physically disabled

person, in violation of all subject laws, and have deterred plaintiff from the right to use XYZ's public facilities on a "full and equal" basis with the general public. Plaintiff seeks statutory damages and actual damages, treble damages, injunctive relief, and reasonable attorney fees, litigation expenses and costs, all as further specifically requested hereinbelow.

23. The discriminatory acts as pled herein and defendants' specific discriminatory policies prevent plaintiff from equal use of the premises and thus continue to discriminate against plaintiff and to deny him "full and equal access" on a daily basis at all times since his visit on or about January 1, 20__. Further, any violation of the Americans With Disabilities Act of 1990 (as pled in the Third Cause of Action hereinbelow, the contents of which are repled and incorporated herein, word for word, as if separately repled) also constitutes a violation of Civil Code §§ 54(c) and § 54.1(d), thus independently justifying an award of damages and injunctive relief pursuant to California law, including but not limited to Civil Code §§ 54.1, 54.2, 54.3 and 55.

24. As a result of defendants' acts and omissions in this regard, plaintiff Darren K. has been required to incur legal expenses and attorney fees, as provided by statute, in order to enforce plaintiff's rights and to enforce provisions of the law protecting access for disabled persons and prohibiting discrimination against disabled persons. Plaintiff therefore seeks recovery of all reasonable attorney fees and costs, pursuant to the provisions of Civil Code §§ 54.1, 54.2 and 54.3. Additionally, plaintiff's lawsuit is intended not only to obtain compensation for damages to plaintiff, but also to require the defendants to make their facilities accessible to all disabled members of the public, and to cease the specific discriminatory policies against disabled persons, thereby justifying "public interest" attorney fees, litigation expenses and costs pursuant to the provisions of California Code of Civil Procedure § 1021.5.

25. On information and belief, plaintiff alleges that at all times

relevant to this complaint defendants were made aware of their duties under the Americans With Disabilities Act of 1990 and California law to refrain from establishing discriminatory policies against physically disabled persons, prior to the filing of this complaint. Defendants' establishment of their discriminatory policy to deny entry to persons with service animals, and their implementation of such a discriminatory policy against plaintiff, as well as their specific illegal and discriminatory conduct on or about January 1, 20__, indicate actual and implied malice toward plaintiff and despicable conduct carried out by defendants with a conscious disregard for the rights of plaintiff, and justify an award of punitive and exemplary damages pursuant to California Civil Code § 3294, in an amount sufficient to make an example of defendants, according to proof.

26. Defendants' actions were knowingly illegal and in violation of the Penal Code. At all times relevant to this action, California Penal Code section 365.5(b) stated:

> (b) No blind person, deaf person, or disabled person and his or her specially trained guide dog, signal dog, or service dog shall be denied admittance to accommodations, advantages, facilities, medical facilities, including hospitals, clinics, and physicians' offices, telephone facilities, adoption agencies, private schools, hotels, lodging places, places of public accommodation, amusement, or resort, and other places to which the general public is invited within this state because of that guide dog, signal dog, or service dog.

Defendants' commission of a Penal Code-prohibited crime, of which plaintiff was the victim, is an additional basis for imposition of treble and punitive damages.

27. Plaintiff has been damaged by defendants' discriminatory conduct barring his entry of a public facility, and seeks the relief that is afforded by Civil Code §§ 54.1, 54.2, 54.3 and 55. Plaintiff seeks actual damages, treble damages, exemplary damages, and preliminary and permanent injunctive relief to enjoin and eliminate the discriminatory practices of defendants respecting denial of equal access for disabled persons, and seeks an award of reasonable attorney

fees, litigation expenses and costs.

28. <u>Request for Injunctive Relief</u>: The acts and omissions of defendants as complained of herein are continuing on a day-by-day basis to have the effect of willfully and wrongfully excluding plaintiff and any other members of the public who are similarly disabled and/or who require the assistance of service animals from full and equal access to that public business establishment and public accommodation known as the XYZ Restaurant. On information and belief the actions of defendants excluding plaintiff from this restaurant are an expression of the policy of defendants, and defendant _____, the parent company of XYZ, and may be reflected at their other restaurants. Such acts and omissions are the cause of fear, intimidation, humiliation and mental and emotional suffering of plaintiff in that these actions continue to treat plaintiff as an inferior and second class citizen and serve to discriminate against him on the sole basis that he is a person with a disability. Plaintiff wishes to return to and patronize this public accommodation. However, plaintiff is unable, so long as such acts and omissions of defendants continue, to achieve equal access to and use of this business establishment and public accommodation, and is intimidated and deterred from patronizing this or any other XYZ restaurant. The acts of defendants have proximately caused and will continue to cause irreparable injury to plaintiff if not enjoined by this Court.

29. Wherefore, plaintiff asks this Court to preliminarily and permanently enjoin any refusal by defendants to grant full access to plaintiff or to retaliate against plaintiff in any way, and to require defendants to comply forthwith with the applicable statutory requirements relating to access for disabled persons. California Civil Code §§ 54.1, 54.2, and 55 provide such injunctive relief. Plaintiff further requests that the Court award statutory costs and attorney fees to plaintiff pursuant to Civil Code §§ 52.2, 54.3, and 55, and Code of Civil Procedure § 1021.5, all as hereinafter prayed for.

Wherefore, plaintiff prays for damages and injunctive relief as hereinafter stated.

SECOND CAUSE OF ACTION: VIOLATION OF UNRUH CIVIL RIGHTS ACT, CALIFORNIA CIVIL CODE SECTIONS 51 AND 52, ON THE BASIS OF DISABILITY

30. Plaintiff repleads and incorporates by reference, as if fully set forth again herein, the factual allegations contained in Paragraphs 1 through 29, above, and incorporates them herein by reference as if separately repled hereafter.

31. At all times herein mentioned, the Unruh Civil Rights Act, California Civil Code §51(b), provided that:

> All persons within the jurisdiction of this state are free and equal, and no matter what their sex, race, color, religion, ancestry, national origin, disability, or medical condition are entitled to the full and equal accommodations, advantages, facilities, privileges, or services in all business establishments of every kind whatsoever.

Per §51(f),

> A violation of the right of any individual under the Americans With Disabilities Act of 1990 (Public Law 101-336) shall also constitute a violation of this section.

32. Plaintiff suffered damages as above described as a result of defendants' violation of California Civil Code §§ 51(b) and 51(f) in multiple regards, including but not limited to violations of the ADA, as described in the Third Cause of Action, *infra*, the contents of which cause of action is incorporated herein as if separately repled. California Civil Code §52(a) provides that each such violation entitles plaintiff to "the actual damages, and any amount that may be determined by a jury, or a court sitting without a jury, up to a maximum of three times the amount of actual damage but in no case less than four thousand dollars ($4,000), and any attorney's fees that may be determined by the court in addition thereto...."

WHEREFORE, plaintiff prays for damages and injunctive relief as hereinafter stated.

THIRD CAUSE OF ACTION:
VIOLATION OF THE AMERICANS WITH DISABILITIES ACT OF 1990
(42 USC §§ 12101 et seq.)

33. Plaintiff repleads and incorporates by reference, as if fully set forth again herein, the allegations contained in Paragraphs 1 through 32 of this Complaint, and incorporates them herein as if separately repled.

34. Pursuant to law, in 1990 the United States Congress made findings per 42 US § 12101 regarding physically disabled persons, finding that laws were needed to more fully protect "some 43 million Americans with one or more physical or mental disabilities; that historically society has tended to isolate and segregate individuals with disabilities;" that "such forms of discrimination against individuals with disabilities continue to be a serious and pervasive social problem"; that "the Nation's proper goals regarding individuals with disabilities are to assure equality of opportunity, full participation, independent living and economic self sufficiency for such individuals"; and that "the continuing existence of unfair and unnecessary discrimination and prejudice denies people with disabilities the opportunity to compete on an equal basis and to pursue those opportunities for which our free society is justifiably famous...." On information and belief the number of Americans entitled to protection by the ADA in 2006 is in excess of 50 million persons.

35. Congress stated as its purpose in passing the Americans With Disabilities Act (42 USC § 12101(b)):

It is the purpose of this act

(1) to provide a clear and comprehensive national mandate for the elimination of discrimination against individuals with disabilities;

(2) to provide clear, strong, consistent, enforceable standards addressing discrimination against individuals with disabilities;

(3) to ensure that the Federal government plays a central role in enforcing the standards established in this act on behalf of individuals with disabilities; and

(4) to invoke the sweep of Congressional authority, including the

power to enforce the 14th Amendment and to regulate commerce, in order to address the major areas of discrimination faced day to day by people with disabilities. [Emphasis added.]

36. As part of the Americans With Disabilities Act of 1990, Public Law 101-336, Congress passed "Title III - Public Accommodations and Services Operated by Private Entities" (42 USC §12181 et seq.). Among "private entities" which are considered "public accommodations" for purposes of this title are "a restaurant, bar or other establishment serving food or drink" (42 USC §12181(7)(B)).

37. Pursuant to 42 USC § 12182, Title III, § 302, "No individual shall be discriminated against on the basis of disability in the full and equal enjoyment of the goods, services, facilities, privileges, advantages, or accommodations of any place of public accommodation by any person who owns, leases, or leases to, or operates a place of public accommodation."

38. Among the specific prohibitions against discrimination were included:

§ 302(b)(2)(A)(ii): "failure to make reasonable modifications in policies, practices or procedures when such modifications are necessary to afford such goods, services, facilities, privileges, advantages or accommodations to individuals with disabilities....

39. Also, pursuant to § 302(b)(2)(A)(iv), discrimination includes "a failure to remove architectural barriers ... where such removal is readily achievable." On information and belief, removal of all architectural barriers that may adversely affect plaintiff on any future visit to the subject XYZ premises is "readily achievable."

40. On information and belief, as of the date of plaintiff's visit on or about January 1, 20___, and thereafter, and as of the date of the filing of this Complaint, defendants continue to deny full and equal access to plaintiff and to discriminate against plaintiff on the basis of his disabilities, thus wrongfully denying to plaintiff the full and equal enjoyment of the goods, services, facilities,

-16-

privileges, advantages and accommodations of defendants' premises, in violation of Title III, § 302 of the ADA, 42 USC § 12182. Further, the changes in policy requested and the removal of the architectural barriers to access complained of are all "readily achievable" pursuant to §§ 301(9) and 302(b)(2)(A)(iv) of the ADA, according to proof.

41. Pursuant to the Americans With Disabilities Act of 1990 (42 USC § 12188ff), plaintiff is entitled to the remedies and procedures set forth in § 204(a) of the Civil Rights Act of 1964 (42 USC § 2000(a)-3(a)), as plaintiff is being subjected to discrimination on the basis of his disability in violation of this title. On information and belief, defendants have continued to violate the law and deny the rights of plaintiff and of other disabled persons to access this public accommodation since on or before January 1, 20___. Plaintiff also seeks a specific prohibition against defendants maintaining or enforcing their discriminatory policy toward disabled persons who are accompanied by service animals, as above described. Plaintiff also seeks the removal of all architectural barriers at the subject XYZ premises, the removal of which is "readily achievable," according to proof.

42. Plaintiff seeks relief pursuant to remedies set forth in section 204(a) of the Civil Rights Act of 1964 (42 USC § 2000(a)-3(a)), and pursuant to Federal Regulations adopted to implement the Americans With Disabilities Act of 1990. Plaintiff is a qualified "person with a disability" for purposes of section 308(a) of the ADA (42 USC § 12188) who is being subjected to discrimination on the basis of disability in violation of Title III and who has reasonable grounds for believing he will be subjected to such discrimination each time that he may attempt to patronize XYZ. Plaintiff intends to return to this public accommodation but cannot do so until defendants cease their discriminatory practices.

Wherefore, plaintiff prays for relief as hereinafter stated.

PRAYER
FIRST AND SECOND CAUSES OF ACTION

1. For general, compensatory and statutory damages in an amount within the jurisdiction of this Court;

2. For treble damages pursuant to California Civil Code §§ 52 and 54.3;

3. For punitive and exemplary damages in an amount sufficient to deter such wrongful conduct and make an example of defendants pursuant to California Civil Code § 3294;

4. For injunctive relief prohibiting operation of this restaurant as a public accommodation until it provides full and equal access to disabled persons, and requiring that such access be immediately provided pursuant to California law;

5. For injunctive relief ordering defendants to immediately cease their policy of barring plaintiff or other disabled persons who use service animals from their premises;

6. For attorney fees and costs pursuant to California Civil Code §§ 52, 54.3 and 55, and attorney fees, litigation expenses and costs pursuant to California Code of Civil Procedure § 1021.5;

7. For all costs of suit;

9. For pre-judgment interest pursuant to California Civil Code § 3291;

10. For such other and further relief as the Court may deem just and proper.

THIRD CAUSE OF ACTION

1. For injunctive relief under the Americans With Disabilities Act of 1990, including ordering defendants to cease their discriminatory treatment of plaintiff Darren K. and requiring that defendants provide full and equal access to

their facilities to plaintiff and all other disabled persons, including blind persons and other disabled persons who require the use of service animals, including guide dogs;

  2. For injunctive relief requiring defendants to remove all "readily achievable" architectural barriers to access;

  3. For attorney fees, litigation expenses and costs of suit, per § 505 of the Americans With Disabilities Act of 1990;

  4. For such other and further relief as the Court may deem proper.

Dated: _____, 20__ PAUL L. REIN
          LAW OFFICES OF PAUL L. REIN

         _____
         Attorneys for Plaintiff
         DARREN K.

DEMAND FOR JURY TRIAL

  Plaintiff hereby demands a jury for all claims for which a jury is permitted.

Dated: _____, 20__ PAUL L. REIN
          LAW OFFICES OF PAUL L. REIN

         _____
         Attorneys for Plaintiff
         DARREN K.

(APPENDIX H)

GENERAL ORDER No. 56
AMERICANS WITH DISABILITIES ACT ACCESS LITIGATION

In any action which asserts denial of a right of access protected by Titles II or III of the Americans with Disabilities Act, 42 USC §§ 12131-89, pursuant to Federal Rule of Civil Procedure 16, the Court **ORDERS** that the following shall apply:

1. Pursuant to Federal Rule of Civil Procedure 4(m), plaintiff shall forthwith complete service on all necessary defendants. A plaintiff who is unable to complete service on all necessary defendants within 63 days may, prior to the expiration of that period, file a Motion For Administrative Relief pursuant to Civil Local Rule 7-11 requesting an extension of the schedule required by this Order.

2. Initial disclosures required by Federal Rule of Civil Procedure 26(a) shall be completed no later than 7 days prior to the joint inspection and review required by ¶3. For example, in a Title III action, if defendant intends to dispute liability based on the construction or alteration history of the subject premises, defendant shall disclose all information in defendant's possession or control regarding the construction or alteration history of the subject premises. In a Title II action, if defendant intends to dispute liability based on overall programmatic compliance, a transition plan, or a self-evaluation plan, defendant shall disclose all information in defendant's possession or control regarding such programmatic compliance, transition plan, or self-evaluation plan. If plaintiff claims damages under California law, plaintiff shall include in the initial disclosures the damages computation required by Rule 26(a)(1)(A)(iii), but need not include attorney's fees and costs. All other discovery and proceedings are STAYED unless the assigned judge orders otherwise. Notwithstanding any other provision of this General Order, any dispute concerning the adequacy of the Rule 26(a) disclosures may be submitted to the court under Civil Local Rule 7.

3. No later than 105 days after filing the complaint, the parties and their counsel, accompanied by their experts if the parties so elect, shall meet in person at the subject premises. If plaintiff alleges only programmatic or policy violations, the parties and their counsel may meet in person at any mutually agreeable location. They shall jointly inspect the portions of the

subject premises, and shall review any programmatic or policy issues, which are claimed to violate the Americans with Disabilities Act.

4. At the joint inspection and review required under ¶3, or within 28 days thereafter, the parties, and their experts if the parties so elect, shall meet in person and confer regarding settlement of the action. The meet and confer obligation cannot be satisfied by telephone or by exchanging letters. At the conference, the parties shall discuss all claimed access violations. Plaintiff shall specify all claimed access violations and the corrective actions requested of defendant. With respect to each claimed violation, defendant shall specify whether defendant is willing to undertake the requested corrective actions or has an alternate proposal. If defendant claims any proposed corrective action is not readily achievable under Title III or otherwise required by law, defendant shall specify the factual basis for this claim.

5. This General Order does not require any party to engage an expert. In simpler cases it may be possible for parties to reach agreement regarding corrective actions without engaging experts, or without the preparation of written expert reports. If written expert reports are prepared, they shall be exchanged. In a case which the parties conclude would benefit from expert assistance, the Court encourages the parties to jointly engage an expert.

6. If the parties reach a tentative agreement on injunctive relief, plaintiff shall forthwith provide defendant with a statement of costs and attorney's fees incurred to date, and make a demand for settlement of the case in its entirety (including any additional damages not included in the Rule 26(a) disclosures). Plaintiff should forthwith not require execution of a formal agreement regarding injunctive relief as a precondition to providing defendant with the statement of costs and attorney's fees, and additional damages. If requested by defendant, plaintiff should provide documentation and support for its attorney's fees similar to what an attorney would provide in a billing statement to a client.

7. If within 42 days from the joint site inspection and review, the parties cannot reach an agreement on injunctive relief, or cannot settle the damages and fees claims, plaintiff shall file a "Notice of Need for Mediation" in the form set forth on the Court's ADR Internet site www.adr.cand.uscourts.gov and on the ECF Website www.ecf.cand.uscourts.gov. The matter

will then be automatically referred to mediation and the ADR Program will arrange for a mediation session to be scheduled as soon as feasible, and in no event later that 90 days from the date the Notice of Need for Mediation is filed, unless otherwise ordered by the assigned judge. The mediator shall have the authority to preside over settlement negotiations that address all issues presented by this matter, including requests for injunctive relief, damages and attorney's fees. Should a settlement be reached, the mediator shall ensure that the parties make a written or audio record of the essential terms of the settlement sufficient to permit any party to move to enforce the settlement should it not be consummated according to its terms. Should any settlement be conditioned upon future conduct such as remediation, the assigned judge will retain jurisdiction to enforce that component of the settlement.

8. If the case does not resolve at mediation within 7 days of the mediator's filing of a Certification of ADR Session reporting that the mediation process is concluded, plaintiff shall file a Motion For Administrative Relief pursuant to Civil Local Rule 7-11 requesting a Case Management Conference.

9. Any party who wishes to be relieved of any requirement of this order or to adjust the schedule set forth herein may file a Motion for Administrative Relief pursuant to Civil Local Rule 7-11.

ADOPTED: June 21, 2005
AMENDED: February 17, 2009
AMENDED: November 5, 2009
AMENDED: May 29, 2012

FOR THE COURT:

_____
JAMES WARE
Chief Judge

(APPENDIX I)

PAUL L. REIN, Esq. (SBN 43053)
CELIA MCGUINNESS, Esq. (SBN
LAW OFFICES OF PAUL L. REIN
200 Lakeside Dr., Suite A
Oakland, CA 94612
(510) 832-5001

JULIE A. OSTIL, Esq. (SBN 215202)
LAW OFFICE OF JULIE A. OSTIL
2010 Crow Canyon Place, Suite 100
San Ramon, CA 94583
(925) 265-8257

Attorneys for Plaintiffs
NICOLE BROWN-BOOKER and JANA OVERBO

M. BRETT BURNS, Esq.
HUNTON & WILLIAMS, LLP
575 Market St., Suite 3700
San Francisco, CA 94105
(415) 975-3700

Attorney for Defendants
LOEWS CALIFORNIA THEATERS, INC. dba AMC
LOEWS METREON 16 IMAX; WESTFIELD
CORPORATION

UNITED STATES DISTRICT COURT
NORTHERN DISTRICT OF CALIFORNIA

NICOLE BROWN-BOOKER and JANA OVERBO,	CASE NO. C07-5368 MHP/JCS
	Civil Rights
Plaintiffs,	
v.	**CONSENT DECREE AND [PROPOSED] ORDER**
LOEWS CALIFORNIA THEATERS, INC. dba AMC LOEWS METREON 16 IMAX; WESTFIELD CORPORATION; and DOES 1-10, inclusive,	
Defendants.	

CONSENT DECREE AND ORDER

1. Plaintiffs NICOLE BROWN-BOOKER and JANA OVERBO, filed a Complaint in this action on October 19, 2007 under the Americans with Disabilities Act of 1990 ("ADA"), 42 U.S.C. §§ 12101 et seq., and California civil rights laws against Defendants, LOEWS CALIFORNIA THEATERS, INC. dba AMC LOEWS METREON 16 IMAX (for which the proper

Defendant entity is American Multi-Cinema, Inc.) ("Defendant AMC"); WESTFIELD CORPORATION (for which the proper Defendant entity is Westfield, LLC); and DOES 1-10, inclusive. Plaintiffs alleged that Defendants violated Title III of the ADA and sections 51, 52, 54, 54.1, 54.3 and 55 of the California Civil Code, and sections 19955 *et seq.*, of the California Health and Safety Code by failing to provide full and equal access to their facilities at the Metreon IMAX 16 Theater at 101 4th Street, San Francisco, California.

2. Defendants at all times denied any violation of law and nothing in this Consent Order constitutes an admission by AMC of any violation under Title III of the Americans with Disabilities Act, its enabling regulations, California state law, or of any of the allegations made by Plaintiffs in this lawsuit.

3. Defendant AMC and Plaintiffs (hereinafter referred to collectively as "the Signing Parties") hereby enter into this Consent Decree and Order for the purpose of resolving this lawsuit without the need for protracted litigation, and without the admission of any liability.

JURISDICTION:

4. The Court has jurisdiction of this matter pursuant to 28 U.S.C. § 1331 for alleged violations of the Americans with Disabilities Act of 1990, 42 U.S.C. 12101 *et seq.* and supplemental jurisdiction for alleged violations of California Health & Safety Code §19955 *et seq.*, including §19959; Title 24 California Code of Regulations; and California Civil Code §§51; 52; 54; 54.1; §54.3; and 55.

SETTLEMENT OF INJUNCTIVE RELIEF:

5. This Order shall be a full, complete, and final disposition and settlement of Plaintiffs' claims for relief that have arisen out of the subject Complaint. The Signing Parties agree that there has been no admission or finding of liability or violation of the ADA and/or California civil rights laws and other applicable laws, codes, regulations, and ordinances, and this Consent Decree and Order should not be construed as such.

6. The Signing Parties agree and stipulate that the corrective work will be performed in compliance with the standards and specifications as set forth in the California Code of Regulations,

Title 24-2, the Americans with Disabilities Act Accessibility Guidelines, and other applicable laws, codes, regulations, and ordinances, unless other standards agreed to in this Consent Decree. If a conflict of law or regulation arises under this Section, the meet and confer procedure outlined below shall be followed.

    a)   Remedial Measures: The corrective work agreed upon by the Signing Parties is attached here to as **Attachment A**. Defendant AMC agree to undertake all of the remedial work set forth therein.

    b)   Timing of Injunctive Relief: Defendant AMC will submit plans for all corrective work to the appropriate governmental agencies within 30 days of entry of this Consent Decree and Order by the court, will commence work within 30 days of receiving approval from the appropriate agencies, and will complete all work within 30 days of commencement. For work not requiring building permits, the work will be completed within 30 days of entry of this Consent Decree and Order by the court. In the event that unforeseen difficulties prevent Defendant AMC from completing any of the agreed-upon injunctive relief, Defendant AMC or its counsel will notify Plaintiffs' counsel in writing within 15 days of discovering the delay. Defendant AMC or its counsel will notify Plaintiffs' counsel when the corrective work is completed, and in any case will provide a status report no later than 120 days from the entry of this Consent Decree.

    c)   Notice and Opportunity to Cure: If Plaintiffs or their counsel believe that this agreement has not been complied with, they will provide notice and an opportunity to cure to Defendant AMC as herein described. Plaintiffs' counsel will provide written notice of any alleged violation of the agreement to Defendant AMC's counsel. Within 20 days of receiving such notice, Defendant AMC or its counsel will either notify Plaintiffs' counsel that the alleged defect has been cured and allow Plaintiffs or their representatives an opportunity to verify that the defect has been corrected, or else will hold a "meet and confer" conference with Plaintiffs' counsel, either by telephone or in person. The Signing Parties will make a good faith effort to resolve any issue regarding compliance with this Consent Decree during the meet and confer. If the Signing Parties are unable to resolve the issue on their own, then Plaintiffs will file a motion with the Court to

Consent Decree and [Proposed] Order
C07-5368 MHP/JCS

enforce compliance with the Consent Decree. If the Signing Parties are able to resolve the issue without court intervention, Plaintiffs will not make any claim for attorney fees or for statutory damages (Plaintiffs do not, however, waive personal injury damages if injured). If Plaintiffs file a motion, they reserve the right to seek attorney fees in connection with the enforcement proceedings, if any.

   d) <u>Notices</u>: All notices, correspondences and reports required by this Order shall be sent by overnight courier to the Signing Parties at the following addresses or to such other person as the Signing Parties may designate in writing in the future:

<u>For notices to the Plaintiffs</u>:

Paul L. Rein, Esq.
Law Offices Of Paul L. Rein
200 Lakeside Dr., Suite A
Oakland, CA 94612
(510) 832-5001

<u>For notices to American Multi-Cinema, Inc.</u>

Edwin F. Gladbach, Esq.
Vice President, Legal
AMC Entertainment Inc.
920 Main Street
Kansas City, MO 64105

and

M. Brett Burns
Hunton & Williams, LLP
575 Market Street, Suite 3700
San Francisco, CA 94105

   e) <u>Delays or Modifications Caused by City, State or Local Authorities</u>: Defendant AMC will make reasonable good faith efforts to obtain permits and authorizations including, without limitation, building permits and certificates of occupancy that may be required under local law, ordinance, or other applicable law in order to accomplish the modifications required under this Order. If a city or other applicable state or local authority does not provide the permits or authorizations in a timely manner, and such delay impacts Defendant AMC's ability to make any of the modifications set forth in the Order within any of the time periods set forth herein, the applicable time period(s) for Defendant AMC to make the modification(s) at issue shall be automatically extended by the period of the delay. Defendant AMC shall notify Plaintiffs' counsel of such delay and the reasons therefore. If a city or other applicable state or local authority refuses to provide permits or authorizations needed to accomplish any modification required under this Order, or conditions the issuance of any such permit or authorization on Defendant AMC's making modifications in addition to those required by the Order, Defendant AMC's obligation to make the modifications(s) will be suspended while Defendant AMC's counsel and Plaintiffs' counsel meet in a good faith effort to agree on a comparable substitute modification(s).

DAMAGES, ATTORNEY FEES, LITIGATION EXPENSES, AND COSTS:

7. The Signing Parties have reached a separate settlement agreement regarding Plaintiffs' claims for damages. The Signing Parties agree that Plaintiffs' claims for attorney fees, litigation expenses, and costs will be submitted to the Court for resolution upon a mutually agreeable schedule.

ENTIRE CONSENT ORDER:

8. This Consent Decree and Order and **Attachment A** to this Consent Decree, which is incorporated herein by reference as if fully set forth in this document, constitutes the entire agreement between the Signing Parties on the matters of injunctive relief, and no other statement, promise, or agreement, either written or oral, made by any of the Signing Parties or agents of any of the Signing Parties, that is not contained in this written Consent Decree and Order, shall be enforceable regarding the matters described herein.

CONSENT ORDER BINDING ON SIGNING PARTIES AND SUCCESSORS IN INTEREST:

9. This Consent Decree and Order shall be binding on Plaintiffs, Defendant AMC, and any successors in interest. The Signing Parties have a duty to so notify all such successors in interest

of the existence and terms of this Consent Decree and Order during the period of the Court's jurisdiction of this Consent Decree and Order.

MUTUAL RELEASE AND WAIVER OF CIVIL CODE SECTION 1542:

10. Each of the Signing Parties to this Consent Decree understands and agrees that there is a risk and possibility that, subsequent to the execution of this Consent Decree, any or all of them will incur, suffer, or experience some further loss or damage with respect to the Lawsuit which are unknown or unanticipated at the time this Consent Decree is signed. Except for all obligations required in this Consent Decree, the Signing Parties intend that this Consent Decree apply to all such further loss with respect to the Lawsuit, except those caused by the Signing Parties subsequent to the execution of this Consent Decree. Therefore, except for all obligations required in this Consent Decree, this Consent Decree shall apply to and cover any and all claims, demands, actions and causes of action by the Signing Parties to this Consent Decree with respect to the Lawsuit, whether the same are known, unknown or hereafter discovered or ascertained, and the provisions of Section 1542 of the California Civil Code are hereby expressly waived. Section 1542 provides as follows:

> A GENERAL RELEASE DOES NOT EXTEND TO CLAIMS WHICH THE CREDITOR DOES NOT KNOW OR SUSPECT TO EXIST IN HIS OR HER FAVOR AT THE TIME OF EXECUTING THE RELEASE, WHICH IF KNOWN BY HIM OR HER MUST HAVE MATERIALLY AFFECTED HIS OR HER SETTLEMENT WITH THE DEBTOR.

11. Except for all obligations required in this Consent Decree and the obligations in the separate settlement agreement, and excluding Plaintiffs' claims for attorney fees, litigation expenses, and costs, as referenced in Section 7, above, each of the Signing Parties to this Consent Decree, on behalf of each, their respective agents, representatives, predecessors, successors, heirs, partners and assigns, releases and forever discharges each other Party and all officers, directors, shareholders, subsidiaries, joint venturers, stockholders, partners, parent companies, employees, agents, attorneys,

insurance carriers, heirs, predecessors, and representatives of each other Party, from all claims, demands, actions, and causes of action of whatever kind or nature, presently known or unknown, arising out of or in any way connected with the Lawsuit.

TERM OF THE CONSENT DECREE AND ORDER:

12. This Consent Decree and Order shall be in full force and effect for a period of six months after the injunctive relief contemplated by this Order is completed. The Court shall retain jurisdiction of this action to enforce provisions of this Order during the aforementioned term.

SEVERABILITY:

13. If any term of this Consent Decree and Order is determined by any court to be unenforceable, the other terms of this Consent Decree and Order shall nonetheless remain in full force and effect.

SIGNATORIES BIND SIGNING PARTIES:

14. Signatories on the behalf of the Signing Parties represent that they are authorized to bind the Signing Parties to this Consent Decree and Order. This Consent Decree and Order may be signed in counterparts and a facsimile signature shall have the same force and effect as an original signature.

Dated: February 10, 2010

Nicole Brown-Booker by Paul L Rein, per written authorization
Plaintiff NICOLE BROWN-BOOKER

Dated: February 10, 2010

Jana Overbo, per Paul L Rein, per written authorization
Plaintiff JANA OVERBO

Dated: February 10, 2010

[signature] Vice President, Legal
Defendant AMERICAN MULTI-CINEMA, INC.

APPROVED AS TO FORM:

Dated: February 10, 2010

PAUL L. REIN
CELIA MCGUINNESS
LAW OFFICES OF PAUL L. REIN

JULIE A. OSTIL
LAW OFFICE OF JULIE A. OSTIL

Paul L Rein
Attorneys for Plaintiffs
NICOLE BROWN-BOOKER and JANA OVERBO

Dated: February 10, 2010

M. BRETT BURNS
HUNTON & WILLIAMS LLP

M Brett Burns
Attorney for Defendant
AMERICAN MULTI-CINEMA, INC.

ORDER

Pursuant to stipulation, and for good cause shown, IT IS SO ORDERED.

Dated: 2/18/10

[signature]
MARILYN HALL PATEL
United States District Judge

Attachment A to Consent Decree and Order
Case No. C07-5368 MHP/JCS

Defendant AMC shall perform the following remedial work, according to the conditions specified in the Consent Decree and Order. For the avoidance of doubt, Defendant AMC shall not be required to make any modifications as to item 10, below, not identified in Plaintiffs' expert report.

1. **Queue-line on First Floor**: Defendant AMC will cause the Q-line stanchions to be placed not less than 36" apart and will ensure that the stanchions are maintained in an accessible position at all times.

2. **Customer Service/Ticket Window Counter on First Floor**: Defendant AMC will adopt a policy to ensure that the lowered counter is in use any time the theater is open, and will institute training procedures to ensure that its employees understand this policy.

3. **Concession Service Counter on First Floor**: Defendant AMC will adopt a policy to ensure that any and all concessions offered by the theater (including ice cream) are available to disabled patrons at the lowered portion of the counter, and will institute training procedures to ensure that its employees understand this policy.

4. **Popcorn Butter Dispenser on First Floor**: Defendant AMC will modify the dispenser so that the operable portion of the mechanism does not exceed 48" above the finished floor.

5. **Women's Restroom**: Defendant AMC will:
    (a) Provide accessible signage pursuant to ADAAG and Title 24;
    (b) Move trash receptacles so that they do not obstruct any required path of travel or clear floor space, and maintain them in such condition;
    (c) Relocate the sanitary toilet seat cover dispenser in the accessible stalls to be mounted no higher than 40" above the finished floor and adjacent to a 30" x 48" clear space;
    (d) Relocate grab bars in accessible stalls as necessary so that they are no higher than 33" above the finished floor and project a minimum of 24" in front of the toilet;
    (e) Reconfigure the semi-ambulatory stall so that it is no less than 36" wide.

EXHIBIT "A"

6. **Door pressure for theater entry doors and other interior doors**: Defendant AMC will adjust the door pressure for the theater doors so that it does not exceed 8 lbs. of pressure to open any unlatched door along an accessible route, and will maintain this pressure by checking and adjusting monthly.

7. **Door landing in Theater 15**: Defendant AMC will provide a compliant 48" landing at the door to Theater 15 (currently a theater seat encroaches).

8. **Door unobstructed surfaces**: Defendant AMC will remove doorstops and any other obstructions along the bottom 12" of the door leading to the wheelchair lift in Theater 13, and in the corridor doors in Theaters 14 and 15.

9. **Ramp slopes in Individual Theaters**: Defendant AMC will remedy the following ramp slopes and ensure that they are not more than 8.33%:

    (a) Theater 4, ramp on left side

    (b) Theater 7, ramp on right side

    (c) Theater 12, entry aisle on left side

10. **Ramp handrails in individual theaters**: Defendant AMC will provide fully ADAAG and Title 24-compliant handrails, including compliant knuckle space and handrail extensions, in the following theaters: Theater 1, Theater 5, Theater 7, Theater 8, Theater 9, Theater 11, Theater 12, Theater 14, and Theater 15.

11. **Vertical rise at bottom of ramps**: Defendant AMC will remedy the ramps so that the vertical rise at the top and bottom of the ramps do not exceed ¼" on the left side in Theaters 1 and 2, and on both sides in Theater 7.

12. **Edge protection at ramps**: Defendant AMC will provide compliant edge treatment at both ramps in Theaters 5 and 6.

13. **Landing at Ramp**: Defendant will provide a compliant landing at the bottom of the ramp in Theater 12.

14. **Unassisted use of wheelchair lift/elevator access**: Defendant AMC will institute policies and procedures to allow disabled patrons unassisted use of the wheelchair lift/elevator,

ATTACHMENT A TO CONSENT DECREE AND ORDER

including providing a key card, code, or other method of operating any locked doors in the designated path of travel to accessible seating in any and all theaters, and will institute training procedures so that its employees understand these policies and procedures. As to the service elevator, Defendant AMC will institute policies and procedures to allow disabled patrons assisted use of the elevator as a temporary measure, with a permanent solution on mutually agreeable terms to be defined at a later date.

15. **Slip Resistance in Path of Travel to Theater 15**: Defendant AMC will provide a slip-resistant treatment on the ramp on the upper level of the path of travel from the elevator to Theater 15.

16. **Accessible seating in all theaters**: Defendant AMC will reconfigure accessible seating as necessary to ensure that no accessible seating or companion seating is provided on any surface with a slope exceeding 2% in any direction. Defendants will reconfigure accessible seating as necessary to ensure that all accessible seating spaces are a minimum of 84" long.

17. **Accessible Seating in IMAX Theater**: Defendant AMC will provide fully compliant accessible seating spaces and adjacent companion seating, for a total of 7 accessible seats and 7 companion seats.

18. **Accessible Seating at the Top of Theater 13**: Defendant AMC will ensure that the distance between the companion seating space and the edge of the top of the stairway is at least 33" wide.

19. **Accessible Seating in Theaters 1-4**: Defendant AMC will provide 1 accessible seating space and adjacent companion seat in row 2 and 4 accessible seating spaces and 3 adjacent companion seats in row 3, for a total of 5 accessible seats and 4 companion seats.

20. **Accessible Seating in Theater 5**: Defendant AMC will provide 1 accessible seating space and adjacent companion seat in row 2 and 4 accessible seating spaces in row 3 with adjacent companion seats at a ratio of one companion seat for each accessible seating space, for a total of 5 accessible seats and 5 companion seats.

21. **Accessible Seating in Theater 6**: Defendant AMC will provide accessible seating spaces in row 3, with adjacent companion seats at a ratio of one companion seat for each accessible seating space, for a total of 5 accessible seats and 5 companion seats.

22. **Accessible Seating in Theaters 7-11**: Defendant AMC will provide accessible seating spaces in row 3, with adjacent companion seats at a ratio of one companion seat for each accessible seating space, for a total of 5 accessible seats and 5 companion seats.

23. **Accessible Seating in Theater 12**: Defendant AMC will provide two accessible seating spaces in the back row, and five accessible seating spaces in the third row, with adjacent companion seats, for a total of 7 accessible seats and 7 companion seats.

24. **Accessible Seating in Theater 13**: Defendant AMC will provide three accessible seating spaces in the back of the theater, and three accessible seating spaces in the 8th row with adjacent companion seats, for a total of 6 accessible seats and 6 companion seats.

25. **Accessible Seating in Theaters 14 and 15**: Defendant AMC will provide one accessible seating space in the fourth row, and six accessible spaces in the back row, with adjacent companion seats, for a total of 7 accessible seats and 7 companion seats.

26. **Public Information Regarding Accessible Seating**: Defendants will institute policies and procedures to inform the public of accessible seating locations in each theater via written pamphlet and internet, and to inform the public of which movies are being shown in which theaters via telephone. Defendants will institute training to ensure that their employees understand these policies and procedures.

ATTACHMENT A TO CONSENT DECREE AND ORDER

(Appendix J)

Sacramento Community Center Theater

Composite Photo from Sacramento Convention Center Website (http://www.sacramentoconventioncenter.com/venues/communityCenterTheater/gallery.cfm)

(APPENDIX K)
Senate Bill No. 1186

CHAPTER 383

An act to amend, repeal, and add Section 6106.2 of the Business and Professions Code, to amend Sections 55.3, 55.52, 55.53, 55.54, and 55.56 of, to add Sections 55.31, 55.545, and 1938 to, and to add, repeal, and add Section 55.32 of, the Civil Code, to add Section 425.50 to the Code of Civil Procedure, to amend Sections 4459.8 and 8299.05 of, to add Chapter 7.5 (commencing with Section 4465) to Division 5 of Title 1 of, and to repeal and add Sections 8299.06, 8299.07, and 8299.08 of, the Government Code, and to add and repeal Section 18944.5 of the Health and Safety Code, relating to disability access, making an appropriation therefor, and declaring the urgency thereof, to take effect immediately.

[Approved by Governor September 19, 2012. Filed with Secretary of State September 19, 2012.]

LEGISLATIVE COUNSEL'S DIGEST

SB 1186, Steinberg. Disability access.

(1) Existing law requires an attorney to provide a written advisory to a building owner or tenant with each demand for money or complaint for any construction-related accessibility claim, as specified. A violation of this requirement may subject the attorney to disciplinary action.

This bill would, instead, require an attorney to provide a written advisory with each demand letter or complaint, as defined, sent to or served upon a defendant or potential defendant for any construction-related accessibility claim, as specified. The bill would require the Judicial Council to update the form that may be used by attorneys to comply with this requirement on or before July 1, 2013. The bill would require an allegation of a construction-related accessibility claim in a demand letter or complaint to state facts sufficient to allow a reasonable person to identify the basis for the claim. The bill would require any complaint alleging a construction-related accessibility claim to be verified by the plaintiff, and would make any complaint filed without verification subject to a motion to strike. The bill would prohibit a demand letter from including a request or demand for money or an offer or agreement to accept money. The bill also would prohibit an attorney, or other person acting at the direction of an attorney, from issuing a demand for money to a building owner or tenant, or an agent or employee of a building owner or tenant, on the basis of one or more construction-related accessibility violations, as specified. The bill would require an attorney to include his or her State Bar license number in a demand letter, and to submit copies of the demand letter to the California Commission on Disability Access and, until January 1, 2016, to the State Bar. The bill also would require, until January 1, 2016, an attorney to submit a copy of a complaint to the commission. The bill would provide that a violation of these requirements may subject the attorney to disciplinary action, as specified.

This bill would require the commission to review and report on the demand letters and complaints it receives until January 1, 2016. The bill also would require the State Bar, commencing July 31, 2013, and annually each July 31 thereafter, to report specified information to the Legislature regarding the demand letters that it receives.

(2) Existing law provides, upon being served with a summons and complaint asserting a construction-related accessibility claim, a qualified defendant, as defined, may file a request for a court stay and early evaluation conference in the proceedings, as specified. Existing law requires the Judicial Council to prepare and post on its Internet Web site instructions and a form for a qualified defendant to use to file an application for stay and early evaluation conference pursuant to this provision.

This bill would permit other defendants to file a request for a court stay and early evaluation conference pursuant to this provision, including (A) a defendant, until January 1, 2018, whose site's new construction or improvement on or after January 1, 2008, and before January 1, 2016, was approved pursuant to the local building permit and inspection process, (B) a defendant whose site's new construction or improvement was approved by a local public building department inspector who is a certified access specialist, and (C) a defendant who is a small business, as described. The bill would require the Judicial Council to prepare and post a form for filing an application for stay and early evaluation conference for use by qualified defendants and these additional defendants, and any additional forms appropriate to implement these provisions, as specified. The bill also would authorize a defendant who does not qualify for an early evaluation conference pursuant to these provisions, or who forgoes those provisions, to request a mandatory evaluation conference, as specified. The bill would authorize a plaintiff to make that request if the defendant does not make that request.

(3) Existing law provides statutory damages in a construction-related accessibility claim against a place of public accommodation if a violation of construction-related accessibility standards denied the plaintiff full and equal access to that site on a particular occasion. A plaintiff is denied full and equal access only if, on a particular occasion, the plaintiff personally encountered the violation or was deterred from accessing the site. These statutory damages are in the amount of actual damages and any additional amount determined by a jury or the court up to a maximum of 3 times the amount of actual damages but not less than $4,000, or, for certain violations, $1,000.

This bill would require the court, in assessing liability in any action alleging multiple claims for the same construction-related accessibility violation on different particular occasions, to consider the reasonableness of the plaintiff's conduct in light of the plaintiff's obligation, if any, to mitigate damages. The bill would reduce a defendant's minimum liability for statutory damages in a construction-related accessibility claim against a place of public accommodation to $1,000 for each offense if the defendant has corrected all construction-related violations that are the basis of the claim within 60 days of being served with the complaint and other specified conditions apply, and would reduce that minimum liability to $2,000 for each offense if the defendant has corrected all construction-related violations that are the basis of the claim within 30 days of being served with the complaint and the defendant is a small business, as specified. The bill would require the Department of General Services to make a biannual adjustment to financial criteria defining a small business for these purposes, and to post those adjusted amounts on its Internet Web site.

(4) Existing law requires the State Architect to develop and submit for approval and adoption building standards for making buildings, structures, sidewalks, curbs, and related facilities accessible to, and usable by, persons with disabilities, as specified. Existing law provides for the inspection of places of public accommodation by certified access specialists to determine if the sites meet all applicable construction-related accessibility standards, and the provision of specified certificates and reports regarding those inspections. Existing law regulates the hiring of real property.

This bill would require a commercial property owner to state on a lease form or rental agreement executed on or after July 1, 2013, if the property being leased or rented has undergone inspection by a certified access specialist.

(5) The federal Americans with Disabilities Act of 1990 and the California Building Standards Code require that specified buildings, structures, and facilities be accessible to, and usable by, persons with disabilities. Existing law establishes in the Department of General Services, the Division of the State Architect with responsibilities relating to architectural services, state buildings, and disability access. Existing law requires the State Architect to establish a certified access specialist program for voluntary certification by the state of any person who meets specified criteria as a certified access specialist. Existing law authorizes the State Architect to require applicants for certification and renewal of certification under the certified access specialist program to pay specified fees, including an application fee, a course fee, and an examination fee, at a level sufficient to meet the costs of administering the program, for deposit into the Certified Access Specialist Fund.

In administering the certified access specialist program, this bill would require the State Architect to periodically review its schedule of fees for certification under the program to ensure that the fees are not excessive. The bill would prohibit the State Architect from charging a California licensed architect, landscape architect, civil engineer, or structural engineer, an application fee for certification that exceeds $250.

This bill would impose, on and after January 1, 2013, and until December 31, 2018, an additional state fee of $1 on any applicant for a local business license or equivalent instrument or permit, or renewal thereof, for purposes of increasing disability access and compliance with construction-related accessibility requirements and developing educational resources for businesses to facilitate compliance with federal and state disability laws, as specified. The bill would divide those moneys for the state between the local entity that collected the moneys and the Division of the State Architect, pursuant to specified percentages. The bill would create a continuously appropriated fund, the Disability Access and Education Revolving Fund, for the deposit of funds to be transferred to the Division of the State Architect, thereby making an appropriation. The bill would make an appropriation by authorizing local government entities to retain 70% of the fees imposed.

By adding to the duties of a local entity, this bill would impose a state-mandated local program.

(6) Existing law establishes the California Commission on Disability Access for purposes of developing recommendations to enable persons with disabilities to exercise their right to full and equal access to public facilities and facilitating business compliance with the laws and regulations to avoid unnecessary litigation. Existing law sets forth the powers and duties of the commission, as specified. Existing law requires the commission to study and make reports to the Legislature regarding disability access laws and compliance, as specified. Existing law requires the commission to act as an information center on the status of compliance with disability access laws, to publish a biennial report, and to coordinate with other state agencies and local building departments to ensure the uniformity of information provided to the public on disability access.

This bill would revise and recast those duties and powers, as specified, and eliminate the biennial reporting requirement. The bill would instead provide that a priority of the commission shall be the development and dissemination of educational materials and information to promote and facilitate disability access compliance, including a requirement that the commission work with the Division of the State Architect and the Department of Rehabilitation to develop educational materials for use by businesses. The bill would require the commission to post specified information on its Internet Web site, including, but not limited to, educational materials and information that will assist business owners. The bill would require the commission to report to the Legislature on its implementation by a specified date. The bill would require the commission to compile data with respect to any demand letter or complaint sent to the commission and post that information on its Internet Web site.

(7) Existing law, the California Building Standards Law, requires a state agency responsible for the adoption of building standards to submit its standards to the California Building Standards Commission for review and approval, subject to specified procedures and a triennial code adoption cycle. Existing law requires the commission to codify and publish approved standards in the California Building Code, as set forth in Title 24 of the California Code of Regulations. Existing law provides that building standards become effective 180 days after its publication, as specified.

This bill would provide, for the purpose of an alleged violation of a construction-related accessibility standard, that upon publication of the 2013

California Building Standards Code, but prior to its effective date, as specified, compliance with the building standards for disabled accessibility in the 2013 California Building Standards Code is authorized as an alternative method of compliance.

(8) The California Constitution requires the state to reimburse local agencies and school districts for certain costs mandated by the state. Statutory provisions establish procedures for making that reimbursement.

This bill would provide that, if the Commission on State Mandates determines that the bill contains costs mandated by the state, reimbursement for those costs shall be made pursuant to these statutory provisions.

(9) This bill would declare that it is to take effect immediately as an urgency statute.

Appropriation: yes.

The people of the State of California do enact as follows:

SECTION 1. Section 6106.2 of the Business and Professions Code is amended to read:

6106.2. (a) It shall constitute cause for the imposition of discipline of an attorney within the meaning of this chapter for an attorney to engage in any conduct in violation of Section 55.3 of the Civil Code.

(b) Commencing January 1, 2013, it shall constitute cause for the imposition of discipline of an attorney within the meaning of this chapter for an attorney to engage in any conduct in violation of subdivision (b) or (c) of Section 55.31, or paragraph (3) of subdivision (a) or subdivision (b) of Section 55.32 of the Civil Code, or paragraph (2) of subdivision (a) of Section 55.32 of the Civil Code as provided in subdivision (c) of that section.

(c) This section shall remain in effect only until January 1, 2016, and as of that date is repealed, unless a later enacted statute, that is enacted before January 1, 2016, deletes or extends that date.

SEC. 2. Section 6106.2 is added to the Business and Professions Code, to read:

6106.2. (a) It shall constitute cause for the imposition of discipline of an attorney within the meaning of this chapter for an attorney to engage in any conduct in violation of Section 55.3, subdivision (b) or (c) of Section 55.31, or paragraph (2) of subdivision (a) or subdivision (b) of Section 55.32 of the Civil Code.

(b) This section shall become operative on January 1, 2016.

SEC. 3. Section 55.3 of the Civil Code is amended to read:

55.3. (a) For purposes of this section, the following shall apply:

(1) "Complaint" means a civil complaint that is filed or is to be filed with a court and is sent to or served upon a defendant on the basis of one or more construction-related accessibility claims, as defined in this section.

(2) "Construction-related accessibility claim" means any claim of a violation of any construction-related accessibility standard, as defined by paragraph (6) of subdivision (a) of Section 55.52, with respect to a place of

public accommodation. "Construction-related accessibility claim" does not include a claim of interference with housing within the meaning of paragraph (2) of subdivision (b) of Section 54.1, or any claim of interference caused by something other than the construction-related accessibility condition of the property, including, but not limited to, the conduct of any person.

(3) "Demand for money" means a prelitigation written document or oral statement that is provided or issued to a building owner or tenant, or the owner's or tenant's agent or employee, that does all of the following:

(A) Alleges that the site is in violation of one or more construction-related accessibility standards, as defined in paragraph (6) of subdivision (a) of Section 55.52, or alleges one or more construction-related accessibility claims, as defined in paragraph (2).

(B) Contains or makes a request or demand for money or an offer or agreement to accept money.

(C) Is provided or issued whether or not the attorney intends to file a complaint, or eventually files a complaint, in state or federal court.

(4) "Demand letter" means a prelitigation written document that is provided to a building owner or tenant, or the owner's or tenant's agent or employee, that alleges the site is in violation of one or more construction-related accessibility standards, as defined in paragraph (6) of subdivision (a) of Section 55.52, or alleges one or more construction-related accessibility claims, as defined in paragraph (2), and is provided whether or not the attorney intends to file a complaint, or eventually files a complaint, in state or federal court.

(b) An attorney shall provide a written advisory on the form described in subdivision (c), or, until that form is available, on a separate page or pages that are clearly distinguishable from the demand letter or complaint, with each demand letter or complaint sent to or served upon a defendant or potential defendant. The advisory shall not be required in subsequent communications following the initial demand letter or initial complaint unless a new construction-related accessibility claim is asserted in the subsequent demand letter or amended complaint. The advisory shall state as follows:

STATE LAW REQUIRES THAT YOU GET THIS IMPORTANT ADVISORY INFORMATION FOR BUILDING OWNERS AND TENANTS

This information is available in English, Spanish, Chinese, Vietnamese, and Korean through the Judicial Council of California. Persons with visual impairments can get assistance in viewing this form through the Judicial Council Internet Web site at www.courts.ca.gov.

California law requires that you receive this information because the demand letter or court complaint you received with this document claims that your building or property does not comply with one or more existing construction-related accessibility laws or regulations protecting the civil rights of persons with disabilities to access public places.

YOU HAVE IMPORTANT LEGAL OBLIGATIONS. Compliance with disability access laws is a serious and significant responsibility that applies to all California building owners and tenants with buildings open for business to the public. You may obtain information about your legal obligations and how to comply with disability access laws through the Division of the State Architect at www.dgs.ca.gov. Information is also available from the California Commission on Disability Access at www.ccda.ca.gov/guide.htm.

YOU HAVE IMPORTANT LEGAL RIGHTS. The allegations made in the accompanying demand letter or court complaint do not mean that you are required to pay any money unless and until a court finds you liable. Moreover, RECEIPT OF A DEMAND LETTER OR COURT COMPLAINT AND THIS ADVISORY DOES NOT NECESSARILY MEAN YOU WILL BE FOUND LIABLE FOR ANYTHING. You will have the right if you are later sued to fully present your explanation why you believe you have not in fact violated disability access laws or have corrected the violation or violations giving rise to the claim.

You have the right to seek assistance or advice about this demand letter or court complaint from any person of your choice. If you have insurance, you may also wish to contact your insurance provider. Your best interest may be served by seeking legal advice or representation from an attorney, but you may also represent yourself and file the necessary court papers to protect your interests if you are served with a court complaint. If you have hired an attorney to represent you, you should immediately notify your attorney.

If a court complaint has been served on you, you will get a separate advisory notice with the complaint advising you of special options and procedures available to you under certain conditions.

ADDITIONAL THINGS YOU SHOULD KNOW: If the document accompanying this notice is a demand letter from a lawyer and not a formal court complaint, the lawyer is generally required by law to also provide a copy of it to the State Bar of California, until January 1, 2016, in order that the State Bar may determine whether the demand letter complies with legal requirements, INCLUDING THAT THE DEMAND LETTER MAY NOT MAKE A REQUEST OR DEMAND FOR MONEY OR AN OFFER OR AGREEMENT TO ACCEPT MONEY. Any demand letter or court complaint must list the lawyer's State Bar license number on the document.

You are encouraged, but are not required, to provide the State Bar with a copy of the demand letter so the State Bar is aware that you received this demand letter and may determine whether it is in compliance with specified legal requirements. A copy of the letter can be sent to the State Bar by facsimile transmission to 1-415-538-2171, or by mail to the State Bar of California, 180 Howard Street, San Francisco, CA, 94105, Attention: Professional Competence.

(c) On or before July 1, 2013, the Judicial Council shall update the form that may be used by attorneys to comply with the requirements of subdivision (b). The form shall be in substantially the same format and include all of the text set forth in subdivision (b). The form shall be available in English, Spanish, Chinese, Vietnamese, and Korean, and shall include a statement that the form is available in additional languages, and the Judicial Council Internet Web site address where the different versions of the form may be located. The form shall include Internet Web site information for the Division of the State Architect and the California Commission on Disability Access.

(d) Subdivision (b) shall apply only to a demand letter or complaint made by an attorney. Nothing in this section is intended to affect the right to file a civil complaint under any other law or regulation protecting the physical access rights of persons with disabilities. Additionally, nothing in this section requires a party to provide or send a demand letter to another party before proceeding against that party with a civil complaint.

(e) This section shall not apply to any action brought by the Attorney General, or by any district attorney, city attorney, or county counsel.

SEC. 4. Section 55.31 is added to the Civil Code, to read:

55.31. (a) Commencing January 1, 2013, a demand letter alleging a construction-related accessibility claim, as defined in subdivision (a) of Section 55.3, shall state facts sufficient to allow a reasonable person to identify the basis of the violation or violations supporting the claim, including all of the following:

(1) A plain language explanation of the specific access barrier or barriers the individual encountered, or by which the individual alleges he or she was deterred, with sufficient information about the location of the barrier to enable a reasonable person to identify the access barrier.

(2) The way in which the barrier encountered interfered with the individual's full and equal use or access, or in which it deterred the individual, on each particular occasion.

(3) The date or dates of each particular occasion on which the individual encountered the specific access barrier, or on which he or she was deterred.

(b) A demand letter may offer prelitigation settlement negotiations, but shall not include a request or demand for money or an offer or agreement to accept money.

(1) With respect to potential monetary damages for an alleged construction-related accessibility claim or claims, a demand letter shall not state any specific potential monetary liability for any asserted claim or claims, and may only state: "The property owner or tenant, or both, may be civilly liable for actual and statutory damages for a violation of a construction-related accessibility requirement."

(2) Notwithstanding any other law, a demand letter meeting the requirements of this section shall be deemed to satisfy the requirements for prelitigation notice of a potential claim when prelitigation notice is required by statute or common law for an award of attorney's fees.

(3) This subdivision and subdivision (a) do not apply to a demand for money, which is governed by subdivision (c).

(c) An attorney, or a person acting at the direction of an attorney, shall not issue a demand for money as defined in subdivision (a) of Section 55.3.

This subdivision does not apply to a demand letter as defined in subdivision (a) of Section 55.3.

(d) (1) A violation of subdivision (b) or (c) constitutes cause for the imposition of discipline of an attorney. Subdivisions (b) and (c) do not prohibit an attorney from presenting a settlement figure or specification of damages in response to a request from the building owner or tenant, or the owner's or tenant's authorized agent or employee, following a demand letter provided pursuant to Section 55.3.

(2) Any liability for a violation of subdivision (c) is as provided in paragraph (1) of this subdivision. A violation of subdivision (c) does not create a new cause of action.

(e) Subdivision (c) does not prohibit any prelitigation settlement discussion of liability for damages and attorney's fees that occurs after a written or oral agreement is reached between the parties for the repair or correction of the alleged violation or violations of a construction-related accessibility standard.

(f) Subdivision (c) shall not apply to a claim involving physical injury and resulting special damages, but a demand for money relating to that claim that is sent shall otherwise comply with the requirements of subdivision (a) and Section 55.32.

(g) Nothing in this section shall apply to a demand or statement of alleged damages made in a prelitigation claim presented to a governmental entity as required by state or federal law, including, but not limited to, claims made under Part 3 (commencing with Section 900) of Division 3.6 of the Government Code.

(h) If subdivision (c) is not operative or becomes inoperative for any reason, the requirements of subdivision (a) and Section 55.32 shall apply to any written demand for money.

SEC. 5. Section 55.32 is added to the Civil Code, to read:

55.32. (a) An attorney who provides a demand letter, as defined in subdivision (a) of Section 55.3, shall do all of the following:

(1) Include the attorney's State Bar license number in the demand letter.

(2) Contemporaneously with providing the demand letter, send a copy of the demand letter to the State Bar of California by facsimile transmission at 1-415-538-2171, or by mail to 180 Howard Street, San Francisco, CA, 94105, Attention: Professional Competence.

(3) Within five business days of providing the demand letter, send a copy of the demand letter to the California Commission on Disability Access.

(b) An attorney who sends or serves a complaint, as defined in subdivision (a) of Section 55.3, shall send a copy of the complaint to the California Commission on Disability Access within five business days of sending or serving the complaint.

(c) A violation of paragraph (2) or (3) of subdivision (a) or subdivision (b) shall constitute cause for the imposition of discipline of an attorney where a copy of the complaint or demand letter is not sent to the California Commission on Disability Access within five business days, or a copy of the demand letter is not sent to the State Bar within five business days. In the event the State Bar receives information indicating that an attorney has failed to send a copy of the complaint or demand letter to the California Commission on Disability Access within five business days, the State Bar shall investigate to determine whether paragraph (3) of subdivision (a) or subdivision (b) has been violated.

(d) Notwithstanding subdivisions (a) and (b), an attorney is not required to send to the State Bar of California or the California Commission on Disability Access a copy of any subsequent demand letter or amended complaint in the same dispute following the initial demand letter or complaint, unless that subsequent demand letter or amended complaint alleges a new construction-related accessibility claim.

(e) A demand letter or complaint sent to the California Commission on Disability Access shall be for the informational purposes of Section 8299.08 of the Government Code. A demand letter received by the State Bar from either the sender or recipient of the demand letter shall be reviewed by the State Bar to determine whether subdivision (b) or (c) of Section 55.31 has been violated.

(f) (1) Commencing July 31, 2013, and annually each July 31 thereafter, the State Bar shall report to the Legislature and the Chairs of the Senate and Assembly Committees on Judiciary, both of the following with respect to demand letters received by the State Bar:

(A) The number of investigations opened to date on a suspected violation of subdivision (b) or (c) of Section 55.31.

(B) Whether any disciplinary action resulted from the investigation, and the results of that disciplinary action.

(2) A report to be submitted pursuant to this subdivision shall be submitted in compliance with Section 9795 of the Government Code.

(g) The California Commission on Disability Access shall review and report on the demand letters and complaints it receives as provided in Section 8299.08 of the Government Code.

(h) Paragraphs (2) and (3) of subdivision (a) and subdivision (b) shall not apply to a demand letter or complaint sent or filed by an attorney employed or retained by a qualified legal services project or a qualified support center, as defined in Section 6213 of the Business and Professions Code, when acting within the scope of employment in asserting a construction-related accessibility claim. The Legislature finds and declares that qualified legal services projects and support centers are extensively regulated by the State Bar of California, and that there is no evidence of any abusive use of demand letters or complaints by these organizations. The Legislature further finds that, in light of the evidence of the extraordinarily small number of construction-related accessibility cases brought by regulated legal services programs, and given the resources of those programs, exempting regulated legal services programs from the requirements of this section to report to the California Commission on Disability Access will not affect the purpose of the reporting to, and tabulation by, the commission of all other construction-related accessibility claims.

(i) This section shall become operative on January 1, 2013.

(j) This section shall remain in effect only until January 1, 2016, and as of that date is repealed, unless a later enacted statute, that is enacted before January 1, 2016, deletes or extends that date.

SEC. 6. Section 55.32 is added to the Civil Code, to read:

55.32. (a) An attorney who provides a demand letter, as defined in subdivision (a) of Section 55.3, shall do all of the following:

(1) Include the attorney's State Bar license number in the demand letter.

(2) Within five business days of providing the demand letter, send a copy of the demand letter to the California Commission on Disability Access.

(b) An attorney who sends or serves a complaint, as defined in subdivision (a) of Section 55.3, shall send a copy of the complaint to the California Commission on Disability Access within five business days of sending or serving the complaint.

(c) A violation of paragraph (2) of subdivision (a) or subdivision (b) shall constitute cause for the imposition of discipline of an attorney if a copy of the demand letter or complaint is not sent to the California Commission on Disability Access within five business days. In the event the State Bar receives information indicating that an attorney has failed to send a copy of the demand letter or complaint to the California Commission on Disability Access within five business days, the State Bar shall investigate to determine whether paragraph (2) of subdivision (a) or subdivision (b) has been violated.

(d) Notwithstanding subdivisions (a) and (b), an attorney is not required to send to the California Commission on Disability Access a copy of any subsequent demand letter or amended complaint in the same dispute following the initial demand letter or complaint, unless that subsequent demand letter or amended complaint alleges a new construction-related accessibility claim.

(e) A demand letter sent to the California Commission on Disability Access shall be for the informational purposes of Section 8299.08 of the Government Code. A demand letter received by the State Bar from the recipient of the demand letter shall be reviewed by the State Bar to determine whether subdivision (b) or (c) of Section 55.31 has been violated.

(f) (1) Notwithstanding Section 10231.5 of the Government Code, on or before July 31, 2016, and annually thereafter, the State Bar shall report to the Legislature and the Chairs of the Senate and Assembly Judiciary Committees, both of the following with respect to demand letters received by the State Bar:

(A) The number of investigations opened to date on a suspected violation of subdivision (b) or (c) of Section 55.31.

(B) Whether any disciplinary action resulted from the investigation, and the results of that disciplinary action.

(2) A report to be submitted pursuant to this subdivision shall be submitted in compliance with Section 9795 of the Government Code.

(g) The California Commission on Disability Access shall review and report on the demand letters and complaints it receives as provided in Section 8299.08 of the Government Code.

(h) The expiration of any ground for discipline of an attorney shall not affect the imposition of discipline for any act prior to the expiration. An act or omission that constituted cause for imposition of discipline of an attorney when committed or omitted prior to January 1, 2016, shall continue to constitute cause for the imposition of discipline of that attorney on and after January 1, 2016.

(i) Paragraph (2) of subdivision (a) and subdivision (b) shall not apply to a demand letter or complaint sent or filed by an attorney employed or retained by a qualified legal services project or a qualified support center, as defined in Section 6213 of the Business and Professions Code, when acting within the scope of employment in asserting a construction-related accessibility claim. The Legislature finds and declares that qualified legal services projects and support centers are extensively regulated by the State Bar of California, and that there is no evidence of any abusive use of demand letters or complaints by these organizations. The Legislature further finds that, in light of the evidence of the extraordinarily small number of construction-related accessibility cases brought by regulated legal services programs, and given the resources of those programs, exempting regulated legal services programs from the requirements of this section to report to the California Commission on Disability Access will not affect the purpose of the reporting to, and tabulation by, the commission of all other construction-related accessibility claims.

(j) This section shall become operative on January 1, 2016.

SEC. 7. Section 55.52 of the Civil Code is amended to read:

55.52. (a) For purposes of this part, the following definitions apply:

(1) "Construction-related accessibility claim" means any civil claim in a civil action with respect to a place of public accommodation, including, but not limited to, a claim brought under Section 51, 54, 54.1, or 55, based wholly or in part on an alleged violation of any construction-related accessibility standard, as defined in paragraph (6).

(2) "Application for stay and early evaluation conference" means an application to be filed with the court that meets the requirements of subdivision (c) of Section 55.54.

(3) "Certified access specialist" or "CASp" means any person who has been certified pursuant to Section 4459.5 of the Government Code.

(4) "Meets applicable standards" means the site was inspected by a CASp and determined to meet all applicable construction-related accessibility standards pursuant to paragraph (1) of subdivision (a) of Section 55.53. A site that is "CASp inspected" on or before the effective date of the amendments made to this section by Senate Bill 1186 of the 2011–12 Regular Session of the Legislature means that the site "meets applicable standards."

(5) "Inspected by a CASp" means the site was inspected by a CASp and is pending a determination by the CASp that the site meets applicable construction-related accessibility standards pursuant to paragraph (2) of subdivision (a) of Section 55.53. A site that is "CASp determination pending" on or before the effective date of the amendments made to this section by

Senate Bill 1186 of the 2011–12 Regular Session of the Legislature means that the site was "inspected by a CASp."

(6) "Construction-related accessibility standard" means a provision, standard, or regulation under state or federal law requiring compliance with standards for making new construction and existing facilities accessible to persons with disabilities, including, but not limited to, any provision, standard, or regulation set forth in Section 51, 54, 54.1, or 55 of this code, Section 19955.5 of the Health and Safety Code, the California Building Standards Code (Title 24 of the California Code of Regulations), the federal Americans with Disabilities Act of 1990 (Public Law 101-336; 42 U.S.C. Sec. 12101 et seq.), and the federal Americans with Disabilities Act Accessibility Guidelines (Appendix A to Part 36 of Title 28 of the Code of Federal Regulations).

(7) "Place of public accommodation" has the same meaning as "public accommodation," as set forth in Section 12181(7) of Title 42 of the United States Code and the federal regulations adopted pursuant to that section.

(8) "Qualified defendant" means a defendant in an action that includes a construction-related accessibility claim that is asserted against a place of public accommodation that met the requirements of "meets applicable standards" or "inspected by a CASp" prior to the date the defendant was served with the summons and complaint in that action. To be a qualified defendant, the defendant is not required to have been the party who hired any CASp, so long as the basis of the alleged liability of the defendant is a construction-related accessibility claim. To determine whether a defendant is a qualified defendant, the court need not make a finding that the place of public accommodation complies with all applicable construction-related accessibility standards as a matter of law. The court need only determine that the place of public accommodation has a status of "meets applicable standards" or "inspected by a CASp."

(9) "Site" means a place of public accommodation.

(b) Unless otherwise indicated, terms used in this part relating to civil procedure have the same meanings that those terms have in the Code of Civil Procedure.

SEC. 8. Section 55.53 of the Civil Code is amended to read:

55.53. (a) For purposes of this part, a certified access specialist shall, upon completion of the inspection of a site, comply with the following:

(1) For a meets applicable standards site, if the CASp determines the site meets all applicable construction-related accessibility standards, the CASp shall provide a written inspection report to the requesting party that includes both of the following:

(A) An identification and description of the inspected structures and areas of the site.

(B) A signed and dated statement that includes both of the following:

(i) A statement that, in the opinion of the CASp, the inspected structures and areas of the site meet construction-related accessibility standards. The statement shall clearly indicate whether the determination of the CASp includes an assessment of readily achievable barrier removal.

(ii) If corrections were made as a result of the CASp inspection, an itemized list of all corrections and dates of completion.

(2) For an inspected by a CASp site, if the CASp determines that corrections are needed to the site in order for the site to meet all applicable construction-related accessibility standards, the CASp shall provide a signed and dated written inspection report to the requesting party that includes all of the following:

(A) An identification and description of the inspected structures and areas of the site.

(B) A statement that, in the opinion of the CASp, the inspected structures and areas of the site need correction to meet construction-related accessibility standards. This statement shall clearly indicate whether the determination of the CASp includes an assessment of readily achievable barrier removal.

(C) An identification and description of the structures or areas of the site that need correction and the correction needed.

(D) A schedule of completion for each of the corrections within a reasonable timeframe.

(b) For purposes of this section, in determining whether the site meets applicable construction-related accessibility standards when there is a conflict or difference between a state and federal provision, standard, or regulation, the state provision, standard, or regulation shall apply unless the federal provision, standard, or regulation is more protective of accessibility rights.

(c) Every CASp who conducts an inspection of a place of public accommodation shall, upon completing the inspection of the site, provide the building owner or tenant who requested the inspection with the following notice, which the State Architect shall make available as a form on the State Architect's Internet Web site:

NOTICE TO PRIVATE PROPERTY OWNER/TENANT:

YOU ARE ADVISED TO KEEP IN YOUR RECORDS ANY WRITTEN INSPECTION REPORT AND ANY OTHER DOCUMENTATION CONCERNING YOUR PROPERTY SITE THAT IS GIVEN TO YOU BY A CERTIFIED ACCESS SPECIALIST.

IF YOU BECOME A DEFENDANT IN A LAWSUIT THAT INCLUDES A CLAIM CONCERNING A SITE INSPECTED BY A CERTIFIED ACCESS SPECIALIST, YOU MAY BE ENTITLED TO A COURT STAY (AN ORDER TEMPORARILY STOPPING ANY LAWSUIT) OF THE CLAIM AND AN EARLY EVALUATION CONFERENCE.

IN ORDER TO REQUEST THE STAY AND EARLY EVALUATION CONFERENCE, YOU WILL NEED TO VERIFY THAT A CERTIFIED ACCESS SPECIALIST HAS INSPECTED THE SITE THAT IS THE SUBJECT OF THE CLAIM. YOU WILL ALSO BE REQUIRED TO PROVIDE THE COURT AND THE PLAINTIFF WITH THE COPY OF A WRITTEN INSPECTION REPORT BY THE CERTIFIED ACCESS SPECIALIST, AS SET FORTH IN CIVIL CODE SECTION 55.54. THE APPLICATION FORM AND INFORMATION ON HOW TO REQUEST

A STAY AND EARLY EVALUATION CONFERENCE MAY BE OBTAINED AT www.courts.ca.gov/selfhelp-start.htm.

YOU ARE ENTITLED TO REQUEST, FROM A CERTIFIED ACCESS SPECIALIST WHO HAS CONDUCTED AN INSPECTION OF YOUR PROPERTY, A WRITTEN INSPECTION REPORT AND OTHER DOCUMENTATION AS SET FORTH IN CIVIL CODE SECTION 55.53. YOU ARE ALSO ENTITLED TO REQUEST THE ISSUANCE OF A DISABILITY ACCESS INSPECTION CERTIFICATE, WHICH YOU MAY POST ON YOUR PROPERTY.

(d) (1) Commencing July 1, 2010, a local agency shall employ or retain at least one building inspector who is a certified access specialist. The certified access specialist shall provide consultation to the local agency, permit applicants, and members of the public on compliance with state construction-related accessibility standards with respect to inspections of a place of public accommodation that relate to permitting, plan checks, or new construction, including, but not limited to, inspections relating to tenant improvements that may impact access. If a local agency employs or retains two or more certified access specialists to comply with this subdivision, at least one-half of the certified access specialists shall be building inspectors who are certified access specialists.

(2) Commencing January 1, 2014, a local agency shall employ or retain a sufficient number of building inspectors who are certified access specialists to conduct permitting and plan check services to review for compliance with state construction-related accessibility standards by a place of public accommodation with respect to new construction, including, but not limited to, projects relating to tenant improvements that may impact access. If a local agency employs or retains two or more certified access specialists to comply with this subdivision, at least one-half of the certified access specialists shall be building inspectors who are certified access specialists.

(3) If a permit applicant or member of the public requests consultation from a certified access specialist, the local agency may charge an amount limited to a reasonable hourly rate, an estimate of which shall be provided upon request in advance of the consultation. A local government may additionally charge or increase permitting, plan check, or inspection fees to the extent necessary to offset the costs of complying with this subdivision. Any revenues generated from an hourly or other charge or fee increase under this subdivision shall be used solely to offset the costs incurred to comply with this subdivision. A CASp inspection pursuant to subdivision (a) by a building inspector who is a certified access specialist shall be treated equally for legal and evidentiary purposes as an inspection conducted by a private CASp. Nothing in this subdivision shall preclude permit applicants or any other person with a legal interest in the property from retaining a private CASp at any time.

(e) (1) Every CASp who completes an inspection of a place of public accommodation shall, upon a determination that the site meets applicable standards pursuant to paragraph (1) of subdivision (a) or is inspected by a CASp pursuant to paragraph (2) of subdivision (a), provide the building owner or tenant requesting the inspection with a numbered disability access inspection certificate indicating that the site has undergone inspection by a certified access specialist. The disability access inspection certificate shall be dated and signed by the CASp inspector, and shall contain the inspector's name and license number. Upon issuance of a certificate, the CASp shall record the issuance of the numbered certificate, the name and address of the recipient, and the type of report issued pursuant to subdivision (a) in a record book the CASp shall maintain for that purpose.

(2) Beginning March 1, 2009, the State Architect shall make available for purchase by any local building department or CASp sequentially numbered disability access inspection certificates that are printed with a watermark or other feature to deter forgery and that comply with the information requirements specified in subdivision (a).

(3) The disability access inspection certificate may be posted on the premises of the place of public accommodation, unless, following the date of inspection, the inspected site has been modified or construction has commenced to modify the inspected site in a way that may impact compliance with construction-related accessibility standards.

(f) Nothing in this section or any other law is intended to require a property owner or tenant to hire a CASp. A property owner's or tenant's election not to hire a CASp shall not be admissible to prove that person's lack of intent to comply with the law.

SEC. 9. Section 55.54 of the Civil Code is amended to read:

55.54. (a) (1) An attorney who causes a summons and complaint to be served in an action that includes a construction-related accessibility claim, including, but not limited to, a claim brought under Section 51, 54, 54.1, or 55, shall, at the same time, cause to be served a copy of the application form specified in subdivision (c) and a copy of the following notice, including, until January 1, 2013, the bracketed text, to the defendant on separate papers that shall be served with the summons and complaint:

ADVISORY NOTICE TO DEFENDANT

YOU MAY BE ENTITLED TO ASK FOR A COURT STAY (AN ORDER TEMPORARILY STOPPING ANY LAWSUIT) AND EARLY EVALUATION CONFERENCE IN THIS LAWSUIT AND MAY BE ASSESSED REDUCED STATUTORY DAMAGES IF YOU MEET CERTAIN CONDITIONS.

If the construction-related accessibility claim pertains to a site that has a Certified Access Specialist (CASp) inspection report for that site, or to a site where new construction or improvement was approved after January 1, 2008, by the local building permit and inspection process, you may make an immediate request for a court stay and early evaluation conference in the construction-related accessibility claim by filing the attached application form with the court. You may be entitled to the court stay and early evaluation conference regarding the accessibility claim only if ALL of the statements in the application form applicable to you are true.

FURTHER, if you are a defendant described above (with a CASp inspection report or with new construction after January 1, 2008), and, to the best of your knowledge, there have been no modifications or alterations completed or commenced since the CASp report or building department approval of the new construction or improvement that impacted compliance with construction-related accessibility standards with respect to the plaintiff's claim, your liability for minimum statutory damages may be reduced to $1,000 for each offense, unless the violation was intentional, and if all construction-related accessibility violations giving rise to the claim are corrected within 60 days of being served with this complaint.

IN ADDITION, if your business is a small business that, over the previous three years, or the existence of the business if less than three years, employs 25 or fewer employees on average over that time period and meets specified gross receipts criteria, you may also be entitled to the court stay and early evaluation conference and your minimum statutory damages for each claim may be reduced to $2,000 for each offense, unless the violation was intentional, and if all the alleged construction-related accessibility violations are corrected within 30 days of being served with the complaint.

If you plan to correct the violations giving rise to the claim, you should take pictures and measurements or similar action to document the condition of the physical barrier asserted to be the basis for a violation before undertaking any corrective action in case a court needs to see the condition of a barrier before it was corrected.

The court will schedule the conference to be held within 70 days after you file the attached application form.

[If you are not a defendant with a CASp inspection report, until a form is adopted by the Judicial Council, you may use the attached form if you modify the form and supplement it with your declaration stating any one of the following:

(1) Until January 1, 2018, that the site's new construction or improvement on or after January 1, 2008, and before January 1, 2016, was approved pursuant to the local building permit and inspection process; that, to the best of your knowledge, there have been no modifications or alterations completed or commenced since the building department approval that impacted compliance with construction-related accessibility standards with respect to the plaintiff's claim; and that all violations giving rise to the claim have been corrected, or will be corrected within 60 days of the complaint being served.

(2) That the site's new construction or improvement passed inspection by a local building department inspector who is a certified access specialist; that, to the best of your knowledge, there have been no modifications or alterations completed or commenced since that inspection approval that impacted compliance with construction-related

accessibility standards with respect to the plaintiff's claim; and that all violations giving rise to the claim have been corrected, or will be corrected within 60 days of the complaint being served.

(3) That your business is a small business with 25 or fewer employees and meets the gross receipts criteria set out in Section 55.56 of the Civil Code, and that all violations giving rise to the claim have been corrected, or will be corrected within 30 days of being served with the complaint.]

The court will also issue an immediate stay of the proceedings unless the plaintiff has obtained a temporary restraining order in the construction-related accessibility claim. You may obtain a copy of the application form, filing instructions, and additional information about the stay and early evaluation conference through the Judicial Council Internet Web site at www.courts.ca.gov/selfhelp-start.htm.

You may file the application after you are served with a summons and complaint, but no later than your first court pleading or appearance in this case, which is due within 30 days after you receive the summons and complaint. If you do not file the application, you will still need to file your reply to the lawsuit within 30 days after you receive the summons and complaint to contest it. You may obtain more information about how to represent yourself and how to file a reply without hiring an attorney at www.courts.ca.gov/selfhelp-start.htm.

You may file the application without the assistance of an attorney, but it may be in your best interest to immediately seek the assistance of an attorney experienced in disability access laws when you receive a summons and complaint. You may make an offer to settle the case, and it may be in your interest to put that offer in writing so that it may be considered under Section 55.55 of the Civil Code.

(2) An attorney who files a Notice of Substitution of Counsel to appear as counsel for a plaintiff who, acting in propria persona, had previously filed a complaint in an action that includes a construction-related accessibility claim, including, but not limited to, a claim brought under Section 51, 54, 54.1, or 55, shall, at the same time, cause to be served a copy of the application form specified in subdivision (c) and a copy of the notice specified in paragraph (1) upon the defendant on separate pages that shall be attached to the Notice of Substitution of Counsel.

(b) (1) Notwithstanding any other law, upon being served with a summons and complaint asserting a construction-related accessibility claim, including, but not limited to, a claim brought under Section 51, 54, 54.1, or 55, a qualified defendant, or other defendant as defined in paragraph (2), may file a request for a court stay and early evaluation conference in the proceedings of that claim prior to or simultaneous with that defendant's responsive pleading or other initial appearance in the action that includes the claim. If that defendant filed a timely request for stay and early evaluation conference before a responsive pleading was due, the period for filing a responsive pleading shall be tolled until the stay is lifted. Any responsive pleading filed simultaneously with a request for stay and early evaluation conference may be amended without prejudice, and the period for filing that amendment shall be tolled until the stay is lifted.

(2) This subdivision shall also apply to a defendant if any of the following apply:

(A) Until January 1, 2018, the site's new construction or improvement on or after January 1, 2008, and before January 1, 2016, was approved pursuant to the local building permit and inspection process, and the defendant declares with the application that, to the best of the defendant's knowledge, there have been no modifications or alterations completed or commenced since that approval that impacted compliance with construction-related accessibility standards with respect to the plaintiff's claim, and that all violations have been corrected, or will be corrected within 60 days of being served with the complaint.

(B) The site's new construction or improvement was approved by a local public building department inspector who is a certified access specialist, and the defendant declares with the application that, to the best of the defendant's knowledge, there have been no modifications or alterations completed or commenced since that approval that impacted compliance with construction-related accessibility standards with respect to the plaintiff's claim, and that all violations have been corrected, or will be corrected within 60 days of being served with the complaint.

(C) The defendant is a small business described in subdivision (f) of Section 55.56, and the defendant declares with the application that all violations have been corrected, or will be corrected within 30 days of being served with the complaint.

(3) Notwithstanding any other law, if the plaintiff had acted in propria persona in filing a complaint that includes a construction-related accessibility claim, including, but not limited to, a claim brought under Section 51, 54, 54.1, or 55, a qualified defendant, or a defendant described by paragraph (2), who is served with a Notice of Substitution of Counsel shall have 30 days to file an application for a stay and an early evaluation conference. The application may be filed prior to or after the defendant's filing of a responsive pleading or other initial appearance in the action that includes the claim, except that an application may not be filed in a claim in which an early evaluation conference or settlement conference has already been held on the claim.

(c) (1) An application for an early evaluation conference and stay by a qualified defendant shall include a signed declaration that states both of the following:

(A) The site identified in the complaint has been CASp-inspected or meets applicable standards, or is CASp determination pending or has been inspected by a CASp, and if the site is CASp-inspected or meets applicable standards, there have been no modifications completed or commenced since the date of inspection that may impact compliance with construction-related accessibility standards to the best of the defendant's knowledge.

(B) An inspection report pertaining to the site has been issued by a CASp. The inspection report shall be provided to the court and the plaintiff at least 15 days prior to the court date set for the early evaluation conference.

(2) An application for an early evaluation conference and stay by a defendant described by subparagraph (A) of paragraph (2) of subdivision (b), which may be filed until January 1, 2018, shall include a signed declaration that states all of the following:

(A) The site's new construction or improvement was approved pursuant to the local building permit and inspection process on or after January 1, 2008, and before January 1, 2016.

(B) To the best of the defendant's knowledge there have been no modifications or alterations completed or commenced since that approval that impacted compliance with construction-related accessibility standards with respect to the plaintiff's claim.

(C) All construction-related violations giving rise to the claim have been corrected, or will be corrected within 60 days of the complaint being served upon the defendant.

(3) An application for an early evaluation conference and stay by a defendant described in subparagraph (B) of paragraph (2) of subdivision (b) shall include a signed declaration that states all of the following:

(A) The site's new construction or improvement was approved by a local building department inspector who is a certified access specialist.

(B) To the best of the defendant's knowledge there have been no modifications or alterations completed or commenced since that approval that impacted compliance with construction-related accessibility standards with respect to the plaintiff's claim.

(C) All construction related violations giving rise to the claim have been corrected, or will be corrected within 60 days of the complaint being served upon the defendant.

(4) An application for an early evaluation conference and stay by a defendant described by subparagraph (C) of paragraph (2) of subdivision (b) shall include the materials listed in paragraphs (5) and (6) of this subdivision, and shall include a signed declaration that states both of the following:

(A) The defendant is a small business that employs 25 or fewer employees and meets the gross receipts eligibility criteria provided in paragraph (2) of subdivision (f) of Section 55.56.

(B) All construction-related violations giving rise to the claim have been corrected, or will be corrected within 30 days of the complaint being served upon the defendant.

(5) An application for an early evaluation conference and stay by a small business defendant under paragraph (4) shall include evidence showing correction of all violations within 30 days of the service of the complaint and served upon the plaintiff with the reply unless the application is filed prior to completion of the corrections. In that event, the evidence shall be provided to the court and served upon the plaintiff within 10 days of the court order as provided in paragraph (4) of subdivision (d). This paragraph

shall not be construed to extend the permissible time under subdivision (f) of Section 55.56 to make the corrections.

(6) An application for an early evaluation conference and stay by a small business defendant under paragraph (4) shall also include both of the following, which shall be confidential documents filed only with the court and not served upon or available to the plaintiff:

(A) Proof of the defendant's number of employees, as shown by wage report forms filed with the Employment Development Department.

(B) Proof of the defendant's average gross receipts for the previous three years, or for the existence of the business if less than three years, as shown by a federal or state tax document.

(7) The following provisional request and notice forms may be used and filed by a qualified defendant until forms are adopted by the Judicial Council for those purposes pursuant to subdivision (*l*):

ATTORNEY OR PARTY WITHOUT ATTORNEY (Name, State Bar number if attorney, and address):	FOR COURT USE ONLY
TELEPHONE NO.: FAX NO. (Optional):	
E-MAIL ADDRESS (Optional):	
ATTORNEY FOR (Name):	

SUPERIOR COURT OF CALIFORNIA, COUNTY OF _____

STREET ADDRESS:

MAILING ADDRESS:

CITY AND ZIP CODE:

BRANCH NAME:

PLAINTIFF:

DEFENDANT:

DEFENDANT'S APPLICATION FOR STAY AND EARLY EVALUATION CONFERENCE PURSUANT TO CIVIL CODE SECTION 55.54 (CONSTRUCTION-RELATED ACCESSIBILITY CLAIM)	CASE NUMBER:

(Information about this application and the filing instructions may be obtained at http:// www.courtinfo.ca.gov/selfhelp/.)

1. Defendant (name)_____ requests a stay of proceedings and early evaluation conference pursuant to Civil Code Section 55.54.

2. The complaint in this case alleges a construction-related accessibility claim as defined under Civil Code Section 55.52(a)(1).

3. The claim concerns a site that (check the box if the statement is true):
   a. _____ Has been inspected by a Certified Access Specialist (CASp) and determined to be CASp inspected or CASp determination pending and, if CASp inspected, there have been no modifications completed or commenced since the date of inspection that may impact compliance with construction-related accessibility standards to the best of defendant's knowledge; and
   b. _____ An inspection report by a Certified Access Specialist (CASp) relating to the site has been issued.
   (Both (a) and (b) must be met for the court to order a Stay and Early Evaluation Conference.)

4. I am requesting the court to:
   a. Stay the proceedings relating to the construction-related accessibility claim.
   b. Schedule an Early Evaluation Conference.
   c. Order Defendant to file a confidential copy of the Certified Access Specialist (CASp) report with the court and serve a copy of the report on the Plaintiff at least fifteen (15) days before the Early Evaluation Conference date.
   d. Order Plaintiff to file the statement required by Civil Code Section 55.54(d)(6)(A)–(D) with the court and serve a copy of the statement on the Defendant at least fifteen (15) days before the date of the Early Evaluation Conference.

I declare under penalty of perjury under the laws of the State of California that the foregoing is true and correct.

Date:

_____   _____
(TYPE OR PRINT NAME OF DECLARANT)   (SIGNATURE OF DECLARANT)

_____
(TITLE OF DECLARANT)

DEFENDANT'S APPLICATION FOR EARLY EVALUATION CONFERENCE AND STAY OF PROCEEDINGS
(Construction-related Accessibility Claim)   Provisional Form

— 23 — Ch. 383

ATTORNEY OR PARTY WITHOUT ATTORNEY (Name, State Bar number if attorney, and address):	FOR COURT USE ONLY
TELEPHONE NO.: FAX NO. (Optional): E-MAIL ADDRESS (Optional): ATTORNEY FOR (Name):	
SUPERIOR COURT OF CALIFORNIA, COUNTY OF _____ STREET ADDRESS: MAILING ADDRESS: CITY AND ZIP CODE: BRANCH NAME:	
PLAINTIFF: DEFENDANT:	
NOTICE OF STAY OR PROCEEDINGS AND EARLY EVALUATION CONFERENCE (CONSTRUCTION-RELATED ACCESSIBILITY CLAIM)	CASE NUMBER:

Stay of Proceedings

For a period of 90 days from the date of the filing of this court notice, unless otherwise ordered by the court, the parties are stayed from taking any further action relating to the construction-related accessibility claim or claims in this case.

This stay does not apply to any construction-related accessibility claim in which the plaintiff has obtained temporary injunctive relief which is still in place.

Notice of Early Evaluation Conference

1. This action includes a construction-related accessibility claim under Civil Code Section 55.52(a)(1) or other provision of law.

2. A defendant has requested an early evaluation conference and a stay of proceedings under Civil Code Section 55.54.

3. The early evaluation conference is scheduled as follows:

    a. Date: Time: Dept. Room:

    b. The conference will be held at _____ the court address shown above, or _____ at:

4. The plaintiff and defendant shall attend with any other person needed for settlement of the case unless, with court approval, a party's disability requires the party's participation by a telephone appearance or other alternate means or through the personal appearance of an authorized representative.

5. The defendant that requested the conference and stay of proceedings must file with the court and serve on all parties a copy of the CASp report for the site that is the subject of the construction-related accessibility claim at least fifteen (15) days before the date set for the early evaluation conference. The CASp report is confidential and only available as set forth below and in Civil Code Section 55.54(d)(4).

6. The CASp report shall be marked "CONFIDENTIAL" and may be disclosed only to counsel, the parties to the action, the parties' attorneys, those individuals employed or retained by the attorneys to assist in the litigation, and insurance representatives or others involved in the evaluation and settlement of the case.

7. The plaintiff shall file with the court and serve on all parties at least fifteen (15) days before the date set for the early evaluation conference a statement of, to the extent known, all of the following:
    a. An itemized list of specific issues on the subject premises that are the basis of the claimed construction-related accessibility violations in the plaintiff's complaint;
    b. The amount of damages claimed;
    c. The amount of attorney's fees and costs incurred to date, if any, that are being claimed; and
    d. Any demand for settlement of the case in its entirety.

hand delivering it or mailing it to the address listed on the complaint on the same date that the court issues this Notice and Order of Stay of Proceedings and Early Evaluation Conference.

Date: _____   Clerk, by _____ , Deputy

More information about this Notice and Order and the defendant's application, and instructions to assist plaintiff and defendants in complying with this Notice and Order, may be obtained at http://www.courtinfo.ca.gov/selfhelp/.)

Requests for Accommodation

Assistive listening systems, computer-assisted real-time captioning, or sign language interpreter services are available if you ask at least 5 days before the date on which you are to appear. Contact the clerk's office or go to www.courtinfo.ca.gov/forms for Request for Accommodations by Persons with Disabilities and Order (form MC-410). (Civil Code Section 54.8)

Proof of Service
(Required from Defendant Filing Application for Stay and Early Evaluation Conference)

I served a copy of the defendant's Application For Stay and Early Evaluation Conference Pursuant To Civil Code Section 55.54 and the court Notice and Order of Stay of Proceedings and Early Evaluation Conference (check one):

_____ On the Plaintiff's attorney

_____ On the Plaintiff who is not represented by an attorney

By hand delivering it or mailing it to the address listed on the complaint on the day the court issued this Notice and Order of Stay of Proceedings and Early Evaluation Conference.

I declare under penalty of perjury of the laws of the State of California that the foregoing is true and correct.

Dated: _____

_____   _____
Type or Print Name   Signature

_____
Address of named person

NOTICE OF STAY OF PROCEEDINGS AND EARLY EVALUATION CONFERENCE
(Construction-related Accessibility Claim)   Provisional Form

(8) The provisional forms and any replacement Judicial Council forms shall include the defendant's declaration of proof of service of the application, the notice of the court's order, and the court's order pursuant to subdivision (d).

(d) Upon the filing of an application for stay and early evaluation conference by a qualified defendant, or a defendant described by paragraph (2) of subdivision (b), the court shall immediately issue an order that does all of the following:

(1) Grants a 90-day stay of the proceedings with respect to the construction-related accessibility claim, unless the plaintiff has obtained temporary injunctive relief that is still in place for the construction-related accessibility claim.

(2) Schedules a mandatory early evaluation conference for a date as soon as possible from the date of the order, but in no event later than 70 days after issuance of the order, and in no event earlier than 50 days after the filing of the request.

(3) Directs the parties, and any other person whose authority is required to negotiate and enter into settlement, to appear in person at the time set for the conference. Appearance by counsel shall not satisfy the requirement that the parties or those with negotiation and settlement authority personally appear, provided, however, that the court may allow a party who is unable to attend in person due to his or her disability to participate in the hearing by telephone or other alternative means or through a representative authorized to settle the case.

(4) (A) Directs the qualified defendant to file with the court and serve on the plaintiff a copy of any relevant CASp inspection report at least 15 days before the date of the conference. The CASp inspection report is confidential and is available only as set forth in paragraph (5) of this subdivision and in paragraph (4) of subdivision (e).

(B) Directs a defendant described by subparagraph (A) or (B) of paragraph (2) of subdivision (b) who has filed a declaration stating that the violation or violations have been corrected, or will be corrected within 60 days of service of the complaint to file with the court and serve on the plaintiff evidence showing correction of the violation or violations within 10 calendar days after the completion of the corrections.

(C) Directs a defendant described by subparagraph (C) of paragraph (2) of subdivision (b) who has filed a declaration stating that the violation or violations have been corrected, or will be corrected within 30 days of service of the complaint to file with the court and serve on the plaintiff within 10 days after issuance of the court order evidence of correction of the violation or violations, if that evidence showing correction was not filed previously with the application and served on the plaintiff.

(5) Directs the parties that the CASp inspection report may be disclosed only to the court, the parties to the action, the parties' attorneys, those individuals employed or retained by the attorneys to assist in the litigation, and insurance representatives or others involved in the evaluation and settlement of the case.

(6) Directs the plaintiff to file with the court and serve on the defendant at least 15 days before the date of the conference a statement that includes, to the extent reasonably known, for use solely for the purpose of the early evaluation conference, all of the following:

(A) An itemized list of specific conditions on the subject premises that are the basis of the claimed violations of construction-related accessibility standards in the plaintiff's complaint.

(B) The amount of damages claimed.

(C) The amount of attorney's fees and costs incurred to date, if any, that are being claimed.

(D) Any demand for settlement of the case in its entirety.

(e) (1) A party failing to comply with any court order may be subject to court sanction at the court's discretion.

(2) (A) The court shall lift the stay when the defendant has failed to file and serve the CASp inspection report prior to the early evaluation conference and has failed also to produce the report at the time of the early evaluation conference, unless the defendant shows good cause for that failure.

(B) The court shall lift the stay when a defendant described by paragraph (2) of subdivision (b) has failed to file and serve the evidence showing correction of the violation or violations as required by law.

(3) The court may lift the stay at the conclusion of the early evaluation conference upon a showing of good cause by the plaintiff. Good cause may include the defendant's failure to make reasonably timely progress toward completion of corrections noted by a CASp.

(4) The CASp inspection report filed and served pursuant to subdivision (d) shall remain confidential throughout the stay and shall continue to be confidential until the conclusion of the claim, whether by dismissal, settlement, or final judgment, unless there is a showing of good cause by any party. Good cause may include the defendant's failure to make reasonably timely progress toward completion of corrections noted by a CASp. The confidentiality of the inspection report shall terminate upon the conclusion of the claim, unless the owner of the report obtains a court order pursuant to the California Rules of Court to seal the record.

(f) All discussions at the early evaluation conference shall be subject to Section 1152 of the Evidence Code. It is the intent of the Legislature that the purpose of the evaluation conference shall include, but not be limited to, evaluation of all of the following, as applicable:

(1) Whether the defendant is entitled to the 90-day stay for some or all of the identified issues in the case, as a qualified defendant.

(2) The current condition of the site and the status of any plan of corrections, including whether the qualified defendant has corrected or is willing to correct the alleged violations, and the timeline for doing so.

(3) Whether subdivision (f) of Section 55.56 may be applicable to the case, and whether all violations giving rise to the claim have been corrected within the specified time periods.

(4) Whether the case, including any claim for damages or injunctive relief, can be settled in whole or in part.

(5) Whether the parties should share other information that may facilitate early evaluation and resolution of the dispute.

(g) Nothing in this section precludes any party from making an offer to compromise pursuant to Section 998 of the Code of Civil Procedure.

(h) For a claim involving a qualified defendant, as provided in paragraph (1) of subdivision (b), the court may schedule additional conferences and may extend the 90-day stay for good cause shown, but not to exceed one additional 90-day extension.

(i) Early evaluation conferences shall be conducted by a superior court judge or commissioner, or a court early evaluation conference officer. A commissioner shall not be qualified to conduct early evaluation conferences pursuant to this subdivision unless he or she has received training regarding disability access requirements imposed by the federal Americans with Disabilities Act of 1990 (Public Law 101-336; 42 U.S.C. Sec. 12101 et seq.), state laws that govern access to public facilities, and federal and state regulations adopted pursuant to those laws. For purposes of this subdivision, a "court early evaluation conference officer" means an attorney employed by the court who has received training regarding disability access requirements imposed by the federal Americans with Disabilities Act of 1990, state laws that govern access to public facilities, and federal and state regulations adopted pursuant to those laws. Attorneys serving in this capacity may also be utilized by the court for other purposes not related to these proceedings.

(j) Nothing in this part shall be deemed to make any inspection report, opinion, statement, or other finding or conclusion of a CASp binding on the court, or to abrogate in any manner the ultimate authority of the court to make all appropriate findings of fact and law. The CASp inspection report and any opinion, statement, finding, or conclusion therein shall be given the weight the trier of fact finds that it deserves.

(k) Nothing in this part shall be construed to invalidate or limit any California construction-related accessibility standard that provides greater or equal protection for the rights of individuals with disabilities than is afforded by the federal Americans with Disabilities Act (Public Law 101-336; 42 U.S.C. Sec. 12101 et seq.) and the federal regulations adopted pursuant to that act.

(*l*) (1) The Judicial Council shall, by January 1, 2013, prepare and post on its Internet Web site instructions and a form for use by a qualified defendant, or other defendant described by paragraph (2) of subdivision (b), to file an application for stay and early evaluation conference as provided in subdivisions (b) and (c), a form for the court's notice of stay and early evaluation conference, and any other forms appropriate to implement the provisions relating to early evaluation conferences. Until those forms are adopted, the Judicial Council shall post on its Internet Web site the provisional forms set forth in subdivision (c).

(2) Until the adoption of the forms as provided in paragraph (1), the provisional application form may be used by a defendant described by paragraph (2) of subdivision (b).

(3) In lieu of the provisions specified in number 3 of page 1 of the application form set forth in paragraph (7) of subdivision (c), the application shall include one of the following declarations of the defendant as to the basis for the application, as follows:

(A) That all of the following apply to a defendant described by subparagraph (A) of paragraph (2) of subdivision (b):

(i) The site's new construction or improvement was approved pursuant to the local building permit and inspection process on or after January 1, 2008, and before January 1, 2016.

(ii) To the best of the defendant's knowledge there have been no modifications or alterations completed or commenced since that approval that impacted compliance with construction-related accessibility standards with respect to the plaintiff's claim.

(iii) All the violations giving rise to the claim have been corrected, or will be corrected within 60 days of the complaint being served.

(B) That all of the following apply to a defendant described by subparagraph (B) of paragraph (2) of subdivision (b):

(i) The site's new construction or improvement was approved by a local public building department inspector who is a certified access specialist.

(ii) To the best of the defendant's knowledge there have been no modifications or alterations completed or commenced since that approval that impacted compliance with construction-related accessibility standards with respect to the plaintiff's claim.

(iii) All the violations giving rise to the claim have been corrected, or will be corrected within 60 days of the complaint being served.

(C) That both of the following apply to a defendant described by subparagraph (C) of paragraph (2) of subdivision (b):

(i) The defendant is a small business described in paragraph (2) of subdivision (f) of Section 55.56.

(ii) The violation or violations giving rise to the claim have been corrected, or will be corrected within 30 days of the complaint being served.

(4) In lieu of the provision specified in number 4(c) of page 1 of the application form set forth in paragraph (7) of subdivision (c), the application shall include a request that the court order the defendant to do either of the following:

(A) For a defendant who has filed a declaration stating that all violations have been corrected, or will be corrected within 60 days of service of the complaint, file with the court and serve on the plaintiff evidence showing correction of the violation or violations within 10 calendar days of the completion of the corrections.

(B) For a defendant who is a small business that has filed a declaration stating that all the violations have been corrected, or will be corrected within 30 days of the service of the complaint, file with the court and serve on the plaintiff evidence showing correction of the violation or violations within 10 calendar days after issuance of the court order, if that evidence showing correction was not filed previously with the application and served on the plaintiff.

(5) The Judicial Council shall also prepare and post on its Internet Web site instructions and cover pages to assist plaintiffs and defendants, respectively, to comply with their filing responsibilities under subdivision (d). The cover pages shall also provide for the party's declaration of proof of service of the pertinent document served under the court order.

(m) The stay provisions shall not apply to any construction-related accessibility claim in which the plaintiff has been granted temporary injunctive relief that remains in place.

(n) This section shall not apply to any action brought by the Attorney General, or by any district attorney, city attorney, or county counsel.

(o) The amendments to this section made by Senate Bill 1186 of the 2011–12 Regular Session of the Legislature shall apply only to claims filed on or after the operative date of that act. Nothing in this part is intended to affect any complaint filed before that date.

(p) Nothing in this part is intended to affect existing law regarding class action requirements.

SEC. 10. Section 55.545 is added to the Civil Code, to read:

55.545. (a) A defendant who does not qualify for an early evaluation conference pursuant Section 55.54, or who forgoes the provisions of Section 55.54, may request a mandatory evaluation conference. A plaintiff may, if the defendant does not make the request with the filing of the responsive pleadings, request a mandatory evaluation conference by filing an application within 15 days of the defendant's filing of responsive pleadings.

(b) Upon being served with a summons and complaint asserting a construction-related accessibility claim, including, but not limited to, a claim brought under Section 51, 54, 54.1, or 55, a defendant may file an application for a mandatory evaluation conference in the proceedings of that claim simultaneous with the defendant's responsive pleading or other initial appearance in the action that includes the claim. Until the application form for the mandatory evaluation conference is developed by the Judicial Council and posted on its Internet Web site pursuant to subdivision (j), a defendant may request the calendaring of the mandatory evaluation conference in a separate application filed with the defendant's responsive pleadings.

(c) Upon the filing of a request or application for a mandatory evaluation conference by a defendant or plaintiff, the court shall schedule a mandatory evaluation conference for a date as soon as possible from the date of the request or application, but in no event later than 180 days after the date of request or application, or earlier than 120 days after the filing of the request or application. Upon mutual stipulation for an extension of the conference date, the mandatory evaluation conference may be extended for up to 30 days. The court's notice of conference shall also do all of the following:

(1) Direct the parties, and any other person whose authority is required to negotiate and enter into settlement, to appear in person at the time set for the conference. Appearance by counsel shall not satisfy the requirement that the parties, or those with negotiation and settlement authority, personally appear. However, the court may allow a party who is unable to attend in person due to his or her disability to participate in the hearing by telephone

or other alternative means, or through a representative authorized to settle the case.

(2) Direct the plaintiff to file with the court and serve on the defendant, at least 30 days before the date of mandatory evaluation conference, a statement that includes, to the extent reasonably known, for use solely for the purpose of the mandatory evaluation conference, all of the following:

(A) An itemized list of specific conditions on the site that are the basis of the claimed violations of construction-related accessibility standards in the plaintiff's complaint.

(B) The amount of damages claimed.

(C) The amount of attorney's fees and costs incurred to date, if any, that are being claimed.

(D) Any demand for settlement of the case in its entirety.

(3) Direct the defendant to file with the court and serve on the plaintiff, at least 30 days before the date of the mandatory evaluation conference, a statement of the defendant detailing any remedial action or remedial correction plan undertaken, or to be undertaken, by the defendant to correct the alleged violations.

(d) A party failing to comply with any court order is subject to court sanction at the court's discretion.

(e) All discussions at the mandatory evaluation conference shall be subject to Section 1152 of the Evidence Code. It is the intent of the Legislature that the purpose of the evaluation conference shall include, but not be limited to, evaluation of all of the following:

(1) The current condition of the site and the status of any plan of correction, including whether the defendant has corrected, or is willing to correct, the alleged violations, and the timeline for doing so.

(2) Whether the case, including any claim for damages or injunctive relief, can be settled in whole or in part.

(3) Whether the parties should share other information that may facilitate evaluation and resolution of the dispute.

(f) Nothing in this section precludes any party from making an offer to compromise pursuant to Section 998 of the Code of Civil Procedure.

(g) The court may schedule additional conferences.

(h) Mandatory evaluation conferences shall be conducted by a superior court judge or commissioner, or by a court early evaluation conference officer as provided in subdivision (i) of Section 55.54.

(i) If an inspection report by a certified access specialist is offered by the defendant, the provisions of Section 55.54 relating to the use and confidentiality of that report shall apply.

(j) (1) The Judicial Council shall prepare and post on its Internet Web site instructions and a form for a party to use to file an application for a mandatory evaluation conference and a form for the court's notice of the mandatory evaluation conference. Until those forms are adopted, a party and the court may use an ad hoc form that complies with the requirements of this section.

(2) The Judicial Council shall also prepare and post on its Internet Web site instructions and cover pages to assist plaintiffs and defendants, respectively, to comply with their filing responsibilities under subdivision (c).

(k) The mandatory evaluation conference may, at the court's discretion, be scheduled or combined with the case management conference within the time period specified in subdivision (c).

(*l*) This section shall not apply to any action brought by the Attorney General, or by any district attorney, city attorney, or county counsel.

(m) This section shall apply only to claims filed on or after January 1, 2013. Nothing in this section is intended to affect any complaint filed before that date.

SEC. 11. Section 55.56 of the Civil Code is amended to read:

55.56. (a) Statutory damages under either subdivision (a) of Section 52 or subdivision (a) of Section 54.3 may be recovered in a construction-related accessibility claim against a place of public accommodation only if a violation or violations of one or more construction-related accessibility standards denied the plaintiff full and equal access to the place of public accommodation on a particular occasion.

(b) A plaintiff is denied full and equal access only if the plaintiff personally encountered the violation on a particular occasion, or the plaintiff was deterred from accessing a place of public accommodation on a particular occasion.

(c) A violation personally encountered by a plaintiff may be sufficient to cause a denial of full and equal access if the plaintiff experienced difficulty, discomfort, or embarrassment because of the violation.

(d) A plaintiff demonstrates that he or she was deterred from accessing a place of public accommodation on a particular occasion only if both of the following apply:

(1) The plaintiff had actual knowledge of a violation or violations that prevented or reasonably dissuaded the plaintiff from accessing a place of public accommodation that the plaintiff intended to use on a particular occasion.

(2) The violation or violations would have actually denied the plaintiff full and equal access if the plaintiff had accessed the place of public accommodation on that particular occasion.

(e) Statutory damages may be assessed pursuant to subdivision (a) based on each particular occasion that the plaintiff was denied full and equal access, and not upon the number of violations of construction-related accessibility standards identified at the place of public accommodation where the denial of full and equal access occurred. If the place of public accommodation consists of distinct facilities that offer distinct services, statutory damages may be assessed based on each denial of full and equal access to the distinct facility, and not upon the number of violations of construction-related accessibility standards identified at the place of public accommodation where the denial of full and equal access occurred.

(f) (1) Notwithstanding any other law, a defendant's liability for statutory damages in a construction-related accessibility claim against a place of public accommodation is reduced to a minimum of one thousand dollars ($1,000) for each offense if the defendant demonstrates that it has corrected all construction-related violations that are the basis of a claim within 60 days of being served with the complaint, and the defendant demonstrates any of the following:

(A) The structure or area of the alleged violation was determined to be "CASp-inspected" or "meets applicable standards" and, to the best of the defendant's knowledge, there were no modifications or alterations that impacted compliance with construction-related accessibility standards with respect to the plaintiff's claim that were completed or commenced between the date of that determination and the particular occasion on which the plaintiff was allegedly denied full and equal access.

(B) The structure or area of the alleged violation was the subject of an inspection report indicating "CASp determination pending" or "Inspected by a CASp," and the defendant has either implemented reasonable measures to correct the alleged violation prior to the particular occasion on which the plaintiff was allegedly denied full and equal access, or the defendant was in the process of correcting the alleged violation within a reasonable time and manner prior to the particular occasion on which the plaintiff was allegedly denied full and equal access.

(C) For a claim alleging a construction-related accessibility violation filed before January 1, 2018, the structure or area of the alleged violation was a new construction or an improvement that was approved by, and passed inspection by, the local building department permit and inspection process on or after January 1, 2008, and before January 1, 2016, and, to the best of the defendant's knowledge, there were no modifications or alterations that impacted compliance with respect to the plaintiff's claim that were completed or commenced between the completion date of the new construction or improvement and the particular occasion on which the plaintiff was allegedly denied full and equal access.

(D) The structure or area of the alleged violation was new construction or an improvement that was approved by, and passed inspection by a local building department official who is a certified access specialist, and, to the best of the defendant's knowledge, there were no modifications or alterations that affected compliance with respect to the plaintiff's claim that were completed or commenced between the completion date of the new construction or improvement and the particular occasion on which the plaintiff was allegedly denied full and equal access.

(2) Notwithstanding any other law, a defendant's liability for statutory damages in a construction-related accessibility claim against a place of public accommodation is reduced to a minimum of two thousand dollars ($2,000) for each offense if the defendant demonstrates both of the following:

(A) The defendant has corrected all construction-related violations that are the basis of a claim within 30 days of being served with the complaint.

(B) The defendant is a small business that has employed 25 or fewer employees on average over the past three years, or for the years it has been in existence if less than three years, as evidenced by wage report forms filed with the Economic Development Department, and has average annual gross receipts of less than three million five hundred thousand dollars ($3,500,000) over the previous three years, or for the years it has been in existence if less than three years, as evidenced by federal or state income tax returns. The average annual gross receipts dollar amount shall be adjusted biannually by the Department of General Services for changes in the California Consumer Price Index for All Urban Consumers, as compiled by the Department of Industrial Relations. The Department of General Services shall post that adjusted amount on its Internet Web site.

(3) This subdivision shall not be applicable to intentional violations.

(4) Nothing in this subdivision affects the awarding of actual damages, or affects the awarding of treble actual damages.

(5) This subdivision shall apply only to claims filed on or after the effective date of Senate Bill 1186 of the 2011–12 Regular Session of the Legislature. Nothing in this subdivision is intended to affect a complaint filed before that date.

(g) This section does not alter the applicable law for the awarding of injunctive or other equitable relief for a violation or violations of one or more construction-related accessibility standards, nor alter any legal obligation of a party to mitigate damages.

(h) In assessing liability under subdivision (d), in any action alleging multiple claims for the same construction-related accessibility violation on different particular occasions, the court shall consider the reasonableness of the plaintiff's conduct in light of the plaintiff's obligation, if any, to mitigate damages.

SEC. 12. Section 1938 is added to the Civil Code, to read:

1938. A commercial property owner or lessor shall state on every lease form or rental agreement executed on or after July 1, 2013, whether the property being leased or rented has undergone inspection by a Certified Access Specialist (CASp), and, if so, whether the property has or has not been determined to meet all applicable construction-related accessibility standards pursuant to Section 55.53.

SEC. 13. Section 425.50 is added to the Code of Civil Procedure, to read:

425.50. (a) An allegation of a construction-related accessibility claim in a complaint, as defined in subdivision (a) of Section 55.52 of the Civil Code, shall state facts sufficient to allow a reasonable person to identify the basis of the violation or violations supporting the claim, including all of the following:

(1) A plain language explanation of the specific access barrier or barriers the individual encountered, or by which the individual alleges he or she was deterred, with sufficient information about the location of the alleged barrier to enable a reasonable person to identify the access barrier.

(2) The way in which the barrier denied the individual full and equal use or access, or in which it deterred the individual, on each particular occasion.

(3) The date or dates of each particular occasion on which the claimant encountered the specific access barrier, or on which he or she was deterred.

(b) Any complaint alleging a construction-related accessibility claim, as those terms are defined in subdivision (a) of Section 55.3 of the Civil Code, shall be verified by the plaintiff. A complaint filed without verification shall be subject to a motion to strike.

(c) Nothing in this section shall limit the right of a plaintiff to amend a complaint under Section 472, or with leave of court under Section 473. However, any amended pleading alleging a construction-related accessibility claim shall be pled as required by subdivision (a).

(d) This section shall become operative on January 1, 2013.

SEC. 14. Section 4459.8 of the Government Code is amended to read:

4459.8. (a) The certification authorized by Section 4459.5 is effective for three years from the date of initial certification and expires if not renewed. The State Architect, upon consideration of any factual complaints regarding the work of a certified access specialist or of other relevant information, may suspend certification or deny renewal of certification.

(b) (1) The State Architect shall require each applicant for certification as a certified access specialist to pay fees, including an application and course fee and an examination fee, at a level sufficient to meet the costs of application processing, registration, publishing a list, and other activities that are reasonably necessary to implement and administer the certified access specialist program. The State Architect shall require each applicant for renewal of certification to pay a fee sufficient to cover the reasonable costs of reassessing qualifications of renewal applicants.

(2) The State Architect shall periodically review its schedule of fees to ensure that its fees for certification are not excessive while covering the costs to administer the certified access specialist program. The application fee for a California licensed architect, landscape architect, civil engineer, or structural engineer shall not exceed two hundred fifty dollars ($250).

(c) All fees collected pursuant to this section shall be deposited into the Certified Access Specialist Fund, which is hereby created in the State Treasury. Notwithstanding Section 13340, this fund is continuously appropriated without regard to fiscal years for use by the State Architect to implement Sections 4459.5 to 4459.8, inclusive.

SEC. 15. Chapter 7.5 (commencing with Section 4465) is added to Division 5 of Title 1 of the Government Code, to read:

CHAPTER 7.5. DISABILITY ACCESS AND EDUCATION

4465. (a) There is hereby established in the Division of the State Architect a Disability Access and Education Revolving Fund, as set forth in Section 4470, for the purpose of increasing disability access and compliance with construction-related accessibility requirements by the following means:

(1) Increasing the number of private and public certified access specialists available to assist building owners and tenants to understand and comply with construction-related accessibility requirements by using some of the funds to moderate some of the costs of certification and testing.

(2) Establishing and maintaining oversight of the certified access specialist program, including, but not limited to, adopting best practices guidelines for certified access specialists, providing continuing education on construction-related accessibility requirements, and performing its audit and discipline functions under Sections 4459.7 and 4459.8.

(3) Increasing outreach efforts and developing educational resources for persons with disabilities and businesses to facilitate compliance with the federal Americans with Disabilities Act of 1990 (42 U.S.C. Sec. 12101 et seq.), the Unruh Civil Rights Act (Section 51 of the Civil Code), and Title 24 of the California Code of Regulations, as they relate to providing full and equal access to public facilities for persons with disabilities.

(b) In developing educational resources with this fund, emphasis shall be placed on the development and dissemination of educational materials, such as toolkits, modules, and checklists, as appropriate, to facilitate a commercial property owner's or tenant's understanding of, and compliance with, the construction-related accessibility requirements.

(c) In developing and disseminating educational resources with this fund, the Division of the State Architect shall consult and work with the Department of Rehabilitation and the California Commission on Disability Access, and may contract with those agencies to develop educational resources. It is the intent of the Legislature that any development or dissemination of educational resources under this section shall be coordinated with educational efforts by other state agencies so as to expand the reach and effectiveness of each effort or the combined efforts.

4467. (a) On and after January 1, 2013, and until December 31, 2018, any applicant for a local business license or equivalent instrument or permit, and from any applicant for the renewal of a business license or equivalent instrument or permit, shall pay an additional fee of one dollar ($1) for that license, instrument, or permit, which shall be collected by the city, county, or city and county that issued the license, instrument, or permit.

(b) The city, county, or city and county shall retain 70 percent of the fees collected under this section, of which up to 5 percent of the retained moneys may be used for related administrative costs of this chapter. The remaining moneys shall be used to fund increased certified access specialist (CASp) services in that jurisdiction for the public and to facilitate compliance with construction-related accessibility requirements. The highest priority shall be given to the training and retention of certified access specialists to meet the needs of the public in the jurisdiction as provided in Section 55.53 of the Civil Code.

(c) The remaining 30 percent of all fees collected under this section shall be transmitted on a quarterly basis to the Division of the State Architect for deposit in the Disability Access and Education Revolving Fund established under Sections 4465 and 4470. The funds shall be transmitted within 15 days of the last day of the fiscal quarter. The Division of the State Architect shall develop and post on its Internet Web site a standard reporting form for use by all local jurisdictions. Up to 75 percent of the collected funds in the Disability Access and Education Revolving Fund shall be used to establish and maintain oversight of the CASp program and to moderate the expense of CASp certification and testing.

(d) Each city, county, or city and county shall make an annual report, commencing March 1, 2014, to the Legislature and to the Chairs of the Senate and Assembly Committees on Judiciary, and the Chair of the Senate Committee on Budget and Fiscal Review and the Chair of the Assembly Committee on Budget, of the total fees collected in the previous calendar year and of its distribution, including the moneys spent on administrative services, the moneys spent to increase CASp services, the moneys spent to fund programs to facilitate compliance, and the moneys transmitted to the Disability Access and Education Revolving Fund. A report to be submitted pursuant to this subdivision shall be submitted in compliance with Section 9795.

4469. On and after January 1, 2013, each city, county, or city and county shall provide to an applicant for a business license or equivalent instrument or permit and to an applicant for the renewal of a business license or equivalent instrument or permit, the following information:

"Under federal and state law, compliance with disability access laws is a serious and significant responsibility that applies to all California building owners and tenants with buildings open to the public. You may obtain information about your legal obligations and how to comply with disability access laws at the following agencies:

The Division of the State Architect at www.dgs.ca.gov/dsa/Home.aspx.
The Department of Rehabilitation at www.rehab.cahwnet.gov.
The California Commission on Disability Access at www.ccda.ca.gov."

4470. (a) All funds received by the Division of the State Architect under this chapter shall be deposited in the Disability Access and Education Revolving Fund, which is hereby established in the State Treasury.

(b) Notwithstanding Section 13340, moneys deposited in the fund are hereby continuously appropriated without regard to fiscal years to the Division of the State Architect for purposes of this chapter.

(c) Notwithstanding Section 10231.5, the State Architect shall make an annual report, commencing March 1, 2014, to the Legislature and to the Chairs of the Senate and Assembly Committees on Judiciary, and the Chair of the Senate Committee on Budget and Fiscal Review and the Chair of the Assembly Committee on Budget, of the total fees transmitted to the fund in the previous calendar year and of its distribution, including the moneys spent on administrative services, the moneys spent to moderate certification and examination fees for the certified access specialist program, the moneys spent on establishing and maintaining oversight of the certified access specialist program, and the moneys spent on developing and disseminating educational materials to facilitate compliance. A report to be submitted pursuant to this subdivision, shall be submitted in compliance with Section 9795.

SEC. 16. Section 8299.05 of the Government Code is amended to read:

8299.05. (a) The commission may recommend, develop, prepare, or coordinate materials, projects, or other activities, as appropriate, relating to any subject within its jurisdiction.

(b) The commission shall provide, within its resources, information regarding any of the following:

(1) Preventing or minimizing problems of compliance by California businesses by providing educational services, including outreach efforts, and by preparing and hosting on its Internet Web site a Guide to Compliance with State Laws and Regulations Regarding Disability Access Requirements.

(2) Recommending programs to enable persons with disabilities to obtain full and equal access to public facilities.

(3) Providing information as requested by the Legislature on disability access issues and compliance.

SEC. 17. Section 8299.06 of the Government Code is repealed.

SEC. 18. Section 8299.06 is added to the Government Code, to read:

8299.06. (a) A priority of the commission shall be the development and dissemination of educational materials and information to promote and facilitate disability access compliance.

(b) The commission shall work with other state agencies, including the Division of the State Architect and the Department of Rehabilitation, to develop educational materials and information for use by businesses to understand its obligations to provide disability access and to facilitate compliance with construction-related accessibility standards.

(c) The commission shall develop and make available on its Internet Web site, or make available on its Internet Web site if developed by another governmental agency, including Americans with Disabilities Act centers, toolkits or educational modules to assist a California business to understand its obligations under the law and to facilitate compliance with respect to the top 10 alleged construction-related violations, by type, as specified in subdivision (a) of Section 8299.08. Upon completion of this requirement, the commission shall develop and make available on its Internet Web site, or work with another agency to develop, other toolkits or educational modules that would educate businesses of the accessibility requirements and to facilitate compliance with that requirement.

(d) The commission shall post on its Internet Web site educational materials and information that will assist building owners, tenants, building officials, and building inspectors to understand the disability accessibility requirements and to facilitate compliance with disability access laws. The commission shall at least annually review the educational materials and information on disability access requirements and compliance available on the Internet Web site of other local, state, or federal agencies, including

Americans with Disabilities Act centers, to augment the educational materials and information developed by the commission.

(e) The commission shall, to the extent feasible, coordinate with other state agencies and local building departments to ensure that information provided to the public on disability access requirements is uniform and complete.

SEC. 19. Section 8299.07 of the Government Code is repealed.

SEC. 20. Section 8299.07 is added to the Government Code, to read:

8299.07. (a) On or before April 15, 2013, the commission shall report to the Legislature, and to the Chairs of the Senate and Assembly Committees on Judiciary, of its activities and efforts since the commission was established to implement Sections 8299.05 and 8299.06, including the provisions that were law prior to amendment or repeal in the 2011–12 Regular Session. Commencing in 2014, and notwithstanding Section 10231.5, the commission shall report on or before January 31 and annually thereafter to the Legislature, and to the Chairs of the Senate and Assembly Committees on Judiciary, of its ongoing efforts to implement Sections 8299.05 and 8299.06, as amended in the 2011–12 Regular Session.

(b) A report to be submitted pursuant to subdivision (a) shall be submitted in compliance with Section 9795.

SEC. 21. Section 8299.08 of the Government Code is repealed.

SEC. 22. Section 8299.08 is added to the Government Code, to read:

8299.08. The commission shall compile the following data with respect to any demand letter or complaint sent to the commission pursuant to Section 53.32 of the Civil Code and post the information on its Internet Web site, pursuant to the following:

(a) The commission shall identify the various types of construction-related physical access violations alleged in the demand letters and in the complaints, respectively, and shall tabulate the number of claims alleged for each type of violation in the demand letters and complaints, respectively. For purposes of this subdivision, any demand for money letters shall be grouped as demand letters.

(b) Periodically, but not less than every six months beginning July 31, 2013, the commission shall post on its Internet Web site a list, by type, of the 10 most frequent types of accessibility violations alleged in the demand letters and in the complaints, respectively, and the numbers of alleged violations for each listed type of violation for the prior two quarters.

(c) The commission shall, on a quarterly basis, identify and tabulate the number of demand letters and complaints received by the commission. The commission shall further ascertain whether a complaint was filed in state or federal court and tabulate the number of complaints filed in state or federal court, respectively. This data shall be posted on the commission's Internet Web site periodically, but not less than every six months beginning July 31, 2013.

(d) Commencing in 2014, and notwithstanding Section 10231.5, the commission shall make an annual report to the Legislature and the Chairs of the Senate and Assembly Committees on Judiciary by January 31 of each year of the tabulated data for the preceding calendar year as set forth in subdivisions (a) to (c), inclusive. A report to be submitted pursuant to this subdivision shall be submitted in compliance with Section 9795.

SEC. 23. Section 18944.15 is added to the Health and Safety Code, to read:

18944.15. (a) Upon the publication date of the 2013 California Building Standards Code as adopted by the commission as part of the 2012 triennial code adoption cycle, for the purpose of any claim brought under Section 51, 54, 54.1, or 55 of the Civil Code based in whole, or in part, on an alleged violation of a construction-related accessibility standard, compliance with the building standards for disabled accessibility as provided in Chapter 11B of Part 2 of Title 24 of the 2013 California Building Standards Code shall be authorized as an alternative method of compliance.

(b) Subdivision (a) shall become inoperative when the provisions of the 2013 California Building Standards Code become effective pursuant to Section 18938.

(c) This section shall become operative on January 1, 2013.

(d) This section shall remain in effect only until January 1, 2015, and as of that date is repealed, unless a later enacted statute, that is enacted before January 1, 2015, deletes or extends that date.

SEC. 24. The Legislature finds and declares that a very small number of plaintiffs' attorneys have been abusing the right of petition under Sections 52 and 54.3 of the Civil Code by issuing a demand for money to a California business owner that demands the owner pay a quick settlement of the attorney's alleged claim under those laws or else incur greater liability and legal costs if a lawsuit is filed. These demands for money allege one or more, but frequently multiple, claims for asserted violations of a construction-related accessibility standard and often demand a quick money settlement based on the alleged multiple claims without seeking and obtaining actual repair or correction of the alleged violations on the site. These "pay me now or pay me more" demands are used to scare businesses into paying quick settlements that only financially enrich the attorney and claimant and do not promote accessibility either for the claimant or the disability community as a whole. These practices, often involving a series of demand for money letters sent to numerous businesses, do not promote compliance with the accessibility requirements and erode public support for and confidence in our laws. Therefore, the Legislature finds and declares that it is necessary and appropriate to enact Sections 55.31 and 55.32 of the Civil Code, and Section 425.50 of the Code of Civil Procedure to protect the public's confidence and support of the right to petition under Sections 52 and 54.3 of the Civil Code.

SEC. 25. The Legislature finds and declares all of the following:

(a) Subdivision (h) of Section 55.56 of the Civil Code, as added by Section 11 of this act, is intended to address the misuse of Sections 52 and 54.3 of the Civil Code by a small minority of disability rights lawyers and plaintiffs. These lawyers and plaintiffs have alleged in demand letters and complaints that they were deterred on repeated occasions by the same violation of a construction-related accessibility standard and thereby assert multiple claims for the same violation without a reasonable explanation for the repeated conduct in light of the obligation to mitigate damages. Their assertions of these "stacked" multiple claims for the same construction-related accessibility violation on different occasions are made to substantially increase the purported statutory liability of a defendant in order to intimidate and pressure the defendant into making a quick monetary settlement. The provisions of subdivision (h) of Section 55.56 of the Civil Code reiterate that where multiple claims for the same construction-related accessibility violation on separate particular occasions are alleged, a plaintiff's conduct must have a reasonable explanation for the asserted need for multiple visits to a site where a known barrier violation would deny full and equal access, in light of the obligation to mitigate damages.

(b) Correspondingly, if there is a reasonable explanation in light of the obligation to mitigate damages for the need to make multiple visits to a site where a known barrier violation would deny full and equal access, a multiple claim for repeated violations of the same construction-related accessibility standard may properly lie. In addition, there may be clear instances when the needs of a person with a disability and circumstances may make mitigation efforts impossible or futile in cases involving multiple instances of deterrence on separate particular occasions where the individual has a reasonable explanation for the need for multiple visits to the same site.

(c) Further, nothing in subdivision (h) of Section 55.56 of the Civil Code is intended to change existing law with respect to the fact that an alleged failure to mitigate damages is pled and proven as an affirmative defense.

SEC. 26. The provisions of this act are severable. If any provision of this act or its application is held invalid, that invalidity shall not affect other provisions or applications that can be given effect without the invalid provision or application.

SEC. 27. The Legislature finds and declares that promoting uniform statewide compliance with construction-related accessibility requirements set forth in the federal Americans with Disabilities Act of 1990 (42 U.S.C. Sec. 12101 et seq.) and the California Building Standards Code is a matter of statewide concern and is not a municipal affair as that term is used in Section 5 of Article XI of the California Constitution. Therefore, this act shall apply to all cities, including charter cities.

SEC. 28. If the Commission on State Mandates determines that this act contains costs mandated by the state, reimbursement to local agencies and school districts for those costs shall be made pursuant to Part 7 (commencing with Section 17500) of Division 4 of Title 2 of the Government Code.

SEC. 29. This act is an urgency statute necessary for the immediate preservation of the public peace, health, or safety within the meaning of Article IV of the Constitution and shall go into immediate effect. The facts constituting the necessity are:

In order to avoid unnecessary litigation and to facilitate compliance with the disability access law, it is necessary that this act take effect immediately.

INDEX

Abuses of the ADA? 338*ff*

- Advanced Notice not Required 342-343
- Attorney Fees as Congressional Incentive for ADA Enforcement 338-341
- Checklist Re: "Abusive" Actions...349
- Existing Court Remedies for "Abuse" 344-345
- Fraudulent Conduct can be punished under existing law 341
- No Standing for Defendants in "Other" Cases.......................................346, 348
- Number of lawsuits not itself vexatious or frivolous......................................347
- SB1608 in California gave state court defendants procedural protections 348
- Section 503 protects plaintiff's "good faith" 348
- "Serial Litigation" 338-341
- Weakening Access laws would destroy ADA Enforceability 342

Access triggered by Alterations 41, 49, 69

Accessibility (defined by regulations) 35

Alterations, structural repairs, additions 33-39

- Triggered access..34, 43, 232

Americans with Disabilities Act of 1990

- ADA Title II.. 215-219
- ADA Title III 232*ff*
- ADA Requirements incorporated into California Civil Code...77, 232, 237, 238
- ADA Compromise: private lawsuit enforcement.................................232, 235
- ADA Purposes and Supremacy (but no preemption of State law).......... 233-235
- Injunctive Relief and Attorney Fees 232
- "Private Attorney General..235
- Public Policy to Encourage "private A.G." Enforcement....................... 236-237
- Removal of ADA actions from State to Federal Court........................... 238-241
- Readily Achievable Standards 241*ff*
- State Regulations, ADA, Whichever Stronger...69

Appendix: See "Appendix Index" at end of this index

"ASA" Regulations (1970 – 1982) 30, 31, 37

Attorney Fees

- ADA Title II Attorney Fees 231
- California Statutory Attorney Fees 166*ff*
- "Catalyst" fees... 122, 170, 290
- "Court Enforceable" Settlement Agreement...288
- Consent Decree 423
- Damages amount not a limitation 180
- Defendants Fees (See "Prevailing")....................................... 190-196, 300-309
- Defendants hours not relevant..179
- Defendants Conduct Increasing Fees... 181-182
- Delayed Payment, basis for current rates...178, 189
- "Duplicative Efforts" sometimes needed 185
- Enforcing Compliance 183
- Federal Fees per ADA Section 505...166, 288*ff*
- Litigation Expenses and Costs (ADA)..288
- Market Rate Standards 169, 189
- "Mootness," effect (discretionary) on ADA federal jurisdiction 187
- Multipliers, enhancement (risk) 175-177
- No Fees against "good faith" plaintiff (in federal court, but beware Jankey v. Lee in state court per section 55 Civil Code 195
- No "pre-litigation" notice required (unless "Catalyst" basis, California law) 172
- "Prevailing" Defendants Fees Against Plaintiff in State Court (Jankey)........307
- "Prevailing Party" standards, ADA 288
- Public Policy, Private Attorney General 168, 169, 173-174
- Staffing and Billing Judgment 187
- Time reasonably needed for quality representation 186
- Threat Against Plaintiff, Dangers 15, 116
- Verified time statements 180
- Written Settlement offers effect, California Statute...............................173, 196

Attorney Fees under the ADA... 288*ff*

- Christianburg Rule in Federal Civil Rights Cases 300
    - o Hubbard v. Sobreck (Fed. Ct.) 307
    - o Litigation Expenses and Costs 301
        - Brown v. Lucky Stores 301
        - DOJ Regulations Protect Plaintiff..302
- Damages low do not reduce fees..291

- Demand for Fees Against Plaintiff 302-304
  - Section 503 ADA Threat?
- Fees not available to prevailing defendant under Section 55 Civil Code in Federal Court (Hubbard v. Sobreck) against "good faith" plaintiff 307
- Fox v. Vice, Limits Defendant Fees to "Frivolous Claims" 308-309
- Harris v. Maricopa County, limited defense fees 307
- Hubbard v. SoBreck, federal courts will follow, reject Jankey v. Lee 307
- Market Rate Standards (Moreno) 298
- Message to Defendants, Attorneys Fees as a 312
- Landlord/Tenant, Joint and Several Liability 309
- Moreno: prevailing market rates 298-299
  - "Lawyers must eat" 296-298
  - Need for adequate Civil Rights fees 296-298
  - Multiple Lawsuits by plaintiff irrelevant 304-305
  - Public Policy to encourage ADA suits (Carnival) 291-292
  - "Serial Lawsuits" may be justified 306
  - Staffing decisions by plaintiff 299

Building Departments

- Authority of Court as final 90
- Not stopped from enforcement 83
- Lack of enforcement not a defense 54, 81, 86
- Permit does not approve violations of access laws (UBC 302-3) 54, 86
- Burden of Production and Burden of Proof 241-217

California State Law 17*ff*

- Damages only under state law 23*ff*
- Public Policy 26, 28
- Statutory Scheme 33
- ADA incorporated into State Law 77
- "Che" case standards 59-62

Class Actions 332*ff*

- ADA limited to injunction and fees 333
- Caveat possible effect on individual actions 335
- Caveat "sweetheart" settlement deals 335
- Disclaimer 332

- Examples of Class Actions for injunctive relief only 333
    - o Denny's 334
    - o Jack in the Box 334
    - o BP Service Stations 334
    - o Greyhound Bus Stations 335
- Injunctive relief only as option 333
- Publicity as positive effect 337

Civil Rights (Race) Cases, Analogies 247

Companion Seating (theaters) 276

Complaint, objectives 23

Crosswalks 72

Damages (California law) 23*ff*

- "Daily Damages" 141-143
- Defined by Civil Code 55.56 127
- Deterrence as basis 126, 127
- Deterrence: <u>Arnold v. United Artists</u> 67
- Examples of damages 121-123
- For denial of "Full and Equal" access 120
- Governments: no punitive damages 226
- "Per visit" 144
- Prior lawsuits, effect? 129-131
- Statutory "minimum" damages 121-123

Defenses, Rebutting common 79*ff*

"Demonstrate" "Not Readily Achievable" (Defendants' Burden) 248-249

Dimensional Tolerances 73-75

Disclaimer (book's legal disclaimer) 7

Discretion, Abuse of (and see "CHE") 97

"Equivalent facilitation," as necessary condition for exception 46, 48, 49, 50, 51

- Required by Government Code 4450 *ff*, and Health and Safety code 19957
  .... 79, 88, 98

Experts: opinions not binding re: compliance 71

Exceptions – "Unreasonable" hardship 41

- Burden of proof on proponent 44, 49
- Equivalent facilitation needed 46, 48-50, 51
- Hardship Exceptions 44-50, 51, 87, 88
- None retroactive 101
- Written findings required by Title 24 .... 51, 96

Federal Jurisdiction, bases, discretionary 78, 79, 285

"Full and Equal" Access Required 135-136

General Order 56 (G.O. 56, Northern District, California procedures) 328, 420

Government Claim (re: damages) six month statute of limitations 197, 215

Government Code sections 4450 ff re: construction or alteration (1968) (and see appendix at 361) 32, 204

Government Entities .... 204 ff

- ADA violations incorporated into California law 224
- ADA Title II 215-219
- Affirmative Steps required 221-223
- Alterations under ASA (1970-1982) 209
- Alterations, 1982 to present 207
- Attorney Fees under ADA Title II 23
- "ASA" or "ANSI" standards 209-211
- "ASA" path of travel standards, "CHE" case 211-213
- Burden of Proof, affirmative defenses 230-231
- California law Access requirements 204ff
- Construction or alteration triggers 207
- Damages under Title II: "intentional" 224
- "Deliberate Indifference" defined as "intentional" discrimination 224
- Disparate impact on disabled (Example: Crowder v. Kitigawa) 226
- Government Code section 11135, policy 214
- Injunctive Relief 219-220
- Jails 228, 229
- Liability of government as owners, operators, lessor, or lessee 227, 228

- No punitive damages v. government..226
- Public Entities under Title II..204 ff, 226
    - Example: Colleges..227
    - Example: Courthouse access..226
    - Public property rented to private company..227
- Public Policy..205
- Rehabilitation Act of 1973, Section 504..215
- Transportation Services under Title II ADA..224

Hankins v. El Torito..132-135

Health and Safety Code (California)..33

Hardships (See "Exceptions" - "Unreasonable Hardship")..46, 50, 51

Historical Building Standards..120

Injunctive Relief..111

- Mootness..112

Intent, wrongful (none needed for liability)..24, 25, 26

- But may be relevant for treble damages..139

Interpretations, Broad to maximize access..26, 107

- Public policy and purpose of laws..32-36, 132-138

Investigations (& discovery, re: history of alterations)..33-36

Joint and Several Liability for Attorney Fees..95, 283

Jurisdiction, Federal – discretionary to retain..79

- "Mootness," effect (discretionary) on ADA federal jurisdiction..187
- Not created by incorporation of ADA into California statutes..78
- Supplemental Jurisdiction..285

Kellum, Keith..2

Kitchen Alterations..103, 104

Landlords and Tenants Liability..282-284

- Joint and several liability 95, 282-283
- Joint and several attorney fees liability 282, 283, 284

Legal Disclaimer 7

Legislative Counsel's 1979 Opinion (on accessible path of travel under ASA) 56

Legislation, New in California (2012) 15, 198-203, 436-476

Lifts, independent operation issues 115

- Ramp usually preferable to lift 116

Limits on Book's Coverage 7, 13

"Line of Sight," theater seating requirements 285

Mootness 112, 113

- "Maintain accessible facilities," use in order to avoid mootness 113

New Legislation (2012) in California .... 15, 198-203, Appendix 436-476

No "Notice" Required under ADA 276

- Botosan: No pre-suit notice required 276
- DOJ administrative determination 281
- No prejudice from lack of notice to local government authorities 282
- Pre-Botosan District Court decisions 277
- Skaff v. Meridian (9th Cir.) no pre-suit notice required 276
- Voluntary Notice 278
- Waiver of any "Notice" defense 277

Nuisance, Public (lack of access) 90

Objectives of Complaint 23

"Opposing Disabled Access: Money, Prejudice, and Ignorance" 351

Owners, successor liability 90, 92, 93, 94

Parent Company Financial Resources 254-256

Path of Travel, accessible required 54-56

- Accessible to and useable by disabled 56-59
- Access required when money spent 67
- ASA standards 64, 213
- Attorney General Opinion, September 17, 1992 .... 68, 382
- Defined by Title-24 Regulations 65
- Donald v. Sacramento Valley Bank 64
- Legislative Counsel Opinion (1979) 213
- Private Attorney Generals, public interest 294-296
- Private Lawsuits, Enforcement by 17, 20, 52, 54
- Public buildings (see "Government Entities") .... 204 *ff*

"Policy" Violations 110, 132, 133

- "Employee Only" restrooms (Hankins v. El Torito) 257-258
- Insurance rates 257-258
- Travel agency inaccurate information 258

Point of Sale Machines 166

Private Attorney Generals, "public interest enforcement" by 17, 20, 52, 54, 294-296

Public Restrooms (Sanitary Facilitation) 76, 77

- Restrooms for restaurants, unisex as readily achievable solution 117-119

Public Policy 17-21, 45, 105, 138, 264, 294

- To maximize integration of disabled 21, 105

"Prior lawsuits," effect of 155, 156-160

Punitive Damages 143-152

Purpose – maximizing accessibility 26, 28, 30, 98

- Of this book 11
- Of ASA Regulations 30, 31
- Of Title 24 Regulations 40

Readily Achievable 250

- ADAAG 4.1.7 set "readily achievable" standards 256
- "Alternative Methods," facilities made accessible through 256

- Botosan v. McNally set 9th Circuit Standards 253
- Burden of Proof 241
- Caveat "Mom and Pop" financial claims 253
- Discovery to compare costs of access v. "overall financial resources" 252
- DOJ regulations 28 CFR 36.304 priorities and examples 258-259
- Parent Company Financial Resources 254-256
- Pinnock upheld ADA constitutionality and set standards 250-252
- Statutory standards .... 250 ff

Rein, Erma 6

Regulations given great weight (interpretations) 67

Remedies, other 331ff

Retaliation .... 260 ff

- Against ADA Enforcers 293
- Burden of Proof 263
- Damages for retaliation 262
- DOJ regulations 263-264
- Discovery by defense counsel about prior ADA actions 264
- Public policy to encourage ADA lawsuits 264-265
- Retaliation or harassment 260-262

Restrooms (see "Public Restrooms")

Roberts, Ed 3

"Second Floor" Standards 108-110

"Serial" lawsuits 156

Service animals 161-164, 284

"SB 1186" (2012) 198-203, 436-476

Settlement: Practical Approaches, Notice, and Cooperation .... 311 ff

- Confidentiality 324
  - Free speech 326
  - Public policy 325
  - Resist as settlement condition 327

- Early communication with defendants 311-312
    - Protect public interest 312
- Early investigation, research and preparation to ensure good faith cases 313
- Expert, Consult before filing 322
- General Order 56 in Northern District 322, 328
- Other remedies 331
    - Small Claims Court 331
    - Class actions .... 332 *ff*
- No notice required for prevailing party attorney fees to plaintiff 321
- Tactical Considerations .... 314 ff
    - Advance Notice 314
        - Catalyst fees under California law 319
        - Government Claim as notice 321
    - "Win-win" settlement approach 321

Standing

- ADAAG section 36.501 specifies standing 269-272
- Chapman and Doran: Broad standing standards 273-275
- Companion seating (theaters) 276
- Congressional Intent 268
- No futile act required 267, 269
- Public Policy: Broad Standing 267-268
- Skaff v. Meridian clarified standing 272-273

State Architect Manual (California) 37

Statute of Limitations 165, 197

Title 24 Regulations (California) 1982-Present 33, 39

Treble Damages and Potential 139-140

"Twenty Percent" rule, re: hardships 100

Uniform Building Code (UBC) 86

Unisex Restrooms (See Public Restrooms)

Unruh Act (California Civil Code sections 51 and 52)

- Incorporation of ADA 79

- No intent needed (Munson) if based on ADA 25, 125

"Unreasonable Hardship" Exceptions (See "Exceptions") 46, 50, 51

"Whites Only" (analogy) 17, 91, 281

Win-Win situation, access as 356

Index of Appendix

ASA Regulations..363

Attorney General Opinions (California) .... 382 *ff*

- September 17, 1992 – Directive to Building Officials...................................282
- July 14, 1993 – (ADA only by DOJ and private lawsuits) 391
- August 4, 2003 – (No "Advance Notice" laws are needed)..........................399

Complaint Sample: Federal Court, ADA & California law 402

Composite Photo: Sacramento Community Theater..435

Consent Decree (Sample)..423

General Order 56 (N.D. California) 470

Government Code Section 4450 *ff* (circa 1968)..361

Leading Access Cases 357

Office of California Legislative Council (March 31, 1979 Opinion re: Path of Travel Requirements under the ASA...375

Resources for Disabled Persons 358

Senate (California) Bill 1186 (2012) Text 436-475

Index of People

Barry Atwood 69, 70, 72, 74, 75

Jonathan Adler 47, 71, 138, 359

Patty Berne 116, 117

Aaron Clefton 1

Sidney Cohen 70, 134, 173, 277

Jim Donald 1, 5, 19, 23, 24, 45, 46, 227

Concetta Jorgenson 326, 334

Clint Eastwood 19, 20, 316, 318, 345

Tom Frankovich 262, 339

Judge Phyllis Hamilton 44, 45, 164, 185

Judge Thelton Henderson .. 30, 53, 67, 98, 108, 111, 123, 126, 140, 156, 168, 180, 186, 187, 233, 236, 257, 265, 267, 271, 292, 294

Lynn Hubbard 346, 347

Judge Lawrence Karlton 26, 81, 84, 125, 142, 143, 144, 248, 311, 346, 348

Peter Margen 71, 115, 130, 148, 230

Larry Paradis 148, 204, 216, 332, 334, 352

Keith Kellum 112, 58, 82, 85

Erma Rein 2, 5, 6

Paul Rein 23, 29, 134, 186

Steve Rein 1

Ed Roberts 1, 3, 4, 358

Sid Wolinsky 24, 130, 147, 148, 332

WA